The Later Lectures of
# Ralph Waldo Emerson
## 1843–1871

# The Later Lectures of
# Ralph Waldo Emerson
# 1843–1871

*Volume 1: 1843–1854*

EDITED BY

Ronald A. Bosco and Joel Myerson

The University of Georgia Press

*Athens and London*

The preparation of this volume was made possible in part by
grants from the Editing and Collaborative Research programs of the
National Endowment for the Humanities, an independent Federal agency.

Paperback edition, 2010
© 2001 by the University of Georgia Press
Athens, Georgia 30602
www.ugapress.org
Set in Ehrhardt by G & S Typesetters

Printed digitally in the United States of America

The Library of Congress has cataloged the hardcover
edition of this book as follows:

Emerson, Ralph Waldo, 1803–1882.
[Speeches. Selections]
The later lectures of Ralph Waldo Emerson, 1843–1871 / edited by
Ronald A. Bosco and Joel Myerson.
2 v. ; 25 cm.
Includes bibliographical references and indexes.
ISBN 0-8203-2295-4 (alk. paper)
1. Speeches, addresses, etc., American.  I. Bosco, Ronald A.
II. Myerson, Joel.  III. Title.
PS1616.B67 2001
815'.3—dc21          00-064880

Paperback ISBN-13: 978-0-8203-3462-2 (vol. 1)
ISBN-10: 0-8203-3462-6 (vol. 1)
ISBN-13: 978-0-8203-3470-7 (vol. 2)
ISBN-10: 0-8203-3470-7 (vol. 2)

British Library Cataloging-in-Publication Data available

*For Bernadette and Greta*

# Contents

# Preface

THE APPEARANCE OF these two volumes of *The Later Lectures of Ralph Waldo Emerson, 1843–1871* continues an extraordinary cycle of recovery and publication from manuscript of primary sources from the hand of the individual who is arguably the foremost intellectual architect of American culture. That cycle began in 1939, when Ralph L. Rusk published the first six volumes of Emerson's *Letters*, to which Joseph Slater added *The Correspondence of Emerson and Carlyle* in one volume in 1964 and Eleanor M. Tilton added an additional four volumes of *Letters* between 1990 and 1995. The cycle continued with a generation of editors who in the 1950s turned their attention to Emerson's early lectures and journals. Emerson's *Early Lectures*, under the editorship of Stephen E. Whicher, Robert E. Spiller, and Wallace E. Williams, appeared in three volumes between 1959 and 1972, and his *Journals and Miscellaneous Notebooks*, under the chief editorship first of William H. Gilman and then of Ralph H. Orth, appeared in sixteen volumes between 1960 and 1982. After the completion of the edition of Emerson's *Journals and Miscellaneous Notebooks*, the cycle continued with a new generation of editors who had been recruited by Mr. Gilman and Mr. Orth to carry on the work of the first generation of Emerson editors, many of whom had passed away by the 1980s. Under Mr. Orth's chief editorship, that new generation of editors, several of whom had worked on the *Journals and Miscellaneous Notebooks*, prepared the one-volume edition of Emerson's *Poetry Notebooks* for publication in 1986 and the three-volume edition of his *Topical Notebooks*, which appeared between 1990 and 1994. Finally, under the chief editorship of Albert J. von Frank, a four-volume edition of Emerson's *Complete Sermons* was published between 1989 and 1992.

This publication process would never have been possible without the care with which, early on, Emerson's children and first editors—Ellen and Edward Waldo Emerson along with James Elliot Cabot, Emerson's literary executor—preserved the manuscripts on which these editions have been based and with which, under the agency of the Ralph Waldo Emerson Memorial Association, the manuscripts were subsequently collected and preserved at the Houghton Library of Harvard University and made available to scholars. And with respect to the cycle of recovery, while numbers alone cannot tell the whole story of the genesis of these editions or the extent to which they sustained scholarly inquiry into Emerson's mind and legacy as they increasingly became available in print, the numbers are impressive. Over the course of the past sixty years, more than thirty editors crossing multiple generational lines have produced a magnificent archaeology of Emerson's thought in thirty-eight volumes, and these volumes have instigated—and, we trust, with the addition of these two volumes of *Later Lectures* will continue to instigate—an outpouring of scholarly, biographical, and textual studies that is unprecedented for an American author. As these volumes of Emerson's later lectures go into press, and especially as computer technology advances, the work of individual scholars studying and writing on Emerson will be assisted by searchable databases on which all editions of Emerson's writings will eventually be mounted. From these databases, scholars will be able to create their own definitive topical concordances to Emerson's writings as well as comprehensive lists of "parallel passages" (that is, lists that indicate and cross-reference Emerson's use of expressions, ranging in length from a phrase to entire paragraphs in his journals, notebooks, letters, sermons, and published writings), both of which will add immeasurably to the thoroughness and accuracy of their research. Anticipating these advances in technology and, admittedly, also as a matter of economy, we have, as we explain in our introduction, not prepared the parallel passages apparatus sometimes found in editions of Emerson's writings; as we also indicate in our introduction, we have prepared and mounted all textual notes associated with our edition on the following website: www.walden.org/emerson/Writings/Later_Lectures. Additional concordance materials concerning Emerson in general and the *Later Lectures* in particular may also be found at this site.

Our work on *The Later Lectures of Ralph Waldo Emerson, 1843–1871* has been supported by a number of institutions and individuals. The Ralph Waldo Emerson Memorial Association provided us with a generous start-up grant, and the association continued to provide us with tangible and moral support throughout our work on this edition; for these we thank Margaret E. Bancroft, president of the association, and Roger L. Gregg. Both the University at Albany, State University of New York, and the University of South Carolina provided us with research leaves; the Faculty Research Awards Program at Albany also provided a research grant at the outset of our work on this edition. Major funding for this edition was provided by grants from the Editing and Collaborative Research programs of the National Endowment for the Humanities (NEH), an independent federal agency; we thank Douglas Arnold and Margot Backas at NEH for their assistance throughout the grant processes. We gratefully acknowledge the Ralph Waldo Emerson Memorial Association and the Houghton Library of Harvard University for permission to publish Emerson's later lectures.

We also acknowledge the assistance of the staffs of the following libraries at which we worked: the Boston Public Library, the British Library, the Concord Free Public Library, the Edinburgh Public Library, the Houghton and Widener libraries of Harvard University, the Massachusetts Historical Society, the National Library of Scotland, and the libraries of the University at Albany and the University of South Carolina. The Houghton Library of Harvard University extended to us the usual splendid courtesies with which the staff of that library has supported Emerson editors over several decades; for these courtesies, we should like to thank Leslie A. Morris, curator of manuscripts, and Susan Halpert, Denison Beach, Tom Ford, Jennie Rathbun, Virginia Smyers, Emily Walhout, and Melanie Wisner. Also, we would like to thank Bradley P. Dean of The Thoreau Institute in Lincoln, Massachusetts, for his expert assistance in facilitating the mounting of our textual notes to this edition on the website that he oversees.

All scholarship is collaborative; as the record of Emerson editions published over the past six decades suggests, scholarly collaboration has been a necessary condition of all editorial work on Emerson's manuscripts, and it has always been graciously offered by specialists in the study of Emerson, by textual specialists, and by archival specialists. We are grateful to the following persons for their assistance at various stages of this project: Lawrence Buell, David R. Chesnutt, Phyllis Cole, Joseph Gerber, Armida Gilbert, Len Gougeon, Nathaniel Lewis, Marcia Moss, Wesley T. Mott, Ralph H. Orth, Barbara L. Packer, Robert D. Richardson Jr., David M. Robinson, Merton M. Sealts Jr., Peter L. Shillingsburg, James L. W. West III, Douglas Emory Wilson, Leslie Perrin Wilson, and Thomas Wortham. James Justus, executor of Wallace E. Williams's estate, generously sent us all the working materials that Williams had assembled during his work on Emerson's lectures. Eric Roman provided essential assistance both during our computerization of this edition and during our work on the lecture "France, or Urbanity." Michael McLoughlin not only assisted in the preparation of annotations but was also invaluable in helping us to create a concordance for Emerson's writings (with the help of Mr. Roman) and in preparing all our computer applications for this edition. Finally, we are especially indebted to these three persons: Helen R. Deese, for her expert review of the manuscript of this edition and timely suggestions for its improvement; Nancy Craig Simmons, for her generosity in sharing with us the results of her research on Emerson's later career as a lecturer, for her thoughtful reading of our introduction and headnotes, and, in particular, for her guidance through the maze of Emerson's deliveries of his *New England* lecture series; and Albert J. von Frank, for sharing with us his extensive knowledge of and resources for the study of Emerson and his times.

Nancy Grayson, formerly of the University of Georgia Press, was the first editor to have faith in us, and we thank her for her early support. At the University of Georgia Press, Karen Orchard and David E. Des Jardines made sure that these volumes were published, and we are grateful to them for their sustained efforts on our behalf.

Wallace E. Williams began his career as an editor of Emerson's *Early Lectures,* and he had been planning, along with James Justus, to finish editing additional Emerson lectures after his retirement. Williams's sudden death in 1990 left his project in an unfinished state, with only unverified transcriptions of selected lecture manuscripts completed, as we discovered when Justus sent us Williams's working materials. Because both the transcriptions and Williams's notes on them were preliminary rather than finished, we decided to perform our own exhaustive survey of all manuscripts relating to Emerson's later lectures at the Houghton Library and to prepare our own transcriptions directly from those manuscripts. While we have on occasion used Williams's work to check our own, we are fully responsible for all transcriptions and editorial decisions in this edition.

Mr. Bosco thanks Louis Roberts, interim chair of the Department of English, and Cyril H. Knoblauch, interim dean of the College of Arts and Sciences, for their support at crucial stages of this edition and gratefully acknowledges Provost Judy L. Genshaft and President Karen R. Hitchcock of the University at Albany for providing him with the intellectual space to complete work on this edition. The following research assistants at Albany did invaluable work over the life of this project: Nadya J. Lawson in verifying transcriptions and assisting with collations of Emerson's lectures with his published works, and Henry Hays Crimmel in assisting with computer applications.

Mr. Myerson thanks Bert Dillon and especially Robert Newman, chairs of the Department of English at the University of South Carolina, for their support of this edition. The following research assistants at South Carolina did invaluable work over the life of this project: Alan Brasher in helping to start it up; Jennifer Hynes in collating Emerson's lectures with his published works; and Chris Nesmith in assisting with proofreading.

We finished this project with hardly a day to spare before our wives threatened to leave us. They have been remarkably patient as over the past eight years Emerson and mounds of paper associated with his later lectures first moved into, then took over, our homes and lives. Their love and support have, as always, made it possible for us to do our work and keep relatively sane in the process. We consider our recovery and publication of Emerson's later lectures to have been very important work, so naturally, and with profound gratitude, we dedicate these volumes to Bernadette M. Bosco and Greta D. Little.

Ronald A. Bosco and Joel Myerson
Concord, Massachusetts
January 2000

# Works Frequently Cited

"Account Books"    Ralph Waldo Emerson's account books (1836–72), bMS Am 1280 H112a–j, Houghton Library, Harvard University.

Cabot, "Blue Books"    James Elliot Cabot's collection of notes on and occasional newspaper reports of Ralph Waldo Emerson's lectures and publications, bMS Am 1280.235 (711), 7 boxes, Houghton Library, Harvard University.

Cabot, *A Memoir*    James Elliot Cabot. *A Memoir of Ralph Waldo Emerson.* 2 vols. Boston and New York: Houghton Mifflin, 1887.

*CEC*    *The Correspondence of Emerson and Carlyle.* Edited by Joseph Slater. New York: Columbia University Press, 1964.

Charvat    William Charvat. *Emerson's American Lecture Engagements.* New York: New York Public Library, 1961.

*Complete Sermons*    *The Complete Sermons of Ralph Waldo Emerson.* Albert J. von Frank, chief editor; Ronald A. Bosco, Andrew H. Delbanco, Wesley T. Mott, Teresa Toulouse, editors; David M. Robinson, Wallace E. Williams, and Douglas Emory Wilson, contributing editors. 4 vols. Columbia: University of Missouri Press, 1989–92.

*CW*    *The Collected Works of Ralph Waldo Emerson.* Alfred R. Ferguson and Joseph Slater, general editors; Douglas Emory Wilson, textual editor; Robert E. Burkholder, Jean Ferguson Carr, Philip Nicoloff, Robert E. Spiller, and Wallace E. Williams, editors. 5 vols. to date. Cambridge, Mass.: Harvard University Press, 1971–.

*Early Lectures*            *The Early Lectures of Ralph Waldo Emerson.* Edited by
                            Stephen E. Whicher, Robert E. Spiller, and Wallace E.
                            Williams. 3 vols. Cambridge, Mass.: Harvard Univer-
                            sity Press, 1959–72.

*Emerson Among His*         *Emerson Among His Contemporaries.* Edited by Ken-
*Contemporaries*            neth Walter Cameron. Hartford, Conn.: Transcenden-
                            tal Books, 1967.

*Emerson and Thoreau*       *Emerson and Thoreau Speak: Lecturing in Concord and*
*Speak*                     *Lincoln during the American Renaissance: Chapters from*
                            *"The Massachusetts Lyceum."* Edited by Kenneth Wal-
                            ter Cameron. Hartford, Conn.: Transcendental Books,
                            1972.

Emerson's *Antislavery*     *Emerson's Antislavery Writings.* Edited by Len Gougeon
*Writings*                  and Joel Myerson. New Haven, Conn.: Yale University
                            Press, 1995.

Emerson's *University*      Ronald A. Bosco. *"His Lectures Were Poetry, His Teach-*
*Lectures*                  *ing the Music of the Spheres": Annie Adams Fields and*
                            *Francis Greenwood Peabody on Emerson's "Natural His-*
                            *tory of the Intellect" University Lectures at Harvard in*
                            *1870. Harvard Library Bulletin,* n.s. 8 (Summer 1997).

*JMN*                       *The Journals and Miscellaneous Notebooks of Ralph Waldo*
                            *Emerson.* William H. Gilman and Ralph H. Orth, chief
                            editors; Linda Allardt, Ronald A. Bosco, George P.
                            Clark, Merrell R. Davis, Harrison Hayford, David W.
                            Hill, Glen M. Johnson, J. E. Parsons, A. W. Plumstead,
                            Merton M. Sealts Jr., and Susan Sutton Smith, editors;
                            Ruth H. Bennett, associate editor. 16 vols. Cambridge,
                            Mass.: Harvard University Press, 1960–82.

*Letters*                   *The Letters of Ralph Waldo Emerson.* Edited by Ralph L.
                            Rusk (vols. 1–6) and Eleanor M. Tilton (vols. 7–10).
                            New York: Columbia University Press, 1939, 1990–95.

*Letters, ETE*              *The Letters of Ellen Tucker Emerson.* Edited by Edith E.
                            W. Gregg. 2 vols. Kent, Ohio: Kent State University
                            Press, 1982.

Letters, *LJE*　　　　　　*The Selected Letters of Lidian Jackson Emerson.* Edited by Delores Bird Carpenter. Columbia: University of Missouri Press, 1987.

Mead, *Yankee*　　　　　David Mead. *Yankee Eloquence in the Middle West: The*
*Eloquence in the*　　　　*Ohio Lyceum 1850–1870.* East Lansing: Michigan State
*Middle West*　　　　　　College Press, 1951.

Simmons, "Arranging　　Nancy Craig Simmons. "Arranging the Sibylline
the Sibylline Leaves"　　Leaves: James Elliot Cabot's Work as Emerson's Literary Executor." In *Studies in the American Renaissance 1983.* Edited by Joel Myerson. Charlottesville: University Press of Virginia, 1983, 335–89.

Simmons, "Emerson's　Nancy Craig Simmons. "Practicing Ecstasy: Emer-
1843–1844 New　　　son's 1843–1844 New England Lectures as Process."
England Lectures"　　　Forthcoming.

*TN*　　　　　　　　　*The Topical Notebooks of Ralph Waldo Emerson.* Ralph H. Orth, chief editor; Ronald A. Bosco, Glen M. Johnson, and Susan Sutton Smith, editors; Douglas Emory Wilson, consulting editor. 3 vols. Columbia: University of Missouri Press, 1990–94.

*Transcendental Log*　　*Transcendental Log: Fresh Discoveries in Newspapers Concerning Emerson, Thoreau, Alcott, and Others of the American Literary Renaissance, Arranged Chronologically for Half a Century from 1832.* Edited by Kenneth Walter Cameron. Hartford, Conn.: Transcendental Books, 1973.

*Uncollected Lectures*　　*Uncollected Lectures by Ralph Waldo Emerson.* Edited by Clarence Gohdes. New York: William Edwin Rudge, 1932.

von Frank　　　　　　Albert J. von Frank. *An Emerson Chronology.* New York: G. K. Hall, 1994.

*W*　　　　　　　　　*The Complete Works of Ralph Waldo Emerson.* Edited by Edward Waldo Emerson. Centenary Edition. 12 vols. Boston and New York: Houghton Mifflin, 1903–4.

# Historical and Textual Introduction

## I. EMERSON AT THE LECTERN

Grace Greenwood tells of an interesting afternoon in the Old Corner Bookstore in Boston, when [Bayard] Taylor, in a weary and a somewhat petulant mood, dissuaded her from lecturing, saying that it was an occupation full of misery, that he himself detested it, and that an audience seemed to him no other thing than a collection of cabbage-heads. A few minutes later Mr. Emerson congratulated her upon the thought of lecturing, saying that there was recompense for all the hardships of the work in the kind words and the smiling faces and the bright eyes of the audience. —Albert H. Smythe, *Bayard Taylor* (Boston, 1896), 103

[T]he sermon I heard from Mr Finney [in 1829 or 1830] was in Park Street Church . . . from the text "The wages of sin is death[.]" . . . He [later] came to Boston & I took courage & went. His text was, "The wages of sin is death," and I recognized in succession all the topics & treatment. . . . It was twenty five years later, . . . when I next saw Mr Finney, soon after his return from London, that I found myself on a Sunday in Rome, New York, & learned that he was to preach there. I went, & his text was "The Wages of sin is death" & the sermon in the main & I suppose in all the particulars the same. . . . It was plain that he was as bad as a hack lecturer like myself. —Emerson to Edward Everett Hale, 30? June? 1870?, *Letters,* 6:123

'Twas tedious the obstructions & squalor of travel. The advantage of their offers at Chicago made it needful to go. It was in short this dragging a decorous old gentleman out of home, & out of position, to this juvenile career tantamount to this: "I'll bet you fifty dollars a day for three weeks, that you will not leave your library & wade & freeze & ride & run, & suffer all manner of indignities, & stand up for an hour each night reading in a hall:" and I answer, "I'll bet I will," I do it & win the $900. —Emerson, 15 February 1865, *JMN,* 15:457

When I handed him a check for twelve hundred dollars for his six lectures, "What a swindle! ' was his exclamation. —William Henry Furness, "Random Reminiscences of Emerson,' *Atlantic Monthly,* 71 (March 1893): 348

THERE ARE NOT many studies of Emerson as a lecturer. The reasons for this neglect, we believe, are threefold: first, only his surviving lectures from 1833 to 1842 have been published; second, the remaining lectures exist in manuscript in varying stages of disarray; and third, there are so many accounts of Emerson's lecturing in major and minor newspapers that the idea of tracing his platform career through a search of these sources is daunting. The information now known about him as a lecturer is, as the comments printed above suggest, often contradictory.

The biographical and intellectual gaps in our knowledge of Emerson caused by the lack of these studies are unfortunate, because he spent over half a century in front of public audiences sharpening his ideas and his style. If, as Bliss Perry has so famously stated, Emerson's journals were the "savings bank" into which he deposited the ideas for his essays and other writings, then his lectures were where he first gave public expression to these ideas once he had withdrawn them from his account.[1] Again and again we see Emerson's writings develop from journal entry to lecture to published work; indeed, a number of his lecture series became books, such as *Representative Men* (1850), *English Traits* (1856), and *The Conduct of Life* (1860), while several of his lecture series on philosophy provided the basis for a posthumous work, *Natural History of Intellect* (1891), edited, if not actually created, first by his literary executor, James Elliot Cabot, then supplemented by his son, Edward Waldo Emerson, Cabot's successor.

But Emerson tried out not only his ideas and his style on the lecture platform, he tried out "Ralph Waldo Emerson," the public persona he both adopted and was forced into by his audiences. We know that Emerson essayed a number of careers in his life, including minister, married man, lecturer, Concordian, author, publishing agent, editor, landowner, traveler, family man, and, finally, being one of the most famous men in America. He also took on a number of formal personae, going through turns as "Ralph" to his family and friends (before becoming "Waldo"), the anonymous author of *Nature* (1836) and of articles and poems in the *Dial* (1840–44), "R. Waldo Emerson" in formal correspondence, and "Ralph Waldo Emerson" on the title pages of his books and pamphlets, a signature that soon became interchangeable with the image of the "Sage of Concord." Significantly, his most important and extensive statements on such subjects as abolitionism, women's rights, and temperance came on the lecture platform, not on the printed page. His career as a lecturer provided an integral component to this constant reinvention of public self. Indeed, Stephen Railton argues that the lecture platform was necessary not only for Emerson's continual self-invention but also for its ability to provide him with a constant reminder of his success in doing exactly that: "Thus while the thematic goal of Emerson's oratory was to announce the omnipotence of each listener's self, the dramatic goal of each such performance was to confirm his own."[2]

Scholars usually assume that Emerson spent so much time as a lecturer because he needed the money and was well paid for his efforts. In some ways, the

---

1. See Perry, "Emerson's Savings Bank," *Nation*, 24 September 1914, 371–73.
2. Stephen Railton, *Authorship and Audience: Literary Performance in the American Renaissance* (Princeton, N.J.: Princeton University Press, 1991), 32.

statistics might bear them out, as in this summary by Robert D. Richardson Jr. of Emerson's lecturing career:

> Over his active career of four decades, Emerson gave some 1,500 public lectures Lecturing was a major part of his life and a major source of income. For twenty-five years he was out and away from home lecturing for four, five or even six months out of each year, every year. He traveled as far west as St. Louis, Des Moines, Minneapolis, and eventually California; he gave 17 lectures in Canada but almost none south of the Ohio River. He delivered the great majority of his lectures in Massachusetts. He gave 157 lectures in New York state. He gave more lectures in Maine than in New Hampshire (35 to 27) and many more in Illinois (49), Ohio (56), Pennsylvania (42), and Wisconsin (29) than in Connecticut, . . . where he spoke only 18 times in his entire career.[3]

Although Emerson was dependent on lecturing for his (and his family's) livelihood in his early life, after the settlement of his first wife's estate in the mid-1830s, his early profits as a lecturer and as an author, and his shrewd investment of his monies, Emerson's finances became secure, to the point that in 1851 he was listed in *The Rich Men of Massachusetts* as possessing $50,000.[4] And after he changed his publishers in 1860 to Ticknor and Fields, the most prestigious Boston firm of the time, his royalty income increased markedly. To Emerson, then, lecturing was significantly more than just a means to obtain money, more than a financially driven alternative career.

The editors of the *Early Lectures*, in dealing with no more than five years' worth of lectures in each of their volumes, were able to give detailed summaries of Emerson's lecturing career during those periods. We, however, print nearly thirty years of Emerson's lectures, from his beginnings as an entrepreneurial individual who performed every task from arranging for the hall in which to give the lecture to writing the notices for it in the local newspapers, through the time when he was so popular that series of private lectures were arranged for him. To try to present anything like a full survey of Emerson's career as a lecturer in this short space is to do him an injustice. Accordingly, this introduction attempts to say something about why lecturing was so important to Emerson, and why the study of Emerson's lecturing is so important to us when we, as readers, approach him. A complete study of Emerson's career as a lecturer must await some future scholar and some future time, when someone has searched for accounts of Emerson both in the many famous national newspapers as well as in obscure local newspapers that followed his career.

3. Robert D. Richardson Jr., *Emerson: The Mind on Fire* (Berkeley: University of California Press, 1995), 418–19.
4. A. Forbes and J. W. Greene, *The Rich Men of Massachusetts* (Boston: V. V. Spencer, 1851), 101.

To understand Emerson's writings, one must first see him at work as a lecturer. This role was crucial to Emerson, as he himself commented:

> I look on the Lecture Room as the true Church of the coming time, and as the home of a richer eloquence than Faneuil Hall or the Capitol ever knew. For here is all that the true orator will ask, namely, a convertible audience,—an audience coming up to the house, not knowing what shall befall them there, but uncommitted and willing victims to reason and love. There is no topic that may not be treated, and no method excluded. *Here,* everything is admissible, philosophy, ethics, divinity, criticism, poetry, humor, anecdote, mimicry,—ventriloquism almost,—all the breadth and versatility of the most liberal conversation, and of the highest, lowest, personal, and local topics—all are permitted, and all may be combined in one speech. It is a panharmonicon combining every note on the longest gamut, from the explosion of cannon to the tinkle of a guitar. . . .
>     . . . Here, the American orator shall find the theatre he needs; here, he may lay himself out utterly large, prodigal, enormous, on the subject of the hour. Here, he may dare to hope for the higher inspiration and a total transfusion of himself into the minds of men.[5]

By examining the lectures and how they were delivered, we can look into the laboratory of Emerson's composing process and see his published writings gestating. And perhaps the most important thing to remember is that we need to study not just the words but the manner in which they were delivered.

As a minister, Emerson liked preaching far more than he did his technical or pastoral ministerial duties. There was something about appearing before an audience that appealed to him, something in him that recognized the importance of language and, as his contemporaries reported it, an "earnest and magnetic" presence in moral suasion. As John McAleer astutely comments, "Rather than being a preacher who came before his audiences in the guise of a lecturer, Emerson had begun his career as a lecturer who came before his congregations in the guise of a preacher."[6] Being a lecturer not only allowed Emerson to spread his doctrines and to work on his writings, but it also gave him opportunities to pursue his life-long task of personal growth. As Barbara Packer has shown, Emerson's early public performances were "mediated through institutions—the church, the lyceum, or the speaker's platform at some ceremonial occasion." When he went out on his own as a lecturer, though, "Emerson for the first time found himself speaking to an audience whose only reason for coming was to hear *him* and whose only reason for staying was that they were interested in what they heard."[7] What this

5. See *New England,* Lecture III: "New England: Genius, Manners, and Customs," in this volume.

6. John McAleer, *Ralph Waldo Emerson: Days of Encounter* (Boston: Little, Brown, 1984), 487.

7. Barbara L. Packer, "The Transcendentalists," in *The Cambridge History of American Literature,* ed. Sacvan Bercovitch, 2 vols. (Cambridge: Cambridge University Press, 1995), 2:394.

meant, according to Stephen Railton, was that "henceforward he would meet his potential congregation as Ralph Waldo Emerson, not as a minister." Finding himself now viewed as a person and not as a type, standing without "a commissioned role, with no institutional authority to speak from, with neither Bible nor liturgy to refer to, he took it upon himself—his presence and his language—to work out the terms of a public identity. The people who filled the hall met only on the common ground that Emerson could supply in his text for the evening."[8] It is by looking at Emerson's platform performances, as described by his contemporaries, that we can better understand what Packer and Railton are describing.

Emerson's first biographer, George Willis Cooke, has left a general description of Emerson's lecturing habits that is worth quoting at length:

> On the lecture platform Emerson seems to be unconscious of his audience, is not disturbed by interruptions of any kind, by hisses, or by the departure of disappointed listeners. He always reads his lectures, though he is not always confined to his manuscript; while he often misplaces his sheets, and stumbles over the chirography. He usually begins in a slow and spiritless manner, in a low tone; and he is not fluent of speech, or passionate in manner. As he proceeds, he becomes earnest and magnetic; while the thrilling intensity of his voice deeply affects and rivets the attention of his audience. He is full of mannerisms in expression and in bodily attitude, seldom makes a gesture, and has little variation of voice. He secures the interest of his hearers by the simple grandeur of his thought, the inspiration of his moral genius, the conviction and manliness which his words express, and by the silvery enchantment of his voice. The glow of his face, the mobile expressiveness of his features, the charm of his smile, add to the interest created by his thought. It is the quality of his ideas, however, which attracts his hearers. His thought often rises to the heights of the purest eloquence. Such passages are sure to command the closest attention. It is the glowing faith and the moral intensity of the seer which gives them their power.[9]

Here we see the basic elements of Emerson's posture as a lecturer: he ignores the audience, he shuffles the pages of his manuscript, his voice is not impressive, and his physical gestures are negligible, yet the audience follows him with rapt attention and goes away inspired. What is happening here? How can Emerson be the subject of such comments as this one from the *Boston Post* in 1849?

> It is quite out of character to say Mr. Emerson lectures—he does no such thing. He drops nectar—he chips out sparks—he exhales odors—he lets off mental skyrockets and fireworks—he spouts fire, and conjurer-like, draws ribbons out of his

---

8. Railton, *Authorship and Audience*, 29.

9. George Willis Cooke, *Ralph Waldo Emerson: His Life, Writings, and Philosophy* (Boston: James R. Osgood, 1881), 258–59.

mouth. He smokes, he sparkles, he improvises, he shouts, he sings, he explodes like a bundle of crackers, he goes off in fiery eruptions like a volcano, but he does not *lecture*.[10]

Lecturing styles in the mid–nineteenth century were classical in origin, formal in practice, Latinate rather than Saxon in word choice, and long in delivery. Elocution, not ideas, was the standard of the day, and Emerson was always dubious of its value. The historical process by which American oratory was changed from neoclassical to popular models was timed perfectly for Emerson's own beliefs, for this was a man who wrote, "Ought not the scholar to convey his meaning in terms as short & strong as the truckman uses to convey his?"

> The language of the street is always strong. . . . I feel too the force of the double negative, though clean contrary to our grammar rules. And I confess to some pleasure from the stinging rhetoric of a rattling oath in the mouth of truckmen & teamsters. How laconic & brisk it is by the side of a page of the North American Review. Cut these words & they would bleed; they are vascular & alive; they walk & run. . . . It is a shower of bullets, whilst Cambridge men & Yale men correct themselves & begin again at every half sentence.[11]

Writing critically in 1828 about his brother Charles, who had just delivered the valedictory oration to his class at Harvard College, Emerson states that "the vice of [Charles's] oratory lies here—he is a *spectacle* instead of being an *engine;* a fine show at which we look, instead of an agent that moves us." By concentrating solely on the technical aspects of his presentation, Charles was like someone who has "chalked around him a circle on the floor & within that he exhibits these various excellences to all the curious." The result is, therefore, that instead of "feeling that his audience was an object of attention from him, he felt that he was an object of attention to the audience." This, Emerson notes, is "the reverse of what it should be. Instead of finding his audience . . . an angry master who is to be pacified, or a sturdy master who is to be cajoled,—&, in any case, one whose difficult regard is to be won,—he takes it for granted that he has the command." And in his final lesson drawn from the example of Charles's oratory, Emerson also criticizes one of the best-known orators of the day, Edward Everett: "Let him feel his situation. Let him remember that the true orator must not wrap himself in himself, but most wholly abandon himself to the sentiment he utters, & the multitude he address;—must become their property, to the end that *they may be-*

---

10. *Boston Post*, 25 January 1849, 2.

11. For the first quotation, see *TN*, 2:149, and for the second, dated June 1840, see *JMN*, 7:374. For more on the changes in American oratory during Emerson's time, see Kenneth Cmiel, *Democratic Eloquence: The Fight over Popular Speech in Nineteenth-Century America* (New York: William Morrow, 1990).

*come his*. Like Pericles, let him 'thunder & lighten.' Let him for a moment forget himself, & then, assuredly, he will not be forgotten."[12]

Contemporary accounts indicate that Emerson himself took the advice he had given to Charles. After all, it was natural for the man whose 1837 address on "The American Scholar" called for a truly American literature to also call for an indigenous American oratory. But this lack of flash and spectacle has led some scholars to ask why Emerson *was* successful; as one modern critic concludes in puzzlement, "He never altered his manner on the platform and as he relied on no gimmicks, physical or oratorical, his ability to captivate an audience remains somewhat mysterious."[13]

The accounts of Emerson as a lecturer that were published over the half-century span of his career parallel those judgments of his printed works set forth over the same period of time: he goes from being attacked as a radical whose writings have no discernible organizing principles to, in his middle and especially later years, a great American whose ideas and brilliancies transcend a style that is often difficult to follow. And just as the radical print Emerson became standardized in later years as his books went through numerous reprintings and showed up in leather-bound volumes in the best homes, the radical lecturer Emerson was tamed by audiences. The reformer Sallie Holley recalled an occasion when the "hall was crowded with the beauty and chivalry of Rochester. How queerly fashion regulates some things in the world! Here was a man of the most ultra radical views, a Garrisonian abolitionist, a Unitarian minister of the worst heretical stamp, a disunionist, a transcendentalist, etc., etc. Yet the very sanctity, piety, patriotism, and boasted conservatism were all present, dressed in their most good-humoured smiles!"[14] However, commentators on Emerson's articles and books could not see his writing process at work: they did not have access to the nearly thirty published volumes of letters, journals, and topical notebooks that modern scholars are able to consult. The audiences for Emerson's lectures, on the other hand, could gather firsthand evidence, in Emerson's appearance and delivery, as to how his work was being created in front of a future group of readers. In general, echoing Cooke's description, they note that Emerson did not make much of a physical impression; shuffled and searched his papers during his presentation; spoke in a discontinuous, even abrupt, fashion; and puzzled his audience by delivering lectures they did not consider to be logically organized.

Emerson's physical presence on the platform was unimposing. Many ac-

---

12. Emerson to Charles Chauncy Emerson, 15 July 1828, *Letters*, 1:238–40.

13. Alfred F. Rosa, "Emerson and the Salem Lyceum," *Essex Institute Historical Collections* 110 (April 1974): 77.

14. Letter of 10 February 1850, in *A Life for Liberty: Anti-Slavery and Other Letters of Sallie Holley*, ed. John White Chadwick (New York: Putnam's, 1899), 68.

counts note his plain, black (almost clerical) garb, often commenting on its old-fashioned cut or on how poorly it fit him. He possessed no flamboyant gestures, but he did demonstrate two oddities that audiences noticed. One was "the motion of the left hand at his side, as if the intensity of his thought were escaping, like the electricity of a battery at that point," or, as another person described it, he used the hand "with unconscious earnestness in driving imaginary stakes."[15] This was combined with a "rocking motion" that "originated in Emerson's unconscious habit of periodically lifting himself up on his toes, as a form of emphasis."[16] The elder Henry James was able to notice that this unprepossessing appearance had a purpose:

> His deferential entrance upon the scene, his look of inquiry at the desk and chair, his resolute rummaging among his embarrassed papers, the air of sudden recollection with which he would plunge into his pockets for what he must have known had never been put there, for his uncertainty and irresolution as he arose to speak, [became] his deep relieved inspiration as he got well from under the burning glass of his auditor's eyes, and addressed himself at length to their docile ears instead.[17]

Clearly, then, Emerson's lack of physical gestures and flourishes forced the audience to concentrate on his words, not his performance.

Numerous commentators noted how Emerson shuffled his manuscripts. This was in large part due to the way in which the lectures were written after the mid-1840s; in later years, it was due both to Emerson's declining eyesight and the gradual decline of his memory.[18] Although the pages of a few of his lecture manuscripts from the 1840s, 1850s, and 1860s are sewn together and appear reasonably neat and finished, the vast majority of lecture manuscripts from these decades consist of heavily emended unsewn leaves. With numerous revisions undertaken on pages worn thin by repeated use, with new prose added on relatively fresh pages of varying paper stocks interleaved among the worn pages, and with multiple sequences of page numbers, these manuscripts survive as concrete evidence that Emerson created lectures incrementally and by organizing them around discrete thoughts occasionally strung together with transitional prose.

Most auditors considered Emerson's shuffling through his manuscripts to be

---

15. *Cincinnati Daily Times,* 28 January 1857, quoted in Mead, *Yankee Eloquence in the Middle West,* 43; John Townsend Trowbridge, *My Own Story with Recollections of Noted Persons* (Boston: Houghton Mifflin, 1903), 348.

16. McAleer, *Ralph Waldo Emerson,* 492.

17. Henry James Sr., "Emerson," *Atlantic Monthly* 94 (December 1904): 741.

18. For details of Emerson's composition of lectures after the mid-1840s, see part 2 of this introduction. In his later years, Emerson was quite explicit in directions to his hosts on how he wished his platform lighted to accommodate his failing eyesight. For instance, he wrote to Samuel Longfellow, "my manuscript should be well lighted for my old eyes; for I sometimes find immoveable gas burners two or three feet from the desk." See Emerson to Samuel Longfellow, 28 January 1868(?), *Letters,* 9:303–4.

a fault: even old friends like Bronson Alcott commented on "his perilous passages from paragraph to paragraph of manuscript, [that] we have almost learned
to like."[19] Others were more astute and found a method to Emerson's apparent
confusion: "His peculiar manner of reading a few pages, and then shuffling his
papers, as though they were inextricably mixed, was embarrassing at first, but
when it was found that he was not disturbed by it, and that it was not the result
of an accident, but a characteristic manner of delivery, the audience withheld its
sympathy and rather enjoyed the novelty and the feeling of uncertainty as to what
would come next."[20]

The disorganization of and the constant searching through his manuscripts
exacerbated the problem many found with Emerson's delivery, that of speaking
in a discontinuous, even abrupt, fashion. Not everyone appreciated his "peculiar,
emphatic, abrupt, sharp, impressive and oracular" elocution, and few would
agree with John Jay Chapman that "in some of Emerson's more important lectures the logical scheme is more perfect than in his essays. . . . [I]n the process of
working up and perfecting his writings, in revising and filling his sentences, the
logical scheme became more and more obliterated."[21] The comments of a Marietta, Ohio, reporter in 1867 are more representative of the problems auditors had
with the organization of Emerson's lectures and his delivery of them: "the Lecturer could begin in the middle, and work forward or backward; or go to the
end first, and take his beginning last; or strike this paragraph or that one, this or
that sentence—go through or between, above or below—and the Lecture be as
complete in any case, even though the half were left out, or more patched on."[22]
Another midwestern reporter describes the problem in this fashion:

> Ralph Waldo Emerson's lecture on Eloquence reminded us of the way it is said
> vessels are built on the St. Lawrence—by the mile, and then cut off to suit orders.
> Mr. Emerson turns over about six sheets where he reads one, and it is of no conse-
> quence where his turning over stops; one place to splice on, or to leave off, is just as
> good as another. His lecture, called "On Eloquence," or by any other name, would
> pass as well, while, no doubt, from that cord of manuscript before him, he could ex-
> tract any required number of lectures, on any required subjects, just as a magician
> can draw all sorts of liquors, on demand, from the same bottle.[23]

19. A. Bronson Alcott, *Concord Days* (Boston: Roberts Brothers, 1872), 26.

20. A description of Emerson lecturing in 1871 by Charles A. Murdock in *A Backward Glance at
Eighty* (1921), quoted in William Hawley Davis, "Emerson the Lecturer in California," *California Historical Society Quarterly* 20 (March 1941): 4.

21. The first quotation is from the *Cincinnati Daily Times*, 28 January 1857, quoted in Mead, *Yankee
Eloquence in the Middle West*, 43; the second is from John Jay Chapman, "Emerson, Sixty Years After,"
*Atlantic Monthly* 79 (January 1897): 34.

22. *Marietta Register*, 21 March 1867, quoted in Mead, *Yankee Eloquence in the Middle West*, 57–58.

23. *Morning Cleveland Herald*, 5 December 1867, quoted in Mead, *Yankee Eloquence in the Middle
West*, 58.

Emerson's friend, the minister and Harvard Divinity School professor Convers Francis, had similar reservations:

> His style is too fragmentary and sententious. It wants the requisite words or phrases of connection and transition from one thought to another; but has unequalled precision and beauty in single sentences. This defect, and his habit of expressing a common truth in some uncommon (is it not sometimes slightly fantastic?) way of his own, are the reasons perhaps why it is so difficult to retain and carry away what he says. I find that his beautiful things are *slippery,* and will not stay in my mind.[24]

Even Emerson himself, in complaining about newspaper reports of his lectures, wrote that the "fault of the reporters is doubtless owing to the lecture itself which lacks any method, or any that is easily apprehensible."[25]

But others found his delivery, while initially problematic, finally to be crafted with a purpose. Abigail May (Mrs. Bronson) Alcott wrote after hearing Emerson lecture: "He is abrupt—disjointed fragmentary but you are arrested by a truth which like a cut diamond sparkles and radiates—you forget the rubbishy stuff which covered it in its normal state—the transition from Scenes of Misery to the Banquet of Beauty was too much—my brain reeled with it.—"[26] Oliver Wendell Holmes is less dramatic but equally favorable: commenting on how Emerson's slow delivery is the result of his careful choice of words, he praises "the delicate way [Emerson] steps about among the words of his vocabulary—if you have ever seen a cat picking her footsteps in wet weather, you have seen the picture of Emerson's exquisite intelligence, feeling for his phrase or epithet."[27]

Some commentators were able to appreciate Emerson's presentation as a whole. A reporter for the *Milwaukee Sentinel* noted that the

> style of the speaker is that which is frequently observed in great thinkers—a certain nervousness of expression, now rapid in motion, now impressively—almost painfully—slow; paying little or no regard to customary punctuation, grammatical or rhetorical; now carrying out a word with great care before he lets it fall, and now splintering them off with much greater rapidity; and in this being governed not at all by the importance of the words, but rather by the motions of his own thoughts.[28]

A Baltimore reporter complains that Emerson "goes fumbling through his manscript picking out a page here and there, and making an awkward pause till

---

24. Convers Francis, journal entry, 16 February 1837, quoted in Joel Myerson, "Convers Francis and Emerson," *American Literature* 30 (March 1978): 24.

25. Emerson to James Bradley Thayer, 16 December 1864, *Letters,* 5:394.

26. Abigail May Alcott, journal entry (January 1849), Houghton Library, Harvard University, *59M-311 (2), folder 4.

27. Quoted in Edward Waldo Emerson, *The Early Years of the Saturday Club 1855–1870* (Boston: Houghton Mifflin, 1918), 477.

28. *Milwaukee Sentinel,* 24 January 1865, quoted in Hubert H. Hoeltje, "Ralph Waldo Emerson in Minnesota," *Minnesota History* 11 (June 1930): 152.

he finds it," but as he does, then, when he "takes off his eye-glasses and extemporizes a sentence or two he has the air of a careful apothecary who is compounding a prescription behind a pair of delicate scales."[29]

Again, George Willis Cooke shows himself to be a perceptive observer of Emerson's lecturing style, when he describes what he considers to be the basis for Emerson's platform style:

> He hesitates for words, and seems to find it difficult to secure the precise expression he desires. He speaks on the lecture-platform much as he converses. . . . In his conversation, there is the same antithesis and abrupt transition to be found as in his books. He does not think continuously; he does not in conversation follow a subject through, but hesitates, skips intervening ideas, is unable, apparently, to hold his mind to all the links of thought. It is not natural for him to do so. He does not think logically, but intuitively, sees and seizes at a glance, in bold generalizations, but is unable to follow and arrange the intervening steps from premise to conclusion.[30]

What Cooke describes as Emerson's conversational style is something that has also been seen in his published works: a loose, apparently disorganized presentation that nevertheless invites the listener or reader to follow the author's own thought processes as he works toward his conclusions. Indeed, it was a style that Emerson quite self-consciously projected, as he himself admitted in 1870 while looking back at the success of his career as a lecturer and writer:

> The reason of a new philosophy or philosopher is ever that a man of thought finds he cannot read in the old books. I can't read Hegel, or Schelling, or find interest in what is told me from them, so I persist in my own idle & easy way, & write down my thoughts, & find presently that there are congenial persons who like them, so I persist, until some sort of outline or system grows. 'Tis the common course: Ever a new bias. It happened to each of these, Heraclitus, or Hegel, or whosoever.[31]

Emerson was a genius in creating a sense of spontaneity on the platform; James Russell Lowell claims to have seen "how artfully (for Emerson is a long-studied artist in these things) does the deliberate utterance, that seems to wait for the first word, seem to admit us partners in the labor of thought, and make us feel as if the glance of humor were a sudden suggestion; as if the perfect phrase lying written there on the desk were as unexpected to him as to us!"[32] Lowell described this effect more succinctly another time: "He somehow managed to combine the charm of unpremeditated discourse with the visible existence of carefully written

---

29. *Baltimore American*, 2 January 1872, quoted in *Mr. Emerson Lectures at the Peabody Institute* (Baltimore, Md.: Peabody Institute Library, 1949), 10–11.

30. Cooke, *Ralph Waldo Emerson*, 264.

31. *JMN*, 16:189.

32. James Russell Lowell, "Mr. Emerson's New Course of Lectures," *Nation*, 12 November 1868, 389–90.

manuscript lying before him on the desk." [33] By inviting his audience to join with him in the pursuit of ideas, Emerson became, as one reporter noted, "the personification of 'man thinking.' The angular gestures, the awkward poses, the shuffling pages—all these were forgotten the moment the audience felt that it was in the presence of ideas in process of creation. Here, fresh from the depths of a great mind, was thought taking form before one's very eyes." [34]

One reason for Emerson's spontaneity was that his lectures were nearly always in the process of becoming. He once wrote that he regretted staying with a friend while lecturing, "in spite of my almost uniform practice of choosing the hotel when I read lectures, for the reason that my lecture is never finished, but always needs a super-final attention." [35] Not only were the lectures constantly being written under deadline, they were rewritten throughout Emerson's career as well, for multiple deliveries, for wholesale revision and incorporation into other lectures, and as practice for what would become book chapters. Emerson's first stage of composition always occurred in his journals and notebooks, where he recorded everything from his waking thoughts, to texts copied from his voluminous readings, to passages translated from his favorite classical and modern writers, to snippets of correspondence received from select friends, to modest prose drafts that were either original with him or syntheses—"assimilations," to use his term—drawn out of one or more of the foregoing sources. Out of those entries, Emerson constructed lecture prose, virtually sentence by sentence. Throughout his career, the major portion of Emerson's actual lecture-writing time was devoted first to his creation of elaborate indices to journal and notebook sources on specific topics, and then to his adaptation of extant journal and notebook prose appropriate to the topics for use at the lectern. This was his version of process writing, and as his second stage of composition it yielded freestanding lectures on individual topics as well as lectures on related topics for series. Whether freestanding or parts of series, Emerson's lectures grew in length with repeated reading and became increasingly sharpened in thesis and scope with each successive delivery. They were then revised again, in much the same way, for publication.

Small wonder, then, that Emerson disliked having his lectures reported on by the newspapers. "These new lectures are rather studies than finished discourses," he wrote one newspaperman, "and I hope, one day, to complete, revise, & print them, or the substance of them." [36] "I am exceedingly vexed," he wrote

33. Quoted in Richard Garnett, *Life of Ralph Waldo Emerson* (London: Walter Scott, 1888), 170.

34. *Milwaukee Sentinel,* 24 January 1865, quoted in Hoeltje, "Ralph Waldo Emerson in Minnesota," 153.

35. Emerson to W. H. Furness, 10 February 1875, *Letters,* 10:153.

36. Emerson to Epes Sargent, 13 January 1849, *Letters,* 7:203.

the editor of the *Boston Commonwealth*, "by finding in your paper this morning, precisely such a report of one of my lectures, as I wrote to you a fortnight since to entreat you to defend me from." "My lectures are written to be read as lectures in different places," Emerson explains, "& then to be reported by myself. To-morrow, I was to have read this very lecture in Salem, & your reporter does all he can to kill the thing to every hearer, by putting him in the possession beforehand of the words of each statement that struck him, as nearly as he could copy them." Emerson does not want to be a censor, but he does wish to maintain his intellec-tual and financial property rights in his words: "Abuse me, & welcome, but do not transcribe me." [37] And to a third editor he complains, "This particular lec-ture was read in a most unfinished state[,] its statements all crude & not properly connected[,] some veiled sketches of private persons whose modesty would be painfully wounded could they be read in print." [38]

Some reporters agreed that they did Emerson a disservice by putting down the texts of his lectures in print. According to one, Emerson's lecture is "not to be re-ported—without his own language, his manner, his delivery it would be little—to essay to reproduce it, would be like carrying soda-water to a friend the morn-ing after it was drawn, and asking him how he relished it." [39] Even Franklin Benjamin Sanborn, a newspaperman and longtime acquaintance, confessed, "I have always thought the reports of Mr. Emerson's lectures most unsatisfactory, and I find my own no exception. The truth is, in listening one perceives a coher-ence of thought lying back of the isolated statements—like a vast encircling dome where lamps hang; in Mr. Emerson's presence one feels the great dim curve which surrounds all—but afterwards it is only the separate glancing lights one recalls." [40]

But Emerson had more than artistic reasons for not wanting to be reported. Put simply, if people could read his lectures for free, they would be less likely to pay to hear him in person. An important reason why Emerson wrote so many newspaper editors to forbear printing transcriptions of his lectures was to con-vince them all to agree to the practice; whenever one refused, responses such as this were typical:

Mr. Emerson delivered his lecture at Horticultural Hall yesterday in the very earnestly expressed "hope" that it might not be reported. Had there been a reason-able probability that this wish would command universal acquiescence from the

37. Emerson to Elizur Wright, 7 January 1852, *Letters*, 4:272–73.

38. Emerson to John Russell Young, 27 October 1868, *Letters*, 9:322.

39. *Cincinnati Daily Times*, 28 January 1857, quoted in Mead, *Yankee Eloquence in the Middle West*, 43.

40. [F. B. Sanborn], "Emerson at Horticultural Hall—The Problem of Reporting Him," *Springfield Daily Republican*, 10 April 1869, 2.

press, we should cheerfully have acceded to the request, at the cost of disappointing our own readers, and making our columns so far an incomplete record of the note-worthy public utterances of the day. But repeated experience has showed that the result of such appeals has been that while we, in common with other Boston papers, have respected the wishes of fastidious speakers, the press outside the city has utterly disregarded them, published such grossly imperfect reports as to deserve all the detestation which Mr. Emerson feels for them, and then sneered at the "lack of enterprise" of the local journals. We have therefore thought that we should best meet the spirit of the eminent philosopher's desire in the matter by making our report as faithful and accurate as possible, in the space at our disposal.[41]

In his later years, Emerson's lectures became harder to report because they used more and more quotations from other sources. Just as Emerson had earlier argued that we should "read for the lustres," now his lectures consisted more and more of personal "lustres," or individual aphorisms and quotations.[42] In writing to someone organizing a private class for him, Emerson comments, "I fancy that, like every old scholar, I have points of rest & emphasis in literature. I know what books I have found unforgettable, & what passages in books. It will be most agree-able to me to indicate such. I should like, in poetry, especially, to mark certain authors & certain passages which I prize, & to state on what grounds I prize them."[43] As usual, perhaps the best statement of Emerson's compositional de-sires and habits comes from him. In his introduction to "Genius and Tempera-ment," written especially for a delivery before a regular audience at Meionaon Hall, Boston, in 1861, he says:

> I cannot tell you with how much satisfaction I meet once more this company. In all other audiences, I have a painful sense of my deficiencies,—real enough, and everywhere to be deplored,—but forced on my own attention elsewhere by the necessity of meeting the expectation and general average of an assembly to whom I am partially known. But here I have no such embarrassment. The company,—sub-stantially the same persons for so many years,—know what to look for and what to pardon, when they come to the class, and do not demand of me,—what they might of another,—a more formal and precise external method,—but are content that I should use my own, knowing that I value a thought or a scientific law, for itself, without insisting that it should stand in a syllogism. They know that a scholar loves any piece of truth better than the most coherent system, because he well knows that every truth is one face of the world.

Still, Emerson knows that he has been asked to appear for a purpose, and though in "the best company, good sense is taken for granted, and we are contented not

41. *Boston Daily Advertiser,* 13 March 1871, 2.
42. "Nominalist and Realist," in *Essays: Second Series, CW,* 3:137.
43. Emerson to James Bradley Thayer, 22 November 1868, *Letters,* 6:43.

to shine," he recognizes that, of course, "I wish to justify the inviting of a class, by offering you thoughts and facts which may have struck my own mind with force in the late months; but I shall think I pay my audience a just compliment if I state them carelessly and incidentally, so only that I state them, as knowing that they will detect fast enough what is important, without too much pains to give it perspective." [44]

Audiences who saw blandness and disorganization in Emerson's platform style left disappointed; those who saw originality and subtle interconnectedness went away inspired, including Henry Clay Folger, who heard Emerson lecture on Shakespeare and then devoted his life to putting together the greatest collection of Shakespeariana in the world, now housed in the library bearing his name in Washington, D.C. Emerson's success as a lecturer was due in part to a major reason why he is still a popular author today: both auditors and readers find in Emerson's works resonances of their own ideas and beliefs. As a preacher and as a lecturer during the 1830s and 1840s at the height of criticism of his religious views, Emerson could appear to the conservatives in his audience as a dangerous radical and to the liberals as a sweet voice of reason—and this would be at the same sermon or lecture. [45]

Modern scholarship has provided us with various means with which to evaluate Emerson's effect upon his audiences, and it comes to pretty much the same conclusions as did his contemporaries. Writers employing reader-response criticism, for example, argue that Emerson's lectures gained meaning not so much through his own intentions as through what his audiences made of them. Writing about Emerson's western New York lectures, Sallee Fox Engstrom suggests "that the text, delivery, and reputation of Emerson as lecturer were dialogic in nature, so that his known views supporting individualism, anti-traditionalism, and, most recently, social reform combined with his presence here to create a symbiotic relationship with audiences in this place at this time." The philosophy of Emerson's message brought "something elevating" into the lives of his audience that "they were eager to hear, something that matched the fervor of individualism already present in the reforming spirit of these communities, even if they did not fully comprehend what they were hearing." [46] Others heard in Emerson's calls for self-reliance and individualism just the opposite: a justifi-

44. See *Life and Literature*, Lecture I: "Genius and Temperament," in volume 2.

45. For more on how auditors and readers saw different versions of Emerson in the same text, see Sarah Ann Wider, *Anna Tilden· Unitarian Culture and the Problem of Self-Representation* (Athens: University of Georgia Press, 1997), and *Emerson and Thoreau: The Contemporary Reviews*, ed. Joel Myerson (New York: Cambridge University Press, 1992).

46. Sallee Fox Engstrom, *The Infinitude of the Private Man: Emerson's Presence in Western New York, 1851–1861* (New York: Peter Lang, 1997), 3, 86–87.

cation for growing capitalism as the century progressed. As Mary Kupiec Cayton notes, the basis for Emerson's lectures was "the radically idealist cosmology sketched out in *Nature* and further elaborated in the spoken and published lectures of the early period," and whatever language or analogies he employed to reach his audience, he saw himself as preaching "a message of moral reform whose warrant was a unique spiritual understanding of nature and nature's laws." However, his audience often "heard the warrant to be a set of already familiar, pragmatic, common-sense rules for attaining individual financial and social success. The Emerson whose anecdotes and aphorisms are understood but whose larger method is not becomes the epitome of the commercial values prized by the audiences who invited him."[47]

Those contemporaries who truly appreciated Emerson's appearance as a lecturer would have agreed with this description by John Jay Chapman that, we believe, succinctly states the reasons for Emerson's genius and his appeal:

> It was the platform which determined Emerson's style. He was not a writer, but a speaker. On the platform his manner of speech was a living part of his words. The pauses and hesitation, the abstraction, the searching, the balancing, the turning forward and back of the leaves of his lecture, and then the discovery, the illumination, the gleam of lightning which you saw before your eyes descend into a man of genius—all this was Emerson. He invented this style of speaking.[48]

And, we might add, he helped to invent this style of reading, for just as Emerson's lectures urged audiences to participate intellectually in his oral discussions, so too do his writings invite us to interact with the development and bases of the ideas and thoughts found there. Emerson the lecturer, then, is not only worthy of study himself but also serves as the midwife to Emerson the essayist.

## 2. THE TEXTS OF EMERSON'S LATER LECTURES

This edition of *The Later Lectures of Ralph Waldo Emerson* begins where the three volumes of *The Early Lectures of Ralph Waldo Emerson*, edited by Stephen E. Whicher, Robert E. Spiller, and Wallace E. Williams, ended in 1972. Although collected as his "later" lectures, in effect the two volumes of this edition present

---

47. Mary Kupiec Cayton, "The Making of an American Prophet: Emerson, His Audiences, and the Rise of the Culture Industry in Nineteenth-Century America," *American Historical Review* 92 (June 1987): 614; for how Emersonian ideas have been misappropriated, see Howard Horwitz, "The Standard Oil Trust as Emersonian Hero," *Raritan* 6, no. 4 (Spring 1987): 97–119, expanded in his *By the Law of Nature: Form and Value in Nineteenth-Century America* (New York: Oxford University Press, 1991), 171–91.

48. Chapman, "Emerson, Sixty Years After," 36.

the clear texts of forty-eight complete lectures that Emerson wrote and delivered over the middle and later years of his career.[49] The copy-texts for all lectures printed in this edition are the manuscripts deposited in the Houghton Library of Harvard University by the Ralph Waldo Emerson Memorial Association.

The distinction between Emerson's middle and later years is important to make at the outset. Some readers of Emerson, especially those who favor the position advanced by Stephen E. Whicher in *Freedom and Fate: An Inner Life of Ralph Waldo Emerson* (1953), a study that dominated Emerson criticism in the second half of the twentieth century, may wish to see Emerson's intellectual life as dividing more or less neatly only between his early, idealistic years, represented by the appearance of *Nature* (1836), "The American Scholar" (1837), "The Divinity School Address" (1838), and *Essays: First Series* (1841) and *Essays: Second Series* (1844), and his later, progressively naturalistic or skeptical years, represented by *Representative Men* (1850), *English Traits* (1856), *The Conduct of Life* (1860), and *Society and Solitude* (1870).[50] Other readers are increasingly arguing for a chronology that coincides with ours, although they may break Emerson's life into segments a few years on either side of the dates we follow in the division of these volumes. These readers, whose position we share, acknowledge shifts in Emerson's intellectual views not only from the mid-1840s to the 1870s but also from the beginning of his public career as a schoolmaster and minister in the 1820s and early 1830s through his dramatic rise as a public figure in Boston, Cambridge, and Concord in the late 1830s and early 1840s. These readers see the shifts in Emerson's intellectual views as sometimes subtle, sometimes quite strong, and they attribute them variously to the circumstances of his personal life such as his loss by death of family members and close friends, to the disruption of the delicate balance revealed in Emerson's sermons and later philosophic lectures and writings between the rational and antirational sides of his nature, and to the persistence of cultural materialism as well as social conditions

49. Throughout this introduction, we refer to this edition as printing clear texts of forty-eight of Emerson's later lectures. In actuality, as explained below, in these volumes we print forty-nine lectures in clear text, of which one lacks concrete evidence of having been delivered. Also, in the electronic textual notes we have prepared for this edition, we print in genetic text four additional lectures from which Emerson read and one complete predelivery draft of a lecture from which Emerson did not read.

50. Stephen E. Whicher, *Freedom and Fate: An Inner Life of Ralph Waldo Emerson* (Philadelphia: University of Pennsylvania Press, 1953). Whicher's thesis undoubtedly informed his approach to the editing of Emerson's *Early Lectures*, and it may have influenced the approaches of his coeditors, especially Wallace Williams, as well. With little modification, Williams carried Whicher's thesis forward into the 1980s in his "Historical Introduction" to the Harvard edition of Emerson's *Representative Men* (*CW*, 4:xi–lxv). Major studies that have subscribed to Whicher's thesis include Philip L. Nicoloff's *Emerson on Race and History: An Examination of "English Traits"* (New York: Columbia University Press, 1961), and John Michael's *Emerson and Skepticism: The Cipher of the World* (Baltimore, Md.: Johns Hopkins University Press, 1988).

such as slavery in American society, all of which result in Emerson's having had to reassess the justice of his early, idealistic views throughout his life. But on the whole, these readers reject claims of Emerson's descent into complete naturalism or skepticism after the mid-1840s, viewing, instead, Emerson's life as his own version of "the scholar": the person who stands by his order—intellectual, social, or otherwise—while constantly, in his early or middle years or in his later life, re-examining the terms of his character and the moral ground of his own and his contemporaries' conduct.[51] Admittedly, these shifts, with their corresponding moments of intellectual reassessment on Emerson's part, will be seen across the 1854/1855 line that temporally divides the volumes of the present edition; however, all readers will also find in the lectures collected here as compelling a body of evidence for seeing Emerson as an idealist throughout his career as some readers have found in the decline of Emerson's idealism seemingly signaled by the ending of the *Early Lectures* in 1842.

In the first part of our introduction, we drew principally on evidence supplied by Emerson's contemporaries, by later scholars and readers of Emerson, and, of course, by Emerson himself to discuss the importance of lecturing as the crucial middle stage of his creative compositional and intellectual processes. Throughout his career, the speaker's platform served as Emerson's principal means to fashion, test, and clarify or emend as appropriate his evolving ideas, prose, and public personae. In this part of our introduction, we describe the textual rationale governing our selection, editing, and presentation of Emerson's later lectures. As with Emerson's ideas, prose, and public personae, our rationale has been the subject of considerable evolution, for while at the outset we happily acknowledge our debt to the high standard of practice followed by the editors of Emerson's *Early Lectures* and *Complete Sermons* in the presentation of their respective texts, we must state that we have had to deal with texts far more fluid in their evolution and unstable in their preserved manuscript state than the texts collected in either of those editions. Owing to Emerson's compositional practices and the multiple uses he and his literary executors, James Elliot Cabot and Ed-

---

51. For recent studies that take this view of Emerson, see Evelyn Barish, *Emerson: The Roots of Prophecy* (Princeton, N.J.: Princeton University Press, 1989); Len Gougeon, *Virtue's Hero: Emerson, Antislavery, and Reform* (Athens: University of Georgia Press, 1990); McAleer, *Ralph Waldo Emerson;* Richardson, *Emerson: The Mind on Fire;* David M. Robinson, *Emerson and the Conduct of Life: Pragmatism and Ethical Purpose in the Later Work* (Cambridge: Cambridge University Press, 1993); and Merton M. Sealts Jr., *Emerson on the Scholar* (Columbia: University of Missouri Press, 1992). See also Albert J. von Frank, "'Build Therefore Your Own World': Emerson's Constructions of the 'Intimate Sphere,'" Lawrence Buell, "Emerson's Fate," and Ronald A. Bosco, "The 'Somewhat Spheral and Infinite' in Every Man: Emerson's Theory of Biography," in *Emersonian Circles: Essays in Honor of Joel Myerson,* ed. Wesley T. Mott and Robert E. Burkholder (Rochester, N.Y.: University of Rochester Press, 1997), 1–10, 11–28, and 67–103, respectively; Emerson's *Antislavery Writings;* and Emerson's *University Lectures.*

ward Waldo Emerson, exacted of our manuscript sources, we have not been able
to adopt completely the editorial rationale of either the *Early Lectures* or the *Complete Sermons* to our work. Instead, we have had to develop an editorial rationale
that begins with theirs but is flexible enough to accommodate our printing of
what is arguably the most textually complex (if not actually tortured) body of
Emerson manuscript sources.

IN THEIR RESPECTIVE statements of editorial policy, the editors of Emerson's
*Early Lectures* and *Complete Sermons* outline the series of steps they followed in
their selection, editing, and presentation of Emerson's texts. Working with copy-
texts that are very stable and fixed in time of presentation inasmuch as they are
virtually all complete and sewn together, the editors of those volumes reasonably
subscribe to the position that Emerson's unit of composition at this early point
in his career is the work as a whole and not the sentence or incomplete paragraph as some readers of Emerson have supposed, although they also acknowledge the presence of Emerson's rushed working outlines of lectures and sermons
in his journals and notebooks and, occasionally, in the copy-texts of the lectures
and sermons themselves. Both sets of editors began their respective editorial
process with their preparation of a genetic text of copy-text, that is, with their
preparation of a text that shows all authorial alterations in the manuscript—all
authorial insertions, cancellations, variants, and transpositions, usually represented by and enclosed within a uniform set of editorial symbols. Then, from
their genetic text, the editors prepared a clear text of each lecture or sermon
intended to restore it to the earliest state of delivery, relegating all authorial
emendation of copy-text to textual notes that accompany each clear text and
distinguishing in their textual introductions between editorial emendations of
the copy-text that are reported in textual notes and those that are "silent."

In both cases, the editors' preference for clear text rather than genetic text in
their presentation of Emerson's writings is completely consistent with modern
editorial practices. These practices treat an author's published works, as well as
in this case his lectures or sermons, as public performances and documents. Indeed, readers of modern editions of Emerson's writings have long been accustomed to the distinction editors have drawn between Emerson's "private" and
"public" texts. In approaching the editions of Emerson's *Journals and Miscellaneous Notebooks* (*JMN*), *Poetry Notebooks*, or *Topical Notebooks* (*TN*), for instance, readers are predisposed to regard Emerson's texts as personal and private
and to read them for, among other things, what their genetic texts disclose of
his compositional and intellectual processes.[52] On the other hand, readers of

52. *The Poetry Notebooks of Ralph Waldo Emerson*, ed. Ralph H. Orth, Albert J. von Frank, Linda
Allardt, and David W. Hill (Columbia: University of Missouri Press, 1986).

Emerson's *Early Lectures* and *Complete Sermons* are conditioned to see Emerson's delivery of a sermon from the pulpit or of a lecture from the speaker's platform as analogous to, if not identical with, public presentation through publication.[53]

Whereas the editors of Emerson's *Early Lectures* and *Complete Sermons* could advance and adhere to the editorial policies just described throughout their editions, the condition of the manuscripts with which we have been working and the attitude toward them exhibited by Emerson and his literary executors have forced us to modify the editorial policies of our predecessors. As we describe their condition in the first part of our introduction, the manuscripts of Emerson's lectures from 1843 through the 1870s exhibit compositional and organizational characteristics that set these later writings completely apart from his early lectures and sermons. While the pages of a few of Emerson's later lecture manuscripts are sewn together, the vast majority consist of heavily emended leaves that were never sewn together. Emerson undertook numerous revisions on many leaves that are worn thin by his repeated use of them in the individual lecture manuscript with which they are gathered today or by his shuffling of them between lecture manuscripts. At the same time, there is ample evidence throughout the later lecture manuscripts of Emerson's having interleaved relatively fresh pages of prose among his worn pages over successive deliveries of a lecture and, as his multiple pagination sequences inscribed in various locations on each recto suggest, of his having moved text around both within individual lectures and between individual lectures as a way to test his own sense of the cogency of and the public's reception to those ideas he set in prose.

---

53. For their respective statements of editorial policy, see the editors' textual introductions in *Early Lectures,* 1 : xxii–xxvii, 2 : xv–xx, and 3 : xvii–xxiv, and *Complete Sermons,* 1 : 33–39. While the editors of the *Complete Sermons* enunciate and follow a clear statement of policy from the outset of their four-volume edition, the editors of the *Early Lectures* subject their policy to subtle revision with the appearance of each of their three volumes. Possessing manuscript copy-texts that are sewn together and almost all complete, both sets of editors construct a policy that accommodates occasional fragmentary texts in their volumes, and they agree completely on what constituted Emerson's basic unit of composition during this early stage of his career and on how Emerson's texts ought to appear in print—as clear texts. However, as we notice later in our textual introduction, either because of the progressively difficult condition of the manuscripts with which they were working or because of the framework Professors Whicher and Williams imposed on Emerson's intellectual life, the editors of the *Early Lectures* moved their proposed end date for their volumes five years back (from 1847 to 1842) between the appearance of volume 1 and their preparation of volume 3. The editors of the *Early Lectures* are never explicit about the reasons for their change of end dates, nor, except in scholarly writings apart from their introductions to and presentation of texts in the *Early Lectures,* are they ever completely forthcoming about the critical biases respecting Emerson's intellectual life that undoubtedly informed their reading and preparation of his lecture texts (see note 50).

For a fully developed rationale for the presentation of Emerson's public texts such as his sermons and lectures in clear text accompanied by textual notes that represent the condition of manuscript copy-text, see Albert J. von Frank, "Genetic versus Clear Texts: Reading and Writing Emerson," *Documentary Editing* 9 (December 1987): 5–9.

Put simply, the principal differences between Emerson's later lecture manuscripts and the manuscripts of his sermons and early lectures are, first, their physical representation of a major shift in his compositional practices during and after the mid-1840s and, second, their representation of Emerson's wholesale adaptation and readaptation of text within and outside of his deliveries of an individual lecture. These manuscripts make clear that, after the mid-1840s, Emerson's unit of composition became the sentence and the paragraph as inscribed on the individual manuscript page and occasional bifolio leaf, not the work as a whole; that he created lectures incrementally and organized them around discrete thoughts sometimes, but not always, strung together with transitional prose; and that he viewed units of prose as completely fluid and available to perform service in various places within a given lecture, outside of a given lecture in other lectures in which he developed topics that invited his appropriation of already used text, or in text that was slowly making its way toward finished prose ready for print.

Thus, the condition in which our manuscript copy-texts survive has forced upon us the need to modify significantly the editorial practices of the editors of Emerson's early lectures and sermons to suit the state in which our sources are preserved. We, like they, began with genetic texts of those complete lecture manuscripts that we found, but as the following account should make clear, the fluidity of our sources has made us think of our genetic texts and the clear texts of Emerson's lectures that we have drawn from them in quite different terms. At the same time, whereas the editors of Emerson's early lectures and sermons could advertise their work as relatively complete and comprehensive (the recent edition of the sermons is, after all, entitled *The Complete Sermons of Ralph Waldo Emerson*), the degree of completeness and inclusion represented in this edition of Emerson's later lectures requires some explanation. For while the starting point of this edition is self-explanatory (we begin, once again, in the year following the last lecture printed in the *Early Lectures*), our end date of 1871 and our inclusion of a relatively small number of lectures given the extent of Emerson's lecture engagements in America and abroad between 1843 and 1871 may, on the surface, seem arbitrary—and especially so since Emerson's career as a lecturer extended well into the 1870s. However, our end date and our decision to include only forty-eight lectures in these volumes follow responsible editorial judgment and common sense. Indeed, by ending in 1871 we acknowledge two important facts, each of which our extensive and repeated surveys of all available later lecture manuscript sources have borne out.

First, the years between 1843 and, roughly, the mid-1850s account for the period when Emerson achieved maturity and visibility as a lecturer and a writer, although lack of access to his lectures of this period has thus far prevented scholars from performing detailed analyses of the lectures themselves and from treating their relation to and influence on other aspects of Emerson's career and writings. Here, as the editors of the *Early Lectures* suggest in a statement closing the third volume of their edition, the lectern served as Emerson's site for the stylistic innovation and experimentation that enabled him to shed the hortatory pulpit eloquence characteristic of his sermons and many of his early lectures (as well as his early essays) and to project a new style based in part on what he thought of as a less formal relationship with his audience and in part on his increasing reliance on lectures as occasions to test literarily and intellectually material he might wish later to develop and refine as essays.[54] Particularly in the 1840s and 1850s, his "new style," Emerson found, was equally suited to literary and biographical lectures, lectures on the history of philosophy, and lectures on what he progressively called the "Natural History of the Intellect," to lectures in which he elaborated on the differences between English or Continental and American life or in which he celebrated his native New England as the cradle of American culture, and to lectures in which he drew from his personal observation of social and political events near and far in order to provide candid commentary on, for instance, temperance, American slavery, the women's rights movement, and the central role of the scholar in effecting social action and change in America. Among the most tangible validations Emerson received for his new style were ever appreciative and eager audiences and repeated invitations to lecture in large American cities (in New York, Providence, Philadelphia, Cincinnati, Chicago, Washington, and, of course, Boston) and in England. It is certainly during this period that Emerson achieved status as a household name throughout America as well as broad respect in literary and intellectual circles abroad, and his successes as a lecturer and writer at this time established the conditions for his popularity and presence at the lectern as an authoritative commentator on philosophy and American culture, broadly construed, for the remainder of his productive life.

Second, while virtually all extant lecture manuscripts after the mid-1850s were mined, some in their entirety, for essays that Emerson or his literary executors, Cabot and Edward Waldo Emerson, subsequently published, many lectures survive not only in their entirety but also, and more important for our purpose, without having been mined in this fashion.[55] The suspicion long circulating in Emerson editing circles has been that it would be impossible to reconstruct Emerson's lectures in any complete or responsible fashion from the point where the *Early Lectures* ended. For three decades, Emersonians have routinely re-

---

54. *Early Lectures*, 3:342–45.

55. For the respective roles played in the mining of Emerson's lecture manuscripts by Cabot and Edward Waldo Emerson, see Emerson's *University Lectures* and Simmons, "Arranging the Sibylline Leaves."

inforced this suspicion, first by pointing to the failure of the editors of the *Early Lectures* to prepare the balance of Emerson's lectures for publication and then, more recently, by negative reports respecting their condition and completeness by some scholars who, for the purpose of intellectual biography or of critical study, have looked into the manuscripts of Emerson's lectures from the early 1840s through the end of his lecturing career in the 1870s.[56] Yet our systematic surveys of lecture manuscripts from the early 1840s through the 1870s disclosed that a considerable body of lectures from the mid- to late 1840s, from throughout the 1850s, and from the 1860s (included among which are several lectures that continued to serve Emerson into the 1870s) could be responsibly edited, whereas the concerns so often cited by others really do not present insurmountable editorial problems until the late 1860s and 1870s.[57]

In addition to the lectures comprising Emerson's introduction and biographical essays in *Representative Men* that were incorporated into the copy-text for that volume as published in Harvard's *Collected Works* series in 1987, a number of lectures from the 1850s that are accounted for by the editors of *English Traits* published in the same series in 1994, and several lectures that served as printer's copy for Emerson's publication of them as essays before he revised them for inclusion in *The Conduct of Life, Society and Solitude,* and *Letters and Social Aims* (1876)—all of which the editors of those forthcoming volumes in the Harvard series will have to inspect and account for as pre-copy-text sources—there is a substantial body of lectures that Emerson first delivered between 1843 and 1867 and, in some instances, revised for delivery into the 1870s that are complete and exist only in manuscript. The forty-eight lectures printed in these volumes

56. Following their survey of all manuscripts collected in the Houghton Library, the editors of the *Early Lectures* provide this assessment of the state of Emerson's lecture manuscripts: "Those of 1833–1839 offer no serious obstacle to publication; those of 1840–1847 are discouraging, but still offer some reward to the reader; only after 1847 does the restoration of a single text become almost impossible." Of their decision—apparently an *initial* decision to end their volumes in 1847—they state: "There is justification [only] for a printed text of the early lectures, even though such an edition must stop at an arbitrary point at which rewards are no longer commensurate with editorial effort" (*Early Lectures,* 1:xiv). While not directly acknowledging the point, by ending their third volume in 1842, not in 1847, the editors of the *Early Lectures* effectively confessed their overly pessimistic view of how far their editorial rationale and the state of Emerson scholarship at the time could carry them toward the ideal conclusion of Emerson's "earlier' lectures. In the years between 1972 and his death in 1990, Wallace E. Williams, an editor of the *Early Lectures,* repeatedly expressed confidence that, by following an editorial rationale more liberal than that to which the editors of the *Early Lectures* subscribed and by tracing the evolution of Emerson's lectures in newspaper accounts of their various deliveries (the last is a view we reject), a partial collection of Emerson's "later" lectures could indeed be edited.

57. Our inspection of all available manuscript sources of Emerson's later lectures puts us in a position to lend authority to the statements or speculations of those who argue that his creative powers go into steep and irreversible decline after 1871. At this point in Emerson's life, an entry he casually made in his journal for 1866 comes to personal fruition: "I find it a great & fatal difference whether I court the

come from this body of unpublished manuscripts. Because in our estimation no responsible purpose would be served by our publishing materials already fully accessible in print, we do not include lectures that Emerson printed wholesale or without substantive revision from their lecture state as essays in *Representative Men, English Traits, The Conduct of Life, Society and Solitude,* and *Letters and Social Aims.*

For the record, following our survey of all available manuscript lecture sources, it is also our conclusion that the state of lecture manuscripts following 1871 that we inspected does, indeed, make impossible the preparation and publication of Emerson's lectures after that date in any coherent and responsible fashion. Not only have all the manuscripts been previously mined for publication, but also all the manuscripts are variously incomplete and either disorganized or pieced together (again, by Emerson and/or his executors) to an extent that defies their reconstruction. It is clear to us that the suspicion among Emersonians noted above respecting the condition and use of Emerson's later lecture manuscripts is right on the mark, especially with texts from after 1871, but it is also evident to us that the originals of many once-complete lectures from the 1860s and from 1870 and 1871 are irretrievably lost. These include the six lectures that Emerson delivered in his *Philosophy for the People* series in Boston between 14 April and 19 May 1866, the sixteen lectures that he delivered in his *Natural History of the Intellect* series at Harvard between 26 April and 2 June 1870, and the seventeen lectures that he delivered in a reprise of the series at Harvard between 14 February and 7 April 1871.[58] To be sure, all of these materials

---

Muse, or the Muse courts me: That is the ugly disparity between age & youth" (*JMN*, 16:25). While Emerson continued to lecture and engage audiences in private "conversations" on literature or philosophy after 1871, he no longer was able to draft new lecture prose; instead, in delivering lectures and engaging audiences in "conversations," he read from lecture manuscripts from which he had read before, and these lectures or "conversations," as a number of our headnotes to lectures printed in this edition indicate, were all carefully orchestrated by his daughter Ellen. Apart from age (he was approaching his seventies, an advanced age for a person in the nineteenth century), at least these four other experiences forced Emerson to concede "the ugly disparity between youth and age" at this time: (1) his failure, as Notebook PH ("Philosophy") clearly shows, to develop new prose for lectures out of his notebooks or journals; (2) his perception of having given a dismal and personally humiliating performance in the University Lecture series at Harvard in 1870 and 1871; (3) his difficulty in rebounding mentally or physically from witnessing his house in Concord partially destroyed by fire in 1872; and (4) his inability to complete either *Parnassus* (1875), an edition of poems and poetic excerpts that over some fifty years he drew from the writings of others, without the assistance of his daughter Edith Emerson Forbes, or *Letters and Social Aims* (1876) without the assistance of James Elliot Cabot and Ellen Emerson. For details, see Ronald A. Bosco, "'Poetry for the World of Readers' and 'Poetry for Bards Proper': Poetic Theory and Textual Integrity in Emerson's *Parnassus*," in *Studies in the American Renaissance 1989*, ed. Joel Myerson (Charlottesville: University Press of Virginia, 1989), 257–312; Emerson's *University Lectures;* and Simmons, "Arranging the Sibylline Leaves." For Emerson's Notebook PH, see *TN*, 2:330–84.

58. For details of Emerson's, Cabot's, and Edward Waldo Emerson's mining of the *Philosophy for the People* and *Natural History of the Intellect* lectures, see Emerson's *University Lectures.*

will have to be accounted for by the editors of later volumes in Harvard's *Collected Works* (*CW*). They will find in the shards we surveyed occasional paragraphs and large portions of essays Emerson included in *Society and Solitude* and in *Letters and Social Aims*, which was itself really a collaborative effort among Emerson, his daughter Ellen, and Cabot; they will also find there remnants of sources for essays that Emerson's executors composed and included in the three miscellanies volumes that conclude the 1903–4 *Complete Works of Ralph Waldo Emerson* edited by Edward Waldo Emerson, including several essays they created out of the manuscripts of Emerson's *Philosophy for the People* and *Natural History of the Intellect* series. And, finally, they will find scattered in Emerson's post-1855 lecture manuscripts periodic notes by Edward to indicate his taking of anywhere from ten to fifty sheets of unspecified lecture manuscript material for a variety of not altogether clear purposes. The sheets that Edward borrowed apparently no longer survive, although we do know that he used and dispersed some of them in the so-called Autograph Centenary Edition of his father's writings (1903–4). We would note here that we are not editing any lectures for which we have concrete evidence of Edward's (or anyone else's) removal of numerous manuscript sheets from our source(s).

THE FOREGOING IS necessary background to what we consider to be the three hallmark features of the editorial rationale governing our selection, editing, and presentation of Emerson's later lectures in these volumes. First, we have selected only complete and on the whole unpublished lectures for inclusion in this edition. Second, we have edited only texts that survive entirely in Emerson's hand, rejecting without notice, as explained below, all emendations in the copy-text by Cabot, Ellen Emerson, and Edward Waldo Emerson. Third, and in perhaps our most significant departure from the practices of the editors of Emerson's *Early Lectures* and *Complete Sermons*, of necessity we have treated each lecture as Emerson's "work in progress."

While in theory we, like the editors of the *Early Lectures* and the *Complete Sermons* who presented texts that were conceived and executed by Emerson as a whole, might have reason to assume that in presenting the text of a lecture that Emerson delivered only once we are close to or are exactly representing the state of the lecture's earliest delivery, in practice, given Emerson's and his executors' extraordinarily casual, almost cavalier arrangement of the loose pages of his texts, we cannot with certainty make such a claim even for those lectures he delivered only once. The situation is exacerbated for those lectures that Emerson delivered on multiple occasions, and especially so for those he delivered over periods of time that extend from a few months, to a few years, to a decade. Consequently, our practice throughout these volumes has been to assume that we are editing the latest version of Emerson's delivery of a lecture, and we have treated our copy-texts accordingly. Unless we are in the possession of evidence internal to the manuscript that leads us to assume otherwise (we always note these instances when we introduce a lecture), we have consistently prepared clear texts as our copy-text indicates they were last delivered by Emerson.

THUS, BEGINNING IN 1843, the year after the final lecture printed in the *Early Lectures,* and continuing through 1854, volume 1 contains twenty-one complete and on the whole unpublished lectures drawn from manuscript copy-texts, each of which (unless otherwise specified in our introductory headnote) is also Emerson's latest surviving version of a particular lecture. Of these, ten lectures were primarily associated with three lecture series that Emerson delivered during this period: *New England* ("The Genius and National Character of the Anglo-Saxon Race," "The Trade of New England," "New England: Genius, Manners, and Customs," and "New England: Recent Literary and Spiritual Influences"), *Mind and Manners of the Nineteenth Century* ("The Powers and Laws of Thought," "The Relation of Intellect to Natural Science," and "The Tendencies and Duties of Men of Thought"), and *Conduct of Life* ("Wealth," "Economy," and "Fate"). One lecture, "England," which Emerson eventually incorporated into his *Conduct of Life* series, performed far greater service as an independent lecture than as a part of that series; consequently, it has been treated as an independent lecture in this edition. Two lectures were academic addresses ("Discourse Read Before the Philomathesian Society of Middlebury College in Vermont" and "An Address to the Adelphic Union of Williamstown College"), two lectures were antislavery addresses ("Address to the Citizens of Concord on the Fugitive Slave Law" and "Seventh of March Speech on the Fugitive Slave Law"), one lecture was delivered as a temperance discourse ("Address to the Temperance Society at Harvard, Massachusetts"), and the remaining five lectures ("The Spirit of the Times," "London," "The Anglo-American," "Poetry and English Poetry," and "France, or Urbanity") were variously delivered as independent lectures or as lectures gathered among others in one or more series of lectures on unconnected topics.

Beginning in 1855 and continuing through the effective close of Emerson's active career in preparing (as opposed to delivering) lectures in 1871, volume 2 contains twenty-seven complete and on the whole unpublished lectures drawn from manuscript copy-texts, each of which unless otherwise specified in our introductory headnote is also Emerson's latest surviving version of the lecture. Of these, eight lectures were primarily associated with two lecture series that Emerson delivered during this period: *Natural Method of Mental Philosophy* ("Country Life," "Powers of the Mind," "The Natural Method of Mental Philosophy," "Memory," and "Self-Possession") and *Life and Literature* ("Genius and Temperament," "Art," and "Some Good Books"). Two lectures, "Resources" and "Table Talk," which Emerson initially presented in his *American Life* series in the mid-1860s, performed considerable service as independent lectures apart from that series; consequently, they have been treated as independent lectures in this edition. Nine lectures dealing variously with character, moral philosophy, and religion in the context of social conditions in America in the late 1850s and early 1860s are also included in volume 2. Emerson prepared six ("Moral Sense," "Reform," "Natural Religion," "Truth," "Essential Principles of Religion," and "Moral Forces") of these nine lectures for delivery on Sundays before Theodore Parker's Twenty-Eighth Congregational Society at the Music Hall in Boston, and he prepared the remaining three lectures ("Classes of Men," "Perpetual Forces," and "Fortune of the Republic") for delivery on Tuesdays in a lyceum series hosted by the Parker Fraternity at the Tremont Temple in Boston; of these, the three lectures Emerson initially delivered before the Parker Fraternity became popular independent lectures beyond their initial occasion. Finally, of the remaining seven lectures printed in volume 2, two lectures were academic addresses ("Celebration of Intellect: An Address at Tufts College" and "The Scholar"); one lecture was an antislavery address ("American Slavery"); two lectures were public addresses on momentous occasions, one of which was national ("Address at the Woman's Rights Convention, 20 September 1855"), the other of which was local ("Address to the Inhabitants of Concord, at the Consecration of Sleepy Hollow, 29 September 1855"); and three lectures were delivered as independent lectures ("Country Life [Concord]," "Morals," and "The Rule of Life").

In addition to the forty-eight lectures presented in clear text in the two volumes of *The Later Lectures of Ralph Waldo Emerson*, six additional complete lectures have been prepared in connection with this edition. Five of these lectures are printed as genetic texts in the electronic textual notes prepared for the lectures printed in volume 1. These include (1–2) Emerson's 1848 and 1849 versions of *Mind and Manners of the Nineteenth Century*, Lecture I: "The Powers and Laws of Thought," for which his version of 1850 supplies the copy-text used in this edition; (3) Emerson's 1847 or 1848 version of *Mind and Manners of the Nineteenth Century*, Lecture II: "The Relation of Intellect to Natural Science," for which his version of 1849 or 1850 supplies the copy-text used in this edition; (4) Emerson's 1848 version of *Mind and Manners of the Nineteenth Century*, Lecture III: "The Tendencies and Duties of Men of Thought," for which his version of 1849 supplies the copy-text used in this edition; and (5) Emerson's complete predelivery draft of his "Address to the Citizens of Concord on the Fugitive Slave Law, 3 May 1851," for which the version from which he read in 1851 supplies the copy-text used in this edition. A sixth lecture, "Discours

Manqué," which is a very brief but complete lecture that Emerson clearly drew from his "Address at the Woman's Rights Convention, 20 September 1855," for delivery before a women's audience late in the 1860s, is printed in volume 2 in clear text in the introductory headnote to Emerson's 1855 address.[59]

In sum, then, we have prepared a total of fifty-four lectures for *The Later Lectures of Ralph Waldo Emerson, 1843–1871;* forty-nine lectures (including "Discours Manqué") are printed in clear text in the two volumes of this edition, and five lectures are printed only in genetic text in the electronic textual notes to the edition. Significantly, although we have not been able to establish with certainty that he actually read from "Discours Manqué," and while manuscript evidence makes it obvious that he never read from the predelivery draft of his "Address to the Citizens of Concord on the Fugitive Slave Law, 3 May 1851," Emerson did read from the manuscripts of each of the lectures from his *Mind and Manners of the Nineteenth Century* series that we print as genetic texts. We provide all known details of these lectures, including their origins and date(s) of delivery, in our introductory headnotes to each lecture printed from that series.

## Presentation of the Texts of Emerson's Later Lectures

The format we have designed for the presentation of lectures in these volumes and for the presentation of the electronic textual notes that accompany this edition provides readers with several types of accessible information. Emerson's lectures are arranged in these volumes in the order of their first date of delivery, even though, as we indicate above, we typically have edited each lecture as last delivered by Emerson. Lectures within a series are printed together, with the date of delivery of the first lecture in a series determining the series' position in the overall arrangement of the volumes. The only exceptions to this rule are "England," "Resources," and "Table Talk," which, although associated with lecture series, performed extensive service as lectures apart from those series and consequently are treated as independent lectures here.

As with "England," "Resources," and "Table Talk," Emerson often moved lectures in and out of series; this appears to be a function not only of a lecture's audience appeal but also of necessity, since he hardly could offer the same audience a successful lecture from a series in one season and the whole series in the next. Although he may have changed their contents, Emerson rarely changed the titles of the five series from which a total of eighteen lectures are drawn in these volumes: *New England, Mind and Manners of the Nineteenth Century, Conduct of*

59. Electronic textual notes prepared for this edition have been mounted on this website: http://www.walden.org/emerson/Writings/Later_Lectures/.

*Life, Natural Method of Mental Philosophy*, and *Life and Literature*.[60] Each series is introduced with a headnote; the range of years during which Emerson delivered the series follows the title of the series.

Lecture titles used to introduce a lecture in the body of these volumes or in the electronic textual notes are generally those last used by Emerson, if he gave the lecture a title at all; all additional titles given to a lecture by Emerson are reported in the headnote to each lecture. When no title by Emerson has been found for a lecture in the manuscripts, titles derived from Emerson's correspondence, from some comparable authority, or from newspaper accounts of his delivery of a lecture are used. The date following each lecture title is the first date of delivery; for lectures that Emerson repeated over more than one calendar year, the range of years of delivery dates is indicated in parentheses below the title and the first date of delivery. Because lectures first delivered in series performed service beyond Emerson's deliveries of the series, occasionally, as with the three lectures printed in this edition from the *Mind and Manners of the Nineteenth Century* series, the range of dates following the title and first delivery date of a lecture may differ from the range of dates indicated in the headnote title for the series. In those instances when Emerson delivered a lecture only once, the date of delivery has been incorporated into the title.

Sometimes Emerson followed a numbered pattern of order in delivering lectures in series; in those series in which his placement of lectures followed a set pattern, his lecture numbers have been used in this edition, whereas in series such as *Conduct of Life* in which individual lectures were placed in different sequences over repeated deliveries of the series, lecture numbers have not been used in this edition. Emerson's own exact series titles and lecture number(s) as well as lecture title(s) and date(s) for lectures delivered within or outside of series are reported as they occur in the electronic textual notes to each lecture; he invariably inscribed all such information on the opening page or pages of a lecture.

---

60. The notable exception to this rule is *Mind and Manners of the Nineteenth Century*. Throughout this edition we use this title, which is the one Emerson first gave to the series and which he most often used in reference to it. This is also the title used in contemporary newspaper reports on the series. After first delivering the series in London in June 1848, Emerson occasionally called it "Mind and Manners in the Nineteenth Century," a title that several scholars, including Charvat and von Frank, have adopted. Further complicating Emerson's use of this series title is the title under which he often grouped the first three lectures in the series: "Natural History of the Intellect." The three lectures included under this title are "The Powers and Laws of Thought," "The Relation of Intellect to Natural Science," and "The Tendencies and Duties of Men of Thought," and, as shown in the textual notes, this is the title that appears on most manuscripts of these lectures, not *Mind and Manners of* [or *in*] *the Nineteenth Century*. Since Emerson also used this title for his series of University Lectures at Harvard in 1870 and 1871, we distinguish between Emerson's two uses of this title by reporting his first (for the subset of *Mind and Manners of the Nineteenth Century* lectures) in quotation marks and his second (for the series at Harvard) in italics.

Except in the body of lectures and of textual notes, throughout this edition dates have been regularized to day, month, year order.

Thus, a heading such as this,

*New England*, Lecture I: "The Genius and National
Character of the Anglo-Saxon Race"
10 January 1843
(1843–1844)

supplies the following information for a lecture. The lecture was delivered as part of a series (*New England*) in which it consistently served as Emerson's first lecture (Lecture I). The title Emerson used for the lecture in the delivery of the series recovered in this edition was "The Genius and National Character of the Anglo-Saxon Race." Emerson's first delivery of the lecture occurred on 10 January 1843, and he delivered the lecture on at least one more occasion in the period we designate "1843–1844." In contrast, a heading such as this,

"France, or Urbanity"
17 January 1854
(1854–1856)

supplies the following information for a lecture. The lecture was delivered independent of any lecture series. The last title Emerson used for the lecture was "France, or Urbanity." Emerson's first delivery of the lecture occurred on 17 January 1854, and he delivered the lecture on at least one more occasion in the period we designate "1854–1856." Finally, headings such as these,

"London"
3 January 1849

"Poetry and English Poetry"
10 January 1854"

"Classes of Men"
20 November 1860
(1860–1870)

supply the following information for the lectures. Each lecture was delivered independent of any lecture series. The last titles Emerson used for the lectures were "London," "Poetry and English Poetry," and "Classes of Men," respectively. Emerson's first delivery of each lecture occurred as follows: "London" on 3 January 1849, "Poetry and English Poetry" on 10 January 1854, and "Classes of Men" on 20 November 1860. Since the date of Emerson's first delivery of "Poetry and English Poetry" is enclosed within quotation marks along with the lecture title, the lecture was delivered only once—on the date specified. Since the date of Emerson's first delivery of "London" is not enclosed within quotation marks along with the lecture title, and since no range of dates is enclosed in parentheses after the date of Emerson's first delivery of "London," the lecture was delivered two or more times only in 1849. And, as the range of dates enclosed in parentheses following the first date of delivery of "Classes of Men" suggests, Emerson repeated this lecture on several occasions over the decade between 1860 and 1870.

Headnotes follow immediately after each lecture's title and date(s). While of necessity some will be more detailed and lengthy than others, each headnote introduces the reader to the occasion(s) surrounding Emerson's composition and delivery or deliveries of a lecture, indicates the fees that he may have received for the lecture, and describes all peculiarities of the copy-text not otherwise accounted for in the present essay as commonplace features of the copy-texts of Emerson's later lectures. Here, we report responses to Emerson's performance or topic that we have found in the personal writings of members of his audience or in newspaper accounts of the lecture. With respect to newspaper and other accounts, in headnotes, as in our introduction to these volumes, we generally cite and direct readers only to substantive reports of Emerson's lectures and evaluative reports on his performance, not to the numerous brief or passing notices we have found of his appearance at some specified time and place to deliver a lecture. Indeed, newspaper reports of Emerson's lectures become increasingly insubstantial during and after the mid-1850s; their scant content is, we believe, a function more of Emerson's attitude toward reporters covering his lectures than of the reporters' or their readers' lack of interest in having access to firsthand information on Emerson's lecturing.[61] Finally, at the conclusion of each headnote we direct readers to adaptations of the lecture in whole or in part in publications by Emerson, by his literary executors, or by later scholars.

The editors of Emerson's *Early Lectures, Journals and Miscellaneous Notebooks, Topical Notebooks*, and *Collected Works* prepared, in annotations or appendixes, listings of where Emerson reused material from one work in another. We have reluctantly decided against preparing such listings for our edition. First, in a series of lectures spanning nearly thirty years, the genealogy of individual passages can become labyrinthine, as Emerson occasionally redeploys (and continually revises) a sentence from his journal to a lecture, to another lecture, to his topical notebooks, to yet another lecture, to his published works (and often his literary collaborators and/or executors copy the sentence into a work published in the

---

61. For additional details of Emerson's attitude toward newspaper coverage of his lectures, see our discussion of "Emerson at the Lectern" above.

years of Emerson's declining mental powers and/or posthumously). Second, and as a result of the first reason, such a listing of parallel passages as earlier editions presented would in these volumes extend to several hundred printed pages, and, forced to choose by reasons of space between printing Emerson's lectures or our parallel passages, we have chosen to print Emerson's texts. As computer technology advances, individual scholars will be able to create their own lists of parallel passages in significantly less time and with more comprehensiveness and accuracy than are possible today by using searchable databases of Emerson's writings such as the one on which we have placed the electronic textual notes to this edition.

Editorial annotations in this edition appear in the form of footnotes to the lecture texts. Footnotes have also been used in the introduction; however, for readers' ease of reference, multiple sources reported in the headnotes to lecture series and lectures have been cited as parenthetical notes. Footnotes, which have purposely been kept to a minimum in this edition, identify Emerson's allusions to persons, places, occasions, quotations, and books as they *first* occur in the text of either volume 1 or volume 2; such universally known figures as Plato, Confucius, and Shakespeare have not been identified. Once persons, places, occasions, quotations, and books have been identified, we do not repeat that information in or between lectures in a volume or between the two volumes of this edition. The only exceptions to this rule are in our identification of Emerson's allusions to some persons and to his repeated use of certain quotations. In one lecture, his allusion to a person may represent nothing more than a casual aside to that person by name, while his allusion to that same person in another lecture may take on significance by virtue of the context in which the allusion is made. In such instances as they occur, we have supplied an additional note specifying the significance of Emerson's allusion in context. Similarly, throughout the lectures included in these volumes, Emerson will be found repeating quotations from favorite writers such as Plato, Zoroaster, and others. Especially in those instances where Emerson applies a quotation to a purpose different from a previous application, we have supplied an additional note indicating the source of the quotations. For the convenience of readers, we have printed a list of works frequently cited at the beginning of volume 1 of this edition. At the end of volume 2, "Manuscript Sources of Emerson's Later Lectures in the Houghton Library of Harvard University" lists by Houghton Library call number the source(s) for each lecture printed in this edition; volume 2 also contains an index to both volumes of this edition.

Finally, we would recommend the following research sources to readers of these volumes who wish to perform detailed analyses of the texts printed in them or who may desire more extensive evidence of Emerson's compositional practices than is represented in his creation of the later lectures. In our estimation, the Harvard editions of Emerson's *Early Lectures* and *Journals and Miscellaneous Notebooks*, the Missouri editions of his *Poetry Notebooks, Complete Sermons*, and *Topical Notebooks*, and the Columbia edition of his *Letters* are indispensable to both enterprises. To these we would add four recent publications: Ronald A. Bosco's treatment of Emerson's *University Lectures* (1997) and Albert J. von Frank's *An Emerson Chronology* (1994), as well as the *Biographical Dictionary of Transcendentalism* and the *Encyclopedia of Transcendentalism*, both edited by Wesley T. Mott.[62]

## Presentation of Textual Notes to Emerson's Later Lectures at http://www.walden.org/emerson/Writings/Later_Lectures/

Textual notes to this edition have been mounted on the website cited above and report all authorial revisions of the copy-text—insertions, cancellations, variants, and transpositions—as well as all editorial emendations of copy-text, save for "silent" emendations, which are accounted for below. No editorial emendations, silent or otherwise, have been introduced into the genetic body of the textual notes, since the purpose of the notes is always to give the exact situation in the manuscript using those symbols that have become commonplace in editions of Emerson's writings:

| | |
|---|---|
| < > | cancellation |
| ↑ ↓ | insertion |
| / / / | variant |
| [[ ]] | Emerson's square brackets |
| ¶ | paragraph |
| { } | manuscript page numbers |

A single set of square brackets ([ ]) encloses editorial commentary in the textual notes. Text that follows immediately after a cancellation without a space or the symbol for insertion should be read as having been written directly over the canceled text (as in "<my>mine"). Authorial and editorial emendations are usually introduced in these notes by two or three key words left unemended by Emerson.

Textual notes for each lecture are headed by the identical title(s) and date(s) used to head lecture texts (see our description of these above). Following the heading, the source or sources of copy-text and of other texts printed in textual notes are given using Houghton Library call numbers. Typically, there are two

62. *Biographical Dictionary of Transcendentalism*, ed. Wesley T. Mott (Westport, Conn.: Greenwood Press, 1996); *Encyclopedia of Transcendentalism*, ed. Wesley T. Mott (Westport, Conn.: Greenwood Press, 1996).

reasons for our listing of more than one source in these notes. First, as in the case of those six lectures described above that we print in addition to the forty-eight lectures that constitute the body of this edition, we occasionally treat more than one text in our textual notes to a lecture. Second, following Emerson's directions in the copy-text that we are editing in which he instructs himself to "insert" or read from the pages of some other lecture or text that he specifies, we also treat pages drawn from sources other than the principal copy-text in our textual notes to a lecture. An editors' note has been used at the end of the Houghton Library call number(s) in those cases where a manuscript is sewn together. Finally, in a departure from the practice in editions of Emerson's writings that use textual notes for the same purposes we do, we have organized entries not by page and line numbers but by paragraph breaks corresponding to those in the clear text printed of each lecture (see our comment on paragraph indentations in our discussion of silent emendations below). For ease of reference in the notes, paragraphs that open with cancellations, variants, or some form of authorial emendation other than an insertion are always run in with the paragraph(s) preceding them and marked with the symbol ¶. Throughout the notes, ellipses indicate text left unrevised by Emerson, and, as explained below, manuscript page numbers, which are here enclosed in braces ({ }), are those assigned by the Houghton Library when the manuscripts were first deposited there. Thus, for the reader who may wish to read a lecture and follow its development in a manner that approximates a reader's access to the manuscript, our format provides a convenient means of simultaneously reading several clear-text paragraphs and their corresponding sources in Emerson's manuscript simply by moving back and forth between the clear texts of this letterpress edition and the electronic textual notes.

## Emerson's Emendation of Copy-text

Emerson's emendation of copy-text takes four principal forms: insertions, cancellations, variants, and transpositions.

Emerson's most typical manner of insertion is to interline the word, the expression, or, sometimes, the larger text to be inserted above the point in his text where he intends the new inscription to be inserted. Occasionally, Emerson inserts a word in the left or right margin of the page, and on such occasions, the insertion's content usually makes its placement self-evident. As in the copy-texts of the *Complete Sermons* and *Early Lectures,* throughout these lecture manuscripts Emerson often interlines an expression such as "Insert A" or simply inscribes an "A" (or another letter or an asterisk) at a point in his text. In all cases, the inscription, whether or not interlined, indicates his placement of text at the point where the phrase, letter, or asterisk is inscribed from elsewhere on the page or in the manuscript. Regardless of where it is located in the manuscript, text that Emerson moves in this manner is always marked with a corresponding direction such as "Insert A" or an "A." Sometimes text so marked represents a genuine insertion, but just as often it represents a stage of Emerson's revisionary process wherein he moves an already inscribed sentence or more of text from one place in the manuscript to another. Editorial commentary in the textual notes distinguishes between these two situations; commentary also describes any additional markings by Emerson in the text such as hands pointing or lines drawn between directions such as "Insert A" and the insertion itself on a facing page.

Emerson's cancellation of text usually takes one of four forms; sometimes, his cancellations combine more than one of these forms. His most common forms of cancellation are to line-through horizontally, to finger-wipe, or to write over text he wishes to cancel On other occasions, he strikes an expression or passage through with one or more vertical or diagonal lines or with crossed lines that make an "X." This fourth form, which sometimes represents a cancellation and sometimes represents a different kind of emendation, has been subject to various interpretations by the editors of Emerson's writings and requires explanation.

Beginning with his composition of the early lectures and with his keeping of journals and notebooks in the 1830s that chronologically correspond to those lectures, Emerson routinely adopted a not altogether clear or consistent system of striking through text. He persisted in this practice throughout the remainder of his life. His purpose for this emendation seems most often to be one of the following: (1) to cancel text so marked; (2) to indicate that the text so marked occurs elsewhere in a lecture or in a journal or notebook; or (3) to indicate that he has used the text so marked in some form of publication. The editors of the *Early Lectures* uniformly treated these strike-throughs as subject to editorial interpretation: in those instances where a passage so marked occurred elsewhere in the copy-text of the lecture they were editing and where the second passage was not so marked, they typically treated the struck-through passage as a cancellation; in those instances where a passage so marked did not occur in any form elsewhere in the copy-text of the lecture they were editing, they typically treated the strike-through as Emerson's shorthand to himself that he had used (or would use) the passage in another lecture or for publication, and they incorporated the passage struck through in their texts. The editors of the *Journals and Miscellaneous Notebooks* almost always treated this inscription as Emerson's "use mark," not his cancellation, and they went to great lengths to indicate whether Emerson's strike-through was vertical or diagonal. (In *JMN*, strike-throughs at angles of 10 degrees or more are noted as diagonal.) On the other hand, the editors of the *Topical Notebooks*—all of whom had been editors of the *Journals and Miscellaneous Notebooks*—dispensed with such subtleties altogether and routinely noted

Emerson's striking through of a passage as "struck through [some number of times]" or "struck through [some number of times] to cancel." The implications of the practice of the editors of the *Topical Notebooks* most closely approximate those of the editors of the *Early Lectures*.

In their respective statements of editorial policies governing their editions, the editors of the *Early Lectures, Journals and Miscellaneous Notebooks,* and *Topical Notebooks* notice, in varying degrees of detail, a set of factors that, beyond those already addressed, thoroughly complicates editorial treatment of strike-throughs in an Emerson copy-text. The factors are these: (1) Emerson's erratic use of parentheses or of his own square brackets ("[[ ]]") to set off a passage that has been struck through and his inscription of parentheses or square brackets sometimes in ink, sometimes in pencil, and sometimes in both ink and pencil; and (2) the presence in the copy-text of comparable inscriptions (strike-throughs, parentheses, *and* square brackets) made by Cabot or Edward Waldo Emerson.

Since the editors of the *Journals and Miscellaneous Notebooks* and *Topical Notebooks* printed genetic texts of their copy-text, the presence of Emerson's parentheses or square brackets had to be noted in the body of the text. Their presence was not subject to editorial interpretation as to their function by the editors of the *Journals and Miscellaneous Notebooks* inasmuch as the editors treated the strike-throughs that parentheses or square brackets enclosed as Emerson's "use marks." As already noted, however, the editors of the *Topical Notebooks* dispensed with the prior practice of treating Emerson's strike-throughs as "use marks," and, consequently, they were bound to distinguish between passages merely struck through or struck through for the purpose of cancellation. The practice of these editors was to treat Emerson's parentheses or square brackets that set off a struck-through passage as integral to the struck-through passage and to represent them either as part of a passage merely struck through or as part of a passage struck through for the purpose of cancellation.

Our purpose here is certainly not to quarrel with the respective practices of the editors of Emerson's *Early Lectures, Journals and Miscellaneous Notebooks,* and *Topical Notebooks* with regard to their treatment of Emerson's strike-throughs and his use of parentheses or square brackets. In our estimation, each edition announced and consistently applied practices that on the whole were appropriate to the texts the editors were editing and to the formats in which they printed texts (clear text or genetic text). But a significant complication for our editing of Emerson's later lectures, a complication with which the editors of the *Early Lectures* also had to contend but to an extent far less than we, is the presence in the manuscripts of comparable marks (strike-throughs, parentheses, and square brackets) made by Cabot or Edward Waldo Emerson.

As we have already commented in detail, following Emerson's own mining of his later lecture manuscripts for publication in essays throughout the 1850s and

1860s and into the 1870s, Cabot and Edward each read and mined these manuscripts for additional publications under Emerson's name. Cabot was assisted in his review and mining of the later lecture manuscripts by Emerson's daughter Ellen, and evidence in the manuscripts shows that he, Ellen, and Edward each returned to these manuscripts on multiple occasions. Whereas Ellen's intrusion into a manuscript is invariably marked by her comments in the margin of a page that the page seemed to her to contain material either already published or available for new publications, Cabot and Edward usually struck through passages that Emerson had used elsewhere in his lectures or for publication in black, blue, or red pencil, often also adding commentary but sometimes not. While their purpose was clearly to indicate that a passage had been used by Emerson, they also used this system to mark passages that they were appropriating for new publication in essays. Further, both Cabot and Edward often set off such passages (both those used by Emerson and those that they used) with parentheses or square brackets inscribed in black, blue, or red pencil. While Emerson often struck through passages in ink and inscribed parentheses or square brackets in ink, he also, unfortunately, used pencil—usually black pencil, but also, we believe, blue and red pencil and sometimes green pencil.

This overlapping use of comparable markings by Emerson and by Cabot and Edward has created an editorial problem that may never be completely or even satisfactorily resolved. Often—too often for an editor to make sweeping claims about these emendation practices with absolute certainty—the copy-text presents an ambiguous situation wherein one is not entirely sure that strikethroughs, parentheses, and square brackets are Emerson's, Cabot's, or Edward's and whether their purpose is to cancel text so marked or to indicate that the text so marked has been used by one or the other person in some form of publication. Since Emerson most often inscribed and emended texts in ink, it seems reasonable to assume that emendations of this form in ink are his. However, unless a passage so emended occurs elsewhere in the copy-text of a lecture or in a journal or notebook without these emendations, that assumption still leaves open to question whether Emerson's purpose for such emendation was, in fact, to cancel the text so marked. Since Cabot and Edward typically emended Emerson's texts in some color of pencil, it seems reasonable to assume that *most* such emendations in pencil are theirs for one of the purposes stated above. In the case of the manuscripts of Emerson's later lectures, however, the presence of wholesale strike-throughs, parentheses, and square brackets is sufficient to make us wonder whether Cabot and Edward may not themselves have occasionally emended these texts in ink.

In this edition, we have consistently treated strike-throughs, parentheses, and square brackets in the following manner. All those inscribed in ink we attribute to Emerson and, consequently, report them in the textual notes; those inscribed in pencil we on the whole attribute to Cabot and Edward and do not report them in the textual notes, since our intention throughout this edition is to represent Emerson's, not his executors', creation of texts. In fact, Cabot's and Edward's typical form of intrusion into these manuscripts has enabled us to maintain and consistently apply this policy, for, like Ellen, they often provide some commentary in their own hands in the margins of pages on which they write in pencil to indicate the purpose of their markings: that a passage so marked duplicates a passage found elsewhere in the manuscript or has been printed by Emerson, or that a passage so marked is being appropriated by them for publication. When such straightforward evidence of the purpose for the pencil markings coming from Cabot or Edward is lacking in the copy-text, we report the marks in the textual notes on the assumption that they are as likely to be Emerson's as Cabot's or Edward's. Also, our practice has consistently been not to treat any such emended passages as Emerson's cancellations but to retain them in our clear texts unless we have found obvious reasons—that a passage so marked is revised in the manuscript or that a passage so marked is duplicated elsewhere in the manuscript—to treat them as Emerson's cancellations. Textual notes always report the number of times Emerson struck through a passage; although they are not incorporated into clear texts, Emerson's parentheses or square brackets are also always reported in the textual notes.

Although at times cumbersome to account for in notes, Emerson's revisions of his later lecture manuscripts with variants and transpositions usually follow a straightforward and consistent pattern. His variants most often consist of an alternate word or phrase interlined above an uncanceled corresponding word or phrase in his initial inscription. Emerson's variants are reported in the textual notes in the following form: /first word or phrase/interlined word or phrase/. The clear text regularly adopts the interlined inscription in a pair of variants, unless doing so is objectionable on self-evident grounds of grammar, context, or sense; editorial commentary is always provided to notice those cases where the first, rather than the second, inscription in a pair of variants has been adopted. In several instances scattered throughout the later lecture manuscripts, Emerson inscribes an alternate word or phrase on the same line or in prose consecutive with an uncanceled corresponding word or phrase in his initial inscription. These situations have been editorially treated in the same manner as Emerson's more common variants, and editorial commentary is always provided to describe the situation. Finally, in several lecture manuscripts Emerson effectively created variants that extend in length from one paragraph to two or three paragraphs by revising text for delivery on new sheets of paper without having canceled his initial inscription of the same. This situation, which is most commonly found in those manuscripts of lectures that he delivered with some frequency, has been editorially treated in the same manner as Emerson's other forms of variants, except that in these instances editorial commentary has been used to inform readers of the opening and closing of each part of the variant and to indicate exactly where within the manuscript the variants are inscribed.

Emerson's transpositions in the later lectures take the form of a word, phrase, sentence, or sentences enclosed in parentheses or his square brackets and labeled with subscript numbers 1 and 2 to show the order in which the transposed matter is to be read. The clear text adopts the transposed order; the original order, along with Emerson's parentheses or square brackets and subscripts, is reported in the textual notes.

## Editorial Emendation of Copy-text

Several forms of editorial emendation of the copy-text of Emerson's later lectures have already been announced. Following directly from our expressed intention to represent only Emerson's part in the creation of his lecture texts, we have naturally not considered for adoption any writing in the manuscript by persons other than Emerson, and we have done so without specific notice of that writing in the textual notes.[63] Second, while we always report in the textual notes Emerson's inscription of lecture title(s), date(s), and similar information on the opening page or pages of the copy-text, we have prepared uniform headings for each lecture that specify lecture series titles and lecture numbers (as appropriate), lecture titles, date of first delivery, and range of years of delivery, although this information is rarely present in the copy-text. Third, while we have always noted Emerson's use of parentheses and square brackets in our textual notes, we never incorporate his square brackets into clear texts, and only occasionally do we retain his parentheses in clear texts. And, fourth, except in the body of lectures and of textual notes, throughout this edition dates have been regularized to day, month, year order.

Because we have understood Emerson's later lectures as works in progress and not as finished texts that he was ready to submit for publication, we have had to walk a fine line between overregularization of a text Emerson prepared for oral

---

63. The only exception to this rule is a brief passage in Emerson's lecture on "Natural Religion," which he first delivered on 3 February 1861. As reported in the electronic textual notes, on pages {90r}–{90v} of the manuscript a brief passage occurs in Ellen Emerson's hand, not her father's. It is doubtful that the text was copied by Ellen contemporaneously with her father's delivery of this lecture; rather, she probably copied his original text in the mid-1870s, when she was assisting Cabot in the preparation of her father's papers for publication. The original of Emerson's text has not been found with the manuscript; however, since Ellen's text ends and her father's begins midsentence on {90v}, we print it on the assumption that it is likely a faithful representation of the original.

delivery and underregularization of texts that, inasmuch as they betray a host of idiosyncrasies that result from both the rushed conditions under which Emerson wrote them and his own inconsistent stylistic practices, would be difficult, if not in some cases impossible, to read in clear text. Many of Emerson's practices we let stand in the clear texts without notice or comment in the textual notes. For instance, we preserve his erratic use of capitals following colons and semicolons and following commas, colons, and semicolons followed by a dash. We also preserve his inconsistent use of British and American forms of words as well as all of his unusual but typical word constructions, including his use of what would today be regarded as unacceptable forms for plural nouns, verbals, the comparative and superlative forms of adjectives and adverbs, and terms improvised from science, other disciplines, and languages other than English. However, for the sake of grammar, style, sense, and context, other of Emerson's practices in copy-text we emend and report in the textual notes, where, unless otherwise indicated below, our emendations are always enclosed in editorial brackets. These include:

1. Editorial insertions. In a few instances, our need to insert a particular word or phrase is explicitly noticed as an editorial insertion in the textual notes. Otherwise, in addition to a letter or letters missing within a word Emerson has inscribed, the following individual words or combinations thereof are reported in the notes within editorial brackets but without further comment: a, affect, ages, all, also, an, and, another, are, as, at, be, becomes, but, by, can, directed, do, even, felt, first, for, France, he, here, honor, I (first-person singular), in, is, it, like, many, men, not, of, on, once, one, or, other(s), our, read, relates, said, say, see, shall, should, so, Taylor (for Thomas Taylor, the Platonist), than, that, the, their, them, then, there, these, they, this, to, too, upon, us, value, voting, was, we, when, which, while, who, with, yet, your.

2. Editorial deletions. Certain types of editorial deletions are fully reported in the textual notes, where they are explicitly noticed as either "deleted" or as "canceled." Editorial deletions that are reported include extraneous words; Emerson's working numerical divisions for sections of a lecture; sentence fragments that may represent the false start of a sentence or a passage; and sentence fragments or sentences that, when they occur at the top of a page, may represent text left uncanceled by Emerson when he borrowed the page from another manuscript source but did not also borrow the page preceding it or that, when they occur at the bottom of a page, may represent text left uncanceled by Emerson when he borrowed the page from another manuscript source but did not also borrow the page following it. Editorial cancellations typically involve a word or words accidentally left uncanceled by Emerson within a larger canceled passage; in a few instances, repeated paragraphs that are not demonstrably variants are also editorially canceled.

In contrast, two forms of editorial deletion are not explicitly noticed in the textual notes as deleted:

First, as we comment above, the manuscript pages of Emerson's later lectures are inscribed with multiple pagination sequences. These sequences occur on recto pages only; verso pages are, on the whole, unnumbered. Some page numbers were inscribed by Emerson in ink or in pencil or both; other page numbers were inscribed by Cabot or Edward Waldo Emerson in pencil. It is not at all unusual to find as many as five pagination sequences, some in ink and some in pencil, inscribed on a page by multiple hands. We have neither followed nor reported these sequences; instead, we have uniformly numbered each page, using Houghton Library page numbers. These occur in pencil in the lower left-hand corner of each manuscript recto page, where they were inscribed at the time the manuscripts were deposited in the Houghton Library by the Ralph Waldo Emerson Memorial Association. Verso pages were not numbered in this manner; consequently, we have supplied page numbers for each page of copy-text thus: using the Houghton Library page numbers, we have numbered the pages "[#|r" or "[#]v," thereby showing numbers for both recto and verso pages. We should also note that neither the numbers inscribed in multiple pagination sequences nor the Houghton Library numbers as we have used them should be taken as authoritative indicators of the order in which Emerson composed a lecture. Indeed, multiple pagination sequences only give some indication of the amount of service a page of text may have performed within or outside of the present state of the copy-text of a lecture; the Houghton Library page numbers, on the other hand, only report the order in which the loose pages of Emerson's lecture manuscripts were assembled at the time they were deposited in the Houghton Library.

Second, Emerson's doubling of words and his use of occasional catchwords as well as his numerous instructions to himself, including those that call for the insertion of additional text from a manuscript source other than that which serves as principal copy-text for a lecture, are shown in the textual notes as they occur but receive no further comment. The text of these should always be understood as editorially deleted in clear text.

3. Editorial restoration of text canceled by Emerson. All editorial restorations of text canceled by Emerson are reported in the textual notes, where they are explicitly noticed as "canceled [Emerson's text] restored."

4. Editorial emendation of Emerson's spelling. Words misspelled by Emerson are corrected and reported in the textual notes. Except for those situations involving spelling that have been described above or are described under "Silent Emendations" below, no attempt has been made to revise Emerson's use of odd or archaic spellings when contemporary authority for them has been found in dictionaries of the period or in the *Oxford English Dictionary.*

5. Editorial emendation of Emerson's punctuation. Except for those situations involving punctuation that are described under "Silent Emendations" below, all editorial emendation of Emerson's punctuation in copy-text is reported in the textual notes. We show Emerson's original punctuation but without further comment.

6. Editorial transposition of Emerson's text. In a very few instances, we have had to transpose Emerson's text in a sentence or across sentences in a paragraph to bring clarity and order to the development of his prose. All editorial transpositions of Emerson's text are reported in the textual notes, and their original position in Emerson's inscription is always noticed. We have not commented on the self-evident situation where a leaf was reversed before it came to the Houghton Library, resulting in the recto following the verso.

7. Editorial emendation of Emerson's notes. Throughout the later lecture manuscripts, Emerson inscribes notes in one of three ways: as footnotes to a text (often indicated by an asterisk), as parenthetical notes within a text, or as notes incorporated into his continuous prose. Most of his notes indicate sources of sayings and quotations, sometimes by reference to a book, sometimes by reference only to a person; his other notes take the form of brief explanatory notes. Regardless of their type or position in copy-text, Emerson's notes do not appear in clear texts. They are reported in the textual notes to show their position relative to the rest of the text; when they provide information not otherwise available, they are referenced in the editors' footnotes to the clear text, where they are acknowledged as Emerson's note.

8. Editorial omissions.[64] Two substantial categories of Emerson text are reported but only briefly noticed in the textual notes. The first and most common editorial omission is of Emerson's working notes. These include everything from his indices of journal and notebook materials variously arranged by journal and notebook name, page number(s), and prose text passages to his random gatherings of unconnected and often incomplete prose. Editorial omission of such material is reported as "Emerson's working note [notes] omitted." A second kind of editorial omission involves passages that range in length from one page, to a few pages, to several pages that have been judged extraneous to the copy-text. Given the presence not only of Emerson's hand but also of Cabot's, Ellen Emerson's, and Edward Waldo Emerson's hands in the preservation and arrangement of text in each lecture manuscript source, the precise origin or purpose of extraneous pages is impossible to reconstruct. Sometimes, as when the text inscribed on such pages bears absolutely no relation to the topic Emerson is developing, the extra-

---

64. As with our decision discussed above concerning parallel passages, we have created this particular category of editorial emendation as a matter of economy; our failure to have devised this category would have added some several hundred pages to the body of the textual notes.

neous nature of the material is obvious at first glance; at other times, as when Emerson appears to be process writing and seeing how many ways he can adapt prose already used in the lecture to some other unspecified end, our determination of the material as extraneous is, admittedly, a judgment call on our part. In all cases, editorial omission of such material is reported as "Page [Pages] omitted as extraneous to this lecture."

In contrast to these two substantial categories of editorial omission, which are reported in the textual notes, a third and relatively minor category of editorial omission is not reported in the textual notes. This category takes into account Emerson's occasional use of headers and marginal notes to himself (or to Cabot) indicating that a passage or page is a duplicate of another passage or page or has been printed.

## Silent Emendations

Modern practice allows editors to employ varyingly elaborate systems of silent emendation in order to bring clarity and a degree of regularity to their texts, as well as to unclutter and make manageable the size of textual apparatus. For some editors, silent emendation has served as a means to modernize a text; that is, it has been used to bring the presentation of a text composed, say, during an earlier century into conformity with modern grammatical and other forms of usage. Contemporary editors of Emerson's writings have always rejected this form of silent emendation; we do so as well. Yet as the example of the clear texts of Emerson's writings printed in the *Early Lectures* and *Complete Sermons* shows, printed versions of texts that Emerson composed for oral delivery require and profit from a judicious system of silent emendation. We thus have routinely made silent emendations in the preparation of clear texts; however, no silent emendations in any form occur in the textual notes. The categories of silent emendation we have followed in this edition come directly from those used by the editors of the *Early Lectures* and *Complete Sermons;* they include:

1. Regularization of proper names. The following proper names frequently cited by Emerson have been regularized in clear texts: Anthony à Wood; Béranger (Pierre Jean de Béranger); Boccaccio (Giovanni Boccaccio); Bussy-Rabutin (Roger de Rabutin, comte de Bussy); Comines (Philip de Comines); Fénelon (François de Salignac de La Mothe-Fénelon); Geoffroy Saint-Hilaire or Saint-Hilaire (Etienne Geoffroy Saint-Hilaire); Gortchakov (Prince Mikhail Dmitrievich Gortchakov); Guyon (Jeanne Marie de la Motte-Guyon); Lalarde (Joseph Jérôme Le Français de Lalande); Lemaître (Antoine Louis Prosper Lemaître); Madame or Mme de Staël (Anne Louise Germaine, baronne de Staël-Holstein); Madame Récamier (Jeanne François Julie Adélaïde Récamier); Mar-

quis and Marquise or Madame de Sévigné; Max Müller (Friedrich Max Müller); Molière (Jean Baptiste Poquelin); Père La Chaise (François d'Aix de La Chaise); Rouget de Lisle (Claude Joseph Rouget de Lisle); Saint-Evremond (Charles de Marguetel de Saint-Denis, seigneur de Saint-Evremond); Saint-Pierre (Jacques Henri Bernadin de Saint-Pierre); Sainte-Beuve (Charles Augustin Sainte-Beuve); Théophile Gautier; Thomas à Kempis.

The names of the states of Arkansas, Connecticut, Minnesota, and Mississippi, the city name Uppsala (in Sweden), and the Tuileries (in France) have been regularized in clear texts to current-day spelling even though Emerson's variant spellings of them as "Missisippi," "Arkansaw," "Connecticutt," "Minesota," "Upsal," and "Tuilleries" were appropriate spellings in the nineteenth century. The city name Nantes (in France) has been regularized in clear texts from Emerson's spelling of it as "Nantz."

2. Regularization of numeral, capitalization and lowercase, punctuation, and paragraph forms. Most numeral forms used by Emerson have been spelled out, as in "3rd" (third) or "17th" (seventeenth). His numerals, which are part of the text that he presumably read, have been spelled out according to context; thus, his "1" may be spelled out as "one" or "first." Numbers of six or more digits have usually been written in arabic numerals.

Emerson's capitalization or lack thereof has been regularized in clear texts, as in the use of capitals for words beginning a sentence and for proper nouns. In Emerson editing circles, several of Emerson's initial letters in words in the body of a sentence have always been recognized as problematic with respect to capitalization, namely, his A's, C's, G's, N's, P's, S's, and U's. We have printed capitals where they seem to occur in Emerson's hand for certain emphatic abstractions (as in "Nature" and "Spirit"), but we have eliminated possible capitalization where it seems to occur merely as an eccentricity of orthography. Although the situation is of necessity reported in the textual notes, it is worth our adding here that Emerson's unemended initial capital for words beginning a sentence has been regularly reduced to lowercase when a new opening word or expression has been inserted by Emerson into the sentence.

Periods, question marks, exclamation points, commas, colons, semicolons, dashes, and accent marks have been silently supplied where they are unquestionably needed, as at the end of sentences, inside closing quotation marks, to separate items in a series, to introduce quotations, to set off appositional or subordinate phrases and clauses where the construction requires, and to regularize words and expressions taken from a language other than English. Periods have also been silently supplied for the titles Dr., Mr., Mrs., and M. (Monsieur). Emerson's use of the apostrophe to show possession has not presented any problems in the copytext; however, because his use of apostrophes in contractions is erratic, apostrophe use in contractions has been silently regularized. Emerson's inconsistent use of single and double quotation marks is preserved without imposing uniformity, but omitted marks in a pair have been silently supplied, mismatched marks have been silently made to agree, and quotes within quotes have been silently regularized to double quotation marks for the quote as a whole and single quotation marks for the quote within the larger quotation.

We have followed the manuscript for compound and hyphenated words, yet, as we have had to recognize, Emerson's practice here—especially as it evolves over nearly thirty years—is relatively meaningless; thus, we have invoked common sense in our preparation of clear texts. Indeed, Emerson's omission of many hyphens and his completely inconsistent spelling out of compounds as one or two words (even on the same line of inscription) appear to be more matters of penmanship and the pressure he felt to finish his text than matters of policy.

Emerson's use of underlining is regularized as italicization only in the clear texts. The titles of books, journals, newspapers, poems, and plays are left in the clear text as Emerson wrote them in the copy-text *if* he either underlined them or enclosed them within single or double quotation marks. When no punctuation has been supplied by Emerson, the title or portion thereof in his text has been italicized. With books, full titles are given in a footnote with bibliographic details drawn from editions in Emerson's library or from his reading when he is known to have owned a particular book or withdrawn it from a library; otherwise a book's original date of publication is given.[65] The title of the English magazine *Punch* is regularized as *Punch*.

Emerson's inconsistent practice with long quotations has been regularized thus: quoted passages of 100 or more words are printed as block quotes. His use of "xxx" for ellipses in quotations, whether long or short, has been regularized as ellipses. In this edition, all quotations from Emerson's published and unpublished journals and notebooks, correspondence, lectures, and miscellaneous manuscripts have been regularized to show only his final level of inscription.

Emerson's paragraphing requires special notice, particularly since we have used paragraphs to organize the textual notes. His use of an indentation in his text to indicate the opening of a paragraph or some other intended (but not altogether clear) break in the text is inconsistent in practice and more often than not impossible to represent meaningfully on the printed page of a lecture. In some lecture manuscripts, Emerson's prose continues for up to ten pages without a break of any kind—a sure sign, we believe, that he is copying his text from another manu-

---

65. We have followed the standard sources for determining Emerson's ownership or borrowing of a book: *Emerson's Library*, ed. Walter Harding (Charlottesville: University Press of Virginia, 1967), and *Emerson's Reading*, ed. Kenneth Walter Cameron (Raleigh, N.C.: Thistle Press, 1941).

script source. From the outset of our work on the later lectures, we have had to use our judgment in paragraphing, and that judgment is represented in the paragraphing form used in clear texts and in textual notes.

3. Expansion of abbreviations. Emerson's ampersands (&) have been regularized to "and"; his various uses of "&c," "&c.," "&c &c," "&c, &c." have been all regularized to "and so forth"; and his abbreviations for months of the year have been expanded. Additionally, the following abbreviations regularly used by Emerson have been expanded in clear texts: Abp. (Archbishop); agric. (agricultural); Benj. (Benjamin); brot, bro't (brought); Capt. (Captain); cd. (could); Col. (Colonel); e.g. (for example); Eng, Engl (English—the people or as a modifier, as in "English opinion"); Engd, Eng$^d$, Eng$^d$. (England); essent. (essential); Fr, Fr. (French—the people, the language, or as a modifier, as in "the French Revolution"); ft, ft. (feet—unit of measurement); Gen. (General); Geo (George); gov. (governing); Gov$^r$, Gov. (Governor); govt, gov't, govt. (government); hist, hist. (history); ie, i.e. (that is); int, int., intel, intel. (intellect or intellectual); Ky. (Kentucky); lit. (literary); Mass, Mass., Mass$^{tts}$, Mass.$^{tts}$ (Massachusetts); mod. (modern); mt, mt. (might); Nat, Nat. (Natural); Nat. Hist (Natural History); Nat. Hist of Int (Natural History of Intellect); NE, N.E, NE., N.E., N England, N. England (New England); N. Hampshire (New Hampshire); N.W (Northwest); N.Y, N.Y., N. York (New York); Penn$^a$ (Pennsylvania); phil, phil. (philosophical or philosophy); Phila. (Philadelphia); P.M. (afternoon); princ, princ. (principle or principles); Reg$^t$. (Regiment); rel, rel. (religion); Rev. (Reverend); S. America (South America); S. Carolina (South Carolina); shd, shd. (should); St. (Saint); tho, tho' (though); thot, tho't (thought); thotful, tho'tful (thoughtful); tho'ts (thoughts); thro, thro' (through); U. S. (United States); U. S. A. (United States of America); wd, wd. (would); wh, wh. (which); W. Indies (West Indies); and, except in quotations, y$^e$ (the), y$^m$ (them), and y$^t$ (that).

# New England,
# 1843–1844

EMERSON DELIVERED his lecture series on *New England* in a number of formats in a number of cities: on 10 and 17 January 1843 in two lectures before the Mercantile Library Association in Baltimore, between 23 January and 1 February as a series of five lectures in Philadelphia, on 7 and 9 February in two lectures that were part of an aborted series of five lectures before the Berean Society at the Universalist Church in New York City, between 11 and 22 February as a series of five lectures at the New York Society Library in New York City, and between 8 and 19 January 1844 as a series of four lectures before the Franklin Lyceum at Westminster Hall in Providence, Rhode Island.

Of the five lectures collectively associated with the *New England* series, four follow in this edition, while the fifth, delivered last in order as "Tendencies" in Philadelphia and as "Results and Tendencies" at the New York Society Library, does not survive as a complete lecture. At the Houghton Library of Harvard University, Emerson's lectures for the *New England* series are arranged in five labeled folders: (1) "New England I. [Origin. Genius of the Anglo-Saxon Race. Feb. 1843]"; (2) "New England II. [Traits. Trade. 1843]"; (3) "New England [III. Manners. 1843]"; (4) "New England. IV. [Literature. 1843]"; and (5) "New England. V. [Results. 1843]." The Houghton Library arrangement of the manuscripts reflects Emerson's delivery of the *New England* series at the New York Society Library in New York City in February 1843, not his last delivery of the series before the Franklin Lyceum in Providence in January 1844. Indeed, prior to Emerson's delivery of the *New England* series in four lectures in Providence, he had delivered the lecture in the Houghton Library's folder 3—"New England [III. Manners. 1843]"—on 6 December 1843 before the Franklin Lyceum as "New England," as, in other words, a lecture separate from, and a full month before he began, the series in Providence. On the basis of the December 1843 lecture, he was invited to give the *New England* series in Providence on 8, 9, 15, and 19 January 1844, an invitation Emerson confirmed in writing to Thomas L. Dunnell, president of the Franklin Lyceum, on 4 January 1844: "For subjects, the general subject is New England. Lecture I. Origin & national genius of the New England people; Lecture II. Trade, Manners & Customs; III. (was read at Providence) IV. Political & social causes now active: and, V. Recent literary & spiritual influences operating on the mind of New England" (*Letters*, 3:233). Although Emerson followed this topical outline for the first two lectures of the *New England* series, by the time he delivered the third and fourth lectures of the series before the Franklin Lyceum he had substantially rearranged the titles and content of those lectures from the outline he had provided to Dunnell.

As Nancy Craig Simmons has reconstructed their delivery, the first two of the four lectures of Emerson's *New England* series in Providence in 1844 consisted of the first two lectures Emerson had delivered at the New York Society Library in 1843; the third lecture of the series was some form of "Literary and Spiritual Influences" (that is, *New England*, Lecture IV: "New England: Recent Literary and Spiritual Influences"), the lecture that, in fact, Emerson had written to Dunnell that he would deliver last; while the fourth and last lecture of the series was some form of "Political and Social Causes Now Active," the lecture that Emerson had written to Dunnell that he would deliver third in the series. Simmons convincingly argues that Emerson's fourth and last lecture before the Franklin Lyceum was an early version of what became between January and March 1844 "New England Reformers," a lecture that Emerson delivered on 3 March 1844 at Amory Hall in Boston and then revised for inclusion in *Essays: Second Series* in 1844 (*CW*, 3:147–67; for additional details, see Simmons, "Emerson's 1843–1844 New England Lectures").

In this edition, we have followed the Houghton Library arrangement of the series—and thus our arrangement of the *New England* series represents the series as Emerson delivered it at the New York Society Library in 1843—for three reasons: first, this is the most stable arrangement of the lectures that is recoverable; second, this arrangement follows Emerson's own outline of the series as he typically described it to his brother William and others in correspondence (see below); and third, since Emerson's is the only hand apparent in the arrangement of the manuscripts themselves, most likely he, and he alone, restored them to the New York Society Library order after rearranging pages among the lectures and rearranging the order of his delivery of the lectures when he gave the series in Providence in 1844.

The complex genealogy of the *New England* series brings into stark relief the difference between Emerson's early and later lecturing practices. Whereas, as we comment in our introduction to this edition, Emerson typically lectured from relatively stable texts up to and through 1842, the majority of lectures in the present edition shows him engaged in wholesale reworking of individual lectures and in wholesale rethinking and reordering of lectures within and outside of series between the mid-1840s and the close of his career as a lecturer in the 1870s. As Simmons has shown, the *New England* series represents a bridge between these two major phases of Emerson's career as a lecturer. As a bridge, the *New England* series is significant not only as a means to distinguish Emerson's early lecturing practices from his later ones but also, in our estimation, as an illustration of the degree of self-consciousness with which Emerson remade himself as a lecturer in order to gain wider public exposure for his ideas.

Emerson was working on the *New England* series by November 1842, when he wrote his brother William, "I have been trying my hand lately at setting down notes with a view to some set of Lectures that I could call 'New England,' that should be good enough to bring to the Southerner: but am not yet perfect in it" (*Letters*, 3:100). Writing a newsy letter to his friend Charles Stearns Wheeler in Germany, Emerson described his series, which he said he hoped to "spin . . . into four or five Lectures," in these terms: "My subject is 'New England,' which pleases me well, as it gives place & value to a hundred things which I have to say. English character & the relation of new to old England is a rich topic, & not letting alone the West & the Future of both [of] which, we Yankees are so fond. Recent spiritual influences in New England culture—unlock all the questions one would care to think of" (13 December 1842, *Letters*, 7:518). By the end of the year, he could write Margaret Fuller that "I have in my portfolio the value of three pretty good lectures on New England, which may become five before they get spoken; say 1. Religion; 2. Agriculture & Trade; 3 Genius & Manners; 4 Recent Spiritual influences; 5. Climate, or Relations or Politics or Future or Miscellaneous" (31 December 1842, *Letters*, 3:107–8). Still, Emerson worked slowly, and even while in New York, when engaged in the second and third deliveries of the series, he could complain to Fuller, "I have written (what I call written) three of my lectures (of Five) at Phila. & here; to a great loss of good time" (23 February 1843, *Letters*, 3:149). But, writing to Thomas Carlyle only two months later, Emerson expressed satisfaction with the overall result of his intense effort on the *New England* series, and he confided a previously unacknowledged motivation for the series and the new lecturing practices it represented:

> Since I last wrote to you, I found it needful . . . to set some new lectures in order, & go to new congregations of men. I live so much alone, shrinking almost cowardly from the contact of worldly and public men, that I need more than others to quit home sometimes, & roll with the river of travellers, & live in hotels. I went to Baltimore, where I had an invitation, & read two lectures on New England. On my return, I stopped at Philadelphia, & my Course being now grown to four [*sic*] lectures, read them there. At New York, my snowball was larger, and I read five lectures on New England. 1, Religion; 2, Trade; 3 Genius, Manners, & customs. 4, Recent literary & spiritual influences from abroad. 5 spiritual history.— Perhaps I have not quite done with them yet, but may make them the block of a new & somewhat larger structure . . . next winter. (29 April 1843, *CEC*, 341)

Emerson was gratified by responses to his Philadelphia series, which he delivered at the Chinese Museum. Writing to Lidian on 25 January 1843 that "it is time to tell you how I fare," Emerson described his success: "Why well enough in the good affection of the young & the intellectual and that special parish of mine the religious infidels. . . . The first evening I thought the audience very small, perhaps 200 but they told me it was made of some of their best people. This night the audience was considerably increased, possibly there were 300; And they listen intelligently enough, nay declare that they are delighted" (*Letters*, 3:133).

Emerson was even moved to write Fuller, "I think the right way to practice this new profession of the Lecture, with effect, would be to come at leisure into such a metropolis as this, and read a pretty long series of connected discourses"; he added that among the advantages he personally enjoyed on this lecture tour was his contact with a whole new audience of listeners and conversationalists:

> I admire the merchants; I think they shame the scholars[.] They understand & do their work greatly better than these do theirs. They take up & consume a great deal more vital force, and the conversations of the hotels are much better exhibitions of manly power than any I hear in libraries. I admire their manners and their docility: so many scholars are made of buckram in mind as well as body, [but] these men . . . are ductile ample liberal natures. (31 January–2 February 1843, *Letters,* 3:137–38)

Emerson's experiences in New York were varied. He had been approached while in Philadelphia by the Berean Society to give his series at their Universalist Church. They promised him an average audience of one thousand people, plus "half the clear proceeds of each lecture" after about $15 had been subtracted for expenses. Emerson arranged with his brother William, who lived on Staten Island, to finalize the arrangements, from which Emerson expected at least $50 per lecture (*Letters,* 3:134–35). Unfortunately, the church in the Bowery section was not easily accessible and the weather was bad, both resulting in a small audience, and Emerson canceled the series after the first two lectures ("Mr. Emerson's Lecture," *New-York Daily Tribune,* 8 February 1843, 2). Emerson started the series over again at the New York Society Library to greater crowds, but he netted only $9 per lecture because of the expenses associated with his extended stay in the city (*Letters,* 3:150).

As part of his effort to remake himself as a lecturer and find, as he wrote to Carlyle, "new congregations" for his ideas, Emerson delivered individual lectures from the *New England* series on numerous separate occasions during and after the period 1843–44. Because Emerson rarely provided discrete titles for these particular deliveries, readers will find that the titles under which they have been reported in Charvat and von Frank are sometimes at variance with one another, as well as with the titles used in this edition. In the headnotes that follow, the majority of titles used to report Emerson's delivery of individual lectures drawn from the *New England* series are those provided by Simmons in her reconstruction from contemporary newspaper accounts of their respective topic(s) (see "Emerson's 1843–1844 New England Lectures").

As with many of his lectures, Emerson mined the *New England* series for use in his other works, most notably "New England Reformers." He did not publish any lecture in the series separately, although he did try unsuccessfully to get Horace Greeley to place his "Introductory Lecture on New England" for publication in *Graham's Magazine* for $50 (see 7 April 1843, *Letters,* 3:164).

# *New England,* Lecture I: "The Genius and National Character of the Anglo-Saxon Race" 10 January 1843 (1843–1844)

Emerson first delivered this lecture as "New England" on 10 January 1843 as the first of two lectures from the *New England* series before the Mercantile Library Association in Baltimore. He received $100 for the series (*Letters*, 3:150). He repeated it on 23 January 1843 as the first of five lectures in a *New England* series at the Chinese Museum in Philadelphia, for which he received no more than $100 (*Letters*, 3:139); on 1 March 1843 before the Mercantile Association in Newark, New Jersey; and on 24 April 1852 as the sixth in a series of six lectures on the *Conduct of Life* before the Mercantile Library Association at Bonsecours Hall in Montreal, for which he received $120 for the series ("Account Books"). In Baltimore the *American & Commercial Daily Advertiser* praised the first lecture in general terms (12 January 1843, *Letters*, 3:117).

Emerson then delivered this lecture under the title "The Origins of New England Character" on 7 February 1843 as the first of an intended five lectures in a *New England* series before the Berean Society at the Universalist Church in the Bowery in New York City. He canceled the series after two lectures because of inclement weather and the difficulty audiences had in finding the church (see *Letters*, 3:143n). Nevertheless, the *New-York Daily Tribune* favorably summarized the lecture in a slightly more than one column report (8 February 1843, 2).

In New York Emerson started again by delivering this lecture as "The Genius and National Character of the Anglo-Saxon Race" on 11 February 1843 as the first of five lectures in a *New England* series at the New York Society Library. After expenses, he was able to clear $9 per lecture (*Letters*, 3:150). He repeated it as "Traits and Genius of the Anglo-Saxon Race" on 25 November 1852 before the Young Men's Association in Troy, New York, for which he received $40 ("Account Books").

Emerson also delivered this lecture as "Origin and National Genius of the People" on 8 January 1844 as the first of four lectures in a *New England* series before the Franklin Lyceum at Westminster Hall in Providence, Rhode Island, receiving $80 for the series (Cabot, "Blue Books"; see Simmons, "Emerson's 1843–1844 New England Lectures"). He was praised for his "accurate observation and vigorous common sense" in a six-paragraph summary in the *Public Ledger* (10 January 1844, 2).

For the reasons given in the headnote to Emerson's *New England* series (see above), the title used for this lecture in this edition is taken from the title under which the lecture was advertised when Emerson delivered it on 11 February 1843 at the New York Society

Library. The text of this lecture has never been published under any of the titles associated with it.


I N CONSIDERING WHAT topic I might best select as a channel for such thoughts
as I had to offer you, none occurred to me as more fit than the name of New
England, connected as it is with this city and with your institution by many ties,
and apt to furnish me in its inward and outward aspects, in its genius and manners, its employments and customs, and especially in its recent spiritual history
with valuable thoughts.

It cannot but happen that in what I have to say of that country, I may say many
things equally true of other, especially Atlantic, states and of Maryland. That is
the reason why the topic is fit. In a country like this, where the locomotive and
the steamboat, like enormous shuttles, shoot every day across the thousand various threads of national descent and employment and bind them fast into one web,
an hourly assimilation is going on, and it is folly to exaggerate peculiarities. You
will consider, then, that I only use the name of New England—not to arrogate
to that district a special praise, nor to exclude other parts of the country from
criticism, but to lessen the chances of misstatement. I shall look in succession
at the descent of the people of New England, at their leading national features,
and, if time is allowed me, at some of the intellectual and moral influences which
have recently operated and are still active in their culture.

They are not a people of yesterday, but their character still preserves a stern
unity which allies them through their progenitors to the oldest families of the
globe. The inhabitants of the United States, especially of the northern portion,
are descended from the people of England, and have inherited the traits of their
national character. It is sometimes said that the American character is only the
English character exaggerated. Are they lovers of freedom? We more. Are they
lovers of commerce? We more. Are they lovers of utility? We more.

It is remarkable that the traits of national character are almost as permanent
as the grander natural forms of a country: the mountains, rivers, and plains.
Through all the manifold causes that have operated for centuries to change their
laws, manners, and customs, the English of the present day bear the same marks
by which their ancestors are described by Caesar and Tacitus eighteen hundred
years ago, *viz.*: "that they were blue-eyed men, lovers of liberty, yielding more to
authority than to command, and respecting the female sex."[1]

The Scots exhibit at the present day a strong likeness to the portrait sketched

---

1. Gaius Julius Caesar (100 – 44 B.C.), Roman general and statesman, and Cornelius Tacitus (ca. 55 –
ca. 117), Roman historian and orator.

of them by Servetus three centuries ago. "The Scots are of rapid genius, quick at revenge, and fierce. Brave in war; patient of the open air, watching, and frost; of comely person, but careless of dress; naturally envious and despisers of other men; very fond of showing their long descent, and in the greatest poverty, tracing themselves to a royal line. They are, moreover, fond of dialectics, and acute at an argument." [2]

The historical virtues and vices of the French nation, at least as their enemies represent them, were sharply set down by Vopiscus and Salvian before the middle of the third century.

> *Francis familiare estridendo fidem frangere:* The Franks are false but hospitable.
> "It is common with the Franks to break their faith and laugh at it." [3]
> "They esteem perjury a figure of speech and not a crime." [4]

An union of laughter and crime, of deceit and politeness, is the unfavorable picture of the French character drawn by the English, and Germans, and even by the French themselves. In Rabelais, the good Gymnast is made to say, "My sovereign lord, such is the nature and complexion of the French, that they are worth nothing but at the first push." [5] (The French have no word for *to stand,* but must express it by a phrase.) Montaigne endorses the remark with one of the same purport. [6] And all the modern performance and failure of that lively nation, have exhibited this union of social talent, with deficiency of the moral sentiment; of skill to live and skill to work, with absence of remote aim; of delirious courage in attack, with levity and want of reserved force, which these old observers recorded.

The British family is expanded but not altered. The national traits are the same for centuries. We see at this moment, only the demonstration of the thoughts which were already ripe in the beginning of the seventeenth century, when the Religious War drove the Puritans to America. The two main points by which the English nation was then distinguished, the two points by which they attached themselves to the heavens and the earth, to the mind and to matter, namely, Conscience and Common Sense, or in view of their objects, the love of Religion and the love of Commerce, Religion and Trade, are still the two hands by which they hold the dominion of the globe.

The English race, in all times of their history, have held a high moral rank:

2. Quoted from Michael Servetus (1511–33), Spanish theologian and physician.
3. Quoted from Flavius Vopiscus, fourth-century Roman historian.
4. Quoted from Salvianus, fifth-century Christian religious figure and writer.
5. François Rabelais (ca. 1494–1553), French satirist.
6. Michel Eyquem de Montaigne (1533–92), French essayist and philosopher, usually identified with skepticism.

earnest, capable of belief, of religion, and, though not prone to it, yet capable of enthusiasm. The wonderful power of that Jewish idea which has so written itself on the nations, has had its full force in the Saxon race. In England, a strong religious nature received Christianity at its first planting, and dearly cherished it. Foxe's *Book of Martyrs,* Southey's *Book of the Church,* the *Acta Sanctorum,* and the Saxon *Chronicles* can testify how well.[7] Faithful work has been done here, for conscience's sake, by men, too, who did not take counsel of flesh and blood, and knew not what they did. For a thousand years, the history of England is a religious history. All the early historians are the religious orders, and the cause of popular rights, of popular education, is maintained by the clerisy, against the brutal power of the king and barons.

The Commonwealth emerges every year into new consequence as one of the great epochs in the spiritual history of mankind. All the contemporary records betray their sense of its peculiar life. I think of George Fox, of Sewel's *History,* of Milton's description of the city of London when besieged.[8]

Sewel, the historian of the Quakers, speaking of the state of England in the year 1648, writes, "About this time, there were abundance of people in England, who, having searched all sects, could nowhere find satisfaction for their hungry souls. And these now understanding that God by his light was so near in their hearts, began to take heed thereunto."

Now hear what Milton says about the same date of the interior character of the time.[9] He speaks of the city of London in the time of the Long Parliament.

> "Behold now this vast city, a city of refuge, the mansion house of liberty, encompassed and surrounded with his protection; the shop of war hath not there more anvils and hammers waking to fashion out the plates and instruments of armed justice in defence of beleaguered truth, than there be pens and heads there sitting by their studious lamps, musing, searching, revolving new motions and ideas wherewith to present as with their homage and their fealty the approaching reformation; others as fast reading, trying all things, assenting to the force of reason and convincement."

Hear further the reason with which he persuades himself of the good issue to humanity of the Civil War.

7. Emerson's references are to *Actes and Monuments* (1563) by John Foxe (1516–87), popularly known as *The Book of Martyrs*; *The Book of the Church* (1824) by Robert Southey (1774–1843); *Acta Sanctorum,* or *Lives of the Saints,* which the Flemish Jesuit hagiologist Jean de Bolland (1596–1665) began editing and which was continued by the "Bollandists," his collaborators and successors.

8. George Fox (1624–91), founder of the Society of Friends (Quakers); *The History of the Rise, Increase, and Progress of the Christian People Called Quakers* by William Sewel (1654–1720), English Quaker historian.

9. John Milton (1608–74), English poet and political writer.

"When a city shall be, as it were, besieged and blocked about, her navigable river infested, inroads and incursions round, defiance and battle oft rumoured to be marching up even to her walls and suburb trenches, that then, the people, or the greater part, more than at other times, wholly taken up with the study of highest and most important matters to be reformed, should be disputing, reasoning, reading, inventing, discoursing, even to a rarity and admiration, things not before discoursed or written of, it betokens a people destined to become great and honorable in these latter ages."

Precisely at this moment, when this most energetic of all the mysterious impulses which agitate man, was in its activity, the colony was detached which planted America. Hence may proceed the more ideal character of the New England race. The people driven out of the country were precisely the idealists of England, the most religious in a religious era.

The flagrant feature in our history down to a quite recent period was its religious character. How richly this old stream of antique faith descended into New England, every town, almost every family, will bear witness. That country forty or fifty years ago was imbued with a certain normal piety, a levitical education which, falling on fit subjects, gave often advantages which, only rarely, devout genius could countervail. It still stands in contrast with the comparatively cold instruction of the theological institutions, like a religion in the blood. The depth of the religious sentiment, as it may still be remembered in individuals imbuing all their genius and derived to them from hoarded family traditions, from so many godly lives and godly deaths of sainted kindred, was itself an education. It raised every trivial incident to a celestial dignity. I heard with awe in my youth of the pale stranger, who, at the time one of these fathers in God, lay on his deathbed, tapped at the window, and asked to come in. The dying man said, 'Open the door;' but the family were timid; Immediately, he breathed his last, and they said one to another, 'It was the angel of death.' Another of these elect souls when near his end had lost the power of speech, and his minister came to him and said, "If the Lord Christ is with you, hold up your hand;" and he stretched both arms aloft and died. In every town in Maine you may still hear of the charities and of the commanding administration of his holy office, of Father Moody of Agamenticus.[10] When the offended parishioners, wounded by his pointed preaching, would rise to go out of church, he cried out, "Come back you graceless sinner, come back." And when his parishioners began to fall into ill customs and ventured into the ale house on a Saturday night, the valiant pastor went in

10. This entire section was inspired by the tales of Mary Moody Emerson (1774–1863), Emerson's aunt (see *JMN*, 5:323–24). Samuel Moody (1676–1747), minister at York, Maine, and Emerson's great-great-grandfather.

after them, collared the sinners, dragged them forth, and sent them home with rousing admonitions. Charity then went hand in hand with Zeal. They gave alms profusely and the barrel of meal wasted not. One of this venerable line the minister of Malden, Massachusetts, whilst his house was burning, stood apart with some of his church and sang, "There is a house not made with hands." His successor was wont to go into the road whenever a traveller passed on Sunday, and entreat him to tarry with him during holy time himself furnishing food for the man and beast.[11] Religion was their occupation, and the prophetic and apocalyptic ejaculations of these worthies still colour the language of devotion in the American churches. In the departure of this faith, see what a vast body of religious writings which came down to this generation as an inestimable treasure— the whole body, I mean, of English and early American sermons and practical divinity—have been suddenly found to be unreadable and consigned to remediless neglect. The result was proportioned to the intensity of this faith.

These Puritans,—however, in the last days they have declined into ritualists,—solemnized the hey-day of their strength by the planting and the liberating of America. Great grim, earnest men! I belong by natural affinity to other thoughts and schools than yours, but my affection hovers respectfully about your retiring footsteps, your unpainted churches, strict platforms and sad offices, the iron gray deacon and the wearisome prayer rich with the diction of ages.

The new is only the seed of the old. What is this abolition, non-resistance, and temperance but the continuation of Puritanism, though it operate the destruction of the church in which it grew as the new is always making the old superfluous.

As an instance of strong attachment in these days to the old forms, I knew an old man who was born and bred in the old New England faith and whose infirmities of late years incapacitated him from attending the parish church, but as I was told by the sole attendant of his last years, that, on the first Sunday of each month, when it was, as we call it, Communion Day, he was accustomed to have a little bread and wine laid in his apartment, and he spent the day alone and in his chamber, where the loneliness of extreme age was added to the loneliness of place, and performed by himself all the parts of his wonted service with great comfort and affection.

"In consequence of Archbishop Laud's famous proclamation setting up certain novelties in the rites of public worship, fifty godly ministers were suspended for contumacy in the course of two years and a half.[12] Hindered from speaking, some of these dared to print the reasons of their dissent and were punished

---

11. Joseph Emerson (1700–1767), minister at Malden, Massachusetts, and Emerson's great-grandfather.

12. William Laud (1573–1645), archbishop of Canterbury (1633–45).

with imprisonment or mutilation. This severity brought some of the best men in England to overcome that natural repugnance to emigration which holds the serious and moderate of every nation to their own soil." Those who had estates turned them into money, and those who had none, by that love which persecution provokes among its victims, easily found means to join the troop of emigrants who were coming among the American savages to plant a church in the snows.

I will not recapitulate the familiar incidents of their history. And yet, in New England, every snowstorm, every December wind, still recites to us the hardships they bore and the alleviations which Nature herself provided. For meat, they had none except when they could barter with the Indians for venison and raccoons. But the rivers and sea swarmed with fish. Indian corn, even the coarsest, made as pleasant a meal as rice. "And let no man," writes their chronicler, "make a jest of pumpkins, for with this fruit the Lord was pleased to feed his people, until their corn and cattle were increased." The land was healthy, and if they found the air of America very cold, they might say with Higginson after his description of the other elements, that, "New England may boast of the element of fire more than all the rest; for all Europe is not able to afford to make so great fires as New England. A poor servant that is to possess but fifty acres, may afford to give more wood for fire, as good as the world yields, than many noblemen in England."[13]

Many wants, had they, but more satisfactions. The light struggled in through windows of oiled paper, but they read the word of God by it. They were fair to make use of their knees for a table, but their limbs were their own. Hard labor and spare diet they had, and off wooden trenchers, but they had peace and freedom, and the wailing of the tempest in the woods sounded kindlier in their ear than the smooth voice of the prelates at home in England. "There is no people," said the pastor to one of these flocks of exiles who had emigrated with him to a little interior town of New England, "but will strive to excel in something. What can we excel in, if not in holiness? If we look to number, we are the fewest; if to strength, we are the weakest; if to wealth and riches, we are the poorest of all the people of God through the whole world. We cannot excel, nor so much as equal other people in these things; and if we come short in grace and holiness too, we are the most despicable people under heaven. Strive we, therefore, herein to excel, and suffer not this crown to be taken away from us."[14] As the preacher spoke, the people heard. And, as we are informed, "The edge of their appetite was greater to spiritual duties at their first coming, in time of wants, than afterwards."

---

13. Francis Higginson (1586–1630), clergyman and author of the popular *New England's Plantation, or, a Short and True Description of the Commodities and Discommodities of that Country* (1630).

14. Peter Bulkeley (ca. 1582–ca. 1658), one of the founders of Concord, Massachusetts.

I dwell on this subject, because I am very well convinced that the history of what is best in New England is the unfolding of this sentiment. The jets of this central fire are institutions, books, men: it is the most creative energy in our experience. As it has constituted the history of past centuries, so its withdrawal, its apparent repose and its transition into new organs, makes what is best in recent history. I doubt if the interior and spiritual history of New England could be truelier told than through the exhibition of town-, of village-, of family-history, in which, for the last twenty years, would everywhere appear the conflict of the new and the old ideas.

I picture New England to myself as a mother, sitting amidst her thousand churches, heir of whatever was rich, and profound, and efficient in thought and emotion in the old religion which planted and peopled this land, and strangely uniting to this passionate piety the fatal gift of penetration; a love of philosophy, an impatience of words, and thus becoming at once religious and skeptical—a most religious infidel. She holds on with both hands to the faith of the past generation, as to the palladium of all that was good in the physical and metaphysical worlds, and extolled and poetised in this beloved Calvinism. Yet all the time, she doubted and denied it, and could not tell whether to be more glad or sorry to find that her thousand sons were irremediably born to the adoption and furtherance of the new ideas. She is like Margaret Graeme, the enthusiast in Scott's romance, who lives to infuse into young Roland her enthusiasm for the Roman Church, only that *our* Margaret doubted whilst she loved, yet loved whilst she doubted.[15]

The farmer is naturally religious, and the peculiarity of his employments, which isolate him every day and drive him into some remote meadow or wood lot to spend the entire day in solitary labor, comes to the assistance of this sentiment. If, as may easily happen, his mind be of a profounder mould, he becomes contemplative and devout, and resists the restless disposition of his countrymen. Trade is of no country, but wanders easily through all. Religion disposes a man to stay at home and consecrates the nearest objects. Religion serves a farther purpose of constantly civilizing and refining men, of resisting degrading influences, and giving an upward look to every hour and every action.

Beside the direct culture of the conscience and the general probity which this hereditary religious sentiment generates, I trace to this deep religious sentiment and to its culture other great and salutary results to the character of the people of New England: First, namely, the culture of the intellect, which has always been found in the Calvinistic Church. The religious are always disposed to give to their children a more liberal discipline of books, of schools, and of superior con-

15. Emerson's description of New England as a "mother" is developed out of a character portrait of his aunt Mary Moody Emerson. Magdalen—not "Margaret"—Graeme is a character in *The Abbot* (1820) by Sir Walter Scott (1771–1832), prolific Scottish novelist.

versation—a fact borne out by all history but especially by the history of New England. The colony was planted in 1620; in 1636 Harvard College was founded. The General Court of Massachusetts in 1647, "To the end that learning may not be buried in the graves of our forefathers, *ordered;* that every township, after the Lord had increased them to the number of fifty householders, shall appoint one to teach all children to write and read; and where any town shall increase to the number of one hundred families, they shall set up a grammar school, the masters thereof being able to instruct youth so far as they may be fitted for the university."

Many and rich are the fruits of that simple statute. The universality of an elementary education in New England is her praise and her power in the whole world. To the school succeeds the village Lyceum, now very general throughout all the country towns of New England, where, every week through the winter, lectures are read and debates sustained which prove a college for the young rustic. Hence, it happens that the young farmers and mechanics who work all summer in the field or shop, in the winter often go into a neighboring town to teach the district school arithmetic and grammar. As you know too, New England supplies annually a large detachment of preachers, and school-masters, and private tutors, to the interior of the South and West. Great numbers, less critically instructed, yet still with some smattering of letters, are employed by the Connecticut bookdealers as book agents to travel in the interior and vend their editions. And, it sometimes happens that a poor man's son in Connecticut, whose intellect is superior, who would fain go to college but has not the means, escapes from hard labor for which his finer organization unfits him, finds someone to trust him with wares, and goes as a pedlar into Virginia and Carolina, that so he may at a small expense see the world, converse with men, and by intercourse with more polished persons than his native village can exhibit, supply the defects of his limited and humble training. One of the most intellectual men I have ever seen had his training so.[16]

It is a remark frequently made by those who are conversant with New England, that, such is the value universally attached to a superior education, that no political or religious prejudices are suffered to stand in its way. If the Catholics have a good school, or if the Unitarians have a good college, the most devoted adherents of other and conflicting sects will send their daughters or sons to these seminaries. It only needs a confidence that a superior culture is really to be had there, to bring as many pupils as are desired.

This is precisely the most agreeable picture which the Northern portion of the country has to show, the universality of a good elementary culture. If you ask me

16. This is Amos Bronson Alcott (1799–1888), Emerson's longtime friend and Concord neighbor.

for the best result in that country, I shall point you to a very common but always affecting spectacle—the poor but educated family. Who can see unmoved the eager blushing boys discharging, as they can, their household chores, and hastening into the sitting-room to the study of tomorrow's merciless lesson, yet stealing time to read a novel hardly smuggled into the tolerance of father and mother: atoning for the same by some pages of Plutarch or Goldsmith; the warm sympathy with which they kindle each other in schoolyard or in barn and wood-shed with scraps of the last oration or mimicry of the orator; the youthful criticism on Sunday of the sermons; the school declamation faithfully rehearsed at home, to the vexation more frequently than to the admiration of sisters; the first solitary joys of literary vanity, when the translation or the theme has been completed, sitting alone near the top of the house; the cautious comparison of the attractive advertisement of the arrival of Kean or Kemble, or of the discourse of a well-known speaker, with the expense of attending the same; the warm, affectionate delight with which they greet the return of each, after the early separations which school or business require; the foresight with which during such absences they hive the honey which opportunity offers for the ear and imagination of the others, and the unrestrained glee with which they disburden themselves of their early mental treasures, when the holidays bring them again together.[17]

What is the hoop that holds them staunch? It is the iron band of poverty, of necessity, of austerity, which, excluding them from the sensual enjoyments which make other boys too early old, has directed their activity in safe and right channels, and made them, spite of themselves, reverers of the grand, the beautiful, and the good. Ah, shortsighted students of books, of nature, and of man! too happy could they know their advantages. They pine for freedom from that mild parental yoke; they sigh for fine clothes; for rides; for the theatre, and premature freedom, and dissipation which others possess. Wo to them, if their wishes were crowned. The angels that dwell with them and are weaving laurels of life for their youthful brows, are Toil and Want, and Truth and Mutual Faith. In the language of Michel Angelo, himself one of the holiest of the masters of beauty,

> As from fire heat cannot be divided,
> No more can beauty from the Eternal.[18]

---

17. Plutarch (ca. 46–ca. 120), Greek historian best known for his series of "lives" of famous Greek and Roman figures; Oliver Goldsmith (1728–74), multifaceted English writer; Edmund Kean (1787–1833), English stage actor who toured America; Frances Anne ("Fanny") Kemble (1809–93), English actress and author who visited the United States.

18. Michelangelo Buonarroti (1475–1564), Italian painter, sculptor, and poet, also called "Angelo" by Emerson, quoted from Sonnet VI in *Rime de Michelangelo Buonorrati il vecchio*, ed. Giambattista Biagioli (1821).

This purer fire was more than elsewhere needed in the utilitarian race I speak of. New England is situated in those cold and hostile latitudes which, by shutting men up in houses and tight and heated rooms a large part of the year, and then again shutting up the body still closer in flannel and leather, defrauds the human being in some degree of his relations to external nature, takes from the muscles their suppleness;—from the skin its exposure to the air; and the New Englander, like every other northerner, lacks that beauty and grace which the habit of living much in the air, and the activity of the limbs not in labor but in grateful exercise, tends to produce in climates nearer to the sun. Then, the necessity which always presses the northerner of providing fuel, and many clothes, and tight houses, and much food against the long winter makes him anxiously frugal, and generates in him that spirit of detail, which is not grand and enlarging, but which goes, rather, to pinch the features and degrade the character. As an antidote to the spirit of commerce and of economy, the religious spirit—always enlarging, firing man, prompting the pursuit of the vast, the beautiful, the unattainable—was especially necessary to the culture of New England. In the midst of her laborious, and economical, and rude, and awkward population, where is little elegance and no facility;—with great accuracy in details, little spirit of society or knowledge of the world, you shall yet not unfrequently meet that refinement which no education and no habit of society can bestow, which makes the elegance of wealth look stupid, and which unites itself by natural affinity to the highest minds of the world, and nourishes itself on Plato, and Dante, and Michel Angelo, and Milton; on whatever is pure and sublime in art, and, I may say, which gave a hospitality in this country to the spirit of Coleridge and Wordsworth, and now to the music of Beethoven, before yet their genius had found "a hearty welcome in Great Britain." [19]

There is a comparative innocence in this country and a correspondent health. We do not see bald boys and gray-haired girls, children who are victims of gout and apoplexy. The street is not full of near-sighted people, nor do we see those horrid mutilations and disgusting forms of disease, leprosy, and undescribed varieties of plague, which European streets exhibit in the stumps of men. How often in Rome or Naples, one sees a fragment of a man sitting all day on a stone in some public crossing place to beg with a plate with covered head, and only some sign of dreadful meaning peeping under his cowl, as if day was not to see such rottenness. An American is struck in England with the appearance in all companies of a great deal of hereditary disease and misses the innocent, rustic complexions

19. Dante Alighieri (1265–1321), Italian poet and Christian humanist; Samuel Taylor Coleridge (1772–1834), English poet and philosopher, and William Wordsworth (1770–1850), British poet, co-founders of the Romantic movement; Ludwig van Beethoven (1770–1827), German composer.

which abound here. There is a certain hard finish about the Englishman, an air of the world, which contrasts with this plain, simple, boundless Jonathan, a little silex which makes a good edge, and protects them like a coat of mail. Whilst the Yankee is apt to make up his want of address by main strength, so that the characteristic of the American in Europe is pretension.

There is a general innocence and health, and with that, a general correctness of thought. We have innocence in our manners and habits, but not a vigorous virtue which dares all and performs all. In like manner, we have a general correctness of thought, but we have no mastery. We are still the disciples of other lands—we, who sometimes think we have broken every yoke.

Something of the physical perfection of the heroic age is exhibited by the Indian in the woods, but without the ardent temperament, and without the taste of the Greek. We feel that he stands in stricter relations with Nature than other persons, and possesses a portion of her majesty. Like the moose and bison which he hunts, he belongs to the order of the world. He is part of the morning and evening, of forest and mountain, and is provided for as the ravens are. It was a just remark of Talleyrand that to go from the American coast one or two thousand miles into the wilderness was like going back one or two thousand years in time.[20] You pass in both from the extreme of civilization to the extreme of barbarism.

20. Charles Maurice de Talleyrand-Périgord, prince de Bénévent (1754–1838), French statesman known for his lack of commitment to established principles.

# *New England,* Lecture II:
# "The Trade of New England"
# 17 January 1843
# (1843–1844)

Emerson first delivered this lecture as "Customs, Genius and Trade of New England" on 17 January 1843 as the second of two lectures in a *New England* series before the Mercantile Library Association in Baltimore. He received $100 for the series (*Letters,* 3 : 130). The *Baltimore Sun* gave the lecture a favorable summary of nearly a full column (19 January 1843, 1).

Under the title of "The Trade of New England," Emerson repeated this lecture on 25 January 1843 as the second of five lectures in a *New England* series at the Chinese Museum in Philadelphia, for which he received no more than $100 (*Letters,* 3 : 139); on 9 February 1843 as the second of an intended five lectures in a *New England* series before the Berean Society at the Universalist Church in the Bowery in New York City; and on 15 February 1843 as the second of five lectures in a *New England* series at the New York Society Library in New York City. Emerson canceled the series before the Berean Society after two lectures because of inclement weather and the difficulty audiences had in finding the church; the *New-York Daily Tribune,* in a one-paragraph favorable description of the Berean lecture, noted that Emerson had "been persuaded to choose a lecture-room more convenient of access and commence his Course afresh" (10 February 1843, 2). After expenses, Emerson was able to clear $9 per lecture from the series at the New York Society Library (*Letters,* 3 : 150).

Under the title "The Trade of New England," Emerson delivered this lecture on 3 February 1843 before the Mercantile Library Association in Philadelphia, which had invited him for one lecture on short notice (*Letters,* 3 : 140). Finally, Emerson delivered this lecture as "Trade, Manners and Customs" of New England on 9 January 1844 as the second of four lectures in a *New England* series before the Franklin Lyceum at Westminster Hall in Providence, Rhode Island, receiving $80 for the series (Cabot, "Blue Books"; for both lectures, see Simmons, "Emerson's 1843–1844 New England Lectures"). Emerson received a favorable thirteen-paragraph summary of his delivery before the Franklin Lyceum in the *Providence Daily Journal* (11 January 1844, 2).

For the reasons given in the headnote to Emerson's *New England* series (see above), the title used for this lecture in this edition is taken from the title under which the lecture was advertised when Emerson delivered it on 15 February 1843 at the New York Society Library. The text of this lecture has never been published under any of the titles associated with it.

I N MY LAST lecture, I described the conscience as one of the two capital powers of the English and the Anglo-American mind leading them to the cultivation of Religion and of Education. I traced the unfolding of that element in the settlement and in the growth of this country. I may once more repeat the remark that, whilst for convenience, and to avoid error, I use the name of New England, I am well aware that most of the statements I make are equally true of all the Atlantic States as of the northern section.

An element in the English mind which has coloured and characterized the whole history and settlement of this country is the strong religious sentiment. There is no end to the important consequences which have flowed into all our institutions from this source. The question of history is, what each generation has done with its surplus produce? One bought games and amphitheatres; one, crusades; one, churches; one, villas; one, horses; one, operas; one, tulips; ours buys railroads, ships, mills, and observatories.

The other element which we marked as conspicuous in the English mind was that determination of blood to the hand, that strong determination of the faculties on the external world, which is called commonsense: and which, I think, would be ascribed to the English race in both hemispheres, not only over all nations that are now, but also over all that ever were in the planet. This trait makes them excellent in business, in farming, mechanic arts, and trade. The favorite employment of these nations is trade. A very small class whom the intellectual tastes possess and direct, are scholars, or find purely clerical employment. A larger but still comparatively small class who unite the practical and the intellectual power enter the profession of the law, and through the law enter the career of politics; but the great body of the energetic class will be found in the ranks of Trade. The English, Napoleon said, are a nation of shopkeepers, and the English in America are shopkeepers. Trade flagellates that melancholy temperament into health and contentment by its incessant stimulus. Its objects are at once sufficiently gross to satisfy their robust and active constitution, and the combination of means to remote ends furnishes that excitement to the intellect which this intellectual population needs. The earliest laws of England have the interests of the merchant in view.

The Atlantic cities, and New England perhaps most of all, have done and are doing whatever analysis can achieve. Minute division, and economy, and personal cares, and the power of the intellect applied to external wealth, are the active principles that generate every hour new masses of power and capital; and I offer these sketches as the best picture which history can furnish of these results. I own I have had my pride as a native of New England gratified by the redundant signs of her prosperity, by the increase of her wealth at each new valuation of ten years, in specifications where the augmentation of capital could not be ascribed to geographical advantages, but only to the invention and industry of her children. But in calmer hours, these things do not content me. They ought not to satisfy her sons. Man exists for his own sake, and not to add a laborer to the state.

I cannot deny my interest in every triumph of the Understanding. I love the ship, and the railroad; but I please myself more with the reactions against the spirit of commerce in New England; with the dawning of a great light of Reform which goes to revise all our modes of life and action. I please myself not with the results of her combination, with trade corporations and road-, canal-, and insurance-companies, or even with her benevolent associations for every object, but with what is not combination, with whatever goes to separate a man, and draw from him the unmixed suggestion of the private mind.

But it is too obvious that all the tendency of the popular mind of this country is to rely on the means provided by the Understanding for the aid and defence of man, and not on the simplest action of the man himself. We are men of expedients, and not of principles. Man in New England, man in this Republic, wants that grandeur of repose which most becomes him.

It seems as if history gave no intimation of any society in which despondency came so readily to heart as we see it and feel it in ours. Young men, young women, at thirty, and even earlier, lose all spring and vivacity, and if they fail in their first enterprize, throw up the game. Our people are surrounded with a greater external prosperity than Indians or Saxons, more resources, outlets, asylums, yet we are sad, and these were not. "A cloud always hangs over an American's brow," says De Tocqueville.[1] The whole American race sit on the anxious benches.

The famous compend of the Saxon laws prepared in the *Harleian Miscellaries* shows the principle of progress which was the genius of their institutions: how a church should become a lord, and an undertheyn, a theyn:

> It was sometimes in yᵉ English laws yᵗ yᵉ people and yᵉ laws were in reputation and then were yᵉ wisest of yᵉ people worship worthy each in his degree Lorle and Chorle, Theyn and Undertheyne.
>
> And if a Chorle so thrived that he had full five hides of his own land, a church and a kitchen, a bell-house and a gate, a seat and several offices in the King's hall: then was he thenceforth the Theyn's right worthy.
>
> And if a Theyn so thrived that he served yᵉ King and on his message or journey rode in his household; if then he had a Theyn that him followed, who to the King's expedition five hide had, and in yᵉ King's palace his lord served, and therewith his errand had gone to yᵉ King, he might afterward with his fore-oath his lord's part play at any need.

1. Alexis de Tocqueville (1805–59), French traveler to the United States best known for his two-volume *Democracy in America* (1835–40).

And if a Theyn so thrived that he became an Earl, then was he right forth an earl right worthy.

And if a Merchant so thrived that he passed over the wide sea, of his own craft, he was thenceforth the Theyn's right worthy.

And if a scholar so thrived through learning that he had degree and served Christ, he was thenceforth of dignity and peace so much worthy as thereto belonged unless he forfeited, so that the use of his dignity might be taken from him.[2]

To this day, though the title of nobility is not quite so summarily conferred, yet it is a well-known fact that the great majority of English nobles are of recent creation from the class of merchants or the sons of merchants.

Of course, the basis of trade must be agriculture, and what agriculture is to trade, that is the agricultural population to the maritime towns. It is the root of the tree. It is the mother-power. It furnishes the rude stock out of which the rich flowers and fruits of power, art, and civility, are matured. The rural population of New England are a hardy race, poor or slowly thriving, and it is commonly said that farming renders a return of only four per cent. It is common for a farmer to hire the money with which he buys his land, and to pay the interest all his lifetime. But, meantime, beside paying the interest, his farm has maintained a large family to whom he has given a good education, sent one boy to college, and one or two into trade in Boston, and the land and buildings are steadily increased in value, every year. As he grows old, his children assume the debt, which the enhanced estate will easily pay.

Farming in New England is a cold, surly business: no Arcadian affair, no piping shepherds, no dancing milkmaids, but a hard tug, and an incessant care. The farmer's gains are slow and pitiful, and got between snowbanks, and in laying heavy stone walls, and in ploughing in early spring with coat and mittens in a raw and biting north wind; at midsummer, sweltering in a hay field, or digging peat in a swamp all day, when days are fifteen hours long; and, in winter, chopping down trees in the woods, with the feet all day in the snow. Very hard work, very ill rewarded, and it naturally follows that the farmer is narrow and selfish in his trade, looks long after a cent, not at all glib or complaisant in his speech.

His dress is plain and of the color of the earth. His motions are slow and grave, his face hard and bronzed, his conversation usually sensible and honest, but without vivacity and inclining to the petty economies of good husbandry. His liberal topics are the town-affairs, general politics, and religion.

A constant, pressing poverty close behind him makes him industrious and saving, but he wants largeness of invention and generosity in his economy. He seldom deviates in any important step from the custom of his ancestors, and still

2. Quoted from the *Harleian Miscellany* (1808–11), ed. John Malham.

more seldom revises for himself his whole condition, or adventures a new way of living. In New England, we have little that can be called heroic farming no invention, no generalship, no humanity, but drudge follows drudge. Thus, it is thought that we devote so much attention to the raising of stock for which a great deal of land is required, that the poor man is degraded into a horse or cow feeder. In Massachusetts, the pig sells well in the market; the whole plantation and economy turns on that excellent animal as on a pivot. The produce is raised to feed pig; the pig again manures the new crop, which enables the farmer to keep more pigs—so that the poor farmer is in danger of becoming a swineherd.

Another injury to the agricultural interest is the continual draining of the best of its class. The constant intercourse with the city brings into every mountain village, into every river meadow, the tidings of the success of some young adventurer who has gone thither from the country to push his fortune in trade, or politics, or in professional life. The failures are not told: the victories are. And this acts as a perpetual bribe to every able and ambitious young man in the country to make him restless and discontented with the dull and poor certainties of rural labor. There are in the agricultural class occasionally to be met with good and great men who would rank with the best of any class, but as a general experience, it is to be considered that when any large brain is born in all this wide inland, it is sent at sixteen or twenty years to Boston or New York, and the country is tilled only by the inferior class of the people, reducing, of course, by so much, the energy and the elevation of the agricultural class. Hence, all the whole districts of shiftless, poverty-struck pig farms. In Europe, where society has an aristocratic structure, the land is full of men of the best stock and the best culture, whose interest and pride it is to remain half of the year at least, on their estates, and to fill these with every convenience and ornament. Of course, these make model farms and model architecture, and are a constant education to the eye and hand of the surrounding population.

There is still another evil which begins to be felt in our rural population, the same, namely, in far less degree which is recently alleged to be the undoing of the English yeomanry, namely, the influx of Irish laborers, a low and semi-barbarous legion, who can subsist almost on offal, and be clothed almost by rags, and can, therefore, easily undersell the labor of the native American, who with all his frugality is a much more costly and expensive person, with his physical, metaphysical, social, literary, and political wants: so that the only alternative left for the proud Caucasian race is to flee before the Irishman.

And, yet, though I have heard this evil stated by intelligent farmers as one already a matter of experience, yet, I own, it does not appear to me real. There are only a few things which these cheap and rude laborers can do. They are good to dig, not so good to hoe, not usually good to mow or to chop wood advantageously, and good for nothing in the garden. In our factories, it is found that educated labor always is valuable, and well-bred persons lose no time by deranging the machine or making blunders, and so their earnings are greater. It is settled law, that you must either lay to more strength, or you must sharpen the edge of your knife. Wit always will be a substitute for drudgery; not for labor, but for drudgery or excess of labor. For wit selects the right point whereon my stroke shall be bestowed, and so saves all the supernumerary strokes.

A dimsighted man strikes with his hammer here and there: a good eye hits the nail on the head. Jock calls on twenty men to help him. Dick calls to the right man that can help him. One sends information to several persons. The other to the newspaper, and it goes at once to twenty thousand.

These causes meantime operate to check, but not to enervate, the country. It has great powers and great virtues; It is sound, hardy, industrious, innocent, reflecting, and wise. They have the repose of strength and of rectitude. Men who know every secret of hardship and therefore are not to be terrified by common dangers. Men who have often turned the frozen soil into corn and wheaten cakes will never feel that terror of starvation which overpowers an inhabitant of cities. Their love of liberty is very marked. In our division of parties, the country is universally found to have a democratic tendency. The rich are timid; the poor are bold and nonchalant, negligent too of each other's opposition, for they see the amount of it and know its limits which the proprietor does not.

Especially the poorest and most laborious class carry this to petulance and are full of rebellion. The teamsters write on their teams, "No monopoly. Old Union Line to Portland or to Bennington." On the guideboards they paint, "Free trade and teamsters' rights." And if you go into the tavern and listen to the talk, you may persuade yourself that this country is far enough from a dominion of the aristocracy; is in much more danger of a Cacocracy; and is really governed in Bar-rooms.

The farmers' festivals and holidays are full of strong and determined freedom. The annual cattle shows will bring into the most secluded village in a few hours an army of wagons, gigs, carry-alls, horsemen, and footmen, and boys who shall in a very peaceful, if in a noisy, manner spend the day together inspecting the animals in the pens, attending the ploughing match, examining the home manufactures, hearing the awards of premiums by committees on butter, and beef, and apples—rugs and cloth, buying trinkets and books. At the booth of an auctioneer, hearing a public "Discourse on Book Farming," and eating gingerbread, and shall empty the village at night without a brawl, or the presence of a police officer.

In the autumn, our villages often hold a more decided holiday called a Cornwallis, as it seems really to have grown out of anniversary celebrations of the

victory at Yorktown.[3] The joke of this festival is to come dressed as much as possible in the style of the Revolutionary War; the troops are arranged in two parties, all the oddities and rags, of course, being put on the American side, a sham
fight follows, and Cornwallis surrenders. The day is ushered in with booming of
cannon, and clatter of bells, and whooping of boys. The motley recruits begin
early to appear in every antique and ludicrous costume that old presses and the
coarsest fun can furnish, and each hoary sinner and village debauchee is clamor-
ously whooped and greeted as he rides or runs into town. On the field, it appears
to be the high tide of nonsense, and, indeed, all the rag and tag of the county are
there in all the wigs, old hats, old firelocks, and aged finery of the last generation.
If there is any grotesque piece of humanity within twenty miles round, it is sure
to be on the ground. So that frequently the faces are like the dresses, such exaggerated noses, chins, and mouths that one could not reconcile them with any
other dress than that frippery they wear. But the officer instantly appears through
all this masquerade and buffoonery. The man of skill, the man of will, makes his
jacket invisible. Two or three natural soldiers among these merry captains play
out their habitual energy so well, that order and reason appear as much at home
in the farce as in the gravest meeting. Military order is really kept: the plan agreed
on by the officers in the morning, is punctually executed. And buffoons at a sham
fight are quickly as tedious as they are in a legislature.

In the little interior town in Massachusetts where I reside, I listen by night,
I gaze by day, at the endless procession of wagons loaded with the wealth of all
regions of England, of China, of Turkey, of the Indies, which from Boston creep
by my gate to all the towns of New Hampshire and Vermont. With creaking
wheels at midsummer and crunching the snows on huge sledges in January, the
train goes forward at all hours bearing this cargo of inexhaustible comfort and
luxury to every cabin in the hills, and thus everywhere is the country fastened to
the town by threads incessantly spun.

There are also masters of their art, men who combine the works of farm, nursery, and garden, and who carry these with a wonderful energy and success. Look
over the fence and see that plain, heavy man in a coat of no colours. No music you
would say there, and no enchantments, yet there is a musician who knows how to
make men run and leap for him in all weathers, and all sorts of men—paddies,
felons, farmers, carpenters, painters—yes, and trees, and grapes, and ice, and
stone, hot days, cold days, all must do the bidding of this *ménétrier de Meudon*.[4]

3. Charles, second earl of Cornwallis (1738–1805), lost the Battle of Yorktown in 1781; the holiday
is undoubtedly named after him and the occasion.

4. Le Ménétrier de Meudon, a figure in *Chansons: nouvelles et dernières* (1833) by French lyric poet
Pierre Jean de Béranger (1780–1857), is a fiddler who "could even make the mourners in a funeral
dance" (see *JMN*, 10:77).

With one stroke of his instrument, he danced a thousand tons of gravel from yonder blowing sand heap onto the bog meadow beneath, where now the English grass is waving in countless acres. With another, he terraced the sand hill and covered it with peaches and grapes. With another, he sends his lowing cattle every spring to the mountain pastures in Nashua and Contocook county.

He economizes every drop of sap in his trees as if it were wine. A few years ago, these trees were whipsticks. Now, every one of them is worth a hundred dollars. Look at their form: Not a branch or a twig is to spare. They look as if they were arms, and hands, and fingers holding out to you the fruit of the Hesperides. This land, when he took it, was a cold swamp impassable to the feet and hateful to the eyes: not worth many shillings the acre. He has drained, and ploughed, and spaded, and rotted, and contrived to make in a few years a soft, warm, smooth, friable soil covered with beautiful crops and inviting to the eyes and feet of every passenger.

Go into his barns and pens, see his swine, his cows, his horses. You shall find the best breeds, and he has a good deal to tell you of every one. His are the woods, the hills, the meadows, the waters: All are husbanded.— And now, since the railroad has reached him, his wood goes by the trains every day to town, the ice in his pond goes to England for a market.

This broad district of rural New England lies there, rough with aboriginal forests, towering into granite peaks, sinking into deep valleys, watered with sounding streams which form rich alluvial bottoms;—this great country lies there, mother of men, for the formation of simple and brave modes of living, and for the repairing by austere discipline the blood and the reason of those spoiled children whom the cities have thrown back upon it as an asylum, yet always it is sending its flower and first fruit into the city. As a fact, it must be conceded that the city draws into itself what is best from the fields. The city is continually recruited from the country. Far the largest part of our best known statesmen, lawyers, and merchants, and manufacturers are country boys, who came up rather late to town from the banks of the Merrimac or the Connecticut, from Moosehead Lake or the roots of Monadnoc, they came to fetch milk or cheese to market, or to get a place in the store of some elder and fortunate townsman, or only from curiosity, having a chance to ride on some uncle's cart or sleigh, and found very quickly how to make themselves useful to others and, so, to themselves. For I suppose that as a class, in natural astuteness and skill to take care of themselves, and get a foothold wherever they chance to be thrown, no people excel the people of New England.

This is their praise and blame everywhere. According to popular notions, the Yankee is one, who, if he once gets his teeth set on a thing, all creation cannot make him let go; who, if he can but grasp anywhere at a rope's end or a spar, will make it carry him; if he can find but so much as a stump or a pine log, will hold on to it and whittle out of it a house and barn, a farm and stock, mill-seat and village, a railroad and bank, a seat in Congress and a mission to England, and various other things equally useful and entertaining. These things are said, and many the like, but these no doubt are inventions of the enemy.

It is undoubtedly true that this people possess great enterprize and acuteness, that finding themselves on the water's edge with excellent ship-timber in the woods, they have built watercraft of all kinds and have, with tallow, hoop poles, shingles, shooks, wooden clocks, shoes, cheese, beef, or, if they could find no other freight, ice and stone, taken to the water and sailed it in every possible direction for a port and a market: and this in a manner so simple and cheap as to undersell almost all other marines. They are rash and run great, perhaps inexcusable, risks. Two or three men or two men and a boy will take a vessel from Maine to the West Indies.

Round every fireside in New England are told the feats of young men who at sea, or in foreign parts, or at home have at the right moment conceived and executed the critical deed which has opened for them a sure road to success.

"The vessels of the U.S. can cross the seas at a cheaper rate than any other vessels in the world. . . . The European sailor navigates with prudence; he only sets sail when the weather is favorable; if an unforeseen accident befals him, he puts into port; at night, he furls a part of his canvass, and, when the whitening billows intimate the vicinity of land, he checks his way and takes an observation of the sun.

But the American neglects these cautions and braves these dangers. He weighs anchor in the midst of tempestuous gales by night, and by day he spreads his sheets to the wind; he repairs, as he goes along, such damage as his vessel may have sustained from the storm; and when, at last, he approaches the term of his voyage, he darts onward to the shore as if he already descried a port. The Americans are often shipwrecked, but no trader crosses the seas so rapidly. And as they perform the distance in a shorter time, they can perform it at a cheaper rate.

The European touches several times at different ports in the course of a long voyage; he loses a good deal of precious time in making the harbor, or in waiting for a favorable wind to leave it, and he pays daily dues to be allowed to remain there. The American starts from Boston to go to purchase tea in China: he arrives at Canton, stays there a few days, and then returns. In less than two years, he has sailed as far as the entire circumference of the globe, and he has seen land but once. It is true that during a voyage of eight or ten months he has drunk brackish water and lived upon salt meat, that he has been in a continual contest with the sea, with disease, and with the tedium of monotony, but upon his return, he can sell a pound of his tea for a halfpenny less than the English merchant, and his purpose is accomplished."[5]

5. Quoted from Tocqueville, *Democracy in America*.

Equally with the farmer, and in New England more than the farmer, the merchant may be taken as the type of the population; the leading and characterizing figure in our society.

He is the mediator or broker of all the farmers on earth. To exchange for them the harvests which under all latitudes they have gathered out of the water, and the earth. He is the practical geographer: he learns where the cotton, the logwood, corn and tea, hides and drugs are to be found, and what fruits and wares the owners of these will barter them for. His eyes are turned to all regions. His warehouse is full of productions of distant places. His pigeonholes are stuffed with letters in all languages from every nation. His head is a map of all seaports; his thoughts are at London, at Havre, and at Canton: his head is the history of the world under one aspect, that of production. He has in every event that occurs, far or near, some interest;—in a revolution, in an election, in a fire, in a freshet, in a frost, in the discovery of a mine or an economical invention, in a new road or a new mode of travelling, in the migration of the herring and the multiplication of whales.

He is a very far-reaching person, and his power is felt in the marts of every civilized country. His rewards are very splendid at home, and sometimes a few years suffice to build up one of those monumental fortunes which found the social and political importance of families and the prosperity of colleges, churches, and charities which our merchants have established. Nay, what is one of our large and suddenly expanded cities, Baltimore, Philadelphia, New York, Boston, along the Atlantic shore, but a club of merchants larger and less, and all this splendor is the result which they have combined to fetch home and spread around them.

Let me, then, come a little nearer to the fine worm that wove all this silk, and read his secret if we can. A great merchant is a very considerable person and by no means very common. Of those who trade in State Street or in Wall Street, Mr. Barnard asserts ninety fail—some say ninety five fail—for one who succeeds. Commerce is sometimes said to have grown so savage that it is next door to piracy. It is only a varioloid of cannibalism: "Eat or be eaten," is its law of nature. As the pike eats up the pickerel, so every great merchant has devoured nine or ten little ones; sometimes, the old ones a great many more. One sees very well in these complaints what the facts are; that commerce is a game of great skill, which every man cannot play, which very few men can play well; the right merchant is a man in whom this average of faculties which we call commonsense, exists in a great and commanding degree. A man of steadiness and penetration, who proceeds only on facts, never on hearsay; who makes up his decision on what he has seen and not on what others think. He is a person thoroughly persuaded of the truths of arithmetic, and he acts upon them always. He believes in General

Jackson's maxim, that nobody breaks who ought not to break.[6] Always there is a reason discoverable in the man for his good or ill fortune, and so in making money. Men think there is some magic about this, as they believe in magic, indeed, in all parts of life. He knows that all goes on the old trot, dollar for dollar, cent for cent; for every effect a perfect cause, and that good luck is another name for industry and economy *unremitted*, as Napoleon replied to one who ascribed a victory to the favor of Providence, that he had noticed that Providence always favors the heaviest battalion.[7] Believing thus in law and not in luck, he runs no risks, he insures himself in every transaction, and contents himself with the small and sure gains of his trade, the regular commissions of his business, believes and knows that his wealth is to come not by gambling which risks all, but by these steady rills which are secure, by these and by *never losing,* he builds up the solid foundations of his credit and daily leaves behind him in the race those, who, tempted by great hopes of gain, ventured when he denied himself and held back. This makes his credit, which is real and robust, and not that fantastic, dreamlike all-or-nothing, which swaggers today and perishes tomorrow in the Merchants' Exchange. Moral considerations give currency every day to notes of hand. This man during the land-fever bought no acre in Maine or in Michigan. His notes have a better currency as long as he lives. That man is a commission merchant, and in the midst of a vast business does not trade on his own account to the amount of a dollar. Everybody gladly buys his paper.

This taste for reality and application of arithmetic with his own eyes and hands to the whole length of each affair with which he deals, is the basis of his success; on which every great and durable fabric of trade has stood, whether that of the Fuggers of Augsburgh, the Medici of Florence, the Rothschilds of London, or the institutors of the whale trade, the cod fishery, the carrying trade, the India trade, the ice trade, in this country.[8]

There are, however, all degrees in the skill and success of this profession. Probity and closeness to the facts are the foundation, but those who are masters in the art add to these powers the long arithmetic, the power of remote combination, and accurate tactics, which make commerce as complex, as extended, and as difficult a game in its larger operations as the game of war played by Marlborough or Napoleon.[9] The problem is to combine many and remote operations with the

6. Andrew Jackson (1767–1845), seventh president of the United States (1829–37).

7. Napoleon Bonaparte (1769–1821), French general and ruler of France.

8. The Fuggers of Augsburg, Germany, were merchants and moneylenders; the Medici of Florence were merchants and rulers of that city and Tuscany; and the Rothschilds of London were bankers.

9. John Churchill, first duke of Marlborough (1655–1722), British statesman and military commander.

same accuracy and scrupulous adherence to the facts as is easy in near and small transactions, so to arrive at gigantic results without any compromise of safety. It is by this unbelief in luck, by this belief in cause and effect, by this assurance that large gains come of many small gains, and the continued application of this faith to operations however extended, and to gains grown enormous, that the Yankee merchant is made.

I look with great interest at the merchant, because his whole character and success seems to me a homage to law. It may easily happen that the devotion of the merchant to his pursuit should appear extreme. But it should be remembered that he has put more than labor, he has put character and ambition into his fortune, and is like a general who needs victory to justify his tactics to himself as well as to others. The recluse thinks he should have been contented with moderate certainties.

But the merchant is Man seeking to carry out by works to a magnitude and success adequate to his powers. Tobacco, cotton, teas, indigo, coffee are the counters with which he plays his game. But his skill, his sense of power acknowledged by all men, that is his reward. In every corporation meeting, in every conversation, almost in every passing salute in the street, he feels his own and his neighbor's measure. He looks on a man's property as a medal of skill; he looks on a great capital not as of evil or dishonorable influence, he does not regard its influence as built on the weakness or sycophancy of men, but as a certificate of great faculty and of virtues of a certain sort.

The merchant and his commerce depend on another very important class, the sailors. Ever since the Puritans of Massachusetts built and launched their first smack and called it "the Blessing of the Bay," they have followed a trade with all nations, and by their native skill in seafaring and by their economy and audacity have managed to live and thrive where the marine of other nations could not prosper.[10] The indentations of the seacoast make them maritime; the fisheries are a nursery of sailors, whom the severity of the climate and the constant competition of active and intelligent countrymen make hardy and daring. So that the seafaring class form a very important element of the population and a genuine fruit of the natural and moral condition of New England. There is something very instructive in the life and manners of the seaman, as he is that man who has carried farthest the confidence in human resources as a match and an overmatch to the power of the great agents of nature. The seaman has acquired by experience a confidence in the proportioned strength of spars and rigging to the ordinary forces of wind and water, so as by means of his little ark of boards and ropes with

10. *The Blessing of the Bay,* a thirty-ton bark launched at Medford, Massachusetts, in 1631.

three or four men and boys to bring any quantity of property through all the whirlwinds of the tropics, the squalls of the gulf, and the freezing west winds that blow off America in winter, into his distant port.

Let us look a little into one of these solitary barks that go tilting over the January ocean and see the inmate. He is the pensioner of the wind; his prosperity and his toil come and go with the fickle air. If the wind forget to blow, he must eat his masts. Presently, on the soft breeze blows a hurricane, and the safety of all makes a perfect despotism. The sailor's obedience is prompt as a soldier's, willing as a child's. He is the man of his hands; man of all work, all eye, all finger, muscle, skill, and endurance; a tailor, a carpenter, a cooper, stevedore, clerk, and astronomer. He is a great saver of orbs and ends, and a great quiddle by the necessity of his situation. No man well knows how many fingers he has, nor what are the faculties of a knife and a needle, or the capabilities of a pine board, until he has seen the expedients and ambidexter ingenuity of Jack Tar.[11] Here, the poor lad whose education was neglected ashore is sure to learn courage and invention. One lesson the sea thunders through the throat of all its winds, this namely, that there is no knowledge that is not valuable. In this little balloon so far from the human family, and their sages, and colleges, and factories, and hotels, every natural or acquired talent, every piece of information, is sometime in request, and a short voyage will show the difference between the man and the apprentice as surely as it will show the superior value of beef and bread to lemons and sugar plums. Evermore on board ship is there honor to the man of action, for the brain in the hand. The stout master is worth a thousand philosophers: a man who can strike a porpoise at the ship's bows; make oil out of his blubber, and steak out of his meat; who can thump a mutineer into duty in two minutes; who can bleed his sick sailor, and mend the box of his pump, and ship a new rudder in a storm when the old is broke, and ride out the roughest gale that roars about the capes; and with the sun, and a chart, and a three-cornered bit of wood, with a roll of cord, can find his way across three or four thousand miles of salt water into some imperceptible gut of inland sea with as much precision as if led by a clue.

Behold the result in the cities that line the Atlantic coast from Portland to Savannah: Boston; New York; Philadelphia; Baltimore; and Charleston; new but great, and growing—God only knows to what immense enlargement. Scarcely two centuries old, yet related by commerce to all the world. The sea is the ring by which the nations are married, and these cities are the altars and temples of the marriage rite. These great markets need no special acuteness to discern their greatness. They intrude and encroach on us with claims not to be put by; they

11. Jack Tar is a popular name for a sailor.

draw and dazzle us; they tyrannize over us. It is as much and more than we can do to resist them and hold our own. He is a good philosopher whom New York does not dispossess of any of his stoicism and power of abstraction.

These great metropolises of the senses, the senses must even rule. Here, Trade is the God and walks supreme in his streets and wharves. Here we must needs see its immense and growing empire. It perforates the world with roads. The old bonds of language, country, and king give way to the new connexions of trade. It destroys patriotism and substitutes cosmopolitanism. It makes peace and keeps peace. The citizens of every nation own property in the territory of every other nation. It crams the city with every species of wealth from every corner of the planet. Nothing is too far, or too difficult, or too insignificant for some adventurer to bring home. The kelp which grew neglected on the roaring sea-beach of the Orkney Islands now comes to the shops; the seal, the otter, the ermine that no man saw but the Indian in the Rocky Mountains—they must come to Long Wharf. The sea-shells, strombus, turbo, and pearl that hid them a hundred fathoms down in the warm waters of the gulf—they must take the bait, and leave their silent depths, and come to Long Wharf also. The New Bedford sailors tell us that the very savage on the Northwest coast of America, has learned to hold up his sea-shell in his hands, and cry "a Dollar!" to the passing mariner. Even the ducks of Labrador that laid their eggs for ages on the rocks, must send their green eggs now to Long Wharf.

More remarkable are the motley sights afforded by one of these towns which mingles all nations in its marts. What picturesque contrasts are crowded on us. We have the beautiful costume of the Hindoo, the Chinese, and the Turk in our streets. Our domestic labor is done by the African, our trench dug by the Irish. The Kanàka from the South Sea is on the wharf, the Penobscot squaw sells mats and baskets at our doors. It is not very long since in our northern metropolis a delegation of the Sacs and Foxes and of the Sioux and Ioways were quartered in Faneuil Hall with a partition erected between the two tribes because these tribes were at war.[12] In the State House they were addressed by Governor Everett, who gave them presents in the name of the Commonwealth.[13] Our Picts in their savage head-dresses and painted nakedness showed as if the bears and catamounts had sent a deputation. Roaring Thunder wore on his head the skin of a buffalo's head with the horns attached; Black Hawk, the skin of his bird with outspread wings. They were very muscular, broad-shouldered, formidable persons. The Governor cautioned us of the gravity of the tribe and that we should beware of any expression of the ridiculous; and, indeed, the citizens seemed inclined to

12. Faneuil Hall in Boston, first built in 1742, served as the city's town hall.

13. Edward Everett (1794–1865), Unitarian minister, Harvard professor, orator, and governor of Massachusetts (1835–39).

treat their red guests gingerly, as the keepers of lions and jaguars do those creatures whose taming is not yet quite trustworthy. They danced a war dance on Boston Common, in the centre of an immense crowd.[14]

The contrasts which commerce so fast abolishes are still to be found within short distances of more softness and refinement than was in Syria or Rome, justifying the remark of Talleyrand that in America to travel inland one or two thousand miles was the same thing as to traverse in history one or two thousand years. You pass from the extreme of refinement to that of barbarism. Sequel of the same commercial revolution, the foundations of cities to which the course of rivers, the richness of soils, and the meridians of climate predict enormous growth, we see laid. We see the camp pitched and the fire lighted which shall never be struck and never extinguished until great revolutions set a limit to human empire.

I own I am not very partial to cities, yet it is to be remembered in their praise that every great metropolis has certain virtues as a museum of the arts. In Boston, the parlours of private collectors, the Athenaeum Gallery, and the college become the City of the City. Whatever is excellent in each kind is gradually collected there. I remember that the reason offered in our Massachusetts Legislature why the state should not give money to Harvard College to build a new Library was that Harvard had so much already. But that is the very reason why it should have more. That certainly is its strongest claim. If you have a valuable antique in your possession, you would not give it to a stage driver, but to some collector who had already a cabinet; Better yet, to a state, or a national cabinet,—for then it would be seen by the greatest number of those whom it concerned. In this manner, the city continually accumulates whatever is most precious in the arts at a geometrical rate of increase, because these things, like silver and gold, draw to their kind. Observe too, that whatever is most beautiful in architecture or in political or social institutions endures. All else soon comes to nought. So that the antiquities and what is most permanent in each city are good and fine.

In Boston, in most respects, the true proficiency and genius of the New England people are adequately represented. Its college in the suburbs, its Athenaeum founded and endowed by the merchants, its sixty churches, its scientific and literary societies with their libraries, its annual courses of lectures which every winter evening fill four or five large halls or theatres at the same hour with audiences amounting to several thousands of persons, and its various political and commercial Reading Rooms and the great concourse of scholars now to be found in its neighborhood make this town a great university for the semination and spread of all knowledge.

14. This event is described in "The Indians," *Boston Daily Advertiser and Patriot,* 30 October 1837, 2.

At the present moment, Boston happens to enjoy some singular advantages amidst the retarded prosperity of the country in general. And this impulse is an unlooked for consequence of steam communication. The frightful expenses of steam make the greater neighborhood of Boston to Europe a circumstance of commanding importance, and the ports of Havre and Liverpool are a day or two nearer to Boston than to New York. This preference as the steam port, added to the contemporaneous opening of its three great lines of railroad, south, west, and north, like iron rivers, which already are making it a depot for flour from western New York, Michigan, and Illinois, promise a great growth to a city which was dwindling before the overpowering expansion of New York.

The historian will hereafter find the office of the New England people in all parts consistent with the faculties we have ascribed to them. They have clear perceptions and an activity which must be employed. In the lowest class, this appears as cleverness and love of labour; in the more informed, as a high intellectual skill. There is in the whole Anglo-Saxon race great ripeness of the active and practical faculties, and a great patience of labour. And there is no country which exhibits more results of skilful labor than New England. In ignorant and semi-barbarous communities,—I am afraid in many portions of this country,— the question concerning any man is, How can he fight? In other companies the question is, Has he money? But in every society of right-minded men, the question is, What can he do? I cannot but think that we in New England have a great advantage in respect to the national feeling on this point over every other people of equal cultivation. We have not the fatal pride of idleness. This country is full of people whose fathers were judges, generals, and corporation presidents, and whose grandfathers were founders of colonies and states, and if all their boys should give themselves airs thereon, and rest hence forth on the oars of their fathers' reputation, we should be a sad, hungry generation. It is our best birthright that our people are not crippled by family and official pride, that the best broadcloth coat is still often put off to put on a blue frock, that the best man in the town may hold his plough-handles or drive his own cart. There is a great deal of work in our men, and a false pride has not yet made them idle or ashamed.

I hope New England will come to have its pride in being a nation of servants, and not like the planting states, a nation of the served. How can men have any other ambition where the reason has not suffered a disastrous eclipse? Whilst every man can say, I serve: To the whole extent of my being I apply my faculty to the service of mankind in my especial place, he therein sees and shows a reason for his being in the world and is not a moth or incumbrance in it.

But it is said that from climate, or temperament, or other cause the activity of the Americans is preternaturally great and disproportioned, and that our people pass their lives in a certain hurry and excitement. It is said that our people have not that steadfastness that can be calculated on. They are not sacramented to their place and career, as in England. "I cannot calculate on your countrymen as on mine," said an Englishman to me; "Your friend, whom now they reckon a liberalist of the most impracticable cast, may turn out a trader, or soldier, or a priest."

The circumstances of the American, explain much of this restlessness. The inhabitant of England or Germany, who comes here and makes this observation on the headiness of our people, comes from a country in which a dense population allows to each man a very narrow space to walk in and little choice of labors. He must do one thing with the utmost steadiness of routine and with a perfection of finish or he will starve. He contents himself with small gains and endless routine. His information is limited; his powers of varied activity never invited forth, but paralyzed, the nerve killed; his talent as a legislator, as a metaphysician, a reformer never known, but the stocking-weaver must from day to day, from year to year, make stockings. Another spends all the best years of his rational existence in polishing a pin. Another sticks them on papers. So with the button maker, the glass blower, the weaver, the smith, and so on. Steadiness of eye and hand, habits of saving, steadiness of carriage, and punctuality are acquired: the brain is not tasked to the verge of insanity: nor the hand spoiled for excellence in one work by too frequent a change of employment: results admirable chiefly to those who have a better taste in pins, or buttons, or cloths than in men.

But the same workman is set down in infancy in this country. A thin population, every one of whom is a candidate for the very highest prizes in a boundless territory where land is cheap and broad. Where whole states have started into full maturity, and the most rapid expansion on land which was Indian hunting ground within forty years. Where cities rise which are markets for all the European fabrics of luxury and taste,—meats, liquors, confections, lace, silk, merino, optical and philosophical instruments, books, pictures, and statues,—on ground where the roots of the new fallen forest are still smoking.

The land is filled with discussion on every topic of ethics, of politics, of science, of taste, of traffic, and especially the topic of new avenues for industry, new *chances* (as our word is) for young men. Every table is spread with newspapers; and, wherever he goes, his vote, his opinion, is made of consequence to him, by the eagerness with which it is solicited. Opportunity is given to every young person of energy to try his hand at several employments. Changes that are ludicrous to every other countryman are in this country matters of course. He begins as a farmer, then he tries teaming, then house painting, next portrait painting, keeps a school, then a tavern, and next year is a judge. When he wishes to go into trade, he finds little difficulty in procuring unlimited credits, for the new state of things in America has accustomed the European as well as the American capitalist to advance goods on the probabilities of talent and success.

Add that he finds himself part of a community of activity, and expansion unprecedented, and till now incredible that the most jocose and fabulous projects
have succeeded, and are matters of course. And that the land still opens westward—far west and farther west—into magnificent, yet real and infallible, extent of country. The column of our population on the western frontier from Lake
Superior to the Gulf of Mexico (twelve hundred miles as the bird flies) advances
every year a mean distance of seventeen miles. "This gradual and continuous
progress of the European race towards the Rocky Mountains has the solemnity of
a providential event. It is like a deluge of men rising unabatedly and daily driven
onward by the hand of God."[15]

But when we have said all this for the genius of the people of New England, it
yet remains to ask whether they have played a great and high part in the history
of man: whether they have done anything for the greatest and highest. There is
a speedy limit to the advantages which flow from Trade, be they never so many.
And in this country, the dangers that menace the manly character are from our
success, from our absorbing devotion to the works of Trade.

These things which make the conversation of all hotels and railroad cars, are
symptomatic of the disease of the people. That repose which is the ornament and
ripeness of man, is not in New England, is not in America. That repose which indicates a faith in the laws of the Universe; a faith that they will fulfil themselves,
and are not to be transgressed, or accelerated. It is too obvious that the tendency
of the popular mind in this country is to rely on means provided by the understanding for the aid and defence of man, and not on the simplest action of the man
himself; on the cannon, and not on the heart of the soldier, on the statute, and not
on the rectitude of the citizen; on expedients, and not on principles.

The power by which man contemplates the Necessary, the True, the Good, or
what we call absolute truth, seems to stand in a wonderful antagonism with the
power by which he apprehends particular facts and applies means to ends. When
the latter is most active, the former is most withdrawn. The first we call Reason,
or Sentiment, or the Soul: the second we call the Understanding. Now the world
consents to acknowledge him the greatest man, and that age the happiest era,
when the sentiments have been most active; when the sentiments have predomi-
nated; when a sentiment led his active powers and not his activity overpowered
his sentiment.

Man is whole as long as the active powers are directed by the soul. A nation
governed by the religious sentiment, by the parental sentiment, by the love of
military glory (which is only an impure greatness, since it proceeds from a self-
trust and excess of manly force), or by the love of art, is still capable of extraor-

15. Quoted from Tocqueville, *Democracy in America*.

dinary deeds. But an activity of the lower powers, once absolved from the dominion of these sentiments, makes life and man mean.

The understanding becomes more acute as the aim is humbler, and in its activity, it weans man from the sentiments which make his greatness and, surrounding him with the fruits of his own industry, makes him at once proud and poor. That which characterises recent history in this country is the extreme activity of the understanding without the check of the sentiments. Commerce is the child and again the tutor of the understanding. Hence, the perfection of the maritime nations in commonsense and acuteness. The Mediterranean Sea has been the school of Europe, and the Atlantic Ocean has been ours.[16] The endless division of labor which commerce operates: whilst it augmented wonderfully the arts and conveniences of life, it sacrificed man by breaking him into particles

Commerce has no reverence: Prayer and prophecy are irrelevant to its bargain. It encroaches on all sides. "Business before friends," is its byword. It puts by the state. The state is subordinate, and only an office of trade, one department of commerce filled with virtual merchants who are there to be rich, and conscious of their parentage or filled with the spirit of the time; government is administered for the protection of trade. Law is interpreted and executed on the principle that a man's enjoyment of his estate is its main end. Education is degraded. It aims to make good merchants only, and Religion even is a lever out of the spiritual world to work upon this. Commerce, dazzling us with the perpetual discovery of new facts, of new particulars of power, has availed so far to transfer the devotion of men from the Living Cause to the material in which it works.

But the Universe must still be propitiated, let the members gain what they may. Being divided, the man's aims are steadily baulked. Commerce has subdued the world, holds all nature in fee, and yet the merchant is not more a man than the farmer and soldier he has supplanted. Meantime, analysis has its extremes, and then its reaction. Forever springs in the soul of man the gracious effort to unite nature,—to see one cause. When the novelty of Commerce, charming men by the number and magnitude of transactions, is a little worn off, men see that the heart is no gainer, that man is a drudge, and they come back lowly and self-abandoning to the eternal sentiments of Love and Truth.

The time will come when the looms of Lowell and the presses of Cambridge will stand still, when the masts of Boston and New York shall rot at their wharves, when great national or great natural changes will have made that region, already on the borders of the Arctic climate, uninhabitable. At that time, this trade, and swarming population, and immense industry will leave no trace; but every moral

16. Emerson suggests that the Mediterranean Sea, by being the home of the Greeks and Romans and an avenue of commerce, helped to school Europe.

trait, every burst of genius, every impulse of humanity and love which fired some lonely heart among those granite hills, will still live and warm the human race.

Amid those decays of old tradition to which I have adverted, I rejoice in the new and growing reverence for character; the increasing influence of character, which will be the religion of the coming age.— Let these be New England's glories, and not new cities and an enlarging census. Truly seen, her honor and hope is now perhaps a deposit in the heart of few and humble men; but a spiritual impulse is always a new quality with which quantities cannot contend. If any revelation of truth, if any sentiment of justice, honor, and self-trust shall go forth from her White Hills, from the banks of the Connecticut or of the Charles River, into the country and the world, she will have served them better than by all her wit and all her accumulation.

# *New England,* Lecture III: "New England: Genius, Manners, and Customs" 28 January 1843 (1843–1844)

Emerson first delivered this lecture as "Manners and Customs of New England" on 28 January 1843 as the third of five lectures in a *New England* series at the Chinese Museum in Philadelphia, for which he received no more than $100 (*Letters,* 3:139). He repeated this lecture as "New England: Genius, Manners, and Customs" on 17 February 1843 as the third of five lectures in a *New England* series at the New York Society Library in New York City. After expenses in New York, he was able to clear $9 per lecture (*Letters,* 3:150). Emerson received a favorable summary of his delivery before the New York Society Library in two full columns in the *New-York Daily Tribune* ("Mr. Emerson's Third Lecture," 18 February 1843, 2).

"New England: Genius, Manners, and Customs" was the most popular of the five lectures associated with the *New England* series, and on several occasions Emerson delivered it under various titles as a lecture independent of the series. He delivered this lecture as "The Genius, Manners and Character of the New England People" on 23 February 1843 before the Hamilton Society in South Brooklyn, New York, for which he received $10 (*Letters,* 3:150n); as "New England Character" on either 15 November 1843 or 4 January 1844 before the Concord Lyceum in Concord, Massachusetts (see *Emerson and Thoreau Speak,* 158); as "The Characteristics of New England" on 5 December 1843 in Woonsocket, Rhode Island, for which he received $15; as "New England" on 6 December 1843 before the Franklin Lyceum in Providence, Rhode Island, for which he received $25; under an unknown title on 8 December 1843 before the Newburyport Lyceum in Newburyport, Rhode Island, for which he received $15; as "The New England Man" on 10 January 1844 before the Salem Lyceum in Salem, Massachusetts, for which he received $20; and as "New England Character" on 16 April 1844 before the Billerica Lyceum in Billerica, Massachusetts, for which he received $8 (except as noted, lecture fees are from the "Account Books"; for Emerson's lecture before the Billerica Lyceum, see Joel Myerson, "The Dating of Emerson's Lecture at Billerica in 1844," in *Studies in English and American Literature: A Supplement to American Notes and Queries,* ed. John L. Cutler and Lawrence S. Thompson [Troy, N.Y.: Whitston, 1978], 246; for additional details on all of these deliveries of "New England: Genius, Manners, and Customs" as a lecture independent of the *New England* series, see Simmons, "Emerson's 1843–1844 New England Lectures").

For the reasons given in the headnote to Emerson's *New England* series (see above), the title used for this lecture in this edition is taken from the title under which the lecture was advertised when Emerson delivered it on 17 February 1843 at the New York Society Library. The text of this lecture has never been published under any of the titles associated with it.

I N MY LAST lecture, I attempted to sketch some of the historical manifestations of the spirit of commerce which so strongly characterizes the English race in both hemispheres, and I enumerated the good results with their limitations which have flowed therefrom in New England. In the present lecture, I proceed to add some details that may still farther fill up the portrait of this race. Many of my remarks are of a miscellaneous character. I am not careful that they are not. A principal object with me is to name, (in any order), if I can, the chief facts in the recent literary and spiritual history of New England, believing that if we can rightly select those, we write the history of history: for it is to these that the mere recorder of facts must come at last. Neither is it to me of any importance to confine my sketches to a geographical section, for I am well aware that as soon as we say anything deep and true, it keeps no territorial limits. The heart is the citizen of every country, and so is strength of character. National characteristics, as soon as a man is well awake, give way to individual ones: as physicians say that fever in every new constitution is a new malady.

The national traits which have for ages distinguished the English race are for the most part very obvious in the New England character, only qualified by the new circumstances of a wide land, a sparse population, and a democratic government. The traits of the Englishman are found throughout America, so that to foreign nations it very naturally appears only an extension of the same people. In New England, where the population is most homogeneous and most English, they are very purely preserved, so as to give rise to the remark, that the Yankee is double distilled English. The British family is expanded, but not altered. The national traits are the same for centuries. We see at this moment only the demonstration of the thoughts which were already ripe in the beginning of the seventeenth century, when the Religious War drove the Puritans to America. The two main points by which the English nation was then distinguished, the two points by which they attached themselves to the heavens and the earth, to the mind and to matter, namely, Conscience and Common Sense, or, in view of their objects, the love of Religion and the love of Commerce,—Religion and Trade,—are still the two hands by which they hold the dominion of the globe.

I have elsewhere had occasion to speak at length of these two topics, the Religion and the Trade of New England; I shall not engage in their development this evening. My aim is to attempt some sketches of some remarkable particulars in the character and tendencies of the New England Man.

He is the old England man in a new place and new duties; and it is very easy to see the influence of his geographical position as a native of the seashore, and of a high latitude, in the modification of his character, distinguishing him not only from the European, but also from his fellow citizen of the interior and of the southern states.

A person of strong understanding, working to surround himself with defences against an extreme climate and a niggard soil, and gaining his victories over nature by successive expedients, as, by clothing, by warm building, by stove and furnace, and improved husbandry, his behaviour does not bely him. The Indian who puts out his fire, and hunts, eats, and sleeps in the snow; or the emigrant who quits a northern parallel and takes up his abode in a warmer clime,—these may be said each *at a single stroke* to relieve themselves of the long war with the elements, which the northern white man sustains. He, on the other hand, contests the field by inches, and his mind acquires the habit of detail, and his strength is that of caution, of forecast, of arithmetic, which accomplishes wonders, at last, by means of aggregation; builds a city, for example,—a noble and dazzling result, by a continual repetition of very easy acts. But the Indian who flings himself into the snow, or the Southerner who resigns himself to the grand influences of nature with boundless leisure to enjoy them, becomes more easily the home of great and generous sentiments. He is not accustomed to check his charitable or his romantic purpose by too narrow a computation of the methods, and he is a much more natural, graceful, and heroic actor, inasmuch as he is more impulsive. This contrast of character is exhibited very strongly every day wherever the Northerner and Southerner meet; not only in results—tabulated results of trade, manufactures, of civil and criminal legislation,—but especially where the races face each other, as in the northern colleges, where young men from different sections often meet; and, most of all, in the city of Washington, where they face each other full-grown, and these contrasts are seen in full breadth. The Southerner lives for the moment, relies on himself, and conquers by personal address. He is wholly there in that thing which is now to be done. The Northerner lives for the year, and does not rely on himself, but on the whole apparatus of means he is wont to employ, and is only half-present when he comes in person: he has a great reserved force which is coming up. The result corresponds. The Southerner is haughty, wilful, generous, unscrupulous,—who will have his way, and has it. The Northerner must think the thing over, and his conscience and his commonsense throw a thousand obstacles between him and his wishes, which perplex his decision and unsettle his behaviour. The Northerner always has the advantage of the Southerner at the end of ten years; and the Southerner always has the advantage today.

I am far from wishing to exaggerate the peculiarities of districts of the country; the grand principles of probity and of beauty are far deeper in man than that a line or two of latitude or a difference of employment will make any important change. They underlie the differences of habit I have spoken of, and the great ideas of modern times are equally honoured with slight differences of costume throughout the Republic.

The traits which I prefer to consider are those moral agents which have been of importance in the history of our people as restraints on the spirit of economy and commerce, which their position generated. The flagrant feature in our history down to a quite recent period, was its religious character, as indeed the planting of New England was the work of the most religious nation in their most religious epoch.

Beside the direct culture of the conscience and the general probity which this hereditary religious sentiment generates, I trace to this strong Calvinism other great and salutary results to the character of the New England people. First, namely, the culture of the intellect, which has always been found in the Calvinistic Church. The religious are always disposed to give to their children a more liberal discipline of books, of schools, and of liberal conversation, a fact borne out by all history—but especially by the history of New England. The Colony was planted in 1620: In 1638, Harvard College was founded.

The General Court of Massachusetts in 1647, "To the end that learning may not perish in the graves of our forefathers, *Ordered;* that every township after the Lord had increased them to the number of fifty householders shall appoint one to teach all children to write and read; and where any town shall increase to the number of one hundred families, they shall set up a grammar school, the masters thereof being able to instruct youth so far as they may be fitted for the university." Many and rich are the fruits of that simple statute. The universality of an elementary education in New England is her praise and her power in the whole world.

To the school succeeds the village Lyceum, now very general throughout the country towns, where every week through the winter lectures are read and debates sustained which prove a college for the young farmer. Hence, it happens that young farmers and mechanics who work all summer in the field or shop, in the winter often go into a neighbouring town to teach the district school arithmetic and grammar. As you know, New England supplies annually a large detachment of preachers, and schoolmasters, and private tutors to the interior of the South and West. Great numbers less critically instructed, yet still with some smattering of letters, are employed by the Connecticut bookdealers as book agents to travel in the interior and vend their editions. And it sometimes happens that a poor man's son in Connecticut, whose intellect is superior, who would fain go to college, but has not money, escapes from hard labour for which his finer organization unfits him, finds someone to trust him with wares, and goes as a pedlar into Virginia and Carolina that so he may, at a small expense, see the world, converse with men, and by intercourse with more polished persons than his native village can exhibit, supply the defects of his limited and humble training. One of the most intellectual men I have ever seen had his training so.[1]

It is a remark frequently made by those who are conversant with New England that such is the high value universally attached to a superior education, that no political or religious prejudices are suffered to stand in its way. If the Catholics have a good school, or if the Unitarians have a good college, the most devoted adherents of other and conflicting sects will send their daughters or sons to these seminaries. It only needs a confidence that a superior culture is really to be had there, to bring as many pupils as are desired.

This is precisely the most agreeable picture which the Northern portion of the country has to show, the universality of a good elementary culture. If you ask me for the best result in this region, compared with the best advantages of other nations, I shall point you to a very common but always affecting spectacle,— the poor but educated family. Who can see unmoved the eager blushing boys discharging, as they can, their household chores, and hastening into the sitting-room to the study of tomorrow's merciless lesson: yet stealing time to read a novel hardly smuggled into the tolerance of father and mother: atoning for the same by some pages of Plutarch or Goldsmith; the warm sympathy with which they kindle each other in schoolyard or in barn and wood-shed.

If in New England the climate and the commerce powerfully tended to generate that spirit of detail which is not grand and enlarging, but which goes rather to pinch the features and degrade the character, the religious spirit, always enlarging, firing man, prompting the pursuit of the vast, the beautiful, the unattainable, was especially necessary as an antidote. In the midst of our laborious, and economical, and rude, and awkward population, where is little elegance and no facility, with great accuracy in details, little spirit of society, or knowledge of the world, you shall yet not unfrequently meet that refinement which no education and no habit of society can confer, which makes the elegance of wealth look stupid, and which unites itself by natural affinity to the highest minds of the world, and nourishes itself on Plato and Dante, Michel Angelo and Milton; on whatever is pure and sublime in art, and I may say, which gave a hospitality in that country to the spirit of Coleridge and Wordsworth, and now to the music of Beethoven, before yet their genius had found a hearty welcome in Great Britain.

I pass now to a topic not remotely related to the last,—to consider, namely, the taste for eloquence, native to every people, and in which every man is a competitor, but always favoured by the institutions of republics.

The thirst of our people for eloquence is often remarked, and in the cities of

---

1. This is Amos Bronson Alcott.

New England it finds every year more opportunities of gratification. Faneuil Hall is one of our best schools. Join the dark and closing groups that gather in the old house when fate hangs on the vote of the morrow. As the crowd grows and the hall fills, behold that solid block of life,—few old men, mostly young and middle aged, with shining heads and swollen veins. Much of the speaking shall no doubt be slovenly and tiresome. Then, the excited multitude predominates, is all the time interlocutor, and the air grows electric, and the multitude appear or disappear according to the success of the speaker. The pinched, wedged, elbowed, sweltering assembly, as soon as the speaker loses their ear, by the tameness of his harangue, feel sorely how ill accommodated they are, forget all politics and patriotism, and attend only to themselves and the coarse outcries which are made all around them. They back, push, resist, and fill the hall with cries of tumult. The speaker stops; the moderator persuades, commands, entreats; the speaker at length gives way. At last, the chosen man rises, the soul of the people, in whose bosom beats audibly the common heart. With his first words he strikes a note which all know. As he catches the light spirit of the occasion, his voice alters, vibrates, pierces the private ear of everyone: the mob quiets itself somehow,—everyone being magnetized, and the house hangs waiting on the lips of one man. Each man whilst he hears, thinks he too can speak, and, in the pauses of the orator, bursts forth the splendid voice of four or five thousand men in full cry,—the grandest sound in nature. If a dull speaker come again, instantly our poor wedges begin to feel their pains, and strive and cry.

New England is faithfully represented in her orators. The person most dear to the Yankees, of course, must be a person of very commanding understanding with every talent for its adequate expression. 'The American,' foreigners say, 'always reasons,' and their orator is the most American of the Americans. He should be a man of great good sense, always pertinent to time and place, with an eye to the simple facts of nature, the hour of the day, the neighborhood of the mountains or the sea, yet with sparing notice of these things, whilst he clings closely to the business-part of his speech; a man of gravity who trusts to his plain strength of statement for the attention of his assembly; a man of great fairness in debate, and who deserves his success by always carrying his points from his adversary by really taking higher ground than he: "I do not inflame, I do not exaggerate, I avoid all incendiary allusion."[2] He is one who is not at all magnetic, but the strongest intellect applied to business—intellect applied to affairs; the greatest of lawyers, and one who should rather carry points with the bench than with the jury or the caucus, and, therefore, carries points with a New England caucus. He shall have no puerilities, no tricks, no academical play in any of his speeches, but as it was

2. Emerson quotes Daniel Webster (1782–1852), statesman and orator.

said of the orations of Demosthenes that they were soldiers, so the speeches of the Yankee orator should all be men of business.[3] No following shall this man have, no troop of friends except those whose intellect he fires. No sweaty mob will carry him on their shoulders. And, yet, all New England to the remotest farmhouse or lumberer's camp in the woods of Maine delights to tell and hear anecdotes of his forensic power.

But a new field for eloquence has been opened in the Lyceum, an institution not a quarter of a century old, yet singularly agreeable to the taste and habits of the New England people, and extending every year to the south and west. It is of so recent origin, that, although it is beginning already like the invention of railways, to make a new profession, we have most of us seen all the steps of its progress. In New England it had its origin in as marked a manner as such things admit of being marked, from the genius of one distinguished person, who, after his connexion with the University, read public courses of literary lectures in Boston. And as this was an epoch of much note in the recent literary history of all that portion of the country, I shall ask leave to pause a little on the recollection. That individual has passed long since into new employments, so that the influence he then exerted and which was a capital fact in the literary annals of the country, now fairly belongs to the past; and one of his old scholars will be indulged in recalling an image so pleasing.[4]

There was an influence on the young people from the genius of this eminent scholar which was almost comparable to that of Pericles in Athens.[5] He had an inspiration which did not go beyond his head, but which made him the master of elegance. If any of my audience were at that period in Boston or Cambridge, they will easily remember, his radiant beauty of person, of a classic style; his heavy, large eye; marble lids, which gave the impression of mass which the slightness of his form needed; sculptured lips; a voice of such rich tones, such precise and perfect utterance, that, although slightly nasal, it was the most mellow, and beautiful, and correct of all the instruments of the time. The word that he spoke, in the manner in which he spoke it, became current and classical in New England.

He had in common with other distinguished members of his family, a great talent for collecting facts, and for bringing those he had to bear with ingenious felicity on the topic of the moment. Let him rise to speak on what occasion soever, a fact had always just transpired which composed with some other fact well known to the audience the most pregnant and happy coincidence. It was remarked that for a man who threw out so many facts, he was seldom convicted of a blunder.

3. Demosthenes (b. ca. 385–322 B.C.), the most famous of the Greek orators.
4. Emerson refers to Edward Everett (see *W*, 10:330).
5. Pericles (ca. 495–429 B.C.), Athenian statesman and orator.

He had a good deal of special learning, and all his learning was available for purposes of the hour. It was all new learning, that wonderfully took and stimulated the young men. It was so coldly and weightily communicated from so commanding a platform,—as if in the consciousness and consideration of all history and all learning,—adorned with so many simple and austere beauties of expression, and enriched with so many excellent digressions and significant quotations, that, though nothing could be conceived beforehand less attractive or, indeed, less fit for green boys from Connecticut, New Hampshire, and Massachusetts, with their unripe Latin and Greek reading, than exegetical discourses in the style of Hug, and Wolf, and Ruhnken on the Orphic and Ante-Homeric remains, yet this learning instantly took the highest place to our imagination in our unoccupied American Parnassus.[6] All his auditors felt the extreme beauty and dignity of the manner, and even the coarsest were contented to go punctually to listen for the manner, when they had found out that the subject matter was not for them. In the lecture room, he abstained from all ornament and pleased himself with the play of detailing erudition in a style of perfect simplicity. In the pulpit, for he was then a clergyman, he made amends to himself and his auditor for the self-denial of the professor's chair, and with an infantine simplicity still of manner, he gave the reins to his florid, quaint, and affluent fancy.

Then was exhibited all the richness of a rhetoric which we have never seen rivalled in this country. Wonderful, how memorable were words made which were only pleasing pictures, and covered no new or valid thoughts. He abounded in sentences, in wit, in satire, in splendid allusion, in quotation impossible to forget, in daring imagery, in parable, and even in a sort of defying experiment of his own wit and skill in giving an oracular weight to Hebrew or Rabbinical words, as *Selah, Ichabod, Tekel, Mene, Upharsin,* and the like—feats which no man could better accomplish, such was his self-command and the security of his manner. All his speech was music, and with such variety and invention, that the ear was never tired. Especially beautiful were his poetic quotations. He delighted in Milton, more rarely in Byron, and sometimes in a verse from Watts, and with such sweet modulation, that he seemed to give as much beauty as he borrowed; and whatever he has quoted will be remembered by any who heard him with inseparable association with his voice and genius.[7] This eminently beautiful person was followed from church to church, wherever the fame that he would preach led, by all the most cultivated and intelligent youths with grateful admiration. He had nothing in common with vulgarity and infirmity, but speaking, walking, sitting was

6. Johann Leonhard Hug (1765–1846), German biblical scholar; Friedrich August Wolf (1759–1824), German philologist; David Ruhnken (1723–98), German classical scholar.

7. George Gordon, Lord Byron (1788–1824), English Romantic poet; Isaac Watts (1674–1748), English hymnologist.

as much aloof and uncommon as a star. The smallest anecdote of his behaviour or conversation was eagerly caught and repeated; and every young scholar could recite brilliant sentences from his sermons with mimicry good or bad of his voice. This influence went much farther; for he who was heard with such throbbing hearts and sparkling eyes, in the lighted and crowded churches, did not let go his hearer when the church was dismissed; but the bright image of that eloquent form followed the boy home to his bed chamber; and not a sentence was written in academic exercises, not a declamation attempted in the college chapel, but showed omnipresence of his genius to youthful heads. He thus raised the standard of writing and speaking in New England. This made every youth his defender, and boys filled their mouths with arguments to prove that the orator had a heart.

This was a triumph of Rhetoric. It was not the intellectual or the moral principles which he had to teach. It was not thoughts. When Massachusetts was full of his fame, it was not contended that he had thrown any truths into circulation. But his power lay in the magic of form; it was in the graces of manner, in a new perception of Grecian Beauty to which he had opened our eyes. And it was commonly said that he would be willing that every hearer should have a copy of his speech in his pocket: he would still be just as secure of their attention.

There was that finish about this person which is about women, and which distinguishes every piece of genius from the works of talent: that these last are more or less matured in every degree of completeness according to the time bestowed on them, but works of genius in their first and slightest form are still wholes. In every public discourse, there was nothing left for the indulgence of his hearer, no marks of late hours and anxious unfinished study, but the goddess of grace had breathed on the work a last fragrancy and glitter.

By a series of lectures largely and fashionably attended for two winters in Boston, this individual made a beginning of popular literary and miscellaneous lectures which in that region, at least, had important results. It is acquiring greater importance every day and becoming a national institution.

But a field for eloquence higher and deeper seems to me already opened in the Lyceum, an institution now in its infancy, yet growing every year into use and favor in the Atlantic cities, as our present meeting bears witness. It answers the purpose of a social meeting for both sexes in a very convenient manner, involving no expense, and no dissipation, and especially of giving an evening occupation to young men in the counting house, and so supplants the theatre and the ballroom. It gives an hour's discourse on some topic not far from the ordinary range, and by continually introducing new speakers, furnishes new topics to conversation with new means of comparison, every week. But these are the beginnings of its use. I set a higher value on it than amusement or the statement of valuable facts. I look upon it as a vent for new and higher communications than any to which we have been wont to listen. I see with pleasure that the first men in the country are put under contribution by this institution, for services which they cheerfully render, led, as I believe, by an instinct of its importance.

For this is precisely the most elastic and capacious theatre of eloquence,— absolutely unrestricted. Is it not plain that not in senates and courts, which only treat of a very narrow range of external rights, but in the depths of philosophy and poetry, the eloquence must be found that can agitate, convict, inspire, and possess us and guide men to a true peace? I look on the Lecture Room as the true Church of the coming time, and as the home of a richer eloquence than Faneuil Hall or the Capitol ever knew. For here is all that the true orator will ask, namely, a convertible audience,—an audience coming up to the house, not knowing what shall befall them there, but uncommitted and willing victims to reason and love. There is no topic that may not be treated, and no method excluded. *Here,* everything is admissible, philosophy, ethics, divinity, criticism, poetry, humor, anecdote, mimicry,—ventriloquism almost,—all the breadth and versatility of the most liberal conversation, and of the highest, lowest, personal, and local topics— all are permitted, and all may be combined in one speech. It is a panharmonicon combining every note on the longest gamut, from the explosion of cannon to the tinkle of a guitar.

It deserves the attention of such as have any truth to offer to men and will soon draw the best powers of the country to its aid. Let us, if we have any thought in our mind, try if Folly, Custom, Convention, and Phlegm cannot hear our sharp artillery. Here is a pulpit that makes the other chairs of instruction cold and ineffectual with their customary preparation for a delivery: the most decorous with fine things, pretty things, wise things, but no arrows, no axes, no nectar, no transpiercing, no loving, no enchantment. Here, the American orator shall find the theatre he needs; here, he may lay himself out utterly large, prodigal, enormous, on the subject of the hour. Here, he may dare to hope for the higher inspiration and a total transfusion of himself into the minds of men.

I please myself with the thought that this may yet be an organ of unparalleled power for the elevation of sentiment and enlargement of knowledge. Why should it not be capable of all the range whereof music is capable, and, as other nations have each their favorite instrument, as Spain her guitar, and Scotland her pibroch, and Italy a viol, and as we go eastward, cymbals and song, let the reasoning, fact loving, and moral American, not by nature a musician, yet with a hunger for eloquence, find his national music in halls opened for discourse and debate, the one leading to the other? Will you let me say that I think the country will so give hospitality and hearing to its men of thought; and, as in former periods, the poet travelled as a harper from town to town, and from castle to castle, the bearer of thought and exhilaration, so now, in a manner fitting the habit of our institutions, the man of ideas and lover of beauty shall find a ready ear from his countrymen for those secrets which in the solitudes of nature the muse whispered in his walks? The lover of men shall find his office foreshown by the master of English song:

> Before the starry threshold of Jove's Court
> My mansion is, where those immortal shapes
> Of bright aerial spirits live insphered
> In regions mild of calm and serene air,
> Above the smoke and stir of this dim spot
> Which men call Earth, and with low thoughted care
> Confined and pestered in this pinfold here
> Strive to keep up a frail and feverish being,
> Unmindful of the crown that virtue gives,
> After this mortal change, to her true servants
> Amongst the enthroned gods on sainted seats.
> Yet some there be, that by due steps aspire
> To lay their just hands on the golden key
> That opes the palace of eternity;
> To such my errand is.[8]

It will use less strict conventions than other assemblies or pulpits,—and invite, perhaps a bolder exercise of thought; for, with all deference to the lovers of precision and method, I think that the best method will always be a new one, new with each speaker, and proper to that which he has to say. There are, as I think, greatly higher merits than easiness of being reported. The great merit is power to excite the slumbering intellect, make it a party to the speaker's thought, and by hints and whispers even, if no more can be, from a great interior world, leave it with a renewed assurance that that world exists—and for him.

This institution, as a school of thought and reason, has vast importance as a check on the vices and insanities of the time. I have said that from the planting of New England down to a recent period, this country has been tinged with a religious spirit. But the boundless opportunity of labor and the rewards of labor opened before us have rapidly changed the genius of the people.

There is in the Anglo-Saxon race a great power of labor, and no country exhibits more results of incessant labor than New England. But is it climate, or is it hereditary temperament—the love of labour becomes usually in our people a certain fury, a storm of activity, and a necessity of excitement. Unhappily, the feature of the times seems to be a great sensualism, a headlong devotion to trade

8. John Milton, "Comus," ll. 1–15.

and to the conquest of the continent, and to each man as large a share of the same as he can carve for himself, and an extravagant confidence in our gregarious activity which becomes, whilst successful, a scornful materialism, but with the fatal fault of that habitude, of course, that it has no depth, no reserved force whereon to fall back when a reverse comes.

Our countrymen love intoxication of some sort. There is no repose in their character. All foreigners and we ourselves observe the sort of hunger, the voracity for excitement, which haunts us. Is it for food? Is it for news? Is it for money? Is it for stimulation in any form? One is drunk with rum, and one with politics, and one with barter, and one with impossible projects. Our trade is wild and incalculable. Our people are wide travellers; our steamboats explode; our ships are known at sea by the quantity of canvass they carry; our people eat fast; our houses tumble; our enterprizes are rash; our legislation fluctuating. The cases of insanity in this country are said greatly to outnumber the patients in Europe. The last President could not stand the excitement of seventeen millions of people, but died of the presidency in one month.[9] A man should have a heart and a trunk vascular and on the scale of the Croton Aqueducts or the Cloaca Maxima at Rome to bear the friction of such a Mississippi stream.[10]

We want steadiness and repose. We are too rash and sanguine to the verge of insanity. We are all resting our confidence on new arts which have been invented: on new machinery, on steam, on the glimpses of mechanical power to be derived from electricity or galvanism; on photogenic drawing, on india-rubber clothing, on lamps that shine without shadow, on stoves that burn without fuel; on clocks to be wound by the tide; on iron boats; and cast steel tools; on steam batteries, life-preservers, and diving bells.

This fury is heated by the peculiar skill and genius of the time. The great achievements that distinguish this age are its mechanical inventions. It is the age of tools. *Now*, the standing topic in all stage coaches and railroad cars, is the improved means of conveyance; and continual impatience is expressed at the slow rate of travelling; twenty five miles the hour is mere creeping; the travelling public will not long submit to such baggage-wagon pace, and wonderful are the plans of the projectors which fill the columns of the daily press.

The men and women shall be galvanically conveyed, or may be put in large quills and propelled across the Atlantic by the pressure of the atmosphere; or dressed in diving-suits manufactured (No. 6 Tremont Street, Boston) by the

9. William Henry Harrison (1773–1841), ninth American president, did die within a month of taking office.

10. The Croton Aqueduct (built 1834–42) extended from southeastern New York State into New York City and brought in approximately 70 million gallons of water daily; the Cloaca Maxima was the primary drainage system of ancient Rome.

Roxbury Company, and conveyed by submarine siphons, and come up near Liverpool in fountains spouting men and women; or a tunnel may run under the sea, and they may go dry-shod. In order to avoid the danger of submarine volcanoes, strenuous measures are to be adopted by the countries abutting on the two ends of the canal. It is disgraceful that every few years an earthquake should be allowed from mere want of proper ventilation to swallow a town like a custard. It only needs timely and vigorous attention from the Congress of Nations. Every boy can take out the pulp and seeds of a pumpkin and make a useful lanthorn of the same. The earth should be properly bored with an artesian well of five hundred miles diameter at the mouth and running down to the depth of three thousand, then by means of steam excavator, the mephitic gases and whatever combustibles, should be brought to the surface and sold to the gas company. And a wholesome and agreeable circulation of air should be kept up.

It may hereafter be found best, when the structure of the human body is better understood and the science of anatomy is perfect, to take passengers to pieces and transport them in the air or under the sea *in parts* chemically packed to be put together by the Transportation Company on the other side at the depot, and the greatest care given to keep the packages *identical*. These marvellous expedients are but a specimen or symbol. In like manner, a certain hurry and impatience leads our people to short ways in every department of life: in short ways to science, to religion, to literature. The race of scholars, of laborious investigators will come to an end. Our people are insatiable readers of newspapers. What acres of these sheets they run through and spend several months of the year in that pastime. And so in their intellectual and scientific training. The vice of the American is that he is too easily pleased. A curious fact in the last ten or twelve years has been the dedication of this country to the study of phrenology, proved by its modification of the language and introduction into general use of as many words as the use of steam by land and water has added.[11] I do not think this is to be wholly attributed to the facility of our people and their deceivability, but partly to the fact that the system, however rudely and coarsely, was a return to a natural instinct; it brought observation to a noble and fit object, to which too much study cannot be given. It betrayed the instinctive belief that under all these dismal masks of men, masks which we wear and which we meet, the form of man was something sacred and beautiful which should yet appear; and it showed the thirst of men for a teaching nearer to their business and bosom than any they enjoyed. Had it confined itself to a reverent accumulation of the facts, it would have been a good hint, but would have had no world's renown; but now with its speedy

11. Phrenology, a popular pseudo-science that held that a person's character could be "read" by examining the bumps on his or her head. These bumps corresponded to areas of "influence" in the brain.

ascent by one jump into the chair of science, it has become a symbol of the times. Is it that we have found quicker than others the real poverty at the bottom of all this seeming affluence of life; the headlong speed with which each seeing soul comes straight through all the thin masquerade on the old fact; is it the disgust at this indigence of nature which makes these raging livers drive their steeds so hard, in the fury of living to forget the soup maigre of life?

Phrenology especially seems to have been invented for the American people with its swift and shallow mode of disposing of the sacred secrets of nature: a man shall be a mystery no more; let me put my hand on his forehead and his hindhead; give me a pair of dividers and a foot rule, and nature cannot hide his genius where I cannot find it by inches and seconds; the recesses of human power and probity are laid open to my fingers. Character is as easily read as a placard, and the fortunes of a man are reduced to an arithmetic problem. Genius is an inflammation of the brain and conscience, a secretion of the left lobe of the heart.

Yet phrenology was modest compared with the pretensions of mesmerism.[12] The ignorant are always on the watch how to cheat nature, and, if all the stories are true, here seemed a chance to occur. Mankind were no longer to labor to come at their ends, nor to abridge their labor by dexterous physical combinations, nor to overpower physical opposition by moral force, but by a third power, by gentle touching of the knuckles, and by persuasive passes, and by coaxing, beckoning, and ogling of fingers, we could hope to raise the state of man to rare and transcendant degrees. The most stupid and perverse man when awake, once get him fast asleep in his chair, shall become an angel of light, a learned physician, a surpassing astronomer, and a telegraph so subtle and swift that he is the Paul Pry of the universe.[13]

And this is the way we will outwit the laws of Nature. With unwashed hands, and our whole day's task unattempted before us, we are grasping after new powers like some Aesop's dog snatching at the shadow of our bone.[14] We would be magians and somnambulists and see with elbows, and know the architecture in Orion, and tunnel the earth to come into pagodas of Pekin. And on the first hint of such powers being attained, we will enter heaven and enter hell, go to the poles and the antipodes so, and dodge the laws and the Fates, the powers of perseverance, the graces, the virtues, all angels, all heroes, all qualities, all gods, and pierce

12. Mesmerism is a type of hypnotism.

13. Paul Pry is the title character of a play (produced in 1825) by the English dramatist John Poole (ca. 1786–1872); his name came to stand for a troublesome adventurer.

14. Aesop, a legendary Greek fabulist of the sixth century B.C. In his fable of the dog and the shadow, a dog crossed a bridge over a stream with a piece of meat in his mouth, saw his own shadow in the water, and thought it another dog with a piece of meat double his own in size. Immediately letting go of his own and fiercely attacking the other dog to get his larger piece from him, he thus lost both, because the dog in the water was a reflection, and his own meat was swept away by the stream.

to the courts of power and light by this dull trick. The wise gods must needs laugh heartily this once.

That nature should have subtile compensations for infirmity, and morbid actions of natural organs, and even from all this profuse treasure house of power and organization some overflowings of light and vitality into crevices and chinks, is not to be doubted; but for men to choose these exceptions and anomalies instead of the law, and prefer these haloes and meteors to the sun and moon, does not do them much honor. By Lake Winnepesaukee, a man lost his feet and learned to walk on his thumbs, and now all New Hampshire is learning to walk on its thumbs, and it will presently take a great genius to convince men that feet were made to walk with.

What is most noticeable is that men who never wondered at anything, who had thought it the most natural thing in the world that they should exist in this orderly and replenished world, have been unable to suppress their amazement at the disclosures of the somnambulist. The peculiarity of mesmerism is that it drew in as inquirers and students a class of persons never on any other occasion known as students and inquirers. Of course, the inquiry is pursued on low principles. Mesmerism peeps. It becomes a black art. The uses of the thing, the commodity, the power, at once come to mind and direct the course of inquiry. It seemed to open again that door which was open to the fancy of childhood: of magicians, and faeries, and lamps of Aladdin and travelling cloaks that were to satisfy the utmost wish of the senses without danger or one drop of sweat. But as Nature can never be outwitted, as no man was ever known to get a cent's worth without paying in some form or other the cent, so this prodigious promiser ends always, and always will, as sorcery and alchemy have done before, in very small and smoky performance.

It is so wonderful that a man can see without his eyes, that it never occurs to the adept that it is just as wonderful that he should see with them. And that is ever the difference between the wise and the unwise: the latter wonders at what is unusual; the wise man wonders at the usual. Well, these things are only symptomatic of the disease of the people. That repose which is the ornament and the ripeness of man is not in New England, is not in America, but hurry, and partiality, and impatience are in its room.

The whole generation is discontented with the tardy rate of growth which contents every European community. America is, therefore, the country of small adventures, of short plans, of daring risks—not of patience, not of great combinations, not of long, persistent, close-woven schemes demanding the utmost fortitude, temper, faith, and poverty. Our books are fast changing to newspapers; our reformers are slight and wearisome talkers, not man-subduing, immutable— all attracting their own task, and so charming the eye with dread and persuading without knowing that they do so. We have no Duke Wellingtons, no George Washingtons, no Miltons, Bentleys, or Seldens among our rapid and dashing race, but abundance of Murats, of Rienzis, of Wallers, and that slight race who put their whole stake on the first die they cast.[15] The great men bequeath never their projects to their sons to finish. These eat too much pound cake. Wordsworth said,

> 'Tis the most difficult of tasks to keep
> Heights which the soul is competent to gain,

and these lines are a sort of elegy on these times, and hardly less in the clerisy or scholastic class than in the practical.[16] If we read in the books of one of the great masters of thought, in Plato, in Aristotle, or in the great thinkers of the age of Elizabeth, we are astonished at the vigor and breadth of the performance. Here is no short breath and short flight, but an Atlantic strength which is everywhere equal to itself and dares great attempts because of the life with which it feels itself filled.

See the impatience of our people to rush into the lists without enduring the training. The Americans are too easily pleased and remind us of what was said of the Empire of Russia: that it was a fine fruit spoiled before it had ripened. Our people are too slight and vain. They are easily elated and easily depressed. See how fast they extend the fleeting fabric of their trade, not at all considering the remote reaction and bankruptcy, but with the same abandonment to the moment and the facts of the hour as the Esquimaux when he offers to sell his bed in the morning. An old merchant said to me that he had learned that he could not learn by experience; for, ten times he had been taught by hard times not to extend himself again, yet always a new crisis took him by surprise, and he was as unprepared as ever. They act on the moment and from external impulse. They all lean on some other, and this superstitiously and not from insight of his merit. They follow a fact, they follow success, and not skill. Therefore, as soon as the success stops, fails, and the admirable man blunders, they quit him; already they remember that long ago they suspected his judgment, and they transfer the repute of judgment to the next prosperous person who has not yet blundered. Of course, this levity makes them as easily despond. It seems as if history gave no account of any society in which despondency came so readily to heart as we see it and feel

---

15. Arthur Wellesley, first duke of Wellington (1769–1852), served in Britain's armies for nearly fifty years; Richard Bentley (1664–1742), English cleric and classical scholar; John Selden (1584–1654), English jurist, historian, and author; Joachim Murat (1771–1815), king of Naples and brother-in-law of Napoleon; Cola di Rienzi (ca. 1313–54), Italian popular leader and patriot; William Waller (ca. 1597–1668), English general in the Thirty Years War.

16. William Wordsworth, *The Excursion*, IV, 138–39.

it in ours. Young men at thirty, and even earlier, lose all spring and vivacity, and if they fail in their first enterprize, throw up the game.

I think we have no worse trait, as far as it is a national one, than this levity, than this idolatry of success, this fear to fail. We shall never have heroes, until we have learned that it is impossible to fail. Of course, this timidity about reputation, this terror of a disaster comes of looking at opinion as the measure of character, instead of seeing that character judges opinion. In the brave West, I rejoice to see symptoms of a more man-like sentiment than this timid asking leave to live of other men. The frank Kentuckian has a way of thinking concerning his reception by his friend that makes him whole: Here I am. If you do not appreciate me, the worse for you. And the great Indian sages had a lesson for the Bramin which every day returns to mind: "All that depends on another gives pain. All that depends on himself gives pleasure. In these few words is the definition of pleasure and of pain."[17] We must learn, too, failure is a part of success. Prosperity and pound cake are for very young gentlemen whom such things content: but a hero's, a man's success is made up of failures, because he experiments and ventures every day, and the more falls he gets, moves faster on: defeated all the time, and yet to victory born. I have heard that in horsemanship he is not the good rider who never was thrown, but that, rather, a man never will be a good rider until he is thrown; then, he will not be haunted any longer by the terror that he shall tumble, and *will ride,*—that is his business, *to ride,* whether with falls, or whether with none, *to ride unto the place whither he is bound.*

The noble Phocion, him of whom it has been so truly said, that, "Phocion haranguing the Athenian *Demos* was as solitary as a ship on the stormy Atlantic," was afraid of applause.[18] For a true man feels that he has quite another office than to tickle or flatter. He is here to bite and to stab, to inflict wounds on self-love and easy, prosperous falsehood, which shall not quickly heal. Demosthenes, when the people hissed him for his ragged and untuneable voice, cried out, "You are to judge players, indeed, by their sweet voices, but orators by the gravity and power of their sentences."

It would seem as if history were full of tributes to the unrivalled ascendency of personal qualities. He is the hero who conquers alone.

"In that immense crowd which throngs the avenues to power in the United States, I found very few men who displayed any of that manly candor and that masculine independence of opinion which frequently distinguished the Americans in former times, and which constitute the leading feature in distinguished charac-

17. Attributed to *The Laws of Menu* (or *Manu*), Indian commentaries on religious laws and social obligations, compiled between 200 B.C. and A.D. 200 (see *TN*, 3:269).

18. Phocion (ca. 402–317 B C.), Athenian general and statesman.

ters wherever they may be found. It seems at first sight as if all the minds of the Americans were formed on one model, so accurately do they correspond in their manner of judging.

A stranger does indeed sometimes meet with Americans who dissent from these rigorous formularies; with men who deplore the defects of the laws, the mutability and the ignorance of democracy; who even go so far as to observe the evil tendencies which impair the national character and to point out such remedies as it might be possible to apply: but no one is there to hear these things beside yourself, and you to whom these secret reflections are confided, are a stranger and a bird of passage." [19]

Is not this tragic in so far as it is true, that this great country, hospitable to all nations, opened for the experiment of new ideas, now in the decrepitude and downfall of the old mythologies of church and state in Asia and Europe,—should be a country of dwarfs; cities and nations of democrats, and never an upright man? That our famous Equality should be a fear of all men; and our famous Liberty should be a servitude to millions; a despicable, skipping expediency; a base availableness, ducking with servile cap to the lowest and worst? I do not wonder that the well-disposed but slow of faith begin to look with wishful eyes to the decorum and police of monarchy, as the poetic and imaginative but drowsy mind is driven by the cold disputation of the Protestant to the stability and veneration of the Roman Church. Some of the most intelligent and virtuous foreigners who have been among us, and those who have surveyed us from afar, have expressed the feeling that the antidote to our excessive spirit of socialism must be found in a class of gentlemen or men of honor,—which, yet, they thought, our institutions did not go to form.

19. Quoted from Tocqueville, *Democracy in America.*

# *New England*, Lecture IV: "New England: Recent Literary and Spiritual Influences" 30 January 1843 (1843–1844)

Emerson first delivered this lecture as "Recent Literary and Spiritual Influences Felt in New England" on 30 January 1843 as the fourth of five lectures in a *New England* series at the Chinese Museum in Philadelphia, for which he received no more than $100 (*Letters*, 3:139). He repeated this lecture as "New England: Recent Literary and Spiritual Influences" on 20 February 1843 as the fourth of five lectures in a *New England* series at the New York Society Library in New York City. After expenses in New York, he was able to clear $9 per lecture (*Letters*, 3:150). He received a favorable one-paragraph review in the *New-York Daily Tribune* (21 February 1843, 2).

Although the occasion was not reported on in any Providence newspapers, Emerson may also have delivered some form of this lecture on 15 January 1844 as the third of four lectures in a *New England* series before the Franklin Lyceum at Westminster Hall in Providence, Rhode Island, receiving $80 for the series (Cabot, "Blue Books"; see Simmons, "Emerson's 1843–1844 New England Lectures").

For the reasons given in the headnote to Emerson's *New England* series (see above), the title used for this lecture in this edition is taken from the title under which the lecture was advertised when Emerson delivered it on 20 February 1843 at the New York Society Library. The text of this lecture has never been published under any of the titles associated with it.

Pity that in this continent where nature is so grand, genius should be so tame: not one unchallengeable reputation. Our painters are fine colorists, not good draughtsmen. One is a beautiful draughtsman, but the soul of his picture is *imputed* by the spectator. His merit is like that of Kean's recitation, merely out-linear, emptied of all obtrusive individuality, but a vase to receive, not a fountain to impart character. So of our best poems, chaste, faultless, beautiful, but uncharacterised. So of our sculpture, picturesque, not creative, and in the affirmative style of old art. So of our preaching and senatorial eloquence: all *feminine* or receptive, not masculine or creative.

We go to school to Europe. We imbibe an European taste: our education, so called—our drilling at college and our reading since—has been European, and we write on the English culture, and to an English public, in America and in Europe. Our eyes presently will be turned westward and a new and stronger tone will be the result. The Kentucky stumporatory, the exploits of Boone and David Crockett and the *Letters of Jack Downing*, are genuine growths and are sought with avidity in Europe, where our European-like books are of no value.[1] Indeed, it is easy to see that soon the centre of gravity, which long ago begun its travels and which now is still on the eastern shore, will shortly hover midway over the Atlantic main and then, as certainly, fall within the American shore, so that the writers of the English tongue shall write to the American and not to the island public, and then will the great Yankee be born.

The people of New England are more addicted even than the rest of their countrymen to travel. It is a part of a liberal education to visit London, Paris, and Rome, if not Athens and Constantinople too. This practice cannot prevail to its actual extent without deeply tinging the minds of the most active and forcible young men with a strong respect for their foreign masters and giving a ready audience to such opinions as come to us from the philosophers and poets of Europe.

A great influence on the present generation in New England was that of Coleridge's genius. As another proof of the greater idealism, the keener taste for mysticism and spiritualism in New than in Old England, witness the readier reception his genius has always found here and the tardiness of its acceptance at home. Many editions of his *Friend*, of his *Literary Biography*, of his *Aids to Reflection*, and of his poems have been exhausted in this country.[2] And with what joy received, with what preference and eminence valued, the best minds in the country will avow. There was a time when he was the representative of all highest and best of contemporary thought.

Since that time, the general study of German, which suggested the reading of Goethe, Schiller, Novalis, and Jean Paul, the study of Kant, Schelling, and Hegel, and the popularity of Carlyle, have somewhat thrown Coleridge into the shade; but one advantage he possesses: that of being the only inlet of liberal and philosophical thought into the orthodox schools.[3] In Andover, and New Haven,

---

1. Daniel Boone (1734–1820) and Davy Crockett (1786–1836), both frontiersmen about whom a literature of tall tales grew; *The Select Letters of Major Jack Downing . . . Written by Himself* (1834) by Seba Smith (1792–1868), a Maine humorist.

2. The works by Coleridge referred to are *The Friend: . . . Essays . . . to Aid in the Formulation of Fixed Principles in Politics, Morals and Religion* (1812), *Biographia Literaria; or Biographical Sketches of My Literary Life and Opinions* (1817), and *Aids to Reflection* (1824).

3. Johann Wolfgang von Goethe (1749–1832), Germany's most famous writer and a great favorite of Emerson; the German philosophers Johann Christoph Friedrich von Schiller (1759–1805), Novalis (pseudonym for Baron Friedrich von Hardenberg) (1772–1801), Immanuel Kant (1724–1804), Friedrich Wilhelm Joseph von Schelling (1775–1854), and Georg Wilhelm Friedrich Hegel (1770–1831); Jean Paul Friedrich Richter (1763–1825), German humorist; Thomas Carlyle (1795–1881), prolific Scottish writer who was Emerson's lifelong friend and correspondent.

and other northern Calvinistic seminaries, all the more intelligent and liberal rally round Coleridge, and shelves full of his books are sold in those towns by the book dealers every year.

Coleridge's merit must at last stand as not that of poetry nor philosophy, but as that of criticism. He is the most eloquent of critics. Plato said, "He shall be as a god to me who shall rightly define and divide," and this is the service which Coleridge has rendered to the scholar. He has given the best definitions of many of the leading words of the age. Instance his definition of the Church and the State; of an Idea; of a Law; of Genius, as distinguished from Talent; his essay on Method, and his speculations on the literature, and theology, and politics of the present day, which will usually reward the reader in proportion to the depth of his own mind. For he drew his definition from the laws of thought and not of life, and, at last, in legislation. Here in America, it very early found a stronghold, and its effect may be traced in all the poetry both of England and America.

Coleridge served an important office in giving new *éclat* to many precious old books which were quite overlaid with dust and forgetfulness: such as, Donne, Drayton, Daniel, George Herbert, not to mention George Fox and Jacob Behmen.[4] And so he made known by his praise an influence not less important than his own: that of Wordsworth.

The genius of both Coleridge and Wordsworth was eagerly decryed on the first introduction of their works into this country, but an early and genuine voice of welcome was here spoken. They have long since been allowed to take their place in the higher niches of our Temple of Fame as approved masters. But there are more recent competitors for naturalization in our House of Fame, who claim by the fact of having spoken to the heart of the youth of this country and of having stimulated the intellect to an activity which is yet far from reaching its term. And in enumerating the spiritual agents who have operated on the New England mind, it would be affectation to omit the name of Carlyle.

Mr. Carlyle's genius is a genuine fruit of the nineteenth century. Every line he writes indicates his time and his place. His page is the redolence of London; of London, the centre of Christendom, the Congress of Mankind—wherein all arts, all actions, all conditions coexist; where every human interest sends its organ, and where a nation is gathered as within four walls; where, by day and by night from a thousand thoroughfares of land and water, the couriers of the earth go and come with tidings in every tongue. Such another London is this style,— so vast, enormous, related to all the world, and so endless in details. It is overloaded with allusion to all regions of geography, to all manual arts, to all the

4. John Donne (1573–1631) and George Herbert (1593–1633), the most famous of the English metaphysical poets; Michael Drayton (1563–1631) and Samuel Daniel (1562–1619), English poets; Jakob Behmen (or Jakob Böhme) (1575–1624), German pantheist.

annals of time. Such is its extent of view, such the microscopic observation of particulars. He sees every hill and river and not less every street, church, park, parliament-house, barrack, baker's shop, mutton-stall, forge, wharf, and ship, and whatever stands, creeps, rolls, or swims thereabouts, and makes them his own. Hence, his encyclopediacal allusion to all knowables, and the virtues and vices of his panoramic style.

The events of the last forty years have not been without their effect on litera-ture; but no writer has been so sensible to their impressions as he. His birth and breeding have chanced when the old walls of language, religion, and politics Napoleon had broken down, and by himself or against himself had set all Europe in movement and drawn closer the ties of neighborhood; and when, greater than Napoleon, Trade, with teams and locomotives had crossed the military lines, bridged the pass, broken the bastion, and by dint of trampling with hoofs and wheels worn a road through every fortification.

With these favorable fortunes of place and time for extended observation, his own literary culture conspired. For ten years, Carlyle was a translator and critic of the German authors. Whilst the literature of England is not marked in our times for a bold taste or philosophy, that of Germany is the most catholic in its tone and tendency that ever existed. Goethe, in a paper in which he introduced to the notice of his countrymen a work of Mr. Carlyle, speaks of the literatures of different countries.

> "A true universal toleration is surest attained when we give entire allowance to the peculiarities of individuals and of nations, yet adhere to the conviction that true merit is known by this mark, that it has equal interest for all men. The Germans have now for a long time made themselves useful as a sort of brokers in effecting the exchange of literature. Whoever understands and studies German finds himself in the market where all nations offer their wares: he plays the interpreter, and, in the meantime, he enriches himself. In like manner, every translator should consider that he labors as a mediator of this universal intellectual commerce, and makes it his af-fair to forward the traffic; since, say what you will of the insufficiency of translation, it is and will be one of the most important and honorable offices in the business of the world.
>
> The Koran says, 'God has given to every people a prophet in its own speech.' So is every translator a prophet to his people."

And Mr. Carlyle, whose faculties of acquisition are at least as vigorous as any he possesses, read their great writers with that good will which leads to in-sight. The English and American public have yet no criticisms of the works of Werner, Novalis, Richter, Schiller, and Goethe, that can compare in the mass of information communicated, or the depth of the commentary, with the papers bearing those titles which he contributed to the early numbers of the *Foreign*

*Review.*[5] He went back to the sources of the German poetry, to Hans Sachs, and to the religious poems of Luther; in the "German Romance," he reviewed the whole series of recent romantic writers, nor thought his circle of study complete, until he had made acquaintance also with Kant and Fichte, the philoso-phers of the Transcendental School.[6] But above all, as was unavoidable, the influence of Goethe sank deep into his mind, a writer by far the most dangerous of all his contemporaries to the originality of young men, as I take it for granted that no scholar under forty, of ordinary intelligence, can be familiar with his writ-ings without the most sensible effect being wrought upon his own modes of thought. He leaves no man as he found him. Carlyle sat for a time at his feet, find-ing him, to use his own words, "the most healthy mind that had appeared in the world for many generations." He entered into correspondence with the poet, and translated *Wilhelm Meister,* beside a multitude of passages from other works.[7] It is easy to see in his own writings the influences of this master, not only in the smiling tolerance for every species of merit down to that of a good stock or stone, or even to that of a liar or a scoundrel who is thorough in his way,—but also in the direction of his inquiry, and the choice of his topics.

Goethe had always regarded with lively solicitude the actors and events of the French Revolution. "Hence," he says, on one occasion,

> "the interest with which for many years my mind was directed to the French Revo-lution, and so I explain my incessant endeavor to master as a poet that tremen-dous event in its causes and sequel. If I look back many years, I see clearly how an adherence to that immeasureable object so long consumed my poetic faculty quite to no purpose; and yet has that impression got so deep root in me, that I cannot deny how much I still muse on a continuation of 'The Natural Daughter,' paint out this strange production in my thought, without power to bring myself to execute it in details."

Goethe, a contemporary, a spectator, and, with his native prince, a sufferer from the inundation of French war, lived too near the events, and was not per-haps able to give them an ideal arrangement for the purposes of composition. That which he vainly sighed to do, it was reserved for his emulous scholar to per-form. Possibly the interest exhibited by Goethe led Carlyle at this time to turn his critical studies to the French Philosophism. His German papers were alter-nated and followed by more brilliant essays on Voltaire, Diderot, Mirabeau,

5. Possibly Friedrich Ludwig Zacharias Werner (1768–1823), German poet and dramatist.

6. Hans Sachs (1494–1576), German poet and the most famous of the Meistersingers; Martin Luther (1483–1546), famous German prelate; Johann Gottlieb Fichte (1762–1814), German meta-physician.

7. Thomas Carlyle's translations of Goethe's *Wilhelm Meister's Apprenticeship* and *Travels* appeared in 1824 and 1827, respectively.

and the *Diamond Necklace*.[8] His power of critical analysis; his independence of all canons; his sympathy with every form of life; his ready appeal to the laws of nature; and the scope of his mind, which is like the cap of an observatory commanding an entire horizon,—the earth below, the heaven above,—are rare merits. A new value of these disquisitions presently appeared, as they were the stations to and around which he made the excavations and run the galleries which enabled him to furnish, at last, a ground plan and elevation of that tower of dread which France exhibited to the nations at the close of the last century.

This foreign culture, falling on such a mind, emancipated Mr. Carlyle from the exclusively classical training of English scholars, and enabled him to look at books and men with as bold and cheerful a brow as we have ever detected in a scholar's closet. He has the air of one who, having 'seen many men and many manners,' knows a man, whether Frank, Arab, or Canàka, and rates him exactly at his worth. Great is his reverence for realities, for all such traits as spring from the intrinsic nature of the actor. He humors this into the idolatry of strength. A strong nature has a charm for him, previous, it would seem, to all inquiry whether the force be divine or diabolic. In his studies of Mirabeau, what gigantic portrait painting![9] How he gropes with muscular fingers into the obscure recesses of power in human will, and makes us feel the might that resides in our freedom. He preaches, as by cannonade, the doctrine that every noble nature was made by God and contains, if savage passions, also fit checks and grand impulses, and however extravagant, will keep its orbit, and return from far. This passion for strength pervades all his productions. Here is the antagonism between Mr. Carlyle's mind and the state of English society which retarded so long his reception at home. In the elevation of his views and the stern demand he makes for the highest attributes, England, absorbed entirely in the two great parties of Radicalism and Conservativism, enrolling every journal and every scholar on the one or the other side, could have little sympathy. Nor could that decorum which is the idol of an Englishman, and in attaining which the English man exceeds all nations, win from him any obeisance. He is eaten up with indignation against such a desire to make a fair show in the flesh.

Combined with this warfare on respectabilities, and, indeed, pointing all his satire, is the severity of his moral sentiment. He is thoroughly in earnest in his reverence for a virtuous action. In proportion to the peals of laughter amid which he strips the plumes of a pretender, and shows the lean hypocrisy to every van-

8. The Frenchmen Voltaire (François Marie Arouet) (1694–1778), author and intellectual; Denis Diderot (1713–84), philosopher and man of letters; and Comte de Mirabeau (1749–91), statesman and orator of the Revolution. Carlyle's "The Diamond Necklace" appeared in *Fraser's Magazine* (January–February 1837).

9. Thomas Carlyle, "Memoirs of Mirabeau," *London and Westminster Review* (January 1837).

tage of ridicule, does he worship whatever enthusiasm, fortitude, love, or other sign of a good nature is in a man. His hatred of cant makes him lean a little the other way, and affect to be a worse man than he is. For this very reason, his praise *is* praise, and reminds us of Johnson's surly eulogies of Milton which transcend all the honey of his panegyrists and still characterise the poet to his warmest admirers.[10] Mr. Carlyle is one of those writers who know how to quicken the pulse of virtuous sentiment. Bating a little for that indiscriminate worship of strength, he is keenly alive to every act of courage, of self-devotion, of kindness, nor is he misled by any popular measures from looking at crimes according to their intrinsic dye, and not their rate in law. And to this merit is due much of the enthusiasm which his genius has awakened in many young men.

A remarkable characteristic of Mr. Carlyle's mind, and one which has contributed as much as anything to his popularity, is his omnipresent Humour. There is nothing deeper in his constitution than his Humour, than the considerate, condescending good nature with which he looks at every object in existence as a man might look at a mouse; enjoys the figure which each self-satisfied particular creature makes in the unrespecting All, and dismisses it with a benison. The ghastly horrors of the Reign of Terror cannot overpower his infinite elasticity. At times, he reminds us of those formidable tribes at the sources of the Nile, who ran to battle with explosions of laughter. He feels that the perfection of health is sportiveness, and will not look grave even at dulness or tragedy. All the daughters of Memory seem to have come in aid of this propensity. He knows every joke that ever was cracked, every side-shaking comedy, public or private, that ever befel.

His style offends at the first encounter from its want of simplicity and from a certain air of defiance to all rhetorical forms and conventions. It is as if one should ask for a lamp and receive a shower of rockets, or inquire for the air of a song and be stunned by an oratorio. The parts are not always subordinated to aid the effect of the whole. One is forever stopping in mid-career to pick up and examine these golden apples. But the redundancy of ornament is no veneering or varnishing; the beauty is in the grain, and demonstrates the matchless virtue and fruitfulness of the root. Mr. Carlyle's facility of association is not more wonderful than the variety and curiosity of his acquired knowledge. His readers are like travellers encumbered by the beautiful obstructions of the groves of Cumana, where the palm and the mahogany burden the ground with their living columns, and vines, like enormous serpents, interweave acres into solid mats of vegetation. We remember many passages where the reader is cloyed with richness, and where the plainest statement would be worth more than all the commentary. In "The

10. Samuel Johnson (1709–84), English lexicographer, editor, and critic.

Diamond Necklace," we doubt not we have the sifted story, the veritable fact as it fell out, yet it is so strangely revealed to us by a profusion of brilliant pictures, that the eye of an accurate inquirer is speedily confused out of all power of distinct vision, and in many places in the *History* before us, we think that every reader would be refreshed and assisted by greater plainness of speech.[11] No living writer has shown equal acquaintance with the resources of the English tongue. He crowds meaning into all the nooks and corners of his periods. He is never encumbered by the particles and circumlocutions of speech, but inflates them all with his soul, so that his sentence is like a bird distended with air to the extremity of every bone and plumule of the body. Once read, he is but half-read. Much of his power is to be attributed to the fact, that he has explored the inexhaustible mine of the language of conversation. He does not use the written dialect of the day, in which scholars, pamphleteers, and the clergy write; nor the parliamentary dialect of lawyers, statesmen, and the better newspapers; but he draws strength and motherwit out of a poetic use of the spoken vocabulary, so that his paragraphs are all a sort of splendid conversation.

The greatest force of Carlyle seems to me like that of Burke: to reside rather in the Form.[12] Neither of them is a poet born to announce the will of the god, but each is a splendid rhetoric wherein to clothe the truth. Carlyle shall make a statement of a fact, shall draw a portrait, shall inlay nice shades of meaning, shall banter, shall insinuate, shall paralyze with sarcasm, shall sing a Tyrtaean song, and speak out like the Liturgy or the old English Pentateuch all the secrets of manhood. This he shall do, and much more, being an upright, plain-dealing, hearty, loving soul of the clearest eye, and of infinite wit, and using the language like a protean engine which can cut, thrust, saw, rasp, tickle, or pulverize, as occasion may require.

He is not a philosopher; his strength does not lie in the statement of abstract truth. His contemplation has no wings. He exhausts his topic. There is no more to be said when he has ended. He is not suggestive, but every new history that shall be written will have owed a hint to him. It is plain that the historian must go now a little nearer to men's shops and sittingrooms. What he has said shall be proverb, and no man shall be able to say it otherwise. One is reminded of the inscription on the Eastern pyramid: "I, King Saib, when I had built this pyramid, covered it with satin. Let him that cometh after me and says he is equal to me cover it with mats."

The power of those devouring eyes, of that portraying hand, was felt by all the youth of New England. They could not forget any word that he had spoken: and

---

11. Carlyle published *The French Revolution* in 1837.
12. Edmund Burke (1729–97), Irish politician and natural philosopher.

his words spake to their condition. Honesty he taught, and courage, and the dignity of self-trust, and he prepared the way for the higher and the highest lessons which he did not offer to read. He gave an impulse to the study of the German writers and mainly of Goethe, which has done much to elevate the reading, not only of the study, but of the sittingroom. His insight and dramatic talent realized his own remark, that "all history is poetry were it rightly told;" and he actually found friends—as many readers among women as among men—and his books threatened for a time to put to flight the wretched swarms of novels which followed the disappearance of Scott. Indeed, it was high time that a book at once attractive and stimulating, but treating of deeper yet familiar experiences, should come into the parlour which was filled only with frivolous literature.

The fertility of these books and the multiplication of them by the new cheap press make them play a certain part in the training of our people. So much novel reading ought not to leave the readers quite unaffected, and doubtless it does work to give a romantic tinge to their daily life. They must study noble behaviour. And we must pause a moment to indicate the divisions of modern romance. They are in the main of two kinds: first, the novels of Costume, which is the old style, and vastly the most numerous still, and second, the novels of Character.

Every story partakes of both these elements, and each ranges itself under one or the other class according to the defect or the excess of the high element. Thus Manzoni's novel, "I promessi sposi," though in form obeying the conventions of the novels of costume, in substance raises itself out of all relation to them in the depth of the resources from which it draws, in the splendour with which the moral sentiment transfigures the face and form of the saintly hero and imparadises the reader in a stream of holy sentiment which he neither will nor can forget.[13] *Spiridion* of George Sand and Balzac's *Livre Mystique* and *La recherche de l'Absolu* are novels of character.[14] The novels of fashion of Disraeli, Bulwer-Lytton, Mrs. Gore, Mr. Ward, belong to the class of Novels of Circumstance or Costume, because the aim in them all is at a purely external success.[15] Of this latter section,—the Tale of Fashionable Life,—by far the most agreeable and the most efficient was *Vivian Grey*.[16] Young men were and still are the readers and victims. Byron ruled for a time, but Vivian with no tithe of Byron's genius

13. *I promessi sposi: storia milanese del secolo XVII* (1825–27) by Alessandro Manzoni (1785–1873), Italian poet and novelist.

14. *Spiridion* (1839) by George Sand, Baronne Dudevant (1804–76), French author whose personal life scandalized Paris; *Le Livre mystique* (1835) and *La Recherche de l'absolu* (1834) by Honoré de Balzac (1799–1850), prolific French novelist.

15. These English novelists are Benjamin Disraeli (1804–81), also a statesman; Edward George Earle Lytton Bulwer-Lytton (1803–73); Catherine Grace Francis Gore (1799–1861); and Robert Plumer Ward (1765–1846).

16. Benjamin Disraeli, *Vivian Grey* (1826).

rules longer. One can distinguish at sight the Vivians in all companies. They would quiz their father, and mother, and lover, and friend. They discuss sun and planets, liberty and fate, love and death over the soup. They never sleep, go nowhere, stay nowhere, eat nothing, and know nobody: but are up to anything, though it were the Genesis of Nature or the Last Cataclasm, Festus-like, Faust-like, Jove-like, and could write an *Iliad* any rainy morning, if fame were not such a bore.[17] Men, women, though the greatest and fairest, are stupid things, but a rifle and a mild pleasant gunpowder, a spaniel, and a cigar are themes for all companies.

But there is an ethical element in the mind of our people that will never let them long rest without finding exercise for the deeper thoughts. In every company there are always a certain number who pine to ask the last questions of human nature: Whence? and What? as well as How?—and the rest of the company can very easily be drawn in. The mind of New England, beginning to agitate the primary questions of intellect, and of morals, the nature of conscience, the foundations of government, of property, and of social institutions, very soon found both Wordsworth and Carlyle insufficient for their end and begun to look wider to the profoundest moralists of ancient and of recent times. The criticism which began to be felt upon our Church generally was that *it was poor,* that it did not represent the deepest Idea in man, that the instructions of the Church have no adequate breadth. It speaks in a dialect. It refers to a narrow circle of experiences, persons, and a literature of its own. What I hear of there, I never meet elsewhere. I cannot make it sufficient to me but by contracting myself. It does not explain to me my fortune, nor my form, nor my affections, my talent, my trade, my disease. I see it not in the sunset: I hear it not in music. If I glance from the catechism to natural history, the connexion of the two things is not quite obvious. The thermometer and microscope have a very unbelieving look.

Now, it is plain that the mark of a truth is that it is rich, all related, all explaining. It was a feeling like this that led and still is leading a large number of active and thoughtful men to the study of the writings of Swedenborg. They classified the world for the receiver, explained his habit, his marriage, his dreams, his fever, his insanity, his vocation, his presentiments, his life and death. This he did in strange prose poems which he called *The Apocalypse Revealed, Heaven and Hell, The Heavenly Secrets, The Doctrine of the Lord,* and the like.[18]

17. All three characters are known for their attempts to gain knowledge: the title character of *Festus* (1839) by Philip James Bailey (1816–1902), an English poet; the title character of Goethe's *Faust* (1808, 1833), who sells his soul to the devil for knowledge; and Jove or Jupiter, the central deity of the Roman religious world.

18. Emanuel Swedenborg (1688–1772), Swedish scientist, theologian, and mystic whose works include *The Apocalypse Revealed* (1836), *A Treatise Concerning Heaven and Its Wonders, and Also Concerning Hell* (1823), *Heavenly Arcana* (1837–48), and *The Doctrine of the New Jerusalem Concerning the Lord* (1833).

Those who converse on beauty and who are esteemed umpires of taste are generally persons who have acquired some knowledge of admired pictures or sculptures and have a love for whatever is elegant and selected, but if you inquire whether they are beautiful souls, and whether their own acts are like fair pictures, you learn they are not, but they are cold, selfish, and sensual. Their cultivation is local, as if you should rub a log of dry wood in one spot to produce fire, all the rest remaining as before. Their knowledge of fine arts is some repetition of rules and particulars, or some limited judgment of color or form, which is practiced for amusement or display. But the laws of Beauty are very deep, and a knowledge of them can only come from a pure, intelligent, and noble mind.

It is a proof of this shallowness of the Doctrine of Beauty in these days that men seem to have lost the perception of the instant dependence of form upon soul. It is thought fanatical to suppose that the forms about us mean anything directly. We were put into our bodies as fire is put into a pan to be carried about, but there is no accurate adjustment between the spirit and the body. And so with the objects that surround us, the intellectual men do not believe in any essential dependence of the material world on thought and volition. The poets who please the ear of this generation wish to lead a life of timid conformity and to write poems not from the life, but from the fancy, the farther away from themselves the better. Theologians think it a pretty air-castle enough to talk of the spiritual meaning of a ship, or a cloud,—of an art, or a trade,—but they prefer to set on the solid ground of historical evidence.

But not so the great poets of the world. The highest minds of the race have been those who did deeply feel and enjoy the double meaning of every sensuous fact—Plato, and Plutarch, and all the masters of sculpture, picture, and poetry.

Every line you can draw on paper has expression. All form is an effect of character; all condition, of the quality of the life; all body, of spirit; all beauty, of truth; all outward harmony, of inward health; and a perception of outward beauty should be sympathetic. The Beautiful rests forever on the foundations of the Necessary. Beauty is the flowering of virtue. Beauty is the pilot which guides to the healthful and good. A beautiful person, among the ancients, was thought to betray by this sign some secret favour of the immortal gods. "As heat cannot be separated from fire, no more can beauty from the Eternal," said Angelo.[19] The soul makes the body.

> "So every spirit as it is most pure
> And hath in it the more of heavenly light,
> So it the fairer body doth procure
> To habit in, and it more fairly dight
> With cheerful grace and amiable sight;

19. Quoted from Michelangelo Buonarroti, Sonnet VI.

> For of the soul, the body form doth take,
> For soul is form and doth the body make." [20]

We shun to record a familiar circumstance; for example, the clergyman, his Unitarian association, his *Christian Register,* his exchanges and his pecuniary, and social, and amiable or odious relations to his parish. And in like manner, each of us so much of his hodiernal economy as occupies most of his time and thoughts; but if we consider how fast the wheel of nature revolves, we shall know that very soon this will be irrevocably gone, intrusive and unpleasing as it now appears. Yet how gladly we would learn from Shakspeare, gladly from Chaucer, from Plato, those daily facts. At a distance, it will appear to ourselves also what was the significance of these employments and meannesses as symbolical. At a distance, we shall see the character overpowering the condition and giving its quality to all the parts. In the perspective of ages and orbs, your daily employment will appear the fit fable of which you are the moral.

It needed some great poet to marry nature again to the mind for men who had lost the link. And this service the next ages will probably owe to Emanuel Swedenborg.

God gave him the fatal gift of penetration. The poet could not see the poorest culinary stove, but he saw its relation to the charity which is the fountain of nature. Swedenborg, of all men in the recent ages, stands eminently for the translator of nature into thought. I do not know the man in history to whom things stood so uniformly for words. Before him the metamorphosis continually plays. If there be in Heaven museums of psychology, the most scientific angel could scarcely find a better example than the brain of Swedenborg of the tendency to signify the moral by the material. Everything is fluid to his eye and obeys the impulses of moral nature. The figs become grapes whilst he eats them. When some angels who held boughs of laurel on one occasion, "The twig blossomed in their hands." [21] The noise seemed at a distance like gnashing and thumping, but coming nearer it was the voice of disputants. The men seemed like dragons in the heavenly light and in darkness, but to each other they appeared as men, and when light from the heavens shone into their cabin, they complained of the darkness, and were compelled to shut the window that they might see.

There was this perception in him which makes the poet or perceiver an object of awe and terror, namely, that the same man or society of men may wear an aspect to themselves and those in like state with them, and a different aspect to higher intelligences. Certain priests, whom he describes as conversing very

---

20. "A Hymme in Honour of Beautie," ll. 127–33, by Edmund Spenser (ca. 1552–99), English poet best known for *The Faerie Queene* (1590).

21. Quoted from Emanuel Swedenborg, *The Apocalypse Revealed* (1836).

learnedly together, appeared to the children, who were at some distance, like dead horses: and many the like misappearances. And, instantly, the mind inquires whether these fishes that swim under the bridge, these oxen that low in the pasture, these dogs that bark in the yard are verily fixed in changeable fishes, oxen, and dogs, or only so appear to me, and perchance to themselves appear upright men; and whether I appear as man to all eyes.

So thought the Brahmin and Pythagoras, and many a poet has doubted or has witnessed the transformation.[22] But the man who sees through the flowing rest the firm nature, and can declare it, will draw us with love and terror. Swedenborg taught a great system of natural ethics, founded on the laws of the human mind, but by him strangely illustrated by narratives of angels whom he had seen and conversed with on their manners, habits, and occupations. For the most part, the conclusions are profoundly true, however he came at them, and will still be true to those who suppose his mind was morbid and self-deceived. The delusion, if such it was, under which he labored, of seeing his thoughts in pictures, was common to him with Martin Luther.

There are certain deductions to be made. Swedenborg had this vice: that he nailed one sense to each image; one and no more. But in nature, every word we speak is million-faced or convertible to an indefinite number of applications If it were not so, we could read no book. For each sentence would only fit the single case which the author had in view. Dante, who described his circumstance, would be unintelligible now. But a thousand readers, in a thousand different years and towns, shall read his story and find it a version of their story by making a new application of every word.

Nature mixes facts and thought to evoke a poem from the poet, but our philosophy would be androgynous and itself generate poems without the aid of experience. For the same reason, Swedenborg's mythus is so coherent, and vital, and true to those who dwell within; so arrogant and sanitary to those without. There is nothing that comes out of the human heart—the deep, aboriginal region—that is not spheral, mundane, thousand-faced—so that if, perchance, strong light falls on it and much study be given to it, it will admit of being shown to be related to all things. The rose is a type of youth and mirth to one eye, of profound melancholy, of fever, of rushing fate, to another. There is nothing in nature which is not an exponent of nature.

The sense of nature is inexhaustible. You think you know the meaning of these tropes of nature, and today you come into a new thought, and so all nature converts itself instantly into a symbol of that; and you see it has been chaunting that song like a cricket ever since the creation. Nature is a tablet on which any sense

22. Pythagoras (d. 497 B.C.), Greek philosopher who raised mathematics to a science.

may be inscribed, only not anything cunning and consciously vicious. Draw the moral of the river, the rock, and the ocean. The river, the rock, and the ocean say, "Guess again."

Swedenborg's interlocutors all Swedenborgize: Sir Isaac Newton, Sir Hans Sloane, King George II, and all angels.[23] The universe in his poem suffers under a magnetic sleep, and only reflects the mind of the magnetizer. Only when Cicero comes by, the good Baron sticks a little at saying he talked with Cicero, but with a human modesty remarks, "One whom it was given me to believe was Cicero;" and when the *soi-disant* Roman opens his mouth, all Rome, all ancient eloquence, has quite departed: it is plain Swedenborg like the rest.[24]

With these deductions, I think the influence of Swedenborg an uncomputed force on the mind of this age and his genius still unmeasured. He redeemed the thoughtful and the profound from the iron dogmatics of Calvinism and from the cold antagonism which rested with denying the popular faith. He brought religion into use as the explainer of life. All these familiar facts were pregnant symbols, and a new value was given to every trivial action. Yet as far as so new and grand a doctrine can yet be tested by its effects, I should say that for a time it exerts the best effect in the culture of the intellect, but as I suppose the mind of the master himself, though grand, was morbid, so I think it a dangerous study to any but a mind of great elasticity. Like Napoleon as a military leader, a master of such extraordinary extent of nature and not to be acted on by any other, that he must needs be a god to the young and enthusiastic.

He will render the greatest service to criticism which has been known for ages who shall draw the line of relation that subsists between Shakspeare and Swedenborg. For here stands the human mind ever in the old perplexity, demanding intellect, demanding conscience, impatient equally of either without the other. There is always this Woman as well as this Man in the mind, affection as well as intellect. And yet no man expresses them both. That great Reconciler has not yet appeared. Partiality of any kind we hate; and when we are weary of the saints, Saint Augustine—Thomas à Kempis, as we so quickly are, Shakspeare is our City of Refuge.[25] And yet the instincts of man presently teach him that the problem of Essence is the one which must take precedence of all others; the questions of Whence? and What?—that the solution of these must be in a life, not in a book; that the best poem or drama is only a proximate or oblique reply; but the Pythagoras, and Menu, and Jesus work directly on this problem. We are alike impatient of the partiality of the one class, and the superficiality of the other.

23. Sir Isaac Newton (1642–1727), English mathematician and natural philosopher; Sir Hans Sloane (1660–1753), English naturalist and physician; George II (1683–1760), king of England (1727–60).

24. *soi-disant,* "so-called"; Marcus Tullius Cicero (106–43 B.C.), Roman philosopher and statesman.

25. Saint Augustine (354–430), early Christian church father and philosopher; Thomas à Kempis (ca. 1380–1471), German mystic and writer.

# "Address to the Temperance Society at Harvard, Massachusetts, 4 July 1843"

Emerson delivered his untitled address to a temperance society in Harvard, Massachusetts, on 4 July 1843. There are no contemporary accounts of the event. This lecture has never been published.

Emerson had been accompanied by William Ellery Channing on his visit, during which they also stopped by to see Bronson Alcott and Charles Lane at their utopian venture, Fruitlands, but he failed to comment directly on his address (see *JMN*, 8:433; *Letters*, 3:184).

I RECEIVED ONLY yesterday your invitation to join you in this festival and to speak to this meeting. I am come hither, not because I was prepared to address an assembly associated for the promotion of Temperance; for, in truth, I was very unready, quite unacquainted with the statistics of the Temperance movement in the Commonwealth, and have never before had the honour to address any society in the state on this subject. But I came, because when challenged, I was ashamed not to come. The Good Spirit which animates all, and me also, seemed to say to me, My son, to what purpose hast thou had bed and board in this world of mine all these years, and protection from so many cares which molest other men, and exemption from hard labor which others endure, whilst thou hast leisure for study and thought,—to what purpose,—if, when thy brothers wish to unite in the praise and furthering of a temperate life, thou hast no word in thy mouth that thou canst speak?

To a thought like this, there was but one reply. We seem to have rights over each other and are each other's, as soon as we meet to a moral end. Though we have never met before or seen each other's faces, we are not strangers. We are instantly domesticated by any manifestation of the moral sentiment. And though a man should go among strangers or to the antipodes and find himself among just men, he would at once find himself more at home than among his acquaintances and kindred.

And still another reason that drew me to this boldness, when I had so little or nothing to say that might be expected on this occasion, was this, that I fancied

I might in this company chance to speak to some one or more persons—to some-one, whose life is rather solitary than social, to some scholar, some bookworm, or what is more likely, to some dreamer and hoper of better times and better men to come, to some lover of his Bible, to some lover of thought, to some believer that the race of man is meant for more, far more, than it has yet shown itself fit, and by speaking, I should encourage that heart in this good hope.

And truly, Gentlemen, it seems to me that this meeting with this object is a fit celebration of the national anniversary. Our people are charged in foreign nations with great want of imagination; with too much devotion to the useful; with lov-ing dollars better than flowers; and the example of the understanding more than the gratification of the sentiments. I think, however, they must have the credit of having exhibited a marked fondness for holidays, and of having shown a quite inventive and graceful skill in public celebrations. The jubilee of Lafayette; the two magnificent processions at the foundation and the completion of Bunker Hill Monument; the floral processions in the city on this anniversary; and many of our Fairs and Sunday School meetings, have been managed with much spirit and beauty.[1]

Especially, I think it a wise use which we are learning to make of this national festival. The Fourth of July has long lost all its ancient interest, and is now a sort of niche or ample vase into which any ornamental ceremony can be laid. It is like the apostle's sheet let down by the four corners out of heaven, into which all manner of honest food may be put for the sustenance of the faithful: and has become the holiday of Temperance, Peace, Antislavery, and Education societies and of other peaceful and moral associations.

This is fit for the time and the country. Such blameless triumphs are in har-mony with the land and the face of nature, and proper to this continent. Who can see without immense hope, the great auguries of this country, as they write themselves on the broad landscape around us? With joy I see its rapid peopling, its rapid roadmaking—We, Gentlemen, shall be nearer neighbors in a twelve-month; this vast country hospitable to the nations; the poor crowded Ireland, and England, and Germany, emptying themselves of their redundant crowds of adult men into America, to render the most valuable services to this recent wilderness. I see the immense improvements begun.

But, Man the Improver must first be improved. We must begin at the begin-ning. And here and now I see the day of the Declaration of Independence turned to a new and nobler use. War is well nigh over; getting out of date. The drum is good only for boys and holidays; the militia is very innocent, and getting a little

1. The Marquis de Lafayette (1757–1834), a hero of the American Revolution, had participated in ceremonies at the laying of the cornerstone for the Bunker Hill Monument in Charlestown, Massa-chusetts, on 17 June 1825; the monument was completed on 17 June 1843.

ridiculous. To be sure, what has once existed will not be destroyed. War is over, but the elements of War are real, and must forever remain; nothing is lost, only it is changed. The antagonism has shifted to higher and higher ground. We do not tear each other as tigers. We have got a little schooling, and it has mended our manners. War is not now foreign, but civil; not civil, but domestic; not domestic, but personal. A man's foes are of his own household, within his own skin, under his own hat; War between the belly and the brains; between the body and the soul.

Let us, then, use the privilege to speak for Man and for Temperance; but let us do it worthily. I cannot disconnect and subdivide the topic. I will not treat of drinks alone or of meats alone; but of the whole subject of that beautiful self-command by which alone a man's life is worth keeping and transmitting. And what is more pleasing testimony to the sanity of each of these humane efforts at Reform, which have so conspicuously marked the present time, than the circumstance everywhere noted that each one admitted, leads in the others by the hand? The same class of persons are the honorable workers in all. If a man becomes engaged in one part of philanthropy, he is pretty sure to be soon active in all the related duties. It reminds me of a most ancient proverb which is said to be current in the houses of heaven: "The more angels, the more room."[2]

Every man that loves his race must rejoice in the love which has engaged so much attention to the subject of Temperance in this country in the last twenty years. Whatever opinion we may entertain of the particular rules that have been recommended, every man must rejoice in the general design. The man shall be master of his organs, master of his mouth. Every unperverted man must see that the increase of temperance is the addition of so much reason to the community. I know how apt we are to have squeamish ears when this subject is handled and to call it coarse and trite. Be it so. But surely vice itself is coarser and triter than the worst speech on it can be. And the humblest attempt to face and subdue it deserves some favor,—is, at any rate, a very small sin.

I admit that there are higher virtues than Temperance. Perhaps Temperance is the lowest of all the virtues. Yet standing in human nature, as it does, at the very doors of the temple of the body, so that without this virtue there is no room for any other to enter, and no exclusion for any vice, and the temptations to violate it are so many, and so instant, that I think the most delicate and squeamish of us all must endure the discussion at least once in a year. We have got tired, perhaps disgusted, with the exaggeration and monotony of well-meaning advocates of partial reforms; but shall it be said of us that we opposed all the contemporary good, because it was not grand? Let us get their humble good, and catch the

2. Quoted from Emanuel Swedenborg, *A Treatise Concerning Heaven and Its Wonders, and Also Concerning Hell* (1823).

golden boon of purity, temperance, and mercy from these poor buffeted men of one idea.

The grounds on which Temperance commends itself to each soul, will vary according to the progress of the soul. Let me enumerate some of them, beginning with the lowest.

First. Health is the last and not a little good. There is a Persian proverb, that "it is the same thing to him whose foot is covered with a shoe, as if the surface of the earth were covered with leather." [3] Shall we not say the same thing of health? I spread my health over the whole world, and make it strong, happy, and service-able, but to a sick man the world is but a medicine chest. Well, Temperance is health, and Intemperance is disease, not disease ripe, but disease in the making.

The question forever recurs to the young man, the young woman, in their hopeful religious hour, Cannot this blood which in all men rolls with such a bur-den of disease, roll pure? Might not a simpler and shorter meal leave me a clearer head, and a kindlier heart, and an unclouded afternoon? Is not water friendlier to the atoms of which my body is built up, than the concoctions of the malt-house, the mill, and the still? And an universal experience all too firm and clear to be doubted, replies. The beasts of the field, those famed water drinkers in their un-broken health, reply. The spoiled children of cities, the eaters of pound cake, the sitters at the wine party, reply.

The celebrated Cornaro, who was broken down in his youth by his intemper-ance, renounced the use of all stimulating liquors and accustomed himself to eleven or twelve ounces of solid food per day, and so restored the powers of his constitution and enjoyed uninterrupted health of mind and body beyond the age of a hundred years. [4] It was his maxim—"That part of your meal which you do not eat, does you the most good." It is the well-known practice of the trainers, as they are called in England, who prepare the combatants for boxing matches, to prescribe accurately the quantity and quality of food for every day, and to put the appetite under great restraint. And I think every person must notice an increas-ing sensitiveness in our community on the subject of health and sickness. People are beginning to be heartily ashamed of being sick and are very plainly becoming conscious that they are somehow accessories before the fact.

Second. Then, Temperance is an estate. The reason of our respect for the rich, is the latent conviction in every man, that he ought to be rich, or able to come at his ends. There are two ways of getting rich; one by making our means more; the other by making our wants less. Socrates, when he saw the luxuries of the Athenians, said, "How many things do I not want!" [5]

3. Quoted from *The Hĕĕtōpădĕs of Vĕĕshnŏŏ-Sărmă* (1787).
4. Luigi Cornaro (ca. 1467–ca. 1566), Venetian known for his diet and longevity.
5. Socrates (ca. 470–399 B.C.), one of the most famous Greek philosophers whose dialogic method of teaching gained many adherents.

The temperate man you cannot make poor: every place yields what he wants. He is not hunted by creditors. The red flag of the auctioneer is not in his farmyard, nor his furniture pawned at the shops. His temperance keeps his children at school, finds his family in books, and brings his aid to the men and institutions he would support. Temperance is a double economist: it saves the time and cost of the debauch, and also the stupor and sleep of the indigestion. Other property may decline in value; it pays a tax to the government. Temperance never declines in value, and never pays any tax.

Third. But to come a little higher; it is Beauty. Our wish to please, to please honestly, not by what is gay, but by what is good, is a legitimate desire and comes out of the heart of love. And it is worth the thought of all persons who are fond of ornaments, and who love to please, that there is not in the world any more elegant ornament than this virtue. It is continually worn, and all men are judges of it. If you go into another country, your words need to be translated, in order to be understood. But your temperance will not need any explanation, but will be admired by savages, by kings, by nobles, by the multitude, and by wise men  It is a universal sign by which we communicate with the pure of every sect and tongue. A diamond breastpin is a pretty ornament and often pleases the eye, but a thief may pilfer it. The kingly decoration of a temperate habit no man can take from you, and no law compel you to conceal. No change of fashion can diminish its current value: like personal beauty, and more lasting than personal beauty. 'Tis a perpetual letter of recommendation wherever you go. In the old nations, they used to sell amulets, which were bought at great price, and kept about the person, as they were supposed to have the power of making the person who carried them, healthful and beloved. If any person who hears me wishes to buy such an amulet, I can tell him where it may be found. It is made chiefly of unbolted wheat and water.

Yes, I praise Temperance for its beauty to the young and the noble, sure beforehand of their sympathy. No man likes anybody's intemperance but his own. And as Temperance is so chief an elegance, is not Intemperance also the only vulgarity? How can he be noble whose brow, eye, face, and whole expression are continually degraded to his appetite? I notice too that it is always handsome and picturesque to see a man in the house or in the street eat fruit or bread or drink water, but to see him consume other victuals is less grateful to the eye. I notice the agreeable circumstance in the life of the poet Shelley that he was fond of all kinds of bread, and his path might be traced in the street by the crumbs which he dropped.[6] I notice the pleasure, and more the hint, which we always derive from the austere lives of the self-commanders.

Demosthenes, the greatest orator of the world, tells us of himself that he al-

6. Percy Bysshe Shelley (1792–1822), English Romantic poet.

ways drank fair water. I read with pleasure that Protogenes, the painter of ancient Rhodes, when he had undertaken to paint his picture of Ialysus for that city, lived on lupines that his judgment might not be clouded by luxurious diet; that Domenichino, the Italian painter whose picture of the *Communion of St. Jerome* hangs in the Vatican as a rival beside Raphael's *Transfiguration,* used the same diet whilst he painted that piece; that when the Persian ambassadors came to negociate with the Roman Emperor Carus at his camp, they found him sitting on the ground eating his dinner of stale bacon and dried pease, and being convinced that gold could not corrupt a man of such habits, they submitted to his terms; that, Franklin lived on bread and water.[7] I quote these old texts because I never hear them and the like without pleasure and profit.

I cannot help repeating, though the story is so old, what is reported of Andrew Marvell, the friend of Milton, that the court of Charles II were so struck with the eloquence of his invectives in Parliament, that they wished to buy him. And Lord Danby climbed up one day his dark staircase to the narrow garret in which he lived, to ask him how the King could serve him. The Lord Treasurer then offered him from King Charles a present of 1,000 guineas as a testimony of his majesty's respect for his virtue and talents. Marvell called in the boy that served him, and in the presence of the minister asked him, "John, what had I for dinner, yesterday?" "That small shoulder of mutton, Sir." "And what today?" "The rest of the same, sir." "And what shall I have tomorrow?" "The bones, Sir." "You see then, my Lord," said Marvell, "that a man who lives in this manner cannot have any use for 1,000 guineas."[8]

One more ground, let me add, on which this mastery of appetite may be sought. Temperance is power, namely, manly power. The time will come to every man who practices this virtue in the love of the virtue, when he will see that the reason why he should be temperate, is, because he belongs to the race of man; because he belongs to himself, and to the soul of his soul; and intemperance forfeits so much of the divine attributes which the Good Spirit within, communicates to these organizations of ours. It deserves thought, that ancient observation has shown a mysterious yet habitual connexion between sensuality and all that is most hideous in human nature. It has been noticed that there is in history a close connexion between sensuality and cruelty, which though not always distinctly traceable in individuals, is yet very easily seen in large masses of men, and which by an unknown process hidden in the depths of our nature, makes devils of malice out of men who have gratified their pleasant tastes.

---

7. Protogenes, fourth-century B.C. Greek painter of Rhodes; Domenichino (1581–1641), Italian painter of religious subjects and landscapes and for a time the Vatican's chief architect; Raphael (1483–1520), Italian painter whose works adorn the Vatican, also called "Raphaelle" or "Raphaello" by Emerson; Marcus Aurelius Carus (ca. 222–83), emperor of Rome (282–83).

8. Andrew Marvell (1621–78), English poet and satirist.

My brothers! this is the ground on which I plead the cause of Temperance: To ask you to be temperate is to ask you to be men, to bring you home to all the true and great powers of your nature; into sympathy with all those men who have been or who are the ornaments of the species, and into relations of flowing love with that Love by which we live. And it is upon this ground that the argument against the use of ardent spirits presents itself with a force to which language cannot do justice.

I have spoken thus far to the general subject of Temperance or to the government of the animal appetite. But if it chance that I speak to any person who, in the face of the reform that is going forward in the consumption of alcohol, has yet thought he might permit himself in the use of it, let me on this ground, that he is a Man, God's greatest work, beseech him to reconsider the matter. I would implore him to consider whether he does not pay a price out of all comparison too great for his gratification.

But not to pass by too slightly that subject to which I know the efforts of your society are specially directed, I have to say that I suppose intoxicating drinks will be hereafter regarded in history as the most active known enemy of the human intellect; and the period in which the use was indulged and defended as a more extraordinary delusion than those of magic or witchcraft or the self-immolation of the Hindoos.

If distilled spirit were sold at five hundred dollars the quart, I don't think you would buy it or drink it. But now you give more for it and think it cheap. For you would not sell that for five hundred dollars, nor for five hundred thousand dollars, which you give away for the pleasure of tippling. If it were gravely proposed to you to sell your intellect or a portion of it for a certain sum of money,—would you do it? I have never yet met with a man who thought he had any too much knowledge, or prudence, or power of self-command. I never met with one who thought he had any wisdom to spare. I believe there is so much of the man left in the very humblest individual, whoever he be, on this floor, that, if the amplest property in these United States were offered him as a price for that rank which he now holds among God's creatures, and for the sake of being enriched with every luxury he was to descend into the station of a mean, little-minded, faint-hearted wretch, he would reject the proffer with indignation. He would say 'I am a man and by God's help I will remain a man.' Yet here is a sweet-tasted liquor which is known to have the property of sucking out a man's brains, and putting folly and the devil in their stead, and, finally, of throwing him on the ground. And though men will not sell their understanding for five hundred dollars, they will sell it, for the pleasure of sipping this liquid.

There are some who think hard drinking wrong, and to be made dead drunk is one of the worst uses to which a man can be put, yet they think it a very different thing to drink a little.— They say truly; it is a very different thing. Far be it from any of us who are sober, to confound such different things. It is like mistaking the gate for the house, or confounding the tavern with the road that leads to it.

But there are some objections to moderate drinking that I should be glad to offer to the kind consideration of those who think it a question yet open to debate.

In the first place, it leads insensibly to immoderate drinking. Common experience will bear me out in saying that it is easier to be abstinent than to be temperate. It is easier to eat no dinner than to stop eating the moment we have eaten enough for nourishment. It is easier to drink nothing than to drink one glass with a friend and let the second pass. The first indulgence does not help our self-command. The old proverb of the Greeks said, *The belly has no ears,* intimating that you must set down all your rules for it beforehand and not trust your discretion after once you have begun to gratify it.

In the second place, the whole difference of capacity between man and man is a small difference. It is very slight, almost imperceptible degrees that separate the wiser, efficient man from the foolish and inefficient. The capacity of all men is how nearly alike. The wisest sayings of the wisest man are understood by the simplest. It seems to him as if he should have said the same thing, had he thought upon it. We are all so nearly upon a level that it seems as if a little difference in temperament only separated one to greatness and another to mediocrity.

Now it is upon that little difference that the stimulus of intoxicating liquor acts. A man who is reckoned prudent, under the slight stimulus of spirit, will become sanguine; he will utter words which before the glass he would have withholden, and so commit himself to acts which just pass the limits of prudence, and just cross the line and have a bad for a good tendency. Who can draw the line that separates between a wise boldness and rashness? The steps which have led this man to danger and ruin seem only a continuation of the very steps that led that man to success and honor.

It is a very fine line and needs a very cool head exactly to keep it. Steady: Steady: Discourage us, and we shall lose it. Exhilarate us, and we shall lose it. We must keep very cool. And a man who drinks a little every day takes off the clearness of his sight and deprives himself of just that degree of prudence, of superiority in judgment, which would have assured him of success in his enterprizes.

It is said, the master of a vessel finds always the sea smoother after he has taken his glass than before, and ventures to spread another sail—one more sail than the straining mast will carry. The prudent merchant finds the speculation he has been thinking of, less hazardous after dinner than it seemed before, and he ventures to close the bargain which in the morning he judged not worthwhile. And the consequence is that the safety and success which the habitual prudence of these individuals had secured, is now put at stake. The habit of a little indulgence converts the prudent man into an easy man. It produces a small change in all his habits. He is observed not to be quite so punctual,—not quite so judicious in his bargains, not quite so early a riser, not quite so attentive to his business, and, on the whole, all these little differences strike the balance a little against him. And when a man begins to decline, the common course of things goes rather to push him down than to hold him up, as it is much easier to keep a stone firm on the top of a mountain than it is to stop it after it has begun to roll down the side.

Power—manly power—that is Temperance. I do not affect to represent a virtue which is the key to all the others as one of cheap and easy attainment. I remember rather the wise saying of Burke, that "all the class of the severe and restrictive virtues are at a market almost too high for humanity." God will not, the Universe will not have cheap, what is so rich and strong. "Abstinence from low pleasures is the price by which we attain the higher."[9]

There is one point which in closing I wish to press, that, namely, which regards the use of stimulants by scholars and literary men; and which is important because these are always the guides of society; and because every man and every woman is or ought to be a cultivator of study and of thought. And it is fit to know whether the use of stimulants is valuable to this purpose.

The only plea on which sickness and weakness advocate the use of stimulating foods and drinks is that they are intellectual; that they repair the tasked and jaded powers and make the body equal to the excessive demands of the mind. But this is deceptive, and the loss is real. I have the deepest conviction that never can any advantage be taken of nature by a trick. The spirit of the landscape, the great calm presence of the Creator, comes not forth to the sorceries of opium or of wine. The sublime presence comes only to the pure and simple soul in a clean and chaste body. Is it not disgraceful to owe our inspiration to opium and to tea? We do not owe an *inspiration*, but some counterfeit excitement and fury. Milton says that the lyric poet may indeed drink wine and live generously, but the epic poet he who should sing of the gods and their descent into men, must drink water out of a wooden bowl. For I think it is with this as it is with toys: we foolishly fill the hands and nurseries of our children with all manner of trivial toys—dolls, drums, and horses—withdrawing their eyes from the plain face and grave but sufficing objects of nature, the sun and moon, the animals, the water and stones which should be their toys. So the poet's habits should be set on a key so low and plain that the common influences should delight him, and, so to speak, he should be tipsy with water.

I say these things the rather, because it seems to me that the great signs all declare the destiny of this country, and of the generation of men now rising here, to

9. Attributed to Walter Savage Landor (1775–1864), English Romantic poet whom Emerson met in England in 1833, in Emerson's "Walter Savage Landor," *Dial* 2 (October 1841): 270 (where it is cited as "Abstinence from low pleasures is the only means of meriting or of obtaining the higher").

be a more intellectual people than have yet been reared. It seems to me that the Conscience in the coming age is to extend its jurisdiction over the intellectual as over the moral sensibility, and whereas, now, men are only aroused to intellectual labor by appeals to their ambition, the time will come when they shall feel the crime of being ignorant, as now they feel the crime of being fraudulent. For according to the most sacred traditions of the ancient world, it is the law of Adrastia, that in the eternal revolutions of each soul, "whatever soul has perceived anything of truth shall be safe from harm until another period." [10]

If the auguries of good for this country can be trusted, if the faith and hope of wise and good men be entitled to any confidence, it becomes us to be ready for that descent of a purer mind, to be leaders in that new age. This very genius of reform, which in a hundred towns today celebrates the redemption of thousands of men from the ruin of drink, and which rallies other thousands to the most generous exertions to exterminate this barbarous and inhuman practice from American society, is itself the brightest sign, is itself the coming of that kingdom it announces. Yet, let me say it is not in bands, nor by pledges to each other, that the victory will be achieved. Souls are not saved in bundles. Not so, but by the reverse of that; not in societies, but in the isolated will and devotion of each mind, in the resolution to give himself no holidays, no indulgences, no hesitations; in his clear election of the right and rejection of the wrong for himself, and as if there were none in the universe but himself, and the Power which made him, is there safety and peace.

10. Quoted from *Six Books of Proclus . . . on the Theology of Plato* (1816).

# "Discourse Read Before the Philomathesian Society of Middlebury College in Vermont, 22 July 1845"

## and

# "Discourse Read Before the Philorhetorian and Peithologian Societies of Wesleyan College in Connecticut, 6 August 1845"

Emerson delivered his untitled discourse before the Philomathesian Society of Middlebury College in Middlebury, Vermont, on 22 July 1845, substantially repeating it on 6 August before the Philorhetorian and Peithologian Societies of Wesleyan College in Middletown, Connecticut. This lecture has never been published.

As was the usual case with Emerson's college discourses of this period, the initial inquiry came from students, not faculty. The Philomathesian (Lovers of Learning) Society was a group whose interests, at least as reflected in the contents of its library relative to that of the college, were "far more radical" ([Bob Buckeye], "Emerson and Middlebury," *Friends of the Middlebury College Library Newsletter*, no. 2 [Fall 1987]: 1). Silas G. Randall wrote Emerson on 14 November 1844 (bMS Am 1280 [2636], Houghton Library), inviting him to address the group the following July, and Emerson replied on the twenty-fifth that he found the invitation "very agreeable" but could not reply for "three or four weeks" (*Letters*, 7:615). Emerson talked the day before official commencement exercises, and the Society formally resolved to send its "thanks . . . to Mr. Emerson for his able & eloquent address" and requested "a copy of the address . . . for publication" (manuscript records of the Philomathesian Society, Middlebury College Library). He received $20 for expenses for the occasion ("Account Books").

Although Emerson described the discourse as "rather grave & cold" (*Letters*, 8:38), contemporary accounts indicate that it did generate some heat. The *Northern Galaxy* noted that "the manner and style of Mr. Emerson is highly cultivated and polished. His address was of the high transcendental character; and whatever may be said of its literary merits, we know that many christian hearts were pained at some expressions which were nothing short of pantheistic atheism"; fortunately, this writer could deal more favorably with the other address of the day, Dr. Joel Parker's "clear, practical and philosophical discussion of the principles of True Philanthropy" ("Middlebury College," 30 July 1845).

As usual, Horace Greeley's *New-York Daily Tribune* proved a sympathetic forum for Emerson, here with a letter from "N. S. N.," who commented that "notwithstanding the prejudices entertained in this region with regard to the peculiar views of the Transcendentalists, the earnest and eloquent exposition of the 'natural functions of the scholar and educated man,' . . . was listened to with an intensity of interest and pleasure, rarely observed on such an occasion" ("Correspondence of the Tribune," 4 August 1845, 2).

Emerson had been invited to appear at Middletown in early February by a student, Daniel Martindale, after both Rufus Choate and Orville Dewey declined because of health problems (this and other information are drawn from Kenneth Walter Cameron, "Emerson at Wesleyan University, Middletown, Connecticut," *Emerson Society Quarterly*, no. 11 [2nd quarter 1958]: 55–62). Writing to James Elliot Cabot on 3 August, Emerson noted, "I have been making a literary speech to the students of Middlebury College, & have now a similar errand this week at Middletown" (*Letters*, 3:293). Four days later he wrote Lidian of making his "speech, which passed very well, & certainly was all the better for having had a rehearsal at Middlebury"; he continued: "The young men asked a copy for printing, and I then told them its history, & found I was telling them no news, for the New-York Tribune [4 August] had already told them of the oration in Vermont & its subject. Well I assured them that the oration was now enlarged & retrenched for them, & if I printed it I would do it on my own charge & they might order any copies they pleased" (*Letters*, 3:294–95). Emerson considered "a part of the Middletown discourse, which was special to the occasion & to the condition of the societies," written especially for this delivery, but this is not evident from the manuscript (*Letters*, 8:77). He received $30 for his address but returned $10 to the Philorhetorian Society for the purchase of books ("Account Books").

Emerson's address, which was delivered late in the afternoon after the commencement exercises, was positively viewed by the local paper, the *Constitution*, which wrote that his "excellent address" was "received with much favor" (13 August 1845). Indeed, in recalling the event years later, one of the graduates described how "Emerson went on in his sphinxian way, looking serenely into the Infinite, while his enigmatic utterances dropped like bombs right and left," and how the governor of the state "sat open-mouthed and utterly bewildered," but the president of the college, Stephen Olin, was convulsed with laughter and "roared by fits, like a blowing whale" (F. H. Newhall, "Emerson among the Methodists," *Zion's Herald;* reprinted in *Springfield Daily Republican*, 31 October 1876, 3).

Subsequent responses were not as positive. The *Albany Religious Spectator* complained about Transcendentalism in general and of Emerson's hour-long "dreamy, and unintelligible speculations," noting that "shortly after, an aged minister [Stephen Martindale], who had never lived in any other than a world of common sense realities, was called upon to pray, and he devoutly thanked God that the Bible . . . was worth more than all the idealism and transcendentalism in the world" (reprinted in the *Calendar*, 23 August 1845, 135; reprinted in Kenneth Walter Cameron, "Emerson's Lecture at Wesleyan in 1845: What or Who Went Wrong?" *American Renaissance Literary Report* 11 [1997]: 267). Writing in 1882, Alexander Ireland described the scene after Emerson's address thus:

> Then arose a Massachusetts minister, who stepped into the pulpit Mr. Emerson
> had just left, and uttered a remarkable prayer, of which this was one sentence: "We

beseech Thee, O Lord, to deliver us from ever hearing any more such transcendental nonsense as we have just listened to from this sacred desk." After the benedic-
tion, Mr. Emerson asked his next neighbor the name of the officiating clergyman,
and when falteringly answered, with gentle simplicity remarked: "He seemed a very
conscientious, plain-spoken man," and went on his peaceful way. (*Ralph Waldo
Emerson: His Life, Genius, and Writings*, 2d ed. [London: Simpkin, Marshall, 1882],
299–300)

A similar story but placed with the events surrounding the delivery of "The Method of
Nature" (1841) at Waterville, Maine, is reported by Edwin Percy Whipple, who says
Emerson concluded his tale with these words: "The address was really written in the
heat and happiness of what I thought was a real inspiration; but all the warmth was extinguished in that lake of iced water" (*Recollections of Eminent Men* [Boston: Ticknor,
1887], 146).

Even though the college's president, Stephen Olin, wrote Emerson that he had listened with "pleasure and admiration," he went on to say, "You of course know that with
my religious views I cannot embrace some of your opinions." He was especially concerned
that some of Emerson's statements would "give much pain to many of our patrons if published just as you delivered them and so inflict serious injury on our Institution." Fearing
controversy, Olin asked Emerson to "modify your discourse by omitting a few brief passages so very likely to incense our religious friends & so to create prejudices against us as
a college" (8 August 1845, bMS Am 1280 [2328], Houghton Library). Emerson replied,
"I can easily believe that there were some petulances of expression which a more considerate taste would correct. I doubt not that I can remove some expressions that may have
disturbed some of your friends and perhaps thereby improve the fitness & the truth of
the piece" (*Letters*, 3:296). The following year, on 10 June, he wrote Daniel Martindale
again, noting that while he had originally held off printing the address because there were
"some pages in the discourse concerning the 'practical' & the 'speculative man' which
seemed to me incomplete," he had by then used enough of the address in his *Representative Men* lecture series that separate publication was no longer possible (*Letters*, 8:76–77;
he had notified the Philomathesian Society of his refusal to print the address by October 1845, as indicated in the Society's manuscript records at Middlebury College).

Along with Emerson's "Address" delivered before the Adelphic Union of Williamstown College on 15 August 1854 and before the Social Union at Amherst College on
8 August 1855 and "The Scholar" (1863), Cabot, with Ellen Emerson's assistance, mined
this lecture for major portions of an address Emerson delivered at the University of Virginia in 1876. Cabot eventually printed that address as "The Scholar" in *Lectures and
Biographical Sketches* in 1884 (see *W*, 10:259–89).


G ENTLEMEN,
    The Athenians took an oath on a certain crisis in their affairs to esteem
wheat, the vine, and the olive, as the boundaries of Attica. The territory of scholars is yet larger. A stranger but yesterday to every person present, I find myself

already at home; for the society of lettered men is an university which does not bound itself with the walls of one cloister or college, but gathers in the distant and solitary student into its strictest amity. Literary men gladly acknowledge these ties, which find for the homeless and the solitary a welcome where least looked for. But in proportion as we are conversant with the laws of life, we have seen the like: we are used to these surprises. This is but one operation of a more general law. As in coming among strange faces, we find that the love of letters makes us friends, so in strange thoughts, in the worldly habits which harden us, we find with some surprise that learning, and truth, and beauty have not let us go; that the spiritual nature is too strong for us; that those excellent influences which men in all ages have designated by the term *Muse*, or by some kindred name, come in to keep us warm and true; that the face of nature remains irresistibly alluring. We have strayed far from the territorial monuments of Attica, but here still are wheat, and olives, and the vine.

I do not now refer to that intellectual conscience which forms itself in tender natures, and gives us many twinges for our sloth and unfaithfulness:—the influence I speak of is of a higher strain. Stung by this intellectual conscience, we go to measure our tasks as scholars, and screw ourselves up to energy and fidelity, and our sadness is suddenly overshone by a sympathy of blessing. Beauty, the inspirer, the cheerful festal principle, the leader of gods and men, which draws by being beautiful, and not by considerations of advantage, comes in and puts a new face on the world. I think the peculiar office of scholars in a careful and gloomy generation, is to be, as the poets were called in the Middle Ages, Professors of the Joyous Science, detectors and delineators of occult symmetries and unpublished beauties, heralds of civility, nobility, learning, and wisdom: affirmers of the One Law, yet as those who should affirm it in music and dancing: Expressors themselves of that firm and cheerful temper,—infinitely removed from sadness,—which reigns through the kingdoms of chemistry, vegetation, and animal life. Every natural power exhilarates: A true talent delights the possessor first. A celebrated musician was wont to say, that men knew not how much more he delighted himself with his playing, than he did others, for if they knew, his hearers would rather demand of him, than give him a reward. The scholar is here to fill others with love and courage, by confirming their trust in the love and wisdom which are at the heart of all things; to affirm noble sentiments; to hear them wherever spoken, out of the deeps of ages, out of the obscurities of barbarous life, and to republish them:—to untune nobody, but to draw all men after the truth; and to keep the world spiritual and sweet.

I find a provision in the constitution of the world for the class of scholars, for the theorist, the uniter, for him who is to show identity and connexion where men see nothing but fragments, and to supply the axis on which the frame of things turns. In all the tastes and endeavors of men in reference to all that is permanent and causal, we are made to feel that nature has dearly at heart the formation of the speculative man or scholar. It is an end never lost sight of, and is prepared in the original casting of things. There is a certain heat in the breast which attends the perception of a primary truth, which is the shining of the spiritual sun down into the shaft of the mine. Nature will be expressed. Whatever can be thought can be spoken, and still rises for utterance, though to rude and stammering organs. If they cannot say it, it waits, waits and works, until, at last, it moulds them to its perfect will, and is articulated.

This, Gentlemen, is the topic on which I shall speak,—the natural and permanent functions of the scholar, as he is no permissive or accidental appearance, but an organic agent in nature. He is here to be the beholder of the real; self-centered amidst the superficial; here to revere the dominion of a serene necessity, and be its pupil and apprentice, by tracing everything home to a cause: here to be sobered, not by the cares of life, as men say,—no, but by the depth of his draughts of the cup of immortality.

One is tempted to affirm the office and attributes of the scholar a little the more eagerly, because of a frequent perversity of the class itself. Men are ashamed of their intellect. The men committed by profession, as well as by bias, to study,— the clergyman, the chemist, the astronomer, the metaphysician, the poet,—talk hard and worldly, and share the infatuation of cities. The poet and the citizen perfectly agree in conversation on the wise life. The poet counsels his own son as if he were a merchant  The poet with poets betrays no amiable weakness. They all chime in, and are as inexorable as bankers on the subject of real life. They have no toleration for literature,—it is all dilettantism, and disgusts: not Napoleon hated ideologists worse than they. Art is only a fine word for appearance, in default of matter.—And they sit white over their stoves, and talk themselves hoarse over the mischief of books and the effeminacy of bookmakers. But, at a single strain of a bugle out of a grove; at the dashing among the stones, of a brook from the hills; at the sound of some subtle word that falls from the lips of an imaginative person, or even at the reading in solitude of some moving image of a wise poet,—this grave conclusion is blown out of memory; the sun shines, and the worlds roll to music, and the poet replaces all this cowardly self-denial and God-denial of the literary class, with the conviction, that, to one poetic success, the world will surrender on its knees. Instantly, he casts in his lot with the pearl-diver and the diamond-merchant. Like them, he will joyfully lose days, and months, and estates. and credit in the profound hope that one restoring, all-rewarding, immense success will arrive at last, which will give him at one bound an universal dominion. And rightly: for, if his wild prayers are granted, if he is to succeed, his achievement is the piercing of the brass heavens of use and limitation, and letting in a beam of the pure eternity which burns up this limbo of shadows and chimæras in which we dwell. Yes, nature is too strong for us; she will not be denied; she has balsams for our hurts, and hellebores for our insanities; she does not bandy words with us, but comes in with a new ravishing experience and makes the old time ridiculous. Every poet knows the unspeakable hope, and represents its audacity, by throwing it out of all probability in his conversation.

Society at all times has the same want, namely, of one sane man with adequate powers of expression to hold up each new object of monomania in its right relations. The ambitious and mercenary bring their last new mumbo-jumbo, whether it be tariff, or Texas, or mesmerism, or phrenology, or Antimasonry, or Romanism, or railroads, and, by detaching the object from its relations, easily succeed in making it seen in a glare, and a multitude go mad about it, and they are not to be reproved or cured by the opposite multitude who are kept from this particular insanity by an equal frenzy on another crotchet. But let one man have so comprehensive an eye, that he can replace this isolated prodigy in its right neighborhood and bearings, it loses instantly all illusion, and the returning reason of the community thanks the reason of the monitor.

But, as froward boys turn on their tutors, there is always a certain ridicule among superficial people thrown on the scholars or clerisy, which is of no import, unless the scholar heed it. Observe the tone of society among us at the present hour. I am not disposed to magnify temporary differences, but for the moment it appears as if in former times, learning and intellectual accomplishments had secured to the possessor a greater rank and authority. In this country, where so much work solicits the hands of men and the avarice of land and wealth increases with the ease of feeding it, the whole emphasis of conversation and of public opinion commends the practical man, and every scholar is sure to hear the solid and practical portion of the community named with the most significant respect in every circle. If this were only the reaction from excessive expectations from literature, now disappointed,—it were a just censure. It was superstitious to expect too much from philosophers and the literary class. The sophists, the Alexandrian grammarians, the wits of Queen Anne, the French *philosophes,* our Lyceums and Diffusion Societies, have not much helped us. Granted, freely granted. Men run out of one superstition into an opposite superstition, and practical people in America give themselves wonderful airs. The cant of the time inquires superciliously after the new ideas; it believes that ideas do not lead to the owning of stocks; they are perplexing and effeminating; but that the ordering a cargo of goods from New-York to Smyrna, or a return cargo; or the running up and down to procure a company of subscribers to set a-going five or ten thousand spindles; or the negotiation of a caucus, and the practising on the prejudices and facility of country people to secure their votes in November,—this is practical and commendable.

Young men, I warn you against the clamours of these self-praising, frivolous activities; against these busy-bodies; against irrational labor; against chattering, meddlesome, rich, and official people. If their doing came to any good end!— Action is legitimate and good; forever be it honoured, right, original, private, necessary action, proceeding new from the heart of man, and going forth to beneficent and as yet incalculable ends: Yes; but not a petty fingering and running, a senseless repeating of yesterday's fingering and running; an acceptance of the methods and frauds of other men; an over-doing and busy-ness which pretends to the honors of action but resembles the twitches of Saint Vitus.[1] The action of these men, I cannot respect, for they do not respect it themselves. They were better and more respectable abed and asleep. All the best of this class, all who have any insight, or generosity of spirit, are frequently disgusted and fain to put it behind them.

If I were to compare action of a much higher strain than this I speak of, with a life of contemplation, I should not venture to pronounce with much confidence in favor of the former. All mankind have such a deep stake in inward illumination that there is much to be said by the hermit and the monk in defence of his life of thought and prayer. A certain partiality, a certain headiness and loss of balance, is the tax which all action must pay. Act, if you like, but you do it at your peril. Men's actions are too strong for them. Show me a man who has acted and who has not been the victim and slave of his action. What they have done commits and enforces them to do the same again. The first act, which was to be only one of an infinite series, becomes a sacrament. The fiery reformer embodies his aspiration, and he and his friends hold on to the fact, and lose the aspiration. The Quaker has established Quakerism, the Shaker has established his monastery and his dance, and though he prates of spirit, there is spirit no longer, but repetition, which is antispiritual. But where are his new things of today *as bold and surprising?* In actions of enthusiasm, in enterprises of great pith and moment, this drawback appears; but in these lower activities, which have, at last, no higher end than to make us more comfortable and more cowardly; in actions of cunning, actions that steal and lie, actions that skulk and flee before the eye of truth; actions that divorce the speculative from the practical faculty, the hands from the head, and put a ban on the reason and the sentiment,—there is nothing else but drawback and negation.

Let us ascend to a juster judgment: The wise Hindoos write in their sacred

1. Saint Vitus's dance, named after the third-century Christian child martyr, was a nervous disorder with symptoms of involuntary jerky motions similar to chorea.

books, "Children only and not the learned speak of the speculative and practical doctrines as two: they are but one; for both obtain the self-same end, and the place which is gained by the followers of the one, is gained by the followers of the other. That man seeth, who seeth that the speculative and the practical doctrines are one."[2] For great and high action, all which I could extol and be willing to share must draw deeply on the spiritual nature. The measure of action is, the sentiment from which it proceeds,—never the circumstance of numbers or dignity of place. The greatest action may easily be one of the most private circumstance.

Gentlemen, I do not wish to check your impulses to action,—I would not hinder you of one swing of your arm. I do not wish to see you effeminate gownsmen taking hold of the world with the tips of your fingers, or that life should be to you as it is to many, optical, not practical. Far otherwise: I rather wish you to experiment boldly, and give play to your energies, but not, if I could prevail with you,—in conventional ways. I should wish your energy to run in works and emergences growing out of your personal character. Nature will fast enough instruct you in the occasion and the need, and will bring to each of you the crowded hour, the great opportunity. Love, Rectitude, everlasting Fame, will come to each of you in loneliest places with their grand alternatives, and Honor watches to see whether you dare seize the palms.

I have no quarrel with action, only I prefer inaction to misaction. And I reject the abusive application of the term practical to those lower activities. Let us hear no more of the practical men, or I will tell you something of them; this namely; that the practical men, the leaders of their class, the robust gentlemen who stand at the head of their order, share the ideas of the time, and deeply share the ideas which they oppose. They also are sick, if you please to term it so, with this very speculation which so appals you in others. The scholar finds in them unlooked for acceptance of his most paradoxical experience. There is confession in their eyes, and if they parade before him their business and public importance, it is by way of apology and palliation for not being the students and obeyers of those diviner laws. Talk frankly with them and you learn that you have little to tell them, that the Spirit of the Age has been before you with influences impossible to parry or resist. The drygoodsmen and the brokers, the lawyers and the manufacturers, are idealists and only differ from the philosopher in the intensity of the charge. We are all contemporaries and bones of one body. For truly, the population of the globe has its origin in the aims which their existence is to serve, and so with every portion of them. The truth takes flesh in forms that can express and execute it. And, thus, in history an idea always overhangs like the moon and rules the tide which rises simultaneously in all the souls of a generation.

2. Quoted from Charles Wilkins, trans., *The Bhâgvăt-Gēētă* . . . (1785).

This shallow clamor against theoretic men comes from the weak. Able men may sometimes affect a contempt for thought which no able man ever feels. For what alone in the history of this world interests all men in proportion as they are men? What, but the mystic import of one or two words men use,—Genius,—Muse,—Love,—Right? Every man or woman who can voluntarily or involuntarily give them any insight or suggestion on these secrets, they will hearken after. If there is anything which never fails to interest, it is genius,—the seer, the power of seeing and reporting the truth. To genius, everything is permitted, and not only so, but it enters into all other men's labours;—a tyrannous privilege, to convert every man's wisdom or skill, as it would seem, to its own use, or, to show for the first time what all these fine and complex preparations are for. See how many libraries one master absorbs. Who will hereafter go gleaning in those contemporary and anterior books, from each of which he has taken the only grain of truth it had, and has given it tenfold value by placing it? For him, the art of writing, the art of printing, the arts of communicating exist; for him, the railroad was built; for he puts them to their best use. For him, history took all these pains with dates and vouchers. For him, arms, arts, politics, and trade waited like menials,—until the lord of the manor should arrive,—which he quite easily administers. Even the demonstrations of Nature for millenniums seem not to have attained their end, until this interpreter arrives. "I," said the high-spirited Kepler, "may well wait a hundred years for a reader, since God Almighty has waited six thousand years for an observer like myself." [3]

Genius is a poor man, and has no house, but see this proud landlord who has built the palace, and furnished it so delicately, opens it to him, and beseeches him to make it honorable by entering there, and eating bread. There could always be traced in the most barbarous tribes, and also in the most character-destroying civilization, some vestiges of a faith in genius, as, in the exemption of a priesthood, or bards, or artists, from taxes and tolls levied on other men, or, in civic distinction, or enthusiastic homage, or in hospitalities, as if men would signify their sense, that Genius and Virtue should not pay money for house, and land, and bread, because they have a royal right in these, and in all things,—a first mortgage, that takes effect before the right of the present proprietor. For they are the First Good, of which Plato affirms, that "all things are for its sake, and it is the cause of everything beautiful." The heart of mankind would affirm, that he is the rich man only, in whom the people are rich, and he is the poor man, in whom the people are poor.

This reverence is the re-establishment of natural order, for, as the solidest rocks are made up of invisible gases, as the world is made of thickened light, and arrested electricity, so men know that ideas are the parents of men and things;

3. Johannes Kepler (1571–1630), German mathematician and astronomer.

there was never anything that did not proceed from a thought. The scholar has a deep, ideal interest in the moving show around him. He knew the motley system in its egg.

Philosophy overlooks no appearance as trifling. We have,—have we not? a real relation to markets and brokers, to currency and coin. "Gold and silver," says one of the Platonists, "grow in the earth from the celestial gods,—an effluxion from them."[4] The unmentionable dollar itself has at last a high origin in moral and metaphysical nature.

Fitchburg stock is not quite private property, but the quality and essence of the universe is in that also. Have we less interest in ships or in shops, in manual work or in household relations, in any object of nature or in any handiwork of man, in any relation of life, or custom of society? The scholar is to show in each identity and connexion; he is to show its origin in the brain of man, and its secret history and issues. He is the attorney of the world, and can never be superfluous, where so vast a variety of questions are ever coming up to be solved, and for ages.

I proceed to say that the allusions just now made to the extent of his duties, the manner in which every day's events will find him in work, may show that his place is no sinecure.

The scholar, when he comes, will be known by an energy that will animate all who see him. The labour of ambition and avarice will appear lazy beside his. In the right hands, literature is not resorted to as a consolation, and by the broken and decayed, but as a decalogue. In this country we are fond of results and of short ways to them; and most in this department. In our experience, learning is not learned, nor is genius wise. The name of the scholar is taken in vain. We, who should be the channel of that unweariable power which never sleeps, must give our diligence no holidays. Other men are planting and building, baking and tanning, running and sailing, hewing and carrying, each that he may peacefully execute his fine function by which they all are helped. Shall he play, whilst their eyes follow him from far with reverence, attributing to him the delving in great fields of thought, and conversing with supernatural allies? If he is not kindling his torch, or collecting oil, he will fear to go by a workshop, he will not dare to hear the music of a saw or plane, the steam engine will reprimand, the steam-pipe will hiss at him. He cannot look a blacksmith in the eye; in the field he will be shamed by mowers and reapers. The labor in a college should be as strenuous and rugged,—I may say, as audacious, as any labor that is undertaken in agriculture or in war, and the student ought to feel (ought he not?) a poignant shame, if, when he reads the marches of Hannibal or Napoleon across the Alps, or the hardships of Hudson or Parry in Polar voyages, or the patience of Columbus, these eminent

4. Quoted from *The Commentaries of Proclus on the Timaeus of Plato* (1820).

pieces of endurance appear to him to indicate a stouter manhood and resolution, a more incessant industry, or a ruder courage, than that which he exercises in his private library.[5]

Let him value his talent as a door into nature. Let him see his performances only as limitations. Then, over all, let him value the sensibility that receives, that believes, that loves, that dares, that affirms. Let him find his superiority in not wishing superiority; find the riches of love which possesses that which it adores; the riches of poverty; the height of lowliness; the immensity of today; and, in the passing hour, the age of ages.

This guidance is for all the parts of life, and the spirit of it is large and liberal as the sky. It is as varied in tone as the works of men, and is not ecclesiastical any more than it is comic.

Thought is valued for Cornelius Agrippa purposes, but the future of the universe is in it.[6] I wish you better than to be scholars by ambition, for there is an absolute realism that would else deprive you of your crown. Poet ceases to be poet when he sits crowned.

It is he only who has labor, and the spirit to labor, because courage sees he is brave, because he sees the omnipotence of that which inspires him. The speculative man, the scholar, is the right hero. Is there only one courage, and one warfare? I cannot manage sword and rifle; can I not therefore be brave? I thought there were as many courages as men. Is an armed man the only hero? Is a man only the breech of a gun, or the hasp of a bowie-knife? Men of thought fail in fighting down malignity, because they wear other armour than their own.

Let them decline, henceforward, foreign methods and foreign courages. Let them do that which they can do. Let them fight by their strength, not by their weakness. It seems to me that the thoughtful man needs no armour but this one,— concentration. One thing is for him settled, that he is to come at his ends. He is not there to defend himself, but to deliver his message; if his voice is clear, then clearly; if husky, then huskily; if broken, he can at least scream; gag him, he can still write it; bruise, mutilate him, cut off his hands and his feet, he can still crawl towards his object on his stumps. It is the corruption of our generation that men value a long life, and do not esteem life simply as a means of expressing the sentiment. But beauty belongs to the sentiment, and is always departing from those who depart out of that. The hero rises out of all comparison with contemporaries and with ages of men, because he disesteems old age, and lands, and

5. Both Hannibal (247–183 B.C.), Carthaginian general, and Napoleon attacked Italy by crossing the Alps; Henry Hudson (d. 1611), English explorer after whom Hudson Bay and the Hudson River are named; Sir William Edward Parry (1790–1855), English Arctic explorer.

6. Cornelius Heinrich Agrippa, known as Agrippa von Nettesheim (1486–1535), German philosopher interested in alchemy.

money, and power, and will oppose all mankind at the call of that private and perfect Right and Beauty in which he lives.

Man is a torch borne in the wind. The ends I have hinted at made the existence of the scholar or spiritual man an indispensable member of the Republic or Commonwealth of Man. Nature could not leave herself without a seer and expounder. But he could not see or teach without organs. The same necessity, then, that would create him, reappears in his splendid gifts. There is no power in the mind, but in turn becomes an instrument. The descent of genius into talents is part of the natural order and history of the world. The incarnation must be. We cannot eat the granite nor drink hydrogen: they must be decompounded and recompounded into corn and water, before they can enter our flesh. There is a great deal of spiritual energy in the universe, but it is not palpable to us until we can make it up into man. There is plenty of air, but it is worth nothing until we can get it by tools and managing into shape and service, to trundle us, for example, with our baggage on a railroad. Then is it paid for by hundreds and thousands of our money. Plenty of water also, sea-full, sky-full: Who cares for it? But when we can get it where we want it, and in measured portions, on a mill wheel, or boat paddle, we will buy it with millions. There is plenty of wild azote and carbon unappropriated; but it is nought until we have made it up into loaves and soup. So we find it in higher relations. There is plenty of wild wrath, but it steads not, until we can get it racked off, shall I say? and bottled into persons;—a little pure, and not too much to every head. How many aspiring poetic geniuses we have seen, and none but ourselves will ever hear of them for want in them of a little talent.

Ah, Gentlemen, I own I love talents and accomplishments, the feet and hands of genius. As Burke said, "it is not only our duty to make the right known, but to make it prevalent." So I delight to see the godhead in distribution; to see men that can come at their ends. These shrewd faculties which belong to man: I love to see them in play, and to see them trained: this memory, carrying in its caves the pictures of all the past, and rendering them in the instant when they can serve the possessor; the craft of mathematical combination, which carries a working-plan of the heavens and of the earth in a formula. I am apt to believe with the Emperor Charles V, that, "as many languages as a man knows, so many times is he a man." [7] I like to see a man of that virtue that no obscurity or disguise can conceal, who wins all souls to his way of thinking.

I delight in men adorned and weaponed with man-like arts, who could, alone or with a few like them, reproduce Europe and America—the results of our civilization. I delight in Euclid, who is geometry; in Plato, who is philosophy; in Swedenborg, who is symbolism; in Shakspeare, who is imagination and human

7. Charles V (1500–1558), Holy Roman emperor (1519–56).

life; in Raphael, master of all the secrets of form; in Chatham, who is so perfect an expression of the English nationality that he carries joy and rage in his hand and lets forth the one spirit or the other at his pleasure; in Demosthenes, every word of whose mouth was a soldier; in Swift, whose pamphlet is war or peace; in Magliabecchi, whose knowledge was so vast that it was said of him that he had forgot more than most other men ever knew; in Mirandola, who never forgot anything; in Adam Smith, with the *Wealth of Nations* in his understanding; in Napoleon, who carries a campaign of Europe in his head; in Humboldt, who can represent in their order and symmetry the vast and the minute of the system of nature, so that if this world were lost out of space, he could almost report it from his brain.[8] It is excellent when the individual is ripened to that degree that he touches both the centre and the circumference, so that he is not only widely intelligent, but carries a counsel in his breast for the emergency of today, and alternates the contemplation of the fact in pure intellect, and the total conversion of the intellect into energy: Jove, and the thunderbolt launched from his hand. We are touched by the picture which the Italian historian gives of Romeo, a poor scholar and minister of Raymond Berenger, Count of Provence. He managed the affairs of his master so well, that he made each one of Raymond's four daughters a queen. Margaret, the eldest, was married to Louis IX of France; Eleanor, to Henry III of England; Sancha, the third, to Richard, Henry's brother, and King of the Romans; and Beatrice, the youngest, to Charles I, King of Naples and Sicily.[9] The Provençal Barons, enviers of Romeo, instigated his master to demand of him an account of the revenues he had so carefully husbanded, and the prince as lavishly disbursed. Then Romeo demanded the little mule, the staff, and the scrip, with which he had first entered into the count's service, a stranger pilgrim from the Shrine of Saint James in Galicia, and departed as he came, nor was it ever known whence he was, or whither he went.

Perhaps I value the power of achievement a little more, because in America there seems to be a certain indigence of nature in this respect. I think there is no more intellectual people than the people of New England. They are very apprehensive and curious. But there is a sterility of talent. Those iron personalities such as in Greece, and Italy, and once in England were formed to strike fear into kings, and draw the eager service of thousands, rarely appear. We have general

8. Euclid (fl. ca. 323–285 B.C.), Greek founder of geometry; William Pitt, first earl of Chatham (1708–78), thought by many to be England's finest prime minister; Jonathan Swift (1667–1745), Irish satirist; Antonio Magliabechi or Magliabecchi (1633–1714), Italian bibliophile; Pico della Mirandola (1463–94), Italian philosopher and humanist; Adam Smith (1723–90), Scottish economist best known for his *Inquiry into the Nature and Cause of the Wealth of Nations* (1776); Alexander von Humboldt (1769–1859), German traveler and scientist.

9. The husbands of the daughters of Raymond Berenger are Louis IX (1214–70), king of France (1226–70); Henry III (1207–72), king of England (1216–72); Richard (1209–72), king of the Romans; and Charles I (1226–85), king of Naples.

intelligence, but no Cyclop-arms. A very little intellectual force makes a disproportionately great impression, and when one observes how eagerly our people entertain and discuss a new theory, whether home-born or imported from abroad, and, I may say, how little thought operates how great an effect, what deep impression—even of terror—has been made through the most intelligent circles in a wide tract of country when two or three of the most private and retiring men conversed on idealism in their libraries, one would draw a favorable inference as to the intellectual and spiritual tendencies of our people. It seems as if two or three persons coming, who should add to a high spiritual aim, great constructive energy, would carry the country with them.

We want fire, a little less mutton, and a little more genius. In making this claim of costly accomplishments for the scholar, I chiefly wish to infer the dignity of his work by the lustre of his appointments. He is not cheaply equipped. The universe was rifled to furnish him. He is to forge out of coarsest ores the sharpest weapons. But, if the weapons are valued for themselves, if his talents assume an independence, and come to work for ostentation, they cannot serve him. It was said of an eminent Frenchman, that "he was drowned in his talents." [10] The peril of every fine faculty, is, the delight of playing with it for pride. Talent is commonly developed at the expense of character. When a man begins to dedicate himself to a particular function, as, to his logical, or his remembering, or his oratorical, or his arithmetical skill, the advance of his character and genius pauses: he has run to the end of his line; seal the book: the development by that mind is arrested. The scholar is lost in the showman. Society is babyish and is dazzled and deceived by the weapon without inquiry as to the cause for which it is drawn; like boys by the drum and colours of the troops. Talleyrand's question is still the main one to be asked of the scholar: Not, Is he rich? is he committed? is he well-meaning? Has he this or that faculty? Is he of the movement? is he of the establishment?—but, "*is he any body?*" Does he stand for something?

He must be good of his kind. That is all men ask: all that Talleyrand, all that State-street asks. [11] Be real and admirable, not as we know, but as you know. Able men do not care in what kind a man is able, so only that he is able. A master requires a master, and does not stipulate whether it be an artist, a mechanic, or a king. The man of worldly force requires of his priest a talent, a force equal to his own, but wholly applied in a priestly direction. He does not forgive an application in the priest to the merchant's or to the politician's concerns. He wishes him to be such an one as he himself should have been, had he been a churchman. He is sincere and ardent in his vocation—absorbed in it. Let the priest or poet be as valid in theirs. Nobody ever forgives in you any admiration of them, any over-

10. Identified as "Target" in *JMN*, 9:137.
11. State Street, the main commercial center of Boston.

estimate in you of what they do or have. The objection of men of the world to what they call the morbid intellectual tendency in our young men at present, is not a hostility to their truth, but to this—its shortcoming, that the new views unfit their children for business in their sense, and do not qualify them for any complete life of a better kind. They threaten the validity of contracts, but do not prevail so far as to establish the new kingdom which shall supersede contracts, oaths, and property. We have seen to weariness what you cannot do: now show us what you can and will. And with perfect reason: We are not afraid of new truth,— of truth, never, new or old,—no, but of a counterfeit. Everybody hates imbecil- ity and shortcoming, not new methods. The astronomer is not ridiculous inas- much as he is an astronomer, but inasmuch as he is not an astronomer. Be that you are: be that cheerly and sovereignly. Plotinus makes no apologies: He says roundly, "the knowledge of the senses is truly ludicrous." "Body and its proper- ties belong to the region of nonentity: as if more of body was necessarily pro- duced where a defect of being happens in a greater degree." [12]

"Matter," says Plutarch, "is privation." Let the man of ideas at this hour be as direct and as fully committed.

Have you a spark of truth? have you a thought in your heart? There was never such need of it as now. As we read the newspapers, as we see the effrontery with which money and power carry their ends, and ride over honesty and good mean- ing, honesty and religion seem to shriek like ghosts. We will not speak for them, because to speak for them seems so weak and hopeless. We will hold fast our opinion and die in silence. But a true orator will make us feel that the states and kingdoms, that the senators, lawyers, and rich men, are caterpillars' webs and caterpillars, when seen in the light of this despised and imbecile truth. Then we feel what cowards we have been! Truth alone is great. The orator, too, becomes a fool and a shadow before this light which lightens through him. It shines back- ward and forward, diminishes or annihilates everybody, and the prophet so gladly feels his personality lost in this victorious life. The spiritual nature exhibits itself so in its counteraction to any accumulation of material force. There is no mass that can be a counterweight for it. The exertions of this force are the eminent experiences, out of a long life. All that is worth remembering. These are the mo- ments that balance years. This makes one man good against mankind. This is the secret of eloquence, for it is the end of eloquence in a half-hour's discourse or perhaps by a few sentences to persuade a multitude of persons to renounce their opinions, and change the course of life. They go forth not the men they came in, but shriven, convicted, and converted.

The scholar, then, is unfurnished who has only literary weapons. He ought to have as many talents as he can;—memory, arithmetic, practical power, manners,

12. Plotinus (ca. 204–ca. 270), Greek philosopher who set out the basic tenets of Neoplatonism.

temper, lion-heart, are all good things, but these are superficial, and if he has none of them, he can still manage, if he have the main mast, if he is anything. But he must have the resource of resources, and be planted on necessity. For the sure months are bringing him to an examination-day in which nothing is remitted or excused, and for which no tutor, no book, no lectures, and almost no preparation can be of the least avail. He will have to answer certain questions, which, I must plainly tell you, cannot be staved off: for, all men, all women, time, your country, your condition, the invisible world, are the interrogators. Who are you? What do you? Can you obtain what you wish? Is there method in your consciousness? Can you see tendency in your life? Can you help any soul?

Can he answer these questions? Can he dispose of them? Happy if you can answer them mutely in the order and disposition of your life! Happy for more than yourself, a benefactor of men, if you can answer them in works of wisdom, art, or poetry; bestowing on the general mind of men organic creations, to be the guidance and delight of all who know them.

These questions speak to Genius, to that power which is underneath and greater than all talent, and which proceeds out of the constitution of every man:—to Genius, which is an emanation of that it tells of; whose private counsels are not tinged with selfishness, but are laws. Men of talent fill the eye with their pretension; they go out into some camp of their own, and noisily persuade society that this thing which they do is the needful cause of all men. They have talents for contention, and they nourish a small difference into a loud quarrel. But the world is wide. Nobody will go there after tomorrow. The gun they have pointed, can defend nothing but itself, nor itself any longer than the man is by. What is the use of artificial positions? But Genius has no taste for weaving sand or in any trifling; but flings itself on real elemental things, which are powers, self-defensive; which first subsist and then resist unweariably forevermore all that opposes. Genius loves truth and clings to it, so that what it says and does is not in a by-road visited only by curiosity, but on the great highways of nature which were before the Appian way, and which all souls must travel. Genius delights only in statements which are themselves true, which attack and wound any who opposes them, whether he who brought them here remains here or not; which are live men—the statements,—and do daily declare fresh war against all falsehood and custom, and will not let an offender go; which society cannot dispose of or forget, but which abide there, and will not down at anybody's bidding, but stand frowning and formidable, and will and must be finally obeyed and done.

The scholar must be ready for bad weather, poverty, insult, weariness, repute of failure, and many vexations. He must have a great patience, and must ride at anchor, and vanquish every enemy whom his small arms cannot reach by the grand resistance of submission, of ceasing to do. He is to know that in the last resort he is not here to work, but to be worked upon. He is to eat insult, drink insult, be clothed and shod in insult, until he has learned that this bitter bread and shameful dress is also wholesome and warm, is, in short, indifferent; is of the same chemistry as praise and fat living; that they also are disgrace and soreness to him who has them.

I think much may be said to discourage and dissuade the young scholar from his career. Freely be that said. Dissuade all you can from the lists. Sift the wheat, frighten away the lighter souls. Let us keep only the heavy-armed. Let those who come be those who cannot but come, and who see that there is no choice here,— no advantage and no disadvantage compared with other careers. For the great Necessity is our patron, who distributes sun and shade after immutable laws.

Yes, he has his dark days, he has weakness, he has waitings, he has bad company, he is pelted by storms of cares,—untuning cares, untuning company. That is the worst,—they are like some foul beasts of prey who tear and spoil much more than they devour. Well, let him meet them. He has not consented to the frivolity nor to the dispersion. The practical aim is forever higher than the literary aim. He shall not submit to degradation, but shall bear these crosses with what grace he can. He is still to decline how many glittering opportunities and to retreat, and to wait.

It is easy to hide for something, easy to hide now, that we may draw the more admiration anon. 'Tis easy to sit in the shade, if we have a Plato's *Republic* teeming in the brain, which will presently be born for the joy and illumination of men. Easy to withdraw and break somewhat morosely the gentle conventions of society, to visit not, and to refuse visits, if we can make good to others or only to our own heart, a rare promise. But how, if you have no security of such a result? How, if the fruit of your brain is abortive; if cramp and mildew, if dreams and the sons of dreams, if prose and blotted pages unreadable by other men and odious to your own eyes be the issue? How, if you must sit out the day in thoughtful attitude and experiment, and return to the necessities and conversation of the household without the support of any product, and they must believe and you may doubt that this waste cannot be justified? I call you to a confidence which surmounts this painful experience. You are to have a self-support which maintains you not only against all others, but against your own moments of skepticism. Pain, indolence, sterility, endless *ennui,* have also their lesson for the great. The Saharas must be crossed, as well as the Nile. It is easy to live for others: everybody does. I call on you to live for yourself. So shall you find in this penury and absence of thought a purer splendor than ever clothed the exhibitions of wit.

I invite you not to cheap joys, to the flutter of gratified vanity, to a sleek and rosy comfort; no, but to bareness, to power, to enthusiasm, to the mountain of vision, to true and natural supremacy, to the society of the great, and to love.

Give me bareness and poverty, so that I know them as the sure heralds of the muse. Not in plenty, not in a thriving, well-to-do condition she delighteth.

He that would sacrifice at her altar, must not leave a few flowers, an apple, or some symbolic gift. No; he must relinquish orchards and gardens, prosperity and convenience; he may live on a heath without trees; sometimes hungry, and sometimes rheumatic with cold. The fire retreats and concentrates within, into a pure flame, pure as the stars to which it mounts. The solitude of the body is the populousness of the soul.

Shall I advance into this realm of the true place and service of the scholar or spiritual man? His faith measures itself by its power to do without. Great believers are always reckoned infidels; impracticable, fantastic, atheistic, and really men of no account. And, truly, the spiritualist ever finds himself driven to express his faith by a series of skepticisms. Charitable souls come to him with heaps of philanthropic schemes, and ask his cooperation, or at least his assent. How can he hesitate? It is the instinct of man to take on each turn the part of hope; it is the rule of mere comity and courtesy to agree where you can, and to turn your sentence with something auspicious and not sneering and sinister. *But he denies them.* He is forced to say, "O these things will be as they must be. What can you do? You blow against the wind." Texas and Slavery, Dram-drinking, Pauperism, Association, the marriage question, the Social Reform question, Puseyism, Protestantism, and all the other generosities of the day prove such intractable elements for him to work in—the people's questions are not his, their methods are not his—that, against all the dictates of good nature, he is forced to say, he has no pleasure in them.

Even the doctrines dear to the hope of man, the doctrines of the Divine Providence and of the Immortality of the Soul, his neighbors cannot put the statement so, that he shall affirm it. But he denies out of more faith and not less. He denies out of honesty and sincerity of character. He had rather stand charged in your eyes with the melancholy and weakness of skepticism, than with the meanness of an untruth. He will not lie even for righteousness and love.

Will any say, "this is cold and infidel?"—The wise and magnanimous will not say so. They will exult, rather, in his farsighted good will that his heart sees that it can afford to grant to the skeptic all that ground without disturbing the omnipotence of good. It sees to the end of all transgression. George Fox, the fervid Quaker, describing one of his early visions, says, "he saw that there was an ocean of darkness and death, but withal an infinite ocean of light and love which flowed over that of darkness." The scholar's faith avails to the whole emergency of life and objects. He is content with the just and the unjust; with fools and sots; with the triumph of folly and fraud: He is content even with dis-content: with the yawning gulf between the ambition of man and his power of performance; between the demand and the supply of power which makes the tragedy of all souls.

Charles Fourier, the French philosopher, whose social theory has recently drawn such a crowd of disciples, announced as the basis of his doctrines the cheering sentiment, that "the attractions of man are proportional to his destinies," in other words, that every desire predicts its own satisfaction.[13] Yet see everywhere the reverse of this, the incompetency of power to the idea which is the universal grief of young and ardent minds. They accuse the Divine Providence of a certain parsimony in the distribution of power. It has shown the heaven and earth to every child, and filled him with a desire for the whole,—a desire raging, infinite,—a hunger as of space to be filled with planets,—a cry of famine as of devils for souls. Then, for the satisfaction,—to each man is administered a drop, a single drop,—a bead of dew, of vital power per day: a cup as large as space,—and one drop of the water of life in it. Each man woke in the morning with an appetite that could eat the solar system like a cake; a spirit for action and passion without bounds: he could lay his hand on the morning star; he could wrestle with Orion; or try conclusions with gravitation or chemistry; but on the first motion to try his strength, hands, feet, and senses would not serve him. He was an Emperor deserted by his states, and left to whistle by himself—thrust rather into a mob of Emperors, all whistling, and still the sirens sung, "the attractions are proportional to the destinies." In every house, in the heart of every maiden and of every boy, in the soul of the soaring saint, this chasm is found—this chasm between a monstrous promise of ideal power, and this shabby experience.

The expansive nature of truth comes to his succour: elastic, invincible, not to be surrounded. He helps himself by vaster generalizations and exults in the new immensities of his horizon. The lesson of life is *practically to generalize,* to believe what the years and the centuries say against the hours, to resist the usurpation of particulars, and to penetrate to the catholic sense which is really expressed, though occultly, by every particular. Things seem to say one thing, and do say the reverse. The appearance is immoral, the result is moral and immutable. All things seem to tend downward, to justify despondency, to promote rogues, to defeat the just,—and by knaves, as by martyrs, the just cause is carried forward. Although history teaches that knaves win in every political struggle, although society seems to be delivered over from the hands of one set of criminals into the hands of another set of criminals, as fast as the government is changed,—and the march of civilization is an endless train of felonies,—yet general ends are somehow answered;—no thanks to the felon's. We see now as heretofore events forced on, which seem to retard or retrograde the civilization of ages. But the world-spirit

13. François Marie Charles Fourier (1772–1837), French social thinker whose doctrines guided the later period of the Brook Farm community, a utopian venture at West Roxbury, Massachusetts (1841–47).

is a good swimmer, and storms and waves cannot drown him. He snaps his finger at laws. And so, throughout history, Heaven seems to affect low and poor means: "Most poor matters point to rich ends."[14] The needles are nothing, the magnetism is all. Through the years, through the centuries, through evil agents, through toys and atoms, a great and beneficent tendency irresistibly streams. And he who believes the tendency is always right, and will be borne out in his testimony: the Scholar is he.

But, Gentlemen, I see plainly there is no end to these expansions. I have exhausted your patience, and I have only begun. It is time to close. I had perhaps wiselier adhered to my first purpose of confining my illustration to a single topic,—but it is so much easier to say many things than to explain one.

Well, you will see the drift of all my thoughts, this namely, that the scholar must be much more than a scholar: that his ends give value to every means, but he is to subdue and keep down his methods; that his use of books is occasional, and infinitely subordinate; that he should read a little proudly, as one who knows the original, and cannot, therefore, very highly value the copy. In like manner, he is to hold lightly every tradition, every opinion, every person, out of his piety to that Eternal Spirit which dwells unexpressed with him. He shall think very highly of his destiny. He is here to know the secret of Genius, here to become not a reader of poetry, but Homer, Dante, Milton, Shakspeare, Swedenborg, in the fountain, through that. If one man could impart his faith to another, if I could prevail to communicate the incommunicable mysteries, you should see the breadth of your realm; that ever as you ascend in your proper and native path, you receive the keys of nature and of history and rise on the same stairs to science and to piety.

And this, Gentlemen, is that which I came hither to say to those few,—if they be few,—to that one among you,—if there be but one who dares believe it,— namely, that every high thing which you have heard or dreamed of the right and power of the scholar,—however contradicted by the voice of your country or of your own seeming observation and experience,—is verily true. The best, the best is always true. Who is he in all this company of brave young men who dare take home to himself this, that he need not seek anything; that power, and love, and friendship shall come to the great? God saith forever within the heart—Do not believe your eyes; believe your sentiment! and the slow Destinies make good the word.

14. William Shakespeare, *The Tempest*, III, i, 3–4.

# "The Spirit of the Times"
# 15 February 1848
# (1848–1856)

Emerson's lecture on "The Spirit of the Times" has an extended genealogy. Its origin is in the lecture "Introductory," which Emerson delivered on 4 December 1839 as the first in a series of ten lectures on *The Present Age* at the Masonic Temple in Boston; he netted $325 for the series. He probably repeated that lecture as "Analysis, the Character of the Present Age" on 26 or 27 February 1840 before the Salem Lyceum in Salem, Massachusetts ($17) and as "The Character of the Present Age" on 12 March 1840 as the second in a series of three lectures at the New York Mercantile Library in New York City ($150 for the series). He also delivered the lecture on 4 March 1840 as the first in a series of nine lectures on *The Present Age* before the Concord Lyceum in Concord, Massachusetts, and on 20 March 1840 as the first in a series of six lectures on *Human Life* before the Franklin Lyceum in Providence, Rhode Island ($180 for the series; lecture fees are from the "Account Books"); for treatments of the lecture "Introductory" and its service in Emerson's *The Present Age* and *Human Life* series, see *Early Lectures*, 3:185–86; for the lecture, see *Early Lectures*, 3:186–201).

Late in 1847, Emerson returned to the lecture "Introductory" as the basis for his lecture on "The Spirit of the Times." He first read his newly composed discourse during his lecture tour in England in 1847–48, delivering it under the title "Genius of the Present Age" on 15 February 1848 as the second in a series of four lectures before the Philosophical Institution in Edinburgh, Scotland, for which he received £21 for the series (Emerson's payment was recorded on 17 February in the "Minutes of the Board of Management of the Edinburgh Philosophical Institution, 1847–1853," p. 122, in the Edinburgh Public Library; for a bibliographic overview of Emerson in England in 1847–48, see the headnote to "England"). On 21 February 1848 he delivered the lecture as "The Spirit of the Times" at the Watts Institution in Dundee. In America he repeated "The Spirit of the Times" on 10 January 1850 as the second of two lectures before the Young Men's Association in Albany, New York, receiving $50 for the two lectures; on 29 January 1850, in place of "London," as the second of two lectures before the Mercantile Library Association at Clinton Hall in New York City ($100 for the two lectures; see the headnote to "London"); on 30 March 1850 as the sixth in a series of seven lectures at Hope Chapel in New York City ($390 for the series); and on 24 May 1850 as the third in a series of eight lectures at the Universalist Church in Cincinnati, Ohio ($471.71 for the series; lecture fees in America are from the "Account Books").

Emerson's canceled introductory statements on page {2r} of the manuscript, in which he offers to the "candor of the Institute some Considerations on [the] character of the

Present Age," were likely part of his opening remarks when he delivered "Genius of the Present Age" in Edinburgh; however, on page {1r} James Elliot Cabot notes, "part at least was given in the 4th lect[ure] at Marylebone 1848," that is, in "Politics and Socialism," which Emerson gave on 13 June as the fourth in a series of six lectures delivered between 6 and 17 June 1848 on *Mind and Manners of the Nineteenth Century* before the Literary and Scientific Institution in Portman Square in London. Although reports of Emerson's lectures in London do not conclusively establish whether or when he spoke from "The Spirit of the Times" in whole or in part in London, his cancellations and insertions on pages {62r} and {67r}–{67v} of the manuscript indicate that he drew from this lecture to close one or more *Mind and Manners of the Nineteenth Century* series (for additional details, see the headnote to the *Mind and Manners of the Nineteenth Century* series; see also the electronic textual notes).

While lecturing on "The Spirit of the Times" in New York City and elsewhere early in 1850, on 18 February Emerson attended a discussion of "the Times" at the Town and Country Club, which was run by Bronson Alcott and usually met in the club's rooms at 15 Tremont Row in Boston. Though his journal of this period reveals his preoccupation with the subject of "the Times," Emerson apparently neither read from nor drew upon ideas developed in this lecture during the club's meeting. Instead, most journal entries on "the Times" show him working toward prose that he would use in the essay "Fate" published in *The Conduct of Life* in 1860 (*W*, 6:3–49; see *JMN*, 11:215–28). However, when the club took up "the Times" again on 25 February, Emerson, who may not have actually attended the meeting, characterized the members' discussion thus:

> It is not the least characteristic sign of the Times, that Alcott should have been able to collect such a good company of the best heads . . . for the expressed purpose of discussing the Times. What was never done by human beings in another age, was done now; there they met to discuss their own breath, to speculate on their own navels, with eyeglass & solar microscope, and no man wondered at them. But these very men came in the cars by steam-ferry & locomotive to the meeting, & sympathized with engineers & Californians. Mad contradictions flavor all our dishes. (*JMN*, 11:228)

Emerson delivered "The Spirit of the Times" under the title "Signs of the Times" on 17 April 1856 as the fourth in a series of six private lectures at Freeman Place Chapel in Boston, for which he received $772.36 for the series ("Account Books"). Ralph L. Rusk notes that announcements of the series in the *Boston Daily Advertiser* on 14 March and from 27 March to 1 May 1856 indicated that the lectures were "old ones," not previously read in Boston (*Letters*, 5:15n). A half-column report on "Signs of the Times" in the *Boston Daily Evening Transcript* makes clear that this lecture was indeed "The Spirit of the Times" (18 April 1856, 2).

Between leaving off "The Spirit of the Times" in 1850 and returning to it once in 1856, Emerson began to adapt the lecture to a new purpose. His intention is clearly hinted at in the title he inscribed on page {1v} of the manuscript: "Success." Both Charvat and von Frank speculate that Emerson first delivered a lecture entitled "Law of Success" on 21 January 1851 before the Salem Lyceum in Salem, Massachusetts; he received $20 for

the lecture. Emerson delivered the "Law of Success" on 22 March 1851 as the second
in a series of six lectures on the *Conduct of Life* for the Young Men's Mercantile Library
Association in Pittsburgh, for which he received $240 for the series (lecture fees are from
the "Account Books"). When he returned to this topic in 1858, Emerson had recast "The
Spirit of the Times" into a new lecture, which he variously titled "Law of Success" and
"Success." Between 14 December 1858, when he delivered "Success" in Hartford, Connecticut, for which he received $50, and 21 December 1869, when he delivered "Success"
in Westford, Massachusetts, for which he received $20 ("Account Books"), Emerson de-
livered a total of twenty-four lectures under the title "Law of Success" or "Success" (see
von Frank).

    We believe that Emerson used the manuscript of "The Spirit of the Times" for his
lectures on the "Law of Success" in 1851; however, we also believe that by the time he
began to lecture on the "Law of Success" and "Success" in 1858, he had prepared a new
manuscript of the lecture, which, although indebted to "The Spirit of the Times," was
actually the first of what were undoubtedly several lecture manuscripts that saw him
through the 1860s. Emerson eventually adapted these lecture manuscripts as the essay
"Success" published in *Society and Solitude* in 1870 (*W*, 7:283–312). Consequently, we
date "The Spirit of the Times" in this edition 1848–1856. This lecture has never been
published.

    There are several reports of Emerson's deliveries of "The Spirit of the Times" as
"Genius of the Present Age" in Scotland. Detailed treatments of his series of four lec-
tures before the Philosophical Institution in Edinburgh appear in *Emerson's Oration to
the Modern Athenians; or, Pantheism. Being a Glance at the Chimera of the Oracle of the
Woods. By Civis* (Edinburgh: J. E. Elder, 1848) and "Emerson and His Visit to Scotland,"
*Douglas Jerrold's Shilling Magazine*, no. 7 (April 1848): 322–31. While "Civis," whom
George Willis Cooke identifies as Alexander Dunlap (see *A Bibliography of Ralph Waldo
Emerson* [Boston: Houghton Mifflin, 1908], 255), compliments Emerson on his "brilliant"
lecturing style, this writer is nonetheless convinced that in lectures such as the "Genius
of the Present Age" he is a dangerous propagandist for French skepticism; on the other
hand, the report in *Douglas Jerrold's Shilling Magazine* written by "A Student," whom
Robert E. Burkholder and Joel Myerson identify as George Cupples (see *Emerson: An
Annotated Secondary Bibliography* [Pittsburgh: University of Pittsburgh Press, 1985], 57),
is uniformly favorable, and especially so on Emerson's visionary politics. In *The "Philosophical": A Short History of the Edinburgh Philosophical Institution and Its Famous Members and Lecturers* (Edinburgh: C. J. Consland and Sons, [1949]), W. Addis Miller provides
a brief overview of Emerson's lectures and reports the anecdote of Thomas De Quincey's
falling asleep during them, since "the nasal sing-song of the American's speech was too
much for the Opium Eater" (9–10). The *Scotsman* and the *Edinburgh Evening Courant*
report on "Genius of the Present Age" as "The Tendencies of the Present Age," and both
comment on the large audience's general approval of Emerson's performance ("Philosophical Institution," 16 February 1848, 2, and "Philosophical Institution," 17 February
1848, 3, respectively). Finally, the *Dundee, Perth and Cupar Advertiser* found Emerson's
discourse on "The Spirit of the Times" at the Watts Institution a "stirring and eloquent"
testimony to "the growing individualism and analytical spirit of the present age"; the

report also noted that a "numerous audience" listened to the lecture with "breathless attention" (22 February 1848, 2).

When Emerson delivered "The Spirit of the Times" as "Signs of the Times" in Boston in 1856, the reporter for the *Boston Daily Evening Transcript* assessed it "one of [his] best lectures" (18 April 1856, 2). However, that opinion stands at considerable odds with virtually all published reactions to Emerson's delivery of "The Spirit of the Times" in America. For instance, in a detailed report, the *Albany Evening Journal* opened its treatment of Emerson's performance before the Young Men's Association by noting that he "took the occasion to say . . . that 'there are some who seem to have a horror of novelty, and some who snuff up heresy from afar.' The remark was carelessly made, but the allusion was apparent. It was intended for the benefit of all those who are not ready to fall in with the doctrines, or follow the teachings of Mr. Emerson." Then, between paragraphs devoted to an abstract of this lecture, the reporter proceeded to interpret it as an illustration of everything questionable in Emerson's philosophy, platform style, and character:

> Mr. Emerson flatters himself, if he supposes that it is the *novelty* of his views which gives offence: it is their *untruth*. . . . There are always those . . . who have an inordinate admiration of intellectual power; who would be ready to fall down and worship Lucifer, if he would present one of his plausible lies in brilliant form. . . . Mr. Emerson has reason to congratulate himself, that his love of the Unexplored, has given him all the advantages which accrue to a First Discoverer in . . . Metaphysics. But his glory will be as transitory as his philosophy.— And inspired by the spirit of prophecy, which he declared . . . *dwells in every man,* we venture to predict, that . . . he will be remembered only as an erratic man, who squandered a brilliant intellect.
>
> . . . Mr. Emerson . . . rejects all systems of Philosophy and Theology. The only deity he worships is Pan, the God of Nature. He rejects prayer as an evidence of weakness. He scoffs at those who "patronise Providence." He regards every man as naturally virtuous, and declares that "the proposition of depravity is the last profligacy and profanation—there is no Skepticism, no Atheism but that." . . .
>
> We have neither the ability, nor the patience, to follow Mr. Emerson through all his wanderings. He who . . . listens to his lectures, feels like one wandering through the intricate chambers of a labyrinth. . . . [Emerson] is considered, and perhaps is, a man of ability. He sometimes throws off a brilliant thought in a striking manner[,] like the supernatural cunning of an insane man. But as to his philosophy, we believe, and we hazard it is the opinion of all sensible and intelligent persons who [have] heard his lectures in this city, that it is the falsest, most inconsistent, egotistical and selfish, which the ingenious intellect, or the deceitful heart of man, ever devised. ("Ralph Waldo Emerson," 15 January 1850, 2)

Hearing Emerson lecture on "The Spirit of the Times" before the Mercantile Library Association in January 1850, Nathaniel Parker Willis complimented "our Prophet of the Intuitive" on the quality and diversity of his audience ("[f]rom the great miscellany of New York they come selectively out, like steel filings out of a handfull of sand to a

magnet"), and though he stated that he had notes on it "with which to gem a paragra⁅h,"
he wrote that he preferred to await the lecture's publication to review it in full (N. Parker
Willis, "Second Look at Emerson," in *Hurry-Graphs; or, Sketches of Scenery, Celebr⁅ies
and Society, Taken from Life* [New York: Charles Scribner, 1851], reprinted in *Eme⁅son
Among His Contemporaries*, 70). In a report of the same occasion, the *New-York Daily ⁅ri-
bune* gave the lecture a mixed review (30 January 1850; reprinted in Jeanne Kronr⁅an,
"Three Unpublished Lectures of Ralph Waldo Emerson," *New England Quarterly* 19
[March 1946]: 98–110). Following its delivery on 30 March at Hope Chapel, a deta⁅led
report in the *New York Herald* repeatedly mentioned the audience's laughter during the
lecture, a function, it appears, not only of their being "tickled a good deal at the od⁅ity
of [Emerson's] expressions" but also of their inability to comprehend his point, "which
would be difficult enough for them, as he did not understand it himself." That report
summarized "The Spirit of the Times" as a "Pantheistic lecture, worthy of the man ⁅ho
declared that he was an emanation from God, Yea, was God! The Pantheistic doctrine,
however, which he describes as new, is very old. He will find it in Virgil and many o⁅er
heathen writers of antiquity: and it is now the creed of that barbarous race, the Hindo⁅s"
("Emerson's Lecture on the 'Spirit of the Age,'" 3 April 1850, 1). Laughter was also the
audience's response when Emerson delivered "The Spirit of the Times" in Cincinnati on
24 May 1850. In an extensive report, the *Columbian and Great West* accused Emerso⁅ of
not rising "to the full dignity of his theme," "in the handling of which it was within his
power to set men thinking; as it was, he thought proper to do little more than make them
laugh" (1 June 1850, quoted in Mead, *Yankee Eloquence in the Middle West*, 29).

Even when Emerson reworked "The Spirit of the Times" for his lectures on the "Law
of Success" and "Success" in the late 1850s, audience response was not positive, as most
early reports show. For instance, when on 16 December 1858 he lectured on the "Law of
Success" at the People's Institute in Philadelphia, for which he received $100, a brief
report in the *Daily Evening Bulletin* noted that "Emerson's monotone tones and profound
way of saying things not overly new, [do] not impress us very favorably" and commer⁅ed
that while they were "evidently gratified at what they had heard," "[a]s in duty bound,
the audience were sufficiently puzzled by Mr. Emerson" ("Last Evening's Lecture⁅—
Sermon at Jayne's Hall, &c.," 17 December 1858, 1). When Emerson repeated the lecture
a week later before the Ontario Literary Society in Toronto ($75), the *Toronto Globe* re-
ported that the society greeted him "with warm plaudits," but some in the audience found
his explanations of success "somewhat mystical" and left dissatisfied ("Mr. Emerson's
Lecture. The Law of Success," 23 December 1858, 2). But perhaps the most damaging
assessment of Emerson's new lecture came when he delivered the "Law of Success" on
20 January 1859 before the Library Association in Cleveland, Ohio ($50; lecture fees are
from the "Account Books"):

> Ralph Waldo Emerson's lecture in the "Law of Success" was listened to by a re-
> spectable audience at the Melodeon last night. He is a man of massive intellect—
> a great and profound thinker—but is nevertheless illy adapted to the lecture room,
> and . . . last evening was a rather sleepy affair. For our own part, not presuming to
> speak for others, we had quite as lief see a perpendicular coffin behind a lecture-desk

as Emerson. The one would amuse us as much as the other. Mr. Emerson is not one to talk to the people of the West about the "Law of Success." . . . [L]ike many other great scholars, he is impracticable and visionary. Let mankind adopt his ideas (provided always that mankind can understand exactly what his ideas are) and they would live a strange, weird life—the chaotic dream of a lunatic! (*Cleveland Daily Plain Dealer*, 21 January 1859, 3)

Reviewing his father's manuscripts in July 1904 for new materials suitable for publication, Edward Waldo Emerson wrote on this lecture manuscript: "This Spirit of the Age doesn't seem worthwhile publishing[.] Best of it has been used in pub[lication] elsewhere." In addition to the multiple uses cited above that he had already made of this lecture, Emerson also drew from either "The Spirit of the Times" or its later adaptation as the "Law of Success" and "Success" for his series on *Natural History of the Intellect* at Harvard in 1870 and in 1871 (see Emerson's *University Lectures*).


W E SAY THE mind and manners of the Nineteenth Century, or the spirit of the times, a topic of universal pertinence. For what is the life of each one of us, but his own summary on the resources and tendencies of this Epoch? For what is the Age? It is what he is who beholds it. It is transparent in proportion to the powers of the eye. To one, the price current and the newspaper; another sees the roots of today in past centuries, and, beneath the past, in the Necessary and Eternal.

The age is not to be learned by the enumeration of all the traits; that were an inextricable miscellany; but by the eminency of some. No foregoing age but has left some residue and trace of itself; shall we therefore find in modern society no peculiar genius, but specimens of every mode of life and thought that has anywhere prevailed? Is modern society composed of the *débris* of the foregone structures of religion and politics, a mixed mass, just as the soil we till is made up of the degraded mountains of the elder world? No: but the age is to be described by those elements which are new and operative, and by their activity now detaching the future from the past, and exposing the decays of the corpse they consume,—and these are all that require attention.

In the confusion of figures, we have been accustomed to distinguish two parties, to one of which all men belong,—the party of the Past, and the party of the Future:—the movement, and the establishment.— This schism runs under the world, and appears in literature, philosophy, church, state, social customs; a war, it seems, betwixt Intellect and Affection. It is a crack in nature, which has split every church; Christendom, into Papal and Protestant; Calvinism, into old and new schools; Quakerism, into old and new; Methodism, into old and new; England, into Conserver and Reformer; America, into Whig and Democrat. It has reached into the immoveable East, and is renovating Constantinople and Alexandria and threatens China. It has reached into the Indian tribes of North America, and carries better politics of Democracy among the Red men.

If, in our inquiry, we fasten our regard on the second of these parties; if we can appreciate their activity and its causes, we can well spare all attention to the other class, except as illustrative of this.

This habit induces the consciousness of sufficiency in each man. The whole of modern history has an intellectual character. The former generations acted under the belief that a shining social prosperity was the beatitude of man, and sacrificed uniformly the citizen to the state. The modern mind believes that the nation exists for the individual, for the guardianship and education of every man, and speaks of itself, that men are reflective or intellectual.

This idea, which stands roughly written in all the revolutions and national movements, in the mind of the philosopher has far more precision, and is attaining a depth and splendour which win all the intellects of men to its party. In the eye of the philosopher, the individual is the World.

This perception is a sword such as was never drawn before. It divides and detaches bone and marrow, soul and body, yea,—almost the man from himself. It is the Age of Severance, of Dissociation, of Freedom, of Analysis, of Detachment. It is the Age of the first person singular. Every man for himself. The public speaker disclaims speaking for any other; he answers only for himself. The social sentiments are weak. The sentiment of Patriotism is weak. Veneration is low: The natural affections feebler than they were. People grow philosophical about native land, and parents, and relatives. There is an universal resistance to ties and ligaments once supposed essential to civil society. The new race is stiff, heady, and rebellious: they are fanatics in freedom; they hate tolls, taxes, turnpikes, banks, hierarchies, governors, yes,—almost laws. They have neck of unspeakable tenderness; it winces at a hair. They rebel against theological as against political dogmas, against mediation, or saints, or any nobility in the unseen. It tends to Solitude. The Association of the time is accidental, and momentary, and hypocritical: the detachment intrinsic and progressive. The Association is for power merely, for means; the end being the enlargement and independency of the individual. Anciently, society was in the course of things. There was a Sacred Band, a Theban Phalanx. There can be none now. College classes, military corps, or Trades Unions, may fancy themselves indissoluble for a moment, over their wine; but it is a painted hoop, and has no girth.

We say, the age is marked by a certain predominancy of the intellect in the balance of the powers. This has the most positive effects; the warm, swart earth-spirit, which made the strength of the past ages, mightier than it knew, with instincts instead of sciences; like a mother yielding food from her own breast, instead of procuring and preparing it through chemic and culinary skill; warm negro ages of sentiment and vegetation all gone; another hour has struck, and other forms arise. Instead of the social existence, which required no private strength,—by the emergence of the intellect, a slight interval is interposed between all the persons. No two are in contact. It is no longer possible to accept what all say, to accept Tradition,—such detachment has been made, that each is irrevocably solitary, and is driven to find all his resources, his hopes, rewards, society, and deity, within himself.

With this intellectual determination, the wants of man remain as they were, and enforce the direction of these fine energies on their supply. Instead of contenting himself like the first rude races with barbarous morsels got as a beast of prey from the nearest victims, or by main strength from a rude agriculture, he sails to other latitudes, and, by exchanging the products of his own, varies and refines his food. Commerce is the first fruit of the Intellect applied to Labor.

Every man must bear in his own person the badge of his time, grossly or spiritually. The sailor will find it in his boat, the scholar in his college, the statesman in parties. That which may be seen colossally traceable in the movements of masses, assumes another shape among the elegant and educated. And we hear more of it, because they know how to celebrate their wars; whilst the others strive and die unsung.

Among the cultivated is now an excess of the reflective habit, tendency to self-dissection, anatomizing of motives and thoughts, exultation in enfranchisement; reference of all persons and periods to our own. We run not to the cheerful world full of work, and the fraternity of a thousand labourers, but inward, and farther inward, to revolve the matter overmuch. Men are sick, ocular, vain, and vagabond.

The hour comes, when, to the mind of the man, the object disjoins itself from the mood of thought it awakens, and he sees that he owes a debt of emotion and thought to a person or thing, which, at the same time, he second-sees not fully to deserve the thought and emotion they have awakened, so that he loves, yet shrinks from marriage; he detests slavery, but his servant must not dare to be more than a servant; he burns with a wish to spread knowledge like water, but he will not serve in the school committee; he loves the state, but dislikes all the citizens; he transfigures a form of nature or art, and solidly proceeds with his theory of it, whilst he more than suspects that though his theory is sound, this actual form or object is unworthy of his praise; or that its emphasis to his imagination was quite accidental. He exposes with indignation the hollow charities of the day. He feels the education in vogue to be no education; the religion no religion. But he finds in himself no resources for the instruction of the people, when they shall discover that their present guides are blind. His criticism is too much for him. His wit has eaten his heart out. He excites others by thoughts, which do not move his own hand. The least effect of the oration is on the orator,—a slight recoil, a kick of the gun. He contrasts this coldness, with the healthy heart of the farmer and mechanic. In the Church, or public meeting, the rough farmers answer every call of sympathy: their faces soften, and their tears flow; but the old hardened sinners in black coats, the arid educated men and women, sit as dry as the bench. Napoleon, after reducing the sections of the city of Paris, under the Convention, had frequent occasion to harangue at the markets, in the streets, in the sections, in the *faubourgs,* and insisted that he always found the *faubourg* St. Antoine the most ready to listen to reason, and the most susceptible of a generous impulse.

These are the distinctions we have been accustomed to draw in signalising the Century, which has now reached half its term. Before I proceed to trace with a little more precision some traits of our time, and connect them with the past and the future, I have to make the general remark that *all the traits or distinctions of any period co-exist in every period.* All the elements are ever co-present. What is once true is always true. Only what was background once, is foreground now. In truth you cannot banish any element of man. You say the religion is disappearing. I think there is as much now as ever there was; but it is there in new forms; it is there to modify and not to lead. We affirm the eminency or culmination of one quality; but the very exaltation of that element is sure to exasperate the antagonist element. For man is an exaggerator, and extreme reformers make conservatism extreme.

Many distinctions, solid or fanciful, may be set up in history. There are many methods of classifying the nations which have peopled our planet since men were wise enough to record their existence; and every distributor defends his own taste. But many of these civilizations are abortive.

I do not easily distinguish but three periods, among those commonly accepted, as of deep and general significance.

First. The Greek Age, when, with very little science, man accepted nature, as it lay before his senses, and deified it, by only adding the human form to each of its elements. Jove was in the air; Neptune in the sea; Pluto in the mine; naiads in the fountain; faun and dryads in the wood; oreads on the mountain. A happy, beautiful expression of his contentment and admiration of nature: which he simply obeyed in all his performances.

These people had bolder and completer senses than we: their art is inventive, yet so secure. We can only in a quite feminine way approve what they have done, owning that it is good as far as we can judge, and doubting not it is correct where we are not judges.

Second. When, now, the age of sensation, the age of the Gymnasium, of the chariot race, of dancing, of a music, and poetry, and history, addressed to the senses,— or, never overstepping a certain sensual limit, had been exhausted,— arrived the second or *Christian* Age.

The senses having been carried to perfection and exhausted, the moral sentiment, became pronounced, and made everything else sterile. The inexperienced
soul made its sally into the absolute; craved a heaven out of nature, and above it;
looking on nature now as an obstacle, an enemy, a snare. The powers that ruled
the world, were held hostile to the Soul.

Here was a new and strange success; a triumph was achieved for the soul; an
enlargement of region; and new resources were found in the sentiments,—for
art, for architecture, painting, sculpture, poetry, and much more for the mind,
for morals, for social life, for education, and the laws.

Christianity was culture and civilization to Europe, and, in its Asiatic imitation of Mahometism, to Asia and Africa. It had this distinction, that it made religion or the sentiment, the centre of all the institutions of Society. The throne,
the laws, learning, and the arts rested on religion; in Romanism, in Anglicans and
Presbyterian or Scottish Kirk.

The Greek and Roman age are the epoch of man, of virility, the Christian age
the representation of Woman.

But this age exhausted itself also; ran into the excess or partialism of its own
element,—too exclusively ideal, sentimental: fell into monkery, asceticism, for-
malism, and hypocrisy; departed too much from nature into unmanly melancholy, and, as is easy to see in looking back at the ecclesiastical ages, put man in
a false and unreal position to nature, and his duties to the world.

Third. Now, lastly, arises the Modern Age, when the sentiments-become-
sentimentalities of the Christian period force men to retrace their steps and
return to Nature.

Nature which was looked upon as an enemy, and an obstacle,—is so regarded
no more; but more sanely, as the proper home, and theatre, and means, of man's
activity; his aim is now to convert the world into the instrument of right reason.
He believes it to be a magazine of riches inexhaustible; it offers itself to him as
the perfect means of executing his perfect will.

The first age was the Age of Man. The second age was the Age of Woman. The
third is the Marriage of the mind to nature. This appears, in particulars, as the
age of commerce, the age of tools, the age of natural science.

1. Age of Commerce.

I said in the outset that a highly intellectual development marked our times.
This is the cause and effect of commerce. Commerce is the first fruit of intellect
applied to labour. Commerce is at once the child and the nurse and tutor of the
Understanding. Hence the perfection of the maritime nations in commonsense
and acuteness. The Mediterranean Sea was the School of Europe; the Atlantic,
of a still richer culture of the same faculties.

Commerce is only a single fruit of the new habit of thought. Yet such is the predominance that belongs to Trade and its consequences at the present day, that, viewed superficially, the Age might easily be designated as the age of commerce. Trade is the ascendant power, and government only a parachute to this balloon. The state is only one department of commerce, filled with virtual merchants, who are there to be rich, and, conscious of their parentage, or filled with the time-Spirit, Government is administered for the protection of trade. Law is interpreted and executed on the same principle, that a man's enjoyment of his estate is its main end. Education is degraded. It aims to make good citizens on this foundation. The one thing which the careful parent sees that his son shall be taught, is, Arithmetic. And Religion even, is a lever out of the spiritual world to work upon this. It is really commerce which broke the power of the Church; for though trade grew up under the shadow of the Church, and gave gifts, and won a kind of tolerance for itself, it is very easy to see that the merchant and the broker are not the men to exaggerate the sentiments; but Trade is the power which recalls man from the sentiments to earth, and occupies itself with arming him with more material weapons.

Among the marks of the age of cities, must be reckoned conspicuously the universal adoption of cash-payment. Once, it was one of many methods. People bought, but they also borrowed, and received much on various claims: of goodwill, on hospitality, in the name of God, in the interest of party, of letters, of charity. Young men made essay of their talents for proof, for glory, for enthusiasm. on any reasonable call, nothing doubting, that, in one or another way, their hazarded bread would return to them after many days. But in the universal expansion of the city by railroads, the stock-exchange infects our country-fairs, and no service is thought reasonable which does not see a requital in money. Yet where is the service which can by any dodge escape its remuneration? For grandeur, at least, let us once in a while serve God.

2. Age of Tools.

Commerce expresses the application of the intellect to the exchange of fruits and commodities; another great application of the understanding was mechanism, or the invention of tools. All truth is practical. No thought dawns on the intellect, but tends directly to become a mechanic power: and all these wonderful aids and means by which we live, were once simple and poetic acts. Every tool was a stroke of genius.

These tools they have invented,—screw, shears, clock, compass, ship, money, alphabet, decimal figures, the newspaper,—are effigies and statues of men also: their wit, their genius, perpetuated. And he that uses them, becomes a great society of men as wise as himself. All these tools think for us.

The effect of the analytic mind of the age has gone on making tools. But all tools are reagents. Mechanism mechanizes. It is a proverb in America, that the

Union is holden by a cotton thread. These agents are absorbing and aggressive. The weaver becomes a web: the machinist, a machine. If you cannot command the tools, they command you; and the question that arises in the end, is, which is the tool?

It is too obvious that the tendency of the popular mind in this country, is, to rely on means provided by the understanding for the aid and defence of man and not on the simplest action of the man himself.

The life of a man in this country is clothed, fed, forwarded, amused, and, in every particular taken off its feet and supported on these secondaries. He is never suffered to touch the ground. He is superfluously served and prevented. He is cushioned, pampered, policed, coached, cabbed, steamed, and telegraphed, through the world. No mountain stops him, and no sea. The land is tunnelled; the water, bridged. He arrives at the seashore, and a sumptuous ship has floored and carpeted the stormy Atlantic for him, and made it a luxurious hotel amid the horrors of tempests; and steam has annihilated the head-wind. "It is the same to him who wears a shoe, as if the whole earth were covered with leather."[1] The same organising power has subsidized and reconstructed society for his use. The population seems to be all couriers, clerks, reporters, labourers or ministers of luxury for his behoof.

All things feel the encroachments of this iron hand. The social day has come to be divided and arranged by the time-tables of the Railway. See how the clocks of this country have been changed to astronomic-time, and all the sea submits to the invading thrills of the electric telegraph. The globe is now practically a moveable observatory to the astronomer; and the diameter of the solar system is the familiar base of his triangles to compute the parallax of stars. The day is indebted to the penny post, the night to the gas-company. In London, lately, the new electric light puts out the gas light, as that had formerly put out the flame of oil: and the newspapers announce with some pathos, that there will be no more night in London; a state of things which has only this consolation, that a new lamp is a more effective guard against crime than twenty policemen.

Our disease, again, is indebted to ether and chloroform. The physician, the dentist have learned to use the body as piece of mechanism, and with ruder and robuster treatment than formerly. Nay more,—it is very plain that the musician, the churchman, the statesman, the socialist, begin to calculate on us; and, as we make tulips and dahlias to order, and breeds of cattle and swine, so Fourier and Owen are computing new combinations to be realized in human posterity.[2]

Yes, we prosper in point of tools. Things begin to mind us. The steam excava-

---

1. Quoted from *The Hĕĕtŏpădĕs of Vĕĕshnoŏ-Sărmă* (1787).
2. Robert Owen (1771–1858), Welsh social reformer and philanthropist.

tor carries off a hill as if we had a secret for making it liquid, and pumping or draining it. The engineer tunnels a mountain as a joiner puts a gimlet through a deal board. The world obeys, the cars roll, and nature is made a mean to control nature.

The engineering is and continues admirable in what it achieves and in what it projects. The work of the world, the pendulum shall do. This idle gravitation, which offers itself everywhere to pull down,—a famous hand he is at pulling too,—pulls men, and stones, and trees, and planets, and suns down,—be a moth and a sluggard no longer, but shall pull to some useful purpose; and, since he has no living to get of his own, shall get a living for honest, walking, blushing men and women.

We have long ago learned to put brooks and rivers to a profitable industry. Not a stream dares to roar in the highlands of New Hampshire, but an ingenious gentleman hurries to the spot, and saves and sells every inch of the water at the price of wine. The sea, with his vast, unnecessary washing and flowing, hither and back, shall be taught something useful, and shall turn wheels, ring bells, and drive engines, and pay for his salt. The air, a chartered libertine, shall no longer be free; he must put on livery: he shall float as great a fleet of balloons and of flying carriages, as the sea now does of ships.

Why should all these fine, nameless energies of the summer-day be squandered? The railroad has turned all the citizens with all their brains full of traps and contrivances like so many walking machine-shops, into the country, and they rack their wits how to extort out of these poor innocent pastures some dividend and brokerage. We will plant a few square miles of trees, that when the southwind blows, we shall not be warm in our own bodies only, but in ten-thousand limbs and ten-million leaves of blossoming trees, in orchard and forest. The wide-related planter in his groves feels the blood of thousands in his body, and his heart pumps the sap of all this forest of vegetation through his arteries.

Then again, he discovers, that, though he had plumed himself on his arts, he has really only taken the first steps. A few plants, like apple, wheat, cane, rice, tobacco, cotton, he has usurped and multiplied; and on a single plant, as, for instance, cotton, he has concentrated all his talent, arts, institutions, as if it were the tree of life; and empires breathe long or short, as the telegraph reports the worm, or blight, or bloom, of the crop in the sea-island:—*one plant;*—and, when he looks into his botanical manual, there are nearly 100,000 plants registered, each with virtues as precious as the cotton or the cane, on which, as yet, he has not experimented, and which are to characterise other civilizations, as cotton characterises this.

Our powers are great, and we seem to be on the edge of attaining greater. One might expect a great immorality from these suddenly developed powers, as from a pauper come unexpectedly into a great estate. It is a maxim, that all that frees talent without increasing self-command, is noxious. And, one thinks, if you have only armed the burglar and the assassin with more terrific agents, what have we gained? But in our experience, it turns out, that, as these arts are for all, they leave society where they found it.

Our powers are great, nor can it be denied that we seem be on the eve of wonderful additions, through chemistry, magnetism, and, according to extraordinary rumours, through mesmerism also. And yet to me it is very certain, that our hands will not be unbound, until our sanity is quite secure. There must be a relation between power and probity. We have now, no doubt, as much power as we can be trusted with. We seem to have more than we can be trusted with: and this must therefore be esteemed a preparation, I will not say, for a superior race, but for a higher civilization of the next centuries;—and is a higher omen of revolution than any other we have seen.

The new tools which we use, the steamboat, locomotive, and telegraph, are effecting such revolutions, as to induce new measures for every value, and to suggest a regret, which is daily expressed, that we who use them were not born a little later, when these agents, whose first machines we see prepared, should be in full play. We have been educated in stagecoach, spinning-wheel, and old tinder-box times, and we find ourselves compelled to accept new arts, new highways, new markets, and mend our old country-trot to keep up with these swifter-footed days.

These things well deserve all their fame, and their history is the history of this age.

Nor is there any chance in their appearance, but they came in the very point of time when they were due. When the man was ready, the horse was brought.

Thus, the timeliness of the invention of the locomotive must be conceded. It came just at the right moment, for America. The geography of America was in no other way to be subdued, the upward navigation of our great rivers; the dangerous navigation of inland seas. More than this, it is an eminent political aid. We could not, else, have held the vast North America together. It was already agitated seriously, the transfer of the seat of government to the west of the Alleganies. But the railroad, with the telegraph, is making it practicable to travel from the extremes of the Empire, without tedious journeys. The important consideration that the Federal Union takes away from its members is the power of declaring peace and war: and this is the main argument for annexation. So that, let Texas, and California, and Minnesota, and Oregon be never so quarrelsome, once in the Union their hands are tied. This gave vital importance to the new facilities of travel and intercourse.

What significance in all the particulars of this history? The course of national expansion and progress of races had just now made it plain that a road to the

Pacific could not be postponed,—a railroad, a shiproad, telegraph,—complete communication in every manner for all nations.

See how it was secured: The World-Soul knows who and what it has to deal with, and employs cheap means for great effects. Suddenly, the Californian soil is spangled with a little gold dust, here and there, in a mill race,—in a mountain cleft; an Indian picks up a little; a farmer, a millwright, a soldier, each a little; the news flies here and there, to New York; to Maine; to London; and an army of sixty thousand volunteers, the sturdiest and keenest men that could be collected, embark for this desart, carrying tools, instruments, books, and framed houses, with them. Such a well-appointed Colony as never was planted before;—they arrive with the speed of sail and steam on these remote shores, carrying with them all these tools, as I say, the sum and upshot of all our old civilization,—and one weapon more, namely, that every colonist has taken his degrees in the caucus, town meeting, and county convention, at home; so that he knows the whole theory and practice of our politics, and is a walking American Constitution in the diggings of the Sacramento;—these all arrive bringing with them the necessity that their government shall at once proceed to make the road from Washington to San Francisco, which they themselves are all intimately engaged to assist.

I proceed to notice a very natural, but somewhat alarming, extension of this age of tools into the social relations.

Filled with wonder at our own success, in this delegation almost of human reason to our arts and instruments we say, "Come, let us make this dominion of art perfect." If tools have done so much, let us have nothing else. The world shall be as geometrical as a beehive, and the geometry, as with the bees, shall enter into the manners and wills of the population. It is but one step, and a very attractive step to bold and inventive heads, to apply the same engineering which they have found so effective on the face of the earth, to the earth-born,—and to employ men with the same precision and despotism, with which they have used shovels and wheels. Clearly, they say, things are very bad now. Every man is in a false position: how cruel, that, scholar and saint though he be, he should find himself in this most awkward relation to loaves of bread! And, as a civil engineer has proved so indispensable where wheat in the mountains, or lead or coal in mines, was to be brought to market,—so now we want a moral engineer who can dispose of these materials more refractory than granite, gravel, or conglomerate; can bring men up to their highest power, and reward them with the gratification of their legitimate desires. Stephenson, with his locomotive and road, executed the idea of the age in iron:—Who will do it in the social department?[3]

3. Emerson is likely referring to George Stephenson (1781–1848), English inventor and founder of railways; Robert Stephenson (1803–59), his son and occasional assistant, constructed the first railway into London, which was completed in 1838.

And, truly, I honour the generous ideas of the socialists, the magnificence of their theories, and the enthusiasm with which they have been urged.

They are the inspired men of the time. Mr. Owen has preached his doctrine of labour and reward, with the fidelity and devotion of a saint, to the slow ears of this generation.

Fourier,—almost as wonderful an example of the mathematical mind of France as Laplace or Napoleon,—has turned a truly vast arithmetic to the question of social misery, and has put men under the obligation which a generous mind always confers of conceiving magnificent hopes, and making great demands, as the right of man.[4] He took his measure of that which all should and might enjoy, from no soup-society or charity-concert, but from the refinements of palaces, the wealth of universities, and the triumphs of artists.

And when I consider how tragic are the evils to which these men addressed themselves, how grim and narrow the ways of life are grown in France, and in Europe generally, how expensive life is, and how many other calamities besides poverty, embitter it: when I consider how gigantic the problem is, I have no heart to make flippant objections to the plans of these reformers, least of all to assume the chair, and affect to decide the question. They who think and hope well of mankind, put all men under obligation. They who in times of gloom, perplexity, and danger, can pilot the ship into port, shall have the praise of the universe.

I regard these philanthropists as themselves the effects of the age in which we live, and, in common with so many other good facts, the efflorescence of the period, and predicting a good fruit that ripens.

They are not the creators they believe themselves; but they are unconscious prophets of a true state of society; one which the tendencies of nature lead unto; one which always establishes itself for the sane soul, though not in that manner in which they paint it: But they are describers of that which is really being done.

The large cities are phalansteries; and the theorists draw all their argument from facts already taking place in our experience. Especially are they to be heard as the proclaimers of the Gods' justice and love, which, they have courage to believe, will be fulfilled, come what may, in the world.

The socialist, I say, wished to mechanize society. I do not think it quite easy to seize the law which determines the legitimate action of this engineering. But it has its beneficent energy, and it has its limits. The world vegetates, like a bulb or an acorn; and everything in the world shares this vegetative quality. To machinery, also, the same pushing and progress is natural and inevitable. The vegetative quality runs into matter, runs into mind, runs into arts; they grow, too, and ramify, and subdivide, but always with the same tax.

4. Pierre Simon de Laplace (1749–1827), French astronomer and mathematician.

The plant grows with less vigour as it leaves the ground, and passing into stem, leaves, flower, and fruit. arrives, with every step, at a new and finer production, becoming feebler all the time: and animal life, in the geologic ages, is, at first, slow and secular, requiring many thousands of years before an existing genus can modify its habit by developing a new organ, and forming a new species. In the fossil formations, it has cost ages to complete the changes through which the egg of a species will now pass in a few days. The world was then newer: the blood was colder: Life had not yet so fierce a glow.

Well; life is accelerated. That which Linnaeus called *prolepsis* or anticipation, takes place.[5] The species lives six days in one. The new races are more complex, finer, higher. In man it reaches its highest mark; but the term is proportionally shorter.

So is it with civility, and its arts and tools. They are only finer life, but the compensations appear. The giant size is reduced to a modest six feet. The antediluvian age, to a period far less alarming to insurance and annuity offices. Man has filled up his life with arts. Money, labour, is worth more, for there is more to buy. See how much more a dollar is worth in Massachusetts or New York than in Siberia;— or in Massachusetts or New York than in Wisconsin or Minnesota. There, it will buy bad bread, bad cloth, bad shelter, bad riding. Here, it will buy speed, comfort, luxury, books, and the neighborhood of sense, beauty, and refinement.

But one limit this power of arts and instruments has, only one limit to its benefit. You may extend it to any degree, so long as you keep it art and instrument: so long as it serves. Its antagonist force is the private reason and conscience of man; character; the moral sentiment; as it is manifested in the inspiration of each human mind. As the excess of Christianity had been asceticism and sentimentalism, so the excess of tools is the invasion of man, and converting man into tool, as Socialism does in the phalanx, as Government does in the tyranny of majorities, as public opinion does in newspaper and mob. The natural and eternal remedy is the reliance on the private soul. This is that which alone is sacred, which alone is great. When this rules, all goes well. That which made the spring of the last period, is to make the regulator of this.

The aim, the determination must come from the Soul, and too much stress cannot be laid on this. Everything else is accidental.

Nothing is so subtle, and nothing so refractory, as what we call personal power; character and genius. It can use all these aids, or it can counterpoise them all. It rests on inspiration. We say, there exists in every man a privilege of obtaining an infallible verdict on all questions touching the conduct of life. And character

5. Carolus Linnaeus (1707–78), Swedish botanist, is considered one of the founders of modern systematic botany.

or personal power has its strength from its obedience to that. The capital misfortune of Socialism is that when it asks for a verdict, the oracle is dumb. The oracle never answers to corporations, or legislatures, or masses; but only to the privacy of each mind.

I have long ago discovered that I have nothing to do with other people's facts. It is enough for me if I can dispose of my own. And I believe that whilst we see with joy the examples of the power of association, which are multiplying around us, and infer the new applications of a principle of such energy and benefit,— we must not prematurely add to them; we must not be bribed by the splendour of material results, to depart from our only safe guide.

The design is magnificent, but there is always a fatal fault in the execution. The economics which must be incidental come to be paramount. Nature's design is that there be men; a man; but, in execution, the philanthropist unmans them that they may have bread. Then the socialist incurably exaggerates his arrangements, and forgets that the virulence of personal qualities will neutralize all forms: as the King of Naples said, when a new uniform was proposed for his troops, "'T was no matter what dress you put on them, they were sure to run away."

The members of the phalanx will be the same men we know. To put them in or out of a phalanx, will not so much mend matters. In the association, or out of it, it is very certain that a higher law will penetrate, which will make the powers and resources of the institution quite unimportant. It is certain that Nature will work in or out of the institution for the men as units, and by them as units. I suppose, it was not unconsidered, the sending of the youthful soul into this university of the world, and perhaps it must have this drastic treatment of famine and plenty, of insult and rapture, of wisdom and tragedy, of infernal and supernal society; in order to secure that breadth of culture which so long-lived a destiny needs. We talk sadly, but sometimes inconsiderately, of the suffering and starvation of the masses. But it could only be understood by the biographies of all the individuals.

"The evils of popular government seem greater than they are: there is compensation for them in the spirit and energy it awakens."

The knowledge of the particle is the key to the knowledge of the mass. In this age of mutations, every little while people become alarmed at the wrongs in society, and expect a revolution. There will be no revolution, none that deserves to be called so. There may be a scramble for money. But there will be no revolution, until there are revolutionists. As all the people we see, want the things we now have, and not better things, it is very certain that they will, under whatever change of forms, keep the old system. Whoever is skilful in heaping money now, will be skilful in heaping money again. When I see changed men, I shall look for a changed world.

When men say, 'These men occupy my place,' the revolution is near. But I never feel that any men occupy my place, but that the reason why I do not have what I wish, is, that I want the faculty which entitles. All spiritual power makes its own place. Revolutions of violence are scrambles merely.[6]

The importance of sound individuals cannot be overvalued. Whatever may be the cry in books of philosophy or in the public opinion of the hour against the dangers of egotism, the energy and wisdom of the universe express themselves through personalities. It is a power now in its beginning, and its power is not demonstrated. As every house that would be most solid and stable, must be built of square stones; so every society that can be depended on, must be composed of men that are themselves complete. It is vain to attempt anything without them. The communities that are quoted as successful, were nothing but the presence and influence of some superior man, and he owed nothing to the rules of his order.

In the judgment of Socrates, in *Gorgias*, "One wise man is better than ten thousand who are unwise." And it is idle to attempt by any balance of rogues to educe honesty, or by combining follies to make wisdom.

The good town, the good state, quite naturally crystallizes round one healthy heart. Give us one, and the state seems to be redeemed. The majority carry the day because there is no real minority of one. If Lycurgus were here, the majority would not laugh any longer.[7] There is something in him which he cannot be laughed out of, nor argued out of, nor can he be terrified or bought off. I am afraid that in the formal arrangements of the socialists, the spontaneous sentiment of any thoughtful man will find that poetry and sublimity still cleave to the solitary house.

The arrangements of Owen and Fourier are enforced by arithmetic: but all the heroism and all the scope and play of thought cleave to the solitary house. The Spartan broth, the hermit's cell, the lonely farmer's life, are poetic; the phalanstery, the patent village, are culinary and mean. Forever we must say, the hope of the world depends on private independence and sanctity. Individualism never was tried. But now, when it is borne in like prophecy, on a few holy souls to go alone,—now, when a few began to think of such celestial enterprise, sounds this tin trumpet of a French phalanstery, and the newsboys throw up their caps, and cry, "Egotism is exploded, now for Communism!" But all that is valuable there comes of individual integrity. I have no wish to take sides, and make flippant criticisms, but sadly I think you must settle it in your hearts, that, when you get a great man, he will be hard to keep step with; he will not be a very supple member of any quadrangle. Spoons and skimmers may lie very well together, but vases and statues must have each its own pedestal.

---

6. Attributed to Charles Maurice de Talleyrand-Périgord in a biography of him (see *JMN*, 9:103).

7. Lycurgus, according to tradition, was the ninth-century B.C. lawgiver who imposed codes on Sparta designed to produce tough and able warriors.

3. Age of Science.

I say the mind of the age is marked by a return to nature. Natural science is studied, and under the light of ideas. The English mind and the French mind are departmental. And they have long made science barren and repulsive by adding fact to fact superstitiously, and repudiating theory as dangerous. A revolution has come. Modern science, with all its tongues, teaches unity. All our new books trace analogy. Observe the titles of our books: Mrs. Somerville writes the *Connexion of the Sciences*; Humboldt writes the same thing under the name *Kosmos.* The *Vestiges of Creation* respects the same Unity.[8] Endless analogies are hunted out,—between the law that ranges leaves on the stem, and the distances of the planets from the sun; between the spinning of infusory eggs, and the planetary motions.

The phenomena of Sound and of Light were observed to be similar. Both observed the same law of reflection, of radiation, of interference, and of harmony. Two rays of light meeting cause darkness; two beats of sound meeting cause silence. When the eye is affected by one prevailing colour, it sees, at the same time, the accidental colour; and, in music, the ear is sensible, at the same time, to the fundamental note, and its harmonic sounds.

The same laws may be translated into the laws of Heat. Light, Heat, Sound, and the waves of fluids, have the same laws of reflection, and are explained as undulations of an elastic medium. Light and Heat are analogous in their law to Electricity and Magnetism. These are shown to be identical. Then, Davy thought the primary cause of electric and of chemical effects one and the same, one acting on masses, the other on particles. Then, Chladni's experiment seems to me central.[9] He strewed sand on glass and then drew musical tones from the glass, and the sand assumed symmetrical figures. With discords, the sand was thrown about. Orpheus, then, is no fable: Sing, and the rocks will crystallize; Sing, and the plant will organize.[10]

Newton, Hooke, Boscovich, Davy believed that the varied forms of bodies depend on different arrangements of the same particles of matter.[11] Possibly the

8. *The Connection of the Physical Sciences* (1834) by Mary Fairfax Somerville (1780–1872), English mathematician and scientific writer; Alexander von Humboldt, *Kosmos* (1845–62); *Vestiges of the Natural History of Creation* (1844) by Robert Chambers (1802–71), Scottish publisher and evolutionist.

9. Sir Humphry Davy (1778–1829), English chemist who advanced an electrical theory of chemical affinity; Ernst Florens Friedrich Chladni (1756–1824), German physicist and authority on acoustics, invented the euphonium.

10. Orpheus, in the Greek myth, was married to Eurydice. After she died, he was allowed to go to Hades to return her to the world of the living on the condition that neither looked back until they were completely out, but Orpheus, seeing the sun, turned to share his happiness with Eurydice, and she disappeared.

11. Robert Hooke (1635–1703), English experimental philosopher; Ruggiero Giuseppe Boscovich (1711–87), Italian mathematician and physicist.

world will be found to consist of oxygen and hydrogen, and even these two elements are one matter in different states of electricity.

Our own little globe is guide enough to the knowledge of all other globes far
and near. We never come into new laws. We can go nowhere into a foreign country, though we run along the vast diameter of the sidereal spaces. History, in its
largest sense embracing natural, civil, and psychical, is the biography of One
Spirit. Swedenborg said that the societies in heaven appeared to him at a distance
as one man. When he came near, he saw they were made up of multitudes.

We are struck in reading any continuous history, as of England and of France,
with the almost biographical character it assumes. The chronicler is forced to
treat the life of the nation as the life of one man. England is one Englishman. He
has memory: carries all his past history in his head: remembers his laws: remembers the charters granted by his kings: knows all his rights, and when he is
wronged, is always sure of his revenge, though it do not fully come until after
a hundred years. Well, not less is the formation of the globe and of the races, the
biography of one spirit. The lesson of geology is a method, a series, as continuous as the ripening of an apple or the growth of an animal. Geology shows the
gigantic gropings of this embryo in the first plants, the first animals: the advance
and refinement to complex organizations. The science of Cuvier, Oken, and
Owen, shows one hand continuous in time, one thought in the variety of forms:
a stupendous unity, which makes each figure convertible into the other, and
all finding their key in the human mind; Man alone corresponding to, understanding, and using them all.[12]

The world is the body of the mind, the arm of the reason, and natural history and civil history are the life or biography of the Soul of the world; and all
facts and all creatures are the proceeding of the Spirit into reality or into self-
possession. The old way of representing it made us colonists, intruders, squat-
ters; we were the accident of an accident; might have been dropped in Saturn or
Mars, or the Sun, as well: and the powers in play here might prove an overmatch;
the sea might drown, the earthquake swallow, the climate roast or congeal us: to
use a common phrase, "We did not live, we only stayed;" and nothing indicated
adaptation. No adoption of the planet as a home; no patriotism to it; no marriage.
It was all experiment, and might easily be a failure.

To the eye of the Nineteenth Century, it looks differently. Thanks to the *hand*
of science, the earth fits man. He does not ride on it, as a man rides on a horse;
but as a man rides on his own legs. It does not fit him as a farm, or a cave, or a
house fits him,—into which he accommodates himself, but as his body fits his

12.  Baron Georges Léopold Chrétien Frédéric Dagobert Cuvier (1769–1832), French naturalist and
comparative anatomist; Lorenz Oken (1779–1851), German naturalist and philosopher; Sir Richard
Owen (1804–92), English comparative anatomist and zoologist.

mind; as his tongue obeys his thought; as his hands serve his eyes; as his eyes and ears serve his curiosity and his will.

There is not only a return to the study of nature, but to a natural method in the study. A return to nature from the superstition of facts. The people had been excluded. Science was costly, collegiate, with academies and laboratories; worst of all, there was no relation between its facts and the spirit in man.

But Democracy in our days had conquered the State. So humanity rushed into Science. The populace first broke in in Lavater's physiognomy, where the relation of the soul to form was shown: then, in Gall and Spurzheim's phrenology, shoving aside the gownsmen, laying a rough plebeian hand on the mysteries of animal and spiritual nature, and dragging down every sacred secret to a street show.[13] But the movement had much truth in it. It felt connection, where the professors denied it, and proved it by modifying the language, and forcing its phraseology into universal use.

Directly on the heels of this intruder, came mesmerism: like the Jacobins on the Girondists in the French Revolution; and with still more audacity pushed into the very shrines of the Soul; attempted the explanation of miracle and prophecy, as well as of creation. What could be more revolting to the sober, patient, contemplative philosopher?

But a certain success attended it, against all expectation and probability. It was human, it was genial; it affirmed unity, and connection between remote points. While society remained in doubt between the indignation of the old school, and the audacity of the new, suddenly a higher note sounded: unexpected aid from high quarters came in to the mob. The German poet Goethe revolted against the science of the day,—against French science, against English science,—declared war against the great name of Newton, and proposed his own new and simpler optics. Then in Botany he introduced his simple idea of metamorphosis; then he extended it into anatomy and animal life: and his views have been adopted into the orthodox science of Europe and America.

The Revolt became a Revolution; Schelling and Oken in Germany, and afterwards Hegel, introduced their ideal Natural-Philosophy. Hegel extended it to Civil History. Geoffroi Saint-Hilaire expounded it to France in natural science; Cousin in philosophy and history; Owen in anatomy explained it to England; and Agassiz to America.[14]

13. Johann Kaspar Lavater (1741–1801), Swiss poet and mystic, usually credited with founding the pseudoscience of physiognomy; German physicians Franz Joseph Gall (1758–1828) and Johann Kaspar Spurzheim (1776–1832), cofounders of the pseudoscience of phrenology.

14. Etienne Geoffroy Saint-Hilaire (1772–1844), French naturalist, propounded a theory of organic unity; Victor Cousin (1792–1867), French transcendental philosopher; Louis Agassiz (1807–73), Swiss-born American naturalist and zoological explorer, began the collections now at the Harvard Museum of Comparative Zoology.

This science aimed at thoroughness to give a theory to elements, gases, earths, liquids, crystals, plants, animals, men; to show inevitable were all the steps; that a vast plan was successively realised; and that the last types were in view from the beginning, and were approached in all the steps; that each circle of facts, as, chemistry, astronomy, botany, repeated in a new plane the same law; that the same advancement which natural history showed on successive planes, civil history also showed; that event was born of event, that one school of opinion generated another; that the wars of history were inevitable; that victory always fell where it was due; no party conquered that ought not to conquer; for ideas were the real combatants in the field, and the truth was always advancing, and always victorious.

The idea of the age, as we say, was return to nature; conquest of nature; conversion of nature into an instrument; perfect obedience to nature, and thereby perfect command of nature; perfect representation of the human mind in nature.

This, of course, involves again the highest morals. Every immorality is a departure from nature, and is punished by a natural loss and deformity. The popularity of such books as Combe on the "Constitution of Man," (though a very humble book it is,) and the moral tone that appears in the most popular worldly and comic books,—in Dickens, Thackeray, Cruikshank, and in *Punch*,—betray the tendency that I mean, the growing feeling of mankind that the greatest of calamities is moral dereliction, and that moral justice can no more be defied or evaded than Gravitation.[15]

The gracious lesson taught by science to this Century is that the history of nature from first to last is *melioration,* incessant advance from less to more, from rude to finer and finest organisation, the globe of matter thus conspiring with the principle of undying Hope in man. Melioration in nature answers to Culture in man, and when he listens to the impulses of the heart, in him, and sees the progressive refinement in nature, out of him, he cannot resist the belief that every new race and moral quality impresses its own purpose on the atoms of matter, refines and converts them into ministers of human knowledge and virtue; that cultivated bodies, instructed blood, ennobled brains shall yet address themselves to the work of the world, and shall obtain a new command of material elements, and obtain from willing nature more magnificent instrumentalities than have yet been suspected to run on errands still more magnificent.

The task appointed us, however special or humble, borrows the grandeur of the system of which it is a part. Modern Science teaches on a comparing of the

15. *The Constitution of Man* (1828) by George Combe (1788–1858), Scottish phrenologist; the popular English novelists Charles Dickens (1812–70) and William Makepeace Thackeray (1811–63); George Cruikshank (1792–1878), English caricaturist and illustrator; *Punch,* the illustrated London satirical weekly, was started in 1841.

ancient strata with the more perfect animal forms which accompany Man, "that there is a plan successively realized in nature, and the types now in existence were in view at the beginning." Is it less true that the ages are all necessary to each other, and that a slow but vast harmony unites the first and last members of this gigantic procession. Each has somewhat special assigned it, on which it lavishes the thought, and love, and lives of competing myriads. That done, the secret is lost; it is no longer doable; and for us remains that undone something which now hovers before and solicits all the leading minds.

To accept our own, is the truest wisdom. Beauty is in nature the pilot which leads us where health and fitness are found; and that work wherein we are most needed is that which is most desired by us.

It is all idle talking,—as if the motes on the stream should prate of the current that is bearing them on. Let us accept the immense beneficence we behold and share. Slower or faster it moves, the huge company;—suns, and earths, and the creatures that inhabit them,—without hurry, and without a pause. We can never intercalate an hour of respite to take breath, look about us, and form resolutions. This age is ours; is our world. As the wandering sea-bird which crossing the ocean alights on some rock or islet to rest for a moment its wings, and to look back on the wilderness of waves behind, and onward to the wilderness of waters before, so stand we perched on this rock or shoal of time, arrived out of the immensity of the past, and bound and road-ready to plunge into immensity again. What place is here to cavil or repine? What apology, what praise, can equal the fact that here it is; therefore, certainly, in the vast optimism, here it ought to be. Wondering, we came in to this watch tower, this broad horizon; but let us not go hence stupid or ashamed; and doubt never but a good genius brought us in, and will carry us out.

Besides, as I stand hovering over this gloom and deep of the Future, and consider earnestly what it forebodes, I cannot dismiss my joyful auguries. It is a reality arriving. It is also dear. I look not at the work of its hand; I follow ever.

The life of man is the true romance which, when it is valiantly conducted and all the stops of the instrument opened, will go nigh to craze the beholder with anxiety, wonder, and love. Wonderful powers are wrapped up under that coarsest of all mattings called Custom, and all wonder prevented. I have read in a German tale that in a gay company, who were amusing themselves on the lawn before a *chateau*, the master of the feast called for a telescope, and a silent, meagre guest put his hand into the breast-pocket of his grey taffeton coat, took from it a beautiful Dollond, and handed it with a bow to the entertainer.[16] Nobody seemed surprised that so large a machine should come from so tiny a pocket. But soon

16. John Dollond (1706–61), English inventor of the refracting telescope.

after, someone expressed a wish to have Turkey-carpets spread here on the turf which was growing damp, and the man in the grey coat, with modest and humble demeanour, began to draw out a rich, embroidered carpet twenty paces long, and ten broad. Nobody thanked him; only a young lady carelessly asked him if he had a marquee? He put his hand to his pocket, and drew forth canvass, bars, ropes, iron frame, in short, everything belonging to a sumptuous tent, which was erected by the help of the young men. In a little while, a ride was proposed, and he took from his pocket three noble riding horses all saddled and bridled.

Can you read the riddle?

Time is the little grey man who takes out of his breast-pocket first a pocket-book, then a telescope, then a Turkey-carpet, then saddled nags, and a sumptuous canvass tent. We are accustomed to Chemistry, and it does not surprise us. But Chemistry is a name for changes and developments as wonderful as those of this Breast-pocket: what then is *Animation*—this life which opens, and enlarges, and declines?

I have heard, and do sometimes remember, that I was a little chubby boy trundling a hoop on a sidewalk in Boston and spouting poetry at the Latin School. Time, the little grey man, has put away the city from me and taken out of his vest-pocket certain green fields and in a corner of them set a wooden house, in which I live; he has taken out of his pocket several full-grown and several very young persons and seated them close beside me. 'Tis wonderful how much we have to say to each other and how easily we act as if we had always known each other; then he has taken that boyhood and that hoop quite away and left here a lean person, a little grey man like himself. I am sure he has played, or is playing, tricks as extraordinary with each person who hears me. Is there nothing astounding in these changes, and are they only astounding when done fast?

The commonest life is made of miracles; for all the most valuable things in nature are on the highway, and not in rare and extraordinary fortunes. These are peculiarities of the time, but we are too much in the age to see them. Besides, all the peculiarities of any age are superficial: that which is deep and great belongs alike to all ages. As soon as we love, or think profoundly; or pray; or are rapt by music; or by grand works of imagination; or address ourselves to any task which absorbs the mind and heart; we are no longer related to our native village or to the current year and month, but are citizens of the world, and at home in all ages.

*Mind and Manners*
*of the Nineteenth Century,*
1848 – 1849

EMERSON FIRST DELIVERED his series on the *Mind and Manners of the Nine-teenth Century* between 6 and 17 June 1848 before members of the Literary and Scientific Institution in Portman Square in London; he netted £80 from the series instead of the £200 he had expected (see *Letters,* 4:80n, 102–3). The six lectures he delivered in that series were "The Powers and Laws of Thought" on 6 June, "The Relation of Intellect to Natural Science" on 8 June, "The Tendencies and Duties of Men of Thought" on 10 June, "Politics and Socialism" on 13 June, "Poetry and Eloquence" on 15 June, and "Natural Aristocracy" on 17 June. In America Emerson repeated five of the six lectures from the *Mind and Manners of the Nineteenth Century* series between 15 January and 12 February 1849 at the Freeman Place Chapel in Boston; he netted $87 from the series ("Account Books"). Although the titles of the first, second, and fifth lectures are not reported, in all probability Emerson delivered "The Powers and Laws of Thought" on 15 January, "The Relation of Intellect to Natural Science" on 22 January, "The Tendencies and Duties of Men of Thought" on 29 January, "Natural Aristocracy" on 5 February, and either "Politics and Socialism" or "Poetry and Eloquence" on 12 February (see below). Immediately upon finishing the series at the Freeman Place Chapel, Emerson repeated *Mind and Manners of the Nineteenth Century* in six lectures between 16 February and 6 April 1849 in Worcester, Massachusetts; he received $138 for the series ("Account Books"). Although none of the titles under which he lectured in Worcester are reported, in all probability Emerson followed the same order he had followed in London the previous June, delivering "The Powers and Laws of Thought" on 16 February, "The Relation of Intellect to Natural Science" on 21 February, "The Tendencies and Duties of Men of Thought" on 9 March, "Politics and Socialism" on 23 March, "Poetry and Eloquence" on 30 March, and "Natural Aristocracy" on 6 April (see below). Of the six lectures associated with the *Mind and Manners of the Nineteenth Century* series, only three survive in complete lecture manuscripts and are printed in this edition: "The Powers and Laws of Thought," "The Relation of Intellect to Natural Science," and "The Tendencies and Duties of Men of Thought " These lectures have never been published.

The *London Inquirer,* which published detailed reports of only "The Powers and Laws of Thought" and "The Relation of Intellect to Natural Science" as Emerson delivered them in London, lavishly praised Emerson's "many advantages" as a lecturer: "His voice is beautifully clear and distinct. . . . His manner is reserved, but pleasing. His delivery is never emphatic, but is yet impressive, and, at intervals, is animated, and at all times commands attention" ("Mr. Emerson's Lectures," 10 June 1848, 379). Highly favorable, near-verbatim reports of Emerson's entire series as delivered at the Literary and Scientific Institution in Portman Square appeared in *Douglas Jerrold's Weekly Newspaper* ("Mr. Emerson's Lectures," 10 June 1848, 750, treats the first two lectures; "Mr. Emerson's Lectures," 17 June 1848, 790, treats the third and fourth lectures; and "Mr. Emerson's Lectures *Concluded*," 24 June 1848, 821–22, treats the last two lectures). In the first report, Emerson is portrayed to readers as "nobly impressive," and his presence at the lectern is assessed as expressing "an eminent *bonhommie*, earnestness, and sincerity which bespoke sympathy and respect— nay, more, secured veneration." Throughout the reports, the *Mind and Manners of the Nineteenth Century* series is treated as a coherent progression from philosophical investigation of the nature of the intellect to commonsense interpretations of contemporary politics and rhetorical usage. Obviously moved by the reports even though he was in possession of the manuscripts from which Emerson had lectured, James Elliot Cabot pasted all the pages from *Douglas Jerrold's Weekly Newspaper* into his "Blue Books," and in *A Memoir* he drew his abstract of Emerson's series from them rather than from the manuscripts themselves (see 2:557–62, 753).

Whether Cabot also believed that the series had coherence as a whole is unclear, but Emerson, as he explained when negotiating with Edward Everett Hale for his delivery of the series in Worcester, considered *Mind and Manners of the Nineteenth Century* to be actually two series in one. The first three lectures, he wrote, constituted a course on the "'Natural History of the Intellect,'" and they required a class with a taste for philosophy and a "thoughtful ear"; the last three lectures were general treatments of current trends in politics, aesthetics, and social and class theory, and, as Emerson told Hale, they "were not objectionable . . . on the score of taxing too much the attention of [a] class" (28 December 1848, *Letters*, 8:197). Emerson's use of portions of "The Spirit of the Times" to close one (or more) of his deliveries of the series underscores his sense of the miscellaneous character of the second half of the series (see the headnote to "The Spirit of the Times").

Emerson's journals show that he had begun work on the three "Natural History of the Intellect" lectures before leaving America for England in 1847. In Scotland and elsewhere in England in 1847 and early in 1848 he read "The Spirit of the Times," lectures drawn from his *Representative Men* series, and some of the miscellaneous pieces he later used in the *Mind and Manners of the Nineteenth Century* series, and while in London and Paris in the spring of 1848 he wrote steadily on the philosophy lectures (for a bibliographic overview of Emerson in England in 1847–48, see the headnote to "England"). Back in America, Emerson's chief investment of time was in a wholesale rewriting of the three

"Natural History of the Intellect" lectures for delivery in and independent of the *Mind and Manners of the Nineteenth Century* series (for additional information, see the headnotes to each lecture below). In fact, within a week of completing the series in Worcester, Emerson began a series of three lectures before the Concord Lyceum in Concord, Massachusetts, consisting only of the three "Natural History of the Intellect" lectures. As reported in the records of the Concord Lyceum, he spoke on "Laws of the Intellect" on 11, 18, and 25 April 1849 (see *Emerson and Thoreau Speak,* 163).

In conjunction with his remarks to Hale and the evidence that follows, the intense effort Emerson brought to organizing and writing the lectures for this series makes it inconceivable that he would have altered its contents beyond abridging the series into five lectures at the Freeman Place Chapel. Indeed, as he wrote to Hale, "these lectures are a study for me, & . . . require that I stay much at home whilst they are on foot" (*Letters,* 8:197). Among those attending the series at the Freeman Place Chapel, Abigail May (Mrs. Bronson) Alcott was inspired by Emerson's delivery of "The Powers and Laws of Thought" on 15 January: "He is abrupt—disjointed fragmentary but you are arrested by a truth which like a cut diamond sparkles and radiates—you forget the rubbishy stuff which covered it in its normal state—the transition from Scenes of Misery to the Banquet of Beauty was too much—my brain reeled with it" (Journal entry, [January 1849], *59M-311 [2], folder 4, Houghton Library). Henry Wadsworth Longfellow, who attended Emerson's lecture on 22 January, characterized the piece as "Analogies between Mind and Matter" (that is, "The Relation of Intellect to Natural Science"), and he criticized Emerson's delivery as having lost some of its individualism since his return from England (see *Letters,* 4:130n). According to two scholarly sources, Herman Melville attended Emerson's lecture on 5 February, and his favorable remarks lend credence both to Emerson's comment to Hale that the second part of his *Mind and Manners of the Nineteenth Century* series consisted of straightforward lectures and to our conjecture that Emerson delivered "Natural Aristocracy" on this date. Writing to Evert A. Duyckinck on 3 March 1849, Melville confessed that he was "agreeably disappointed" by Emerson's performance: "I had heard of him as full of transcendentalisms, myths & oracular gibberish . . . till I heard him lecture.— To my surprise, I found him quite intelligible, tho' to say truth, they told me that night he was unusually plain" (Harrison Hayford et al., eds., *The Writings of Herman Melville* [Evanston and Chicago: Northwestern University Press and The Newberry Library, 1993], 14:121, see also the editors' note on 14:118; and Merton M. Sealts Jr., *Pursuing Melville, 1940–1980* [Madison: University of Wisconsin Press, 1982], 257–61). Regrettably, no comparable hard evidence has come to light to support our view that Emerson repeated the *Mind and Manners* *of the Nineteenth Century* series in Worcester as he had delivered it earlier in London.

The generally positive reception Emerson enjoyed as a person and, through his lectures, as an intellectual throughout England in 1847 and 1848 enhanced his stature as an international figure. This was precisely what friends such as Alexander Ireland, who had organized many of Emerson's lecture engagements, and Thomas Carlyle had hoped this second visit to England would achieve (see Alexander Ireland, "Recollections of Emerson's Visits to England in 1833, 1847–8, and 1872–3," in *Ralph Waldo Emerson: His Life, Genius, and Writings, a Biographical Sketch* [London: Simpkin, Marshall, 1882], 140–81). Gratifying as this may have been for Emerson, perhaps the greatest satisfaction he took in the tour was the occasion it provided for him to organize his thoughts toward the creation of his "Natural History of the Intellect." His three lectures on the subject in the *Mind and Manners of the Nineteenth Century* series constitute the basis of what Cabot once characterized as the "chief task of [Emerson's] life": a formal accounting of "mind" developed through the scientific classification of its properties in a "Natural History of the Intellect," or, as Emerson also called it, a "New Metaphysics" (see *A Memoir,* 2:633; *TN,* 1:134). In part, as Robert D. Richardson Jr. recently observed, the early "Natural History of the Intellect" lectures "represent Emerson's answer to the challenge of bluff British empiricism and the pervasive materialism of modern England" (*Emerson: The Mind on Fire,* 450). To a greater extent, however, they represent a new stage in Emerson's lifelong adherence to idealism, for by proposing, as they do, a poetic rather than, in the strict sense, a philosophical or scientific construction of the mind, they retain all the enthusiasm out of which Emerson wrote on human and mental "Prospects" in *Nature* in 1836, and they anticipate the confidence with which he defended his brand of enlightened natural science against the positivism of traditional science and metaphysics for the remainder of his life. Indeed, we find Emerson's idealism unchecked in the version of "The Powers and Laws of Thought" from which he read in London in 1848: "The conclusion is irresistible that what is a truth or idea in [the] mind is a Power out there in nature, that whilst [an individual] converses with truths as thoughts, they exist also as plastic powers, as the soul of a man, or the soul of a plant, or the genius or constitution of any part of nature which makes it what it is" (see bMS Am 1280.200 [3], {30r}, in the electronic textual notes to "The Powers and Laws of Thought"). And more than twenty years later, we find Emerson a still fully committed idealist: "All science must be penetrated by poetry. I do not wish to know that my shell is a strombus, or my moth a vanessa, but I wish to unite the shell & the moth to my being: to understand my own pleasure in them; to reach the secret of their charm for me. Reality . . . has a sliding door" (*JMN,* 16:251).

As his lectures on the "Laws of the Intellect" before the Concord Lyceum in April 1849 may suggest, Emerson continued to work on and read from the three "Natural History of the Intellect" lectures immediately after he ceased delivering the *Mind and Manners of the Nineteenth Century* series. Over the winter of 1849–50, he rewrote each of the three lectures for deliveries under new titles in the spring of 1850 (see the headnotes to each lecture below). In a journal entry dated 5 January 1850, Bronson Alcott half-dejectedly noted, Emerson "is now writing on 'The Modern Mind' . . . and the current of discourse set in that direction. But the best of intercourse is the intercourse, and the best of all conversation is the least reportable. Our amanuensis is thus unaccountably shy of us, or, by some freak of fancy or another, is absent altogether" (Odell Shepard, ed., *The Journals of Bronson Alcott* [Boston: Little, Brown, 1938], 219). By the mid-1850s Emerson had begun Notebook IT, which he subtitled "Natural History of Intellect" (see *TN*, 1 : 131–85), and there he named his project the "New Metaphysics," declaring that the New Metaphysicians "are to write a collection of Accepted Ideas, a Table of Constants," a "Farmers Almanac of Mental moods" (*TN*, 1 : 134). Although he never managed to put the complete text of his New Metaphysics before the public in print, he nevertheless brought it to the public in three substantial lecture series: *Natural Method of Mental Philosophy*, first delivered at the Freeman Place Chapel in Boston in 1858, which contained four lectures on "intellectual science"; *Philosophy for the People*, delivered at Chickering Hall in Boston in 1866, which consisted of six philosophical discourses; and *Natural History of the Intellect*, which as first delivered in the University Lectures series at Harvard in 1870 consisted of sixteen lectures and as reprised in the University Lectures in 1871 consisted of seventeen lectures (for additional information, see the headnote to the *Natural Method of Mental Philosophy* series and Emerson's *University Lectures*).

# Mind and Manners of the Nineteenth Century, Lecture I: "The Powers and Laws of Thought" 6 June 1848 (1848–1850)

Emerson delivered "The Powers and Laws of Thought" on 6 June 1848 as the first in a series of six lectures on the *Mind and Manners of the Nineteenth Century* before members of the Literary and Scientific Institution in Portman Square in London; he netted £80 from the series instead of the £200 he had expected (for lecture receipts, see *Letters,* 4:80n, 102–3). In America he repeated "The Powers and Laws of Thought" on 15 January 1849 as the first in a series of five lectures on the *Mind and Manners of the Nineteenth Century* at the Freeman Place Chapel in Boston, netting $87 from the series, and again on 16 February 1849 as the first in a series of six lectures on the *Mind and Manners of the Nineteenth Century* in Worcester, Massachusetts, for which he received $138 for the series (except as noted, lecture fees are from the "Account Books").

As he explained to Edward Everett Hale while negotiating for his delivery of the *Mind and Manners of the Nineteenth Century* series in Worcester, Emerson considered the first three lectures of the series—"The Powers and Laws of Thought," "The Relation of Intellect to Natural Science," and "The Tendencies and Duties of Men of Thought"— to constitute a course on the "'Natural History of the Intellect,'" and they required, he said, a class with a taste for philosophy and a "thoughtful ear" (28 December 1848, *Letters,* 8:197). Within a week of completing the series in Worcester on 6 April 1849, Emerson began a series of three lectures before the Concord Lyceum in Concord, Massachusetts, consisting of the three "Natural History of the Intellect" lectures. The records of the Concord Lyceum indicate that he spoke on "Laws of the Intellect" on 11, 18, and 25 April 1849 (see *Emerson and Thoreau Speak,* 163); undoubtedly, he delivered "The Powers and Laws of Thought" on 11 April 1849 as the first in his series of three lectures on "Laws of the Intellect." Finally, Emerson delivered "The Powers and Laws of Thought" under the title "Natural History of the Intellect" on 30 May 1850 as the sixth in a series of eight lectures at the Universalist Church in Cincinnati, Ohio; he received $471.71 for the series ("Account Books"). This lecture has never been published.

Three manuscripts—two complete and one incomplete—of "The Powers and Laws of Thought" are preserved in the Houghton Library of Harvard University. The manuscript cataloged as bMS Am 1280.200 (3), which is complete, is the earliest version of the lecture and is the manuscript from which Emerson read when he delivered "The Powers and Laws of Thought" before the Literary and Scientific Institution in London in 1848.

Emerson evidently wrote portions of this manuscript in 1847 prior to his trip to England, and he continued to compose it throughout the spring of 1848 while he was in London and Paris preparing lectures for the series at Portman Square. This manuscript is printed in its entirety in the electronic textual notes.

The manuscript cataloged as bMS Am 1280.200 (4), which is incomplete, is a revision of, roughly, the first three fourths of the earliest version of the lecture. Emerson most likely wrote this manuscript in the fall of 1848 in preparation for his lectures in Boston, Worcester, and Concord in the winter and spring of 1849. Though incomplete, the condition of the manuscript makes it clear that Emerson read from it; it too is printed in its entirety in the electronic textual notes. Pages from the 1848 version undoubtedly supplied the conclusion when Emerson delivered "The Powers and Laws of Thought" in 1849; thus, the incomplete 1849 version of this lecture is effectively a variant of the 1848 version through page {31r} of that manuscript.

The manuscript cataloged as bMS Am 1280.200 (5), which is complete, supplies the copy-text for "The Powers and Laws of Thought" in this edition. Emerson composed this version of the lecture during the winter of 1849–50 in anticipation of delivering it in the spring of 1850. As it happened, he did not deliver it until 30 May, when he spoke under the title "Natural History of the Intellect" in Cincinnati; however, as a report of his lecture on "Instinct and Inspiration" on 2 April 1850 at Hope Chapel in New York City printed in the *New York Herald* indicates, Emerson opened that lecture with introductory pages from this manuscript of "The Powers and Laws of Thought" (see "Lecture of Ralph Waldo Emerson. On Instinct and Inspiration," 6 April 1850, 6, and the headnote to "The Tendencies and Duties of Men of Thought").

Responses to "The Powers and Laws of Thought" appear to be uniformly positive. The *London Inquirer,* which published a detailed report of the lecture as Emerson delivered it before the Literary and Scientific Institution in Portman Square, praised Emerson's "advantages" as a lecturer ("Mr. Emerson's Lectures," 10 June 1848, 379); a highly favorable, near-verbatim report of this same delivery appeared in *Douglas Jerrold's Weekly Newspaper* ("Mr. Emerson's Lectures," 10 June 1848, 750). In America Emerson's delivery of "The Powers and Laws of Thought" in Boston in 1849 created a moment of inspiration—a "Banquet of Beauty"—for Abigail May (Mrs. Bronson) Alcott (journal entry, [January 1849], *59M-311 [2], folder 4, Houghton Library). Reporting on both "The Powers and Laws of Thought" and "The Relation of Intellect to Natural Science" as delivered in the *Mind and Manners of the Nineteenth Century* series at the Freeman Place Chapel, the *Boston Post* praised Emerson's efforts in the not always rewarding realm of metaphysical speculation:

> There [are] dimly visible, vague, shadowy substances, a milky way in the distant skies, which overarch the realms of thought. The human intellect is the only power we have to resolve this nebulous matter. The acute, penetrating mind is the only agency with which we can work. The constant effort to accomplish this result in the present age . . . displays the powerful interest and the exalted hopes which attends such investigations. There has ever been a deep and earnest desire to separate and

define certain dim ideas of the human mind, which often go under the denomina-
tions of metaphysical speculations or transcendental fancies. It is, therefore, not
unwise or useless, but, on the contrary, there is very great sense and utility in keeping our most acute minds turned in this direction. . . .

   Mr. Emerson's efforts . . . are of the highest value. And in thus busying himself
in looking after new stars and comets in the vast universe of thought, he may hit
upon some discovery which shall overturn whole systems of knowledge and belief,
expand to an unwonted degree the limits of thought, and illuminate with celestial
radiance the inmost depths of the human soul. ("Mr. Emerson's Lectures, *Again*,"
26 January 1849, 2)

Finally, when Emerson delivered "Natural History of the Intellect" (that is, "The Powers
and Laws of Thought"), "Identity of Thought with Nature" ("The Relation of Intellect
to Natural Science"), and "Inspiration and Instinct" in Cincinnati on 30 and 31 May and
3 June 1850, a reporter for the *Daily Cincinnati Gazette* used the occasion of announcing
"Inspiration and Instinct" to explain the paper's failure to report on the first two lectures
and, as it happened, to justify the paper's failure to report on the third: "The last two lectures have been listened to with great attention . . . but they are of too abstruse a nature,
and altogether too comprehensive in their method, to be characterised in a newspaper
paragraph or two. . . . The nut of the *Nineteenth Century*, which Mr. Emerson has been
cracking, exhibits more and more meat, the more he works at it" ("Mr. Emerson's Lectures," 3 June 1850, 2).

   Both Emerson and his executors made extensive use of "The Powers and Laws of
Thought." Emerson drew from the 1848 and 1850 versions of the lecture throughout lecture series he delivered on philosophy in 1858, 1866, 1870, and 1871. Between 3 March
and 7 April 1858, he delivered a series of six lectures on the *Natural Method of Mental
Philosophy* at the Freeman Place Chapel in Boston, of which four lectures were devoted
to "intellectual science"; he received $883.08 for the series. Between 14 April and
19 May 1866 he delivered six lectures in a *Philosophy for the People* series at Chickering
Hall in Boston, receiving $947 for the series. Between 26 April and 2 June 1870 Emerson
delivered sixteen lectures in a *Natural History of the Intellect* series at Harvard in 1870,
and between 14 February and 7 April 1871 he reprised the series at Harvard in seventeen
lectures. Emerson received $8.75 for each lecture in 1870 (Emerson's *University Lectures*)
and $340 for the series in 1871 (except as noted, lecture fees are from the "Account
Books"; for additional information on all these series, see the headnote to the *Natural
Method of Mental Philosophy* series and Emerson's *University Lectures*). James Elliot Cabot
mined all three manuscript versions of "The Powers and Laws of Thought," but especially the version used here as copy-text, for the essay "Natural History of Intellect" that
he arranged for publication in his *Natural History of Intellect* volume in 1893. Edward
Waldo Emerson retained "Natural History of Intellect" as the title for a three-part essay
he arranged for publication in the Centenary Edition of his father's *Works* (1903–4);
Cabot's essay appears as part 1 under Edward's subtitle, "Powers and Laws of Thought"
(see *W*, 12:3–64).

I HAVE OFTEN USED such opportunity as I have had, and lately in London and Paris, to attend scientific lectures, and, in listening to Richard Owen's masterly enumeration of the parts and laws of the human body, or Michael Faraday's explanation of magnetic powers, or the botanist's description, one could not help admiring the irresponsible security and happiness of the attitude of the naturalist, sure of admiration for his facts, sure of their sufficiency.[1] They ought to interest you: if they do not, the fault lies with you.— Sure too of their immense relations, and of the grandeur of their tendency; and yet himself deriving an honest dignity from the nobility of his studies. They lend him a certain severe charm.

Then I thought,— could not a similar enumeration be made of the laws and powers of the Intellect, and possess the same claims on the student? Why not? These powers and laws are also facts in a Natural History. They also are objects of Science, and may be numbered and recorded like stamens and vertebrae. At the same time, they have deeper interest, as, in the order of nature they lie higher, and are nearer to the mysterious seat of power and creation.

They have however a stupendous peculiarity, of being at once observers and observed, so that it is difficult to hold them fast as objects of examination, or hinder them from turning the professor out of his chair. The wonder of the science of Intellect, is, that the substance with which we deal, is of that subtile and active quality that it intoxicates all who approach it. Gloves on the hands, glass guards over the eyes, wire-gauze masks over the face, volatile salts in the nostril, are no defence against this virus, which comes in as secretly as gravitation, into and through all barriers. Every thing is mover or moved. And this delicacy of the substance does not add to the ease of the analysis.

But what most delighted me and, I observed, deepened the silence in the theatre of the College of Surgeons, was, in every instance the general statement,— the statement of widest application. And, I thought, could we only have a list or a summary of these results of the naturalist! Better still, could we have a summary collected from all the departments of nature, and presented in the same rigorous manner, without any effusion of eloquence!

Could we have, that is, the exhaustive accuracy of distribution which chemists use in their nomenclature, and anatomists in their description applied to a higher class of facts, to those laws, namely, which are common to chemistry, anatomy, astronomy, geometry, intellect, morals, and social life;— laws of the world.

Why not? It is high time it should be done, and only now in the contribution of results from so many Sciences could this at last be done. You will not think

1. Michael Faraday (1791–1867), chemist and physicist, known for his experiments with electromagnetism.

it strange that the list of mental laws, of those laws that elevate themselves like towers in our experience,—the Decalogue of the Intellect,—remains to be written, when you consider that we dull men had walked and sailed under the beautiful cap of the sky for many thousand years, and 'tis only the other day, that Sir John Herschel completed the map of the heavens, by going to the Cape of Good Hope, and publishing a catalogue of the stars of the Southern Hemisphere.[2]

For we cannot, in the Nineteenth Century, keep out of view the disproportion between the length of human life, and the number of knowables and doables. A prompt and peremptory rejection of millions of things one might be happy with, if life were only long, or art, short. We grudge the time to lists of particulars which are only new pounds to our load, and would rather have the new principle, which is to animate and carry them. A great library disheartens us. We compare the rolling ages it requires, with the few minutes we can spend. And the circle of the Sciences disheartens, when it only piles new mountains on the already unmanageable mass of experience.

But when any man observes the genius or tendency of any part of nature, whether of an animal function or of the course of winds or tides, or the principle of heat, sees its activity, its limits and return, and at last reads the law, he adds a power; for fatigue he gives me wings; he robs me of no time and prepares for me no repentance. Best of all, the moment it is announced, I see it over-shoot the sphere or constitution it governs, and apply itself to all other constitutions. The highest value of natural history and of the new inferences from geology, from the discovery of parallax, and the resolution of nebulae, is, their translation into an universal cipher, which will be found to be rules of the intellect, and rules of moral practice.

Language is organic, and the languages of nations, it is alleged, should be studied, not one after another, but at the same time, in their natural order, as dialects of one universal speech. In the same assurance of the unity of nature, which usually accompanies a powerful mind, Kepler pronounced analogically from music on the laws of astronomy, and the French socialist Charles Fourier, whose ambition to distribute and name over again, like a new Adam, the whole catalogue of things, required an encyclopaedia of Science, studied profoundly the theory of music, that he might acquaint himself in one science with the secrets of all, and, it is alleged, that of all the properties which he discovered in sound, he found the analogous in other and remote departments, and was guided by his knowledge of the first, to new and important conclusions in the last.

And, at last, it is only that exceeding and universal part which interests us,— when we shall read in a true history what befals in that kingdom where a thou-

2. John Frederick William Herschel (1792–1871) cataloged the stars at the Cape of Good Hope.

sand years is one day, and see that what is set down is true through all the sciences in the laws of thought as of Chemistry.

That is my design, to make sketches on such a plan of the laws of the Intellect, in the confidence that what is truly observed and related of the eye of the world, will be true also of the world itself. I claim the same irresponsibleness and security with chemist and astronomer. The observer has no duties but fidelity. He simply sets down on tablets the height of the mercury, the variation of the needle, the declination of the star, quite assured that these cold records will be found, when a century or their natural cycle is complete, more beautiful rhythm, a more lovely dance than any invention could have combined. It ought not to be less true of the metaphysician.

Whilst I announce with confidence enough this mode of treatment of the subject,—to take away from metaphysics its reproach;—whilst I wish it put into connection with life and nature of recent ages, I am not so hardy as to think that any single observer, unless born with happiest star, can accomplish this, or write the Natural History of the Intellect, much less that I can. What I am now to attempt is simply, some sketches or studies for such a picture: *Mémoires pour servir* toward a natural history of Intellect. In the first lecture, I wish to speak of the excellence of that element and the great auguries that come from it, notwithstanding the impediments which our sensual civilization puts in the way.

In the next; I treat of the Identity of the Thought with Nature; and I add a rude list of some Bye-laws of the Mind. In the third, I proceed to the fountains of thought in *Instinct* and *Inspiration,* and I also attempt to show this relation of men of thought to the existing religion and civility of the present time.

I suppose I need not go about to prove that such a catalogue of mental laws would be found interesting. For none but shallow persons will dispute the attractiveness of thought. I need not remind you of Hazlitt's saying, that he found his literary friendships held out the best.[3] What but thought deepens life, and makes us better than cow and cat? One would not live with his eyes on a tureen, or a champagne-basket; but on Sun and Star, crystal and chemistry, politics and morals; and this because we are conscious that every step into thought ennobles. But there is besides a proper enjoyment, a thrill of pleasure, connected with a new perception. We are fond of thought, as our bodies are of food. Men are as mad for eloquence, though it is so rare, as in the beginning of the world. Socrates tells Phaedrus, (who has procured a manuscript of Lysias, on the subject of love,) that he, Phaedrus, well knows his infirmity, and, that, as men are wont to make a hungry animal follow them by holding up to him a green bough or a wisp of hay, so, whilst Phaedrus holds up before him this manuscript, he might lead him

---

3. William Hazlitt (1778–1830), English critic and essayist.

to the end of Attica, or farther, if he would. I am quite sure, every one will remember some parallel experience of his own.

'Tis true that the highest life interests all men. See what the theatre applauds, a moral sentiment. See what heals all party discords, and melts into one man a breathless crowd,—a sentiment of justice or of generosity. See the interest of men in all ages in the immortality of the Soul, and next to these, and hardly less, those rare accounts which the human mind has been able to render of itself. Ask the bookseller in the corruptest or in the politest capital, 'What books have numerous editions and the widest sale?' Bibles, Korans, Plato's philosophies, Imitations of Christ, Immortalities of the Soul;—out of all lanes and alleys and cellars, out of middle-class houses, and out of palaces, come the customers to buy these. Observe the audience in the theatre when the anatomical professor has something to tell them of the skull and brain of the higher and ascending organizations; and then of the brain in the races of man. Observe the interest inspired by Zerah Colburn, Young Safford, Crichton, Newton, or any transcendant intellectual power.[4] Look at the homage to imaginative power. What charm transfigures to young and old a face and form which is believed to be inhabited by genius.

Conversation that would really interest me would be those old conundrums which at table the seven or seventy wise masters were wont to crack. What is Intellect? What is Time? What is Memory?

The question I would ask of my friend is, 'Has anything been made clear to you?' 'Is there method in your thought?' 'Does the taper of consciousness shed a ray over proportion, or over confusion?' I will not ask if you see your way out of the labyrinth? But do you find a thread? 'Do you see tendency?' 'What is the religion of 1850?' Or, 'What is the mythology of 1850?' 'Tis very certain that if any man had something sure and certain to tell on these matters the entire population would come out to him.

Why then does n't every body turn metaphysician? Why not recover Occam and the schoolmen? Why not rub off the dust from Aristotle and Ramus?[5] Restore the Scotch school and the German school? Give Kant an English and American fame? Leave Boston and Lowell for Cambridge; leave Liverpool, Sheffield, and Havre, for Oxford and the Sorbonne.

Why not? Not certainly because they do not value thought, but because they

4. Zerah Colburn (1804–39), Vermont minister considered a mathematical prodigy as a youth; Truman Henry Safford (1836–1901), American mathematician, astronomer, and child mathematics prodigy; James Crichton (1560–ca. 1582), Scottish scholar and adventurer known for his knowledge of languages and sciences.

5. William of Occam (ca. 1300–ca. 1349), English philosopher who argued that things must be seen in their simplest terms; Petrus Ramus (1515–72), French philosopher who opposed Aristotelianism.

do not believe it is to be got by going in these directions. They have tried such experiments and they have heavily failed. Who has not looked into a metaphysical book, and what sensible man ever looked twice? What was called Science of the mind was not that; but was the weariest rubbish of useless names.

I put it to the Sense of men, if our science of mind is not most unworthy and not on the high footing. It is the last of sciences, and is yet to be written, if it can be written at all. Is it possible that the globe of light and flame—the human brain in which the universe is reproduced in all its opulence of relations, should be the only arid and revolting study? We know, it is interesting; we know, it must be poetic. It must be humanly and popularly unfolded. Other studies, even the physical, are dull, when badly taught. Look at the Science of Anatomy! How often it has been tried in lecture and demonstration, and the whole constabulary force of Boston could not hold a popular audience together. And if a genial experimenter unfolds the facts under the light and in the order of an idea, the whole mass of facts are lit up with a strange charm. Every man's mind finds a home for them, and every man becomes an anatomist.

Be sure, be sure, if the throng in the wharves and thoroughfares of this city, heartily believed that insight and knowledge could be added to them, that the questions which in sane hours they ask themselves could be answered, that an acceleration of the intellectual processes could be acquired by themselves at the colleges; they would drop their bundles in the street, forget their notes of hand, leave their invoices unread, turn about, throng the bridges, and take the college by storm. The bribe of California gold would be cheap. For, I suppose, nobody doubts, they all love power; love possession of the world; position, and influence on the wills of other men; and their search of gold in California or in Canton, is for power, and possession, and influence. And nobody would go about for indirect means to power, who could come at once at the direct means, namely, commanding insight.

For, is it not true, that out of a few heads come the mythology, divinity, law, and social machinery of the world? Whence came all these tools, inventions, books, laws, parties, kingdoms? Out of the invisible world, through a few brains.

Nineteen-twentieths of their nourishment and of their substance do trees owe to the air. Plant the pitchpine in the sandbank, where is no food, and it grows and thrives, and presently makes a wood of pine trees, and covers the sand with its leaves. Not less are the arts and institutions of men created out of thought. The powers that make the capitalist are metaphysical. The force of method and the force of will makes trade and builds towns. "All conquests that history tells of, will be found to resolve themselves into the superior mental powers of the conquerors;" and the real credentials by which man takes precedence of man and lays his hand on those advantages which confirm and consolidate rank are intellectual.[6]

These are really attractive to us, and of right ought to be. Yet these questions which really interest men, how few can answer. In point of fact there is an universal incompetence to lead in this art. All men are on a low equality, and we must search the nations to find an Oedipus. Here are learned faculties of law and divinity; but would questions like these come into mind when I see them? Here are learned academies and universities. Yet they have not propounded these for any prize. Seek the literary circles, the stars of fame, the men of splendour, of *bonmots*—will they yield me satisfaction? I think no city is big enough to furnish the most desireable of all society. In a great town of 130,000 souls, my friend, a man devoted to books and to thought, said, "There is no chair for me to sit down in; no house into which I can go to speak of the only matters worth speaking of." I think you could not find a club at once acute and liberal enough in the world.

Bring the best wits together, and they are so impatient of each other, so vulgar;—there is so much more than their wit,—such follies, gluttonies, partialities, age, care, and sleep, that you shall have no academy. There is really a large amount of unavailableness, about men of wit. A plain man finds them so heavy, dull, and oppressive, with bad jokes, and conceit, and stupefying individualism, that he comes to write in his tablets, 'Avoid the great man as one who is privileged to be an unprofitable companion.'

For the course of things makes the scholars either egotists or worldly and jocose. In so many hundreds of superior men hardly ten, or five, or two, from whom one can hope for a reasonable word. On the contrary, such monstrous egotisms that one wishes to run. Go into the scientific club, and hearken. Each savant proves in his admirable discourse, that he and he only knows now, or ever did know anything on the subject. Does the gentleman speak of anatomy? I tell that gentleman and the Society that it is my jerboa which the gentleman has stolen, and described in the Society's "Transactions." Who peeped into my box at the Custom House, and then published a drawing of my rat?— Or, is it pretended discoveries of new strata that are before the meeting? The professor hastens to inform us that he knew it all twenty years ago, every series, every fossil, every drift, and is ready to prove that he knew so much then, that all further investigation was quite superfluous; and poor nature, and the sublime law, which is all that our student cares to hear of, is quite omitted in this triumphant vindication.

Was it better when he came to the philosophers, who found everybody wrong; acute and ingenious to lampoon and degrade mankind. Alas! from what worlds of

6. Quoted from *The Heimskringla; or, Chronicle of the Kings of Norway*, translated by Samuel Laing in 1844 (see *JMN*, 11:11).

life the excluder excluded himself! And then was there ever prophet burdened with a message to his people who did not cloud our gratitude by a strange confounding in his own mind of private folly with his public wisdom; the ridiculous perceiver with the wise thing perceived?

Prophets, poets, men of culture must be had, at whatever cost, were it only for ornament. Palaces, fine company, cannot get on without them. But what if you have to push aside the man, in order to get at what he knows?

But, if you like it better, to run away from this besetting sin of sedentary men, you can escape all this insane egotism by running into society, where the manners and estimate of the world have corrected this folly, and effectually suppressed this overweening self-conceit. Here each is to make room for others, and the solidest merits must exist only for the entertainment of all. Here they play the game of conversation, as they play billiards, for pastime and credit.

Conversation! Why that is what we most want. 'Tis the highest felicity which human life admits. I have no book and no pleasure in life comparable to it. Ask any grave man of wide experience, 'What is best in his experience?' He will say, 'A few passages of plain dealing with wise people.' When men are met in the spirit of knowledge, which is serious, trustworthy, we come down to the shore of the sea, and dip our hands in its miraculous waves. We are assured of eternity, and can spare all omens, all prophecies, all legends, for we see and know that which these obscurely and popularly announce.

We are rich with earth and air and heaven. Yes, that was the belief of the student. But here again he was doomed to disappointment. Our conversation in society was found to be on a platform so low as to exclude science, the saint, and the poet. Amid all the gay banter, sentiment can not profane itself and venture out. The reply of old Isocrates came so often to mind, "The things which are now seasonable, I cannot say; and for the things which I can say it is not now the time."[7] Besides, what has cowl and study gown to do here? Who can resist the charm of talent. The lover of truth loves power too. Among the men of wit and learning, he could not withhold his homage from the gaiety, the power of memory, luck, splendour, and speed. Such exploits of discourse, such feats of society. These were new powers, new mines of wealth; but when he came home, his brave sequins were dry leaves. He found, either that the fact which they had thus dizened and adorned, was of no value; or, that he knew already all, and much more than all they told him. He could not find that he was in the smallest degree helped, that he had one thought or principle, one clear fact, one commanding impulse. Great was the dazzle, but the gain was small.

In a country college, the professor was asked, why the water of a river runs

---

7. Isocrates (436–338 B.C.), Athenian orator and rhetorician.

faster by night than by day, the inquiry being founded on the allegation, that the watermill grinds more meal by night than by day. The professor went to the miller; the miller confirmed the statement as well known, and said, that, where, as in some places happened, the privilege was let out to different parties by night and by day, those who had it by day, held it a longer time. The professor measured the waterwheel, counted the revolutions, and at night came again, and, on entering, was surprised to notice the increased rapidity of the flashing spokes; instantly conceded the fact, yes, it was turning at least twice as fast:—he took out his watch, and found that the wheel went round in precisely the same number of seconds, and the additional speed was in our deceiving eyes.[8]

Yes, 'tis a great vice in all countries, the sacrifice of scholars to be courtiers and diners out; to talk for the amusement of those who wish to be amused, though the stars of heaven must be plucked down and packed into rockets to this end. And one sees the frivolous old age without resources, without respect, and really it seems to me, that if the habit of derision grows out of the possession of immense wealth and power, as in England, liberty and empire may cost too much. But how is it to be resisted? We meet it at every turn.[9] I knew a good man who died not long ago, and who was, in his lifetime, in a large and cultivated city its most enlightened citizen, who felt this fatal giddiness and bestirred himself to resist it, and said, "Come, let us have a few words of sense at the close of a day." And he engaged a man of science and of social habits to open his house to a select party of learned and witty people with the view of agreeing on the best mode of conducting the experiment. The friends met,—a well-chosen company, representing various departments of thought and learning;—whilst they were mutually greeting, a side door opened to a room, in which,—whether our scientific friend had wished to mark the extremes of the scale,—but the table was unfortunately covered with bivalves, the company passed into supper, and so ended the scheme for securing intellectual conversation in a city of 120,000 souls.[10]

Yes, conversation of wise men, was the masterpiece of nature; the uniting of costly power and experience with its peer. But in real life it is travestied and resembles the men-singers at the opera, the dancers at the ballet; the old religious and national design of the pomp was long since lost sight of, and these poor eunuchs and harlots can utter to the people no sense or sentiment which has not also lost its virtue and force.

8. Identified as Benjamin Silliman (1816–85), professor of chemistry at Yale, by another hand in the manuscript.

9. Identified as a reference to Brook Farm by another hand in the manuscript.

10. In this anecdote, the "good man" is William Ellery Channing (1780–1842), the most famous Unitarian clergyman of his time; the "man of science" is John Collins Warren (1778–1856), surgeon and professor at the Harvard Medical School (see Emerson's use of this incident in "Historic Notes of Life and Letters in New England," in *W,* 10:340–41).

Yes, what with Egotism on one side, and levity on the other, we shall have no Olympus. But there is still another hindrance, namely, Practicality. The scholar defers to the man of affairs, and accepts the manners and estimate of the world, and plays the merchant and statesman. We must have a special talent; we must be somewhat; bring something to pass. Yes, that is desireable, nay indispensable; but must we necessarily make cart-wheels, or gunstocks, or tin pans? The distinction between speculative and practical seems to me much as if champions should tilt for the superiority respectively of each of the four elements,— except in so far as it covers the difference between seeming and reality.

There are two theories of life,— one, for the demonstration of our talent; and the other, for the elevation of the man. One is activity, the busy-body, the following of that practical talent which we have, in the belief that what is so natural, easy, and pleasant to us, and desireable to others, will surely lead us out safely In this direction lies usefulness, comfort, society, low power of all sorts. The other is trust; religion; consent to be nothing for eternity; entranced waiting; the worship of ideas. It is solitary, grand, secular. These two are in perpetual balance and strife. One is talent; the other, genius; one, skill; the other, character. We are ever tempted to sacrifice genius to talent; the hope and promise of insight through the sole avenue of better being, to the lust of freer demonstration of those gifts we have. We seek that pleasurable excitement which unbinds our faculties, and gives us every advantage for the display of that skill we possess, and we buy this freedom to glitter by the loss of general health.

The demands of the practical faculty were never carried to such a height as at this day, in the predominance of the English race with their prodigious power of performance in all parts of the globe. It was inevitable that a people with such admirable hands should overvalue the hand. Especially is that quality excessive in England itself. The English mind in its proud practicalness, excludes contemplation. Every Englishman is a House of Commons, and expects that you will not end your speech without proposing a measure. The scholars not less: the easy sauntering stargazing habit he cannot forgive. And he does not value the expansive and medicinal influence of intellectual activity, studious of truth, without a rash realization. Plato is only read as a Greek book. Ever since the Norse Heaven made the stern terms of admission, that a man must do something excellent with his hands or feet, or with his voice, eyes, ears, or with his whole body, the same demand has been made in Norse Earth.

But the highest service to be rendered is not a railway, nor even a Rosse telescope, nor a patent village, but a touch of divinity.[11] It is certain that a general and permanent enlargement of the power of sight is better than any one act of vision which it makes possible.

11. William Parsons, third earl of Rosse (1800 – 1867), Irish astronomer and telescope builder.

The grandeur of the impression the stars and heavenly bodies make on us is surely more valuable than our exact perception of a tub or a table on the ground. Wisdom may even be said to consist in keeping the soul liquid, or in resisting the tendency to too rapid petrifaction. For, what we really want, is, not a haste to act, but a certain piety toward the source of action and knowledge. And tender and studious natures, after many experiments on affairs, find themselves desolated and injured by them, they retreat on ideas, where they can read once for all the laws of life which they cannot yet enact without profanation.

The very scale according to which the popular voice ranges the employments of men; the dignity of political employment; the general consent that Lamartine, in leaving the profession of poet for the business of statesman, has risen,—only show how ill the office of intellectual man is served.[12] If there were any who could furnish us with thoughts; if there were potentates of the spiritual nature; if the man who knew the heart of the dice, (to use an eastern expression), and the mind of the player; who carried the epoch in his head and heart; "True Thomas," whose eyes the faeries had washed, and said, "Thou shalt speak never a lie"; a pulse timed to the movement of the world, so that all the world lay figured in his brain, and the future lay in clear landscape before it;—if there were such, be sure, one would know or care little about "provisional" or "republican" or any other sort of government. It is in the general vacancy of real employment, that a mania for tulips, or for tea cups, or for coins, or for playing soldier, or playing at politics, or Poniatowski gems or French politics can exist.[13]

In fact, we have to say, that there is a certain Beatitude,—I can call it nothing less,—to which all men are entitled, tasted by them in different degrees, which is a perfection of their nature, and to which their entrance must be in every way forwarded. Practical men, though they could lift the globe, cannot arrive at this. Something very different from their feats has to be done, the availing ourselves of every impulse of genius,—an emanation of the heaven it tells of,—and the resisting this conspiracy of men and of material things against the salutary and legitimate inspirations of the intellectual nature: and, though to make an apology for the Intellect, may seem to be like drawing with chalk on white paper, I must risk the speaking of the excellency of that Element.

Be quite sure, it is always good to know something. Jove is Jove, because he is the oldest, and knows the most. Knowledge is the only elegance, and the uniform behaviour of all beings, of the ignorant as well as of the wise, is a homage to it. He who knows, is calm and secure, whilst vulgar life is made up of awkward shifts of half-knowledge, or alarums and feints to amuse the eye and conceal the want of

12. Alphonse Marie Louis de Prat de Lamartine (1790–1869), French poet and statesman.
13. A reference to the Poniatowskis, a noble Polish family.

knowledge. One would say, that, whoever had tasted this beatitude, would think all other goods cheap. *Quantum Scimus sumus.*[14] How much we know, so much we are. What is life, but the angle of vision? A man is measured by the angle at which he looks at objects. What is life—but what a man is thinking of all day? This is his fate and his employer. The brain is the man. The eyes outrun the feet, and go where feet and hands will never come; yet it is very certain that the rest of the man will follow his head. The history of intellect will be the best of all chronicles, and quite supersede them. 'Tis true there are quick bounds to our knowledge, but we cannot therefore undervalue what we know. As gems among pebbles catch the savage eye brooding over their mysterious lustre, so over truths we hover and muse, assuring ourselves of their high import. We go on hiving thoughts from year to year, without any precise object, but only from an instinct of their intrinsic worth, and in the belief that they are also to have a new value to us one day as our history opens.

Blessed is the region of Thought. "Calm pleasures there abide, majestic pains."[15] There is a certain medicinal value to every intellectual action. 'Tis fine ablution which chastens and encourages. Affairs make us stout and supple, but engage us in low connexions and compromises, and hurt us. Palaces and luxury degrade and starve us, as much as coarse and excessive work, and the society of the ignorant. Thoughts refresh and dignify us again, and restore price to life. Thought, while it lasts, is the only thing of value, and appears of universal and eternal value. Whatever addresses itself to the Intellect, subordinates the senses. The intellect absorbs so much vital power, that it kills or suspends the senses. This is the meaning of the famous sentence, that, "Vice loses half its evil, by losing all its grossness."[16] In vice, it restores,—in gloom and skepticism, it replaces things.

There is no day so dark, but I know the worst facts will presently appear to me in that higher order which makes skepticism impossible. How can a man of any inwardness not feel the inwardness of the universe. If he is capable of science and moral sentiment, the stability of spiritual nature appears. It is better that races should perish if thereby a new principle be taught. And, in his hour of thought, the world, the galaxy is a scrap before the metaphysical power. I apply to it the words of the Koran, "Verily worlds upon worlds can add nothing to it."

It is the interest of the whole human race. We announce in contradiction to all doubt and all desperation the tidings that the best is to be had; that the best is accessible and cheap. Every man cannot get land or jewels, but every man can get what land and money and rank are valued for, namely, substantial manhood,

---

14. "We are what we know."
15. Emerson quotes himself (see *JMN*, 14:115).
16. Quoted from *Reflections of the Revolution in France* (1790) by Edmund Burke.

thoughts self-realizing and prophetic of the farthest future; thoughts, of which poetry and music are the necessary expression. "The true coin for which all else ought to be changeable, is the right understanding of that which is good." [17]

The thinker is as much prepared in the general plan of things, as the cultivator of the ground. The singing Iopas is quite as much in nature as the sworded Hector.[18] Nature, provided for the communication of thought by the planting with it in the receiving mind a fury to impart it. The man of ideas she fastened to every company in which he finds himself, by two hooks, firstly his thought, and then by his power to understand theirs.

To avoid confusion in speaking of Intellect, we must distinguish three things into which it opens.

We can trace three descents, shall I say, from the mind into nature, assuming identity as the base.

1. Truths as thoughts become perceptions of the mind.

2. What is a truth in his mind is a power in nature.[19]

Whilst the man of ideas converses with truths as thoughts, they exist also as plastic forces, as the soul of a man, the soul of a plant, the genius or constitution of any part of nature, which makes it what it is. Like a fragment of ice in the sea, so man exists in the firmament of truth which made him. He is a thought embodied, and the world of thought exists around him for element. The thought which was in the world, part and parcel of the world, has disengaged itself, and taken an independent existence.

But of those elemental organic thoughts which we involuntarily express in the mould of our features, in the tendency of our characters, there is no measure known to us. The institution draws all its solidity and impressiveness from the virulence and centrality of the thought. The history of the world is nothing but the procession of clothed ideas.

And as we distinguished truths first, as thoughts when they were perceptions of the mind, and second, as species in nature, so third, we see them as powers self-organized into the talents of men: Insight, Memory, Imagination.

Only as power, as weapons, as finer artillery, the mechanics and geometry of this fine function deserve study. A small acceleration of the intellectual processes without loss of continuance would, of course, add indefinite ages to human life and a small increase of perception would be equivalent to a vast increase of power.

The guide who knows the way will go up the mountain in night or in snow.

17. Attributed to Plato, *Phaedrus*, by Emerson in a note in the manuscript.

18. Iopas, in Virgil's *Aeneid*, was known for his lyre playing; Hector, in Homer's *Iliad*, was slain by Achilles at Troy.

19. Although Emerson enumerates only two of three "descents . . . from the mind into nature" here, he notes the third, while reprising the two enumerated here, three paragraphs below.

The pilot who knows the rig and working of his boat, will face a sea which would drown any other sailor. The smallest increments of animal, much more of mental power, in the man, countervail the largest accumulations of physical impediment in the enterprise. Thus if Eric the Northman has slept well, and is at the top of his condition, and thirty years old, he will reach Greenland, and then Labrador.[20] But if you take out Eric, and put in a better man, namely Biorn, he makes nothing of six hundred, a thousand, fifteen hundred miles more, and reaches Massachusetts Bay with his ships.[21] In like manner, the practised mathematician ventures on the instant into problems which dismay an unpractised man. The practised advocate quite unprepared addresses a public meeting and dives into the heart of political questions. Yet these are vulgar examples compared with a true insight which plunges into the solution of great problems of human life and society, secure in the habit of steadily reading the laws of the universe.

Observe the effect upon any mind of being comprehended by another mind, and forced to take a leap forward: the first hint, perhaps, of a larger dialectic. He who has seen one proof, ever so slight, of the terrific powers of this organ, will remember it all the days of his life. The most venerable proser will be surprised into silence. It is like the first hint that the earth moves, or that iron is a conductor of fluids, or that granite is a gas. The solids, the centres, rest itself, fly and skip. Rest is a relation and not rest any longer.

And here is revealed to me some neighboring activity, an immaterial somewhat, some new condition of ideal order, which seems to have clapped wings to solid earth, and solid houses, and real estates, which, like so many nimble musquitoes, do exceedingly leap and fly. How many times, once at least in every man's experience, the influence of an earnest thinker has brought to his lips the question of Callicles, "If you are in earnest, Socrates, and these things which you say are true, is not our human life subverted; and are not all our actions contrary to what they ought to be?" [22] And 'tis curious, that a great charter is allowed a certain universal homage and hospitality follows the extraordinary degrees of intellectual power.

Popes, and Kings, and Councils of Ten are very sharp with their Censorships and Inquisitions, but it is on dull people. Some Dante or Angelo, Machiavel, Shakspeare, Hafiz, Rabelais, Goethe, Beranger, or whatever genuine wit of the

20. Erik the Red, tenth-century Norse explorer, founded the first Norse settlement in Greenland; Leif Eriksson later founded the first Norse settlement in Newfoundland.

21. There are many characters named "Biorn" in the Old Norse *Story of the Ere-Dwellers* (or *Eyrbyggja Saga*).

22. Callicles, who proposed that the selfishness of the strong be made the principle of justice in the world, was answered and countered by his contemporary Plato's picture of the ideal republic.

old inimitable class, is always allowed.[23] Kings feel that this is that which they themselves represent: This is no redshirted rebel, but loyalty, kingship. But if the metaphysicians or learned German doctors mutter and analyse a little, the king cries with Diotima, "None of the gods philosophises," and sends the police to him.[24]

I must think this keen sympathy, this thrill of awe, with which we watch the performance of genius, a sign of our own readiness to exert the like power. I know there is a poor-spirited skepticism in regard to elevated gifts. We unwillingly impute wit to the witty, and set out to explain a great genius with the presumption that he must begin, and ought to begin, stupid. I believe in nature; that there are roses and oranges, peach and pomegranate; and that the very finest combinations are precisely the most probable. I must think we are entitled to powers far transcending any that we possess; that we have in the race, the sketch of a man which no individual comes up to; and, *that* from deficiency of certain points in the organization of each, which are found complete in some other. Let those masters who have shown what of highest the human brain can achieve in each function, be collectively the model. Shall we draw the portrait from the mediocre, or from the best?

I know that the claims of the Intellect have been repulsive in much of our recent philosophy and poetry. It has been pathology. The laws of intellect have been the laws of disease. Very fine romances and poems have had too much affinity with the *Pirate's Own Book*.[25] I leave all that untouched. I speak, of course, of the substance in its purity. What we affirm, we affirm of the unadulterated salt. I accept, once for all, the criticism which the Commonsense of mankind passes upon foolish scholars. They see the narrowness of the man of letters,—how small he looks with his wit and his crotchet; they feel that what we want is a new day; Reason coming with the sun in her hand; wisdom solidly invested, general superiority, character, that, after whatever accumulation of thoughts, we are just as poor creatures as at first, for one thought drives out another, unless we rise to a new principle; that wit is an icy light; that a whole Scotland of argumentation does not really help us; and that a perpetually descending character is compatible with increasing erudition and constant intellectual activity. The men are victims of this partialism, self-indulgent; and the curious rich man concludes, when the idealist drinks madeira, that ideas must be a humbug, as he had already found patriotism to be, when they found office a composing draught to the fieriest elo-

23. Niccolò Machiavelli (1469–1527), Italian statesman and political strategist; Hafiz, fourteenth-century Persian philosopher and poet and a great favorite of Emerson.

24. Diotima, reputed to be the teacher of Socrates.

25. Charles Ellms, *The Pirate's Own Book; or, Authentic Narratives of the Lives, Exploits, and Executions of the Most Celebrated Sea Robbers* (1837).

quence. He should rather learn that that which can attach immeasurable distinction through all ages, to some wretched and vicious mortal, must itself be excellent; and true knowledge of the world teaches to hold fast to that which falls not, even whilst we behold the fall of that which taught us it.

The commonsense of mankind, the general sanity, certainly needs to have its course, and is not to be confounded with particular talents and subtilties, ingenuities, or fine insanities whatsoever. Books written by authors under lock and key; *Coups de force;* hotel poetry; poetry of strong coffee; novels or speeches that are exhalations out of the Pit, by dint of ether and chloroform; somnambulant, mesmeric wisdom; are not it. Beware of the muse which resembles a dragon. These gifts are counterfeits and can never bear the daylight. The only muse I know is Health; which is, the timing, the symmetry, the firm and beautiful coordination of all the faculties, so that the ear is finer, and the eye keener, and all the nimble senses catch reports from things which in ordinary hours they do not render.

The world is always opulent; the oracles are never silent; but it requires that the receiver should by a happy temperance be brought into that top of condition, that frolic health, that he can easily take and give out again these fine communications. The trees in my garden are exposed to innumerable enemies, to blight, cold, insects, wounds; and many arts of cure are practised; but the one royal cure is the thrifty tree, which outgrows blight, insects, and wounds.

Every thing sound, lasting, and fit for men, the divine Power has marked with this stamp. What delights, what Emancipates, not what scares and pains us, is wise and good, in speech, writing, and the arts. For, truly, the Heart at the centre of the Universe, with every throb, hurls the flood of happiness into every artery, and vein, and veinlet, so that the whole system is inundated with the tides of joy. The plenty of the poorest place is too great; the harvest cannot be gathered. Every sound ends in music: The edge of every surface is tinged with prismatic rays.

# Mind and Manners of the Nineteenth Century, Lecture II: "The Relation of Intellect to Natural Science" 8 June 1848 (1848–1850)

Emerson delivered "The Relation of Intellect to Natural Science" on 8 June 1848 as the second in a series of six lectures on the *Mind and Manners of the Nineteenth Century* before members of the Literary and Scientific Institution in Portman Square in London; he netted £80 from the series instead of the £200 he had expected (for lecture receipts, see *Letters*, 4:80n, 102–3). In America he repeated "The Relation of Intellect to Natural Science" on 22 January 1849 as the second in a series of five lectures on the *Mind and Manners of the Nineteenth Century* at the Freeman Place Chapel in Boston, netting $87 from the series, and again on 21 February 1849 as the second in a series of six lectures on the *Mind and Manners of the Nineteenth Century* in Worcester, Massachusetts, for which he received $138 for the series (except as noted, lecture fees are from the "Account Books").

As he explained to Edward Everett Hale while negotiating for his delivery of the *Mind and Manners of the Nineteenth Century* series in Worcester, Emerson considered the first three lectures of the series—"The Powers and Laws of Thought," "The Relation of Intellect to Natural Science," and "The Tendencies and Duties of Men of Thought"—to constitute a course on the "'Natural History of the Intellect,'" and they required, he said, a class with a taste for philosophy and a "thoughtful ear" (28 December 1848, *Letters*, 8:197). Within a week of completing the series in Worcester on 6 April 1849, Emerson began a series of three lectures before the Concord Lyceum in Concord, Massachusetts, consisting of the three "Natural History of the Intellect" lectures. The records of the Concord Lyceum indicate that he spoke on "Laws of the Intellect" on 11, 18, and 25 April 1849 (see *Emerson and Thoreau Speak*, 163); undoubtedly, he delivered "The Relation of Intellect to Natural Science" on 18 April 1849 as the second in his series of three lectures on "Laws of the Intellect." Finally, Emerson delivered "The Relation of Intellect to Natural Science" under the title "Identity of Thought and Nature" on 31 May 1850 as the seventh in a series of eight lectures at the Universalist Church in Cincinnati, Ohio; he received $471.71 for the series ("Account Books"). This lecture has never been published.

The present state of "The Relation of Intellect to Natural Science" manuscripts complicates the reporting of their history. The manuscript cataloged as bMS Am 1280.200 (6) in the Houghton Library of Harvard University is the earliest version of the lecture, composed either in 1847 prior to Emerson's trip to England or in the spring of 1848 while he was in London and Paris preparing lectures for the series at Portman Square. In a departure from Emerson's usual practice with his lecture manuscripts, pages of this manuscript are sewn together with white thread along the left margin; however, the intrusion of multiple hands in the manuscript makes it difficult to determine whether the manuscript was sewn together by Emerson or even under his direct supervision. No dates occur in Emerson's hand in the sewn-together portion of the manuscript; however, on the first page of the first of two loose folios used as wrappers for the manuscript, the following occurs centered on the top of the page in Emerson's hand: "Natural History / of / Intellect. / Lecture II. / 1842–3."

In contrast, the manuscript cataloged as bMS Am 1280.200 (7) in the Houghton Library is an extensive revision of, roughly, the first three fourths of the earliest version of the lecture. Once sewn together (a line of stab holes is evident along the length of the left margin), the manuscript bears no dates in Emerson's hand except for "1843," which occurs as an insertion following this title on the first page of the text: "Natural History of Intellect. / Lecture II." Immediately following the title page, a stray folio occurs, one page of which contains notes in Emerson's hand unrelated to the lecture.

Because there is no correspondence in the spacing of stab holes between this and the earlier manuscript, the manuscripts were certainly never sewn together as one unit, and as is true for the now sewn together text, it is impossible to determine whether the revised manuscript was sewn by Emerson or even under his direct supervision. The condition of the pages in both manuscripts provides ample evidence that Emerson read from both at one time or another.

Taken together, evidence of the present state and condition of the manuscripts suggests the following: first, because Emerson evidently read from both manuscripts in their unsewn state, the last pages of the earliest version, along with two pages prior to the point where the revised version of the lecture breaks off, supplied an internal transition for the revised version of the lecture and the conclusion for both versions of the lecture; second, while it is possible that the respective pages of the separate manuscripts were initially sewn together by Emerson or under his supervision, it is a virtual certainty that the final arrangement of the manuscripts as found in the Houghton Library today comes not from Emerson's hand but from James Elliot Cabot's. Whatever his reasons, which may have been driven by aesthetic concerns as much as by anything else, it was Cabot's decision to preserve the concluding pages of the lecture sewn (or, just as likely, *re*sewn) together with the pages of the earliest version of the lecture. While dates in Emerson's hand in both manuscripts indicate the early 1840s as the time of composition, there is no evidence that Emerson was at work on either version of this lecture before the summer and winter of 1847–48. Emerson's misdating most likely occurred in the 1870s: in 1870 or 1871, when he was drawing on the early "Natural History of the Intellect" lectures for his *Natural History of the Intellect* series at Harvard, or later in the decade, when he was organizing his papers for Cabot's review and possible use in publication. On the dating, Cabot himself noted on the earliest version, "The dates . . . seem to have been put on later, & wrongly."

As with "The Powers and Laws of Thought," the first lecture in his *Mind and Manners of the Nineteenth Century* series. Emerson probably completed the earliest draft of "The Relation of Intellect to Natural Science" just prior to delivering it in England and undertook his revisions as early as 1849, but no later than 1850, for those occasions on which he would reprise the three lectures that initially made up his lectures on "Natural History of the Intellect." Consistent with editorial practice throughout this edition, "The Relation of Intellect to Natural Science" as printed represents Emerson's latest version of the lecture. Of necessity, then, copy-text for the lecture has been drawn from both manuscript sources: bMS Am 1280.200 (7) supplies the introduction and body of the lecture as Emerson last read it, and, as reported in the electronic textual notes, bMS Am 1280.200 (6) supplies the final quarter or conclusion of the lecture from pages that served as the conclusion in Emerson's earliest and revised versions of the lecture, as well as two pages—{26r} and part of {26v}—to complete a transition lacking between pages {33v} and {34r} of the revised text.

The *London Inquirer* published detailed reports of "The Powers and Laws of Thought" and "The Relation of Intellect to Natural Science" as Emerson delivered them before the Literary and Scientific Institution and praised Emerson's "advantages" as a lecturer ("Mr. Emerson's Lectures," 10 June 1848, 379); a highly favorable, near-verbatim report of this delivery of "The Relation of Intellect to Natural Science" also appeared in *Douglas Jerrold's Weekly Newspaper* ("Mr. Emerson's Lectures," 10 June 1848, 750).

In America, however, audiences were not as kindly disposed to "The Relation of Intellect to Natural Science," perhaps because, as the condition of its manuscripts suggests, Emerson had not yet achieved complete mastery of his subject. Henry Wadsworth Longfellow was disappointed by the lecture when he heard it on 22 January 1849 at the Freeman Place Chapel. Characterizing it as "Analogies between Mind and Matter," he even criticized Emerson's delivery as having lost some of its individualism since his return from England (see *Letters*, 4:130n). The *Boston Post* was at a complete loss to report on the substance of this lecture when Emerson delivered it on 22 January 1849, but unlike Longfellow, the *Post* seemed absolutely taken with Emerson's performance:

> We listened to Mr. Ralph Waldo Emerson's second lecture . . . as we always listen to him, with admiration and delight. Yet it is quite out of character to say Mr. Emerson lectures—he does no such thing. He drops nectar—he chips out sparks—he exhales odors—he lets off mental skyrockets and fireworks—he spouts fire, and, conjurer like, draws ribbons out of his mouth. He smokes, he sparkles, he improvises, he shouts, he sings, he explodes like a bundle of crackers, he goes off in fiery eruptions like a volcano, but he does not *lecture*.
>
> . . . He is a vitalized speculation—a talking essence—a sort of celestial emanation—a bit of transparency broken from the spheres—a spiritual prison through which we see all beautiful rays of immaterial existences. His leaping fancy mounts upward like an India rubber ball, and drifts and falls like a snow-flake or a feather. He moves in the regions of similitudes. He comes through the air like a cherubim with a golden trumpet in his mouth, out of which he blows tropes and figures and gossamer transparencies of suggestive fancies. He takes high flights, and sustains himself without ruffling a feather. He inverts the rainbow and uses it for a swing— now sweeping the earth, and now clapping his hands among the stars. (25 January

1849, 2; see also "Mr. Emerson's Lectures, *Again*," *Boston Post,* 26 January 1849, 2, for a serious discussion of Emerson's efforts in both "The Powers and Laws of Thought" and "The Relation of Intellect to Natural Science")

What the *Boston Post* found to compliment in Emerson's performance at the Freeman Place Chapel, the *Boston Daily Evening Transcript* took as an invitation to parody. In a brief piece printed on the front page of its 30 January 1849 issue, the *Transcript* reported, "The Boston Post . . . speaks of one of Mr. Emerson's 'lectures;' the brilliant description is itself an exemplification of the thing described" and then, following this introduction, printed a text nearly identical to that quoted above from the *Post* ("Ralph Waldo Emerson," 1). Nor did the mischief end there. On 6 February the *New-York Tribune* published a satirical cartoon of Emerson that depicted him swinging in an inverted rainbow (see Merton M. Sealts Jr., *Pursuing Melville, 1940–1980* [Madison: University of Wisconsin Press, 1982], 252, for additional discussion).

Finally, when Emerson delivered "The Relation of Intellect to Natural Science" as "Identity of Thought with Nature" in 1850, a reporter for the *Daily Cincinnati Gazette* used the occasion of announcing "Inspiration and Instinct" to explain the paper's failure to report on the first two philosophy lectures and to justify the paper's failure to report on the third, stating, "they are of too abstruse a nature . . . to be characterised in a newspaper paragraph or two" ("Mr. Emerson's Lectures," 3 June 1850, 2).

IN THE LAST lecture, I proposed to attempt a simple enumeration of some of the mental laws; I spoke of their commanding interest for all men, notwithstanding the frequent ruin of the inquirers, through one of the vices insidiously born with him like the weevil in the wheat.[1] I spoke of the Excellency of Knowledge and Thought; of the Intellect pure, whose sign was declared to be Beauty and Cheerfulness. I proceed now with that description and have to consider, first, the Identity of the Intellect with Nature and, second, some of the Statutes or Byelaws of the Mind.

The first fact in the Natural History of the Intellect, is its similarity, in so many remarkable points, to the history of material atoms; indicating a profound identity with all the parts of Nature. All seem to come of one stock. What is the interest of tropes and symbols to men? I think it is that; unexpected relationship. Each remote part corresponds to each other, can represent the other; because all spring from one root. Nature is a chamber lined with mirrors, and look where we will in botany, mechanics, chemistry, numbers, the image of man comes throbbing back to us. From whatever side we look at nature, we seem to be exploring

1. On page {3r} of the early version of this lecture printed in the electronic textual notes, Emerson specifies egotism, satire, and practicality as these "vices."

the figure of a disguised man. We still see the old law gleaming through as the sense of a poem in a language imperfectly understood. Shall I say that the world may be reeled off from any one of its laws like a ball of yarn; that a chemist can explain by his analogies the processes of the Intellect; the physician from his; the geometer, and the mechanician, respectively from theirs?

Thus the idea of Vegetation is irresistible in considering mental activity. Man seems a higher plant. What happens here in mankind, is matched by what happens out there in the history of grass and wheat: an identity long ago observed or, I may say, never not observed, suggesting that the planter among his vines is in the presence of his ancestors; or, shall I say, that the orchardist is a pear raised to the highest power? In this mind, the Persian poet wrote,

> "The gardener's beauty is not of himself,
> His hue the rose's, and his form the palm's."[2]

This curious resemblance to the vegetable pervades human nature, and repeats, in the mental function, the germination, growth, state of melioration, crossings, blights, parasites, and, in short, all the accidents of the plant. The analogy is so thorough, that I shall detain you a few minutes on some of the points.

It appears as if a good work did itself; as if whatever is good, in proportion as it is good, had a certain self-existence or self-organizing power. The new study, the good book, advances, whether the writer is awake or asleep; its subject and order are not chosen, but pre-appointed. It is observed, that our mental processes go forward, even when they seem suspended. Scholars say, that, if they return to the study of a new language after some intermission, the intelligence of it is more and not less. A subject of thought to which we return from month to month, from year to year, has always some ripeness, of which we can give no account. Hence we say, the book grew in the author's mind.

Under every leaf, is the bud of a new leaf; and, not less, under every thought, is a newer thought. Every reform is only a mask, under cover of which a more terrible reform, which dares not yet name itself, advances.

The plant absorbs much nourishment from the ground, in order to repair its own waste by exhalation, and keep itself good. Increase its food, and it becomes fertile. The mind is first only receptive. Surcharge it with thoughts, in which it delights, and it becomes active. The moment a man begins not to be convinced, that moment he begins to convince.

In the orchard, many trees send out a moderate shoot in the first summer heat, and stop. They look, all summer, as if they would presently burst the bud again,

---

2. Quoted from *Practical Philosophy of the Muhammadan People*, trans. W. F. Thompson (1839) (see *JMN*, 9:286).

and grow; but they do not. The fine tree continues to grow. The same thing happens in the man. The commonest remark, if the man could only extend it a little, would make him a genius; but the thought is prematurely checked and grows no more.

All great masters are chiefly distinguished by the power of adding a second, a third, and perhaps a fourth step, in a continuous line. Many a man had taken their first step. With every additional step, you enhance immensely the value of your first. It is like the rising premium which is sometimes set on a horse by farmers. A price is agreed on in the stable; then he is turned into a pasture, and allowed to roll; and every time he shall roll himself quite over, adds ten dollars to the value.

Van Mons, the inventor of pears, discovered that under favorable circumstances, and at a certain age, the tree was in a state of variation, or state of melioration; as Newton had already observed the fits of easy transmission and easy refraction in light.[3] And there is not less in the human mind, in certain favorable times and relations, a creative saliency, a habit of saliency, which is a sort of importation and domestication of the Divine Effort in a man; a habit of originating, a habit of initiating action, instead of following custom.

See how many men are near a capital discovery; or how near all men are, for years, for ages,—and only one man leaps the invisible fence, and arrives at it. Bichat remarks, "Nothing is more simple than the fact discovered yesterday: Nothing more difficult, than that which will be discovered tomorrow."[4]

The botanist discovered long ago, that nature loves mixtures, and nothing grows well on the Crab Stock; but the bloods of two trees being mixed, a new and excellent fruit is produced. Our flower and fruit gardens are the result of that experiment.

And not less in human history, aboriginal races are incapable of improvement; the dull, melancholy Pelasgi arrive at no civility until the Phoenicians and Ionians come in. The Briton, the Pict, is nothing, until the Roman, the Saxon, the Norman arrives. The Indian of North America is barbarous. And, in the conduct of the mind, the blending of two tendencies or streams of thought, the union of two brains, is a happy result. And usually every mind of a remarkable efficiency owes it to some new combination of traits not observed to have met before.

All that delight which the eye owes to complemental colours, for example, those two harmonies of colour which our winter scenery so frequently offers, in the contrast of snow lying under green pine-trees; and of snow lying under the dead oak-leaves; each of which contrasts gives the eye a lively pleasure; and also that delight which the ear owes to the complemental sounds,—the beautiful sur-

3. Jean Baptiste Van Mons (1765–1842), Belgian horticulturalist.
4. Marie François Xavier Bichat (1771–1802), French physiologist and anatomist.

prises of music,—delights us still more in the combinations of human life, and gives rise to love and joy.

It is quite easy to indicate these analogies to any extent, as, for instance, in the special cultivation. The education of the garden is like the education of the college, or the bound apprentice; its aim is to produce, not sap, but plums or quinces; not the health of the tree, but an overgrown pericarp; and it is too apparent in much old history of Universities, not less, which will train a grammarian, though it dry up the man. We will hope that the mended humanity of Republics will save us from this peril.

As thus, it is easy to take vegetation as the type of power; to represent the world as a plant, and the particles plants,—and the vegetable function may be easily traced through all parts of nature, and even in the functions of mind, where Freedom seems to suspend the brute organic action, so it would be easy, with the ancient mythologists, and early theorists, to find the world an animal, which repeats in colossal the economy of animation, which has locomotion, perspiration, inspiring and expiring of air and water, assimilates food, and draws to it with intelligence all that suits its constitution. Its particles were animals, and endowed with appetences, and the whole order of things exhibits the analogy of sex. Kepler looked at the world as a single animal which roared in caverns, and breathed in sea tides; and Goethe represents it as sucking in and ejecting water to make the alternations of weather as well as of tides. It was then, of course, easy to represent all the metaphysical facts by animal analogies; and, indeed, so many of our mental words are derived from the animal body; as, grasp, carry, leap, digest, swallow, run, sleep, wake, hear. It admits too the most exact analogy. Saint Augustine says, "The memory is, as it were, the belly of the mind, and joy and sadness like sweet and bitter food, which, when committed to the memory, are, as it were, passed into the belly, where they may be stowed, but cannot taste. Ridiculous is it to imagine these to be alike, and yet they are not utterly unlike."

It would be as easy to draw our terms of describing mental science from the secret activity of crystallization and its self-determined affinity and form; or, from electricity, which lies already in so many minds as the sufficient theory for explaining creation.

And, in general, all the secrets of natural laws are repeated in mental experience.

Or, the like analogies might be shown between the chemical action of bodies and the intellectual chemistry. The affinity of particles accurately translates the affinity of thoughts; and, what a modern experimenter calls "the contagious influence of chemical action," is so true of minds, that I have only to read the law, that its application may be evident. It is thus. "A body in the act of combination or decomposition, enables another body with which it may be in contact, to enter into the same state."[5] "A substance which would not of itself yield to a particular chemical attraction, will nevertheless do so, if placed in contact with some other body, which is in the act of yielding to the same force."

And if one remembers how contagious are the moral states of men, if one remembers how much we are braced by the presence and actions of any Spartan soul;—it does not need vigour of our own kind; but the spectacle of vigour of any kind, of any prodigious power of performance, wonderfully arms and recruits us.

On the other hand, how many men are degraded only by their sympathies. Their native aims and genius are high enough, but their relation all too tender to the gross people about them.

In unfit company, the finest powers are paralysed. No ambition, no opposition, no friendly attention and fostering kindness, no wine, music, or exhilarating aids, neither warm fireside, nor fresh air, walking, or riding, avail at all to resist the palsy of misassociation. Genius is mute, is dull; there is no Genius. We have tried every variety of appliance, and failed with all, to elicit a spark. Misalliance. Ask your flowers to open, when you have let in on them a freezing wind.

This singular exactness of analogy between all the parts of nature,—this copula or tie between all the sciences,—has been and remains the highest problem which men have to solve. You all know the Platonic solution of the Reminiscence. Show us what facts you will, and we are agitated with dim sentiments that we already know somewhat of this.

The mechanical laws might as easily be shown pervading the kingdom of mind, as the vegetative. A man has been in Spain. The facts and thoughts which the traveller has found in that country gradually settle themselves into a determinate heap of one size and form, and not another. That is what he knows and has to say of Spain. He cannot say it truly, until a sufficient time for the settling and fermenting has passed, and for the disappearing of whatever is accidental and not essential. Then how obvious is the momentum in our mental history! The momentum which increases by exact law in falling bodies, increases by the same rate in the intellectual action. Every scholar knows that he applies himself coldly and slowly at first to his task, but, with the progress of the work, the mind itself becomes heated, and sees far and wide, as it approaches the end of its task: so that it is the common remark of the student, 'Could I only have begun with the same fire which I had on the last day, I should have done something.'

It is true, there is a striking, and, if you will, a certain ridiculous resemblance between a man and a woodchuck; between a man and a pineapple; between a man

5. Quoted from *Chemistry in Its Application to Agriculture and Physiology*, ed. Lyon Playfair (1842), by Baron Justus von Liebig (1803–73), German organic chemist (see *JMN*, 10:104).

and a sponge; or whatever natural creature. The gentleman stands in his garden by his vines; gentleman and vine: the one can make a railroad, or a Canton voyage, or an oration; the other can make a watermelon. Each is a caricature of the other, the man of the vine, the vine of the man. A sort of Hudibrastic rhyme.[6] Well, the man discovers that resemblance in all things he looks at,—the sun, the moon, or the salt, or metal, in his crucible. They all mock him, mimic him;—there is the oddest parody always going forward. What can it mean? Every thing he looks at, seems to be humming,

> "For auld lang syne, my dear,
> For auld lang syne!"

Well, here are two explanations.

Plato explains the intuitive knowledge which all souls have of the truths of geometry, by reminiscence. They have all been through the mill before: they are horribly old: and, on first meeting with a new truth, the soul shakes its head with a knowing look, "Old fellow, I knew your grandfather." And certainly, it were very desirable, as we have histories entitled "Adventures of a cent," "History of a velvet cushion," "Adventures of an old soldier," and the like; that we should have the veracious "Adventures of an old Soul." The history of one of these eternal Jews on the high road of eternity must supersede Malebranche, Locke, Stewart, and Hegel.[7]

That is Plato's doctrine, *that,* the souls learned it all long ago by experience; have been everywhere; and are soaked and saturated with nature, and, in short, have quite sucked the apple of Eden.

The other theory of this relation is the *Omoiomeria* (or like atoms) of Leucippus and Lucretius; the *"leasts"* of Malpighi and Swedenborg; that, fire is made of little fires; and water, of little waters; and man, of manikins; drops make the ocean, sands compose its shores.[8] A drop of water and a grain of sand give you the whole economy. A man is a developed animalcule; animalcule is an arrested Man, but animalcule, again, is made up of atoms, the same atoms of which water, fire, or sand are composed, and, on each atom, the whole atomic power is impressed. A violence of direction is given to it, a genius belongs to it,

6. *Hudibras* (1663–78), satirical poem directed against the Puritans by Samuel Butler (1612–80), English poet.

7. Nicolas de Malebranche (1638–1715), French metaphysician; John Locke (1632–1704), English founder of the sensationalist school of philosophy; Dugald Stewart (1753–1828), Scottish "commonsense" philosopher.

8. In contrast to Plato, who believed that actual things were the copies of transcendent ideas, were Leucippus, fifth-century B.C. Greek philosopher who founded the atomic school of philosophy; Lucretius (ca. 96–55 B.C.), Roman philosophical poet; and Marcello Malpighi (1628–94), Italian physiologist and founder of microscopic anatomy.

which, in all its career of combination, it never loses, but still manages to express in a man, in an orange, in a ruby, in a peacock, in a moss: it is still atom, and holds hard by the honest manners and aims of atom.

It is certain that however we may conceive of the wonderful little bricks of which the world is builded, we must suppose a similarity, and fitting, and identity in their frame. It is necessary to suppose that every hose in nature fits every hydrant; that every atom screws to every atom. So only is combination, chemistry, vegetation, animation, intellection, possible. Without identity at base, chaos must be forever.

Identity at the base. It need not be atoms: Modern theory sets aside atoms as unphilosophical, and the first of English physical philosophers, Faraday, propounds that we do not arrive at last at atoms, but at spherules of force. But, in the initial forms or creations, be they what they may, we must find monads that have already all the properties which in any combination they afterwards exhibit. (And this is the fruitful fact whence the sense of relation and the intellectual facts also must be explained.)

It is very easy to push the doctrine into vagaries and into burlesque. Pythagoras and Plato taught it in grave earnest: The comic Poets and the Hindoo priests exaggerated it into the transmigration of Souls who remembered in one state what befel them in another. But the necessities of the human mind, of logic, and of nature, require the admission of a profound identity at the base of things to account for our skill, and even for our desire of knowledge.

Somewhere, sometime, some eternity, we have played this game before, and have retained some vague memory of the thing, which, though not sufficient to furnish an account of it, yet enables us to understand it better, now that we are here.

If we go through the British Museum, or the *Jardin des Plantes* in Paris, or any cabinet where is some representation of all the kingdoms of nature, we are surprised with occult sympathies, and feel as if looking at our own bone and flesh through colouring and distorting glasses. Is it not a little startling to see with what genius some people take to hunting; with what genius some men fish; what knowledge they still have of the creature they hunt, (the robber, as the police reports say, must have been intimately acquainted with the premises,) how lately the hunter was the poor creature's organic enemy: a presumption *inflamed*, (as lawyers say,)—by observing how many faces in the street still remind us of visages in the forest;—the escape from the quadruped type is not yet perfectly accomplished.

I see the same fact everywhere. The chemist has a frightful intimacy with the secret architecture of bodies; as the fisherman follows the fish, because *he* was *fish;* so the chemist divines the way of alkali, because he was alkali.

As we cannot go into the Zoological Museum without feeling our family ties, and every rhomb, and vesicle, and spicule claiming old acquaintance, so neither can a tender Soul stand under the starry heaven, and explore the solar and stellar arrangements, without the wish to mix with them by knowledge. If men are analogons of acids and salts, and of beast and bird, so are they of geometric laws, and of astronomic galaxies. I have read that "The first of mortals was formed according to all the art, image, and connexion of the world.——"[9]

This knowledge and sympathy only needs augmentation, and it becomes active or creative. The love of the stars becomes inventive and constructive. Descartes, Kepler, Newton, Swedenborg, Laplace, Schelling, wrestle with the problem of genesis, and occupy themselves with constructing cosmogonies.[10]

Nature is saturated with Deity; the particle is saturated with the elixir of the Universe. Little men just born Copernicise.[11] They cannot radiate as suns, or revolve as planets, and so they do it in effigy, by building the orrery in their brain.

Who can see the profuse wealth of Raphaelle's or Angelo's designs, without feeling how near these were to the secret of structure, how little added power it needs to convert this rush of thoughts and forms into bodies? Nay, who can recall the manifold creations of his own fancy in his dreams, without feeling his own readiness to be an artist and creator? And we are very conscious that this identity reaches farther than we know,—has no limits; or none that we can ascertain; as appears in the language men use in regard to men of extraordinary genius. For, the signal performances of great men seem only an extension of the same art that built animal bodies, applied to toys or miniatures. Thus in Laplace and Napoleon, is the old planetary arithmetic now walking in a man: in the builder of Egyptian, or in the designer of Gothic piles, is a reduction of nature's great aspects in caverns and forests, to a scale of human convenience. And there is a conviction in the mind, that some such impulse is constant; that, if the solar system is good art and architecture, the same achievement is in our brain also, if only we can be kept in height of health, and hindered from any interference with our great instincts.

This theory is the root of all the great arts of picture, music, sculpture, architecture, poetry. And the history of the highest genius will warrant the conclusion, that, in proportion as a man's life comes into union with nature, his thoughts run parallel with the creative law.

The act of Imagination is the sharing of the ethereal currents. The poet be-

9. Quoted from Emanuel Swedenborg, *The Principia* . . . (1845–46) (see *JMN*, 10:26).

10. René Descartes (1596–1650), French philosopher and mathematician.

11. Nicolaus Copernicus (1473–1543), Polish astronomer credited with founding the science of modern astronomy who believed that the planets revolved around the sun.

holds the central identity, and sees an ocean of power roll and stream this way and that, through million channels, and, following it, can detect essential resemblances in things never before named together. The poet can distribute things after true classes. His own body also is a fleeing apparition, his personality as fugitive as any type, as fugitive as the trope he employs. In certain hours, we can almost pass our hand through our own bodies. I think the last use or value of poetry to be, the suggestion it affords of the flux or fugaciousness of the poet

The act of Imagination is, the sharing of the real circulations of the Universe; and the value of a symbol or trope, on which, as we know, religions and philosophies are built, is, the evidence it affords that the thought was just.

I had rather have a good symbol of my thought, or a good analogy, than the suffrage of Kant and Plato. If you agree with me, or if Locke, or Montesquieu, or Spinoza agree, I may yet be wrong.[12] But if the elm tree thinks the same thing, if running water, if burning coal; if crystals and alkalies, in their several fashions, say what I say, it must be true.

A good symbol or image therefore is worth more than any argument. A good symbol is a missionary to persuade thousands and millions. The Vedas, the Edda, the Koran, and each new religion and philosophy, what else have they been than the expansion of some happy figure?

Thus, "One touch of nature makes the whole world kin."[13] Intellect agrees with nature. Thought is a finer chemistry, a finer vegetation, a finer animal action. The act of imagination is an obedience of the private spirit to the currents of the world. The act of memory is only the right polarity of the individual or the private mind adjusted to the poles of the world; then it easily commands, as at the centre, the past and the present.

It is not strange that the workman should appear in the work. The world exists for the thought. It is to make appear things which hide. Plants, crystals, animals, are seen; that which makes them such, is not seen. These, then, are "apparent copies of unapparent natures."[14]

Thought agrees also with the moral code of the universe. There is nothing anomalous or antinomian in its higher properties, but as complete a normality or allegiance to general laws, as is shown by the moss or the egg.

The same laws which are kept in the lower parts, in the mines and workshops of nature, are kept in these palaces and council chambers. One police is good for snails and for seraphim. Nature is a shop of one price,—*prix fixé*. Great advan-

12. Baron de La Brède et de Montesquieu (1689–1755), French political philosopher; Baruch Spinoza (1632–77), Dutch philosopher and pantheist.

13. Shakespeare, *Troilus and Cressida*, III, iii, 175.

14. Attributed to Zoroaster sixth-century B.C. Iranian religious philosopher (see *JMN*, 9:81).

tages are bought at great cost. It is good to see the stern terms on which all these high prizes of fortune are obtained, and which parallel in their exactness the rigour of material laws.

If you will suffer me to express somewhat mathematically,—that is, somewhat materially,—the relation of Knowledge, Wisdom, and Virtue, I should say, Knowledge is the straight line, Wisdom is the power of the straight line, that is, the Square. Virtue is the power of the Square, that is, the Solid. A man reads in the "Cultivator," the method of planting and hoeing potatoes, or follows a farmer hoeing along the row of potato hills. That is knowledge. At last, he seizes the hoe, and, at first, with care and heed, pulls up every root of sorrel and witch grass. The day grows hot, the row is long; he says to himself, "This is wisdom,—but one hill is like another,—I have mastered the art: It is trifling to do many times the same thing;" and he desists. But the last lesson was still unlearned. The moral power lay in the continuance, in fortitude, in working against pleasure, to the excellent end, and conquering all opposition. He has knowledge; he has wisdom; but he has missed Virtue, which he only acquires who endures routine, and sweat, and post-ponement of ease, to the achievement of a worthy end.

The whole history of man is a series of conspiracies to win from nature some advantage without paying for it. Especially, the history of Arts, and of Education. We need not go back to old Sophists.[15] We have had some signal instances in our own times.

It is very curious to see what grand powers we have a hint of, and are mad to grasp, yet how slow Heaven is to trust us with edge-tools.

We found insuperable difficulty in the old way to obtain the knowledge which others all around us possessed, and were willing enough to impart, and which we wanted. Barriers of society,—barriers of language,—inadequacy of the channels of communication, all choked up and disused. Lawyers say, Speech is to conceal. Each man has facts I am looking for, and, though I talk with him, I cannot get at them, for want of the clew. I do not know enough to ask the right question. He does not know what to do with his facts. I know, if I could only get them. But I cannot get society on my own terms. If I want his facts, I must use his keys,—his keys,—that is his arrangements and reserves.

Here is all Boston, all railroads, all manufactures and trade, in the head of this merchant at my side. What would I not give for a peep at his rows, and files, and systems of facts?— Cuvier is gone, and Humboldt is gone, but here is another man who is the heir of all their faculty, with the whole theory of anatomy and Nature: I am in his chamber, and I do not know what question to put.—Here

15. Sophists, philosophers who flourished in the fifth century B.C., were noted for their subtle and allegedly spurious reasoning.

is the king of chemists, whom I have known so long, who knows so much; and I through my ignorance of the vocabulary have never been able to get anything truly valuable from him.—

Here is all Fourier, with his brilliant social schemes, in the head of his disciple.—Here is a philologist, who knows all languages.—Here is all anatomy in the mind of Richard Owen, all electromagnetism in Faraday's, all geology in Lyell's, all mechanism in Stephenson's, all Swedenborg in yonder mystic, all American History in Bancroft's or Sumner's head; and I cannot, with all my avarice of these facts, appropriate any fragment of all their experience.[16] I would fain see their picture-books as they see them. Now, said the adept, if I could cast a spell on this man, and see his pictures by myself, without his intervention — I see them, and not he report them,—that were science and power. And, having learned that lesson, then turn the spell on another, lift up the cover of another hive, and see the cells and suck the honey; and then another; and so without limit, they were not the poorer, and I were rich indeed. This was the expedient of mesmerism,—by way of suction-pump to draw the most unwilling and valuable mass of experience from every extraordinary individual at pleasure. It is not to be told with what joy we began to put this experiment in practice. The eyes of Lynceus who saw through the earth the ingots of gold that were lying a rod or two under the surface; or of the diver who comes suddenly down on a bed of pearl-oysters, that were all pearl;—were not to be compared to his, which put him in possession of men. He was the man-diver. He was the thought-vampyre. He became at once ten, twenty, a thousand men, as he stood gorged with knowledges and turning his fierce eyes on the multitude of masters in all departments of human skill, and hesitating on which mass of action and adventure to turn his all-commanding introspection.

Unhappily, on trial, this bubble broke. Nature was too quick for us. It was found, that the old conditions were invariably enforced; that, if he would arrive at their pictures by the short cut proposed, he must still be imprisoned in their minds by dedication to their experience, and lose so much career of his own, or so much sympathy with still higher souls than theirs: that the condition of par-

---

16. Some of these figures were identified by Emerson in an earlier version of this lecture: "the man who is the heir of all their faculty" is Louis Agassiz; "the king of chemists" is Emerson's brother-in-law Charles Thomas Jackson (1805–80), who is generally credited with the first surgical use of ether; Fourier's "disciple" is Albert Brisbane (1809–90), a reformer who helped introduce the Frenchman's ideas to America; Sir Charles Lyell (1797–1875), English geologist, but in the earlier version the geologist was Edward Forbes (1815–54), English naturalist and paleontologist; and "yonder mystic" is Sampson Reed (1800–1880), who promoted Swedenborgianism and, through his writings, helped Emerson to develop the ideas of correspondence and organic form. Also mentioned are George Bancroft (1800–1891), historian noted for his ten-volume *History of the United States*, begun in 1834, and Charles Sumner (1811–74), statesman and abolitionist.

ticipation in any man's thought, is, entering the gate of that life. No man can be intellectually apprehended;—as long as you see only with your eyes, you do not see him. You must be committed, before you shall be intrusted with the secrets of any party.

Besides, he found that really and truly there were no short cuts, that every perception costs houses and lands. Every word of the man of Genius, apprises me how much he has turned his back upon. Every image, every truth, cost him a great neglect; the loss of an estate; the loss of brilliant career opened to him; the loss of friend; wife; child; the flat negation of a duty. Alas! The whole must come by his own proper growth, and not by addition; by education not by induction. If it could be pumped into him, what prices would not be paid! Money, diamonds, houses, counties, for that costly power that commands and creates all these. But no,—the art of arts, the power of thought, Genius, cannot be taught.

In speaking of identity, I said, All things grow; in a living mind, the thoughts live and grow; and what happens in the vegetable happens to them. There are always individuals under generals, not stagnant, not childless, but everything alive reproduces, and each has its progeny which fast emerge into light, or what seemed one truth, presently multiplies itself into many.

Of course, this detachment the intellect contemplates. The intellect forever watches and foresees this detachment.

'Tis an infinite series. Every detachment prepares a new detachment. Of course, the prophecy becomes habitual and reaches to all things. Having seen one thing that once was firmament enter into the kingdom of change and growth, the conclusion is irresistible, there is no fixture in the Universe. Everything was moved, did spin, and will spin again. This changes once for all his view of things. Hint of dialectic: Things appear as seeds of an immense future. Whilst the dull man seems to himself always to live in a finished world, the thinker always finds himself in the early ages; the world lies to him in heaps and gathered materials;— materials of a structure that is yet to be built.

But, what is very curious, this intellect that sees the interval, partakes of it; and the fact of intellectual perception severs, once for all, the man from the things with which he converses. Affection blends, Intellect disjoins the subject and object. For weal or for woe we clear ourselves from the thing we contemplate. We grieve, but are not the grief; we love, but are not love. If we converse with low things, with crimes, with mischances, we are not compromised: and if with high things, with heroic actions, with virtues, the interval becomes a gulf, and we cannot enter into the highest good. "Artist natures do not weep." [17] Goethe, the surpassing intellect of modern times, is spiritual, but not a spiritualist.

17. Emerson quotes himself (see *JMN*, 11:12).

You may see it in any home in which the boy of genius is born: it makes him strange among his housemates. He can take what interest he pleases in their interests and pursuits,—he cannot be mixed with them. He holds a Gyges ring in his hand, and can disappear from them at will.[18]

"Many are the ways," said Mahomet to Ali, "by which men enter into Paradise; but thou, by thy intellect, art created near, and standest above them by many degrees of approach." Bonaparte, by force of intellect, is raised out of all comparison with the strong men around him. His marshals, though able, are as horses and oxen; he alone is a fine tragic figure, related to the daemons, and to all time. Add as much force of intellect again, to repair the large defects of his *morale*, and he would have been in harmony with the ideal world.

This inevitable interval is one of the remarkable facts in the natural history of man; a fact fraught with good and evil. It is only those who have this detachment, who interest us. If we go to any nation, who are those whom we seek? Who, but the men of thought. If we go to any society, though of seraphim, he only would engage us, who comprehended and could interpret the thought and theory of it; and that act does instantly detach him from them. That thought is the unfolding of wings at his shoulders.

The poet, in celebrating his hero, celebrates to the wise ear, his superiority to his hero, and announces to the intelligent the lowness of that he magnifies. Shall I say, 'tis an exquisite luxury,—for so I feel it,—the speech of those who treat of things by the genius of the things, and not by the facts themselves? What is vulgar but the laying of the emphasis on persons and facts, instead of on the quality of the fact?

Mr. Prose and Mr. Hoarse-as-crows inform me that their respected grandmothers died this morning, in this very room, an hour ago. I cannot bring myself to say, Alas! No, not if they should both suffer as their grandmothers did. But an engineer draws my notice to the electricity on a shred of paper; a mote may show the secret of gravity; or one of the masters of the world may show me how a feature of the human face obeys a moral rule; and open to me a new scale of means and agencies.

It is not to be concealed, that the gods have guarded this god-like privilege with costly penalty. This slight discontinuity which perception effects between the mind and the object, paralyses the will. If you cut or break in two a block of wood or stone, and unite the parts, you can indeed bring the particles very near, but never again so near that they shall attract each other, so that you can take up the block as one. That indescribably small interval is as good as a thousand miles, and

18. Gyges, seventh-century B.C. king of Lydia, was supposed to possess a ring that made its wearer invisible.

has forever severed the practical unity. Such too is the immense deduction from power by discontinuity. There is a story in the nursery books (which always seemed to me to be a covert satire directed at the Universities and men of thought,) of Velent, who had a sword so wonderfully sharp, that its entrance into the body was hardly to be perceived.— "I feel thy sword," cried *Æmilius*, "like cold water gliding through my body." "Shake thyself," said Velent; he shook himself, and fell down dead in two pieces.

This interval even comes between the thinker and his conversation,—which he cannot inform with his genius.

There is, indeed, this vice about men of thought, that, you cannot quite trust them, not as much as other men of the same natural probity without intellect, because they have a hankering to play Providence, and make a distinction in favour of themselves, from the rules which they apply to all the human race. The correction for this insubordination is herein,—that religion runs in true and parallel lines, through the Intellect, as through Morals. All the powers and rewards of Faith, which we find in the *Good*, hold equally in the region of the *True*. Integrity is really the fountain of power, in one as in the other.

In regard to a poem of mine in which hints were given how the national Destinies would be likely to work out the problem of Mexican War, I remember something like this was objected.[19]

It is the office of the poet to justify the moral sentiment and establish its eternal independence on demoniacal agencies. It is the merit of New England that it believes and knows, that Slavery must be abolished. That faith and the expression of it, we demand of the poet.

In a poem for modern men, in these days of subserviency and adulation, the possibility of emancipation should have been made indubitable. There is a God to propitiate against this duality in Nature;—and the poet, whilst admitting the facts as they lie in nature, owes to that worship of the Best in the best men, the celebration of his own and the reader's faith in the possible reconciliation of things, that is, the bad force of things, with mankind.

This interval or discontinuity is every way a remarkable trait of intellectual action. I pointed out some of the many analogies between vegetation and intellection. Certainly, this is not the least. In the growth of the plant, cell grows out of cell, the walls bend inwards, and make two. In the instinct of progress, the mind is always passing—by successive leaps,—forward into new states, and, in that transition, is its health and power. The detachment which thought effects is the preparation for this step.

---

19. In "Ode, Inscribed to W. H. Channing" (1847), Emerson wrote "Go, blindworm, go, / Behold the famous States / Harrying Mexico / With rifle and with knife!" (ll. 15–18, *W,* 9:76).

The brain and hands are hardly contemporaries. The brain is the ancestor of the man. The Intellect is the watchman, the Angel in the sun, and announces the far off age. All its laws it can read before yet the happy men arrive who enter into Power. But the rest of men must follow their heads; and if I can see their eyes, I will trust that they will soon be able to disengage their hands.

Every truth tends to become a power. Every idea from the moment of its emergence, begins to gather material forces, and, after a little while makes itself known in the spheres of politics and commerce. It works first on thoughts, then on things; it makes feet, and afterward shoes; first, hands; then, gloves; makes the men, and so the age and its *materiel* soon after. Astronomy is of no use, unless I can carry it into shops and sitting-rooms. He only is immortal to whom all things are immortal.

As certainly as water falls in rain on the tops of mountains, and runs down into valleys, plains, and pits, so does thought fall first on the best minds, and run down from class to class, until it reaches the masses, and works revolution. Let the river roll which way it will, cities will rise on its banks.

Nature obeys a truth. The earth, the stones, stir to own their law. See a political revolution dogging a book. See armies, and institutions, and literatures appearing in the train of some wild Arabian's dream. See all the ponderous instrumentalities which follow a speech in Parliament. What is personal power but the immense terror and love that follow a thought.

From the steamboat I like to mark the long wake in the sea, whitening the water for a mile or two astern. I like that the brain of the animal should be produced to a goodly length of tail. I like long hair, I like longevity, I like every sign of riches and extent of nature in an individual; but most of all, I like a great memory: "Stability of knowledge." I hate this fatal shortness of memory, these docked men whom I behold. We knew of Assyria and Egypt, of Dorians and Etruscans, of Macedon and Rome, and Gaul and England. We knew of geography, and natural philosophy, geology, chemistry, magnetism. We knew of poets and painters, we knew of hundreds of private persons, their lives, relations, fortunes. We gathered up what a rolling snowball as we came along, much of it professedly for the future as capital stock of knowledge.

Where is it all now? Look behind you. I cannot see that your train is any longer than it was in childhood. The facts of the last two or three days are all you have with you: the reading of the last month's books. Your conversation, your action, your face and manners report of no more, of no greater wealth of mind. Alas, you have lost something for every thing you have gained, and cannot grow. You are a lead stone put through steel-shavings, only so much iron will it draw. It gains new particles, all the way, as you move it, but one falls off for every one that adheres. The reason of the short memory is the shallow thought. As deep as the thought, so great is the attraction. An act of the understanding will marshal and concatenate a few facts. A new principle, will thrill, magnetise, and new divide the whole world. Yet 'tis amusing to see the astonishment of people over any new fact, as mesmerism. You would think they knew everything but this one, and there is no one thing they knew.

A deeper thought would hold in solution more facts. It is the law of nature that you shall keep no more than you use. The fishes that swim in the waters of the Mammoth Cave in Kentucky in darkness are blind.[20] When the eye was useless, it ceased to exist. It is the eternal relation between power and use.

A man should not be rich by having what is superfluous, but by having what is essential to him like a manufacturer, or engineer, or astronomer who has a great capital invested in his machines. The question is, How to animate all his possessions? If he have any not animated by his quality and energy, let him sell them and buy things nearer to his nature. Such a rich man excites no envy. He has no more than he needs or uses. Give us a deeper nature, increase our affinities, and you add organs and powers. The oyster has few wants and is a poor creature. The Mammalia with their manifold wants are rich men.

The complex animals are the highest: the more wants the richer men. Men want everything. They are made of hooks and eyes and put the universe under contribution. Man is rich as he is much-related.

The more rich, the more expensive, the better. I would have vaster demands made, and rich men shown how to be rich. I never saw a rich man who was rich enough, as rich as all men ought to be. Rich men are powerless and unskilful spenders. Very few understand that art. It needs truly great wants to be greatly gratified. One would like that thoughts should spend! What an apparatus does not every high genius require! No handloom, no watch-wheel, but wheels that roll like the solar system. I think you must give him gardens, towns, courts, kings, earth itself and astronomies, a freedom of the whole City of God.

I like to see rich men seem rightly rich when I see them take more hold on the world, possess Niagara; possess the sea, the mountains.

Every truth leads in another. The bud extrudes the old leaf, and every truth brings that which will supplant it. In the true and real world the judge sits over the culprit, but in the same hour, the judge also stands as culprit before a true tribunal. Every judge is culprit, every law an abuse. Every fort has been taken. Every scholar has his superior. Life is on platforms. Montaigne kills off bigots as cowage kills worms, but there is a higher muse there, sitting where he durst not soar, of wing so swift and eye so keen, that it can follow the flowing Power,

20. See Emerson's letter to Lidian describing the Mammoth Caves in Kentucky in *Letters*, 4:211–14.

follow that which flies, and report of a realm in which all the wit and learning of the Frenchman is no more than the cunning of a beast.

The ground of hope is in the infinity of the world, which infinity reappears in every particle. The man truly conversant with life, knows against all appearances, that there is a remedy for every wrong, and that every wall is a gate.

Everyone's reading will have furnished him with how many examples of the parentage of those thoughts that make the value of literature. Every thought begets sons and daughters. In like manner, the history of politics, of philan-thropy, for a short term of years shows a rapid filiation. From the Society for Abolition of Slavery sprang within a few years a Temperance, a Non-Resistance, an Anti-Church and Anti-Sabbath Movement.[21]

Every truth is universally applicable, thousand-sided. Every drop of blood has great talents; the original vesicle, the original cellule, seems identical in all ani-mals, and only varied in its growth by the varying circumstance which opens now this kind of cell and now that, causing in the remote effect now horns, now wings, now scales, now hair; and the same numerical atom, it would seem, was equally ready to be a particle of the eye or brain of man, or of the claw of a tiger. In the body of a man, all those terrific energies which belong to it, the capability of being developed into a *saurus,* or a mammoth, a baboon that would twist off heads, or a grampus that tears a square foot of flesh from the whale or grampus that swims by him,—are held in check, and subordinated to the human genius and destiny. But it is ready at any time to pass into other circles and take its part in baser or in better forms. Nay, it seems that the animal and the vegetable tex-ture at last are alike. Well, as thus the drop of blood has many talents lurking in it, so every truth is much more rich.

Every law detected in any part of nature holds in every other part. The law of music is law of anatomy, of algebra, of astronomy, of human life and social order. The Greek statues of the ancient temples of Jove, Mars, Venus, Diana, and Apollo are observed to have a family likeness. It is certain that these laws are all versions of each other. The symmetry and coordination of things is such that from any creature well and inly known the law of any other might be legitimately deduced. Palmistry, phrenology, astrology rest on a real basis. 'Tis certain that there is a relation between the stars and your wedding day, between the lines of your hand and the works done by it, between the activity of your brain and its outward figure,—there is a relation,—though you may easily fail to find it. The world, the Universe, may be reeled off from any idea, like a ball of yarn. Just see how the chemist, how the Christian, how the negro, each disposes of it with the

21. The Non-Resistance Society preached passive resistance to authority.

greatest ease, after his own peculiar habit, and finds all the facts fit and confirm his view.

And each science and law is in like manner prospective and fruitful. Astronomy is not yet astronomy whilst it only counts the stars in the sky. It must come nearer and be related to men and their life, and interpret the moral laws. In learning one thing you learn all. Egg and stratum go together, as the naturalist found that the order of changes in form of the embryo in the egg from day to day determined the right succession of the fossil remains of species which had occupied the surface of the globe for geologic ages.

I had intended to add to these a few examples of specific laws; as, that every thought ranks itself; that there is a constant effort at ascension of state; that a certain motive force is the aim of education: a whip for our top. I but shall continue the inquiry in the next lecture.

# Mind and Manners of the Nineteenth Century, Lecture III: "The Tendencies and Duties of Men of Thought"
## 10 June 1848
## (1848–1850)

Emerson delivered "The Tendencies and Duties of Men of Thought" on 10 June 1848 as the third in a series of six lectures on the *Mind and Manners of the Nineteenth Century* before members of the Literary and Scientific Institution in Portman Square in London; he netted £80 from the series instead of the £200 he had expected (for lecture receipts, see *Letters*, 4:80n, 102–3). In America he repeated "The Tendencies and Duties of Men of Thought" on 29 January 1849 as the third in a series of five lectures on the *Mind and Manners of the Nineteenth Century* at the Freeman Place Chapel in Boston, netting $87 from the series, and again on 9 March 1849 as the second in a series of six lectures on the *Mind and Manners of the Nineteenth Century* in Worcester, Massachusetts, for which he received $138 for the series (except as noted, lecture fees are from the "Account Books ').

As he explained to Edward Everett Hale while negotiating for his delivery of the *Mind and Manners of the Nineteenth Century* series in Worcester, Emerson considered the first three lectures of the series—"The Powers and Laws of Thought," "The Relation of Intellect to Natural Science," and "The Tendencies and Duties of Men of Thought"—to constitute a course on the "'Natural History of the Intellect,'" and they required, he said, a class with a taste for philosophy and a "thoughtful ear" (28 December 1848, *Letters*, 8:197). Within a week of completing the series in Worcester on 6 April 1849, Emerson began a series of three lectures before the Concord Lyceum in Concord, Massachusetts, consisting of the three "Natural History of the Intellect" lectures. The records of the Concord Lyceum indicate that he spoke on "Laws of the Intellect" on 11, 18, and 25 April 1849 (see *Emerson and Thoreau Speak,* 163); undoubtedly, he delivered "The Tendencies and Duties of Men of Thought" on 25 April 1849 as the third in his series of three lectures on "Laws of the Intellect." Emerson also delivered "The Tendencies and Duties of Men of Thought" as "Instinct and Inspiration" on 2 April 1850 as the seventh in a series of seven lectures at the Hope Chapel in New York City, for which he received $390 for the series, and on 9 April 1850 as the fourth in a series of six private lectures in Philadelphia ($180.46 for the series); on 3 June 1850 he repeated the lecture under the title "Inspiration and Instinct" as the eighth in a series of eight lectures at the Universalist Church in Cincinnati, Ohio, receiving $471.71 for the series ("Account Books"). This lecture has never been published.

"The Tendencies and Duties of Men of Thought" is preserved in two manuscripts: the first, composed in 1848, is printed in full in the electronic textual notes to this lecture; the second, composed in 1849–50, provides the copy-text for this edition. It is clear from Emerson's occasional use of the heading "Instinct and Inspiration" in the copy-text that this is the manuscript from which he read in New York City, Philadelphia, and Cincinnati in 1850. His notations on the opening pages of the manuscript indicate that he also read from it on 12 May 1866 when he delivered "Conduct of the Intellect" as the fifth in his series of six lectures on *Philosophy for the People* at Chickering Hall in Boston, for which he received $947 for the series ("Account Books"), and again in 1870 and 1871 in his two series of University Lectures on the *Natural History of the Intellect* at Harvard. At Harvard, this manuscript provided text for "Conduct of Intellect" on 31 May and "Relation of Intellect to Morals" on 2 June 1870, the fifteenth and sixteenth in his series of sixteen lectures that year, and for "Will and Conduct of the Intellect" on 3 April, "Conduct of the Intellect" on 5 April, and "Relation of Intellect to Morals" on 7 April 1871, the fifteenth, sixteenth, and seventeenth in his series of seventeen lectures that year. Emerson received $8.75 for each lecture in 1870 (Emerson's *University Lectures*) and $340 for the series in 1871 ("Account Books").

Edward Waldo Emerson mined both manuscripts of "The Tendencies and Duties of Men of Thought," but particularly the second (that is, our copy-text), less the sections that contributed to the essays "Worship" and "Immortality," for the essay "Instinct and Inspiration," which, in the Centenary Edition of his father's *Works* (1903–4), he added to James Elliot Cabot's arrangement of "Natural History of Intellect" first published in *Natural History of Intellect* in 1893 (for Edward's essay and notes on "Instinct and Inspiration," see *W*, 12:65–89, 442–43, respectively; for "Worship," first published in *The Conduct of Life* in 1860, see *W*, 6:199–242, and for "Immortality," first published in *Letters and Social Aims* in 1876, a volume arranged by Cabot with the assistance of Ellen Emerson, see *W*, 8:321–52; for additional details on Emerson's *Philosophy for the People* and *Natural History of the Intellect* series, see the headnote to the *Natural Method of Mental Philosophy* series and Emerson's *University Lectures*).

A highly favorable, near-verbatim report of Emerson's delivery of "The Tendencies and Duties of Men of Thought" before the Literary and Scientific Institution in London appeared in *Douglas Jerrold's Weekly Newspaper* ("Mr. Emerson's Lectures," 17 June 1848, 790). The *Boston Post* ceased detailed coverage of the *Mind and Manners of the Nineteenth Century* series delivered at the Freeman Place Chapel after the *Boston Daily Evening Transcript* constructed a parody of Emerson's performance from the *Post*'s generally positive review of his delivery of the second lecture in that series (see the headnote to "The Relation of Intellect to Natural Science"). In a brief advertisement printed on 2 April 1850, the *New York Daily Tribune* alerted readers that Emerson proposed to advance "the creed held by Boston Transcendentalists" in a delivery of "Instinct and Inspiration" at Hope Chapel that day ("Mr. Emerson's Lecture," 2). A detailed full-column report of that delivery in the *New York Herald* on 6 April 1850 makes it clear that Emerson opened the lecture with introductory remarks drawn from "The Powers and Laws of Thought" before moving into the body of "Instinct and Inspiration." After reporting on the lecture, the *Herald* concluded,

Now, before a man pretends to lecture on intellect and metaphysics, he ought surely to know something of those who have preceded him—of Aristotle, . . . Locke, Reed, Stuart, Hartley, Hume, Tucker, and others. He ought surely to know something of the subject; and if he had intellect himself, and had gathered knowledge from the labors and experiences of others, he would at least be able to state some one simple proposition, and prove, clearly and consecutively, the parts of his proposition when he had stated it, instead of heaping together an insane mass of crude absurdities and follies—loose, silly and unconnected—yet dogmatic, impudent, bold and pretend-ing. ("Lecture of Ralph Waldo Emerson. On Instinct and Inspiration," 6)

As if this summary negative judgment of Emerson's position in "Instinct and Inspira-tion" left anything to its readers' imagination, the *New York Herald* again attacked Emer-son's performance at Hope Chapel and his character in this report on "Art and Literature" in the same issue of the paper:

[The] transcendental oddities and sparkling hotab-potch sentences of Emerson [are] . . . a waste of breath to read, and a waste of time to listen to. It is astonishing what want of socialism and communism appears manifest in this philosopher and itinerant apostle of socialism. His sentiments, thought, and conceptions, have no cohesion—no social relationship—no affinity. They are unsocial, disunited in the extreme. His style is a mournful picture of the state of society such people seek to create—viz.: confusion, discord, incoherence—no union—no hand of harmony— no connection. (4)

Finally, when Emerson delivered "The Tendencies and Duties of Men of Thought" as "Inspiration and Instinct" in Cincinnati in 1850, the *Daily Cincinnati Gazette* announced the lecture but did not report on it ("Mr. Emerson's Lectures," 3 June 1850, 2).


I N RECKONING THE sources of our mental power, it were fatal to omit that one which pours all the others into mould:—that unknown country in which all the rivers of our knowledge have their fountains, and which by its qualities and structure determines both the nature of the waters, and the direction in which they flow. We have a certain blind wisdom, a brain of the brain, a seminal brain, which has not yet put forth organs, which rests in oversight and presence,—but which seems to sheathe a certain omniscience; and which, in the despair of lan-guage, is commonly called Instinct.

This is that which never pretends: Nothing seems less, nothing is more. Ask what the Instinct declares, and we have little to say; he is no newsmonger, no dis-putant, no talker. Consciousness is but a taper in the great Night; but the taper at which all the illumination of human arts and sciences was kindled. And in each man's experience, from this spark torrents of light have once and again streamed and revealed the dusky landscape of his life.

'Tis very certain that a man's whole possibility is contained in that habitual first look which he casts on all objects. Here alone is the field of metaphysical discovery, yes, and of every religion and civil order that has been or shall be. All that we know are flakes and grains detached from this mountain. None of the metaphysicians have prospered in describing this power, which constitutes sanity; and is the corrector of private excesses and mistakes; public in all its regards, and of a balance which is never lost, not even in the insane.

All men are, in respect to this source of truth, on a certain footing of equality; equal in original science, though against appearance, and 'tis incredible to them. There is a singular credulity which no experience will cure us of, that another man has seen or may see somewhat more than we, of the primary facts; as, for example, of the continuity of the individual; and, eye for eye, object for object, their experience is invariably identical in a million individuals. I know, of course, all the grounds on which any man affirms the immortality of the soul. Fed from one spring, the water-tank is equally full in all the gardens: the difference is in the distribution by pipes and pumps, the difference is in the aqueduct and fine application of it.

Its property is absolute science and an implicit reliance is due to it. Why should I hasten to solve every riddle which life offers me? I am well assured that the Interrogator who brings me so many problems, will bring the answers also in due time. Very rich, very potent, very cheerful Giver that he is! He shall have it all his own way for me. Why should I give up my thought, because I cannot answer an objection to it? Consider only whether it remains in my life the same it was.

All true wisdom of thought and of action comes of deference to this instinct, patience with its delays. We are to know that we are never without a pilot. When we know not how to steer, and dare not hoist a sail, we can drift: The current knows the way, though we do not. When the stars and sun appear, when we have conversed with other navigators who know the coast, we may begin to put out an oar, and trim a sail.

To make a practical use of this instinct in every part of life, constitutes true wisdom. And we must form the habit of preferring in all cases this guidance, which is given as it is used.

To indicate a few examples of our recurrence to instinct, instead of to the understanding: We can only judge safely of a discipline, of a book, of a man, or other influence, by the frame of mind it induces, as whether that be large and serene, or dispiriting and degrading. Then we get a certain habit of the mind as the measure, as Haydon found Voltaire's tales left him melancholy.[1] The eye and

---

1. Benjamin Haydon (1786–1846), English historical painter.

ear have a logic which transcends the skill of the tongue. The ear is not to be cheated. A continuous effect cannot be produced by discontinuous thought, and when the eye cannot detect the juncture of the skilful mosaic, the spirit is apprised of disunion, simply by the failure to affect the spirit.

Objection and loud denial not less prove the reality and conquests of an idea, than the friends and advocates it finds. One often sees in the embittered acuteness of critics snuffing heresy from afar, their own unbelief, and that they pour forth on the innocent promulgator of new doctrine, their anger at that which they vainly resist in their own bosom.

Again, if you go to a gallery of pictures, or other works of fine art, the eye is dazzled and embarrassed by many excellences. The marble imposes on us; the exquisite details impose; we cannot tell if they be good or not: but long after we have quitted the place, the objects begin to take a new order; the inferior recede and are forgotten; and the truly noble forms reappear to the imagination; as a strain of music is heard farther than the noise of carts and drays.

The Instinct begins at this low point at the surface of the earth, and works for the necessities of the human being; then ascends, step by step, to suggestions, which are, when expressed, the intellectual and moral laws.

And what is Inspiration?

It is this Instinct whose normal state is passive, at last put in action. We attributed power, and science, and good will to the Instinct, but we found it dumb and inexorable. If it would but impart itself!— To coax and woo the strong instinct to bestir itself, and work its miracle, is the end of all wise endeavour. It is resistless, and knows the way, is the inventor of all arts, and is melodious, and at all points a god. Could we prick the sides of this slumberous giant; could we break the silence of this oldest Angel, who was with God when the worlds were made! The whole art of man has been an art of excitation, to provoke, to extort speech from the drowsy genius. We ought to know the way to our nectar. We ought to know the way to insight and prophecy, as surely as the plant knows its way to the light; the cow and sheep, to the running brook; or the feaster, to his wine. We believe, the drop of blood has latent power and organs; that the rudest mind has a Delphi and Dodona,—predictions of nature and history in itself, though now dim and hard to read.[2] All depends on some instigation, some impulse. Where is the yeast that will leaven this lump? Where the wine that will warm and open these silent lips? Where the fire that will light this combustible pile?

Here are we with all our world of facts and experience, the spontaneous impressions of nature and men, and the original oracles,—all ready to be uttered if only we could be set a-glow. How much material lies in every man!

2. In Greek mythology, both the cities of Delphi and Dodona had famous oracles who could predict the future.

A cold sluggish blood fancies it has not quite facts enough for the purpose in hand. But they who do speak and act, have no more,—have less. Heat, heat is all; heat, or freedom of motion, gives you all the power of the facts you have. That force or flame is alone to be considered; 'tis indifferent on what fuel it is fed. A snowflake will go through a pine board, if projected with more momentum.

Inspiration is the play of the powers at their highest health; it is the continuation of the divine Effort that built the man.

The same course continues itself in the mind which we have witnessed in nature, namely, the carrying on and completion of the metamorphosis from grub to worm, from worm to fly.

In human thought this process is so often arrested for years and ages. Who knows not the insufficiency of our forces, the solstice of genius? The star climbs for a time the heaven, but never reaches the Zenith; it culminates low, and goes backward whence it came. History of mankind is history of solstice, of arrested growth. The human faculty only warrants inceptions. Even those we call great men, build substructures, and, like Cologne Cathedral, these are never finished. Lord Bacon begins; Behmen begins; Goethe, Fourier, Schelling, Coleridge, they all begin: we, credulous bystanders, believe, of course, that they can finish as they begun.[3] If you press them, they fly to a new topic, and here, again, open a magnificent promise, which serves the turn of interesting us once more, and silencing reproaches, but they never complete their work.

Inspiration is vital and continuous. It is also a public or universal light, and not particular.

There is a conflict between a man's private dexterity or talent, and his access to the free air and light, which wisdom is; conflict too, between wisdom, and the habit and necessity of repeating itself, which belongs to every mind. Peter is the mould into which every thing is poured, like warm wax, and be it astronomy, or railroads, be it French revolution, or botany, it comes out Peter. But there are quick limits to our interest in the personality of people. They are as much alike as their pantries and barns and are soon as stupid and musty. They entertain us for a time. Therefore at the second or third encounter, we have nothing more to learn, and they have grown fulsome. But genius is as weary of his personality, as others are, and he has the royal expedient to thrust nature between him and you, and perpetually to divert attention from himself, by the stream of thoughts, laws, and images.

In the healthy mind, the thought is not a barren thesis, but expands, varies, recruits itself with relations to all nature, paints itself in wonderful symbols, appears in new men, in institutions, in social arrangements, in wood, in stone, in art, in books.

---

3. Roger Bacon (ca. 1214–94), English philosopher and scientist.

The mark and sign of it is newness. The divine energy never rests or repeats itself; but casts its old garb, and reappears, another creature; the old energy in a new form, with all the vigour of the earth; the Ancient of Days in the dew of the morning.

Novelty in the means by which we arrive at the old universal ends, is the test of the presence of the highest power, alike in intellectual and in moral action. How incomparable beyond all price, seem to us a new poem, (say Spenser), or true work of literary genius! In five hundred years, we shall not have a second. We brood on the words or works of our companion, and ask in vain the sources of his information. He exhibits an exotic culture, as if he had his education in another planet. The poet is incredible, inexplicable.

The poet works to an end above his will, and by means, too, which are out of his will. Every part of the poem is therefore a true surprise to the reader, like the parts of the plant, and legitimate as they. The Muse may be defined, *supervoluntary ends effected by supervoluntary means.* No practical rules for the poem, no working-plan was ever drawn up. It is miraculous at all points. The poetic state given, a little more or a good deal more or less performance seems indifferent. It is as impossible for labour to produce a journal of Milton, or a song of Burns, as Shakspeare's *Hamlet;* or the *Iliad.*[4] As we say on the railway, there is much loss in the stops, but the running time need be but little increased, to add great results. One master could so easily be conceived as writing all the books of the world. They are all alike. For it is a power to convert all nature to his use. It is a taproot that sucks all the juices of the earth.

This is work which needs a frolic health to execute. In that prosperity, the artist is sometimes caught up into a perception of methods and materials, of fine machineries, and funds of poetic power, which were unknown to him, and which he can avail himself of, can transfer to mortal canvas, or reduce into iambic or trochaic, into lyric or heroic rhyme. These successes are not less admirable to the poet, than to his audience. He has seen something which all the mathematics and the best industry could never bring him unto: and, like Raffaelle or Michel Angelo, it only shows how near man is to creating. To him, a man as other men, have come new circulations; the marrow of the world is in his bones; the opulence of forms begins to pour into his intellect; and he is permitted to dip his brush into the old paint pot, with which birds, flowers, the human cheek, the living rock, the ocean, the broad landscape, and the eternal sky were painted.

It is this employment of new means,— of means not mechanical, but spontaneously appearing for the new need, and as good as the end,— that denotes the inspired man. This is equally obvious in all the fine arts; and in action, as well as in fine arts. We must try our philanthropists so.

---

4. Robert Burns (1759–96), Scotland's most famous poet.

The reformer comes with many plans of melioration, and the basis on which he wishes to build his new world, a great deal of money. But what is gained? Certain young men or maidens are thus to be screened from the evil influences of trade by force of money. Perhaps that is a benefit; but those who give the money, must be just so much more shrewd, and worldly, and hostile, in order to save so much money. I see not how any virtue is thus gained to society. It is a mere transference. But he will instruct and aid us who shows us how the young may be taught without degrading the old; how the daily sunshine and sap may be made to feed wheat instead of moss and Canada thistle: and, really, the capital discovery of modern agriculture, is, that it costs no more to keep a good tree than a bad one.

But *how,* cries my reformer, is this to be done? *How* can I do it, who have wife and family to keep? The question is most reasonable,—yet proves that you are not the man to do the feat.[5] The mark of the Spirit, is, to know its way, to invent means. It has been in the universe before, of old, and from everlasting, oldest inhabitant, and knows its way up and down. Power is the authentic mark of Spirit. It can come at its ends. The mark of a great man, we say, is to succeed.

I may well say, this is divine, the continuation of the divine effort. Alas! It seems not to be ours, to be quite independent of us. What a revelation of power is music! Yet, when we consider who and what the professors of that art usually are, does it not seem as if music falls accidentally and superficially on its artists? Is it otherwise with poetry? Often, there is so little affinity between the man and his works, that we think the wind must have writ them. Here is a famous ode, which is the first performance of the British mind and lies in all memories as the high water mark in the flood of thought in this age. What does the writer know of that? Converse with him, learn his opinions and hopes: He has long ago passed out of it, and perhaps his only concern with it is some copyright of an edition in which certain pages so-and-so entitled are contained. When a young man asked old Goethe about *Faust,* he replied, "What can I know of this? I ought rather to ask you, who are young, and can enter much better into that feeling." Indeed, I believe, it is true in the experience of all men,—for all are inspirable, and sometimes inspired,—that, for the memorable moments of life, we were in them, and not they in us. We found ourselves, by happy fortune, in an illuminated portion, or meteorous Zone, and passed out of it again; so aloof was it from any will of ours.

"How they entered into me, let them say if they can; for, I have gone over all the avenues of my flesh, and cannot find by which they entered," said Saint Augustine. And the ancient Proclus seems to signify his sense of the same fact, by

---

5. Identified as Amos Bronson Alcott (see *JMN,* 8:310).

saying, "The parts in us are more the property of wholes, and of things above us, than they are our property."[6]

Yes, this wonderful source of knowledge remains a mystery; and its arts and methods of working remain a mystery: it is untameable; the ship of heaven guides itself, and will not accept a wooden rudder.

It must be owned, that what we call Inspiration is coy and capricious; we must lose many days to gain one; and, in order to win infallible verdicts from the inner mind, we must indulge and humour it in every way, and not too exactly task and harness it.

Also its communication from one to another, follows its own law, and refuses our intrusion. It is in one, it belongs to all: yet how to impart it? This makes the perpetual problem of education. How shall I educate my children? Shall I indulge, or shall I controul them? Philosophy replies, Nature is stronger than your will, and, were you never so vigilant, you may rely on it, your nature and genius will certainly give your vigilance the slip, though it had *delirium tremens*, and will educate the children by the inevitable infusions of its quality.[7] You will do as you can. Why then cumber yourself about it, and make believe be better than you are? Our teaching is indeed hazardous and rare. Our only security is in our rectitude, whose influences must be salutary. That virtue which was never taught us, we cannot teach others. They must be taught by the same schoolmaster. And, in spite of our imbecility and terrors, in spite of Boston and London, and universal decay of religion, and so forth, the moral sense reappears forever with the same angelic newness that has been from of old the fountain of poetry and beauty and strength. Nature is forever over education—our famous orchardist once more. Van Mons of Belgium, after all his experiments at crossing and refining his fruit, arrived at last at the most complete trust in the native power. "My secret is to sow, and sow, and resow, and in short do nothing but sow."

It is not in our will. That is the quality of it, that, it commands, and is not commanded. And rarely, and suddenly, and without desert, we are let into the serene upper air. Is it, that we are such mountains of conceit, that Heaven cannot enough mortify and snub us,—I know not,—but there seems a settled determination to break our Spirit. We shall not think of ourselves too highly. Instead of a firmament, which our eyes ask, it is an eggshell which pens us in; we cannot even see what or where our stars of destiny are.

From day to day, for weeks, for months, the capital questions of human life are hidden from our eyes; suddenly, for a moment, they come to view, and, we think, how much good time is gone, that might have been saved and honoured,

6. Proclus (ca. 410–85), Greek Neoplatonic philosopher.
7. The expression "delirium tremens" refers to tremors caused by prolonged abuse of alcohol.

had any hint of these things been shown! A sudden rise in the road shows us the system of mountains, and all the summits, which have been just as near us, all the year, but quite out of mind. The inexorable Laws, the Ideas, the private Fate, the Instinct, the Intellect, Memory, Imagination, Fancy, Number, Inspiration, Nature, Duty.

'Tis very certain that these things have been muffled as under towels and blankets, most part of our days, and, at certain privileged moments, they emerge unaccountably into light. I know not why, but our thoughts have a life of their own, independent of our will.

We call genius, in all our popular and proverbial language, divine; to signify its independence of our will. Every man is a guest in the earth, a guest in his house, and a guest in his thought. Intellect is universal, not individual. Wisdom is like electricity. There is no permanent wise man, but men capable of wisdom, who, being put into certain company, or other favorable conditions, become wise, for a short time; as glasses rubbed acquire electric power for a while.

I think this pathetic,—not to have any wisdom at our own terms, not to have any power of organizing victory.

The only comfort I can lay to my own sorrow, is, that we have a higher than a personal interest, which, in the ruin of the personal, is secured. I see, that all beauty of discourse or of manners lies in launching on the thought, and forgetting ourselves; and, though the beatitude of the Intellect seems to lie out of our volition, and to be unattainable as the sky, yet we can take sight beforehand of a state of being wherein the will shall penetrate and controul what it cannot now reach. The old law of Science, "*Imperat parendo,*" "*We command by obeying,*" is forever true; and, by faithful serving, we shall complete our noviciate to this subtle art.

Yes, and one day, though far off, you will attain the controul of these states; you will enter them at will; you will do what now the Muses only sing. That is the nobility and high prize of the worlds.

And this reminds me to add one more trait of the inspired state, namely, incessant advance,—the forward foot.

For it is the curious property of truth to be uncontainable and ever enlarging. Truth indeed! We talk as if we had it, or sometimes said it, or knew anything about it:—that terrific re-agent. 'Tis a gun with a recoil which will knock down the most nimble artillerist, and therefore is never fired. The *ideal* is as far ahead of the videttes and the van, as it is of the rear. And before the good we aim at, all history is symptomatic, and only a good omen.

And the practical rules of literature ought to follow from these views, namely, that all writing is by the grace of God; that none but a writer should write; that he should write affirmatively, not polemically, or should write nothing that will not help somebody,—as I knew of a good man who held conversations, and wrote on the wall, "that every person might speak to the subject, but no allusion should be made to the opinions of other speakers;"—that we must affirm and affirm, but neither you nor I know the value of what we say, that we must be openers of doors and not a blind alley; that we must hope and strive, for despair is no muse and vigour always liberates.

The whole Ethics of Thought is of this kind, flowing out of reverence of the source, and is a sort of religious office. If there is inspiration, let there be only that. You shall not violate its conditions, but we will by all means invite it. It is a sort of rule in Art, that you shall not speak of any work of art except in its presence; then you will continue to learn something, and will make no blunder. It is not less the rule of this kingdom, that you shall not speak of the mount except on the mount; that there are certain problems one would not willingly open, except when the irresistible oracles broke silence.

He needs all his health and the flower of his faculties for that. All men are inspirable. Whilst they say only the beautiful and sacred words of necessity, there is no weakness, and no repentance. But, the moment they attempt to say these things by memory, Charlatanism begins. I am sorry that we do not receive the higher gifts justly and greatly. The reception should be equal. But the thoughts which wander through our mind, we do not absorb and make flesh of, but we report them as thoughts; we retail them as news, to our lovers and to all Athenians. At a dreadful loss we play this game; for the secret Power will not impart himself to us for tea-table talk; he frowns on moths and puppets, passes by us, and seeks a solitary and religious heart.

All intellectual virtue consists in a reliance on Ideas. It must be carried with a certain magnificence. We must live by our strength not by our weakness. It is the exhortation of Zoroaster, "Let the depth, the immortal depth of your soul lead you." It was the saying of Pythagoras, "Remember to be sober, and to be disposed to believe; for these are the nerves of wisdom."

Why should we be the dupes of our senses, the victims of our own works, and always inferior to ourselves. We do not yet trust the unknown powers of thought. The whole world is nothing but an exhibition of the powers of this principle, which distributes men.

Whence came all these tools, inventions, books, laws, parties, kingdoms? Out of the invisible world, through a few brains. Nineteen-twentieths of their substance do trees draw from the air. Plant the pitch-pine in a sandbank, where is no food, and it thrives, and presently makes a grove, and covers the sand with a soil by shedding its leaves. Not less are the arts and institutions of men created out of thought. The powers that make the capitalist are metaphysical: the force of method and the force of Will makes trade, and builds towns.

"All conquests that history tells of, will be found to resolve themselves into the superior mental powers of the conquerors:" and the real credentials by which man takes precedence of man, and lays his hand on those advantages which confirm and consolidate rank, are intellectual and moral.

The men are all drugged with this liquor of thought, and thereby secured to their several works. It is easy to see that the races of men rise out of the ground preoccupied with a thought which rules them, divided beforehand into parties ready armed and angry to fight for they know not what. They all share to the rankest Philistines the same belief. The haberdashers, and brokers, and attorneys are idealists and only differ in the amount and clearness of their perception. Whether Whiggery, or Chartism, or Church, or a dream of Wealth, fashioned all these resolute bankers, merchants, lawyers, landlords who administer the world of today, as leaves and wood are made of air: an idea fashioned them, and one related to yours.[8]

A stronger idea will subordinate them. Yours, if you see it to be nearer and truer. A man of more comprehensive view can always see with good humour the seeming opposition of a powerful talent which has less comprehension. 'Tis a strong paddy, who, with his burly elbows, is making place and way for him. Trust entirely the thought. Lean upon it; it will bear up thee and thine, and society, and systems, like a scrap of down.

The world is intellectual; and the man is. Every man comes into nature impressed with his own polarity or bias, in obeying which, his power, opportunity, and happiness, reside. He is strong by his genius, gets all his knowledge only through that aperture. Society is unanimous against his project. He never hears it as he knows it. Nevertheless he is right; right against the whole world. All excellence is only an inflamed personality. If he is wrong, increase his determination to his aim, and he is right again.

What is the use of trying to be somewhat else? He has a facility, which costs him nothing, to do somewhat admirable to all men. He is strong by his genius, and happy also by the same. The secret of power is delight in one's work. He takes delight in working, not in having wrought. His workbench he finds everywhere, and his workbench is home, education, power, and patron. Whilst he serves his genius, he works when he stands, when he sits, when he eats, and when he sleeps. The dream which now or lately floated before the eyes of the French nation,— that, every man shall do that which of all things he prefers, and shall have three francs a day for doing that,—is the real law of the world; and all good labour, by which society is really served, will be found to be of that kind.[9]

8. Philistines, people interested in materialism and disdainful of intellectual pursuits; Whigs, conservative politicians, often representing monied interests, who opposed Andrew Jackson; Chartists, English reformers who promoted better conditions for the working classes.

9. Emerson is referring to the revolution in France that in 1848 replaced the monarchy with a republican form of government.

All we ask of any man is to be contented with his own work. An enthusiastic workman dignifies his art and arrives at results. Him we account the fortunate man, whose determination to his aim is sufficiently strong to leave him no doubt.

I am aware that nature does not always pronounce early on this point. Many men are very slow in finding their vocation. It does not at once appear what they were made for. Nature has not made up her mind in regard to her young friend: and when this happens, we feel life to be some failure. Life is not quite desireable to themselves. It uniformly suggests in the conversation of men the presumption of continued life, of which the present is only one term. We must suppose Life to such is a kind of hybernation, and 'tis to be hoped that they will be very fat and energetic in the spring. They ripen too slowly than that the determination should appear in this brief life. As with our Catawbas and Isabellas at the eastward, the season is not quite long enough for them.

This determination of Genius in each is so strong, that, if it were not guarded with powerful checks, it would have made society impossible. As it is, men are best and most, by themselves: and always work in society with great loss of power. They are not timed each to the other: they cannot keep step; and life requires too much compromise.

Men go through the world each musing on a great fable dramatically pictured and rehearsed before him. If you speak to the man, he turns his eyes from his own scene, and, slower or faster, endeavours to comprehend what you say. When you have done speaking, he returns to his private music. Men generally attempt, early in life, to make their brothers, afterwards their wives, acquainted with what is going forward in their private theatre; but they soon desist from the attempt on finding that they also have some farce, or, perhaps some ear- and heart-rending tragedy forward on their secret boards, on which they are intent; and all parties acquiesce, at last, each in a private box, with the whole play performed before himself *solus*.

The source of thought evolves its own rules, its own virtues, its own religion. Its whole equipment is new, and it can only fight with its own weapons. Is there only one courage, one gratitude, one benevolence? No, but as many as there are men. Every constitution has its own health and diseases. A new constitution, a new fever, say the physicians. I think the reason why men fail in their conflicts, is, because they wear other armour than their own. Each must have all, but by no means need he have it in your form. Each must be rich, but not only in money or lands; he may have, instead, the riches of riches,—creative supplying power. He must be armed, not necessarily with musket and pike. Better, if, seeing these, he can feel that he has better muskets and pikes in his energy and constancy. To every creature its own weapon, however skilfully concealed from himself a good while.

His work, his work, is his sword and his shield. Let him accuse no one; let him injure no one. The way to mend the bad world, is to create the right world. The way to conquer the foreign workman, is, not surely to kill him; but every blow of the hammer, every blast of the forge in your own workshop, is conquest.

Within this magical power derived from fidelity to his nature, he adds also the mechanical force of perseverance. He shall keep the law which shall keep him. He shall work in the dark; work in gloom, and sorrow, and faintness. If he is insulted, he can be insulted. All his affair is, not to insult. In persistency, he knows the strength of nature and the immortality of man to lie.

A man must do the work with that faculty he has now. But that faculty is the accumulation of past days. That which you have done long ago, helps you now. No rival can rival backwards. What you have learned and done, is safe and fruitful. Work and learn in evil days, in barren days, in days of depression and calamity. "There is but one only liberator in this life from the daemons that invade us, and that is, Endeavour, earnest, entire, perennial endeavour." Partial activity and occasional impulses set free some part or limb for a short time.

Follow this leading, nor ask too curiously whither. To follow it, is thy part. And what if it lead, as men say, to an excess, to partiality, to individualism: Follow it still. His art shall suffice this artist, his flame this lover, his inspiration this poet. The artist must be sacrificed. Take it sadly home to thy heart,—the artist must pay for his learning and doing with his life. The old Herschel must choose between the night and the day, and draw on his nightcap when the sun rises, and defend his eyes for nocturnal use. Michel Angelo must paint Sistine ceilings, till he can no longer read, except by holding the book over his head. Nature deals with all her children so. See the poor flies, lately so wanton, now fixed to the wall or the tree, exhausted and presently blown away. Men likewise: they put their lives into their deed. What is a man good for, without enthusiasm, and what is enthusiasm, but this daring of ruin for its object? There are thoughts beyond the reaches of our souls. We are not the less drawn to them. The moth flies into the flame of the lamp; Archimedes, Socrates, Behmen, Bruno, Pascal, Swedenborg, must solve the problems, though they be crazed or killed.[10]

It is to be considered that the one secret of power intellectual or physical is concentration, and that all concentration involves a certain narrowness. It is a law of nature that he who looks at one thing must turn his eyes from every other thing in the universe. The horse goes better with blinders, and the man for dedication to his task. And if you ask what compensation is made for the inevitable narrowness: Why this, that, in learning one thing well, you learn all things. Things are coordinated.

10. Archimedes (ca. 287–212 B.C.), Greek mathematician and engineer; Giordano Bruno (ca. 1548–1600), Italian pantheistic philosopher; Blaise Pascal (1623–62), French geometrician.

There is a probity of the Intellect, which demands, if possible, virtues more costly than any Bible has consecrated. It consists in an absolute devotion to truth, founded in a faith in truth. You will say, this is quite axiomatic and a little too true. I do not find it an agreed point. Literary men, for the most part, have a settled despair as to the realization of ideas in their own times. There is in all students a distrust of truth, a timidity about affirming it, a wish to patronize Providence. We lie for the right. We affect a greater hope than we feel. We disown our debt to moral evil.

Society does not love its unmaskers. The virtue of the Intellect is its own, as its courage is of its own kind; and, at last, it will be justified, though for the time it seem hostile to that which it most reveres.

Truth is our only armour in all passages of life and death. The words you spoke are forgotten, but the part you took is organized into the body of the universe. I will speak the truth in my heart, or think the truth against what is called God.

Ignorant people confound the reverence for the intuitions with egotism. This confusion of thought in our vulgar theology argues great inexperience of that which is life to know. There is no confusion in the things themselves. True elevation of mind consists in the perception of law. Its dignity and joy consist in being under a law. Its goodness is the most generous extension of our private interests, the extension of our private interests to the dignity and generosity of ideas. Nothing seems to me so excellent as a belief in the laws. It communicates dignity and, as it were, an asylum in temples, to the loyal soul.

I confess that every thing connected with our personality fails. Nature never spares the individual. We are always baulked of a complete success. No prosperity is promised to that. We have our indemnity only in the sure success of that to which we belong. *That, that* is immortal, and we only through that.

One polarity is impressed on the Universe and on its particles. As the whole has its law, so each individual has his genius. Obedience to its genius, to speak a little scholastically, is the particular of faith; perception that the tendency of the whole is to the benefit of the individual, is the universal of faith.

The soul stipulates for no private good. That which is private, I see not to be good. "If Truth live, I live; if Justice live, I live," said one of the old saints, and the Chinese Confucius said, "Put men to death by the principles which have for their object the preservation of life, and they will not grumble."

Do not truck for your private immortality. If immortality, in the sense in which you seek it, is best, you shall be immortal. If it is up to the dignity of that order of things you know, it is secure. The sky, the sea, the plants, the rocks, astronomy, chemistry, keep their word. Morals and the genius of humanity will also. In short, the whole moral of modern science is the transference of that trust which is felt in Nature's admired arrangements, to the sphere of freedom and of rational life.

But clear your notion of Immortality. Let the life you would continue into immensity, not be something you are ashamed of when it is only a few years long,— a few wearisome personalities, and dull trifles, repeated already much too often. It is a life a good man would not turn on his heel to save. What is called Religion effeminates and demoralizes; such as you are, the gods themselves could not help you. Men are too often unfit to live, from their obvious inequality to their own necessities; or, they suffer from politics, or bad neighbours, or from sickness,— and they would gladly know that they were to be dismissed from the duties of life. But the Intellect asks of these, How will Death help them? These are not dismissed, when they die. You shall not wish for death, out of pusillanimity. The weight of the Universe is pressed down on the shoulders of each slave to hold him to his task. The only path of escape known in all the world of God is performance. You must do your work, before you shall be released.

Men talk as if Victory were something doubtful. Work is Victory. Wherever work is done, victory is obtained. There is no chance, and no blanks: All draw prizes. You want but one verdict. If you have your own, you are secure of the rest. And yet, if witnesses were wanted, witnesses are near. I cannot see, without awe, that no man thinks alone, and no man acts alone; but the divine assessors, who came up with him into life, now under one disguise, now another, like a police in citizens' clothes, walk with him step by step through all the kingdom of time.

These studies seem to me to derive an importance from their bearing on the universal question of modern times, the question of Religion.

We live in a transition period, when the old faiths which have educated, and comforted, and legislated for nations, and not only so, but have made the nations, seem to have spent their force, and to be comparatively powerless on the public and the private mind of Europe and America. Society is full now of fancy faiths, of gentlemen and of nations in search of religions. It seems to me, as if men stood craving a more stringent creed than any of the pale and enervating systems to which they had recourse. The Turk who believes that his doom is written on the iron leaf on the moment when he entered the world, and that he cannot alter it, rushes on the enemy's sword with undivided will. The Buddhist who finds gods masked in all his friends and enemies, and reads the issue of the conflict beforehand in the rank of the actors, is calm. The old Greek was respectable, and we are not yet able to forget his dramas,—who found the genius of tragedy in the conflict between Destiny and the strong *should,* and not like the moderns, in the weak *would.* And the natural remedy against this miscellany of knowledge and aim, this desultory universality of ours, this immense ground-juniper falling abroad, and not gathered up into any columnar tree, is, to substitute realism, for sentimentalism; a recognition of the simple and terrible laws, which, seen or unseen—(seen as they are, or falsely, vicariously, and personally seen)—pervade and govern.

The religion which is to guide and satisfy the present and coming ages, whatever else it be, must be intellectual. The scientific mind must have a faith which is science. "There are two things," said Mahomet, "which I abhor, the learned in his infidelities, and the fool in his devotions." Our times are very impatient of both, and specially of the last. Let us have nothing now which is not its own evidence. There is surely enough for the heart and the imagination. Our books are full of generous biographies of saints, who knew not that they were such; of men and of women who lived for the benefit and healing of nature. But one fact I read in them all,—that, there is a religion which survives immutably all persons and fashions, and is worshipped and pronounced with emphasis again and again by some holy person;—and men, with their weak incapacity for principles, and their passion for persons, have run mad for the pronouncer, and forgot the religion.

But there is surely enough for the heart and the imagination in the religion itself. Let us not be pestered with assertions and half-truths, with emotions and snuffle: "Surely all that is simple is sufficient for all that is good."

There will be a new Church founded on moral science; at first, cold and naked, a babe in a manger, again; the algebra and mathematics of ethical law; the church of men to come; without shawms, or psaltery, or sackbut; but it will have heaven and earth for its beams and rafters; all science for symbol and illustration: it will fast enough gather beauty, music, picture, poetry. Was never Stoicism so stern and exigent as this shall be.[11] It shall send man home to his central solitude, shame these social supplicating manners, and make him know, that, much of the time, he must have himself to his friend. He shall expect no cooperation; he shall walk with no companion. The nameless Thought, the nameless Power, the superpersonal Heart,—I wish him to repose alone on that.

He needs only his own verdict. No good fame can help, no bad fame can hurt him. The Laws are his Consolers: The good Laws themselves are alive: They know if he has kept them. They animate him with the consciousness of great duty and an endless horizon. Honour and fortune are to him who always recognizes the neighbourhood of the great, always feels himself in the presence of high causes. The joy of knowledge, the late discovery that the veil which hid all things from him is really transparent, transparent everywhere to pure eyes, and the heart of trust which every perception fortifies,—renew life for him. He finds, that events spring from the same root as persons; the Universe understands itself, and all the parts play with a sure harmony.

---

11. Stoicism refers to the philosophical school founded in 308 B.C. known for a belief in submitting to necessity.

# "England"
# 5 December 1848
# (1848–1852)

Emerson first delivered "England" under the title "Why England is England" on 5 December 1848 before the Concord Lyceum in Concord, Massachusetts. Two days later, on 7 December 1848, he delivered the lecture as "England" before the Newport Lyceum in Newport, Rhode Island, and received $20. He repeated "England" on 25 December 1848 before the New Bedford Lyceum in New Bedford, Massachusetts, receiving $20; on 27 December 1848 as the first of two lectures before the Mercantile Library Association at Tremont Temple in Boston ($100 for the two lectures); on 20 February 1849 as the first of two lectures in Framingham, Massachusetts ($25 for the two lectures); on 7 March 1849 before the Cambridge Lyceum in Cambridge, Massachusetts ($15); on 22 January 1850 as the first of two lectures before the Mercantile Library Association at Clinton Hall in New York City ($100 for the two lectures); on 26 March 1850 as the fifth in a series of seven lectures at the Hope Chapel in New York City ($390 for the series); on 29 March 1850 as the third in a series of three private lectures at Female Academy Hall in Brooklyn, New York ($116 for the three lectures); on 3 April 1850 as the first in a series of six private lectures in Philadelphia ($180.46 for the series); again, because of inclement weather on 3 April, on 11 April 1850 as the sixth and final lecture in Philadelphia; on 16 May 1850 before the Library Association in Cleveland, Ohio; on 27 May 1850 as the fourth in a series of eight lectures at the Universalist Church in Cincinnati, Ohio ($471.71 for the series); on 6 February 1851 before the Atheneum and Mechanics' Association in Rochester, New York; on 10 February 1851 before the Young Men's Association in Buffalo, New York ($75); on 20 March 1851 as the first in a series of six lectures on the *Conduct of Life* before the Young Men's Mercantile Library Association in Pittsburgh ($240 for the series); and on 19 April 1852 as the first in a series of six lectures on the *Conduct of Life* before the Mercantile Library Association at Bonsecours Hall in Montreal ($120 for the series; lecture fees are from the "Account Books").

On 23 January 1849 Amos Adams, president of the East Lexington Lyceum in East Lexington, Massachusetts, wrote to Emerson specifically requesting "England" (see *Letters*, 8:206); although Emerson did not record his topic, he undoubtedly delivered "England" on 28 February 1849 when he appeared before the East Lexington Lyceum, for which he received $10 ("Account Books").

Emerson ceased using "England" as a title for this lecture after delivering it on 19 April 1852 in Montreal. However, he continued to rely on "England" for lectures he delivered under various titles between 1854 and 1856. On 12 December 1854 Emerson spoke on "English Character and Influence" before the Concord Lyceum in Concord, Massachusetts. He lectured under the title "English Civilization" on 21 November 1854 before the Mechanics' Institute in Portsmouth, New Hampshire, for which he received $30; on 2 March 1855 in Hudson, New York ($25); on 13 March 1855 at the Salem Lyceum in Salem, Massachusetts; and on 27 March 1856 as the first in a series of six private lectures at Freeman Place Chapel in Boston ($772.36 for the series; lecture fees are from the "Account Books").

On 19 December 1854 Emerson delivered "Characteristics of the English" in Littleton, Massachusetts, for which he received $11 (Charvat titles this lecture "Characteristics of the English People"); he again spoke under this title on 26 December 1854 before the East Boston Library Association in Boston, for which he received $20. Returning to the title that he first used on 17 January 1849 when delivering "England" before the Salem Lyceum in Salem, Massachusetts, for which he received $20, Emerson delivered "England and the English" on 1 January 1856 before the Young Men's Library Association at the Baptist Church in Rock Island, Illinois. Finally, on 3 January 1854 Emerson combined "English Influence on Modern Civilization" and "The Norseman" as the first in a series of six private lectures on the *Topics of Modern Times* in Philadelphia ($1,166.34 for the series; lecture fees are from the "Account Books").

Although it has never been published, "England" ranks among Emerson's most important and popular lectures. Emerson first visited England in 1833, and he visited it a third and final time in 1872–73, but his multiply titled versions of "England," as well as his lectures on "London" and "The Anglo-Saxon," have their origin in his lecture tour of the United Kingdom during his second visit in 1847–48 (Emerson's lecture "London" is printed in this edition; for "The Anglo-Saxon," see the headnote to "The Anglo-American"). During that tour, Emerson delivered sixty-four lectures between 2 November 1847 and 24 February 1848 in twenty-five cities and towns in England and Scotland and a series of six lectures on the *Mind and Manners of the Nineteenth Century* between 6 and 17 June 1848 at the Literary and Scientific Institution in Portman Square in London (see Townsend Scudder, "Emerson's British Lecture Tour, 1847–1848, Part I," *American Literature* 7 [March 1935]: 16–36, and "Emerson's British Lecture Tour, 1847–1848, Part II," *American Literature* 7 [May 1935]: 166–80; "A Chronological List of Emerson's Lectures on His British Lecture Tour of 1847–1848," *PMLA* 51 [March 1936]: 242–48; and "Emerson in London and the London Lectures," *American Literature* 8 [March 1936]: 22–36; for additional details on Emerson's lectures before the Literary and Scientific Institution in Portman Square, see the headnote to the *Mind and Manners of the Nineteenth Century* series).

The importance of Emerson's 1847–48 British lecture tour to his national and international reputation as a lecturer, to the shaping of his ideas on English history, manners, and character, and to the fullest expression of his thoughts on England and the English in *English Traits*, published in 1856, has been recounted in many forms. Principal among these are Alexander Ireland's *In Memoriam. Ralph Waldo Emerson: Recollections of His Visits to England in 1833, 1847-8, 1872-3, and Extracts from Unpublished Letters* (London: Simpkin, Marshall, 1882) and his *Ralph Waldo Emerson: His Life, Genius, and Writings* (1882); James Elliot Cabot's treatment of Emerson's "Second Visit to England" in *A Memoir* (2: 501–62); the annotations by Ralph L. Rusk and Eleanor M. Tilton to the letters Emerson wrote from England (see *Letters,* 3, 4, and 8); the letters them-selves, especially those Emerson regularly wrote to Lidian during his trip, many of which he later mined for descriptions of persons, events, and the English landscape, which he recast in his lectures on "England" and "London"; and Emerson's journals and note-books on England, some of which he kept during and some of which he developed after his tour, which have been edited and fully annotated by Merton M. Sealts Jr. (see *JMN,* 10). A number of significant scholarly studies and biographies of Emerson have relied on these primary sources and extended their application. These include Ralph L. Rusk, *The Life of Ralph Waldo Emerson* (New York: Charles Scribner's Sons, 1949), 331–37, 340–46, 351–57; William J. Sowder, *Emerson's Impact on the British Isles and Canada* (Charlottesville: University Press of Virginia, 1966), 1–68; Nicoloff, *Emerson on Race and History: An Examination of "English Traits";* Gay Wilson Allen, *Waldo Emerson: A Biography* (New York: Viking Press, 1981), 491–518; McAleer, *Ralph Waldo Emerson: Days of Encounter,* 430–55, 462–65; Larry J. Reynolds, *European Revo-lutions and the American Literary Renaissance* (New Haven, Conn.: Yale University Press, 1988), 25–43, 179–82; and Richardson, *Emerson: The Mind on Fire,* 441–56. The Harvard University Press edition of *English Traits* (*CW,* 5) supersedes Edward Waldo Emerson's edition of that volume (*W,* 5); published in 1994 with an historical intro-duction by Philip Nicoloff, extensive annotations by Robert E. Burkholder, and texts established and introduced by Douglas Emory Wilson, the Harvard edition provides an authoritative account of the relation between Emerson's visits to England and the devel-opment of his ideas on England in the lectures he began to deliver on his return home in 1848.

Reports of Emerson's multiply titled versions of "England" are on the whole quite positive. Indeed, reporters tended to register their approval of the lecture by ignoring fea-tures of Emerson's platform style that they typically criticized, although in a few instances they chided him for being too partial to English culture. For instance, after Emerson in-troduced the lecture as "England" before the Newport Lyceum in December 1848, the *Boston Daily Evening Transcript* printed this dispatch: "We had last night the pleasure of hearing Mr Ralph Waldo Emerson lecture on the subject of England; in praise of which he could not say too much. He laid it on pretty thick, I assure you" (11 December 1848, quoted in *Letters,* 4:125n). A one-column report in the *Boston Post* of Emerson's delivery of "England" before the Mercantile Library Association at Tremont Temple in Decem-ber 1848 concentrated entirely on the discourse, not on Emerson's manner ("Mercantile Library Association," 29 December 1848, 1). Possibly this was the original of the report of "England" that Carlyle received from Joseph Neuberg in a reprint from the *New-York Tribune,* which Carlyle, in turn, sent off to two English newspapers: "Your beautiful curious little discourse (report of a discourse) was sent to me by Neuberg; I thought it, in my private heart, one of the best words (for *hidden* genius lodged in it) . . . so sent it to the *Examiner,* from which it went to the *Times* and all the other Papers: an excellent sly little word" (Carlyle to Emerson, 19 April 1849, *CEC,* 451–54; the report appeared in the *Lon-don Examiner* on 10 March 1849 and as "An American's Opinion of England" in the *Times* of London on 14 March).

Nathaniel Parker Willis published a witty and positive report of "England" as deliv-

ered in January 1850 before the Mercantile Library Association in New York City in
which he concluded that, for his "Titanic," "prophetic metaphor of England's power,"
"Victoria should name one of her annual babies Emerson" ("Emerson," in *Hurry-Graphs*,
reprinted in *Emerson Among His Contemporaries*, 70). In a detailed account of the same
delivery printed in the *New-York Daily Tribune*, the reporter found Emerson's lecture
"deeply interesting and instructive on England," and he concluded by stating, "Mr. E.
accompanied his descriptions with a great variety of striking illustrations, which can no
more be reported than the colors of the sunset" ("Mercantile Library Lectures," 23 January 1850, 2). A reporter for the *New York Herald* was similarly impressed, opening his
long report by describing Emerson's "high reputation for . . . originality, boldness, and as
some have said, the transcendentalism of his style and ideas. . . . His appearance is pleasing and prepossessing, being modest, simple, and unostentatious; having in his countenance the marks of intellect and benevolence, and in his manners the evidence of quiet
gentility and good breeding" ("Lecture on England, at the Mercantile Library," 23 January 1850, 1). When Emerson again delivered "England" three months later in New York
City, the *New-York Daily Tribune* advertised it as "a delightful and discriminating survey
mainly of the more inviting aspects of British Character and Manners, and richly worth
listening to" ("City Items," 26 March 1850, 2). In May 1850, when Emerson found himself stranded in Cleveland after the steamer on which he had been traveling caught fire,
an invitation was quickly extended to him by the Library Association, which offered "England," "the most popular and applauded" of Emerson's lectures, free to the public
("Ralph Waldo Emerson," 16 May 1850, *Cleveland Daily Plain Dealer*, 2). A report in
the *Cleveland Daily True Democrat* noted that "rarely [had Cleveland] heard any lecturer
more captivating" than Emerson, who "delighted a crowded hall—collected together at
a few hours notice—with his brilliant discourse" (18 May 1850, quoted in Mead, *Yankee
Eloquence in the Middle West*, 27).

   When Emerson delivered "England" in April 1852 as the first lecture in his series on
the *Conduct of Life* in Montreal, the *Montreal Courier* included it in reports of the series.
Calling the series "eloquent," the *Courier* stated that it "had never known anything of the
kind to be so popular in Montreal" (*Letters*, 4:291n). As he continued to lecture about England over the next four years, public response to the topic seems not to have diminished
at all—and Emerson apparently knew it. For instance, when he wrote to William Henry
Furness on 17 October 1853 about his plan to open his series on the *Topics of Modern
Times* in Philadelphia on 3 January 1854 with a text then vaguely titled "Genius of
the Northmen, still operative," Emerson, who undoubtedly knew that he would also be
reading portions of "England" on that occasion, could confidently state, "I flatter myself
that my abstractions will be interesting, & my details significant. . . . But your good will
is so large, that I need not draw on it by bragging" (*Letters*, 4:391). Two years after the
Philadelphia series, when he delivered "England and the English" on 1 January 1856 in
Rock Island, Illinois, Emerson was evidently pleased to find himself advertised in advance
of the lecture as "the celebrated Metaphysician" (*JMN*, 14:26); in her study of Emerson's
lectures in Rock Island in 1856, Eleanor Bryce Scott remarks that Emerson's lecturing left
his audience there "breathless" ("Emerson Wins the Nine Hundred Dollars," *American
Literature* 17 [March 1945]: 78–85).

THE TRAVELLER ON arriving in England is struck at once with the cultivation. On every side, he sees the triumph of labor. Man has subdued and made everything. The country is a garden. Under that ash-coloured sky, the fields are so combed and rolled, that it seems as if they had been finished with a pencil instead of a plough.[1] The structures that compose the towns, have been piled by the wealth and skill of ages. Nothing is left as it was made. Rivers, hills, valleys, the sea all feel the hand of a master. The long habitation of a powerful and ingenious race has turned every rood of land to its best use, has found all the capabilities, all the short cuts, all the arable soil, all the quarriable rock, all the navigable waters; and the new arts of intercourse meet you everywhere, so that England itself is a huge mill, or hotel, or palais-royale, where all that man wants is provided within the precinct. Cushioned and comforted in every manner, the traveller rides everywhere, as on a cannon-ball, high and low, over rivers and towns, and through mountains, in tunnels of three miles and more, at twice the speed, and with half the shaking, of our trains, and reads quietly the *Times* newspaper, which, again, by its wonderful system of correspondence and reporting, seems to have machinized the world for his occasion.

If one remembers here Mr. Landor's exclamation, "Who would live in a new country, that can live in an old?"—especially, he recalls, in the old cities, where the question would find a more unanimous affirmative—no familiarity or long residence can exhaust the advantages of London, because the past as well as the present are always filling the basket faster than any diligence can empty it. Every age since Julius Caesar has left some trace of itself in the building of old King Lud's town, and a certain civility and conservative instinct has kept all in repair.[2] The railway excavations, within this very year, have laid bare a Roman pavement. Fragments of the London wall of that age are still to be found near Ludgate Hill; and so down: Saxon arches, Norman windows, mediæval towers; Westminster Abbey; palaces of Inigo Jones; Saint Paul's Cathedral and fifty-four churches of Christopher Wren; old colleges, immemorial hospitals, immense accommodations which modern commerce has provided for itself, and all the facilities which the wealth of all the monarchs of Europe could not buy, but which are yielded for his small subscription of a few pence or shillings to the private citizen of an old town; facilities that belong to the living on the spot where the great agencies centre and where the ruling men in every kind are found; whence all ships, expresses, roads, and telegraphs radiate for all parts of the world, and where every service you require is rendered by the first masters in that kind. Rothschild or

---

1. This description is drawn from the writings of Count Vittorio Alfieri (1749–1803), Italian dramatist, according to Emerson's note in the manuscript.
2. Lud, the legendary king of England who rebuilt the walls of London.

the Barings are your bankers; Stephenson and Brunel your engineers; Pugin and Barry build; Chadwick makes the aqueduct, Wheatstone the telegraph, Reid ventilates; the military arrangements (and, in April last, they were serious,) are made by the Duke of Wellington; the mighty debate in Parliament by Peel, Russell, Cobden, Brougham, and Stanley; Faraday, and Richard Owen, Sedgwick, and Buckland, are the lecturers in science; Herschel, Airy, and Adams, in the observatory; the great heirs of fame are living and talking in society: Turner and Landseer paint; Wordsworth, Landor, Hallam, Tennyson, Dickens, write; and for your entertainment, Rachel plays, and Macready; Lablache, Grisi, and Jenny Lind sing, Taglioni dances, and Soyer cooks.[3]

Happy is the man who lives where the best is cheap! Life is here in extremes; the traveller goes from show to show; he can be pampered to the highest point; he sits in a cloud of pictures; he eats from off porcelain and plate; his rug is the skin of a lion. Science will quiddle for him: if he will, his light is polarised, his water distilled, he sleeps with a puff of chloroform on water-bed, and all his implements, garments, and trinkets are the work of artists, whose names have been familiar to him for years as the best makers.

But, more than all, the riches of a cultivated population one cannot exaggerate. Every day you may meet a new man who is the centre of a new circle of thought and practice, which, but for what seems an accident, you should never have heard of, in this mob of gifted and educated men. The inequalities of power have their consolation here,—that they are superficial. Everyone can do something. When I see the power that every human being possesses to make himself valued and beloved by making himself useful and necessary to those with whom he finds himself,—I pity him no longer.

3. Inigo Jones (1573–1652) designer of the government buildings at Whitehall in London; Christopher Wren (1632–1723), architect of Saint Paul's Cathedral in London; the Baring Brothers and Company (along with the Rothschilds), a major banking firm of the day; Sir Marc Isambard Brunel (1769–1849) and his son Isambard Kingdom Brunel (1806–59), designers of, respectively, the Thames Tunnel and the Great Western Railway; Augustus Welby Northmore Pugin (1812–52), assistant in building Saint Paul's Cathedral; Sir Charles Barry (1795–1860), builder of the Houses of Parliament; Sir Edwin Chadwick (1800–1890), active in the first sanitary commission of 1839; Sir Charles Wheatstone (1802–75), an inventor of the electric telegraph; Sir William Reid (1791–1858), Scottish meteorologist and author of books on storms; there were uprisings against the British in the spring of 1848 in Ireland and India; Sir Robert Peel (1788–1850), whose reforms split the Tory party; Lord John Russell (1792–1878), introducer of the Reform Bill in 1831; Richard Cobden (1804–65), advocate of free trade and peace; Henry Peter Brougham (1778–1868), Scottish statesman and a founder of the *Edinburgh Review;* Edward George Geoffrey Smith Stanley (1799–1869), three-time premier of England; Adam Sedgwick (1785–1873), professor of geology at Cambridge University; William Buckland (1784–1856), a geologist; Sir William Herschel (1738–1822), discoverer of the planet Uranus; Sir George Biddell Airy (1801–92), director of the Greenwich observatory; John Couch Adams (1819–92), director of the observatory at Cambridge University; Joseph Mallard William Turner (1775–1851), landscape painter known for his experiments with light; Sir Edwin Henry Landseer (1802–73), animal painter; Henry

Some of the causes of the historical importance of England, I shall enumerate. But I premise with this remark, that the praise of England is not that it has freed itself from the evils under which other countries labor, not that England has found out how to create wealth and power without the creation of poverty and crime—No, for all have these griefs and England also; but, that England has with this evil produced, in the last five hundred years, a greater number of strong, wise, educated, and humane men—a greater number of excellent and finished men, than any other nation.

England has the best working climate in the world. It is never hot or cold. There is no hour in the year when one cannot work. Here is no winter, but such days as we have in Massachusetts in November. A climate which makes no exhausting demand on human strength, but allows the fullest development of the form.

Then, England has all the materials of a working country,—all the materials except wood. The constant rain, a rain with every tide in some parts of the island, keeps its multitude of rivers full and swift. It has abundance of water, of stone, of coal, and iron. It is a working country, and everybody works in England. It is computed, that only three or four percent of the whole population are idle.

The only drawback on this advantage that I know is the darkness of its grey sky. The night and day are too nearly of a color. It strains the eyes to read or to write. Add, the smoke of the manufacturing towns, where the *blacks* darken the air, give white sheep precisely the color of black sheep, discolor the human saliva,—and you will know the want of daylight in Leeds and Manchester.

In this climate, (which, however, Ireland also enjoys,) the English appear to possess the advantage of the best blood. Without going into the history,—we may say, the mixture of Britons and Saxons was a good cross. Afterwards, England yielded to the Danes and Northmen in the tenth, and eleventh, and twelfth centuries; and was the receptacle into which all mettle of that strenuous population was poured. It would seem, that, the perpetual supply of the best men in Norway, Sweden, and Denmark to the piratical expeditions of the ninth and tenth centuries, into England, gradually exhausted those countries, like a tree which bears much fruit when young,—and these have been second-rate powers, ever since.

---

Hallam (1777–1859), historian; Alfred, Lord Tennyson (1809–92), named poet laureate in 1850 to succeed Wordsworth; Rachel (1820–58), stage name of Elisa Félix, French actress; William Charles Macready (1793–1873), actor and theater manager who made several tours of America; Luigi Lablache (1794–1858), Italian opera singer who taught singing to Queen Victoria; Emerson is probably thinking of Giulia Grisi (1811–69), an Italian opera singer whom he had seen in London in 1848; Jenny Lind (1820–87), singer known as the Swedish Nightingale, brought to America by P. T. Barnum in 1850–52 for a triumphant tour; Maria Taglioni (1804–84), member of a celebrated European family of dancers; Alexis Benoît Soyer (1809–58), English cook.

Konghelle, the famed town, where the kings of Norway, Sweden, and Denmark, were wont to meet, is now rented to a private English gentleman as a shooting ground.

The English, at the present day, have great vigor of body and endurance. Other countrymen look slight and undersized beside them, and invalids. They are bigger men than the Americans; I suppose, a hundred English, taken at random out of the street, would weigh a fourth more than so many Americans. Yet, I am told, the skeleton is not larger. They are round, ruddy, and handsome; at least, the whole bust is well formed; and there is a tendency to make stout and powerful frames, like castles. This stoutness of shape particularly struck me, on my first landing at Liverpool;—porter, drayman, coachman, guard,—what substantial, respectable, grandfatherly figures, with costume and manners to suit. The American has really arrived at the old mansion-house, and finds himself among his Uncles, Aunts, and Grandmothers. The pictures on the chimney-tiles of his nursery were pictures of these people. Here they are in the identical costumes and air which so took him.

There are two styles of dress here which a traveller in the trains will soon take note of, the tortoise style, and the supple or becoming; the former, wherein the man seems to have obtained by time and pains a sort of house of cloth and buckram built up around him and speaks out of his building, suits English manners well enough.

It is the fault of their forms that they grow stocky, and the women seem to have that defect to their beauty;—few tall, slender persons of flowing shape, but stunted and thickset figures. But they are a very handsome race and always have been. The bronze monuments of Crusaders lying cross-legged in the Temple Church in London and those in Worcester Cathedral which are nine hundred years old are of the same type as the best youthful heads of men now in England, and please by beauty of the same character—a certain expression, namely, of good nature, refinement, and valor, and mainly with that uncorrupt youth in the face of manhood, which is daily seen in the streets of London. They have a vigorous health and last well into middle and old age. The old men are as red as roses, and still handsome. A clean skin, and a peach-bloom complexion, is found all over the island.

The English head is round, and the animal powers are in perfection. Their veins are full of blood, and the people hearty eaters, attaching great importance to a plentiful and nutricious diet. The cyclops operative of England cannot subsist on food less solid than beef, and his performance is not more amazing to the foreign laborer than his diet is. Good mutton, wheat bread, and malt liquors are universal among the first-class laborers. It is curious that Tacitus found the English beer already in use among the Germans: "*Potui humor ex hordeo aut frumento in quandam simililudi nem vini corruptus."*[4] Lord Chief Justice Fortescue, in Henry VI's time, says, "the inhabitants drink no water unless at certain times on a religious score and by way of penance."[5] The extremes of poverty and of ascetic temperance never reach cold water in England. Wood, the antiquary, in describing the poverty and maceration of Father Lacey, an English Jesuit, does not deny him beer.[6] He says, "His bed was under a thatching, and the way to it up a ladder: His face was coarse, his drink of a penny a gaun or gallon."

They have more constitutional energy, physical and moral, than any other people, and this is no whit abated, but in full play at this moment. I find the Englishman to be he of all men who stands firmest in his shoes. They have in themselves what they value in their horses: mettle and bottom. A gentleman on the day of my arrival, in describing the Lord Lieutenant of Ireland, said, "Lord Clarendon has pluck like a cock and will fight till he dies;" and what I heard first, I heard last, and the one thing the English value is pluck. The cabmen have it; the merchants have it; the bishops have it; the women have it; the journals have it; the *Times* newspaper, they say, is the pluckiest thing in England; and little Lord John Russell, the minister, would take the command of the Channel Fleet tomorrow.[7]

It requires, men say, a good constitution to travel in Spain. I say as much of England, simply on account of the vigor and brawn of the people. I know nothing but the most serious business that could give me any counter-weight to these Baresarks, though they were only to order eggs and muffins for their breakfast. The Englishman speaks with all his body; his elocution is stomachic as the American's is labial. The Englishman is very petulant and precise about his accommodation at inns and on the roads; a quiddle about his toast and his chop, and every species of convenience; and loud and pungent in his expressions of impatience at any neglect. He has that *aplomb* which results only from a good adjustment of the moral and physical nature, and the obedience of all the powers to the will. The axes of his eyes are united to his backbone, and only move with the trunk.

When I landed, the times were disastrous, and the commercial and political sky full of gloom.[8] But it was evident, that, let who will fail, England will not. It is plain, from the security of their manners, that these people have sat here a

---

4. "For drink they use the liquid distilled from barley or wheat, after fermentation has given it a certain resemblance to wine," quoted from Tacitus, *Germania,* chap. 23, sec. 1; "simililudi" should be "similitudinem."

5. Sir John Fortescue (ca. 1394–ca. 1476), named chief justice of the King's Bench in 1442.

6. Anthony à Wood (1632–95), British antiquary.

7. George William Frederick Villiers, fourth earl of Clarendon (1800–1870), lord lieutenant of Ireland from 1847 to 1852.

8. Emerson had arrived in England in October 1847 during a period of revolutionary fervor on the Continent; the overthrow of the monarchy in Paris occurred the next year.

thousand years, and here will continue to sit. They will not break up, or arrive at any strange, desperate revolution like their neighbors, for they have as much energy and as much continence of character as they ever had. The immense power and possession which surround them is their own creation, and they exert the same commanding industry at this moment.

In America, we fancy that we live in a new and forming country, but that England was finished long ago. But we find London and England in full growth. The towns are growing, some of them almost at the rate of American towns. Birkenhead, opposite Liverpool, was growing as fast as South Boston. The towns in Lancashire will by and by meet, and make a city, as big as, and bigger than, London. London itself is enlarging at a frightful rate, even to the filling up of Middlesex, and the decoration and repairs in every part of the old city go on day by day. Trafalgar Square was only new finished in April 1848. The British Museum is in full course of growth and activity and projected arrangement; the Vernon Gallery is just added to the National. The London University opens like our mushroom colleges at the West, and the Houses of Parliament are just sending up their proud Victoria tower, four hundred feet into the air. Everything in England bespeaks an immense and energetic population. The buildings are on a scale of size and wealth far beyond ours. The colossal masonry of the docks and of all public buildings attests the multitudes who are to be accommodated by them and who are to pay for them. England could not now build her old castles and abbeys, but what the nineteenth century wants,—club houses, vaults, docks, mills, canals, railways,—she builds fast and well.

A manly ability, a general sufficiency, is the genius of the English. The land and climate are favorable to the breeding of good men; and it was an odd proof of it, that, in my lectures, I hesitated to read many a disparaging phrase which I have been accustomed to throw into my writing, about poor, thin, unable, unsatisfying bipeds,—so much had the fine physique and the personal vigor of this robust race worked on my imagination. This abundant life and vigor betrays itself, at all points, in their manners, in the respiration, and the inarticulate noises they make in clearing the throat, all significant of burly strength. They have stamina; they can take the initiative on all emergences. And the one rule for the traveller in England, is,—This is no country for fainthearted people. Do not creep about diffidently. Make up your mind, take your course, and you shall find respect and furtherance.

This vigour appears in the manners of the people in the complete incuriosity and stony neglect of each to every other. Each man walks, eats, drinks, shaves, dresses, gesticulates, and, in every manner, is, acts, suffers, without reference to the bystanders, and in his own fashion, only careful not to interfere with them, or annoy them. It is not that he is trained to neglect the eyes of his neighbors; he is really occupied with his own affair, and does not think of them. In the first-class carriage, a clergyman takes his stout shoes out of his carpet bag, and puts them on, instead of thin ones, on approaching the station. Every man in this polished country consults only his convenience, as much as a solitary pioneer in Wisconsin. I know not where any personal eccentricity is so freely allowed, and no man gives himself any concern with it. An Englishman walks in a pouring rain swinging his closed umbrella, like a walking stick; wears a wig, or a shawl, or a saddle; or stands on his head; and no remark is made. And, as he has been doing this for several generations, it is now in the blood.

In short, every one of these islanders is an island himself—safe, tranquil, incommunicable. In a company of strangers, you would think him deaf; his eyes never wander from his own table and newspaper; he is never betrayed into any curiosity or unbecoming emotion. They seem all to have been trained in one severe school of manners, and never to put off this iron harness. He does not give his hand. He does not let you meet his eye. It is almost an affront to look a man in the face, before being introduced. In mixed, or in select companies, they do not introduce persons, so that a presentation is a circumstance as valid as a contract. Introductions are sacraments. He withholds his name. At the hotel, if they ask his name at the book office, he stoops, and gives it in a low voice. If he give you his private address on a card, it is like an avowal of friendship; and his bearing, on being introduced, is studiously cold, even though he is seeking your acquaintance, and is studying how he shall serve you.

'Tis no wonder that this rigor astonishes their lively neighbors across the Channel, so strongly contrasted with the social genius of the French, and is the standing theme of French raillery. "The islanders of Albion," says a brilliant French writer,

"carry with them a peculiar fluid, which I shall call the *Britannic fluid*, and, in the midst of which, they travel, as little accessible to the atmosphere of the regions which they traverse, as the mouse at the centre of the exhausted receiver. It is not only to the thousand precautions with which they go surrounded that they owe their eternal impassivity; it is not because they wear three pair of breeches one over the other that they arrive perfectly dry and clean in spite of rain and mud; it is not because they have woolen wigs that their stiff and wiry frisure defies moisture; it is not because they go loaded each with as much pommade, brushes, and soap as would serve to adonize a whole regiment of Bas Breton conscripts that they have always the beard smooth and the nails irreproachable. It is because the external air does not touch them; it is because they walk, drink, eat, and sleep, *in their fluid*, as in a glass bell of twenty feet diameter, and, across which they behold with pity the cavaliers whose hair the wind discomposes, and the foot passenger whose shoes the snow soils."[9]

9. Attributed to George Sand in Emerson's note in the manuscript.

'Tis very certain that the Englishman has a confidence in the power and performance of his nation, which makes him provokingly incurious about other nations. It is a very old remark,—some centuries old,—that he dislikes foreigners. Swedenborg, who visited England many times in the last century, remarks: "There is a similitude of minds among them, in consequence of which, they contract a familiarity with friends who are from their nation, and seldom with others. They are lovers of their country, and zealous for its glory, and they regard foreigners as one looking through a telescope from the top of his palace regards those who dwell or wander about out of the city." But in a much older traveller, the *Relation of England* by a Venetian in 1500, three hundred and fifty years ago, I find a similar testimony: "The English are great lovers of themselves, and of everything belonging to them. They think that there are no other men than themselves, and no other world but England; and whenever they see a handsome foreigner, they say that he looks like an Englishman, and it is a great pity he should not be an Englishman: and when they partake of any delicacy with a foreigner, they ask him whether such a thing is made in *his* country." [10]

It is very certain that this arrogance is really in the true-born Englishman, and all the goodness of heart and studious courtesy that belong to him fail to conceal it. When he accumulates epithets of praise, his climax of commendation is, "*So English*," and when he wishes to pay you the highest compliment, he says, "I should not know you from an Englishman."

At the same time, I know no national pride that is so easily forgiven and so much respected as his, and for the reason that it is so well-founded. The Englishman is proud—Yes, but he is admirable; he knows all things, has all things, and can do all things. How can he not be proud? There is a certain general culture wherein he surpasses other nations. There is no man so equally and harmoniously developed, and hence his easy pride when he finds every other countryman inferior to him as a social man. His wide outlook, his birth and breeding in the commercial and political centre of the world, have accustomed his eye and mind to whatever is best in the planet and made him instantly perceptive of any meanness or fault. A certain liberality and catholicism, an air of having seen much and seen the best, appears in all men. They are bored by anything provincial and detect the smutch of native clay sticking to the clothes of a villager. They notice in the American speech a certain purism, the accent of a man who knows how the word is spelled, rather than the unrestrained expression of a man who is only eager to say what he means.

Besides, it is quite inevitable that this spoiled child of nature and fortune should have the fastidiousness which the habit generates. He talks of his politics

10. Quoted from *A Relation, or Rather a True Account, of the Island of England . . . about the Year 1500,* trans. Charlotte Augusta Sneyd (1847) (see *JMN,* 10:198).

and institutions, but the real thing which he values is his home and that which belongs to it—that general culture and high polish, which, in his experience, no man but the Englishman possesses, and which, he naturally believes, have some essential connexion with his throne and laws.

In all culture, so much depends on sympathy, on a great number who keep each other up to a high point, that, 'tis a pleasure to the traveller in England to know that there is all around him an infinite number of educated and thoughtful people, all quietly and calmly carrying forward every variety of profound and elegant study, with the best aids and materials, though rarely communicating, and, for the most part, each wholly independent and unacquainted with the rest.

And here comes in an element of decisive importance, the existence of a superior or model class, legalised by statute and usage, fostered and privileged from the beginning of the national history, with all the institutions of the country to secure them in their hereditary wealth, owners of all the soil, with the best education to develop and stamp these advantages, and placed in every manner on such high ground, that, whatever benefit the nation reaps with its million arms outstretched from pole to pole,—they more. The finest race of men in the friendliest climate, possessing every natural and accidental advantage and secured in the possession of these by the loyal affection of the people, they easily came to produce sound minds in sound bodies and exhibit more finished men than any other nation.

The favoured class seem to gain as much as they lose by their position. They survey all society as from the top of Saint Paul's, and, if they never hear plain truth from men, as the poor do, they see the best of everything in every kind, and they see things so grouped and amassed, as to infer easily the sum and genius, instead of tedious particularities. Their good behaviour deserves all its fame; and they have, in the highest degree, that simplicity and that air of repose which are such chief ornaments of greatness.

It was inevitable that these people should have a controlling influence on the manners of the people. They naturally furnish the best models of manly behaviour to their country and the world. Moreover, it has come to be the ambition of the English system of education,—of their schools and of the universities,—to turn out gentlemen, rather than scholars or skilful masters in any art; and the like feeling runs into the middle and lower classes.

It is not to be disguised, however, that there is much in this English culture, so much prized at home, so much admired abroad, that will not bear analysis,—is by no means the best thing in the English state; is material; is built on wealth, built on trifles, and certainly has another less reputable face and name as the height of cockneyism. For, it rests on land and money, on birth, on diet, on excellence in horsemanship, on hunting, on dogs, on boxing, on boating, and on betting. The self-command and continuity of will are exerted in affairs,—the bribes of speculation, the panics of trade, the game of party, all powerless,—foiled by an insight which commands the law of the game better than any other player,—it is the guarantee of victory.

They have carried inoffensiveness to a very high point. They have applied their strong understanding and their love of animal comfort to a perfect organization of the details of a domestic day, studiously excluding everything annoying or discordant, and have become superstitiously neat and proper, and orderly, and respectable. Their hat, and shoes, and linen, their horse and gun, their egg, and toast, and soda water, and wine, and politics, and visiting-set, are irreproachable. It is a world of trifles, and seems to argue a mediocrity of intellect in the nation which allows it so much importance. Whilst we pay homage to the indisputable merits of the English people, we must not confound their immense regard to trifles, with their virtues

Their good form and habit are much indebted to the manly exercises to which they are trained from earliest youth. They begin with cricket, archery, and skittles,—in each of which games they acquire some skill at school and at college. They learn the use of oars at Eton and Westminster schools: at Oxford and Cambridge, the boat clubs are in daily practice; and yachting and regattas are favorite amusements of gentlemen in every part of the island where there is water.

Still more universal is their attachment to horses, and to hounds, and to every form of hunting. They are always on horseback, centaurs. Every inn-room is lined with pictures of racers. And expresses bring, every hour, news to London, from Newmarket and Ascot.

The universal practice of betting, too, is not without its uses as it makes the knowledge of all men whom you meet singularly accurate in regard to all common facts. Every distance has been measured in miles, rods, and inches. They know the distance of their towns, the length of their boats, the speed of their horses, the numbers of their partisans, and complain of looseness in the information of other countrymen on these points.

But what I think is the secret of English success, is, a certain balance of qualities in their nature, corresponding to what we call temper in steel. The geographical position of England is excellent; but there are many countries with good seacoasts besides England,—many countries with good climate, which make no pretension to British influence. But here is the best average brain. Men found that this people had a faculty of doing, which others had not. There is an incompatibility in the Italians, in the Spaniards, in the Turks, of dealing with other nations,—of treating with them. But the English brain is of the right temper. Neither too cold, nor too hot; neither too swift, nor too slow.— Calm, energetic, tenacious, just, and wise.

The English metal is not brittle, is not soft, not explosive, but tenacious, incorruptible, and admitting a good working edge: That happy adaptedness to things which makes the ordinary Englishman a skilful and thorough workman, and the higher classes good heads for the combining and arranging of labour. The fabulous Saint George has never seemed to me the patron saint of England; but the scholar, monk, soldier, engineer, lawgiver, Alfred,—working-king; often defeated, never discouraged; patient of defeat, of affront, of labor, and victorious by fortitude and wisdom,—he is the model Englishman. They have many such in their annals. Cromwell is one. One is William of Wykeham,—Bishop of Winchester in the reign of Edward II, Edward III, and Richard II,—a poor boy of obscure parentage, who by study, and practical talent, and sound judgment, and a certain humble magnanimity, conceived and carried out great plans; built roads and causeys; built Windsor Castle; built the sublime Winchester Cathedral; and, observing the gross ignorance of the priesthood, in his times, and, attributing many public evils to that cause,—established a school at Winchester, and livings for seventy boys, to be there trained for the university, at his expense, forever; and then established at Oxford Winchester or New College, with livings for seventy fellows, at his expense forever. In May (1848) I visited Oxford, and Dr. Williams, the polite head of the College, showed me the halls, chapel, library, and common rooms and gardens—over every gate of which was written in stone William of Wykeham's motto, "Manners maketh man"—and assured me that now, after five hundred years, the seventy boys at Winchester school and the seventy fellows at Winchester College, are still maintained on the bounty of the founder.[11]

One of the merits of Wykeham was the stern investigation which he instituted into the embezzlement and perversion of the religious and charitable foundations in his time; especially, the account which he demanded of the revenues of the "Hospital of Saint Cross," where, long before him, Henry of Blois, brother of King Stephen, had founded a charity for the support of a hundred poor, and, with a provision, that a measure of beer and a piece of bread should be given forever to every son of man who should ask for it.[12] As I passed the Hospital of Saint-Cross, on my way from Stonehenge, in July, I knocked at the door, to see if William-of-Wykeham's word was sterling yet in England, and received my horn of beer and my piece of bread, gratuitously, from the charity of a founder who has

11. Saint George (d. 303), Cappadocian military tribune who became the patron saint of England in the fourteenth century; Alfred the Great (849–99), king of England from 871 to his death; Oliver Cromwell (1599–1658), revolutionary who became lord protector of the realm; William of Wykeham (1324–1404), bishop of Winchester from 1367 to his death. Emerson had been shown the grounds of Oxford by David Williams, warder of New College, when he had visited there in May 1848 (see *Letters*, 4:48).

12. Henry II (1133–89), king of England (1154–89), followed Stephen (1097?–1154), the previous king (1135–54).

been dead seven centuries. I hardly think it less honorable that the man whom the English of this age put forward as the type of their race is a man so proverbial for his veracity, perseverance, and moderation as the Duke of Wellington.

I fear, that, in many points, the English tenacity is in strong contrast to American facility. The facile American sheds his Puritanism, when he leaves Cape Cod, runs into all English and French vices, with great zest, and is neither Unitarian, nor Calvinist, nor Catholic, nor Quaker, nor stands for any thought or thing; all which is very distasteful to English honor.

I do not think the English quite capable of doing justice to our countrymen. He is annoyed by the free and easy pretension, the careless manners, and the neglect of certain points of decorum and respect, to which he is accustomed to attach importance; and he does not see, that, this is his own self-reliance transferred to a new theatre, where there is no such division of labor as exists in England, and where every man must help himself in every manner, like an Indian, and remember much which the European more gracefully abandons to his valet.

But the main advantage which the American possesses, is a certain versatility, and, as far as I know, a greater apprehensiveness of mind. He more readily and genially entertains new thoughts, new modes, new books, is more speculative, more contemplative, and is really related to the future, whilst the Englishman seems mortgaged to the past. Each countryman is qualified for the part assigned him in history to play.

In drawing these sketches, I am well aware there is a dark side of England, which, I have not wished to expose. The first effect of the extraordinary determination of the national mind for so many centuries on wealth has been, in developing colossal wealth, to develop hideous pauperism. These fair, ruddy, muscular, well-educated bodies go attended by poor, dwarfed, starved, short-lived skeletons. There are two Englands;—rich, Norman-Saxon, learned, social England,—seated in castles, halls, universities, and middle class houses of admirable completeness and comfort, and poor, Celtic, peasant, drudging, Chartist England, in hovels and workhouses, cowed and hopeless. I only recognize this fact, in passing. It is important that it be stated. It will not help us now to dwell on it.

England is the country of the rich. The great poor man does not yet appear. Whenever he comes, England will fall like France. It would seem, that an organizing talent applied directly to the social problem,—to bring, for example, labor to market; to bring want and supply face to face; would not be so rare. A man like Hudson, like Trevylian, like Cobden, should know something about it.[13] The Reform Bill took in new partners, and Chartism again takes in more.

13. Probably Sir Charles Edward Trevelyan (1807–86), British politician much involved with India.

They are "strange, neat-handed Titans, and, if wanting fire from heaven, make, at least, the cheapest and most polished patent lamps for receiving it, when it shall come." They have propriety and parliamentariness, propriety felt both in what they do not say, and in what they say. The schools and universities cling to them, and give a certain mechanical integrity to their manners and culture and make it impossible to them to make a mistake. In the educated English, one feels the advantage of thorough drill. Eton, and Harrow, and Rugby have done their work; they know prosody, and tread securely through all the humanities.

But the Englishman is the victim of this excellence. The practical and comfortable oppress him with inexorable claims, and the smallest fraction of power remains for heroism and poetry. My own feeling is, that the English have sacrificed their grandeur to their cleverness. They have vaunted their practicalness, until the brain serves the hand, which ought to serve the brain, and until the nobler traits, which, in former times, distinguished the British nation, are disappearing before the indispensable demand of wealth and convenience.

The English boast the grandeur of their national genius; but seem not to observe that a total revolution has taken place in their estimate of mental greatness. The age of their greatness was an ideal and Platonic age: all the great men of the Elizabethan period had that tendency. Now, the intellect of England plumes itself on its limitary and practical turn. Once there was mysticism in the British mind, a deep vein of religion. Once there was Platonism, a profound poetry, and daring sallies into the realm of thought on every side. Now, there is musty, self-conceited decorum—life made up of fictions hating ideas: but not a breath of Olympian air dilates the collapsing lungs. *Now*, we have clever mediocrity: the paragraph writers, the fashionable-romance writers, the elegant travellers, and dapper diners-out, with anecdote and bons mots,—made up men with made up manners,—varied and exact information; facts,—(facts the Englishman delights in all day long;)—humour too, and all that goes to animate conversation. "Conversational powers," says Campbell, "are so much the rage in London, that no reputation is higher than his, who exhibits them to advantage." [14]

We have plenty of derision and worldliness. The genius of the House of Commons is a sneer. "What delights the House," says Fowell Buxton, "is a mixture of good sense and joking." [15] We have no plain-dealing, no abandonment, but every sentence in good society must have a twist—something unexpected, something the reverse of the probable, is required. The day's Englishman must have his joke as duly as his bread. Bold is he and absolute in his narrow circle, versed in all his routine, sure and elegant, his stories are good, his sentences firm, and all

14. Attributed to Thomas Campbell (1777–1844), English poet and critic (see *JMN*, 11:305).
15. Sir Thomas Fowell Buxton (1786–1845), philanthropist.

his statesmen, lawyers, men of letters, and poets, finished and solid as the pavement. But a faith in the laws of the mind like that of Archimedes; belief like
that of Euler and Kepler, that experience must follow and not lead the laws of
the mind; a devotion to the theory of politics, like that of Hooker, Milton, and
Harrington;—the modern English mind repudiates.[16]

I am forced to say that aristocracy requires an intellectual and moral basis, and
that though all the accidents are very well, they indispensably involve real elevation at last. But, in England, one had to humour the society. "It was very well,
*considering*"—as our country people say. Very fine masters, very fine misses,
charming saloons,—but where were the great? The Americans who should succeed in it were the well-bred rich, and not those who make America to me. I am
wearied and inconvenienced by what are called fine people. The moment I meet
a grand person, a man of sense and comprehension, I am emancipated. Such persons I did not find. One would say there was a plentiful sterility of such. One goes
through England making believe that this is good society. It is so old, so much has
been spent on it, the case is so costly, it has such a history around it,—effigies of
a nation of ancestors—or it has so neatly stepped into the history and place of the
real prince, that one easily lets it pass for true, and, nine times out of ten, does not
doubt its legitimacy. But such illusion leads to suicide.— If this is the height of
life, let me die.

Plutarch tells us, "that Archimedes considered the being busied about mechanics, and, in short, every art which is connected with the common purposes
of life, illiberal and ignoble; and those things alone were objects of his ambition,
with which the beautiful and the excellent were present, unmingled with the necessary." I have to say that the whole fabric is wonderful, but has cost too much;
that the higher faculties have been sacrificed. The English mind is less contemplative, less religious, less open, than it was in former periods. Books of larger
scope, as Wordsworth and Coleridge, must come to this country for their fame,
before they gain it in England.

My own impression is, the English mind has more breadth and cosmopolitanism, but no ascending scale. He has not the least interest in speculation. No
men in England are quite ideal, living in an ideal world, and working in politics
and social life, only from that. Her best writer is an earth-son mixed up with politics of the day as a partisan. I suffered myself to be dazzled willingly by the various brilliancy of men of talent. But he who values his days by the number of
insights he gets, will as rarely find a good conversation, a solid dealing, man with
man, in England, as in any country.

16. Leonhard Euler (1707–83), Swiss mathematician; Richard Hooker (ca. 1553–1600), the logian; James Harrington (1611–97), wrote on civil government.

The English are eminently prosaic or unpoetic. All the poetic persons whom I saw, were deviations from the national type. The people have wide range, but no ascending scale in their speculation. An American, like a German, has many platforms of thought. But an Englishman requires to be humored, or treated with tenderness, as an invalid, if you wish him to climb.

Herein England has but obeyed the law, which, in the order of the world, assigns one office to one people. Nature does one thing at a time. If she will have a perfect hand, she makes head and feet pay for it. So now that she is making railroad and telegraph ages, she starves the *spirituel*, to stuff the *materiel* and *industriel*.

But with all the deductions from the picture which truth requires, I find the English to have a thorough good nature; they are a true, benign, gentle, benevolent, hospitable, and pious race, fearing God, and loving man. There is respect for truth, and there is milk of kindness in them; and this in all classes, from the Chartist to the Duke. In the shops, the articles you buy are thoroughly made, and you learn to rely on the probity of the tradesman. Probity is the rule. In the large transactions, it is not less. An eminent merchant, by birth American, whose name is known through the world as partner in one of the first houses in London, said to me, "I have been here thirty years, and no man has ever attempted to cheat me." [17] If you stand at the door of the House of Commons, and look at the faces of the members, as they go in, you will say, these are just, kind, and honorable men, who mean to do right. If you go to Englishmen, properly introduced—which is indispensable in this dense population, with the multitude of strangers, too, from all parts of the earth—if you go to their houses, I do not think there is in the world such sincerity and thoroughness of hospitality. They see you through. They give you real service: they give you their time: they introduce you cordially to their friends: until you ask yourself,—'if they do thus to every stranger, how many hours will be left to them in the day and the year?'

They are as gentle and peaceful, as they are brave and magnanimous. At Oxford, I was told, among twelve hundred young men, comprising the most noble and spirited in the aristocracy, a duel never occurs. In Cambridge, among seventeen hundred, the same is true. And there is a sentiment of justice and honor resident in the people, which is always sure to respond aright, when any private or public wrong has been attempted.

I trace the peculiarities of English manners and English fortune, then, to their working climate, their dense population, the presence of an aristocracy or model class for manners and speech, to their diet generous and orderly taken, to

17. Attributed to Joshua Bates (1788–1864), a partner in the Baring Brothers banking firm (see *JMN*, 10:331).

their force of constitution, to the tenacity or perseverance of their nature, and to their fine moral quality. And these are some of the reasons why England is England. When to this vivacious stock at home, yielding armies of young men, every year, for her business of commercial conquest, all over the globe, you add the steady policy of planting a clear-headed, generous, and energetic gentleman, at every important point, all along their immense colonial territory, in islands and on the main, in the shape of a military, or diplomatic, or, at least, a commercial agent, you have the secret of British history. These Clives, Hastingses, Brookes, Cannings, Ponsonbys, and Hardinges, carry the eye and heart of the best circles of London into the extremities of the earth, and the homes of almost bestial barbarism.[18]

It is common to augur evil of England's future and to forbode her sudden or gradual decline under the load of debt, and pauperism, and the unequal competition with new nations where land is cheap. Certainly, she has enormous burthens to carry and grave difficulties to contend with. And her wisest statesmen incline to call her home from her immense colonial system. But though she may yield to time and change, what a fate is hers! She has planted her banian roots in the ground, they have run under the sea, and the new shoots have sprung in America, in India, in Australia, and she sees the spread of her language and laws over the most part of the world made certain for as distant a future as the science of man can explore.

18. Most of these persons were involved in the British colonization of India: Robert Clive (1725–74) helped to orchestrate the original British settlement of India; Warren Hastings (1732–1818), first governor general (1774); Sir James Brooke (1803–68), first raja of Sarawak, Borneo; George Canning (1770–1827), president of the board of control for India (1816–20); and Sir Henry Hardinge (1785–1856), governor general (1844–48). The line of Ponsonbys included John (1713–89), speaker of the Irish House of Commons for fifteen years; his son George (1755–1817), lord chancellor of Ireland; and his son Sir Frederick Cavendish (1783–1837), a soldier and governor of Malta.

# "London"
# 3 January 1849

Emerson first delivered "London" on 3 January 1849 as the second of two lectures before the Mercantile Library Association at Tremont Temple in Boston, receiving $100 for the two lectures. He repeated the lecture on 7 February 1849 before the Concord Lyceum in Concord, Massachusetts, and on 27 February 1849 as the second of two lectures in Framingham, Massachusetts ($25 for the two lectures; lecture fees are from the "Account Books"). "London" was announced but canceled for 29 January 1850 as the second of two lectures for the Mercantile Library Association at Clinton Hall in New York City; "The Spirit of the Times" was substituted in its place (*New York Evening Post*, 30 January 1850; see *Letters*, 4:177–78n). This lecture has never been published.

Emerson first delivered "London" within a month of first delivering "England." Clearly, his greater investment of time went into composing "England," as many passages in "London" are indebted to it for remarks made there specifically about London and for general remarks about England adapted in "London" to descriptions of the city and the manners and customs of its people. In "London," as in "England," Emerson is on the whole very positive toward English culture. In his comparison of London and Paris, for instance, Paris, with its superficial beauty, falters before London's imaginative practicality. On the other hand, in "London" Emerson is more critical than he is in "England" of English class structures and, especially, of the responsibility of English aristocrats for the nation's poverty. Virtually all of the new writing for "London" occurs in the last third of the lecture—in Emerson's descriptions of London's museums and botanical gardens and in his history of recent museum acquisitions.

Emerson's first delivery of "London" followed his delivery of "England" on 27 December 1849 at Tremont Temple in Boston before the same audience. When he delivered "England" on 20 February 1849 as the first of two lectures in Framingham, he followed with "London" a week later. Although no details of the audience's response to those deliveries of "London" survive, Emerson undoubtedly abandoned "London" after the Framingham lectures because of its closeness to "England," which in its first months of delivery was proving to be a very popular lecture (see the headnote to "England"). Thus, the fact that he delivered "England" on 22 January 1850 as the first of two lectures before the Mercantile Library Association at Clinton Hall in New York City probably explains his decision to replace "London" with "The Spirit of the Times" as his second lecture in New York City.

T HE MOST WONDERFUL thing I saw was London,—immeasurable, plural London, at once seen to be the capital of the world, old, older than all book or tradition; where men have lived ever since there were men; whose only history is in the venerable names which still cleave after ages to the old thoroughfares. London,—King Lud's town—still keeping the hoary name of Ludgate in one of its streets; London, an aggregation of capitals; a nation in brick; with a population larger than that of some European states. There it is with its two and a half millions of souls; with its magazines of wealth; with its centres of power; with its restless, world-embracing machinery; with its senate of kings, hiding its two thousand years of history in the din and grandeur of the present hour. The smoke over the city, through which the sun rarely penetrates, gives a dusky magnificence to the huge piles of buildings in its western part. Martin's pictures of Babylon are faithful copies of the west end—light, darkness, architecture.[1]

There are in London several little nations; a Jew's quarter in Monmouth Street and Holywell; a German quarter in Whitechapel; a French quarter in Spitalfields, where the silk weavers have preserved their own customs ever since the revocation of the Edict of Nantes.

An account of London is a history of England, and the sufficiency of the English people, and the reason why London is London and has all the business and all the money of the world passing through it. There are many countries with good seacoast besides England, many countries with good climate, which make no pretension to the British influence. But here is the best average brain. Men found that this people had a faculty of doing, which others had not. There is an incompatibility in the Italians, in the Spaniards, in the Turks, of dealing with other nations; of treating with them. But the English brain is of the right temper; neither too cold, nor too hot, neither too swift, nor too slow: calm, energetic, tenacious, just, and mild.

It has taken a long time to build London. It was a British town twenty centuries ago. It was enlarged by the Romans, and the old legend gives to Julius Caesar the founding of the Tower. The British town grew again, after the Romans were gone. Then it yielded to the Saxon for four hundred years; then to the Danes or Northmen, in the tenth, eleventh, and twelfth centuries; and was the receptacle into which all the mettle of that strenuous population was poured. It would seem that the perpetual supply of the best men in Norway, Sweden, and Denmark to the piratical expeditions of the ninth and tenth centuries gradually exhausted the country like a tree which bears much fruit when young. And these have been second-rate powers ever since. Konghelle, the famed town where the

---

1. John Martin (1789–1854), historical painter whose works include *The Fall of Nineveh* (1833).

kings of Norway, Sweden, and Denmark were wont to meet, is now rented to a private English gentleman as a shooting ground.

Here all is central, cosmopolitan. The eye is struck with the manners of a great city; with the effect on the men of running in and out constantly amidst the play of centralized forces; the effect to keep them tense and silent, and to mind every one his own. They have all the manners enforced by a dense population. They have a great talent of letting alone everything that does not concern them. They economize speech, and when they speak, clip their words. Ask your way in the streets, of a passenger; probably, he will point in silence.

A certain liberality and catholicism, an air of having seen much, and seen the best, appears in all men. They are bored by everything provincial, and detect the smutch of native clay sticking to the clothes of a villager. They notice in the American speech a certain purism, the accent of a man who knows how the word is spelled, rather than the unrestrained expression of a man who is only eager to say what he means.

In like manner, the London tailor tells you that your coat is of a French or German pattern, and would be noticed. But here is a coat that you may go into any part of the world with, and it will not be noticed. London, in English phrase, is a capital place to take the nonsense out of a man.

Indeed, the necessity of leaving much alone, is quickly apparent. I presently found that the Londoner was, like me, a stranger in London: I had soon much to tell him of it, if he had much to tell me. And there is no man who at all masters or much affects this huge, weltering, self-arranging mass. In London, no man is entitled to do the honours. London is of that size that the Englishman also feels that it is a mart of the world, and that the newest comer is also at home in it, as much as he, and that there would be a kind of impertinence in assuming too civilly to show the place, as if you visited him in his own house in the country. Personal character and real business or relation to great interests constitutes in every great capital the freedom of the city.

But it is by necessity that everyone lets every other one alone. There are all sorts of necessities to be considered. The long distances make short days. It requires decision not to lose a great deal of time. The many miles of street you must traverse on foot or in bus or cab; the despotic limits of office hours, and of ceremonial hours in visits; and the rain which falls at any time almost every day, waste time and soon establish the habit of concentration.

The general appearance of London is not attractive and picturesque like that of Paris. The Seine adorns Paris. The Thames is out of sight in London. The Seine is quayed all the way, so that broad streets, on both sides of the river, as well as gay bridges, have all the good of it: the sun, and moon, and stars look into it, and are reflected. At London, one can hardly remember seeing the river. The houses abut on it; the bridges are the only places where it is visible, and not there easily, over the high parapet. In Paris, are magnificent gardens, neither too large nor too small for the convenience of the whole population who spend every evening in them, gardens with noble and copious fountains, gardens and parks far more available to the pleasure of the people than those of London.

The palaces of France are truly royal. If the Tuileries have cost a great deal of treasure at some time, the French have at least got a palace to show for it. Whilst in London, there is no palace, with all their millions of guineas that have been spent. Compared with the powerful and spirited, ornate architecture of Paris, which is the efflorescence of the French people, London looks heavy and formal.

But a main difference between London and Paris, which recommends Paris to the foreigner, is perhaps less honorable to it: this, namely, that Paris exists for the foreigner; serves him; whilst, in London, it is the Londoner, who is much in the foreigner's way. England has built London for its own use. France has built Paris for the world. The Parisian population seems to devote itself to the pleasure and pride of those who come to it, with money to spend. Whilst the English are not likely to be visited by anybody who has half as much money as hundreds and hundreds of native citizens in the streets of London, and who would hardly feel very sensibly the loss of the foreigners; at least, of those who come for their pleasure.

On inspection, these advantages of Paris disappear; at least, the national character of both countries is shown in their cities; the solid, homely, comfort-seeking Englishman has secured the useful, first. Thus, in the economy of water: In Paris, the stranger is struck with the beautiful fountains on the Place de la Concorde, and gives Paris the preference to London. But this beautiful water is not drinkable; and the houses in Paris have no wells or pumps, and buy all their water by the bucket from water carriers, who bring it from certain springs. In London, every house has some kind of water privilege, as that in which I lived received its water from Hertfordshire, which entered at the top of the house. The walls of a London dwelling-house are perforated with systems of pipes for water—fresh, hot, and waste; for gas; for heat; for sound (the servants in a cellar-kitchen, at a long distance from the matron in the third story, must be informed of the wants of the parlour, after the bell is rung); and, lastly, for light, by means of glass doors, and floors, and skylights. Over the apartment in which I break-fasted daily, was a glass floor one and a quarter inch thick, and over that another before you came to the skylight. One of the most valued engineers of the age, is Mr. Chadwick, who promises to give every house a profusion of pure water,—sixty gallons a day to every head, at one penny a week.

The system of drainage and sewers is receiving extreme attention in these times by the Health of Towns Commissioners. One of my countrymen told me, he saw, one morning, a man issuing out of the ground with a bunch of candles in his hand. Much wondering, he cried out to him, "Good Heavens! Where did you come from?" "O," replied the man, "I've come seven miles under there this morning."[2] And there is a story that Chadwick rode all under London on a Shetland pony.

I stayed in London till I had become acquainted with all the styles of face in the street; till I had seen the museums, the galleries, the lecture rooms, the Royal Institution, the gardens; till I had found the suburbs and the straggling houses at each end of the city; then I took a cab, left my farewell cards, and took the train for Liverpool. To see Paris, is to see France; but to see London, is not to see England. To see all England well, needs three hundred years. For, what they told me was the merit of Sir John Soane's Museum, that "it was admirably packed," is the merit of England, which is crammed full in all corners and crevices with towns, castles, churches, villas, ruins of the old, and factories of the present generation.[3]

But what a fate is that of England. She has planted her banian roots in the ground, they have run under the sea, and the new shoots have sprung in America, in India, in Australia, and she sees the spread of her language and laws over the most part of the world made certain for as distant a future as the science of man can explore.

The first effect of this extraordinary accumulation of wealth at one pole of the state, is, the creation of the worst poverty, at the other. In a simple pastoral state, there is no poverty. Where all men walk on foot, nobody is hurt by a fall; but in a highly artificial state, when some men mount on horses; and mount on chariots; climb locomotives; the introduction of dangerous machinery makes life a more difficult game to play. 'Tis better for those who ride, but if anybody is weak, and gets under the wheels, he must be torn to pieces. We have never yet found the secret of generating vast wealth without generating pauperism.

England rides over every sea and land loaded with debt, sucked by pauperism. Every new earl, were he never so good a one, brings in new imbeciles to the state; indeed, Colonel Thompson's theory of primogeniture is that it is an expedient to make the son so strong that he can force the public to maintain all the rest.[4] Pensioners breed pensioners; prisons, prisons; and paupers, paupers; so that the poor ship gets incrusted with barnacles till it cannot move.

The beggary of England is frightful. In the parish of Westminster, within a mile of the magnificent patrician mob which walk or ride all day and all night on Regent Street or Hyde Park, whole streets are filled with undersized, sickly,

2. Possibly a reference to Henry Colman, a Unitarian minister studying in London (see *JMN*, 10:257).

3. Sir John Soane (1753–1837), collector and antiquary whose house in Lincoln's Inn Fields in London is today a museum holding his collections.

4. Thomas Peronnet Thompson (1783–1869), politician and general.

ragged men and women. Saint Giles is full of gin and putridity. Rag-fair is the
riot and Saturnalia of Want. In Spitalfields, the fever is always lurking, and
prudent men do not willingly go into that quarter. There are districts where the
policeman gets only such obedience as he can. At every crossing, a lascar, or boys
and girls, or old burly tatterdemalion besieges every passenger for a penny. At
night, you shall stumble on a little pile of sleeping children heaped against the
side of a wall. Woman is cheap and vile in every street. Put an empty hogshead
or a sugar puncheon into a London street, and it will instantly be filled with a
family.

In the towns of Manchester, of Liverpool, the beggary is more appalling. At
Liverpool, malignant fevers, cholera, plague, I know not what, are always devouring the starved, emaciated, vicious cellar and suburb population which is always renewed, and Liverpool appears in the bill of mortality the most unhealthy
town in the kingdom. A magistrate told me, that they had a cellar population of
twenty thousand, living in loathsome extremes. The magistrates had voted to
exclude this subterranean tenantry, and shut up their holes. But they bored
and grubbed into them and defied the police. The streets, the towns, the villages
are full of the trades of despair: chiffoniers, dancers, barrel organists, runners,
hangers on, thieves, and searchers of the filth of sewers for rings, shillings, and
teaspoons which have been washed out of sinks.

Of course, as the evil goes on increasing, and the parish burdens are become
intolerable, and as our last news says, many cottages, many of the lower class of
houses, are shut up, the tenants lapsing into the class of paupers, the laws of re-
striction and repression are severe. I read near Stirling on a signboard, "*Notice.
No stranger poor permitted to beg in Clackmannanshire.*"

The hedges of hawthorn and acacia, holly and yew, are the fence of the country. The wet climate of England is as favorable to this species of fence as the
drought of America is unfriendly. The grass covers England with a soft carpet,
the most delicious ornament. At Cambridge, they told me they mowed every
morning till it grows as fine as hair. In the north, between England and Scotland,
I once saw harvests so rich standing that I could almost believe what was pretended: that the land was too precious than that any riches could be spared for
fences.

Pertinacity is a prime element of English power and grandeur. What an eminent example is this catalogue of stars by younger Herschel. His father had done
it for the northern hemisphere. He now expatriates himself and family four
years among Dutchmen and bushmen at Cape of Good Hope, finishes his inven-
tory, comes home, and redacts it, in eight years more; and it will not begin to be
useful for thirty years, and then it will forever be precious. That is true nobility of use.

Walter Scott defined genius as perseverance. The power is used with wantonness. The most absurd violations of good manners are introduced and recommended by these censors of manners. Pückler-Muskau describes in these words the well-known character of the English fashionist: "His highest triumph is to appear with the most wooden manners as little polished as will suffice to avoid castigation; nay, to contrive even his civilities so that they may appear as near as may be to affronts. Instead of a noble, highbred ease to have the courage to offend against every restraint of decorum; to invert the relation in which our sex stand to women, so that they appear the attacking and he the passive or defensive party," and so forth.[5] But this hero with his silent fury and contempt of mankind is sufficiently well known.

The antagonist to the caprices and absurdities of this high-bred and assuming class is the species of gruff Jacobin manners which their extravagances always create and inflame. Surly wealth, which they have excluded and insulted, plebeian power, conscious of its weight and arrayed against the aristocracy, and fanaticism please themselves in treading on its pride. Jack Cade, John Knox, George Fox, the liegers of Ghent, the peasants of Munster, the impracticable goatherds of Switzerland—Goth, Hun, and Dane—orator Hunt, William Cobbett, are an undying party who enjoy their own strength in short speech, strong hand, and stamping with wooden shoes on the soft carpets of palaces.[6] This is the class who, without taste, have strong understanding, and their pride is gratified by the expression of unaffected contempt for the tinsel and trifles which others magnify. Of course, before these burly peasants mere manners, mere conventions, fall like cardhouses. They make etiquette ridiculous. It is of such antagonism that Lord Falkland said, that "for keeping State, there must go two to it, for let the most precise courtier stand ever so nicely upon points of form, a bold and confident man immediately batters down all his fences and reduces him to the plainest dealing."[7] Of course, the being of this party depends on the extravagance and effeminacy of the great whom they oppose, and the attraction which Tell, Luther, Fox, or the Green Mountain Boys possess is in the supposed manhood and plain dealing which their manners express.[8]

5. Quoted from Prince Hermann Ludwig Heinrich von Pückler-Muskau (1785–1871), *Tour in England, Ireland, and France in the Years 1826, 1827, and 1829 . . . by a German Prince* (1833) (see *JMN* 5:119).

6. John (Jack) Cade (d. 1450), leader of a rebellion against the crown and character in Shakespeare's *Henry VI;* John Knox (ca. 1510–72), Scottish architect of the Reformation; William Cobbett (1762–1835), under the pseudonym of "Peter Porcupine," wrote about country life; Henry Hunt (1773–1835), known as "Orator Hunt."

7. Lucius Cary, second viscount Falkland (ca. 1610–43), poet, scholar, and statesman.

8. William Tell, legendary Swiss hero who shot an apple from the head of his son; Green Mountain Boys, name for Vermont soldiers in the American Revolution.

This quality one sees in all the arts and efforts of that people. They clinch every nail they drive. They have no running for luck, no immoderate speed. They spend largely on their labour, and await the slow return. Their leather lies tanning seven years in the vat. At Rogers's mills in Sheffield, where I was shown the process of making a razor and a penknife, I was told, "there is no luck in making good steel;" that they make no mistakes; and every blade in the hundred is good. And that is characteristic of all their work. No more is attempted than is done.

They don't know when they are beaten. It is a certain tenacity of thinking and striving which makes in its excess obstinacy, which has given the English their proverbial nickname, but which, in degree, is an indispensable element of manly character.[9] An incident occurred whilst I was in London which evinces the trait. On the arrival of a distinguished French minister in London on his escape from Paris, many private friends called on him. His name was immediately proposed as an honorary member of the Athenæum, which, you know, is one of the popular and prized of the London clubhouses. The French minister was blackballed. Certainly, they would be proud of his name,—but the Englishman is not fickle. He had really made up his mind now for years, as he read his newspaper, to hate and despise Guizot.[10] And the altered position of the man as an illustrious exile, and a guest in the country, make no difference to him, as they would instantly to an American.

They require the same adherence, through conviction, and reality, in public men. It is the want of character which has made the low reputation of the Irish members, one hundred and twenty seven, all voting like sheep, never proposing anything, and all but four voting the income tax, which was an ill-judged concession of the government to Irish property relieving Irish property from the burdens charged on English. They have a horror of adventurers in Parliament and elsewhere. The ruling passion of Englishmen in these days is a terror of humbug. In the same proportion, they value honesty, and stoutness, and adherence to your own. Nay, I noticed lately that a noted English felon, who was brought to justice in this country, complained loudly of his American accomplices, that "they were not staunch."

I fear, that, in many points, the English tenacity is in strong contrast to American facility. The facile American sheds his Puritanism when he leaves Cape Cod; runs into all English and French vices with great zest; and is neither Unitarian, nor Calvinist, nor Catholic, nor stands for any thought or thing: all which is very distasteful to English honour. It is a bad sign that I have met with many Ameri-

9. Emerson refers to "John Bull," slang for an Englishman.

10. François Pierre Guillaume Guizot (1787–1874), French historian and statesman, served as minister to London in 1840.

cans who flattered themselves that they pass for English. They deceive themselves. I recognize the Americans in the first sentence they speak.

I do not think the English quite capable of doing justice to our countrymen. He is annoyed by the free and easy pretension, the careless manners, and the neglect of certain points of decorum and respect, to which he is accustomed to attach importance, and he does not see that this is his own self-reliance transferred to a new theatre, where there is no such division of labour as exists in England, and where every man must help himself in every manner (like an Indian,) and remember much which the European more gracefully abandons to his valet.

But the main advantage which the American possesses is a certain versatility, and, as far as I know, a greater apprehensiveness of mind. He more readily and genially entertains new thoughts, new modes, new books, is more speculative, more contemplative, and is really related to the future, whilst the Englishman seems mortgaged to the past. Each countryman is qualified for the part assigned him in history.

In drawing these sketches, I am well aware there is a dark side of England which I have not wished to expose. The first effect of the extraordinary determination of the national mind of England, for so many centuries on wealth, has been, in developing colossal wealth, to develop hideous pauperism. These fair, ruddy, muscular, well-educated bodies go attended by poor dwarfed, starved, short-lived skeletons. There are two Englands;—rich, Norman, Saxon, learned, social England,—seated in castles, halls, universities, and middle-class houses of admirable completeness and comfort—and poor, Celtic, peasant, drudging, chartist England, in hovels and workhouses, cowed and hopeless, as Freedom in America has developed two Americas,— one, white and exclusive; and the other, black and excluded. I only recognize this fact in passing: it is important that it be stated;—it will not help us now to dwell on it.

Mr. Landor said well enough, "Who would live in a new country, that can live in an old?" There may easily be two answers. Certainly, a great many people would much prefer the opportunities and plasticity of the new; those who study comfort and luxury will certainly choose the old. But the question were better, "Who would live in a new city, that can live in an old?" What gifts does not every city inherit from each generation that has inhabited it. The genius of many periods, many opinions, many styles of religion and civility, have got inscribed on it, in stone, and iron, and gold; and there they all speak their many languages to the imagination and the senses. Every age since Julius Caesar has left some trace of it in the building of old London, and a certain civility and conservative instinct has kept all in repair. The railway excavations, in this very year, have laid bare a Roman pavement. Fragments of the London wall of that age, are still to be found near Ludgate Hill. And so down; Saxon arches, Norman windows, mediæval towers, Westminster Abbey, palaces of Inigo Jones; Saint Paul's Cathedral, and fifty-four churches of Christopher Wren; old colleges, immemorial hospitals; immense accommodations which modern commerce has provided for itself; and all the facilities which the wealth of a monarch could not buy, but which are yielded for his small subscription of a few pence or shillings to the private citizen of an old town; facilities that belong to the being at the spot where the great agencies centre; where the ruling men in every kind are found; whence all ships, expresses, roads, and telegraphs for all parts of the world start.

Here are ships, if you like them; six or seven thousand vessels belong to this port. Here are single docks covering twenty-five acres. In their vaults, an arithmetical friend of mine told me, he passed through nineteen miles of pipes of wine, piled from floor to ceiling. Here are shops, bursting with opulence into the streets, which tell in the profusion of their costly wares what wealthy customers frequent them. 'Tis very clear, that London has too many glass doors to afford a revolution. A friend who was furnishing his house, told me, that he found piles of plate breast high in many shops on Ludgate Hill. Here is the Bank. Here is the Parliament House covering eight acres. Here is the British Museum and the Hunterian, Kew Gardens and the Zoological, and the parks. Here are the clubhouses.

Here is the collected society of English learning, wit, wealth, and power. The riches of a cultivated population, one cannot exaggerate. Every day, you may meet a new man, centre of a new circle of thought and practice, which, but for what seems an accident, you should never have heard of. What a difference between city and city! What unlike moral values in the crowd of hats one looks down upon from a street window in London, and the turbaned heads one might see from a mosque in Constantinople!

There is an economy in coming into a town, where every service which one requires is rendered by the first masters in that kind. Rothschild is your banker; Stephenson and Brunel your engineers; Pugin and Barry build; Chadwick makes the aqueduct; Reid ventilates; the military arrangements are made by the Duke of Wellington; the nightly debate in Parliament, by Peel, Russell, Cobden, Brougham, and Stanley. Faraday and Richard Owen, Sedgwick and Buckland, are the lecturers in science. Herschel, Airy, and Adams, are in the observatory. The great heirs of fame are living and talking in society. Turner and Landseer paint: Landor, Wordsworth, Hallam, Tennyson, write; and for your entertainment Lablache, Grisi, and Jenny Lind sing; and Taglioni dances; and Soyer cooks.

The best is not too good for you. Happy is the man who lives where the best is cheap. The life of a traveller in London is in extremes: he goes from show to show; he dines every day in a new palace; he is curiously and luxuriously cefended and pampered: he sits in a cloud of pictures; he eats from off porcelain and plate; his rug is the skin of a lion. It is as if everything had a touch of art; Science will quiddle for him if he will, as if all his light was polarized; all his water distilled; he goes to sleep with a puff of chloroform, on water bed, and all his implements, and garments, and trinkets, are the work of artists whose names have been familiar to him for years, as the best makers.

One of the great values of London is the British Museum, a collection of specimens from all the kingdoms of nature, but in this point not perhaps superior to the *Jardin des Plantes;* and needing the addition of the Kew and Zoological Gardens, to rival the completeness of that *Jardin.* But the British Museum adds the best collection of Egyptian sculpture and the spoil of the Pyramids; then of Nineveh and Nimroud; then of Etruscan remains; then of Ionian marbles; then, high above all others, the Elgin Marbles;[11] then of such Greek and Roman remains as the Townley Collection contained.

The British Museum is a national monument. It could only be collected in so short a time by a first-rate power, possessing command and influence in every part of the earth. This is the tribute money of Egypt, of Italy, of Greece, of Turkey, of India, of Australia, of Madagascar and the Mauritius, of Iceland and the Artic and the Antarctic Circles to British supremacy. What is better, England keeps them, with the sanction of every other nation. These Elgin Marbles, or these spoils of Pyramids, for example; Who is not glad that these inimitable works, irreparable documents in the history of mankind, are in the safekeeping of such a treasurer? Had they remained in Egypt, in Greece, they would, before this, have been burned for lime, or discharged as cannon balls, or become materials for the underpinning of houses. Now, they are laid up with reverential care and opened gratuitously to the eyes of all nations. Is not everyone glad that they are in England which, by habit of mind and experience has shown itself the most stable of empires? The conservative of nations, she is the right conservator of the jewels of the world.

It is surely not my intention to bore you with a catalogue of the British Museum. Yet I must say one word of these antique marbles. Everyone knows the history of the Elgins, but another chamber contains the Lycian marbles which have been added within a few years and which I had the privilege of seeing under the immediate guidance of Sir Charles Fellows, the discoverer and donor.[12] He went to Xanthus in the Aegean, and whilst there, a Turk chanced with his staff to scratch the ground on the edge of a block of stone, and so uncovered and showed Mr. Fellows the reliefs sculptured on its face. On examination, he found numer-

11. Between 1801 and 1803, Thomas Bruce, seventh earl of Elgin (1766–1841), brought most of the marble frieze of the Parthenon back to England, where it is now in the British Museum.
12. Sir Charles Fellows (1799–1860).

ous fragments of sculpture, and he procured laborers and set regularly at work to uncover, collect, and arrange them one by one. Gradually, he found all the parts of a triumphal monument, which had been erected in commemoration of the taking of the neighboring city by the Greeks; and which had been thrown down by an earthquake, after it had stood some centuries. Four times he sailed from London to Xanthus, and with infinite pains, and expense, and study, and the study of all other men whom he could engage, he succeeded at last in bringing to London and setting up in the Museum enough of the old monument to make its design, elevation, and details apparent, and drew from it some of the most remarkable confirmations and illustrations of the history of Herodotus, and of Homer, too, that had been given [13] This reconstruction of the Temple was like that of the Dinornis, the antediluvian bird which Owen had sketched from a fragment of a single bone.[14] It is the most beautiful work of archaic science. He had called in the aid of chemists to analyze the pigments, of geology, of history, of the sculptor Gibson, and numismatology; and good sense.[15]

It is important in every way as illustrating the history of Greek art. The temple itself imitates in stone the old carpentry of the country still visible in the huts of the peasantry, and is an ark, with the ends of the poles projecting by which it could be lifted and carried. The peasantry never changes. The women wear the same ornaments; the boys have the same tuft of hair; the horses are harnessed in the same fashion. This temple was built many years before the Parthenon. Yet one or two groups in the friezes of the Parthenon are manifest plagiarisms from this, and many important observations on Greek art and on the transcendant excellence of the Greek senses were suggested by this Lycian monument. Thus, the exact truth and fitness of every particular of Greek ornament; every chamber, cell, angle, column, and every rosette, fillet, ornament, is there for cause as much as the foundation or the roof. If there are ten statues, it is because we learn from the history that there were ten cities; if they stand each on some emblem as a dove, a snake, a crab, it is because we find from the coins of the period that each of these symbols was the appropriate arms of the several cities which sent quotas of troops. The friezes accurately describe the siege and capture of the town.

The inscriptions are calculated for the perspective in the size of the letters, so that when printed line for line, in letters of equal size, they assume a pyramidal form. The architecture of the Parthenon also is perspective and has no straight lines.

13. Herodotus (ca. 484–ca. 425 B.C.), Greek historian best known for his account of the Greco-Persian War.

14. In 1843 Richard Owen reconstructed the "Dinornis," an extinct bird of great size, from remains found in New Zealand.

15. John Gibson (1790–1866), sculptor known for his classical themes.

Some details on this matter may not be uninteresting. The Church of La Madeleine in Paris, you know, is an elegant structure in the Greek model built after the Maison Carrée at Mismas, and exceeding the size and resembling the proportions of the Parthenon. After it was built, there was a sinister rumor that the foundations had settled, and the long line of the frieze had sunk a little in the centre. Architects were consulted, and, on accurate measurement, it was found that it was perfectly true and horizontal, that the sinking in the midst, was only an optical illusion, which must always deform to the eye a building of that length. The question arose, how was this managed in the Parthenon? The Society of Dilettanti in London sent an architect, Mr. Penrose, to Athens, to measure the lines of the Parthenon with very delicate instruments; [16] and, he found, that, there was no straight line in the building; that precisely this optical illusion was allowed for, by making small upward curves, and that the line of the roof, or, what in a wooden building we should call the ridge pole, was an arc of a circle of seven or eight miles circumference.

In like manner, the Panathenaic frieze is beautiful, if lighted from below, as it really is in the Parthenon; otherwise, the feet of the horses are finished and obtrusive, and the heads of the men bald.

Of the Elgin Marbles I have little to say, though they exerted no small part of the attraction that drew me to England. Great pains have been taken in making the best possible arrangement of these in the hall which is devoted to them, and there they lie in beauty so simple, so superior in their rhythmic motion, sitting upon their horses with the grace of riding gods. People go to the Elgin chamber many times, and, at last, the beauty of the whole comes to them at once, like music. A poet remarked to me, in London phrase, one day, that to come out of the next room, where, too, many fine remains of old sculpture are collected, into this, "was like coming from a room full of *snobs,* to a room full of gentlemen."

Yet, though admirable remains of ancient sculpture are here, it must be confessed that the arrangement is surprisingly careless, without any good order or skilful disposition, without names and without numbers. The information in the printed catalogue you buy at the door, is not much more than in an auctioneer's catalogue, and is totally inadequate. The Museum seems in most of the chambers a mere warehouse of old marbles.

I took occasion from this to recommend to one or two friends a new profession. It seemed to me it would be a good undertaking for a young scholar in London to devote himself for a time to the study of Winkelmann and Visconti, then to Denon and Wilkinson, and to make himself master, as far as he could, of the

---

16. Francis Penrose (1817–1903), English architect who devoted a great part of his life to measuring the Parthenon in Athens.

antiques in the British Museum, with the view of explaining them to visiters.[17] He might then advertise himself as Guide to the British Museum, offering his services to those who wished a thorough explanation. It would be most welcome and valuable instruction to the best class of strangers, and would be a very instructive profession to the professor himself, for years; and he would then be well-fitted for higher employment in the Museum, or the Library.

Attached to the Museum and a part of it is the King's Library, where 420,000 printed books and fifty or sixty thousand manuscripts are collected, and second in value only to the King's Library at Paris. The law requires that, of every book printed in England, a copy shall be given to the King's Library. Here the line of loaded shelves runs twelve miles, and the supposed annual increase runs up to twenty thousand volumes.

In Westminster Abbey, I was surprised to find the tombs cut and scrawled with penknives, and even in the coronation chair, in which is contained the royal stone of Scone, and in which, for hundreds of years, kings and queens have been crowned, Mr. Butler, and Mr. Light, and Mr. Abbott have recorded their humble pretensions to be remembered. "I, Butler slept in this chair," is explicitly recorded by that person's penknife on the seat.

Kew Gardens I naturally join to the British Museum, as an essential of the great British conservatory of nature and art and a token of the greatness of London. There is no other place where they would not be a wonder of the world; but here, they are obscure, and, I was told, you shall rarely meet a Londoner who has seen them. They comprise a space of *six* or *eight hundred* acres,—park, conservatory, palm house, and *stores*, as the greenhouses are called. The new glass palm house is three hundred sixty-two feet long, one hundred wide, by sixty-six high, and cost forty thousand pounds. The garden is an admirable work of power and taste. No expense spared; all climates have been searched. The *echino cactus visnager*, which is a thousand years old and perhaps four feet high, cost many hundred pounds to transport it from the mountains in Mexico to the sea. Here was tea, green and black, growing finely; here were clove, cinnamon, chocolate, lotus, caoutchouc, gutta-percha, kava, ivory plant, upas, baobab, orotava, and the papaw, which makes tough meat tender. Here was the papyrus; here the banian. Here was the *Strelitzia Regina*, named for Queen Charlotte, one of the gayest flowers in nature, which looked like a bird, and all but sung.[18] Here the *Graphtophyllum Pictum*, or caricature plant, on whose leaves the yellow spots

17. Johann Joachim Winckelmann (1717–1868), German antiquities expert; Ennio Quirino Visconti (1751–1818), Italian archaeologist in charge of the Capitoline Museum in Rome; Baron Dominique Vivant Denon (1747–1825), French archaeologist who published a book about Egypt; Sir John Gardner Wilkinson (1797–1875), Egyptologist and author of many books on the subject.

18. Queen Charlotte Sophia (1744–1818) was married to George III of England.

form very good *Punch* portraits, which I saw. Lately, there was so good a likeness of Lord Brougham's well-known face, that all men remarked it. Here were tree, shrub and vine, fungus, and a stove full of wonderful orchises, which are the rage of England now.

It would be wrong to pass by the Hunterian Museum and other museums. But I must not stop to describe these. These are valued, and will be visited by all judicious travellers. Yet, I well know, that the American in London will be pretty sure before he visits the Museum, to find the Houses of Parliament. All feet turn to the Senate, the two patrician houses, with no great difference: one of these that are lords, and one of those that shall be.

"I am more cosmopolite than patriot, and great cities appear to me the common country of all independent and civilized men. They are the centre where meet all the talents, all the arts, all the knowledges, all the industry, all the resources of a nation. 'Tis from these great foci of light and activity that issue all the favors which the genius of civilization pleases to pour on the human race."

# Conduct of Life,
# 1851–1853

EMERSON DELIVERED HIS lecture series on the *Conduct of Life* in a number of formats in a number of cities between 1851 and 1853. He first delivered the *Conduct of Life* series in six lectures between 20 March and 1 April 1851 before the Young Men's Mercantile Library Association in Pittsburgh, for which he received $240 ("Account Books"). Responding on 1 February 1851 to an invitation from the Committee of the Association to lecture in Pittsburgh, Emerson wrote, "I have just been preparing some Lectures which at this moment interest me a good deal,—a series of topics on 'the Conduct of Life.' One is 'Power,' one 'Wealth,' one 'Culture,' & so on" (*Letters*, 4:241–42). The lectures he delivered in Pittsburgh were "England" on 20 March, "The Law of Success" on 22 March, "Wealth" on 25 March, "Economy" on 27 March, "Culture" on 29 March, and "Worship" on 1 April. Emerson repeated the *Conduct of Life* series in six lectures between 22 December 1851 and 26 January 1852 at the Masonic Temple in Boston; the "Account Books" show that he netted $144.50 from the series, while Charvat reports that he netted $420.05. The lectures he delivered at that time were "Fate" on 22 December, "Power" on 29 December, "Wealth" on 5 January, "Economy" on 12 January, "Culture" on 19 January, and "Worship" on 26 January.

Between 18 February and 27 March 1852, Emerson delivered a *Conduct of Life* series in four private lectures at Hope Chapel in New York City ($61.18 for the series [Charvat]). The lectures he delivered at Hope Chapel were "Fate" on 18 February, "Economy" on 20 February, "Culture" on 25 March, and "Worship" on 27 March. Before finishing the series at Hope Chapel, Emerson began a *Conduct of Life* series in Medford, Massachusetts ($69 for the series [Charvat]). Emerson delivered six lectures in Medford, and while it is doubtful that he would have significantly changed the content of the series, no record has been found to indicate definitively the order of the lectures he gave or the titles under which he delivered them in Medford on 11 March, 18 March, 28 March (Charvat) or 29 March (von Frank), 1 April, 8 April, and 29 April 1852.

Between his fifth and sixth lectures in Medford, Emerson delivered a *Conduct of Life* series in six lectures before the Mercantile Library Association at Bonsecours Hall in Montreal, for which he received $120 for the series ("Account Books"). In Montreal he delivered "England" on 19 April, "Power" on 20 April, "Wealth" on 21 April, "Economy" on 22 April, "Culture" on 23 April, and "New England" on 24 April.

In December 1852 Emerson delivered a *Conduct of Life* series in six private

lectures in Cincinnati, Ohio, for which he received $362 for the series ("Ac-
count Books"). In Cincinnati he delivered "Power" on 9 December, "Wealth"
on 11 December, "Economy" on both 13 and 15 December (see the headnote to
"Economy"), "Fate" on 17 December, and "Worship" on 20 December.

Leaving Cincinnati, between 27 December 1852 and 7 January 1853 Emerson
delivered a *Conduct of Life* series in seven lectures before the Mercantile Library
Association at Wyman's Hall in St. Louis, Missouri, receiving $500 for the se-
ries ("Account Books"). Adding "The Anglo-Saxon" to the six lectures that
had become the core of his *Conduct of Life* series, Emerson delivered "Power" on
27 December, "Wealth" on 28 December, "The Anglo-Saxon" on 30 December,
"Economy" on 3 January, "Fate" on 4 January, "Culture" on 6 January, and
"Worship" on 7 January.

The *Conduct of Life* series proved to be of immense value to Emerson as a
means of organizing his thoughts toward the volume that he would publish as *The
Conduct of Life* in 1860. Although Charvat reports that Emerson reprised a *Conduct of Life* series one last time in November 1858 in Salem, Massachusetts (see
the headnote to the *Natural Method of Mental Philosophy* series), the St. Louis
series in 1852–53 was, in fact, the last he gave under the title. Nevertheless, all
of the lectures associated at one time or another with the series were popular lectures independent of the series. For instance, Emerson had been delivering
"England" for two years before introducing it into the *Conduct of Life* series
in Pittsburgh, while "Wealth," "Economy," and "The Anglo-Saxon" (which he
eventually titled "The Anglo-American"; see the headnote to that lecture) variously served him in other series or as independent lectures for another lecture
season or two.

Of all the lectures associated with the *Conduct of Life* series, five survive
as complete lecture manuscripts and are printed in this edition. "Wealth,"
"Economy," and "Fate" follow immediately as *Conduct of Life* lectures, while
"England" and "The Anglo-Saxon" (that is, "The Anglo-American") have been
treated as lectures independent of the series. None of these lectures has ever
been published. Their service, along with the service of "Power," "Culture," and
"Worship," to *The Conduct of Life* will be accounted for in the Harvard edition
of that volume (*CW*, 6) forthcoming under the editorship of Barbara L. Packer,
Joseph Slater, and Douglas Emory Wilson.

# Conduct of Life: "Wealth"
# 25 March 1851
# (1851–1854)

EMERSON FIRST DELIVERED "Wealth" on 25 March 1851 as the third in a series of six lectures on the *Conduct of Life* before the Young Men's Mercantile Library Association in Pittsburgh, receiving $240 for the series ("Account Books"). He repeated the lecture on 5 January 1852 as the third in a series of six private lectures on the *Conduct of Life* at the Masonic Temple in Boston ($144.50 for the series ["Account Books"; Charvat reports $420.05 for the series]); on 4 February 1852 before the Young Men's Association in Buffalo, New York ($50); on 16 February 1852 in the Mercantile Library Course at Hope Chapel in New York City ($60); on 21 April 1852 as the third in a series of six lectures on the *Conduct of Life* before the Mercantile Library Association at Bonsecours Hall in Montreal ($120 for the series); on 26 November 1852 before the Young Men's Association of Union College in Schenectady, New York ($25 [Charvat]); on 11 December 1852 as the second in a series of six private lectures on the *Conduct of Life* in Cincinnati, Ohio ($362 for the series); and on 28 December 1852 as the second in a series of seven lectures on the *Conduct of Life* before the Mercantile Library Association at Wyman's Hall in St. Louis, Missouri ($500 for the series; except as noted, lecture fees are from the "Account Books").

On 7 April 1852 Emerson lectured on either "Wealth" or "Power" before the Norwich Lyceum in Norwich, Connecticut, for which he received $30 (see *Letters*, 4:284–85, 287–88, 8:308). In place of "Culture" as originally advertised, he combined "Wealth" and "Economy" to form one lecture for delivery on 9 February 1854 in Ottawa, Illinois ($30; see *JMN*, 13:498, and *Letters* 4:427n). Although no record of the fact has been found, Emerson may have delivered "Wealth" before the Concord Lyceum in Concord, Massachusetts: on page {7v} of the manuscript, he interlined "our own town" above "my village" but did not cancel the latter. It may be, however, that he used pages {7r}–{7v} from "Wealth" in "Economy," which he delivered before the Concord Lyceum on 25 February 1852 (see the electronic textual notes; Emerson's lecture "Economy" is printed in this edition). Finally, Emerson lectured under the title "Wealth" on 1 May 1859 before the Twenty-Eighth Congregational Society at the Music Hall in Boston, for which he received $50 (lecture fees are from the "Account Books"). Because no detailed reports of that delivery have been located, it is unclear whether on that occasion Emerson spoke from this manuscript or from some combination of text from "Wealth" and "Economy" as he had in Ottawa, Illinois, in 1854. The lecture "Wealth" has never been published.

Emerson began to offer "Wealth" regularly as an independent lecture and as part of his series on the *Conduct of Life* in January and early February 1851 (see *Letters*, 4:241–42).

As topics, "wealth" and "economy" were virtually synonymous in Emerson's mind. His lectures on "Wealth" and "Economy" share the theme that organicism is the key to personal or "moral" economics and wealth. This is Emerson's extension of his conception of compound interest, which he believed would double the principal in eleven years (see *JMN*, 10:67).

"Wealth" was generally well received, even though Bronson Alcott was not pleased by Emerson's handling of the subject at the Masonic Temple on 5 January 1852:

> Emerson said fine things last night about "Wealth," but there are finer things to be said in praise of Poverty, which it takes a person superior to Emerson even to say worthily. Thoreau is the better man, perhaps, to celebrate that estate, about which he knows much, and which he wears as an ornament about himself. . . . He can best describe the evils of wealth and the penury it often entails—on owner and trustee. . . .
>
> Eloquent, wise, and witty were the orator's praises of Gold, and just to this transition period of civilization, the merchant's day as none ever before—still the moral laws were too faintly implied, and so left not without detriment in the auditor's mind. (Entry for 6 January 1852, *The Journals of Bronson Alcott*, 261)

A month after Alcott heard this lecture, the *Buffalo Commercial Advertiser* favorably described Emerson's delivery of "Wealth, its purposes and its uses" before the Young Men's Association, stating that the large audience in Buffalo was highly entertained; the reporter also thought that Emerson's "lean and ungainly . . . *physique*" suggested "the idea of a roving reformer, Grahamite, Fourierite, or some other" (4–6 February 1852, quoted in *Letters*, 4:274–75n).

The *New York Times* reported on Emerson's 16 February 1852 delivery of "Wealth" at Hope Chapel in the Mercantile Library Course in a column that also served as an advertisement for the *Conduct of Life* series that opened at Hope Chapel on 18 February but did not include "Wealth":

> The subject—"Wealth, or the Subjugation of Nature to Human Wants." It is superfluous to say that the text was handled in the style of a master. Mr. Emerson abhors common-place. To shun it he occasionally sinks into obscurity of sense. But the perpetual novelty of definition; abruptness of inference from startling premises; quaintness of allusion; unexpectedness of illustration, retain the mind in a state resembling that produced by a narcotic stimulus. Every vibration of the instrument evolves new phases and combinations of beauty, formal and chromatic; and when the exhibition is ended, it is hard to extract the moral, so completely have the perceptions been absorbed in purely sensual enjoyment. ("Mercantile Library Lectures," 17 February 1852, 2)

The following week, the *New York Herald* printed a detailed abstract of that performance ("On Wealth—By Ralph Waldo Emerson," 24 February 1852, 6). Later in the year, the *Schenectady Reflector* reported that inclement weather "prevented a large, but could not prevent a select audience" for Emerson's delivery on 26 November 1852 before the Young

Men's Association of Union College; the reporter added, "Those who went to hear Tran-scendentalism, came away astonished to find that they had understood, admired and most heartily approved [his ideas]" (3 December 1852, quoted in *Letters*, 4:324n). According to Mead, local newspapers reported that Cincinnatians responded favorably to Emerson's "rich intellectual feast" of "Wealth" and "Economy" in December 1852 and that they did not seem put off by the bluntness of his stated assumption that "the Ladies and Gentle-men before him came to think, not to be entertained" (Mead, *Yankee Eloquence in the Middle West*, 35). Although his appearance later that month in St. Louis received only brief announcements in the *Daily Missouri Republican* from 27 December 1853 to 7 Janu-ary 1854, Emerson's lectures there are more fully treated in John Francis McDermott, "Emerson at St. Louis, 1852: Unpublished Letters and Telegrams," *Emerson Society Quarterly*, no. 6 (1st quarter 1957): 7–9. Finally, when Emerson delivered "Wealth" be-fore the Twenty-Eighth Congregational Society in 1859, the *Boston Post* published a brief notice that was more concerned with the decorations of the Music Hall than with Emer-son's lecture: "The Hall was gaily decorated with flags and streamers, and presented quite a Fourth of July appearance. Directly in the centre of the hall was suspended a stuffed spread eagle. The decorations were used at the Howard Fair, which closed [the night be-fore]" ("Mr. Emerson at the Music Hall," 2 May 1859, 1).

W HAT AN IMMENSE body of nonsense the state must absorb and dispose of to get the simplest ends accomplished by its officers. They cut down a whole palm to get the bud in the top. On plantations with twenty slaves in the house, you cannot get a clean plate. If you take a long journey, you carry the horse.

In the house, we spend our money for that which is not bread, for paint and floor cloths, for newspapers, for men-servants and maid-servants, who yield us the smallest fraction of direct advantage. The friction of the social machine is grown enormous and absorbs all the power applied.

Our rich men are not rich, nor our powerful men truly strong,—making the mountains, the woods, the mines, the sea, and the air, subservient to them; mak-ing the planet beautiful with gardens, rich with architecture, full of benefit, twice the home of man, first from nature, then equally so by art. They cannot use things but are used by them. He is only rich who understands it. He only truly possesses anything who knows what to do with it. But I see no rich men who impress me as real masters of the world. They have their wealth as substitute for manhood. What they really wish for is not mill shares, nor bank stock, but to be masterly men, with a counsel in their breast.

Wealth is felt and treated as the national lifeblood. Every man's speech is esteemed as it bears on this. Every government is held responsible to foster trade; and success in trade is the door to the highest rank. If a merchant shall pass twice across the sea in his own ship, he shall be a thane right worthy, and now that calico has come to be an element in England's history. When the elder Peel spoke in Parliament, they considered this man employs fifteen thousand men and pays forty thousand to the excise.[1]

Where there is immense wealth, it will be sure to buy power. Power may always be had by paying for it. And any height of style and state, may be had for the money. An earl, a duke, or a bishop is only a merchant grown rich enough to masquerade it so. Only in England, where is a multitude of rich merchants, it is a thing of degrees, and all the steps cannot be taken in one lifetime. The father takes one or two, the son a third and fourth, and the grandson stands on the steps of the throne with what titles he lists.

Socrates, hearing one of his friends in Athens crying out with joy, "What a glorious city is this! The wine of Chios is sold for a pound; the purple fish, for three; and a pint of honey, for three drachms:"—"Come with me," said Socrates; so he brought him to the miller's, and showed him that a large quantity of the finest flour was sold for a half-penny; 'tis a great frugality; then he brought him to the oilman's, and told him he might have a chœnix full of olives for two farthings; at last, he went to a slop shop, and convinced him that the price of a jerkin without sleeves was only ten drachms: so that from thence he might infer the true felicity of the city.

There is, to be sure, some range for freak and caprice in the expenditure of wealth, and, as there is always a large infusion of folly in the brain, everywhere there is some precious absurdity for which men spend,—as Indians sell a county for a red coat. The people of Southern Europe value an equipage, and will go hungry to secure that. An opera-box is a necessary of life to a French or an Italian family. In the East, they put an estate into a gem or a horse; but under governments, where concealment and portableness are half the value of property, there is more sense in it, than in serious Holland buying tulips with thousands of florins, or solid England spending a couple of thousand guineas on a tall copy of Boccaccio, or a hundred thousand pounds on a gewgaw tournament at Eglintown.[2]

There are these freaks, and every country and every man has his own. Still, there is a general consent on solid values.

Thus, among kinds of property, the instinct, which makes language wise, has always designated estate in land as *real:* and with reason, since, in the homestead, it acquires such high moral values, and, because, while a piece of land seems to make the sun, and air, and sea, which touch and mix with it, ours,—that species of property has values for the imagination, and easily becomes sublime. And,

1. Sir Robert Peel (1750–1830), father of the politician of the same name, was a prosperous English textile manufacturer and a member of Parliament.
2. Giovanni Boccaccio (1313–75), Italian poet.

therefore, rich men, in all ages, have spent vast sums in the planting and decoration of their lands. Parks, gardens, conservatories,—who but must admire the
taste, which, having ample means and labour, creates these delicious homes, and
ornaments, and entertainments for man. Wherever wealth and dense population
are found, these are found. The pride of English villas is Chatsworth, where
the Duke of Devonshire, with the aid of Mr. Paxton, has created magnificent
gardens; stoves; a fountain with a jet of near three hundred feet; an arboretum,
where all the trees of the world may be found; and his agents are crossing all seas,
and climbing all mountains, and wading through the desarts, to supply every rich
and fantastic growth of nature. George Stephenson, the inventor of the locomotive, in his delight at the overflowing conveniences and nobilities of this villa,
said to the Duke, "When your grace goes to Heaven, I don't see that you will have
much more." [3]

In this country, this costly and aristocratic kind of property is the cheapest and
most accessible of all. I could point in my village to more than one plain farmer
who does not imagine he is a rich man, who yet keeps from year to year a lordly
park, washed by the river widening to a lake, that would move the envy of an
English earl, lying idly open to all comers, without crop or rent, with its hedges
of barberry, alder, and hazel, its grapevines, its sumptuous lawns and slopes, its
old orchard, its solemn pines, and its chesnut grove, the mirror at its foot, and the
terraces of coloured autumnal forest on the opposite bank.

What is wealth? I should say, Wealth consists in having at every moment a commanding position as regards your ends. A man in debt, has it not. Every hour
bringing certain opportunities to do somewhat desirable. But we are not free to
use today, or to promise tomorrow, because we are already mortgaged to yesterday, having eaten our cake before we had earned it. Leisure, tranquillity, grace,
and strength belong to economy. My rich neighbor mows his own grass. Philosopher Kant wears the same hat for twenty years. Minott never rides. [4] Redman
stays at home on the farm, if he sends his family abroad. Anderson goes to work
every day, though his contemporaries have retired to their villas. And each of
these men is free and able for the new day, free and great as it; whilst their gay
friend, who indulges himself in debts for his pleasant occasions, is perplexed in
the extreme, and, because he falls in his own esteem, loses rank in the world.

Neither do I see how we can, with the best democracy in the world, quite avoid
the odious inequality of cultivated labour. A superintendent at the mills who sits

3. William George Spencer, sixth duke of Devonshire (1790–1858), English politician and book
collector; Sir Joseph Paxton (1801–65), English architect, appointed supervisor of the gardens at
Chatsworth in 1826.
4. Emerson's neighbor, the farmer George Minott, died on 1 December 1861 at the age of seventy-
eight years and ten months.

in his chair, must have two thousand dollars, whilst the most industrious operative has only four hundred dollars! Yea verily; for, order and administrative faculty are rare as diamonds. Why should not the wheels of the loom say, "See me;
I whirl and buzz with five hundred revolutions a minute, whilst that big waterwheel, below there, only turns five times; I will not go faster than he."

The consideration of inflation goes into all farming value. The farmer earns
two hundred, in the same time that the merchant earns two thousand dollars.
But the farmer's two hundred is safer, and is more likely to remain to him. It
was heavy to lift up from the soil; but it was, for that reason, more carefully bestowed; and will stay where it was put; so, that, the two sums turn out, at last, to
be equivalent.

Indeed, one might question, on this ground, the reliableness of the valuations
of Massachusetts, of Boston, and of New York, for direct comparison. Thus, the
gross numbers of the late census are taken, and we read, that Boston could buy
Maine, and have $80,000,000 left. But the valuations of Boston are variable val-
ues, or fancy stocks, the values of luxuries, furniture, books, and pictures; prices
of inflation, of land, house lots, and houses:—whilst the values of Maine are, for
the most part, low, primary, and necessary, and, therefore, likely to be permanent
under any state of society.

It is true, notwithstanding all the tricks of trade, and all the mishaps of honest
men, that God has made the profitable the inseparable badge of the good. And all
discerning men, and all men in their moments of sanity, are continually arriving
at this immutable fact. Mirabeau was very little of a saint, but being disgusted at
the flimsy deceptions of the bookseller's wife, he said to her, "Madame Jay, If
there were no such thing as probity, it would be invented as a means of getting
rich." Every man learns at last that fraud is shortsighted and suicidal.

The system of wealth being thus a natural product of the wit of man working
on the fruits of the world, wealth and civilization are identical; wealth increases
with the wisdom and probity of men, and, with whatever particular anomalies
and faults, the existing system of property and our system of money must be
looked on as a part of the natural history of the world, or as the best system which
the existing state of things admitted. It is, on the whole, beneficent; It was intended: and it contains and will disclose its own checks or remedies for such evils
as are incidental to it.

In this general consideration, we must find the defence of the existing system
of property, which our laws and traditions support, though we admit many objectionable traits.

For example: Here is a man sitting in his parlour, talking philanthropy, who
has his pocket full of papers representing labour done long ago, not by him, nor
even by his ancestor, but by hands which his ancestor had skill to set at work, and

get the certificates of,—and now, these certificates of the work of long mouldered hands are honoured by all men, and our friend can for them get what vast amounts of work done and value procured, by new young hands, namely, mills, railways, houses, gardens, coaches, pastures, oxen, sheep, and corn! As no man ever detected our philanthropic friend in any labour, this seems not quite just.

Again, wherever money is in hands that earned it, wherever it came by the attraction of personal qualities; wherever the owner exhibits a title to it by eminent personal worth, by accomplishments, by manners, even; by skill and dignity of spending;—it exists with more or less good will of mankind. But, it often falls out, that men blunder into wealth. I chanced lately to go into the western country, and in all the towns, in Rochester, in Buffalo, in Chicago, in Cincinnati, in St. Louis, I heard the like anecdotes, namely, that men of largest property would gladly, a few years before, have sold their land at insignificant prices, but nobody would buy: They were compelled to hold onto it: Now, the land is in the heart of great cities, and the owners, in spite of themselves, are grown rich.— Of course, one could not feel a very high sympathy with the prosperity of this description.

The farmer works very hard and very skilfully to get a good estate, and gets it. But by his skill and diligence, and that of thousands more, his competitors, the wheat and milk which I and others not farmers live by, are made so cheap, that they are within reach of our money; and we are not yet forced to take off our coats, and dig for ourselves. But it is no part of the farmer's design to keep down the price of hay, or wheat, or milk.

There is no end to illustrations of the good of non-interference. Granted, and the defence is, that 'tis essential that property be secure to its owners. If I do not know that I shall control it, I shall not earn it. 'Tis better, therefore, that it sometimes fall to dunces and to sots than, in attempts to give it only to the deserving, that the least insecurity should paralyze the arm of labour. 'Tis with this as it is with laws determining prices. We complain that the flour dealers hoard their flour for high prices, and we ask the state to compel them to sell at fair prices. Do not compel, nor interfere. They will not hold, unless there is likely to be want, and then it is best for all that they should not now sell cheap.

In like manner, the socialists parade the losses of farmers for want of good barns, good bins, scientific treatment, and so forth, and advise that this loss shall be saved to the world by vast granaries, and consociated action, such as Fourier proposes. But it is to be considered, on the other hand, that the harvest will be better preserved and go farther if laid up in private bins, in each farmer's corn barn, and each woman's basket,—than if it were kept in national granaries.

An amount of money will go farther if expended by each man and woman for their own wants, and in the feeling that this is their all, than if expended by a public steward or national commissioner. Take from me the feeling that I must cepend on myself, give me the least hint that I have good friends and backers there in reserve, who will gladly help me, and instantly I relax my diligence. I obey the first impulse of generosity that is to cost me nothing, and a certain slackness will creep over all my conduct of my affairs. Here is a bank note of one hundred dollars. Let it fall into the hands of an easy man who never earned the estate he spends, and see how little difference it will make in his affairs. At the end of the year, he is just as much behind-hand as ever, and could not have done at all, without that hundred. Let it fall into the hands of a poor and prudent woman, and every shilling, and every cent of it goes to reduce debt, or to add to instant and permanent comfort; mends a window, buys a blanket or a shawl, gets an effective stove, instead of the old cavernous fireplace. Committees of philanthropic societies are found to be lavish spenders.

What is the best use of Wealth? And, what are the points of a right Economy? As thus: wealth is the union of mind with nature, is mental; it follows, that mentality is the most potent wealth, and that whatever goes to better the man, is the best riches. For this is immediately reproductive: any prices paid for education are cheap; any addition of intellectual power; for land and money are measures of value, but knowledge is value itself, and exchangeable for every coin of the globe. What price would not a wise man, if he were blind, pay for his eyes, even to the whole of his estate? In like manner, for any new knowledge or art which was as much more valuable than eyes, as eyes are than the groping of the fingers, he might well pay what he had now, and mortgage the income of his labour for years to come. What would he not pay for a power of memory which put all the past perpetually present to him? What for a power of concentration, or of computation like Newton's, or of mechanical combination like Brunel's?

Would not any prudent man afflicted with slow and ineffectual speech sell his cow pasture and his cow, if he could thereby buy a power of good and prevailing speech in town meeting, or in the Senate, or in private society? Would he not, if heavy and repulsive, sell his house and barn, if he could buy good, manly manners and a behaviour that made him at ease, and drew friends around him in all companies?

He might safely, in this world of half-knowledge, put at peril all his livelihood, for any intimate and exact knowledge, if it were only of one of his crops, as of corn, of rye, of the turnip, or the potato; since a hundred fields would be open at once to any man, who, whilst others were guessing their way, and losing by rot or bad season, could, by knowing the cause and the remedy, plant and reap with certain success.

How much more for the higher secrets of chemistry, of botany, of meteorology? A new degree of intellectual power seems cheap at any price. The use of the world is, that, man may learn its laws. And the human race have wisely signified their sense of this, by calling wealth, *means*, man being the end. Language is always wise.

Therefore, I praise New England because it is the country in the world where is the freest expenditure for education. And, when one considers the immense advantage of educated power over rude strength, and the skill that long practice and knowledge of best methods, give to a quite ordinary understanding, we get a pretty good hint in what direction the chief expense should be laid.

I knew a man, who, for incidental purposes, wished to learn the theory of music. He sailed for Europe, and went to the professors of that art in London, and on the Continent, and inquired, Who in Europe had the profoundest science in music? And, being sent up from class to class, was informed by the best artists, that there was in Paris one man, who, having spent his life in the study of the laws of music, was believed by the professors to be acquainted with its secrets more thoroughly than any other. To Paris he went, and to the man, and said; I have six months, or a year of time; I am ready to pay any prices; make your own terms, but you must teach me your science; And, professing his readiness to accept any stipulations, the master received him as a scholar, and showed him to their mutual contentment, all the principles to which he had attained. All that is strange about this example is that it is so rare.

My second corollary, is that each man's wealth should be peculiar or proper to him. Wealth is by the upper road, and must have its measures from his own nature, and not from the brokers. A man's condition should flow from his character; his expense should be for what is essential to him. He should be rich by direct and not by indirect means. Not, certainly, every young and able man ought to go to California. Rather, very few ought to go. It is a very operose and round about way to your ends that you should go round Cape Horn to get money in order to buy something you want here. The great Condé, when his army could get no pay from the public treasury, said, "As long as the state exists, I shall never want for anything", and paid his army out of his own funds.[5] So, every man in his place with a true talent cannot be spared, and must be bought at his own price. A true and thorough workman in any kind is always sure of employment. Great lawyers say, "It is shallow, superficial students who huddle into cities, and think they must board in hotels, and live close by markets; a man who really knows the law, if he should open his office in a shanty, in a pine-barren, will and must be had, and clients will go in troops and fetch him to court."

But, though every man is entitled to a living, by no means must he measure his success by his acres or his stocks, but by his possession of what is proper

5. Quoted from Philip Henry Stanhope, Lord Mahon, *The Life of Louis, Prince of Condé, Surnamed the Great* (1845) (see *JMN*, 11:232). Louis II, duc d'Enghien (1621–86), was the "Great Condé."

and needful to the exercise of his talent. By no means is it true that all men must be large owners. The insurance of the first-class carriages in the railway is the "second-class carriage" which goes with them: and the telegraph lines which convey the messages of Rothschild and Loyd would be surely cut, if it were not known that tidings also of interest to the million, were vibrating invisibly, with these, along the wires.[6]

Dr. Johnson said he had read the story of a traveller in Arabia having a part of the desart to cross, and, being told that it was dangerous, he hired a troop of dragoons and proceeded on his way. Dr. Johnson said, he had never been struck before with the value of wealth. But wealth will buy much better things, when it builds hospitals, when it makes roads, when it establishes schools of science, and sends Dr. Kane to the North Pole, when it uses Arabian hospitality to feed the poor soldier returning wounded and hungry from the war.[7] It will buy noble outfits for young men, and portions for young women, as well as pictures and teacups from Dresden and Japan.

"Without wisdom," said Alfred, "wealth is worth little. Though a man had a hundred and seventy acres sown with gold, and all grew like corn, yet were all that wealth nothing worth, unless, that of an enemy, one could make it become his friend. For what differs gold from a stone, but in discreet using of it?" But wealth, we say, consists in having these auxiliaries of man, in having the planet, at our command, and in having astronomy, and time, and space—the sun, and moon, and star work—for us.

6. Samuel Jones Loyd (1796–1883), Baron Overstone, English economist and financier.
7. Elisha Kent Kane (1820–57), member of expeditions to the North Pole in 1850–51 and 1853–55.

# Conduct of Life: "Economy"
## 27 March 1851
## (1851–1854)

Emerson first delivered "Economy" on 27 March 1851 as the fourth in a series of six lectures on the *Conduct of Life* before the Young Men's Mercantile Library Association in Pittsburgh; he received $240 for the series ("Account Books"). He repeated the lecture on 12 January 1852 as the fourth in a series of six private lectures on the *Conduct of Life* at the Masonic Temple in Boston ($144.50 for the series ["Account Books"; Charvat reports $420.05 for the series]); on 20 February 1852 as the second in a series of four private lectures on the *Conduct of Life* at Hope Chapel in New York City ($61.18 for the series [Charvat]); on 25 February 1852 before the Concord Lyceum in Concord, Massachusetts; on 22 April 1852 as the fourth in a series of six lectures on the *Conduct of Life* before the Mercantile Library Association at Bonsecours Hall in Montreal ($120 for the series); on 13 December 1852 as the third in a series of six private lectures on the *Conduct of Life* in Cincinnati, Ohio ($362 for the series); again, on 15 December 1852 as the fourth in the same series of six private lectures on the *Conduct of Life* in Cincinnati, Ohio (Charvat lists "Fate" on this date, but Emerson delayed that lecture until 17 December; see *Letters*, 4:328n, and the headnote to "Fate"); on 3 January 1853 as the fourth in a series of seven lectures on the *Conduct of Life* before the Mercantile Library Association at Wyman's Hall in St. Louis, Missouri ($500 for the series); and on 9 March 1853 in Gloucester, Massachusetts ($20; except as noted, lecture fees are from the "Account Books").

In place of "Culture" as originally advertised, Emerson combined "Economy" and "Wealth" to form one lecture for delivery on 9 February 1854 in Ottawa, Illinois, for which he received $30 ("Account Books"; see *JMN*, 13:498, and *Letters*, 4:427n). The lecture "Economy" has never been published.

While he was delivering his series on the *Conduct of Life* at the Masonic Temple in Boston, Emerson wrote to his brother William, "The 'Economy' to my surprise turned out attractive to a great house, so that I am not sure of my gravities now that my levities prosper so well" (17 January 1852, extract in Cabot, "Blue Books"; see *Letters*, 8:3c). As topics, "economy" and "wealth" were virtually synonymous in Emerson's mind. His lectures on "Economy" and "Wealth" share the theme that organicism is the key to personal or "moral" economics and wealth. This is Emerson's extension of his conception of compound interest, which he believed would double the principal in eleven years (see *JMN*, 10:67).

On 23 February 1852 the *New-York Daily Tribune* printed an extended abstract of "Economy" from Emerson's delivery of it in his *Conduct of Life* series at Hope Chapel ("The Conduct of Life. Lecture II. By R. W. Emerson," 6; reprinted in Jeanne Kronman,

"Three Unpublished Lectures of Ralph Waldo Emerson," *New England Quarterly* 19 [March 1946]: 98–110). According to Mead, local newspapers reported that Cincinnatians responded favorably to Emerson's "rich intellectual feast" of "Wealth" and "Economy" in December 1852 and that they did not seem put off by the bluntness of his stated assumption that "the Ladies and Gentlemen before him came to think, not to be entertained" (Mead, *Yankee Eloquence in the Middle West*, 35). Although his appearance later that month in St. Louis received only brief announcements in the *Daily Missouri Republican* from 27 December 1853 to 7 January 1854, Emerson's lectures there are more fully treated in John Francis McDermott, "Emerson at St. Louis, 1852: Unpublished Letters and Telegrams," *Emerson Society Quarterly*, no. 6 (1st quarter 1957): 7–9.

SOME PARTICULARS WERE suggested by the general subject of "Wealth" which found no room in that discourse, and which seemed to demand exhibition under the head of "Economy," to which so large a portion of the earlier life of all men is given.

Moral values become money values. As it happened in the rough settlement of the Pilgrims in Massachusetts Bay, when men saw that these people, besides their industry and thrift, had a heart and soul, and would stand by each other at all hazards, they desired to come and live here. A house in Boston was worth as much again as a house just as good in a town of timorous people; because here the neighbors would defend each other against bad governors, and against troops; and, quite naturally, house-rents rose in Boston: much more, when men found, that the inhabitants of this town had better wits and more knowledge and wisdom than other people.

Nature is, in her common chemistry and botany, the first economist. Never a drop of water does she waste, nor the paring of a nail. We burn and throw away. She watches for the crumbling atoms, seizes them as they fall, and redistributes them instantly, into new bodies; as a compositor redistributes his types from the broken form. And her distinction over our clumsy art, is, in the equality of her spending to her income. Her income balances her out-go. She absorbs exactly all her means; could not do with less; nor wants an atom more. This is attained with stupendous skill. Her architecture, her vegetation, crystallizing, anatomy, astronomy, are all cheap,—a system of low fares; the smallest amount of material. The straight line, or, shortest distance is her rule. The cell of the bee is of that angle, geometry found, that gave the greatest capacity, with the least expense of wax. The arch of the skull, the quill of the eagle, the bone of the fish, are patterns of the best form, and cheapest form, for the function.

Read Palladio and Wren, read Ruskin, and you learn that, precisely that secret which makes architecture, or the art of building well, namely, that, by a skilful disposition of material, less material will serve, and the beauty is increased in the degree in which the material is safely diminished, as when you break up a prose wall and leave all the strength of it in the poetry of columns, is the problem which nature solves in every bone and in every orb.[1]

The gods deal very strictly with us: make out quarter-bills and exact specie payment, allow no partnerships, no stock companies, no arrangements,— but hold us personally liable to the last cent and mill. The youth, charmed with his intellectual dream, says, Why must I be annoyed with these impertinent trifles? I can neither do this nor that. My father lived in the care of land, and improvements valued his meadow, his mill dam. Why must I be worried with hay and grass, my cranberry field, my burned woodlot, my broken mill, the rubbish lumber, my grass, my crop, my trees? Can I not have a partner? Why not organize our new society of poets and lovers, and have somebody with talent for business to look after these things;—some deacons of trees, and grass, and buckwheat, and cranberries, and leave me to letters and philosophy? But the nettled gods say, Go to ruin with your arrangements.

You, alone, are to answer for your things. Leases and covenants shall be punctually signed and sealed. Arithmetic, and the practical study of cause and effect in the laws of Indian corn and rye meal, is as useful as betting is in second-class society to teach accuracy of statement, or, duelling, in countries where the perceptions are obtuse, to hold men to courteous behaviour.

To a certain extent, every individual is holden to the study and management of his domestic affairs. It is a peremptory point of virtue that his independence be secured; and there is no more decisive training for all manly habits, than the household.

I said, the other evening, that, Nature peremptorily requires that each man must feed himself. She sends each man into the world armed with some faculty which enables him with ease and pleasure to do something which no other man can do, and so to make himself necessary to society. I have to say this very often, but Nature says it oftener than I. It is a clownish merit to insist on doing all things with one's own hands, as if every man should build a clumsy house, forge his own hammer and nails, knead and bake his dough; another can do it better and cheaper; but it is his essential virtue, to dare to do what he believes and loves, if his skill lie in taming horses, or in laying out gardens, or in sailing a ship, or in writing musical scores, let him leave all and do that.— If he think steamboats, and cities, and the great West to be all a foolish fuss, but a song or a sonnet is the flower and result of the world, let him scorn the Erie Road and the Mississippi

---

1. Andrea Palladio (1508–80), Italian architect after whom the Palladian or classical revival style was named; John Ruskin (1819–1900), English art critic and author of *The Seven Lamps of Architecture* (1849).

River, the Isthmus and the railroad to the Pacific, and breathe his life out in his jingling sonnet. This is the plainest thrift. "I will get you to mow this grass," says the mechanic; "I can earn more in the shop." That is each man's way of helping others, not as they would have him, but as he knows his helpful power to be.

The quality of the soil is not tasted by munching a mouthful of earth, but in the corn, apples, and grapes, that grow in it. So your help to your fellow men and to the state, is not by running bodily to their assistance in the street, or yet in activity at the polls, (some men can be spared from politics,) but by designing a house; by adding a tube to a steam engine; a new reflector to a telescope; correcting the logarithms; by establishing in the courts a just legal distinction; by writing a song, or a musical score.

The first of these measures is, Do your thing: let your expense be for what is proper to you. Let your genius spend to the uttermost. Every man's expense and economy must proceed from his character. A carpenter cannot be a carpenter without his tools, which he must buy, cost what they may; or the engineer, without his theodolite and chain; or the painter, without easel, and pigments, and canvas; or the astronomer, without azimuth and telescope, a farmer without lands, or a manufacturer without mills, nor the scholar without books.

As long as your genius buys, the investment is safe. And great trust must be given to that impulse. For pleasure, buy not; for the eyes of others, buy not; for the chances of gain (unless you are a merchant), buy not; but for the work to which you are born, and which you intermit not, night or day, spend like a monarch. To save, on this particular point, is not economy, but suicide. For, economy does not consist in saving coals or candles, but, in turning the time while they burn into life. One thing is certain, you cannot afford to be a fool.

Spend here, for the economy of economies is to put reality into your expense, to do your work, to put reality into the world. A seaman will not economize by buying rotten rope or rotten canvas if he is to go in the ship. *Do your thing, and spend for your expense.* The economy of every man is different. Columbus must have ships, but he need not have palaces; and an astronomer, telescopes, but he can spare the theatre. The economy of the farmer is to save, but of the merchant to secure the market, and like the Dutch, he may make money by burning half his crop of pepper. The economy of the general is to strike terror and take cities by forced marches, and he burns his ships and throws his baggage-wagons into the river, whilst the wisdom of the flour dealer is to hoard every bushel for high prices.

There is a great deal of economy in spending and destroying. The baggage is gone, but the troop is safe. You have worn out your shoes, but you might measure your health by the shoes, hats, and clothes, you have worn out. You have broken down your oxen at last; but their strength is in the farm. The Cid has foundered five horses in the day; but the battle is his.[2] Extend the same view: You have won and lost many times; made many experiments, spent much treasure, stood the shock of many defeats, made and outlived many connexions, and yet have never lost your faith and firmness, but all the principles of conduct are confirmed for you. Then, all these defeats are the elements of a real prosperity.

The French papers say, that somebody is revolutionizing mechanics by converting the come and go force of the pendulum into a perpetual push, as has been done by steam in the rotation of the paddle-wheel, instead of the oar. Well, this power of the perpetual instead of the spasmodic push is the differencing power of men. However mild and gentle the nature, if it have a steady push in one direction, it is soon a recognized element in society, and is entitled to shake its head at twenty times as much genius or force, of the intermittent kind.

Do your thing: for so only can you be warranted in that persistency to which the palm of the universe is promised.

Do your work, respecting the excellence of the work, and not its acceptableness. This is so much economy, that, rightly read, it is the sum of economy. Profligacy consists not in spending years of time or hundreds of thousands of money,—but in spending them off the line of your career. The crime which eats out the heart of society and bankrupts men, states, and civilization itself, is job-work—declining from your main design, to serve a turn here or there.

The lawyer may well spend a month on a suit of trifling amount, provided it involves history and principles that will be treasures to him a little farther on. That recommends the office of teaching to the young graduate, that it is the rehearsal and reprinting of the elements of grammar and of figures in his memory. The anatomist and chemist may well give their thankless days and nights to carrion and offal, if they are disclosing the secrets of these structures of beauty and power. But the tasks which fashion custom or others' will impose,—aside from a man's native direction, however well paid,—must bankrupt him and make him useless to the world.

Economy is to neutralize all those extraordinary knacks and talents which are distributed among men by which each can do easily some feat quite impossible to any other. Giotto could draw a perfect circle with his pen.[3] There is a man in Clinton to whom you have only to explain what work you wish done, and he can invent you a machine to do it. Mr Stephenson can put you together a locomotive like a watch. Mr. Pook can give you a formula in figures for your ship. Byron valued himself that he could write a poem of which fourteen thousand copies were sold in a day. Leverrier carries the Copernican system in his head, and has rea-

2. The Cid (ca. 1040–99), national hero of Spain who fought the Moors.
3. Giotto di Bondone (ca. 1266–1337), the dominant Italian painter of his time.

soned out the place of a new planet.[4] It is and must be there, though neither I or any man ever saw it. Go, gentlemen, and look for it. They went and found. Here is a shipmaster who has his ships course to an island where eider, duck, and guano are to be found, and inestimable cargos to be gathered, known to him only.

In short, I think we are entitled here to draw a straight line,—hit whom and where it may, and say that society can never prosper, but must always be bankrupt, until every man does that which he can do.

I use the scholar's economy as a good example of the necessity of exclusion and rejection, because, as his pursuits are finer, and require finer organs, a certain delicacy and daintiness is imperative. But in every profession and pursuit, some sturdiness is essential to success. He is to find his house and home in his employment. His heart is so much in that, as to make it insignificant to him where he is, or with whom; so that his work goes forward; as, angry, or enamoured, or insane persons make no account of heat or cold, wet or dry, house or circumstances, that are serious things to others.

Another form in which the same steadiness to the work and indifference to circumstance more universally show themselves, is, in the quality of adhesiveness, which is alone an insurance of success. It is observed as an element of success, in certain individuals, the lichen-like property of adhering where they fall. It needs not gold mines for them. It needs not a rich soil or warm and soft surroundings. They have glue on their feet; and will take root on a slate or a marble slab; and no wind will blow them, no rain wash them away, and no railroad tempt them to wander. If the soil yields less, it poisons less; if the people are fewer, there are fewer competitors. And, by the moderation of their demands, and the skill of their method, they gradually acquire power and stability, until they have created a garden on the adamant. There are insects found living in the polar circles, and on the Himalayan heights; and the Scotchman, the German, and the New England man stand next to these, in the scale of moderate demand.

The native of New England is usually described as one who, for power to help himself, and surmount difficulties, and get a foothold in, is equal to any countryman; *It is said,* he is one, who, if he can catch a rope's end, or a pine log, will hold on to it, and whittle out of it a house and barn, a timber lot and saw mill, a school house and church, a seat in Congress, and a mission to England, and many other things equally useful and entertaining. These things are said.—

This habitativeness is indeed required by the conditions of human life. It is worth remarking, that, though railroads threaten to destroy it, and have really given it a certain enlargement, yet it is still made necessary by the shortness of

4. Erastus Brigham Bigelow (1814–79), inventor of a power loom for his factory in Clinton, Massachusetts (see *JMN*, 11:90); Samuel Hartt Pook (1827–1901), designer of the first New England clipper ship in 1850; Urbain Jean Joseph Leverrier (1811–77), French astronomer and codiscoverer of the planet Neptune.

life. If human life were three hundred years long, we should instantly become travellers. We have often sighed over the brevity of life; yet it is easy to see, that the stability of human beings, and of homes, depends on that limitation. Your climate in Pennsylvania is something to thank God for,—but who would live in Massachusetts, who had heard of Rio Janeiro, of the Sandwich Islands, of Lake Como, of Naples, or the Styrian Alps, or of Valencia?—but that there is not time to establish himself there, without too great a hazard of his power and happiness in the few years that remain. Therefore, we stick where we are, learn accommodation, and leave Cuba, Egypt, and even Italy, and Madeira, unseen.

The man was made for activity, and action to any end has some health and pleasure for him; but when with the modern ways he has come out at last to what is called success, behold he is starved for objects, and seizes a pistol or perhaps some slow poison of dice-box, or alcohol, or ambition in the state.

We must accept without criticism or modification the costume of our times, and be glad we have one care less in our hands, dress, money, language, railroads, taxation, and the civilization generally. The custom of the country will do so much for us. Let it, and be thankful: All the *materiel* is vanquished to your hand; now for the triumphs of the *spirituel*.

Political economy teaches many excellent lessons, and rebukes a good deal of hypocritical nonsense. For instance, it does not teach rotation in office. But we are too good democrats to hear what is told us. Let us apply that favorite rule of ours in industrial matters. You have been watch-maker, long enough. Now, it is my turn to make watches; and you can bake muffins. The carpenter shall cut flint glass, this year; and the glass blower make staircases. The blacksmith is to cut me a coat, and the tailor can take his place and hammer out a locomotive. Here is a senator, who has served thirty years' apprenticeship, has become master of the routine, and is the working member on whom the burden falls; by all means, take him out, and put Johnny Raw in. The senator will make an excellent dentist or portrait painter.

Some men, again, get rich by spending nothing and living a great while: then the laws of compound interest begin early to work on their property, and, as we used to read that a penny put at compound interest at the Christian era, would have accumulated now, to I know not how many globes of gold as big as our planet, so, if these fellows live a great while, they begin to taste the syrups of that blessedness. I was pointed out an old gentleman in England who, having discovered that the annuity tables in use were not correctly computed for old people, but were greatly in their favour, had sold all and bought annuities, and was now living incessantly, being extraordinarily helped and succoured in his longevity by the feeling that he was making by mere continuance an amazing fortune out of the insurance companies.

A deeper thought would hold in solution more facts. It is the law of nature that you shall keep no more than you use. The fishes that swim in the waters of the Mammoth Cave in Kentucky, in darkness, are blind. When the eye was useless, it ceased to exist. It is the eternal relation between power and use. A man should not be rich by having what is superfluous, but by having what is essential to him, like a manufacturer, or engineer, or astronomer, who has a great capital invested in mills, or in the observatory.

The question is, How to animate all his possessions? A rich man who uses all his means excites no envy. Give us a deeper nature, increase our affinities, and you add organs and powers. The oyster is a poor creature who has few wants. The mammalia with their manifold wants are rich capitalists. The complex animals are the highest. The more wants, the richer people.

Men want everything. They are made of hooks and eyes, and do put the universe under contribution. Man is rich as he is much-related. The more rich, the more expensive, the better. I would have vaster demands made; and rich men shown how to be rich. Rich men, for the most part, are powerless and unskilful spenders: Few understand that art. It needs truly great wants to be greatly gratified. One would like that thoughts should spend! What an apparatus does not every high genius require. No hand-loom, no watch-wheel, but wheels that roll like the solar system. I think you must give him gardens, towns, courts, kings, earth itself, astronomies—a freedom of the whole city of God.

Everyone's reading will have furnished him with how many examples of the parentage of those thoughts that make the value of literature. Every thought begets sons and daughters. In like manner, the history of politics, of philanthropy for a short term of years, shows a rapid filiation. The fallacy is that trade is a trick to get money. The reality is that trade is an exchange by skill and labor which has its just price and stands secure on honesty in all the parties.

Newton taught, that the reason why one body was transparent, and another opake, was, that, in one, the particles were homogeneous, and, when a ray of light entered it, being attracted equally in every direction, it was, as if not attracted at all, and passed through: thus the diamond was transparent. But, if the particles of a body were heterogeneous, the ray, entering, was drawn now hither, now that way, and did not pass through. This was the opake body. Well, such a body as the transparent one described, is the universe.

Now, some men are born with a taste for the manners of nature. It is pervaded by nerves. It is the art of art, the geometry of geometry. The crystals of salt, or ice, or the diamond, make no error in their angle, but, in a million gems, or countless millions, have never one fault. So just is the line, so true the shooting of the ray, in this rock of diamonds, this globe of crystal.

The world is a company of individual atoms, where every individual is guaranteed by all the stockholders. The sympathy is entire. Not a particle, but the sun in the ecliptic must answer for, and the sun cannot lose a ray, but every worm will suffer. This experiment in France of telegraphing from Paris to Peru, by means of snails, may be true or false in its details, but is true and less than the whole truth in philosophy. And who dare say how far, how high, this organism may go? All above as below is organized by means of their sympathetic structure.

That thus idle, stupid, and fraudulent people should hold property, is an objection to our system of inheritance, and of money, which theorists have proposed to remove by making the government the only proprietor; by abolishing the laws of inheritance, and making all property revert at the death of the owner to the state; by abolishing the interest of money, and by abolishing money or representative value. But the ground on which the present system rests, notwithstanding these objections, is, that it is essential that property be secure to its owners. It is a greater evil to any state that each citizen should not be secured in his possession, than that there should sometimes be bad or stupid owners. It is essential to the creation of property that property be secure to its owners. If I do not know that I shall control it, I shall not earn it. 'Tis better, therefore, that it sometimes fall to dunces and to sots, than that, in attempts to give it to the deserving, the least insecurity shall paralyze the arm of labour.

To follow nature is indeed a maxim so trite as hardly to admit of being stated, if it were not always gaining a new significance as it jumps out on us, an old friend in a new place, at every corner. Life itself is a balance of old and new, of daring thought and Chinese copying, which mix in every act. The excellence of the ship is the freedom with which it yields throughout its form and equipment to the conditions of wave and wind.

The story itself gives the admirable unity to the epic poem. The part that is built teaches the architect how to build the rest. The streets compress the mob into battalions. Who taught Raffaelle and Correggio how to draw?[5] Was it Signor Quadro, the perspective master, with his rule and dividers? No; it was the weather stains on the wall; the cloud over the house-roof yonder, with that shoulder of Hercules, and brow for Jove. It was the chance outlines observed in marbled paper; it was a lucky scratch with a bit of charcoal, which taught the secret of possibility, and confounded and annihilated Signor Quadro and themselves also.

Benvenuto Cellini, Angelo, Raphael, or any man with a wonderful sense of aptitude and beauty in his head, who can take any pile of bricks or cobblestones and heave them into forms that dispose all men irresistibly to sentiments of tranquillity, of sublimity, of worship, is a person whom kings and states must buy and employ.[6] Not less an eminent capacity for affairs, who can give shape to any jangle and perplexity, and put facts in an order which brings juries to irresistible

5. Correggio (1494–1534), Italian Renaissance painter.
6. Benvenuto Cellini (1500–1571), Italian sculptor and worker in gold and silver.

conclusions. Much more than a good governor, a calculating head which arranges a tumultuous mob into unity and the concentration of action of one man are talents men cannot miss and will pay for with the devotion of their lives. On our knees we tender tithes, halves, nay all our goods, and our bodies also.[7]

The covenant which great souls make one with the other, is, not let us flatter, and tickle, and push forward each other; but let there be truth between us two, so that each can answer for the other as for himself. Such appear best in solitude and poverty. It was said of a Spanish Prince, "the more you took from him, the greater he became."

7. "C. Austin," Emerson's note inserted below this paragraph, may refer to "a certain brilliant" Charles Austin, whom Emerson met in England in 1848 and later described as having "'made £30,000 in one year by his profession,' (of law)" (*Letters*, 4:41).

# Conduct of Life: "Fate"
## 22 December 1851
## (1851–1853)

Emerson first delivered "Fate" on 22 December 1851 as the first in a series of six lectures on the *Conduct of Life* at the Masonic Temple in Boston; he may have received $144.05 for the series ("Account Books"; Charvat reports $420.05 for the series). He repeated the lecture on 18 February 1852 as the first in a series of four private lectures on the *Conduct of Life* at Hope Chapel in New York City ($61.18 for the series [Charvat]); on 17 December 1852 as the fifth in a series of six private lectures on the *Conduct of Life* in Cincinnati, Ohio ($362 for the series); and on 4 January 1853 as the fifth in a series of seven lectures on the *Conduct of Life* before the Mercantile Library Association at Wyman's Hall in St. Louis, Missouri ($500 for the series). Emerson also may have delivered "Fate" on 11 March 1852 as the first in a series of six lectures, probably on the *Conduct of Life*, in Medford, Massachusetts, for which he received $69 (see von Frank and *Letters*, 4:272, 8:314; except as noted, lecture fees are from the "Account Books"). This lecture has never been published.

Emerson's personal writings reveal his preoccupation with fate as a subject in the early 1850s. For instance, as the title "FATE" on its front cover verso indicates, his Notebook EO is devoted almost entirely to the subject, and his letter of 22 July 1853 to Caroline Sturgis Tappan profoundly details his perception of the "heavy cobweb" of "fate": "Friends are few, thoughts are few, facts few—only one: only one fact, now tragically, now tenderly, now exultingly illustrated in sky, in earth, in men & women, Fate, Fate" (see *TN*, 1:58–92, and *Letters*, 8:374–75 [cf. *Letters*, 4:376–77]). Headed "*Fate*.," the following manuscript pages from this period in a file of miscellaneous lecture pages at the Houghton Library of Harvard University also show him grappling with the concept of fate:

We tread the dark bottom of hell with necessities as hard as iron. Pindar (?)

Grey clouds, short days, moonless nights, a drowsy sense of being dragged easily somewhere by that locomotive, Destiny, which, never seen, we yet know must be hitched on to the cars wherein we sit,—that is all that appears in the dark months.

The existence of evil & malignant men does not depend [on] themselves or on men; it seems to indicate a virulence that remains uncured in the Universe,—uncured & corrupting, & hurling out these pestilent rats & tigers, & men rat-like & wolf-like.

The benefit of the doctrine of Fate is that under that form we learn the lesson of the immutability & universality of Law. There are no contingences. And that fact is grateful to the sound mind. If we had not confidence that Law provided for every exigency,—that not an impulse of absolute freedom or autocrasy could exist, we should rush by suicide out of the door of this staggering Temple.

It teaches us that we are to each other results. As your perception or sensibility is exalted, I see the genesis of your action & your thought. I see you in your debt & fountains; & to my eye, instead of a little pond of life, you are a rivulet fed by rills from every plain & height in nature & antiquity, & deriving a remote origin from the source of things.

Reality rules destiny. They may well fear fate who have any infirmity of habit & aim. But he who rests on what he is, is part of destiny & can make mouths at fortune.

Use what language you will, you can never say anything but what you are. We should never feel that any men occupy our place, but that the reason why we do not have what we wish, is, that we want the faculty that entitles to it. All spiritual or real power makes its own place. Revolutions of violence are scrambles merely. (bMS Am 1280.214 [106], {1r}–{4r})

However, Emerson had considerable difficulty in bringing this lecture to completion. A few days after first delivering it, he complained to his brother William, "I have been very busy . . . with a new lecture,—which is always, I fancy, as bad as a huge note to pay in Wall Street" (25 December 1851, *Letters*, 4:269). A year later, while delivering his series on the *Conduct of Life* in Cincinnati, he wrote to Lidian that he was still writing on the lecture because he needed it to help turn a profit for the series: "[Ainsworth Rand] Spofford is heroically endeavoring to make the lectures to which he invited me, pay; which Cincinnati is stoutly resisting. . . . If hereby the 'Fate' chapter gets written, I shall think it worth the coming" (15 December 1852, *Letters*, 4:330). Yet in spite of all his work, the copy-text for "Fate" reveals only Emerson's rushed successive attempts to bring the lecture to completion, not a discourse finished off in his usual style. Throughout, material is inscribed on individual pages which during revisions of his lectures Emerson typically incorporated into more extended statements or modified with transitional prose. In this lecture manuscript, quotations and occasional paragraphs remain inscribed on a variety of worn pages and odd slips of paper, and although they lack transitional or contextual prose, they are integral to the text.

Reports of "Fate" generally indicate that Emerson's audiences were unaware of his difficulties with the lecture. A brief notice in the *New-York Daily Tribune* on the morning after he opened the *Conduct of Life* series at Hope Chapel stated: "The room was fairly filled, not crowded, by an audience who gave their undivided attention to the speaker throughout his discourse. . . . His intellectual fairness, and perception, and precision— the unflinching firmness and justice of his characterization and epithets—his lofty thought and musical style, have long since won from 'mouths of wisest censure,' the confession of his preëminence as a public lecturer" ("Mr. Emerson's Lectures," 19 February 1852, 5). The next day, the *Daily Tribune* published a detailed abstract of "Fate" that was prefaced by Emerson's introduction to the series ("The Conduct of Life. Lecture I," 20 February 1852, 8). Except for his lectures on "Fate" and "Worship," Emerson's *Conduct of Life* series in Cincinnati was covered in detail by the *Daily Cincinnati Gazette* from 4 to 20 December 1852. Ralph L. Rusk attributed the delay of "Fate" reported there to

Emerson's engagement in Dayton, where he delivered "The Anglo-Saxon" on 16 December (*Letters*, 4: 328n); however, Emerson's letter of 15 December to Lidian cited above in which he stated that he was still working on "Fate" provides a more plausible reason for the delay. In Cincinnati the delivery of "Fate" generated a letter to the *Gazette* from "A German" who complained that Emerson "did not take particular pain to reconcile" his conflicting ideas on fate but instead developed random thoughts that "have no bearance upon the subject." The writer ended, saying that Emerson was "entirely Celtic in his philosophy and mode of thinking" (18 December 1852, quoted in Mead, *Yankee Eloquence in the Middle West*, 36). Emerson's *Conduct of Life* series in St. Louis, which received only brief announcements in the *Daily Missouri Republican* from 27 December 1853 to 7 January 1854, is more fully treated in John Francis McDermott, "Emerson at St. Louis, 1852: Unpublished Letters and Telegrams," *Emerson Society Quarterly*, no. 6 (1st quarter 1957): 7–9.

Emerson abandoned "Fate" as a lecture after delivering it in St. Louis in January 1853. He wrote to Carlyle on 19 April 1853 that, expecting to make it into an essay, he was still working on the text of the lecture, and he promised him, "if we all live long enough, that is, you, & I, & the chapter, I hope to send [it to] you in fair print" (*CEC*, 485). Even though his remarks to Carlyle and Edward Waldo Emerson's comments on the essay seem to imply otherwise, this lecture bears minimal relation to the essay "Fate" that Emerson published in *The Conduct of Life* in 1860 (*W*, 6: 1–49; for Edward's comments, see *W*, 6: 337).


T HE EXCELLENCE OF men consists in the completeness with which the lower system is taken up into the higher—a process of much time and delicacy, but in which no point of the lower should be left untranslated, so that the warfare of beasts should be renewed in a finer field, for more excellent victories. Savage war gives place to that of Turenne and Wellington, which has limitations and a code.[1] This war, again, gives place to the finer quarrel of property, where the victory is wealth, and the defeat is poverty. But the ruin here is how much less! Instead of being killed or mutilated, a man is behind-hand in paying his notes, lives in a cheaper street, and walks instead of riding to his work.

The skeptic says, How can any man love any woman except by delusion and ignorance? Brothers do not wish to marry sisters, because they see them too nearly. And all attractiveness, like fame, requires some distance. But the lover of nature loves nature in his mistress or his friend; he sees the faults and absurdities of the individual, as well as you. No familiarity can exhaust the charm. It is not personalities, but universalities that draw him.

The like is true of life. It seems to me that he has learned its lesson, who has

---

1. Vicomte de Turenne (1611–75), French general who served in the army with distinction for nearly fifty years.

come to feel so assured of his well-being as to hold lightly all particulars of today and tomorrow, and to count death amongst the particulars. He must have such a grasp of the whole, as to preserve it when he is ridiculous and unfortunate.

We do acquire some patience, some temper, some power of referring the particular to the general. We acquire perspective so as to rank our experiences and know what is eminent. Life is fictitious, and we would have it real, say what we think, and do only what is fit for us. Then, we must not be such good Americans, and live on the run. We are encumbered by unfit society, obliged by false expectations of people, loaded with debt for that which is not bread; for all which, we may thank our too much hurry. God is great and gives to the great. Method and season are the only true speeds.

Let us, in the one golden hour allowed us, be great and true, be shined upon by the sun and moon, and feel in our pulse circulations from the heart of nature. We shall be more content to be superseded some day, if we have once been clean and permeable channels.

One would think from the talk of men that riches and poverty were a great matter,—whilst they are really a thin costume, and our life, the life of all of us, is identical. For we transcend circumstance continually and taste the real quality of existence as in our employments, which only differ in the manipulation, but express the same laws; or in our thoughts, which wear no broadcloth, and taste no ice-creams. We see God face to face every hour, and know the savour of nature.

Life is a game between God and man. God disparts himself and feigns to divide into individuals. Part he puts into a pomegranate, part in a king's crown, part in a beautiful boy. Instantly, man sees the beautiful things and goes to procure them. As he takes hold of each, God smiles and says, "It is thyself;" and when he has them all, "It is thyself." We love and will die for a beauty, which, we wrong ourselves in thinking alien.

We sit and speculate in glowing hours, and life discloses new and rosy recesses of joy and grace. We quit the fine friend and go to town to pay a debt, or to engage a man to work in the meadow, and all our fine glimpses are become like pictures on the wall, no more valid in the memory.

Today I wrote C. that, 'tis not we, but the elements, the destinies, and conscience, that make places and hours great,—they, the omnipresent;—and, if we will only be careful not to intrude and chatter, the least occasion and the domestic hour will be grand and fateful.[2] We shall one day wonder that we have ever distinguished days, or circumstances, or persons.

---

2. Identified as Caroline Sturgis (1819–88), longtime friend of Emerson and Margaret Fuller, in *JMN*, 7:517; see also Emerson's letter to Sturgis of 5 October 1840 in *Letters*, 2:343.

He is dull who needs distinguished men in order to see grand traits. If there is grandeur in you, you will find grandeur in ditchers and washerwomen. Very fine relations are established between every clear spirit and all bystanders. You are a dull fop if you think there is no tie but your dollar, between you and your land-lord or your merchant. Have these made no distinction between their customers or guests?

What I want to know is the meaning of what I do, believing that any of my current Mondays or Tuesdays is authentic Fate-Book for me, and hints and telegraphic signals are every moment arriving to me out of the interior eternity. I am tormented with impatience to make them out. We meet people who seem to overlook and read us with a smile, but they do not tell us what they read, as economists do by us, starving the imagination and the sentiment. In this impov-erishing animalism, I seem to meet a Hunger, a wolf. Rather let us be alone whilst we live, than encounter these impoverishers. Man should emancipate man. He does so, not by jamming him, but by distancing him. The nearer my friend, the more spacious is our realm, or, the more diameter our spheres have.

We are like rats and mice in a library gnawing and scampering over history and poetry for the sake of the paste in the paper. So these arts and trades, eating and drinking, prospering and failing, conversing with a million materials, and agents, and powers, are, in the whole and in each particular, beaming with wis-dom more worth than all the facts, as the design of a book is superior to the words and letters.

This immense preponderance of the senses, it is the end of culture to balance and redress. Let culture call out the powers. Let the soul awake from its deep sleep, and there shall be new heavens and new earth. Culture should make life appear a gift worthy of omnipotence. Culture should enable one to entertain oneself; culture should teach one to be manly, happy. Culture should make one content with his vocation, his art. Culture should inspire hope; should show good issues remotely proceeding from an evil world; and reconcile cities with thoughts: and the end of culture should be, to make no end. I thank those—that teach me not to be easily depressed. Whatever man acts or speaks out of his mind forgetful of other people—shall yield us a sublime admonition.

But, I confess, that I think we can as yet discern no social measures adapted for this end. We are instantly embarrassed when we attempt to apply a reform to societies of men. Societies are not convertible: to the highest ends societies can-not act. No, I speak to the individual heart. I throw myself on the noble hope that struggles up through obstruction and perplexity in the private soul; I seek to show to one man his possible attainment and to bring to his ear the solicitations of a fairer earth and heaven than that he now inhabits—him to possess and use it. In the presence of the assembly, he has the desire, perhaps for the first time, to

express himself largely, symmetrically, gigantically, not in fragments and miniatures. Shall I call it a lambert flame enlarging, elongating, contracting to a point,
that dances before the eyes of his mind? Ah! could he confine it; could he direct
that wild fire in a blowpipe, he would melt the planet.

That which he wishes, that which eloquence ought to reach, is, not a particular skill, as of telling a good story, or neatly summing up evidence, or arguing
logically, or dextrously, addressing the prejudice of the company; no, but doing
all this, and much more: a universal skill, a taking sovereign possession of the
audience. Him only we call an artist, who should play on an assembly of men as
a master on the keys of the piano; who, seeing the people furious, should soften
and compose them; should draw them, when he would, to laughter and to tears.
Bring him to his audience, and, be they who they may, coarse or refined, pleased
or displeased, sulky or savage, with their opinions in the keeping of a confessor,
or with their opinions in their bank-safes,—he will have them pleased and hu-
moured as he chooses, and they shall carry and execute that which he bids them.

This is that despotism which poets have celebrated in the Pied Piper of
Hamelin, whose music drew like the power of gravitation, drew soldiers and
priests, traders and feasters, women and boys, rats and mice; or that of the
minstrel of Meudon, who made the pallbearers dance around the bier.[3] This is
a power of many degrees, and requiring in the orator a great range of platforms
or experiences; a large composite man, such as nature rarely organizes and en-
dows, so that, in our experience, we are forced to gather up this figure in fragments; here, one talent; there, another.

It is true that which they say of our New England oestrum, which will never
let us stand or sit, but drives us like mad, through the world. The calmest and
most protected life cannot save us. I want some intercalated days, as if I lived in
State Street, to bethink me, and to derive order to my life from the heart. That
should be the use of a reasonable friend, to check this headlong racing, and put
us in possession of ourselves, once more, for love, or for shame. The life lived,
the thing done, is a paltry affair, as far as I know it, though in the presence and
consciousness of the magnificent, yea, the unspeakably great. Yet I love life,—
never little,—and now, I think more and more, entertained and puzzled though
I be, by this lubricity and inaccessibleness of its pith and heart. The variety of
the game delights me. I seem in the bosom of all possibility and have never tried
but one or two trivial experiments. In happy hours it seems as if one could not lie
too lightly on it and like a cloud it would buoy him up and convey him anywhither.
But by infirm faith we lose our delicate balance and flounder down, into the

---

3. The Pied Piper of Hamelin, hero of a poem of the same title published in 1842 by Robert Brown-
ing (1812–89), English poet, who himself drew upon a medieval legend.

realms and under the laws of mud and stones. The depth of the notes which we accidentally sound on the strings of nature is out of all proportion to our taught and ascertained power, and might teach us what strangers and novices we are— vagabond in this universe of pure power to which we have but one key. I will at least be glad of my days,—I, who have so many of them, and, having been informed by God in the casualest manner that my funds are inexhaustible, I will believe it. Let there be no oestrum for me. I think of sculpture and painting only so, that they shall teach us manners, and abolish hurry. I have heard of Niagara, that it falls without speed.[4]

Fate in thoughts: Milton says they are tender things. But these fine fruits of judgment, poesy, and sentiment, when once their hour is struck, and the world is ripe for them, I suppose, know, as well as coarser, how to feed and replenish themselves and maintain their stock alive, and multiply; for roses and violets renew their race like oaks, and flights of painted moths are as old as the Alleghenies. The balance of the world is kept, and his dewdrops and haze, and pencil of light, are as hardy and long-lived as chaos, and night.

They may well fear Fate who have any infirmity of habit or aim. But he who rests on what he is, has a destiny above destiny, and can make mouths at Fortune.

Fate in small things: Pomona complained of flies. How many days are gnawed away by the vermin of Fate! We suffer more from flies and bugs than from dragons; Mischances, things mistimed, annoy the scholar. Yesterday, the carpenter,— today, the painter;—tomorrow, the cook is in a fury; and next day the money must be scraped together to pay the note. Each untunes the day, for freedom, fancy, and invention. Jeannie Deans's rule for housekeeping is as good for the library, that, "Much can be done by timing your turns."[5]

> "Everything which has an intellectual subsistence continues to exist under Providence alone, but everything which has a corporeal subsistence endures under necessity."[6]

> "The soul, when it falls into sense, follows the natures that are beneath it, living with them as with drunken neighbors."[7]

> "Look not on nature; her name is fatal."

> "Nor co-augment Fate, nor become corporeal with the fatal herds."

4. For the text and original occasion of this paragraph, see Emerson to Margaret Fuller, 7 June 1843, *Letters*, 3:178.

5. Jeannie Deans, in Sir Walter Scott, *The Heart of Midlothian* (1818).

6. Quoted from *The Six Books of Proclus . . . on the Theology of Plato*, trans. Thomas Taylor (1816).

7. Emerson may be quoting himself: this quotation appears without attribution in *TN*, 1:79.

"The souls that become venerable by understanding the works of the Father, will escape the fatal wing of Destiny."[8]

For history is the history of ideas. We foolishly fight against James and John, and do not see that they are the frail and casual tents in which certain invulnerable immortal opinions and ideas house for a night. Free-soil liberty, slavery, are affirmative and negative of one idea of Freedom, and it is due and is arrived at this hour of the world in the general human spirit. If Kossuth, if Mazzini, if the brave men in the American Senate and homesteads whom it animates should perish, it would animate others and animate them as well; for it is the bravery of this which makes them brave; it is respect and limitation of this idea, which cripples their bravery.[9] The history of liberty goes on; logical, wide, elemental, like the encroachment of the sun's heat, or of the ripened air, or of the gathered sea, when, in geologic periods, it is changing its bed. One day Gracchus turns from the Senate to the Forum.[10] One day, the kneeling third estate in the Diet of Tours refuses to kneel.[11]

I know that in looking over a man's whole career, we see an agreement between his action and his inherited constitution—his physique, his faults, his lameness, bad eyes, or ears, or stomach, or spleen—so that we think he could not have been essentially different; his opinions were organic.

But where does the consent of mankind lie to the fool, and the Judas, and the counterfeiter? The self-executing laws take effect very fast, and the martyr already wears his crown and the judge who hanged him is already putrid and smells in our nostril. And though we learn to look with charity on each other, and gaze at the old foibles and blunders as the defects of an imperfect machine, yet if these peccadilloes grow to crimes, we again hold the party responsible. Precisely that happens in any private circle which has chanced, in the public opinion, in dealing with crime.

The first results of modern zoology were to establish the tyranny of organism. Each animal was and must be as his organs compelled him to live and act. Man,

8. The last three quotations are attributed to the sixth-century Iranian religious reformer Zoroaster in *The Six Books of Proclus*, trans. Taylor.

9. Lajos Kossuth (1802–94), leader of the Hungarian revolution of 1848–49; Giuseppe Mazzini (1805–72), leader of the Italian revolution of 1848, during which he made Margaret Fuller's acquaintance.

10. Gracchus, the name of a plebeian family of ancient Rome, refers to numerous Roman consuls and statesmen. Although writing in the singular, here Emerson is probably referring to Tiberius Sempronius Gracchus (163–133 B.C.) and his brother Gaius Sempronius Gracchus (153–121 B.C.).

11. The Third Estate, which represented the common people (though composed primarily of lawyers and officials), as opposed to the first two estates, which represented the nobility and the clergy, respectively, participated in the Estates-General of 1789, which led to the formation of a National Assembly and the beginnings of the French Revolution.

too, was the victim of his skeleton and spine. With the deluge of natural science, the moral and political freedom of men came to be treated as an illusion, following the eternal necessity of nature. Thought was degraded to a bodily action. Physiologists made minute observations on the nerves of the brain. Phrenology unfolded the character out of the form of the skull. Kant's categorical imperative was quite forgotten. But, what is noticeable,—with this reform from the natural sciences, quite no change happened in practice.[12] It did happen that heads were examined.[13] In public opinion, in public morals, in civic life, in criminal law, quite no change of the old practice, which was founded on the theory of responsibility and freedom of the will, occurred.

Souls with a certain quantity of light are in excess, and, once for all, belong to the moral class, what animal force they may retain to the contrary notwithstanding. Souls with less light — it is chemically impossible that they be moral,—what talent or good they have to the contrary notwithstanding, and these belong to the world of Fate, or animal good: the minors of the Universe,—not yet twenty-one, not yet voters, not robed in the *toga virilis.*

Nor is it permitted to any soul of the free or of the apprentice, that is, to the free, or to the fated, to cast a vote for the other. The world wants so much alum, so much saccharine, so much iron, so much hemp, so much mahogany, nor could any rebellion or freedom be suffered in atoms without chaos. If coal should undertake to be lemon, or feathers turpentine, we should have a pretty ruin to be sure. And these excesses and defects in you, the determination to the moral or to the animal, are the means by which high Nature works.

By inspiring her purpose above her plane, we, who were her footmen, drays, and porters, became her muses and angels. The fatalist stands on this, that a man cannot jump out of his skin; and well for him that he cannot, if one considers what that at last must mean; for his skin is the world, and the stars of heaven do hold him there: in the folly of men glitters the wisdom of God.

There are no contingences. The doctrine of Fate only masks the lesson of the immutability and universality of Law. If we had not confidence that Law provided for every exigency, that not an impulse of absolute freedom could exist, we should rush by suicide out of the door of the staggering Temple.

Your fate is what you do, because first it is what you are. Nothing befalls us that we do not invite. Wherever there is a wrong, the response is pain. Wherever there is a wrong, the effect is disease. An ugly, an infirm, a vicious person is that.

We are talkative, but Heaven is silent. We puzzle ourselves, with a mob of writers before us, in trying to state the doctrine of Fate. We wish to sum the con-

12. "With the deluge . . . in practice" is Emerson's translation from the German of a passage published in *Atlantis* (July 1856) (see *TN,* 1:81).
13. A reference to phrenology.

flicting impressions by saying, that all point at last to an unity which inspires all, but disdains words, and passes understanding. Our poetry, our religions are its skirts and penumbrae. Yet the charm of life is the hints we derive from this. They overcome us like perfumes from a far off shore of sweetness, and their meaning is, that no tongue shall syllable it without leave; that only itself can name it; that by casting ourselves on it, and being its voice, it rushes each moment to positive commands, creating men and methods, and ties the will of a child to the love of the First Cause. And I can conceive, as soon as it is uttered, it is profaned. The thinker denies personality out of piety, not out of pride. It refuses a personality which is instantly imprisoned in human measures.

"It stands written on the Gate of Heaven, 'Wo to him who suffers himself to be betrayed by Fate.'"[14]

I have heard that they seem fools who allow themselves to be engaged and com-promised in noble undertakings, but that at last it appears quite otherwise, and, to the gods it so appears from the first. I affix a like sense to this text of Hafiz; for he who loves nobly is not betrayed, but makes a fool of Fate.

Let the men be right, and the action be right, and the marriage be right, with humanity in their united heart for motive and genius, and the effect would cor-respond. Let us trust Cause and Effect, with a geometer's or a chemist's trust. Here is a lion-hearted hero, who comes from two nobodies.— His father was an Ethiop; and his mother was a cow,—and perhaps his son will be a jack o'lanthorn again. Yes, but there's a history behind these curtains, a history of each, and the instinct always expects when the intellect will come up with it.[15] Always a truth, always a right, an obeying of the commandment of nature, is at the foundation of every beauty in parts or in wholes. The old geometric morals, the old Rectitude, is there, like astronomy and gravitation, to bring us up at last.

---

14. Attributed to Hafiz in *Der Diwan von Mohammed Schemsed-din Hafis*, trans. Joseph von Hammer (1812–13).

15. Henry David Thoreau is the subject of Emerson's original version of this description of "a lion-hearted hero" and the sentence that follows it on history (see *JMN*, 13:82, 83; *TN*, 1:236, 245).

# "Address to the Citizens of Concord
## on the Fugitive Slave Law,
## 3 May 1851"

Emerson delivered his address on the Fugitive Slave Law on 3 May 1851 to the citizens of his hometown, Concord. He adapted the address on several occasions during May as a campaign stump speech in an unsuccessful attempt to get John Gorham Palfrey elected to Congress from Middlesex County on the Free Soil Ticket: 9 May in Lexington, 14 May at the City Hall in Cambridge (for which he received $4 in expenses), 15 May in Worcester, 16 May in Fitchburg ($2 in expenses), 18 May in Marlborough, 20 May in Sudbury, 21 May in West Cambridge (now Arlington; $1 in expenses), and 22 May in Cambridge again ("Account Books").

Eleanor M. Tilton also argues for a delivery of the address at Waltham, based on an invitation by William Porter of that city dated 8 May, but there is no evidence that Emerson accepted. Tilton also states that Emerson talked in both Cambridge and Cambridgeport, but her case is garbled and the evidence contradictory, and we have rejected it (see *Letters*, 10:235–36).

Because this was a political address rather than a formal lecture, it was not widely reported by the newspapers. A single paragraph account in the *Liberator* describes the address as "a fine intellectual and moral treat" (9 May 1851, 75). The *Liberator* also mentions a delivery of the address in Cambridge on the fourteenth at which Emerson was booed and hissed by unruly Harvard students ("Mr. Emerson's Lecture," 23 May 1851, 3). Edwin Percy Whipple was present at the occasion and gives his account of it in "Some Recollections of Ralph Waldo Emerson," *Harper's New Monthly Magazine* 65 (September 1882): 583–84.

The address was first published as "Fugitive Slave Law" in the Centenary Edition (1904) of *Miscellanies* (*W*, 11:177–214). It was reedited as "Address to the Citizens of Concord" in Emerson's *Antislavery Writings*, 53–72. A complete early draft of the address is printed in the electronic textual notes.

FELLOW CITIZENS,

    I accepted your invitation to speak to you on the great question of these days, with very little consideration of what I might have to offer. For there seems to be no option. The last year has forced us all into politics, and made it a paramount duty to seek what it is often a duty to shun.[1]

We do not breathe well. There is infamy in the air. I have a new experience. I wake in the morning with a painful sensation, which I carry about all day, and which, when traced home, is the odious remembrance of that ignominy which has fallen on Massachusetts, which robs the landscape of beauty, and takes the sunshine out of every hour. I have lived all my life in this State, and never had any experience of personal inconvenience from the laws, until now. They never came near me to my discomfort before. I find the like sensibility in my neighbors, and in that class who take no interest in the ordinary questions of party politics.

There are men who are as sure indexes of the equity of legislation and of the sane state of public feeling, as the barometer is of the weight of the air; and it is a bad sign when these are discontented. For, though they snuff oppression and dishonor at a distance, it is because they are more impressionable: the whole population will in a short time be as painfully affected.

Every hour brings us from distant quarters of the Union the expression of mortification at the late events in Massachusetts, and at the behavior of Boston. The tameness was indeed shocking. Boston, of whose fame for spirit and character we have all been so proud; Boston, whose citizens, intelligent people in England told me, they could always distinguish by their culture among Americans; the Boston of the American Revolution, which figures so proudly in "John Adams's Diary," which the whole country has been reading; Boston, spoiled by prosperity, must bow its ancient honor in the dust, and make us irretrievably ashamed.[2] In Boston,—we have said with such lofty confidence,—no fugitive slave can be arrested;—and now, we must transfer our vaunt to the country, and say with a little less confidence,—no fugitive man can be arrested here;—at least we can brag thus until tomorrow, when the farmers also may be corrupted.

The tameness is indeed complete. It appears, the only haste in Boston, after the rescue of Shadrach last February, was, who should first put his name on the list of volunteers in aid of the marshal.[3] One is only reminded of the Russian poltroonery,—a nation without character, where, when they cheat you, and you show them that they cheat, they reply, "Why, you did not think we were Germans; we are only Russians;" that is, we all cheat. I met the smoothest of Episco-

1. Emerson wrote in his journal of the Fugitive Slave Law: "I will not obey it, by God" (*JMN*, 11:412).

2. John Adams (1735–1826), second president of the United States (1797–1801), whose ten-volume *Works of John Adams* (1850–56), edited by Charles Francis Adams, had just begun publication.

3. The escaped slave Shadrach Minkins had been rescued from custody in Boston on 15 February 1851, an early attempt to prevent the implementation of the Fugitive Slave Law.

pal clergymen the other day, and allusion being made to Mr. Webster's treachery, he blandly replied, "Why, do you know I think *that* the great action of his life." It looked as if, in the city, and the suburbs, all were involved in one hot haste of terror,—presidents of colleges and professors, saints and brokers, insurers, lawyers, importers, and manufacturers;—not an unpleasing sentiment, not a liberal recollection, not so much as a snatch of an old song for freedom, dares intrude on their passive obedience. The panic has paralysed the journals, with the fewest exceptions, so that one cannot open a newspaper, without being disgusted by new records of shame. I cannot read longer even the local good news. When I look down the columns at the titles of paragraphs, "Education in Massachusetts," "Board of Trade," "Art Union," "Revival of Religion," what bitter mockeries!

The very convenience of property, the house and land we occupy, have lost their best value, and a man looks gloomily on his children, and thinks 'What have I done, that you should begin life in dishonor?' Every liberal study is discredited: Literature and science appear effeminate, and the hiding of the head. The college, the churches, the schools, the very shops and factories are discredited; real estate, every kind of wealth, every branch of industry, every avenue to power, suffers injury, and the value of life is reduced. Just now a friend came into my house and said, "If this law shall be repealed, I shall be glad that I have lived; if not, I shall be sorry that I was born." What kind of law is that which extorts language like this from the heart of a free and civilized people?

One intellectual benefit we owe to the late disgraces. The crisis had the illuminating power of a sheet of lightning at midnight. It showed truth. It ended a good deal of nonsense we had been wont to hear and to repeat, on the nineteenth of April, the seventeenth of June, and the fourth of July.[4] It showed the slightness and unreliableness of our social fabric; it showed what stuff reputations are made of; what straws we dignify by office and title, and how competent we are to give counsel and help in a day of trial: It showed the shallowness of leaders; the divergence of parties from their alleged grounds; showed that men would not stick to what they had said: that the resolutions of public bodies, or the pledges never so often given and put on record of public men, will not bind them. The fact comes out more plainly, that you cannot rely on any man for the defence of truth, who is not constitutionally, or by blood and temperament, on that side. A man of a greedy and unscrupulous selfishness may maintain morals when they are in fashion: but he will not stick. However close Mr. Wolf's nails have been pared, however neatly he has been shaved, and tailored, and set up on end, and taught

4. The Battles of Lexington and Concord were fought on 19 April 1775. The Battle of Bunker Hill was waged in Boston on 17 June 1775.

to say, "Virtue and Religion," he cannot be relied on at a pinch: he will say, morality means pricking a vein.

The popular assumption that all men loved freedom, and believed in the Christian religion, was found hollow American brag. Only persons who were known and tried benefactors are found standing for freedom: the sentimentalists went down stream. I question the value of our civilization, when I see that the public mind had never less hold of the strongest of all truths. The sense of injustice is blunted,—a sure sign of the shallowness of our intellect. I cannot accept the railroad and telegraph in exchange for reason and charity. It is not skill in iron locomotives that marks so fine civility as the jealousy of liberty. I cannot think the most judicious tubing a compensation for metaphysical debility. What is the use of admirable law-forms and political forms, if a hurricane of party feeling and a combination of monied interests can beat them to the ground? What is the use of courts, if judges only quote authorities, and no judge exerts original jurisdiction, or recurs to first principles? What is the use of a Federal Bench, if its opinions are the political breath of the hour? And what is the use of constitutions, if all the guaranties provided by the jealousy of ages for the protection of liberty are made of no effect, when a bad act of Congress finds a willing commissioner?

The levity of the public mind has been shown in the past year by the most extravagant actions. Who could have believed it, if foretold, that a hundred guns would be fired in Boston on the passage of the Fugitive Slave bill?[5] Nothing proves the want of all thought, the absence of standard in men's minds, more than the dominion of party. Here are humane people who have tears for misery, an open purse for want, who should have been the defenders of the poor man, but are found his embittered enemies, rejoicing in his rendition,—merely from party ties. I thought none that was not ready to go on all fours, would back this law. And yet here are upright men, *compotes mentis*—husbands, fathers, trustees, and friends, open, generous, and brave—who can see nothing in this claim for bare humanity and the health and honor of their native state, but canting fanaticism, sedition, and "one idea."

Because of this preoccupied mind, the whole wealth and power of Boston,—two hundred thousand souls, and one hundred eighty millions of money,—are thrown into the scale of crime; and the poor black boy, whom the fame of Boston had reached in the recesses of a rice-swamp, or in the alleys of Savannah, on arriving here, finds all this force employed to catch him. The famous town of Boston is his master's hound. The learning of the universities, the culture of ele-

---

5. One hundred guns were fired on the Boston Common after the passage of the Fugitive Slave bill.

gant society, the acumen of lawyers, the majesty of the Bench, the eloquence of the Christian pulpit, the stoutness of Democracy, the respectability of the Whig party, are all combined to kidnap him.

The crisis is interesting as it shows the self-protecting nature of the world, and of the divine laws. It is the law of the world, as much immorality as there is, so much misery. The greatest prosperity will in vain resist the greatest calamity. You borrow the succour of the devil, and he must have his fee. He was never known to abate a penny of his rents. In every nation, all the immorality that exists breeds plagues. Out of the corrupt society that exists, we have never been able to combine any pure prosperity. There is always something in the very advantages of a condition which hurts it. Africa has its malformation; England has its Ireland; Germany, its hatred of classes; France, its love of gunpowder; Italy, its Pope; and America, the most prosperous country in the universe, has the greatest calamity in the universe, negro slavery.

Let me remind you a little in detail how the natural retributions act in reference to the statute which Congress passed a year ago. For these few months have shown very conspicuously its nature and impracticability.

It is contravened,

First. By the sentiment of duty.

An immoral law makes it a man's duty to break it, at every hazard. For Virtue is the very self of every man. It is therefore a principle of law, that an immoral contract is void, and that an immoral statute is void. For, as laws do not make right, but are simply declaratory of a right which already existed, it is not to be presumed that they can so stultify themselves as to command injustice.

It is remarkable how rare in the history of tyrants is an immoral law. Some color, some indirection was always used. If you take up the volumes of the "Universal History," you will find it difficult searching. The precedents are few. It is not easy to parallel the wickedness of this American law. And that is the head and body of this discontent, that the law is immoral. Here is a statute which enacts the crime of kidnapping,—a crime on one footing with arson and murder. A man's right to liberty is as inalienable as his right to life.

Pains seem to have been taken to give us in this statute a wrong pure from any mixture of right. If our resistance to this law is not right, there is no right. This is not meddling with other people's affairs: This is hindering other people from meddling with us. This is not going crusading into Virginia and Georgia after slaves, who, it is alleged, are very comfortable where they are:—that amiable argument falls to the ground: but this is befriending in our own state, on our own farms, a man who has taken the risk of being shot, or burned alive, or cast into the sea, or starved to death, or suffocated in a wooden box, to get away from his driver; and this man who has run the gauntlet of a thousand miles for his free-dom, the statute says, you men of Massachusetts shall hunt, and catch, and send back again to the dog-hutch he fled from.

It is contrary to the primal sentiment of duty, and therefore all men that are born are, in proportion to their power of thought and their moral sensibility, found to be the natural enemies of this law. The resistance of all moral beings is secured to it. I had thought, I confess, what must come at last would come at first, a banding of all men against the authority of this statute. I thought it a point on which all sane men were agreed, that the law must respect the public morality. I thought that all men of all conditions had been made sharers of a cer-tain experience, that in certain rare and retired moments they had been made to see how man is man, or what makes the essence of rational beings, namely, that, whilst animals have to do with eating the fruits of the ground, men have to do with rectitude, with benefit, with truth, with something which *is,* inde-pendent of appearances: and that this tie makes the substantiality of life, this, and not their ploughing or sailing, their trade or the breeding of families. I thought that every time a man goes back to his own thoughts, these angels receive him, talk with him, and, that, in the best hours, he is uplifted in virtue of this es-sence, into a peace and into a power which the material world cannot give: that these moments counterbalance the years of drudgery, and that this owning of a law, be it called morals, religion, or godhead, or what you will, constituted the explanation of life, the excuse and indemnity for the errors and calamities which sadden it. In long years consumed in trifles, they remember these moments, and are consoled.

I thought it was this fair mystery, whose foundations are hidden in eternity, which made the basis of human society, and of law; and that to pretend anything else, as, that the acquisition of property was the end of living, was to confound all distinctions, to make the world a greasy hotel, and, instead of noble motives and inspirations, and a heaven of companions and angels around and before us, to leave us in a grimacing menagerie of monkeys and ideots. All arts, customs, societies, books, and laws, are good as they foster and concur with this spiritual element; all men are beloved as they raise us to it; all are hateful as they deny or resist it. The laws especially draw their obligation only from their concurrence with it.

I am surprised that lawyers can be so blind as to suffer the principles of law to be discredited. A few months ago, in my dismay at hearing that the Higher Law was reckoned a good joke in the courts, I took pains to look into a few law-books. I had often heard that the Bible constituted a part of every technical law-library, and that it was a principle in law that immoral laws are void. I found, accordingly,

that the great jurists—Cicero, Grotius, Coke, Blackstone, Burlamaqui, Montesquieu, Vattel, Burke, Mackintosh, and Jefferson—do all affirm this.[6]

I have no intention to recite these passages I had marked:—such citation indeed seems to be something cowardly—for no reasonable person needs a quotation from Blackstone to convince him that white cannot be legislated to be
black—and shall content myself with reading a single passage.

Blackstone admits the sovereignty—"antecedent to any positive precept of
the law of nature"—among whose principles are, "that we should live honestly,
should hurt nobody, and should render unto every one his due," and so forth.
*"No human laws are of any validity, if contrary to this."* "Nay, if any human law
should allow or enjoin us to commit a crime" (his instance is murder) "we are
bound to transgress that human law; or else we must offend both the natural and
divine." Lord Coke held, that where an act of Parliament is against common right
and reason, the common law shall control it, and adjudge it to be void. Chief
Justice *Hobart,* Chief Justice *Holt,* and Chief Justice *Mansfield* held the same.[7]
Lord Mansfield in the case of the slave Somerset, wherein the *dicta* of Lords Talbot and Hardwicke had been cited to the effect of carrying back the slave to the
West Indies, said, "I care not for the supposed *dicta* of judges, however eminent,
if they be contrary to all principle."[8] Even the *Canon Law* says, *in malis promissis
non expedit servare fidem:* "neither allegiance nor oath can bind to obey that which
is wrong."

> "No engagement (to a sovereign) can oblige or even authorize a man to violate the
> laws of nature. All authors who have any conscience or modesty, agree, that a per-
> son ought not to obey such commands as are evidently contrary to the laws of God.
> Those governors of places who bravely refused to execute the barbarous orders of
> Charles IX to the famous Saint Bartholomew's, have been universally praised; and
> the court did not dare to punish them, at least, openly. 'Sire', said the brave Orte,
> governor of Bayonne, in his letter; 'I have communicated your majesty's command
> to your faithful inhabitants and warriors in the garrison, and I have found there only
> good citizens, and brave soldiers; not one hangman: therefore, both they and I most

6. Hugo Grotius (1583–1645), Dutch jurist; Edward Coke (1552–1634), English lawyer and
attorney-general; William Blackstone (1723–80), English lawyer and author of *Commentaries on the
Laws of England* (1765–69); Jean Jacques Burlamaqui (1694–1748) and Emmerich de Vattel (1714–67),
Swiss jurists; Edmund Burke wrote on individual liberty; James Mackintosh (1765–1832), Scottish
philosopher and lawyer; Thomas Jefferson (1743–1826), third president of the United States (1801–9)
and founder of the University of Virginia.

7. English chief justices Henry Hobart (d. 1625), John Holt (1642–1710), and William Murray, Lord
Mansfield (1705–93).

8. The English jurists Charles Talbot (1685–1737) and Philip Yorke, first earl of Hardwicke (1690–
1764), English lord chancellor who helped establish that country's system of equity.

humbly entreat your majesty, to be pleased to employ your arms and lives in things that are possible, however hazardous they may be, and we will exert ourselves to the last drop of our blood.'"[9]

The practitioners should guard this dogma well, as the palladium of the profession, as their anchor in the respect of mankind; against a principle like this, all the arguments of Mr. Webster are the spray of a child's squirt against a granite wall.

Second. It is contravened by all the sentiments.

How can a law be enforced that fines pity, and imprisons charity? As long as men have bowels, they will disobey. You know that the Act of Congress of September 18, 1850, is a law which every one of you will break on the earliest occasion. There is not a manly whig, or a manly democrat, of whom, if a slave were hidden in one of our houses from the hounds, we should not ask with confidence to lend his wagon in aid of his escape, and he would lend it. The man would be too strong for the partisan.

And here I may say that it is absurd, what I often hear, to accuse the friends of freedom in the north with being the occasion of the new stringency of the southern slave-laws. If you starve or beat the orphan, in my presence, and I accuse your cruelty, can I help it? In the words of Electra, in the Greek tragedy,

"'Tis you that say it, not I. You do the deeds,
And your ungodly deeds find me the words."[10]

Will you blame the ball for rebounding from the floor? blame the air for rushing in where a vacuum is made or the boiler for exploding under pressure of steam? These facts are after laws of the world, and so is it law, that, when justice is violated, anger begins. The very defence which the God of Nature has provided for the innocent against cruelty, is the sentiment of indignation and pity in the bosom of the beholder. Mr. Webster tells the President, that, "he has been in the north, and he has found no man whose opinion is of any weight who is opposed to the law." Ah! Mr. President, trust not the information. The gravid old universe goes spawning on; the womb conceives and the breasts give suck to thousands and millions of hairy babes formed not in the image of your statute, but in the image of the universe; too many to be bought off; too many than that

9. In August 1572, Charles IX of France, following the Saint Bartholomew's Day Massacre of up to 10,000 Huguenots in Paris, wrote to his provincial governors, ordering them to put to death Huguenots who attempted any form of assembly. Several governors refused to obey this edict. There is no hard evidence to confirm the story of Vicomte d'Orthe's response, which may be apocryphal, though in fact no massacre took place in Bayonne.

10. Sophocles (ca. 496–406 B.C.), Greek playwright, probably wrote the play *Electra* at about 430 B.C.; see ll. 626–27.

they can be rich, and therefore peaceable; and necessitated to express first or last every feeling of the heart. You can keep no secret, for, whatever is true, some of them will unseasonably say. You can commit no crime, for they are created in their sentiments conscious of and hostile to it; and, unless you can suppress the newspaper, pass a law against bookshops, gag the English tongue in America, all short of this is futile. This dreadful English speech is saturated with songs, proverbs, and speeches that flatly contradict and defy every line of Mr. Mason's statute.[11] Nay, unless you can draw a sponge over those seditious Ten Commandments which are the root of our European and American civilization, and over that eleventh commandment, "Do unto others as you would have others do to you," your labor is vain.

Third. It is contravened by the written laws themselves, because the sentiments, of course, write the statutes.

Laws are merely declaratory of the natural sentiments of mankind, and the language of all permanent laws will be in contradiction to any immoral enactment: And thus it happens here: statute fights against statute. By the law of Congress March 2, 1807, it is piracy and murder punishable with death, to enslave a man on the coast of Africa.[12] By law of Congress, September 1850, it is a high crime and misdemeanor punishable with fine and imprisonment to resist the re-enslaving a man on the coast of America. Off soundings, it is piracy and murder to enslave him. On soundings, it is fine and prison not to re-enslave. What kind of legislation is this? What kind of Constitution which covers it? And yet the crime which the second law ordains is greater than the crime which the first law forbids under penalty of the gibbet. For it is a greater crime to re-enslave a man who has shown himself fit for freedom, than to enslave him at first, when it might be pretended to be a mitigation of his lot as a captive in war.

Fourth. It is contravened by the mischiefs it operates.

A wicked law cannot be executed by good men, and must be by bad. Flagitious men must be employed, and every act of theirs is a stab at the public peace. It cannot be executed at such a cost, and so it brings a bribe in its hand. This law comes with infamy in it, and out of it. It offers a bribe in its own clauses for the consummation of the crime. To serve it, low and mean people are found by the groping of the government. No government ever found it hard to pick up tools for base actions. If you cannot find them in the huts of the poor, you shall find them in the palaces of the rich. Vanity can buy some, ambition others, and money others. The first execution of the law, as was inevitable, was a little hesitating; the

---

11. James Mason (1798–1871), senator from Virginia, drafted the Fugitive Slave Law.

12. Congress passed a law on 2 March 1807 prohibiting the African slave trade and the importation of slaves into America after 1 January 1808.

second was easier; and the glib officials became, in a few weeks, quite practised
and handy at stealing men.

But worse, not the officials alone are bribed, but the whole community is
solicited. The scowl of the community is attempted to be averted by the mischievous whisper, "Tariff and southern market, if you will be quiet; no tariff and
loss of southern market, if you dare to murmur." I wonder that our acute people,
who have learned that the cheapest police is dear schools, should not find out that
an immoral law costs more than the loss of the custom of a southern city.

The humiliating scandal of great men warping right into wrong was followed
up very fast by the cities. New-York advertised in southern markets, that it would
go for slavery, and posted the names of merchants who would not. Boston,
alarmed, entered into the same design. Philadelphia, more fortunate, had no
conscience at all, and, in this auction of the rights of mankind, rescinded all its
legislation against slavery. And the "Boston Advertiser" and the "Courier," in
these weeks, urge the same course on the people of Massachusetts.[13] Nothing
remains in this race of roguery, but to coax Connecticut or Maine to out-bid us
all by adopting slavery into its constitution.

Great is the mischief of a legal crime. Every person who touches this business
is contaminated. There has not been in our lifetime another moment when public men were personally lowered by their political action. But here are gentlemen
whose believed probity was the confidence and fortification of multitudes, who,
by fear of public opinion, or, through the dangerous ascendancy of southern
manners, have been drawn into the support of this foul business. We poor men in
the country, who might once have thought it an honor to shake hands with them,
or to dine at their boards, would now shrink from their touch, nor could they
enter our humblest doors. You have a law which no man can obey, or abet the
obeying, without loss of self-respect and forfeiture of the name of a gentleman.
What shall we say of the functionary by whom the recent rendition was made?
If he has rightly defined his powers, and has no authority to try the case, but only
to prove the prisoner's identity, and remand him, what office is this for a reputable citizen to hold? No man of honor can sit on that bench. It is the extension
of the planter's whipping-post: and its incumbents must rank with a class from
which the turn-key, the hangman, and the informer are taken,—necessary func-

13. Emerson is referring to such sympathetic editorials as this one on "Fugitive Slave Agitation"
from the *Boston Daily Advertiser:* "The senseless excitement which was raised at New Bedford on Sunday last, by the active circulation of a false report, shows how ready a portion of the public are to become
the dupes of a few designing men. . . . This transaction is a most unfortunate one, from the impression
which it must produce abroad of the character of our community and the fidelity of our people to the
Constitution" (20 March 1851, 2).

tionaries, it may be, in a state, but to whom the dislike and the ban of society universally attaches.

Fifth. These resistances appear in the history of the statute, in the retributions which speak so loud in every part of this business, that I think a tragic poet will know how to make it a lesson for all ages.

Mr. Webster's measure was, he told us, final. It was a pacification, it was a suppression, a measure of conciliation and adjustment. These were his words at different times; "there was to be no parleying more"; it was "irrepealable." Does it look final now? His final settlement has dislocated the foundations. The state house shakes like a tent. His pacification has brought all the honesty in every house, all scrupulous and good-hearted men, all women, and all children, to accuse the law. It has brought United States' swords into the streets, and chains round the court house.

"A measure of pacification and union." What is its effect? To make one sole subject for conversation and painful thought throughout the continent, namely, slavery. There is not a man of thought or of feeling, but is concentrating his mind on it. There is not a clerk, but recites its statistics; not a politician, but is watching its incalculable energy in the elections; not a jurist, but is hunting up precedents; not a moralist, but is prying into its quality; not an economist, but is computing its profit and losses. Mr. Webster can judge whether this sort of solar microscope brought to bear on his law is likely to make opposition less.

The only benefit that has accrued from the law is its service to education. It has been like a university to the entire people. It has turned every dinnertable into a debating club, and made every citizen a student of natural law. When a moral quality comes into politics, when a right is invaded, the discussion draws on deeper sources: general principles are laid bare, which cast light on the whole frame of society. And it is cheering to behold what champions the emergency called to this poor black boy; with what subtlety, what logic, what learning, what exposure of the mischief of the law, and, above all, with what earnestness and dignity the advocates of freedom were inspired. It was one of the best compensations of this calamity.

But the Nemesis works underneath again. It is a power that makes noonday dark, and draws us on to our undoing; and its dismal way is to pillory the offender in the moment of his triumph. The hands that put the chain on the slave are in that moment manacled. Who has seen anything like that which is now done?

The words of John Randolph, wiser than he knew, have been ringing ominously in all echoes for thirty years,—words spoken in the heat of the Missouri debate. "We do not govern the people of the north by our black slaves, but by their own white slaves. We know what we are doing. We have conquered you once, and we can and will conquer you again. Aye, we will drive you to the wall, and when we have you there once more, we will keep you there, and nail you down like base money." [14] These words resounding ever since from California to Oregon, from Cape Florida to Cape Cod, come down now like the cry of Fate, in the moment when they are fulfilled. By white slaves, by a white slave, are we beaten. Who looked for such ghastly fulfilment, or to see what we see? Hills and Hallets, servile editors by the hundred, we could have spared.[15] But him, our best and proudest, the first man of the north in the very moment of mounting the throne, irresistibly taking the bit in his mouth, and the collar on his neck, and harnessing himself to the chariot of the planters?

The fairest American fame ends in this filthy law. Mr. Webster cannot choose but to regret his loss. He must learn that those who make fame accuse him with one voice; that those who have no points to carry, that are not identical with public morals and generous civilization, that the obscure and private who have no voice and care for none, so long as things go well, but who feel the disgrace of the new legislation creeping like a miasma into their homes, and blotting the daylight,—those to whom his name was once dear and honored, as the manly statesman to whom the choicest gifts of nature had been accorded, disown him: that he who was their pride in the woods and mountains of New England, is now their mortification,—they have torn down his picture from the wall, they have thrust his speeches into the chimney. No roars of New York mobs can drown this voice in Mr. Webster's ear. It will outwhisper all the salvos of the "Union Committee's" cannon. But I have said too much on this painful topic. I will not pursue that bitter history.

But passing from these ethical to the political view, I wish to place this statute, and we must use the introducer and substantial author of the bill as an illustration of the history.

I have as much charity for Mr. Webster, I think, as anyone has. I need not say how much I have enjoyed his fame. Who has not helped to praise him? Simply, he was the one eminent American of our time, whom we could produce as a finished work of nature. We delighted in his form and face, in his voice, in his eloquence, in his power of labor, in his concentration, in his large understanding, in his daylight statement and simple force; the facts lay like strata of a cloud, or like the layers of the crust of the globe. He saw things as they were, and he stated them so. He has been by his clear perception and statement, in all these years, the best head in Congress, and the champion of the interests of the northern sea-board.

14. John Randolph (1773–1833), U.S. senator from Virginia (1825–27).

15. Probably Isaac Hill (1789–1851), proslavery New Hampshire editor and politician; Benjamin Franklin Hallet (1797–1862), proslavery editor of the *Boston Post*.

But as the activity and growth of slavery began to be offensively felt by his constituents, the senator became less sensitive to these evils. They were not for him to deal with: he was the commercial representative. He indulged occasionally in excellent expression of the known feeling of the New England people: but, when expected and when pledged, he omitted to speak, and he omitted to throw himself into the movement in those critical moments when his leadership would have turned the scale. At last, at a fatal hour, this sluggishness accumulated to downright counteraction, and, very unexpectedly to the whole Union, on the seventh of March, 1850, in opposition to his education and association, and to all his own most explicit language for thirty years, he crossed the line, and became the head of the slavery party in this country.

Mr. Webster perhaps is only following the laws of his blood and constitution. I suppose his pledges were not quite natural to him. Mr. Webster is a man who lives by his memory, a man of the past, not a man of faith or of hope. He obeys his powerful animal nature;—and his finely developed understanding only works truly and with all its force, when it stands for animal good; that is, for property. He believes, in so many words, that government exists for the protection of property. He looks at the Union as an estate, a large farm, and is excellent in the completeness of his defence of it so far. He adheres to the letter. Happily, he was born late,—after the independence had been declared, the Union agreed to, and the Constitution settled. What he finds already written, he will defend. Lucky that so much had got well-written when he came. For he has no faith in the power of self-government; none whatever in extemporising a government. Not the smallest municipal provision, if it were new, would receive his sanction. In Massachusetts, in 1776, he would, beyond all question, have been a refugee. He praises Adams and Jefferson; but it is a past Adams and Jefferson that his mind can entertain. A present Adams and Jefferson he would denounce.

So with the eulogies of liberty in his writings,—they are sentimentalism and youthful rhetoric. He can celebrate it, but it means as much from him as from Metternich or Talleyrand.[16] This is all inevitable from his constitution. All the drops of his blood have eyes that look downward. It is neither praise nor blame to say that he has no moral perception, no moral sentiment, but, in that *region*, to use the phrase of the phrenologists, a hole in the head. The scraps of morality to be gleaned from his speeches are reflections of the minds of others. He says what he hears said, but often makes signal blunders in their use to open the door of the sea and the fields of the earth, to extemporize government in Texas, in California, and in Oregon, and to make provisional law where statute law is not ready. This liberalism appears in the power of invention, in the freedom of think-

---

16. Prince Klemenz von Metternich of Austria (1773–1859), foreign minister and statesman.

ing, in the readiness for reforms; eagerness for novelty, even for all the follies of false science, in the antipathy to secret societies; in the predominance of the democratic party in the politics of the Union, and in the allowance of the voice of the public, even when irregular and vicious,—the voice of mobs, the voice of Lynch law, because it is thought to be on the whole the verdict, though badly spoken, of the greatest number. All this forwardness and self-reliance covers self-government; proceeds on the belief, that, as the people have made a government, they can make another; that their union and law are not in their memory, but in their blood and condition. If they unmake a law, they can easily make a new one. In Mr. Webster's imagination, the American Union is a huge Prince Rupert's drop, which, if so much as the smallest end be shivered off, the whole will snap into atoms.[17] Now, the fact is quite different from this. The people are loyal, law-loving, law-abiding. They prefer order, and have no taste for misrule and uproar. The destiny of this country is great and liberal, and is to be greatly administered. It is to be administered according to what is, and is to be, and not according to what is dead and gone. The Union of this people is a real thing, an alliance of men of one stock, one language, one religion, one system of manners and ideas. I hold it to be a real and not a statute Union. The people cleave to the union, because they see their advantage in it: the added power of each.

I suppose the Union can be left to take care of itself. As much real Union as there is, the statutes will be sure to express. As much disunion as there is, no statutes can long conceal. Under the Union, I suppose the fact to be that there are really two nations, the north and the south. It is not slavery that severs them, it is climate and temperament. The south does not like the north, slavery or no slavery, and never did. The north likes the south well enough, for it knows its own advantages. I am willing to leave them to the facts. If they continue to have a binding interest, they will be pretty sure to find it out: if not, they will consult their peace in parting.

But one thing appears certain to me, that, as soon as the Constitution ordains an immoral law, it ordains disunion. The law is suicidal, and cannot be obeyed. The Union is at an end as soon as an immoral law is enacted. And he who writes a crime into the statute book, digs under the foundations of the capitol to plant there a powder magazine, and lays a train.

Nothing seems to me more hypocritical than the bluster about the Union. A year ago, we were all lovers of the Union, and valued so dearly what seemed the

17. "Prince Rupert's Drop," a tadpole-shaped solid glass object formed by dropping a small glob of molten glass into cold water and leaving it to cool. This process results in a tremendous stress between the outside layer, which is cooled by water, and the inside, which is still warm. Because of the surface tension, the thick, bulbous end can be struck with a hammer, while even the slightest scratch of the thin tail releases the internal stress so forcefully that the entire piece shatters. These were introduced to England in the 1640s by Prince Rupert of Bavaria (1619–82).

immense destinies of this country, that we reckoned an impiety any act that compromised them. But in the new attitude in which we find ourselves, the personal dishonor which now rests on every family in Massachusetts, the sentiment is changed. No man can look his neighbor in the face. We sneak about with the infamy of crime, and cowardly allowance of it on our parts, and frankly, once for all, the Union, such an Union, is intolerable. The flag is an insult to ourselves. The Union,—I give you the sentiment of every decent citizen: "The Union! O yes, I prized that, other things being equal; but what is the Union to a man self-condemned, with all sense of self-respect and chance of fair fame cut off, with the names of conscience and religion become bitter ironies, and liberty the ghastly mockery which Mr. Webster means by that word? The worst mischiefs that could follow from secession and new combination of the smallest fragments of the wreck, were slight and medicable to the calamity your Union has brought us."

It did not at first appear, and it was incredible, that the passage of the law would so absolutely defeat its proposed objects: but from the day when it was attempted to be executed in Massachusetts, this result has become certain, that the Union is no longer desireable. Whose deed is that?

I pass to say a few words to the question, What shall we do? First, What in our federal capacity in our relation to the nation? And, second, what as citizens of a state?

I am an unionist as we all are, or nearly all, and I strongly share the hope of mankind in the power, and, therefore, in the duties of the Union; and I conceive it demonstrated,—the necessity of commonsense and justice entering into the laws.

What shall we do? First, abrogate this law; Then, proceed to confine slavery to slave states, and help them effectually to make an end of it. Or shall we, as we are advised on all hands, lie by, and wait the progress of the census? But will slavery lie by? I fear not. She is very industrious, gives herself no holidays. No proclamations will put her down. She got Texas, and now will have Cuba, and means to keep her majority. The experience of the past gives us no encouragement to lie by.

Shall we call a new convention, or will any expert statesman furnish us a plan for the summary or gradual winding up of slavery, so far as the Republic is its patron? Where is the South itself? Since it is agreed by all sane men of all parties—or was yesterday—that slavery is mischievous, why does the South itself never offer the smallest counsel of her own? I have never heard in twenty years any project except Mr. Clay's.[18] Let us hear any project with candor and respect.

18. Henry Clay (1777–1852), U.S. secretary of state, was instrumental in preparing the legislation that included the Fugitive Slave Law.

Is it impossible to speak of it with reason and good nature? It is really the project fit for this country to entertain and accomplish.

Everything invites to emancipation. The grandeur of the design; the vast stake we hold; the national domain; the new importance of Liberia; the manifest interest of the slave states; the religious effort of the free states; the public opinion of the world;—all join to demand it.[19]

It is said, it will cost a thousand millions of dollars to buy the slaves,—which sounds like a fabulous price. But if a price were named in good faith,—with the other elements of a practicable treaty in readiness, and with the convictions of mankind on this mischief once well-awake and conspiring, I do not think any amount that figures could tell, founded on an estimate, would be quite unmanageable. Every man in the world might give a week's work to sweep this mountain of calamities out of the earth.

Nothing is impracticable to this nation, which it shall set itself to do. Were ever men so endowed, so placed, so weaponed? Their power of territory is seconded by a genius equal to every work. By new arts the earth is subdued, roaded, tunneled, telegraphed, and gas-lighted; vast amounts of old labor are disused, the sinews of man being relieved by sinews of steam. We are on the brink of more wonders. The sun paints: presently we shall organize the echo, as now we do the shadow. Chemistry is extorting new aids. The genius of this people, it is found, can do anything which can be done by men. These thirty nations are equal to any work, and are every moment stronger. In twenty-five years, they will be fifty millions. Is it not time to do something besides ditching and draining, and making the earth mellow and friable? Let them confront this mountain of poison,—bore, blast, excavate, pulverize, and shovel it once for all, down into the bottomless Pit. A thousand millions were cheap.

But grant that the heart of financiers, accustomed to practical figures, shrinks within them at these colossal amounts, and the embarrassments which complicate the problem. Granting that these contingences are too many to be spanned by any human geometry, and that these evils are to be relieved only by the wisdom of God working in ages,—and by what instruments,—whether Liberia, whether flax-cotton, whether the working out this race by Irish and Germans, none can tell, or by what scourges God has guarded his law; still the question recurs, What must we do?

One thing is plain, we cannot answer for the Union, but we must keep Massachusetts true. It is of unspeakable importance that she play her honest part. She

19. The African nation of Liberia had been founded in 1822 by blacks funded by the American Colonization Society and was declared a republic in 1847. A number of reformers suggested black emigration to Liberia as a solution to the slavery crisis.

must follow no vicious examples. Massachusetts is a little State. Countries have been great by ideas. Europe is little, compared with Asia and Africa. Yet Asia and Africa are its ox and its ass. Europe, the least of all the continents, has almost monopolized for twenty centuries the genius and power of them all. Greece was the least part of Europe. Attica a little part of that,—one-tenth of the size of Massachusetts. Yet that district still rules the intellect of men. Judaea was a petty country. Yet these two, Greece and Judaea, furnish the mind and the heart by which the rest of the world is sustained. And Massachusetts is little, but, if true to itself, can be the brain which turns about the behemoth.

I say Massachusetts, but I mean Massachusetts in all the quarters of her dispersion; Massachusetts, as she is the mother of all the New England states, and as she sees her progeny scattered over the face of the land, in the farthest south and the uttermost west.

The immense power of rectitude is apt to be forgotten in politics. But they who have brought this great wrong on the country have not forgotten it. They avail themselves of the known probity and honor of Massachusetts, to endorse the statute. The ancient maxim still holds, that never was any injustice effected except by the help of justice. The great game of the government has been to win the sanction of Massachusetts to the crime. Hitherto, they have succeeded only so far as to win Boston to a certain extent. The behaviour of Boston was the reverse of what it should have been: it was supple and officious, and it put itself into the base attitude of pander to the crime. It should have placed obstruction at every step. Let the attitude of the state be firm. Let us respect the Union to all honest ends. But also respect an older and wider union, the law of nature and rectitude. Massachusetts is as strong as the universe, when it does that. We will never intermeddle with your slavery,—but you can in no wise be suffered to bring it to Cape Cod and Berkshire. This law must be made inoperative. It must be abrogated and wiped out of the statute book; but, whilst it stands there, it must be disobeyed.

We must make a small State great, by making every man in it true. It was the praise of Athens, "she could not lead countless armies into the field, but she knew how with a little band to defeat those who could." Every Roman reckoned himself at least a match for a province. Every Dorian did. Every Englishman in Australia, in South Africa, in India, or in whatever barbarous country their forts and factories have been set up,—represents London, represents the art, power, and law of Europe. Every man educated at the northern schools carries the like advantages into the south. For it is confounding distinctions to speak of the geographic sections of this country as of equal civilization.

Every nation and every man bows, in spite of himself, to a higher mental and moral existence; and the sting of the late disgraces is, that this royal position of

Massachusetts was foully lost, that the well-known sentiment of her people was not expressed. Let us correct this error. In this one fastness, let truth be spoken, and right done. Here, let there be no confusion in our ideas. Let us not lie, nor steal, nor help to steal; and let us not call stealing by any fine names, such as "union" or "patriotism." Let us know, that not by the public, but by ourselves, our safety must be bought. That is the secret of southern power, that they rest not in meetings, but in private heats and courages. It is very certain from the perfect guaranties in the Constitution, and the high arguments of the defenders of liberty, which the occasion called out, that there is sufficient margin in the statute and the law for the spirit of the magistrate to show itself, and one, two, three occasions have just now occurred and passed, in any of which, if one man had felt the spirit of Coke, or Mansfield, or Parsons, and read the law with the eye of freedom, the dishonor of Massachusetts had been prevented, and a limit set to these encroachments forever.[20]

20. William Parsons (ca. 1570–1650), lord justice of Ireland.

# "The Anglo-American"
## 7 December 1852
## (1852–1855)

Emerson first delivered "The Anglo-American" under the title "The Anglo-Saxon" on 7 December 1852 before the Young Men's Association in Cincinnati, Ohio. Even though it was sometimes reported under some version of the title "Anglo-Saxon Race," Emerson continued to use "The Anglo-Saxon" as his title for the lecture when he delivered it on 16 December 1852 in Dayton, Ohio; on 30 December 1852 as the third of seven lectures in a *Conduct of Life* series before the Mercantile Library Association in St. Louis, Missouri, for which he received $500 for the series; on 10 January 1853 as the first in a series of three lectures in Springfield, Illinois ($110 for the series); on 20 January 1853 as the first of two lectures before the Library Association in Cleveland, Ohio ($60 for the two lectures); on 27 January 1853 at the Bache Institute in Philadelphia ($75); on either 10 February 1853 in Portland, Maine (*JMN*, 13:475) or 11 February 1853 before the Augusta Lyceum in Augusta, Maine ("Account Books"), for which he received $30 in Augusta; and on 24 February 1853 before the Concord Lyceum in Concord, Massachusetts. Emerson undoubtedly used "The Anglo-Saxon" for his lecture on "Traits and Genius of the Anglo-Saxon Race," which he delivered on 25 November 1852 before the Young Men's Association in Troy, New York ($40; lecture fees are from the 'Account Books").

A report in the *Troy Daily Times* on Emerson's delivery of "Traits and Genius of the Anglo-Saxon Race" in November 1852 stated that the lecture "exhibited deep thought, but not sufficient care in its arrangement" (26 November 1852, quoted in *Letters*, 4:32n). In Cincinnati a few weeks later, "The Anglo-Saxon" was "listened to with much attention and interest"; however, the *Cincinnati Daily Enquirer* stated that the topic "was handled in a manner peculiar to the distinguished lecturer," who did "not possess the graces of elocution in any eminent degree—owes nothing to *manner*, and is indebted to his *matter* for his great reputation in the literary world." The *Cincinnati Daily Enquirer*'s report may be a genuine assessment of Emerson's performance, or it may suggest the reporter's pique at Emerson's request, which was printed on 8 December 1852 in Cincinnati's *Daily Gazette* and *Daily Times*, that reporters "forbear making a sketch of his discourse" (the first assessment is quoted from an unidentified source in Mead, *Yankee Eloquence in the Middle West*, 34; the second assessment, from the *Cincinnati Daily Enquirer* of 9 December 1852, is quoted in ibid.; Emerson's request to reporters is quoted in ibid., 34n).

Nevertheless, on the whole Emerson appears to have been pleased with this lecture.

Writing to his brother William from Cincinnati on 17 December 1852, Emerson, impatient to be home, claimed that, along with the other lectures drawn from his experiences in England in 1847–48, "The Anglo-Saxon" had reached a fair state of completion: "You may judge I am tired of hotels & railroad trains, & wish to be at home, where I have now accumulated tasks. For my English notes have now assumed the size of a pretty book, which I am eager to complete" (*Letters*, 4:332; see the headnotes to "England" and "London"). And evidently Emerson was right about the state of his lecture manuscript and its relation to *English Traits*, which, in fact, would not be published until 1856 (*CW*, 5). A one-column biographical sketch printed on 8 January 1853 in Springfield's *Illinois Journal* informed readers of Emerson's approach, stating, "he is not a lecturer—call him rather a public monologist, talking rather to himself, than to his audience, [but] what a quiet, calm, commanding conversation it is!" ("Ralph Waldo Emerson," 2). On 12 January 1853 the *Illinois Journal* reported the lecture's debut in that city in glowing terms: "The Lectures of Ralph Waldo Emerson opened . . . with the '*Anglo-Saxon Race*,' which was a lucid and enchantingly beautiful production—full of fact, rich in instruction, and rare in flowing diction. Such treats of intellectual aliment are not common . . . in the wilds of our prairie home; but as our migrations westward flow onward, we have every reason to anticipate a nearer approach to the rising luminaries of the east" ("A New Era in Springfield," 2). Returning to Emerson's performance in the next day's issue of the *Illinois Journal*, the reporter stated that the lecture "was received with enthusiastic admiration, and the Lecturer at once rose in the minds of his auditory to that elevation, which true genius and splendor of renown can only inspire"; he added that no detailed abstract of the lecture would be forthcoming but made the "gratifying announcement" that "the lecture . . . embraces but a portion of the leaves that will soon appear in a book of notes upon England, by Mr. Emerson" (13 January 1853, 2).

Early in 1853 Emerson began adding new material to this lecture to emphasize its American bias. He first used "The Anglo-American" for its title when he delivered it on 14 March 1853 as the first of two lectures at the Bache Institute in Philadelphia, receiving $150 for the two lectures. He repeated "The Anglo-American" on 1 December 1853 before the Concord Lyceum in Concord, Massachusetts; on 11 January 1854 in the People's Course in Williamsburg (Brooklyn), New York ($50); on 16 February 1854 in Penn Yan, New York ($25); and on 29 January 1855 before the Mercantile Library Association at Tremont Temple in Boston ($50; lecture fees are from the "Account Books").

Emerson drew from "The Anglo-American" for lectures on three additional occasions. On 29 and 30 November 1853 he delivered two lectures on American subjects before the Salem Lyceum in Salem, Massachusetts; Charvat and Tilton (*Letters*, 8:383) report that Emerson delivered "American Character" on both days, while von Frank reports that he possibly delivered "The Anglo-American" on the first day and "American Power" on the second. The "Account Books" show Emerson received $25 from the Salem Lyceum on both dates. On 14 November 1855 Emerson delivered "Anglo-American Character" in South Boston (Mattapan), Massachusetts ($30). Finally, on 14 November 1865 he delivered "American Life" as the sixth in a series of six lectures on *American Life* before the Literary Societies of Williams College in Williamstown, Massachusetts ($240 for the series; lecture fees are from the "Account Books"); Emerson's pocket diary for the date states, "'American Life' compiled from 'Boston,' 'Anglo-America[n]' & 'Fortune of Republic'" (*JMN*, 15:530).

Emerson's lecture on "The Anglo-American" has never been published under this or any of its other titles. To the extent that it was reported on as a lecture, "The Anglo-American" generally garnered responses parallel to its earlier positive service as "The Anglo-Saxon." After delivering it before the Concord Lyceum in December 1853, Emerson chanced to talk to Henry Thoreau about his reaction to the lecture. Thoreau said that he "regrett[ed] that whatever was written for a lecture, or whatever succeeded with the audience was bad." Emerson responded, "I am ambitious to write something which all can read, like Robinson Crusoe," to which "Henry objected . . . & vaunted the better lectures which only reached a few persons" (*JMN*, 13:270). Emerson was rewarded for his position by a large audience in January 1854, when he delivered "The Anglo-American" in Williamsburg, New York (*Letters*, 4:416n), and sterling reviews of one of his last deliveries of this lecture before the Mercantile Library Association in Boston in January 1855. On that occasion, the reporter for the *Boston Post* praised "The Anglo-American" as "not subject to the usual charge made against the distinguished lecturer of being vague and abstruse" and with evident pleasure commented that the lecture "expressed more hopefulness for the future [of America] than is . . . entertained by the unpractical class of men to which [he] belongs" ("Mercantile Library Association," 30 January 1855, 2). The reporter for the *Boston Daily Evening Transcript* agreed, finding the lecture "sententious and piquant, abounding in humor, and underlaid with a veil of the deepest thought and strongest *Emersonian* sense" ("The Anglo-American," 30 January 1855, 2).

E VERYTHING IN AMERICA is at a rapid rate. The next moment eats the last. Whatever we do, suffer, or propose, is for the immediate entertainment of the company. We have a newspaper published every hour of the day, and our whole existence and performance slides into it. When I went to Ohio, I was asked, When were you here before?— Three years ago.— O, that is just one age in Ohio: Let me introduce you to the new generation.

A gentleman in Cincinnati defended his immoveableness by saying, "Sir, I have held that opinion three weeks." There is no difference between boy and man. As soon as a boy is table high, he contradicts his father.

"American" means speedy in Europe, as if the ingenuity of this country were directed on nothing so much. The impediment on the western rivers is the low water, at certain seasons, so they must have light boats. They once had on the Mississippi a boat called "*Skim*," drawing so little water that they said it would sail in a heavy dew, and when it got aground, the crew jumped out and put their shoulders under the boat, and lifted it over the bar. On the sea, the value of freight is the warrant of quick arrival at the market; and the American builds clipper ships which outrun all other craft so far, that they command a higher freight in foreign ports, and the East India Company send home cargoes in American vessels, in preference to their own! The American challenge has not been accepted,—to build and run a freight ship to Canton and home, for a purse of ten thousand pounds to the quickest. Lord DeBlaquiere advertised his yacht to race with all yachts, *not American.*

Everything is sacrificed for speed,—solidity and safety. They would sail in a steamer built of lucifer matches if it would go faster; with spars of the very largest jackstraws.[1] A stability is only to be found in this Country in a few isolated localities as, for example, in Essex, Massachusetts, a little town which builds fishing boats, and where ninety families bear the name of Burnham and all the rest are Cogswells or Choates. Perhaps there is an influence continental, climatic, to modify the race, and free certain forces that lay latent before. The sun of America, and its western wind, as they work on the frame, certainly add vivacity and speed.

This national trait stands in strange contrast with the habit of the land of our forefathers. The English have a Cummerian Conservatism.[2] It is called *the Old Country,* and everything in it is old. Its manufactures reach back beyond the memory of history. Fuller says, "The date of cloth and of civility is one in this island."[3] Sheffield has made knives for five hundred years and more. Staffordshire has made potteries, Cornwall dug its mines, Nottingham woven its laces, for centuries. The Spitalfield weavers still pursue their trade as at the revocation of the Edict of Nantes.

The sun returning to the spring solstice finds each man in England sitting at the same workbench at which he left him on that day twelvemonth. The same tenacity is in families and fames. "The Duke of Buckingham was born," says Wotton, "at Brookely in Leicestershire, where his ancestors had chiefly continued about the space of four hundred years, rather without obscurity, than with any great lustre."[4]

The air and aspect of England are loaded with stability and reverence. Take a map, and read the names. In England, it has taken Cambridge between seven and eight hundred years since the monks of Croyland taught in a farm and in a barn to reach the present wealth of its University. Oxford goes back one thousand years to King Alfred for its charter, and much longer, if, as is pretended, the

1. The fiery and sulphuric burning effect of matches led to their being called "lucifers."

2. "Cummer" is a Scottish word that means godmother, midwife, female friend, or even witch.

3. Attributed to Thomas Fuller (1608–61), English clergyman and chaplain to Charles II (see *JMN,* 13:93).

4. Sir Henry Wotton (1568–1639), English diplomat and author.

Druids had a school on the same spot.[5] In Merton College Library I found books still chained to the shelves to which they were locked centuries ago when books were precious as gold.

But we have changed all that, and, in our new states, we extemporize an University like a picnic. In 1851, I chanced to witness this rapid crystallization at Rochester, New York. There had been some negociation about removing into the city a college which was situated twenty miles off. But the negociations dragged; no satisfactory result was likely to come: So an enterprising citizen (Mr. Wilder) bought a cheap hotel, (once a railroad terminus-station,) turned the dining-room into a chapel, by putting up a pulpit on one side; made the barroom into a Pythologian society's hall; the drawing-room into a library; the chambers, into recitation rooms and professors' apartments; all for seven hundred dollars a year.[6] He called in a painter, sent him up a ladder to paint "University of Rochester," on the wall; sent an omnibus up to Madison, and brought the whole faculty of professors bodily down,—bag and baggage, Greek, Hebrew, Chaldee, Latin, *Belles Lettres*, Mathematics, and all sciences; sent runners out on all roads to catch students: One lad, they said, came in yesterday; another, this morning; "thought they should like it first-rate." Already, the guardians of the institution evidently thought themselves ill used, if they did not add a new student every day, and were confident of graduating a class of ten, by the time green peas were ripe. Well, the next year they graduated fifteen Bachelors of Arts; the Greek professor published a Greek grammar of good pretention. Last year, Neander's Library was offered for sale, at Berlin, in Prussia. Various colleges and private collectors were in treaty for the purchase; but the wide-awake little University said to itself, in the phrase of the country, "the longest pole takes the persimmon,"—had a man on the spot, with his money in his pocket,—bought the library,—and it is now triumphantly mounted on the shelves at Rochester, to be explored, at leisure, as soon as they have learned enough to read it.

In every part of the country this vigorous people have struck out some bold and effectual resource. In the north, the summers were short, the soil sterile, and the crop uncertain. Near the foggy island of Newfoundland is stretched a sand-bank six hundred miles long, and the sea flowing over this vast submarine mountain contains an amount of human food which the nations of Europe and America have for several centuries labored indefatigably to collect with nets, lines, and every process that could be contrived or imagined, and yet not the smallest diminution of fruitfulness has ever been observed. Thither he went, and if one

5. The Druids were ancient Celtic priests.
6. John Nichols Wilder (1814–58), first chair of the board of trustees of the University of Rochester.

should go to the capes of Massachusetts, to Gloucester, to Plymouth, Barnstable, Provincetown, he would find, that poor men, without other capital than their arms, built a boat of sixty or seventy tons,—all the owners went in her,—every man carrying his own little bag of provisions,—(a little salt, molasses, and meal, and pork;—) every man fished for himself; and hence the phrase *on his own hook*. This fishing led to the hunting of the whale by some bold Quakers who lived in Nantucket, and who planted their little shipyards at New Bedford, and built up that gigantic trade.

East of the Penobscot River, the climate changes, and the earth will no longer produce wheat, or corn, or apples. Even the potato now is cut off. The agricultural societies resolved, that the hackmetach root was their best esculent, and the shingle-mill their best orchard. At Bangor, where the summer is only a two months' thaw, they fill the forests of Maine with lumberers; buy and sell townships and all the timber on the St. John's River; keep up a brisk game of saw- and slitting-mills. They drag a pine log to mill, turn a crank, and it comes out chairs, and tables, and pianos.

An American in this ardent climate gets up early some morning, buys a river, advertises for twelve or fifteen hundred Irishmen, digs a new channel for it, brings it to his mills, and has a head of twenty-five feet of water: to give him an appetite for his breakfast, he raises a house; then carves out, within-doors, a quarter township into streets and building lots, tavern, school, and Methodist meetinghouse; sends up an engineer into New Hampshire to see where his water comes from, and, after advising with him, sends a trusty man of business to buy of all the farmers such mill privileges as will serve him among their waste hill and pasture lots, and comes home with glee, announcing that he is now owner of the great Lake Winnepesaukee, as reservoir for his Lowell mills at midsummer. The Lowell people gave $200,000 for one hundred square miles of water.[7] Now, they put up their flashboards when there is too much water; and let them down, when there is too little; and have a just supply all summer.

Plenty of ability for this taming and subduing the land, and for expediting internal intercourse. There is many a man who has built his city with all needful aids of engineering, ship and boat building, surveying, and machine shops at their disposal. Go into each great capital; Go into Wall Street. See how well the city of New York is officered for its wants. What large brains, what forcible and persevering gentlemen: six or eight citizens have pioneered the short way to California, and the short way to Liverpool, and the short railway to the Pacific.

The English slow, sure finish has changed into the irresistibility of the American. The climate itself is in extremes. We get, in summer, the splendor of the

7. Lowell, Massachusetts, was famous for its textile mills, which were water-driven.

equator and a touch of Syria, with enormous productiveness. Nature in this climate, ardent, rushing up, after a shower, into a mat of vegetation. Nature goes
into the genius, as well as into the cucumbers, whilst the poor polar man only gets
the last of it. The man's irresistibility is like nature's. Like nature, he has no conscience. His motto, like her's, is, Our country right or wrong. He builds shingle
palaces, shingle cities, picnic universities; extemporizes a state in California; in
an altered mood, I suppose, he will build stone cities, with equal celerity. Tall,
restless Kentucky strength: good stock;—but, though an admirable fruit, you
shall not find one good sound, well-developed apple on the tree. Nature herself
was in a hurry with these racers, and never finished one.

If you travel in New England, you will find in each town some manufacture
rooted, for which the place offered no special facilities. In one town, there is a
whip factory; in another, jewelry; in a third, church-organs; in a fourth, accor-
dions; in a fifth, shoepegs; in a sixth, planes and case knives; in a seventh, fountain pens, and when you inquire what caused this thriving work which feeds
hundreds and thousands, to grow up here, Why, Mr. Driver moved into the
place, and set up his lathe, and, after a time, one of his men set up another, and
so on. It was not that the leather grew here, or the ivory, or the iron; It was not
nearer to the market; It was not the water power; It was only that here grew
Mr. Driver's brain.

All is hasty, and with the penalty that speed must pay. Time respects nothing
but what himself has made. All is hasty, incomplete, cheap, much of it counterfeit. There is superficial finish, and want of solidity. His leather is not tanned;
his white lead is whiting; his sulphuric acid has half-strength; in architecture, his
pillars are drums; his stone is well-sanded pumpkin-pine; his mahogany is
veneered; and, I am sorry to say, in Philadelphia itself, he has learned to build
marble houses with veneers instead of blocks.

Our newspapers name it as a merit, that the steam engine of our sea steamers
was first put together in the ship. That circumstance will not recommend the
boat to the Englishman who knows that his countrymen do not venture to put
the machine into the ship until it first it has been kept a'going for months in the
works. Instead of the grand old knees of oak which nature has been employed for
seven centuries in the forest to knot and gnarl into rocky strength,—we have
found out, by more dexterous fashion of our saws, to saw, out of refuse sapling
stuff, knees of any shape; if they will hold together till they are nailed, they will
hold till they are screwed, and then covered up with boards and veneered with
bird's-eye maple, and varnished with copal; Who will ever know the difference!
Ah, nobody—Nobody but the ugly Ocean, and the rending and bursting of the
Southwestern Gale, and the drowning passengers.

Rashness of adventure marks all their acts and professions. Their steam-marine outnumbers every other nation's, but it is frail, and recklessly hazarded, burned, snagged, run into, and raced to ruin, and proverbially unsafe. The safety-valve is fastened down with a billet of wood. No eastern man travels on the western rivers, without a life-preserver. And I found, that whilst, on the Mississippi, my companions, who were western merchants, did not take off their clothes or their boots,—until they entered the Ohio; then they undressed, and went to sleep. Forty-seven steamboats were burned at St. Louis in the year 1849–1850.

Another form in which this levity shows itself is a social and public action, in which, the individuals composing the assembly do not feel themselves committed. They are fond of excitement, and like crowds; and will lend their hand and voice to swell the clapping and huzzas that applaud some person or sentiment, on whose merits they have by no means made up their minds. They have a superficial heat, a two-inch enthusiasm, a passing flush and are willing to cry for anything with a million. It is a sort of rose-influenza, epidemic for a day or two, far and wide, and then forgotten. And if some foreign celebrity passes by, as Lafayette, or Kossuth, or Dickens, or Lord Morpeth, or Meagher, or Gavazzi, or Thackeray, the shout of welcome, first from a few voices, is echoed about and caught from city to city, East, West, North, South, until it swells into an oriental superlative of adulation, and deceives the object of it into some belief that he is the man they all were waiting for.[8] And they are only humbugging each other. If Kossuth had received on his landing in England, such a welcome as he found at the city of New York, it might have been relied on, whereas the very actors in the New York scene knew it meant nothing.

"Haste," said Mahomet, "is of the devil; Delay is of the All-giving." The like incompleteness runs into education, into the schools, and the trades and professions: The like into manners and plans of life. Fine manners, fine intercourse, require time, and abhor hurry.

The climate adds vivacity, but exhausts. In this close competition, every man is tasked beyond his strength, and grows early old. Life is a lottery, in which everyone may draw a fortune, or a blank. In California, insanity abounds. It frequently happens, that one man is getting out of his digging twenty dollars a day; another, in the very next beside him, is getting out a thousand dollars a day. Of course, 'tis vain to say, "Gentlemen, in Digging number one, Keep cool! There's plenty of time." No: They work like dogs, because they are expecting every hour that they will strike on the same shelf. How can brains or bodies stand such excitement? Yet what happens in the mines, happens throughout the Union.

8. George William Frederick Howard, Viscount Morpeth (1802–64), English statesman; Thomas Francis Meagher (1823–67), Irish-American general; Alessandro Gavazzi (1809–89), Italian patriot and religious reformer.

The leading features of national character are less glaring in our large and old cities, which have kept much of the European spirit. In the new-planted territory of the West, it found free play, and is seen without disguise. It is said, if you would see the American, you must cross the Alleghanies.

There is a levity of social and public action. I think there is a reaction on the people from the extraordinary advantages and invitations of their condition. In proportion to the personal ability of each man, he feels the invitation and career which the country opens to him. He is easily fed with wheat and game, with Ohio wine; but his brain is also pampered by finer draughts, by political power and by the power in the railroad board, or the mills, or the banks. This elevates his spirits and gives, of course, an easy self-reliance that makes him self-willed and unscrupulous.

I think, when we are most disturbed by their rash and immoral voting, it is not malignity, but recklessness. The people are better than their votes. They are careless of politics, because they do not ever feel seriously threatened; they feel strong and irresistible; they can do and undo; what they have enacted, they can repeal; and they do not entertain the possibility of being seriously caught and endangered in their own legislation. They stay away from the polls, saying, that *one vote can do no good;* and then they take another step, and say, *one vote can do no harm,* and vote for something which they do not approve, because their party or set, votes for it not from malice, but from levity. Of course, this levity puts them in the power of any party which has a steady interest to promote, which does not conflict manifestly with the pecuniary interest of the voters. New England, it is said, on each new political event, resolves itself into a debating society, and is the Germany of the United States.

The men also are uncertain. It is agreed by those who have lived there, that you can form no conclusion to depend upon, from what a man on the prairie says, he will do. He says, he will come on Monday. He will not come on Monday. He may arrive some days later. He says, he will bring twenty hands. Perhaps he will bring three. Entire want of punctuality and business-habit—a principal cause of which is the uncertainty of health. The miasma takes the labourers.

Go to the states on the Mississippi. Your western romance fades into reality of some grimness. Everything wears a raw and ordinary aspect. You find much coarseness in manners; much meanness in politics; much swagger, and vaporing, and low filibusterism; the men have not shed their canine teeth. Well; don't be disgusted: 'tis the work of this river,—this Mississippi River,—that warps the men, warps the nations, and dinges them all with its own mud.

I found a good many burly fellows, with dangerous eyes, on the banks, everyone with his cigar.— What is that man doing? What is that other man's work? And what of this? And this?— "O, they are river-hands; They follow the river."

Never was a truer word. I found it every day more deeply exact, and of thousands and millions. *They follow the river.* They must chop down its woods; kill the alligator; eat the deer; shoot the wolf; mind the boat; plant the Missouri corn; cure, save, and send down stream the wild foison harvest, tilth, and wealth of this huge mud-trough of the two thousand miles or ten thousand miles of river. How can they have a day's leisure for anything but the work of the river? Everyone has the mud up to his knees, and the coal of the country dinges his shirt. How can he know letters, or arts, or sciences?

Centre of all the Valley, and Gate of California, is St. Louis, a little French town when it came into American possession fifty years ago.[9] And I have seen various persons who remember it, when there was only one brick house in it. It has now nearly 100,000 inhabitants, and is a well-built city, with spacious squares, and ample room to grow. The people are fully aware of their advantages: they have long smelled the Pacific Ocean. Cincinnati is a *bagatelle,* and they do not speak with due respect of New York. A certain largeness appears in the designs and enterprise of the people and a generosity. They talk St. Louis in all companies, all day, and great fortunes have been made by such as were wise or lucky enough to hold on to their lands. Governor Edwards, an old pioneer, told me that he remembered when St. Louis consisted of nothing but old tumbledown French houses with their little piazzas, whose columns, rotted away at bottom, and suspended from the top, were swinging in the wind: and that nobody who came here then, would think of buying land, in such a dilapidated place.[10] But a few men had the wisdom to look rather on the map, than in the streets; and they discovered that the two enormous river axes of the Continent, the Mississippi running North and South, and the Ohio and Missouri running East and West, had their practical intersection at St. Louis, and that sixty thousand miles of navigable river were tributary to this town; that this town must come to be "the greatest cross-roads the world ever saw."

I stood at St. Louis and saw the Father of Waters rolling his steady flotilla of cakes and islands of ice, four miles an hour; and, day by day, the stream grew more impressive as one grew better acquainted with it.[11] 'Tis the only divinity that is worshipped on its banks. It is a power not to be trifled with. Here the river is only half a mile wide; But in freshets, it extends from bluff to bluff, or here ten to fifteen miles, and is crossed in steamboats so far. The engineers think the river here unconquerable and that they must follow, not dictate to it. They who know it best, fear it most. If you drive piles into it, to build a dam or pier, you only stir

9. St. Louis had been ceded to America by the French in 1803.

10. Emerson confuses Ninian Wirt Edwards (1809–89), first superintendent of instruction in Illinois, with his father, Ninian Edwards (1775–1833), governor of the Illinois Territory (1809–18) and the state of Illinois, as he had earlier (see *JMN,* 11 : 527).

11. "Father of Waters," loose translation of the Algonquian name for the Mississippi River.

the bottom, which dissolves like sugar, and is all gone. Very laborious and costly constructions have been carried off. Real estate on the shores of Missouri is very floating capital.

Go into the states which make its valley, to know the powers of the river, the insatiate craving for nations of men to reap and cure its harvests, and the conditions it imposes, for it yields to no engineering. The prairie exists to yield the greatest quantity of tallow. For corn makes swine; swine is the export of all the land; and St. Louis, furiously, like some Eblis, vociferates, "Men! Men! more men, for I have more pork to pack." [12]

Cotton has done its office in the South,—cotton and sugar,—but now pig plays his unctuous part, draws his larded sides, like modest Prosperity, through the streets of all cities; grunts softly to nations; grunts melodiously to all who are not preoccupied by the new glitter of California, and seems to say, "My dear men, henceforth owe your aristocracy and civility to me!"

'Tis ever so. What earldoms of Guienne, Champagne, and Bourgogne lay sleeping in the first grape-store that was carried by travelling man or flying bird into the country of the Rhine? What civilization and power in the first grain of wheat on the Nile; in the first orange of Spain; in the tea plant of China; in the coal of England; in the peach-store of New Jersey; in the sugar cane for the shores of the Gulf of Mexico? Thrones, constitutions, cities, states, laws, learning, arts, all dependent on some one plant which they ripen and sell: and not less, in all this prairie, on this modest quadruped. For, though it cannot be disputed that telegraphs are beautiful triumphs of science and art, if you hold your ear close to the poetic wires, the lightning is whispering to the packers, "A penny more on lard! An eighth on candles!"

Such as the people, such is the hero. I asked, "Who was the great man of the prairie?", and was shown a field of corn containing within one fence one thousand acres. The owner of this was the hero: one of themselves, a man who owned forty thousand acres, a cattle dealer who raises three or four thousand head of cattle, who delights to stand in the gap when great droves of cattle are to be separated,— these for the market, and those to pasture. The man who stands in the gap is to choose, on the instant, by their looks, as they come up, which to let through the gate, and which to keep off the other way, and he must be of such a size and look that a buffalo would not run over him. He delights in fat steers. He hardly knows what a bed is, sleeps behind a door, while his horse is baited; lives in the saddle; never knows leisure; eats his mush and milk with two spoons; he laughs at politics, as long as he is absolute in the market towns and cattle yards, and nobody can make money out of him.

I tell this story, because I passed a field alleged to be of these dimensions;

12. Eblis, the prince of the evil spirits.

though it seems, it is something incredible on the Atlantic states. For Mr. Greene of Cincinnati told me he knew of a simple field on the Big Miami River, which contains one thousand acres, and yielded one hundred bushels of corn to the acre.[13] Yet, he says: When he told this story in New England, Gentlemen would always take wine with him.

Narrow views, the narrow trade enforces, and yet the poverty and the habits of the swineherds and cattle dealers are wholesome for liberty. A stern equality is guarded and enjoyed. These men are fierce. Most of them live in loghouses,— the whole family in one room; eat ham and corn cakes; are all day in the open air, and accustomed to serve themselves; their dress is plain, and they pay no regard to a fine coat. Every man alternates the most daring and vigorous exertion, with listless repose.

They are all alike, all in working clothes. The Governor of the state works with his hands, and all the dignitaries must harness their own teams. I called on the Governor of the state at the statehouse, and, whilst I was paying my respects, the Secretary of State came into the room. "Governor," said the Secretary, "Did you take my screwdriver out of my room?" The executive acknowledged the act. It stood confessed, that he had borrowed it for his own uses. Need enough there was to use it: the statehouse was all cracking to pieces. They are all poor country people and live hard. But the sense of freedom and equality is never interrupted. New England men and women said, "We never knew what it was to be free, till we came to Missouri." They affirm, that, after people have been out west, ten years, nothing would draw them back to the old states. An alumnus of Yale, whom I discovered in grey working dress, told me, that, though his eyes ached for the hills when he went back to Connecticut, he could not breathe there;— a man was nothing there,—could not make his mark.

The people are all kings,—if the sceptre is a cattledealer's driving-whip. I noticed an extraordinary firmness, even to ferocity, in the face of many a drover, an air of independence, and lips which expressed more pluck, and perseverance, and wo to all opponents, than could be crowded into a coat of arms.

The condition of the Western states is today what was the condition of all the states fifty or a hundred years ago. It is the country of poor men. Here is practical democracy;—not the old experiment, out of a prostrate humanity, as out of a bank or magazine, to draw materials of culture to a class, and to avenge the injured many by wonderful success in a few; but here is the human race poured out over the continent to do itself justice; all mankind in its shirt-sleeves; not grimacing, like poor rich men in cities, pretending to be rich, but unmistakably taking off its coat, as in California, to hard work, when labor is sure to pay. This

13. William Greene (1797–1881), Cincinnati lawyer.

through all the country. For, really, though you see wealth in the capitals, it is only a sprinkling of rich men in the cities and at sparse points: the bulk of the population is poor. In Maine, every man is a lumberer. In Massachusetts, every twelfth man is a shoemaker and the rest millers, farmers, sailors, or fishermen.

Well, the result is, instead of the doleful experience of the European economist who tells us, "In almost all countries the condition of the great body of the people is poor and miserable," here that same great body has arrived at a sloven plenty;—ham and corn cakes, tight roof and coals enough have been attained an unbuttoned comfort—not clean, not thoughtful, far from polished, without dignity in his repose; the man awkward and restless if he have not something to do; but honest and kind, for the most part; understanding his own rights, and stiff to maintain them; and disposed to give his children a better education than he received.[14]

The Anglo-Saxon race are characterised by their universal interest in politics. The people of England are educated by political discussion. In America, the public topic is not less absorbing; it is the one topic which neither age, nor sex, nor profession can long keep out of any conversation. But in this country a prodigious stride has been taken in practice, through universal suffrage. The fact that everybody elects and everybody is eligible, exasperates the discussion. In England, politics is a monopoly of a few; it is with the people a very distant affair. It is a choice of somebody far above them, and few of them are the choosers. The people whom I saw, eminent people, some of them, had never voted in their lives. But here, it is *you*, and *me*, and *him*, that are immediately concerned.

It were fatal to the happiness of a young man to set out with ultra-conservative notions in this country. He must settle it in his mind that the human race have got possession, and, though they will make many blunders, and do some great wrongs, yet, on the whole, they will consult the interest of the whole.

Practically, the tendency among us, is, to elect middle class men, and, by no means, first class men.

It is certainly desireable that men of capacity and virtue, that the best and wisest, should be entrusted with the helm of power, and the tendency to promote to this charge young men of very imperfect training, is, I know, regretted, and is, on many accounts, a bad feature. But there are certain benefits which mitigate the folly. I said, the people were educated by politics. Well, after a young man of the humblest class has passed through the village school, if he has vivacity and a social talent, and interests himself on the street, and at the railroad station, in talking politics, he is chosen to the Legislature. There, to his great surprise, he

14. The quotation is attributed to John Stuart Mill (1806–73), English philosopher and economist (see *JMN*, 13:82).

finds himself, for a whole winter, in far better company than he ever kept before; subject to social attentions and opportunities such as he never knew; listening (every day) to debates, to which he must listen, because he is to vote, and to give a reason for his vote, at home; and entertaining in his mind, daily, a class of questions wholly new to him, and quite above his habit. If he have capacity, this ordeal cannot fail to work on him, and I have known (it is notorious) an ordinary tavern brawler lose all his profanity and a large part of his other nonsense, and come back at the end of a single winter at the legislature, at least as much improved, as his young townsman from two years at the University.

There was in the Illinois Legislature a member, to whom plainly all parties looked with interest as a man likely to take a leading part. A gentleman who followed him in debate, took occasion to commend his speech, and to congratulate the legislature that this self-made man, so lately retired from a mechanical trade, had forsaken an honorable toil to lend his powerful service to the state. The new member made haste to correct his colleague (who described him as formerly a working man,) by saying, that he was still a mason, had by no means relinquished his trowel, had laid twenty thousand feet of plaster this fall and valued his work as a mason more than his skill in politics.

The American, in view of these great powers, appears passively to yield to this superincumbent Fate. His task is, to educe the capabilities of the Continent,—to make the most of it.

It is the American discovery, that, it is as easy to occupy large space, and do much work, as, to occupy a small space, and do little. And his task is the easier for the wonderful tools he uses. Mr. Webster had a good head, and loved Union; but the telegraph and railroad are better unionists than ten thousand Websters. He has a finer invention. In this age of tools, one of the skilfullest of all machines is this governing machine, rude as it is yet, which the Americans have so far perfected;—the distributing of political electricity over a vast area to avoid explosion. Last November, we had an election day,—and a revolution,—for every election is a revolution,—went off with the quietness of a pic-nic, or a sermon.

Thanks to his telegraph, his Election day, and his newspaper, he looks with a public eye, he works in a public spirit. The young American must know the geography of his continent, as exactly as his father did the streets of his town; such proximity have steam, rails, and telegraphs wrought.

Indeed, he has a wilderness of capabilities. He is versatile; (πολυτροποσ Οδυσσευσ;) [15] has a many-turning Ulyssean culture. He is confident as Jove in his powers and triumph; has a prospering look. He is a good combiner. The stock companies, the mills of the North, owe everything to the good concert of skilful

15. Possibly a reference to the voyages of Ulysses in Homer's *Odyssey*.

men. His eyes run up and down, here and out there, and nothing escapes them. He thinks of Cuba, he thinks of Japan, he thinks of annexing South America, in due course. Nothing is impossible. He is accustomed to see things mind him. He believes, if he should attach his clamps to a granite mountain, and let on the steam, it would follow him like a spaniel round the globe.

The English are stiff to their own ways. As I showed you, the towns are stiff to their old crafts for five centuries. It is the remark of our people employing English workmen, that they show great reluctance to deviate from their own methods, or proper work; whilst an American will turn his hand to anything. The very existence of our manufactures is a proof of aptitude: The stone cutters become sculptors. The house painters take to landscape and portraits. We can make everything but music and poetry. But also he has chambers opened in his mind which the English have not. He is intellectual and speculative, an abstractionist. He has solitude of mind and fruitful dreams. See what good readers of dreamy Germans we are—books which the English cannot bear. Many and many a good thought of some inspired man floats about for a time among studious men, and, not long after, I have noticed it caught up by some of the gladiators at Washington; and, endorsed or, rather, usurped by them, it passes into the newspapers, and, becomes, under these base colours, the property of the million.

This Fate, this natural growth, is really the ground on which the shrewd men of the world fall back, as their remedy for all evils. Such men do not believe much in any special policy, as free trade, nor put much faith in any statute in our capricious and fluctuating legislation; nor are they wont to trust the honesty of people, or to lift their eyes to considerations so large as the self-avenging power that mixes in human affairs, under the name of morals. But analyse what they say, and they do believe in the natural growth of the Republic; and this Fate really involves, in their mind, melioration, or, the self-avenging moral power. Name any benefit; One way or another, they believe the nation arrives at the same thing, which this ingenious person would compass with his law. Thus a strong party is for free trade; and all the reason and humanity is on their side; all the conclusions of history. But the old man shakes his head, and says, Look, You have got free trade in substance, though not in form; free trade with thirty-one nations, reaching through all climates, some of them manufacturing nations; some agricultural; some seafaring; some mining, and some hunting and fishing; all varieties of production, and not a customhouse.[16] You wanted tariff to protect your iron. Well, you did not get it; but, instead of twenty thousand tons, a year ago you manufactured 800,000.

16. The "old man" is identified by Edward Waldo Emerson as Thomas Wren Ward (1786–1858), Boston merchant (see *JMN*, 11:408n).

Peace you want. But Mr. Cobden and Mr. Burritt, however respectable, do not seem to him to say much to the purpose.[17] But trade can't afford to make war, or to suffer war to be made, and every man who has land, or money, or goods is by them bound ever to keep the peace. You talk of annexing new territory. It only adds to your burdens. By reciprocity, or free trade with England, you annex England, without the taxation of England.

Here, gentlemen, is a grave interest, the future of a quarter of the world, and of a race as energetic and as able as any in it: and one cannot help asking, What is to come of it?

Everybody working all day and half the night, and no man in this country knows whither we are driving, or can chant the destiny of the Anglo-American. The solar system, astronomers say, is moving toward a star in the arm of the Constellation Hercules: but whither we are drifting, who can tell.

When a new question is before Congress, or in the Courts, the presumption in all men's minds is that it will not be decided as the man within the breast would decide it, and a verdict on grounds of natural equity gives all men the joy of surprise. On Education; on Temperance; on Copyright; on claims of injured parties, whether states or private citizens; the Anglo-American usually gives a selfish and electioneering verdict. What can be worse than our legislation on Slavery? If there be any worse, be sure we shall find it out, and make that law.

But is this the action of legislatures only? It is also the public opinion as expressed in what are called the respectable journals. The tone of the press is not lower on Slavery than on everything else. Criminal on that point, ready to be criminal on every other. It has no great men. Its able men are not patriots, but simply attorneys of gross sectional interests. Its politics are the politics of trade. It goes for wars, if they be profitable wars. Its argument at the elections, is, "Roast Beef and two dollars a day;" and our people will not go for liberty of other people, no, nor for their own, but for annexation of territory, or a tariff, or whatever promises new chances for young men, more money to men of business.

The gain of the means of living absorbs them to the exclusion of the ends. Nothing but the brandy of politics will wake them from brute life. No song of any muse will they hear.

I know we must speak very modestly of the political good sense of the country and of its virtue. Any action of the well-disposed and intelligent class in its affairs is uniformly reckoned an impertinence, and they are presently whipped back into their libraries and churches and Sunday schools. But drive out nature with a fork, and she presently comes back again. The moral sense is still renewed, and every child that is born is of nature's party.

17. Elihu Burritt (1810–79), linguist and social reformer.

We lack repose. As soon as we stop working, or active thinking, we mope. There is no self-respect, no grand sense of sharing the Divine preference. We are restless, run out and back, talk past, and overdo. When that civilization of their Universities and men of science and thought enters into their politics, I shall think they have made a real advance.

But this perhaps is partial and ungenerous, when we remember the sturdy minority, often for an age the majority, that, in England itself, has striven for the right, and the largest justice, and won so many charters, and still strives there with the lovers of liberty here. Rather, it is right to esteem without regard to geography this industrious liberty-loving Saxon wherever he works,—the Saxon, the colossus who bestrides the narrow Atlantic,—with one foot on England, and one on America,—at home on all land,—at home on all seas, asking no leave to be of any other,—formidable, conquering and to conquer, with his nervous and sufficient civilization weaponed already far beyond his present performing. At least I infer that the decided preference of the Saxon on the whole for civil liberty is the security of the modern world. He is healthy;—nature's democrat, nature's worker;—his instincts and tendencies, sound and right. Only let high and sound counsels be given to these twin nations, admonishing, and holding them up to their highest aim. At present, one hears only the tinkle of preparation. At present, their commerce is but costly trifling belting the world for raisins, oranges, oil, wine, tobacco, gums and drugs, hides and silk. But what for thought? What for humanity? What for the interests of the human soul? Is science, is the head, is the heart, always to be postponed, and only endured or tolerated? And our politics are no better than our trade. Are legislatures convened, with upheaval of the peace of nations in the fury of elections, to any noble, humane purpose? No; but to the most selfish and paltry.

It is impossible that a race so gifted and historied as this, should not presently make good the wonderful education of so many centuries. It is not indiscriminate masses of Europe that are shipped hitherward,—but the Atlantic is a sieve, through which only, or chiefly, the liberal, bold, *America-loving* part of each city, clan, or family, pass. It is mainly the light complexion, the blue eyes of Europe, that come; the black eyes, (the black drop,) the Europe of Europe is left. Still, a portion of both races come, and the old contest of feudalism and of democracy renews itself here on a new battlefield.

That makes sometimes, and, at this moment, the vast interest of American history. Which principle, which branch of this compound English race is here (and now) to triumph? The liberty-loving, the thought-loving, the godly and grand British race, that have fought so many battles, and made so many songs, and created so many reverend laws and charters, and exhibited so much moral grandeur in private and poor men;—or, the England of Kings and Lords; castles and primogeniture; enormous wealth and fierce exclusion? Which is to be planted here? It is wonderful with how much rancour and premeditation at this moment the fight is prepared. Of late years, as I said, England has been materialized by its wealth, and the noble air of other times is gone.

Again, mark the differences more marked in every generation between the English and the Americans. The great majority of the Americans are of pure English descent. In some parts of America, their pedigrees have been well kept in family Bibles and in the town-clerk's office: Yet differences appear in stature, weight, complexion, feature, voice, widening too, in national character. These spring from new conditions, from climate, from the occupancy of wide territory, inducing solitary labor and sloven cultivation; from new staples of tillage and trade, new laws, new enemies. Climate draws the teeth, emaciates the body, spends the constitution, unbuilds and recomposes the bulky compact Briton into the loose-jointed, spare, swaggering Kentuckian. The Englishman, well-made, and even fatted by his climate of clouded sunshine, walks and sits erect, and his chair rests squarely on its legs. The American lolls and leans, tips his chair, adds rockers to it to keep it tipped, but is capable of equal energy in action and the mental powers are not impaired. The difference of manners is marked. The American is demonstrative; the English, shy and reserved.

When Rome has arrived at Cicero and Caesar, it has no more that it can do, and retreats. When Italy has got out Dante and Raffael, all the rest will be rubbish. So that we ought to be thankful that our hero or poet does not hasten to be born in America, but still allows us others to live a little, and warm ourselves at the fire of the sun; for, when he comes, we others must pack our petty trunks and be gone.

'Tis said, that when the Sphinx's riddle is solved, the Sphinx rolls herself off the precipice and falls into the sea.[18] 'Tis said, every race or age ends with the successful man who knots up into himself the genius or idea of his nation, and, that, when the Jews have flowered into their prophet, or cluster of prophets, there is the practical end of the nation. When Greece is complete in Plato, Phidias, Pericles, the race is spent, and rapidly takes itself away.[19]

The Anglo-American is a pushing, versatile, victorious race. Then it has wonderful powers of absorption and appropriating. The Mississippi swallows the Illinois, the Missouri, Ohio, and Red rivers, and does not widen: And this Anglo-American race absorbs into itself thousands and millions of Germans, French, Irish, Norwegians, and Swedes, and remains unchanged.

18. Numerous writers have dealt with the story of travelers being asked a riddle about existence by the Sphinx; for Emerson's attempt, see his poem "The Sphinx" (1841), *W*, 9:20–25, which concludes with the Sphinx saying, "'Who telleth one of my meanings / Is master of all I am.'"

19. Phidias (ca. 500–ca. 430 B.C.), Greek sculptor.

Our young men went to the Rhine to find the German genius which had charmed them and it was not there. Lessing, Herder, Schiller, Goethe, Wieland were all dead.[20] They hunted for it in Heidelberg, in Gottingen, in Halle, in Berlin: no one knew where it was. From Vienna to the frontier, it was not found; and they slowly and mournfully learned, that really America possessed more of that expansive inquisitive spirit, and they must return and look for it in Boston and New York.

The convictions of multitudes are sometimes as well expressed by braggart lips or in jeers that sound blasphemous,—and that word "manifest destiny," often profanely used, yet signifies the sense all men have of the prodigious energy and opportunity lying dormant here. The poor Prussian, or Austrian, or Italian escaping hither discovers that he has been handcuffed, fettered all his early life-time, with monopolies and duties at every tollgate on his little cart of corn, or wine, or wood, or straw, or on his cow or ox or donkey, and his own lips and mind padlocked. No country, no education, no vote,—but passports, police, monks, and foreign soldiers instead.

The wild, exuberant tone of society in California is only an exaggeration of the uniform present condition of America in the excessive attraction of the extraordinary natural wealth. 'Tis doubtful whether London, whether Paris, whether Berlin can answer the questions which now rise in the American mind. American geography and vast population must be considered in all arrangements of commerce and politics, and we are forced, therefore, to make our own precedents. The radiation of character and manners here, the boundless America, gives opportunity as wide as the morning; and the effect is to dig away the peak of the mountain, to change the peak into a vast table-land, where millions can share the privilege of a handful of patricians.

20. In Emerson's youth, many prominent Americans traveled to Germany to seek out the scenes of German literature and the country's major writers and theologians; one of them was Emerson's brother William. The German authors mentioned here are Gotthold Ephraim Lessing (1729–81), critic and dramatist; Johann Gottfried von Herder (1744–1803), critic and poet; and Christoph Martin Wieland (1733–1813), poet and novelist.

# "Poetry and English Poetry
## 10 January 1854"

Emerson delivered "Poetry and English Poetry" only once: on 10 January 1854 as the third in a series of six private lectures on the *Topics of Modern Times* in Philadelphia, for which he netted $1,166.34 for the series ("Account Books"). "Poetry and English Poetry" was one of the new lectures Emerson had promised William Henry Furness for that series when he wrote to him on 17 October 1853, "I flatter myself that my abstractions will be interesting, & my details significant" (*Letters*, 4:391). This lecture has never been published.

Emerson merged "Poetry and English Poetry" with some form of his many lectures on "Genius" to create a version of "Culture," which he delivered on 13 November 1865 as the fifth in a series of six lectures on *American Life* before the Literary Societies of Williams College in Williamstown, Massachusetts; he received $240 for the series ("Account Books"). His pocket diary for that date shows "'Culture' drawn from Lectures on 'Genius' & 'Poetry & Eng. Poetry'" (*JMN*, 15:530), and his insertion of the roman numeral "V." on page {ar} of the manuscript of "Poetry and English Poetry" confirms his use of this text in 1865. However, those notations barely begin to hint at the uses Emerson made of this highly worn manuscript, the introduction to which was found not in the body of the manuscript but in a collection of manuscript pages on poetry marked "Old Copy" by Emerson (see the electronic textual notes).

Poetry was, of course, one of Emerson's favorite topics, as his essay on "The Poet" published in *Essays: Second Series* in 1844 (*CW*, 3:1–24) and his voluminous correspondence, early lectures on literature, journals, and notebooks devoted primarily to poetry suggest (see, for example, "The Poet" [1841] in *Early Lectures*, 3:348–65; *Poetry Notebooks;* and Notebooks Orientalist, PY ["Theory of Poetry"], and ZO in *TN* 2:39–141, 258–329, 3:179–237). Among his lectures, "Poetry and English Poetry" stands approximately midway between Emerson's earliest speculations and pronouncements on poetry and his latest. Beginning with "The Poet" in 1841, Emerson developed his ideas on poetic theory and practice in lectures on "Poetry and Eloquence," which he delivered on 15 June 1848 as the fifth in a series of six lectures on the *Mind and Manners of the Nineteenth Century* at the Literary and Scientific Institution in Portman Square in London, for which he netted £80 for the series (see the headnote to the *Mind and Manners of the Nineteenth Century* series); "Poetry and Criticism in England and America," which he delivered on 8 May 1861 as the fifth in a series of six lectures on *Life and Literature* at Meionaon Hall in Boston, for which he netted $474.10 for the series; "Poetry and Criticism," which he delivered on 19 October 1868 as the second in a series of six private lectures in Boston managed by James T. Fields and Ticknor and Fields ($1,655.75 for the series), on 7 January 1869 as the first in a series of six lectures in Providence, Rhode Island ($300 for the series), and on 13 April 1869 as the second in a series of six lectures in New Bedford, Massachusetts ($300 for the series); and "Imagination" and "Poetry," which he first delivered on 2 January 1872 as a two-part lecture in a series of four lectures at the Peabody Institute in Baltimore ($400 for the series), and again on 22 and 29 April 1872 as his second and third "conversations" in a series of six private "conversations" at Mechanics' Hall in Boston ($1,407 for the series; Charvat reports $1,457 for the series; except as noted, all lecture fees are from the "Account Books").

Emerson's partial drafts of the lectures and conversations on "Poetry" and "Imagination" are not lecture texts in the way lectures have been understood in this edition; rather, they are extraordinarily casual reading texts interspersed with poetic excerpts that Emerson read and lists of poems that he recited from memory during his lectures and conversations in 1872, thereby testing material to include in his poetry anthology *Parnassus* (1875). With the notable exception of these materials, only "The Poet" and "Poetry and English Poetry" survive as complete lecture manuscripts. Except for these two lectures, Emerson successively mined all the lectures on poetry that he delivered before the two-part lectures and conversations on "Poetry" and "Imagination" in order to create each new lecture on poetry and, eventually, the reading texts of "Poetry" and "Imagination." "Poetry" and "Imagination," in turn, constituted the basic copy-texts from which Emerson and James Elliot Cabot with the assistance of Ellen Emerson arranged the essay "Poetry and Imagination" in *Letters and Social Aims* in 1876 (*W*, 8:1–75). Significantly, "Poetry and Imagination" is one of the few essays in that volume that come to us essentially from Emerson's own hand; its genealogy will be presented in the Harvard edition of *Letters and Social Aims* (*CW*, 8), which is forthcoming under the editorship of Ronald A. Bosco and Glen M. Johnson (for additional details on the evolution of "Poetry and Imagination" and of Emerson's various intended uses of the essay, see Bosco, "'Poetry for the World of Readers' and 'Poetry for Bards Proper': Poetic Theory and Textual Integrity in Emerson's *Parnassus*," 257–312; for a chronological accounting of all of Emerson's lectures on poetry, see von Frank).

WHEN SIR ISAAC NEWTON saw in his garden the apple fall from the tree, he said, 'I see it at last; the moon is only a larger apple falling to the earth; the earth a still larger one falling to the sun. I see the law of all nature. Every particle in the Universe gravitates to every other.' But there was a little boy bestriding the garden-fence who had watched the same apple ripening for some days, and now, when it fell, he ran and picked it up, and before the philosopher had finished his reflection, the boy ate the pippin. Of course, if the boy had overheard Sir Isaac's soliloquy, he would have thought it mighty silly. "You are welcome," he would say, "to all that about the moon, and so forth, as long as I've got the apple." And Newton, on his part, was contented that the boy should have orchards of apples, as long as he had the meaning of it.

Well, society has been divided ever since on the question, Who had the apple? Newton? or the Boy? the majority believing that the boy had the substantial apple, and Newton the shadow, whilst a minority believe that Newton had all the reality of the fruit, and the boy merely the form.

But whilst Newton sees in the fall of apple and moon a law of matter,—sees the immense extent, nay, the universality of a law, that perception is only *one* use of the apple, far higher than the boy's use of the apple, namely, for food,— another mind sees in it its analogies, to human life, its growth, its beauty, its odor, its fruit and its decay, and its resurrection in its progeny, and these so various and so perpetually suggested, as to make its habits and forms a kind of language to convey the accidents of man in a more pleasing manner. What is true of the tree is in like manner true of the animals.— In fact, bird, or beast,—do in their forms, habits, and instincts continually suggest parallels to man, though on a lower scale, and make possible the fables of Æsop, where the beasts are used purely to a human purpose.

Now this secondary use by the intellect belongs to all natural facts, nay, to the whole being and behavior of the material universe. And every thought, every experience of man can be represented or languaged by an analogy from brute nature.

Thus, whilst commonsense looks at things, or visible nature,—the ground, the sky, the house, the men and women, and so forth as real and final facts,—Poetry, or the imagination, which dictates it, is a second sight, which looks *through* these, and uses them as types or words for thoughts which they signify. Nor is this a metaphysical whim of modern times, and quite too refined. It is as old as the human mind. Our best definition of poetry is one of the oldest sentences, and claims to come down to us from the Chaldaean Zoroaster, who wrote it thus; "Poets are standing transporters, whose employment consists in speaking to the Father and to Matter; in producing apparent imitations of unapparent Natures, and inscribing things unapparent in the apparent fabrication of the world." [1] In other words,—the world exists for thought. It is to make appear things which hide. Mountains, crystals, plants, animals are seen; that which makes them is jest with us, but is in earnest,—is the house of health and life. In spite of all the joys of poets, and the joys of saints, the most imaginative and abstracted person never makes with impunity the least mistake in this particular, never tries to kindle his oven with water, or seizes his wild charger by the tail. We should not pardon it in another, nor should we endure it in ourselves.

But whilst we deal with this as finality, early hints are given, that we are not to

---

1. Attributed to Zoroaster in Thomas Taylor, "Collection of the Chaldaean Oracles," *Monthly Magazine and British Register* (1797).

stay here; that we must be making ready to go;—a warning that this magnificent hotel and conveniency we call Nature, is not final. First, inuendoes; then, broad hints, then smart taps are given, suggesting that nothing stands still in nature but Death; that the creation is on wheels, in transit, always passing into something else, streaming into something higher, that matter is not what it appears; that chemistry can blow it all into gas. Faraday, the most exact of natural philosophers, taught, that when we should arrive at the monads or primordial elements, the supposed little cubes or prisms of which all matter was built up, we should not find cubes, or prisms, or atoms at all, but spherules of force. It was whispered that the globes of the universe were precipitates of something more subtle; nay, somewhat was murmured in our ear that dwindled astronomy into a toy;—*that*, too, was no finality, only provisional, a makeshift;—under chemistry was power and purpose: Power and purpose ride on matter to the last atom. It was steeped in thought, did everywhere express thought; that, as great conquerors have burned their ships when once they were landed on the wished-for shore, so the noble house of nature we inhabit, has temporary uses, and we can afford to leave it one day. The ends of all are moral, and therefore the beginnings are such.

Thin or solid, everything is in flight. I believe, this conviction makes the charm of chemistry, that we have the same *avoirdupois* matter in an alembic, without a vestige of the old form; and, in animal transformation, not less, as, in grub and fly, in egg and bird, in embryo and man; Everything undressing and stealing away from its form, streaming into something else, and nothing fast but those invisible cords which we call laws, on which all is strung. Then we see that things wear different names and faces, but belong to one family; that these secret cords or laws show their well-known virtue through every variety,—is it animal, is it plant, is it planet,—and the interest is gradually transferred from the forms, to this lurking method. The man finds his own sense written in the drollest variety of disguises all over nature.

This hint, however conveyed, upsets our commonsense systems, upsets our politics, our trade, our customs, our marriages, nay, the commonsense side of religion and of literature, which are all founded on low nature, on the cleanest and most economical mode of administering the material world, considered as final. The admission, never so covertly, that this is a makeshift, sets the dullest brain in ferment. Our little sir, from his first tottering steps, as soon as he can crow, does not like to be practised upon, suspects that someone is "*doing*" him; and at this hint, everything is compromised; gunpowder is laid under every man's breakfast table.

It is curious that the secret of the march of Science in these days, is, the poetic perception of metamorphosis that is the key to Botany; that the same vegetable point or eye which is the unit of the plant can be transformed at pleasure into every part, as leaf, petal, stamen, pistil, bract, or seed. So in animals; that there is one animal, which new conditions infinitely vary and perfect. What an emotion of the sublime was felt in seeing a bough of a fossil tree in the possession of Playfair which was perfect wood at one end and perfect mineral coal at the other.[2]

The poet is he who, knowing that there is a second sense, looking at the same things with other men, presently sees the meaning that gleams through and instantly feels that this is all their value.

Suppose there were in the ocean certain strong currents which drove a ship caught in them, with such force, that no skill with the best wind, and no strength of oars, or sails, or steam, could make any head against them,—any more than against the current of Niagara. Such currents,—so tyrannical,—exist in thoughts, those finest and subtilest of all waters, that, once thought begins, it refuses to remember whose brain it belongs to,—what country, tradition, or religion,—and goes whirling off,—swim we merrily,—in a direction self-chosen, by law of thought, and not by law of kitchen-clock, or county committee. It has its own polarity. One of these vortices, or self-directions of thought, is the impulse to search resemblance, affinity, identity, in all its objects.

Suppose an anatomist should take a particle of gelatine on the end of a glass rod, and, dipping it in water, it should become a fish. Putting it on the top of a mountain, it should become a chamois; on a prairie, it should be a horse; in the forest, a lion; in the mud, a turtle; on the rock, a lizard; in the air, a bird; on a flower, a bee; underground, a worm; or, suppose, that the same particle, under new conditions of food, and sunshine, and freedom, became a Saxon man; And you have the theory of modern anatomy, namely, that there is one animal, which can be improved or retrograded into any other given animal.

Or, if a botanist on the blade of his pen-knife should take a little pollen, and, laying it on a stem, it should become a leaf; laying it at the bottom of the stem, in the ground, it should become root; at the top of the stem, it should become petals pink or purple; laying it on the top of the flower, it should become fruit,— the same imperceptible atom taking these different forms, at pleasure, to serve the end of the plant; and you have the idea of modern Botany.

Camper, the physiologist, was wont to draw on his blackboard the skeleton of man, and by a few strokes transform him into a horse, then into an ox, into a bird, into a fish.[3] We have or had in the Athenæum a series of fifteen or twenty drawings beginning with a toad, and by successive, slight modifications the figure was enlarged and harmonized into the Belvedere Apollo.[4]

2. John Playfair (1749–1819), Scottish natural philosopher.
3. Pieter Camper (1722–89), Dutch physician and comparative anatomist.
4. The Apollo Belvedere, the most famous statue of the Greek god of sun and wisdom, Apollo, is at the Vatican.

"What he would write, he was before he writ."[5]

But I do not wish to find that my poet is not partaker, or that he amuses me with that which does not amuse him. He must believe in his poetry, or I shall soon be cured of my belief in it. Homer, Milton, Hafiz, Herbert, and Wordsworth, are heartily enamored of their sweet thoughts.

The world is thoroughly anthropomorphized, as if it had passed through the body and mind of man, and taken his mould and form. He is advertised, that there is nothing to which he is not related, that every thing is convertible into every other. This is like that. The staff in my hand is the *radius vector* of the sun. The chemistry of this is the chemistry of that. Whatever one thing we do, whatever one thing we learn, we are doing and learning all things;—marching in the direction of universal power. Every man's mind is a true Alexander, or Sesostris, building an universal monarchy.[6]

To this belongs the interest of all fables, and that never-dying fable in all conversation, the humour of calling a man a donkey;—the joke of all mankind, that never wears out, the wit of those who have not any other,—to intimate to your companion, never so slily, that he can bray, or that his ears are long. This ticklishness, (if you will pardon me the word), on the subject, can only be explained on the belief, that there is transformation, that this unadmired quadruped is a poor relation of ours. In the same manner, the interest inspired by the qualities imputed to the lion, is inflamed by the belief that his face is an exaggerated man's face; and, the Arabs say, that the roar of the lion almost articulates the syllables, *Ahna ou el ben mera*, "I, and the son, of the woman," as if he believed only in man and himself.

Chemistry discloses the same self-direction. In the alembic, not only the same atom takes every form,—stone, earth, metal, liquid, and gas,—but, ever since the first experiments, they have been torturing every substance to resolve itself into simpler forms, and they have toiled to change one metal into another, one gas into another, until, at last, they shall find only one, which can at pleasure be transmuted into any other. This is the philosopher's stone.

What is Art, but the translation of one and the same thought into the several

---

5. The line is from "Upon the Report of the Printing of the Dramatical Poems of Master John Fletcher, Never Collected Before, and now Set Forth in one Volume," a "Commendatory Poem" at the beginning of Francis Beaumont and John Fletcher, *Comedies and Tragedies* (1647), by William Cartwright (ca. 1611–43), English dramatist.

6. Alexander the Great (356–323 B.C.), Alexander III of Macedon (336–323 B.C.), conqueror of the known civilized world; Sesostris, the Greek corruption of the Egyptian "Senusret," is the name of three kings of the Twelfth (Theban) Dynasty: Sesostris I (ca. 1980–1935 B.C.), second king of the dynasty; Sesostris II (ca. 1906–1887 B.C.), fourth king of the dynasty; and Sesostris III (ca. 1887–1849 B.C.), fifth king of the dynasty.

languages—of drawing, of sculpture, of architecture, of music, of poetry? Or; analyse the inventions of man, and you find him still brooding on this secret of unity.

Thus, money was an ideal invention. He was poor with all the wheat of Egypt, with all the cedars of Lebanon, with all the land of Asia, marble of Greece, and imagined Aladdin's lamp or Fortunatus' cap, that would bring him, instead of a glut of one thing, the little he wanted of everything.[7] The refined invention of money was Plutus, or Power, to hold all values, all forms, in one value, one form, and convert it at pleasure.

There is one animal, one plant, one chemic matter. Well, the laws of light and of heat translate each other; and so do the laws of sound and of color; and so galvanism, electricity, and magnetism are varied forms of one energy. While he is pondering this strange unity, he observes that all the things in nature, the animals, the mountain, the river, the seasons, wood, iron, stone, vapor,—all have a relation to his thoughts and his life; that all their growths, decays, process, quality, and use so curiously resemble himself, in parts and in wholes, that he is compelled to speak by means of them. All his words and his thoughts are framed by their help. Every word is an image. Nature gives him sometimes in a flattered likeness, sometimes in caricature, a copy of every humor and shade in his character and mind. The world is an immense picture book of every passage in human life.

A central unity inundates nature with itself. Every object he beholds is the mask of a man.

> "The privates of man's heart
> They speken and sound in his ear
> As though they loud winds were,"

for all the Universe is full of echoes of them.[8]

But to grasp and to articulate these identities of which all are obscurely aware, is rare and divine. 'Tis wonderful the difficulty of taking this step. Hundreds, thousands, read Wordsworth or Tennyson with a perfect sympathy. While they read, they think they might write it, but in millions, there is not one who can. A new verse comes once in one hundred years, and, therefore, Pindar, Hafiz, and Herrick speak so proudly of what seems to you cheap tune enough.[9]

Poetry seems to begin in the slightest change of name, or, in detecting identity under variety of surface. Boys please themselves with crying to the coachman,

---

7. Fortunatus, in the Spanish nursery tale, possessed both a bottomless purse and a wishing cap.

8. *Confessio Amantis*, I, ll. 2806–8, by John Gower (ca. 1325–1408), English poet.

9. Pindar (ca. 522–443 B.C.), the greatest of the Greek lyric poets; Robert Herrick (1591–1674), English lyric poet.

"Put on the string"; with calling a fire-engine, a tub; and the firemen, tigers. A boy's game of ball is called "Four Cats." When he is older, he calls money tin; his hat a tile. He likes to say, that boiled potatoes open their jackets. In a ship-wreck, the novelist finds cordilleras of water. They call a losing gamester, a lame duck; a cheated one, plucked. A lady's tippet is a boa, or python; a camel, is a ship of the desert; sand, is the snow of the desert. Martial calls snow the thick fleece of silent waters, *densum tacitarum vellus aquarum.*[10] This metonymy makes the vivacity of all discourse when each speaker hits off the character of the person or thing in question by some symbol which unexpectedly magnifies the trait with more force.

Swedenborg affirms that, "Names, countries, nations, and the like are not at all known to those who are in heaven; they have no idea of such things, but of the realities signified thereby." "When they saw terrestrial objects, they did not think at all about them, but only about those which they signified and represented, which to them were most delightful."

Now, this metonomy, or seeing the same sense in divers things, gives a pure pleasure. Every one of a million times we take pleasure in the metamorphosis. It makes us dance and sing. It delights all. All men are poets. 'Tis idle to tell me they do not like poetry; For they do.

When people tell me they do not like poetry, and bring me Shelley, or Aikin's *Poets,* or I know not what volumes of rhymed English, to show that it is not likeable, I am quite of their mind.[11] But this dislike only proves their liking of poetry. For they relish Æsop, and cannot forget him or not use him; bring them the *Iliad,* and they like that; and the *Cid,* and that goes well;—and read to them from Chaucer, and they reckon him an honest fellow. *Lear,* and *Macbeth,* and *Richard III* they know pretty well without a guide. Give them Robin Hood's ballads, or "Lady Jane," or "Fair Annie," or "Hardiknute," or "Chevy Chase," or "the Cronachs' cried on Bennachie," or Robert Burns, or Beranger, and they like these well enough.[12] Marie Antoinette said, that, when she read Florian, she thought she ate milk porridge.[13] And the London costermongers say, we like to pay our pennies for something that's worth hearing. They like statues; they like to name the stars; they like to talk and hear of Jove, Apollo, Minerva, Venus, and

10. Martial (43–ca. 104), Latin poet.

11. *Select Works of the British Poets* (1820) by John Aiken (1747–1822), English physician and author.

12. Robin Hood, legendary twelfth-century English outlaw and popular hero whose fight against injustice and for the poor gave rise to a series of ballads extolling his virtues; "Lady Jane," "Fair Annie," and "Chevy Chase" were all popular ballads; "Hardiknute" is by Lady Elizabeth Wardlaw (1677–1727), Scottish poet; "Cronach" by Sir Walter Scott is in Emerson's *Parnassus* (1874), 461; "Bennachie" is probably "Benachie," the highest class of ancient Celtic noblemen.

13. Marie Antoinette (1755–93), queen of France from 1774 to her death by the guillotine; Jean Pierre Claris de Florian (1755–94), French writer of romances, plays, and fables.

the Nine. See how tenacious we are of the old names; and our walls are hung with pictures that recall the name of Greece. They like yet better the stars themselves; they like the landscape, the wells of water, the mountain, the plain, sunshine and night; for in these, they obscurely feel the flowings also of their thought.

But the doctrine of poetry reverses the common sense, for it is the doctrine that the soul generates matter. It is the doctrine of the sovereignty of the soul and implies, therefore, all the grandeurs of faith, of love, of duty. Poetry is the speech of man after the ideal. It is the expression of a sound mind speaking after the ideal, and not after the apparent. All becomes poetry when we look from within, and are using all as if the mind made it. All becomes prosaic, when seen from the point of common sense, as if the world existed for material good, or as if matter were a finality.

For events are, not as the brute circumstance that falls, but as the life which they fall upon. The atoms of matter are plastic enough, for they are of us and we of them, and carbon and azote, mountain and planet, play one tune with man and mind. Why we can reach so far to the planets and sun with our short arms, is because we have a pocket edition of the whole. Your brain is timed with the sea-tide, has agreements with the sun.

All this, because Poetry is science, is the breath of the same Spirit by which nature lives, and the Poet is a better logician than the analyzer. His sayings are wise, and to the purpose, and not those of unpoetic men. He sees each fact as an inevitable step in the path of the Creator. He is the right classifier, seeing things grouped, and following the grand way of nature. And never did any science originate, but by a Poetic Perception. "A great natural philosopher without this gift is impossible."[14] The schoolmen think they are logical, and the poet to be whimsical, illogical. Do they think there is any chance or choice in what he sees and says? He knows that he did not make his thought; No, his thought made him, and made the sun and stars also. And it is because his memory is not too strong for him, does not hold him to routine and lists of words, that he is still capable of seeing. For a wise surrender to the currents of nature, a noble passion which will not let us halt, but hurries us into the stream of things, makes us truly know. Passion is logical, and I note that the vine, symbol of the Bacchus which intoxicates the world, is the most geometrical of all plants. And was not this the meaning of Socrates who preferred artists, because they truly knew, and of the tragedians: Horace, and Persius, and Lucretius in the Latin?[15] Dante was faithful, when not carried away by his fierce hatreds.

But if I should count the English poets who have contributed to the bible of

14. Attributed to Johann Wolfgang von Goethe (see *TN*, 3:192).

15. Horace (65–8 B.C.), Roman poet also known for his writings about poetry; Aulus Persius Flaccus (34–62), Roman satirist.

existing England and America, sentences of guidance or consolation, which are
still glowing and effective,—how few! Milton, Shakspeare, Spenser, Herbert,
Jonson, Donne, Dryden, Pope, Young, Cowper, Burns, Wordsworth: What disparity in the names! but these are the authors.[16]

But how shall I find my heavenly bread in the reigning poets? Where is great
design in modern English poetry? Where, with the exception of Wordsworth?
Tennyson is richly endowed precisely in points where Wordsworth wanted.
Since Milton, there was no finer ear, nor more command of the keys of language.
But, he wants a subject. He has climbed no mount of vision, and brought its se-
crets down.

The Poet adopts in every action the method of nature, the most direct; believing, that, in the nature of everything, its own check will appear, and save the
absurdity of artificial checks. Liberty is the doctrine of Poets: Liberty of opinion; Liberty of worship; Liberty of Vote, political, universal suffrage, nonjuring;
Liberty of trade, banking; Liberty of printing, no censure, and no copyright;
even Liberty of Divorce.

Education is better than politics; Race, or native knowledge, than Education. Architecture follows Nature's exact veracity in building for use, and beauty
follows. The Poet, thus beholding laws, is believer and lover. The world to him
is virgin soil. And the men mean well: it is never too late to do right. He affirms
the applicability of the ideal law to this moment, and to the present knot of
affairs. But parties, lawyers, and men of the world, invariably dispute such an
application, as romantic and dangerous. They admit the general truth; but they
and their affair always constitute an exceptional case. Free trade may be very well
as a principle, but it is never quite time for its adoption without prejudicing actual interests. Chastity, Temperance, are very well,—Ethical laws are very well,
which admit no violation;—but so extreme were the times and manners, that you
must admit the miracles of Moses, for the times constituted a case. It is true what
you say, that legends are found in all tribes,—but this legend is different and so
throughout. Poetry affirms eternal laws; prose busies itself with exceptions, with
the local and individual.

The question is often asked, Why no poet appears in America? Other nations
in their early, expanding periods, in their war for existence, have shot forth the
flowers of verse, and created a mythology which continued to charm the imagination of after-men. But we have all manner of ability, except this: we are brave,
victorious; we legislate, trade, plant, build, sail, and combine as well as any oth-

16. The English writers are Ben Jonson (1573–1637), dramatist; John Dryden (1631–1700), meta-
physical poet and dramatist; Alexander Pope (1688–1744), poet who championed the heroic couplet;
Edward Young (1683–1765), poet, dramatist, and literary critic, best known for *The Complaint; or,
Night Thoughts* (1742–45); and William Cowper (1731–1806), poet and satirist.

ers, but we have no imagination, no constructive mind, no affirmative books. We have plenty of criticism; elegant history; all the forms of respectable imitation; but no poet, no affirmer, no grand guiding mind, who intoxicates his countrymen with happy hopes,—makes them self-respecting, with faith that rests in their own minds, and is not imported from abroad.— And,—fruit of all—our lives are impoverished and unpoetic, that is, inhuman.

The answer is, for the time, to be found in the preoccupation of all men. The work of half the world to be done: and it is a hard condition of Nature, that, where one faculty is excessive, it lames all the rest. We are the men of practice, the men of our hands, and, for the time, the brain loses in range what it gains in special skill.

The genius of civilization, except while it is new, is antagonistic to sentiment, utilitarian, and expensive. Taught by England, nay begotten by England, the American mind has learned to call great small, and small things great: Tasteless expense, arts of comfort, and the putting as many impediments as we can between the man and his objects, we have learned; and our arts, and our books, and our characters betray the taming of the Imagination. He does not astonish or intoxicate us much or often. Yet, there is an elasticity in the American mind which may redeem us, and the effect of popular institutions in continually sending back the enervated families into the realities of nature and of toil, may serve the highest medical benefit.

Whilst commonsense draws water, bakes bread, builds houses, keeps shop, and always on the assumption that everything else is a blunder,—in the performing these very works, men are compelled by a certain tyranny which springs up in their own thoughts, to believe in something else. For, their thoughts have an order, and method, and beliefs of their own, very different from the order which this commonsense uses.

Commonsense says, One thing at a time; stick to your fact; keep your cake from burning!— And, meantime, the cake is burning to cinder, whilst the boy's thoughts, to be sure, are running on war and kingdoms, on poetry, on beauty, and the divine life.

As soon as an active mind is born, it is continually comparing its facts, hunting resemblances in them; it is seeking to make things all out of one kind, and it finds them of one kind.

Furthermore, as it is, first, the doctrine of the sovereignty of mind, that Mind makes matter; so second, it is the doctrine of Unity, there are not two things, but one thing. Mind exists; matter has no real existence. Matter is only a rude or temporary form of mind.

Now the doctrine we maintain, is, that the Poet is the healthy, the wise, the fundamental, the only man, the seer of the secret, who sees things after a true scale, sees them as God sees them; in order and beauty. That men who are not yet poets, lack their true humanity. That the children are poets, and the men should be; that politicians, and savans, and critics, and men of business are such in default of real power, that is, because they are out of true relation,—because they fail of being poets,—and these dignities and offices are their poor amends. The flashes of rhetoric and imagination in great orators, Chatham, Burke, Canning, Patrick Henry,—which make them and the nations happy, are the fragments of reason and health which they still retain, and are the last clew, by which, were they logical, they would yet be guided back to the rectitude they have forfeited.[17]

17. Patrick Henry (1736–99), Virginia patriot and statesman.

# "France, or Urbanity"
# 17 January 1854
# (1854–1856)

Emerson delivered "France, or Urbanity" on 17 January 1854, the fifth in a series of six private lectures on the *Topics of Modern Times* in Philadelphia, receiving $1,166.34 for the series ($1,162, according to *Letters*, 8:397n). He repeated it on 31 January 1854 as the second of two lectures before the Young Men's Society in Detroit, Michigan; on 5 April 1854 before the Concord Lyceum in Concord, Massachusetts; on 3 April 1856 as the second in a series of six private lectures at the Freeman Place Chapel in Boston, receiving $772.36 for the series; and as "French Character" on 14 March 1855 before the Salem Lyceum in Salem, Massachusetts, for which he received $25 (Charvat; except as noted, lecture fees are from the "Account Books"). Once, when he proposed the lecture as part of a series, Emerson called it one "with which I like to reward the young people for good behaviour" during the other, "metaphysical lessons" (*Letters*, 5:40). This lecture has never been published.

William Henry Furness—Emerson's cousin, lifelong friend, and minister in Philadelphia—first proposed a lecture series for him in May 1853, and Emerson replied affirmatively in October ("I flatter myself that my abstractions will be interesting, & my details significant"), though "France, or Urbanity" was not one of the six titles listed (*Letters*, 8:368, 4:391). Emerson seems to have been writing the lectures well into January, for he complained to Lidian from Philadelphia on the ninth that "I am confined by the preparation of each lecture" (*Letters*, 4:14); his work schedule had probably been upset by the death of his mother on 16 November 1853. The series was financially successful, netting Emerson over $1,100. According to Furness, when he handed Emerson his check, the lecturer replied, "'What a swindle'" (Furness, "Random Reminiscences of Emerson," *Atlantic Monthly* 71 [March 1893]: 348).

The lecture was next repeated, along with "Culture," in Detroit, with Emerson receiving $100 for the pair ("Account Books"). Although the *Detroit Daily Advertiser* found that the talk contained "many lively characteristic anecdotes," Emerson himself was not as animated: his "personal appearance is not striking, his attitudes and gestures are decidedly awkward, one of them eminently so; he has a habit of holding his hands with the fingers slightly bent, a little above the table, as if he were playing the piano standing. His voice is rough and unmelodious, and his enunciation at times hesitating. . . . But notwithstanding all this you recognize a man of power before he has been many minutes speaking" (1 February 1854; reprinted in C. J. Wasung, "Emerson Comes to Detroit," *Michigan History Magazine* 29 [January–March 1945]: 61, 67).

In Boston the lecture formed part of another financially successful series, from which Emerson garnered $772.36 ("Account Books"). Emerson even asked one of the organizers to arrange for extra chairs to be placed in the aisles for latecomers (*Letters*, 5:20). According to an advance notice in the *Boston Daily Evening Transcript*, it is "said to be one of the most brilliant of his lectures" (3 April 1856, 2). The *Boston Daily Journal* gave it a favorable four-paragraph summary, and the *Boston Daily Evening Transcript* provided a long, three-paragraph summary, concluding that "in Mr. Emerson's lecture compositions, like his other more permanent literary compositions, it is excessively hard to discover the moral" ("Mr. Emerson's Second Lecture," 3 April 1856, 2; "Mr. Emerson's Lecture on France," 4 April 1856, 2). Through the offices of Horatio Woodman, Emerson was able to obtain the Boston papers' consent not to publish accounts of his lectures if he himself provided them with abstracts that "should not exceed *one third* of a column" (S. N. Stockwell to Woodman, 25 March 1856, on page {14v} of the manuscript of this lecture in the electronic textual notes; Woodman, in passing the letter on to Emerson, wrote on it, "I hope you may be able to do this").

In 1872 Emerson proposed to read papers at private conversations, beginning with the lecture on France, about which Ellen commented, "I had never heard of [it]"; there is no evidence that Emerson followed through with this proposal (*Letters, ETE,* 1:657).

Some passages from this lecture were first printed in Lestrois Parish, *Emerson's View of France and the French* (New York: American Society of the French Legion of Honor, 1935), 6–12.

T HE DIVINE PROVIDENCE has distributed man into men; has not chosen to put all the wine in one jar, but has lodged it in many bottles. Of the men that sit here in this hall,—one can sing, and one can cipher, and one can engineer, and one can paint, and one can argue causes, and one can fight, and one can plant trees. You have to run through a city to find all the faculties that belong to one man. The French Fourier said, therefore, "it took 1,728 persons to make a phalanstery," or one man. And, as one man lacks qualities that his neighbor has, so each nation wants some properties which abound in some other people. Each of the nations is one instrument in a full orchestra. Or, as the ancients believed that the world was a huge animal, shall we say, the civility of the world must pass through all the stomachs of the camel to be purified and assimilated.

Italy, Germany, India, America, are the stomachs of Behemoth. In the members of this mundane body, let us see what offices are served by France.

Great cities—you can't compute the influence. In New Orleans, in New York, in Montreal, in Guadaloupe a middle-aged man is just embarking with his property to spend his old age in Paris. From every corner of Europe the like happens, so that a fortune falls on every day. Astronomers, because there find companions Chemist and Geologist; Composers and *Artistes,* because there only are their patrons. An inventor of *ragoût à modiste,* each looks on it at his point of view.[1]

Paris has great merits as a city. The river is made a delight to the eye, by the quays and bridges. In London, they have managed to hide the Thames. In Paris, the gardens or parks are more available to the pleasure of the people. The fountains, the buildings, which are far more spirited and national than the English; the truly palatial Tuileries; Notre Dame; Le Palais de Justice; La Sainte Chapelle; the old Tower St. Jacquerie de la Boucherie; the Hôtel de Ville, and the Panthéon; the Palais Royal, where all that can seduce the sense is found. The Boulevards, lined with cafés, blazing with light, with theatres, with magazines of everything odd, rare, and rich; with music, and swarming with a crowd collected from Europe; the seductive independence of furnished lodgings; the cheapness of good living; the cheap wine, the national beverage; the boundless good humour and politeness; the immense bookstalls in the streets,—maps, pictures, models, busts, sculptures, libraries, spread abroad at the side of the road: the treasures of art opened freely to the passport of the stranger, at all hours, and to all the world on Sunday. Twelve thousand students are connected with the university, from all nations, who listen and hear, without price, lectures from the first professors in all sciences and letters. 'Tis a noble hospitality, and well calculated also, as it brings a great population of young foreigners to spend their money in France.

Then, the manners of the people are full of entertainment, so spirited, chatty, and coquettish, and lively as lizards: the manners of the people, and probably their inferiority as individuals, make it easy to live with them as so many shopkeepers, whose feelings and convenience are nowise to be consulted. Paris and London have this difference, that Paris exists for the foreigner, serves him,—whilst in London, it is the Londoner, who is much in the foreigner's way. England has built London for its own use. France has built Paris for the world.

One is struck with the military air and manners of the Celt. When I was in Paris, in 1848, the whole nation was in uniform, a costume which fits them best. It is not easy to guess at a *table d'hôte* the social rank and employment of the guests. Their manners, their stately bow and salutation, are, like their beards, a screen, which the eye must take time to penetrate. They all have a soldier-like aplomb. Every gamin is drest with a trigness, and a certain fancy-cut, all masculine. Your French tutor is just come from the pistol gallery, and leaves you to go to a barricade. They all take their places so naturally in the line, on the *Fête,*

---

1. A *ragoût à modiste* is a dressmaker.

following the drum-major, a vast man, with baton and a mountain of fur cap, with *sapeurs* and *pompiers*.[2]

Then, these brilliant reading-rooms close by, with their expensive arm chairs! They say in France, that, if "Dunois, himself, the young and brave," were to reappear today, he would not go to Palestine, but would found a journal.[3] The lively *feuilletons* of the journals, in certain respects, are the best in the world.[4] They exceed or exceeded in number those of all other capitals. In 1848, there were two hundred, and gentlemen who wished to keep themselves up with the several sections of party, read twelve every day.

Another attraction of the French capital is the language. The central position of France, its power and activity in the system of Europe, the attractions of the country to travellers and the caravan of people from all parts of the world that is streaming through it, the mathematical clearness of the French mind, expressed again in their language,—have caused this to become the universal medium of conversation. The Latin has long been abandoned; the French adopted. "It was natural, that the language of the most social people, the language of a nation which speaks more than it thinks, a nation which needs to speak in order to think, and which thinks only to speak, ought to be the language of universal conversation."[5] "There is, in the power of the French, in their character, in their tongue above all, a certain proselyting force, which passes imagination."[6]

I remember when I first encountered those merry crowds,—everybody gesticulating, everyone chattering, amid the blaze of shops,—I said, the only thing here which I really wish to buy is very cheap, yet I cannot buy it, namely, their speech. I covet that which the vilest of the people possesses. At the *table d'hôte*, where five hundred French *habitués* daily dined, whatever the ragoûts were, I found the grammar good. The bill of fare said, "bread at discretion;" but I also found the nouns, pronouns, verbs, and interjections furnished gratuitously.

The schools to which we resort for our daily lesson, the theatre where Rachel played Phèdre, and where she then chanted the *Marseillaise*,—pale always, paler with passion, as she shook the tricolor banner in her hand:—the tragic-comedian Lemaître at the Porte St. Martin; the comic Bouffé, at the Variétés; the clubs, which were assemblies of men terribly in earnest, where people gathered in crowds to applaud a stormy eloquence, threatening to tear each other to pieces on

2. A *sapeur* is a member of a military engineer unit that executes field fortification work; it can also mean the engineer who lays, detects, and disarms mines. A *pompier* is a fireman.

3. Jean, comte de Dunois (1402–68), military leader and companion of Joan of Arc as well as the prototype of the noble and courageous knight-prince.

4. *Feuilletons* are newspaper serials.

5. Attributed to Fernando Galiani (1728–87), Italian political economist (see *JMN*, 15:386).

6. Attributed to Galiani in Emerson's note in the manuscript.

any difference of sentiment: men, ostentatiously armed in helmet and cuirass, walked up and down.[7] They came in torch-light processions, with a seek-and-slay look, dripping burning oil, the bearers smiting the torch on the ground, and lifting it into the air. At Blanqui's Club, I listened to one orator in blouse, who said, "Why should the rich fear that we shall not protect their property? We shall guard it with the utmost care, in the belief that it will soon be our own."[8] At any rate, these were schools in which one learned his French very fast.

The spread of their language, the circulation of their *feuilletons* and novels, bind all polite society in its hoop. Each French popular romancer, as Balzac, Dumas, or Mérimée, has Europe for his garden and park.[9] It was said of Balzac, that he did not need the freedom of cities to be presented to him. Wherever, in all Christendom, he chanced to find himself, he had only to select the best-looking house in sight, the first handsome house he came to, knock at the door, and announce his name, to be cheered and welcomed instantly by bands of his friends and admirers. No matter what was the language of the country, in Bohemia, in Poland, in Sweden, in Germany, in Spain, they were *his* people who lived there.

This universality of their language among educated people is a secret of power. "A dangerous book written in French is a declaration of war to Europe," said Bonald.[10]

In France, with the courtesy, and charm, and attractiveness, is an exclusiveness not less extraordinary. "The whole nation is nothing but a vast *propaganda*." The traveller eats lotus all day, and forgets home, forgets time, and other nations, all books, and all topics that once drew him. The lively people ignore all other people, letters, politics, and social forms, but their own, and would fain courteously persuade you, that you have arrived at the metropolis; that you see Rome; there is nothing beyond: Out of Paris, there is no salvation. They have even carried the common pride of nationality one step farther than most peoples, in their proverb that the good God belongs to their tribe: *Le bon Dieu est Français.*

"The French," says M. Guizot, "is the most civilized of civilizations." France lies in light. All that is not French is barbarous. I do not know anything so aggressive and importunate. Is it possible, we shall one day wake up in some other

7. Phèdre, title role in the classical tragedy (1677) by Jean Baptiste Racine (1639–99); Frédérick Lemaître (1800–1876), the greatest actor of his day; Bouffé (1800–1888), actor known for his work in the vaudeville.

8. Louis Auguste Blanqui (1805–81), social reformer whose friends formed the Club des Droits de l'Homme, which Emerson visited.

9. Alexandre Dumas père (1802–70), novelist and dramatist; Prosper Mérimée (1803–70), novelist, historian, and literary critic.

10. Louis de Bonald (1754–1840), aphorist.

country, and be able to put France behind us, and remember that loquacious Paris as a fading dream?

In what I have yet to say of France, I shall not begin by canting. I shall not pretend to more impartiality than my countrymen ordinarily carry thither. I am born, I suppose, to my full share of Saxon nationality; I confess, that I have observed, that all people of Teutonic stock,—Germans, English, Americans,—do at heart regard it as a serious misfortune to be born a French native: that they believe there are certain limits to the Frenchman, not so quickly found in the neighboring race; that he pays for his great advantages of address, by a scale of faculty something less complete. The English head is round, the French head is angular,—and, perhaps, some essential defects are thus coarsely indicated. But whilst these biases must certainly so far impair the value of my testimony, I am wont, for that reason, to distrust my own unsupported impressions. And I design, when I have unfavorable opinions to express, to draw my witnesses from themselves.

The French occupy one of the fairest territories, and have made it the most attractive country for its own merits to travellers from all others. We go to Italy, for the antiquities: we go to France, for what is now there. They are a people singularly affable and courteous. They have a clear intellect and correct taste. They have a strong animal nature; and so, the concentration of their faculty on making things agreeable to the sense; adding the most to the enjoyments of the day,— an immense demand for amusement in their heads,—and all that is done goes to embellish France, embellish Paris, the boulevards, the hotels, the café, the theatre, and draw thither everybody in all the world who wishes to be amused, and has money to spend.

They have good heads; a fine genius for mathematics, which is visible in their great men, and in every man and woman in the streets; and an elegant numerical order. Everything in France is done with a mathematic and military system. It is the leading merit of the French mind. Clearness results, and is what they value. Descartes said, "All clear ideas are true." Voltaire said, "Whatever is not clear is not French." Napoleon said, "Be clear; all the rest will follow." "France," says M. Guizot,

"has been the centre, the focus of European civilization. There has been no great idea, or great principle of civilization, but it has been new prepared in France. And for this reason: there is in the French character something sociable, something sympathetic, something which makes its way with greater facility and effect than does the national genius of any other people.

Is it from our language, or the turn of our mind, of our manners,—certain it is, that our ideas are more popular than those of other people; present themselves more clearly and intelligibly to the masses; and penetrate among them more readily. Perspicuity, Sociability, Sympathy, the Characteristics of France."

Heinrich Heine thinks the office of the French language, to test the sense that is in any philosophy or science. Translate it into French, and you instantly dispel all the smoke and sorcery, and it passes for what it is.[11]

France is the country of method, of numerical order. Everything is centralized, everything geometrical. I think the French muse is Arithmetic. The great men of that country are men of numerical system and superficial analysis in whatever department, and prodigious ciphers, as, Lavoisier in Chemistry; Laplace in Astronomy; Euler in Algebra; Fourier in Social Science; Napoleon in War; Cuvier in Natural History.[12] The Academy of Sciences measured the first degree of the meridian, which gave Newton a correct basis for his theory of gravity. They gave to the world the decimal system of weights and measures, perfect from the start. In the Revolution, they abolished the chronology of mankind, and begun with the year One; for the world is a slate to a Frenchman on which he wipes out all the old marks and lines to work out his whole problem anew.

The French Academy from the time of its institution took the air of founding and ruling literature. They were charged with the duty of making the *Dictionary* of the language.[13] The Institute, which comprises the Academy as one of its five classes, applies the same despotic system and sits as the Parliament of Science, the Supreme Court of Appeal. *La Biographie Universelle* was begun in 1810, finished in 1830, in fifty-two volumes by three hundred of the best writers. Every article signed by its author, and every line submitted to several contributors, and finally the dead are summoned to make corrections before the supplement closes all appeal:

> Silence in the Court! Proclamation was made, that, if any man of old or modern renown, if Solon, or Solomon, or the Cid, or Columbus, or Richard III, or Spinoza, had any friends who thought his fame had suffered, now the assessors were set, the verdict was to be made up: let them speak now, or forever be silent.[14]

---

11. Heinrich Heine (1797–1856), German lyric poet and critic.

12. Antoine Laurent Lavoisier (1743–94), founder of modern chemistry.

13. The *Dictionnaire de l'Académie Française* was first published in 1694. The Academy, which had been founded in 1635, had been charged with making a dictionary that would define the correct, common usage of words in nontechnical French.

14. Quoted from *A Memoir of Sebastian Cabot* (1831), by Nicholas Biddle (1796–1847), lawyer and author (see *TN*, 1:213). Solon (ca. 638–ca. 559 B.C.), Athenian lawgiver; Solomon (ca. 973–ca. 933 B.C.), king of Israel known for his impartial justice; Christopher Columbus (1451–1506), known as the discoverer of America; Richard III (1452–85), king of England (1483–85).

In literature, they have a multitude of lucid and agreeable writers. If life were long enough, we could spend agreeable years in libraries of French *mémoires:* but they have only a few examples of the profounder class: no single example of imagination; and never a poet.

The profounder wits are Rabelais, Montaigne, Pascal, and Montesquieu. But the three first seem to be something less national, and more allied to the Teutonic genius. Molière, we must admit to be French, with his broad commonsense.[15]

Only in our days, has French genius flowered into a poet, in Béranger, and though genuine, not of a high class. Singular, but certain, this absence of poetry in the French. A nation of accurate thinkers, impulsive, generous, and graceful, but, in the art of poetry, arithmetical skill. The very rhythm which Moore cruelly describes to be all contained in a single English line

*"A cobbler there was, and he lived in a stall—"*

is a symbol of its power.[16] There is no motherwit, no jet of fire. No first-class nation was ever so poor in imagination, except our own. In the verse of all other nations one finds flowers, if it were only the breath of arctic plants, mosses, and lichens; but in the French, it is otto of roses and *millefleurs* from the perfumer's shop.

But I may as well, at the risk of error, say out what I think: that I esteem the French mind partial and not symmetrical; the defect in poetry points at the defect in the French race. They have not Imagination, one of the cardinal powers, the true second sight or use of material world as representative. More than that, they have not genius in the high sense, and that because they want the moral element. Genius is a total force, moral and mental. I think the French have not the moral sensibility in equal force to their mental power. It is a half-mind; a half-man. More intellectual than moral; more animal than intellectual. There is always a wonderful externality about them, but the power essential to philosophy, to poetry, to religion they have not. Montesquieu, Pascal, Vauvenargues, and Geoffroy Saint-Hilaire are exceptional.[17] But, when compared with the Germans, who penetrate science, religion, art with central ideas, they are superficial. And *Genius,* they degrade.

The office of France is to popularise ideas, arts, learnings; to be the interpreter, to the masses of Europe, of the wisdom of the few; to give, in an elegant and portable form, the results of the laboratory, of the calculus, of astronomy, chemistry, political economy. What Mme de Staël did by her "Germany",—What

15. Molière (1622–73), dramatist and actor most famous for his comedies.
16. Thomas Moore (1779–1852), Irish poet.
17. Luc de Clapiers, marquis de Vauvenargues (1715–47), writer and moralist.

Cousin did for Hegel,—that France does for western Europe and for America still—all, through her clear and popular mind.[18]

Of the French contributions to the useful arts, and to the arts pertaining to comfort, Sir Francis Head's book contains an excellent account.[19] The exhibition of their wares in the Crystal Palace in London, and in that in New York, have been in a high degree creditable.[20] A native elegance and a fanciful variety. The national genius tends naturally to quality in variety; the English genius to quantity in uniformity.

Their taste is correct and elegant in dress, in furniture, in equipage, in draperies, in festal decoration and arrangement, and in fine ornamental wares, whether webs, or porcelain, or bronzes, or silver and gold: and, in these, the French designers give the fashions to all nations. The prints and designs of England on porcelain, and on woolen and cotton fabrics, are incorrect and heavy. Nice observers say, that in English designs the flower is sometimes set on the stem and leaf of some other plant. The French draughtsman Von Waagen is more correct.[21] New York is reputed to dress better than London, because New York dresses after Paris, and London is headstrong enough to intermix something of its own.

I have been told by persons to whose tastes great deference is due,—that they had found, in careful observation of the fashions, how truly they follow a law of gradation, and are never arbitrary, since the new mode is always only a step farther in the same direction as the last mode; and that a cultivated eye is always prepared for and predicts the new fashion. And this fact suggests the reason of all mistakes, and offence in our own modes. It is necessary, in music, when you strike a discord, to let down the ear, by an intermediate note or two, to the accord again; and many a good experiment born of good sense and destined to succeed, fails, only because it is offensively sudden. I suppose, the Parisian milliner who dresses the world from her imperious boudoir, will know how to make even Bloomer costume good and reconcileable to the eye of mankind, and triumphant over Punch himself, by interposing the just gradations which it has overleaped.[22]

I need not say, how wide the same law ranges, and how much it can be hoped to effect. All that is a little harshly claimed by progressive parties may easily come to be conceded, without question, if this rule be observed. Thus, the circum-

18. *Germany* (1814) by Madame de Staël (1766–1817), French novelist and social critic.

19. Sir Francis Bond Head (1793–1875), English traveler and author of *A Faggot of French Sticks, or Paris in 1851* (1852).

20. The exhibitions held in the metal-and-glass buildings called the Crystal Palace in London (1851) and New York (1853) were the equivalents of today's international expositions and trade fairs.

21. Gustav Friedrich Waagen (1794–1868), German art historian.

22. Amelia Bloomer (1818–94), American temperance and women's rights reformer known for her costume of loose trousers covered by a dress with a short skirt.

stances may easily be imagined, in which woman may speak, vote, legislate, and drive a coach, and all the most naturally in the world—if only it came by degrees. What we call nowadays a swallower of formulas, is one who fails to strike the intervening notes.

Be this as it may, the French fabric is, by its excellence, the right pattern: and the English and American manufacturers, when they affect to make patterns, are only, I am told, collating French patterns, taking a little here, and a little there, to suit the taste of our people. Worst of all, it is whispered, that the French have too correct a taste for our people, and when I have gone to our own mills of calico prints and *mousseline-de-laine,* I have found some of the masters honest enough to own that their designers were occupied not in making the best patterns, but in unmaking or corrupting them, and trying to make something bad enough to catch the eye of customers.

The French excel all nations in dress, in cooking, in dancing, and in police. They do these things well. They do them too well. The decorations or conveniences of life have absorbed the life. The word *Genius* has lost its meaning and scope. It means, in France, a dentist, a hair dresser, a cook, a milliner. And the questions that divide the *beau monde* are of like import. Will they wear strings in their shoes? black scarfs, or colored ones? powder on their hair?

From the Tuileries to the village inn, every evening and every Sunday and *fête* day finds them happy in the dance. France furnishes dancing masters to all the world, and in England and America, the popular idea of a Frenchman is of a man better furnished for this amusement, than for any serious business.

This trait has appeared once or twice in historical moments. The great Condé opened the trenches before Lerida to the sound of violins. And Voltaire related, that, instantly after taking possession of Munich by storm, the French made up a dance. The fact was questioned, and Voltaire was requested to give his authority. He replied, that he had lost his note, but the fact was incontestable, for the French always dance: *parce que les Français dansent toujours.*[23] "The Opera," says Napoleon, "is the very soul of Paris, as Paris is the soul of France." Indeed I believe it has passed into a sort of aesthetic rule in France, that whatever cannot be said can be sung, and whatever cannot be sung can be danced. Alfieri, with more bitterness, gives his version of the same trait: "I have never since known how to dance a half-minuet, and this word alone has always since made me laugh and fret by turns, which are the two effects I have uniformly experienced from the French themselves: for, taken altogether, they are nothing more than an everlasting and often badly danced minuet."

We have a proverb, "Who sings mainly and dances mainly, will not go far."

23. "Because the French find any pretext to organize a dance."

This fascinating amusement encroaches on the day and its duties. It was against the subversive dissipation that Rousseau lifted his voice of warning and that all the graver writers, when first the thunder of the Revolution growled at a distance,—Condorcet, Grimm, Vauvenargues,—expressed their sense that all was leading to ruin.[24] Napoleon was very frank in expressing his contempt of his compatriots. "Tomfoolery," he said, "is characteristic of the nation ever since the days of the Gauls." He added, "they have predominant in them vanity, levity, and caprice, with an unconquerable passion for glory. They will as soon do without bread, as without glory. Badges, ribbons, proclamations, are the rattles by which these mankind are led." The last billet written by Mirabeau, only a few days before his death, ends with these words; "O light-headed, and three-times light-headed nation!"

Of the cookery, I shall say only, They are the best wine-makers in the world. Of the fourth art, the police, that also is not quite pleasing or creditable. Its system and performance are the best in the world. And many good anecdotes are told of it. You know, Fouché, who organized it, was wont to say, "Give me three lines of any man's own hand-writing, and I can bring him to the guillotine."[25] And his means of information were so extraordinary that it began at last to be believed that the Empress herself must be in his pay.

A man denied having received a deposit. M. de Sartine sent for him, and, as he persisted in his denial, he said to him, "I believe you, but, in the circumstances, I must require you to write from this place to your wife, these few words.

*"All is discovered, and I am lost, if you do not instantly bring me the deposit we received."*

At this proposition, the man changed color. He foresaw that his wife, thus surprised, would not fail to betray him. All was in fact discovered, and the truth extorted from a false friend by an expedient comparable to the judgment of Solomon.

They have an immense forgetfulness. The craving for novelty makes the tactics of their governors easy, provided only, they will not contradict the people of Paris in the first twenty-four hours. Everything bubbles up at the surface of that enormous whirlpool for an instant, and gives place as fast to a newer spectacle: today a balloon or a ventriloquist; then a dancer, or a criminal process; then a comet predicted by M. Lalande; then an *ombres chinois;* then Cagliostro; then

24. Jean Jacques Rousseau (1712–78), philosopher and one of the founders of Romanticism; marquis de Condorcet (1743–94), social philosopher and revolutionary arrested by the Jacobins who died in prison; Baron Friedrich Melchior von Grimm (1723–1807), German diplomat who left France when the Revolution began.

25. Joseph Fouché, duc d'Otrante (1763–1820), minister of police under Napoleon.

M. Desforges in an osier gondola clothed with feathers to fly in the air; then a Spanish Saint Peter who walks the water; then the burning of diamonds; then the telegraph of snails; then the transfusion of blood, and the propagation of fishes by spawn.[26]

The motto of the *Mercure de France* was, *Mobilitate Viget,* or, "Luck to the nimble."[27] George Sand celebrates "the immortal inconstancy of the French."[28] 'Tis said of them, that, they would change their constitution as often as their shirt. And it is true, that, their onset in battle was always terrible, but their power of endurance less than others. Caesar said of the *Galli Insubres,* "that, in the beginning, they appeared more than men, but proved, in the end, less than women." Rabelais makes Gymnast say, "My sovereign lord, such is the nature and complexion of the French, that they are worth nothing but at the first push." Montaigne gives the like testimony. For a street-fight, for barricades, and delirious courage in the onset, the *gamins* are famous, but no Frenchman can stand ridicule or solitude. Napoleon said, "They can't understand that the great art is to be governed by time; the Gallic temperament can't submit to wait upon time; and yet, it is by doing so, that I have gained all my success."

It is noticed, in like manner, that they grow early old; that, they are very handsome in the flower of their youth, but, after twenty, presently strike forty in their faces. And their wisdom was noted to be early, but of no continuance.

Each effaces the last, and, if events occur that make the blood boil, a newer vaudeville, a more beautiful dancer, must be found, to sponge out the too tenacious strokes from the slate. Grimm complains of the extreme difficulty of ascertaining the exact facts in any occurrence at Paris. If any quarrel or crime has transpired in any palace or convent,—for two days it makes sensation, and everybody recites, with absolute confidence, the worst details. But try to follow it up to the source, you are baffled; it is totally overlaid and forgotten by everybody, on the third day; no importunacy can recall it to mind.

"You must do something new, every three months, to catch the imagination of the French nation. With it, whoever does not advance, is ruined."[29] The serious men in the nation rely on this levity, as the sole remedy for any abuse, any institution or mode dangerous to the nation: "Well, thank God, they will weary of it in a week or two." Thus of the clubs in 1786.

26. Joseph Jérôme Le Français de Lalande (1732–1807) revised the planetary tables for Halley's Comet; an *ombres chinois* is a shadow show or pantomime; Count Alessandro di Cagliostro (1743–95), Italian adventurer once imprisoned in Paris.

27. The motto of the newspaper *Mercure de France* could be translated more properly as "speed lends her strength" (see Virgil, *Aeneid,* l. 175).

28. Attributed to Sand by Emerson (see *JMN,* 6:353).

29. Attributed to George Sand by Emerson (see *JMN,* 10:69).

France is the empire of *bagatelle*, and one must leave at the frontier the standards of other nations, and be content to take things upside down. To be amused is the purpose of the people. Everything comes to be valued for its entertainment. War itself bribes them on that side; Lamartine, is forced to confess that when the Allied Armies conquered France, and marched into Paris, the citizens who begun the day with terror and mortification,—as the military procession advanced into the city, forgot their defeat in the splendor of the show. "All is spectacle for such a city—even its own humiliation."

They are vain, and live for show. They do everything for effect. An eminent physician told me, how much he admired the swift and penetrating diagnosis of M. Louis, as he followed him, every day, with the students, from bed to bed, through the hospital.[30] But, one day, he went in the afternoon to the hospital, and found the professor secretly visiting the wards with carefullest auscultation and scrutiny, that he might pronounce on the case of each patient with ostentatious promptitude before the class.

A Frenchman who had lost his wife, met one of his friends who offered his condolence and said, he had perceived how keenly he felt his loss. "When and where did you observe my sorrow?" asked the widower. "At the funeral service." "Ah!" replied the disconsolate man, "Ah, *mon ami,* you should have seen me at the grave!"

And so throughout. God will have life to be real; the French will have it theatrical. They attitudinize: they write fustian proclamations: they dramatize their own deaths. Even when the ends are great, the means are ridiculous. A capital discovery, a public benefit, must be got in by intrigue and compliment. Vaccination was introduced into France by the physician of the Duke of Orléans, M. Senac, who having quarrelled with the Faculté de Medicine and wishing to put them down, persuaded M. le Duc d'Orléans to have his eldest son, the Duc de Chartres and Mademoiselle, vaccinated by M. Trouchin.[31] As soon as this was done, the practice found favor at Court, and then through France. The culture of potato came in by intrigue. M. Parmentier persuaded the king to wear a potato blossom in the buttonhole of his coat at a *fête,* and instantly some of the great lords procured the seed and sent it down to their estates, to be planted.[32] Even during the Revolution, he was rejected as a magistrate, because he had invented potatoes. It is also said that M. Parmentier affected to guard his field by day as if the seed were very precious, in hopes that it would be stolen by night.

---

30. This anecdote about Dr. Pierre-Charles-Alexandre Louis was reported to Emerson by his brother-in-law Charles Thomas Jackson (see *JMN,* 10:158).

31. Either Louis Philippe d'Orléans (1725–85) or Louis Philippe Joseph (1747–93), his son.

32. The story of Antoine-Augustin Parmentier is attributed to a biography of Cuvier (see *JMN,* 6:211).

The true test of character is impression. One man remains there entire, refuses to be disposed of. You believe, you have said better things, done better and more than he, but somehow, after all is said and done, there he towers still, unconvinced. And it is the old law of the human mind, in the moment when one is not convinced, in that moment, he begins to convince. I find a secondary tone in everything written in French journals. The national vanity appears,—they write for effect: England is never out of mind. But English journals and Englishmen are very little solicitous what is said about them in France.

"The most dangerous fault of our nation," says Condorcet, "is its taste for imitation. A Frenchman cannot exist or think alone. He holds to a class, or he is of a sect." And Alfieri said, "The French character consists in not having one."

Britain lies close to France, as if to establish this fact by setting the qualities and defects of the race in strong relief. There sit the two nations side by side, age after age, in steep contrast; they call themselves *natural enemies.* I do not know but they exasperate these differences, by pushing each to the verge of its character; each avoiding the other's whim, and hugging its own; perhaps each drawing out of the other nation any talent or taste which suits itself better, and making the contrast broader. In England, they spend for comfort; in France, for pleasure,—and the lighter-minded English go to France or establish a little France in England; and the soberer French, the Huguenot, down to this day, (if one is left,) makes a little England around him in France.

The French have the advantage of other nations in all that goes to the elegance and amenities of social life—to all, that, by eminence, is called *society,* in modern times. Their quick perceptions, their politeness, their love of pleasure, their delight in proprieties, their grace in trifles, their union of courage and kindness, qualified them to be the masters of Europe in whatever relates to etiquette, courtesy, saloons. All these words are theirs. And all this is nothing but the application of good sense to these trifles of every day. It is said, that the French possess vastly more political influence in Europe than the English. What the English have, is by main force of wealth and power: what the French have, is by affinity, and talent, and liking.

France has an advantage in the freedom from the aristocratic morgue, in the tone of society. It is quite easy for any young man of liberal tastes to enter, on a good footing, the best houses. It is not easy in England, not only on account of the English exclusiveness, but also on account of English expensiveness. There is in France, in all times, a true respect for science, and for learning, and for more simple and sensible modes.

The French have no domestic manners or life. There are no homes. If they have families, the boys are sent away to school in the country, the girls to a convent for their education, and the husband and, perhaps, the wife find their dinner at the restaurant more agreeable than in their own apartments. Thus, living in public, they have no time for the formation of private manners and character. Paris is France, and every café in the kingdom is a little Paris again.

When convention and dissipation become general, there are no more manners or character. In a party of a dozen persons, everyone talks the same jargon. All are alike. But in this too social living, in the *soirées*, masked balls, little suppers, and dancing gardens of this perpetual carnival, the women secure the opportunity of establishing their empire.

The grace and air of the French woman, the security and piquancy of her manners, and her unrivalled *toilette*,—I leave to younger eyes. They have much better graces. "There is a quality in which no woman in the world can compare with a French woman: it is in the power of intellectual invitation. She will draw wit out of a fool. She strikes with such address the chords of self-love, that she gives unexpected vigor and agility to fancy, and electrifies a body that appeared nonelectric."[33]

They despise books. "When I asked a reason for his opinion," said a French lady, "he advised me to read a certain work, which had just appeared." "Read! I read! Never. As many facts as you like, but the reason, I read only in my own head." But for the picture of the French woman, they have drawn it themselves in so many *mémoires* and romances, and in the lively heads which hang in shop windows, all through America. I am sorry to say they are not famed for preserving their empire over their giddy lovers.

Madame Sand celebrates the immortal inconstancy of the French. Regnard says, "There are great revolutions in one night in a French head."[34] And Bussy-Rabutin says of his mistress, "I could not endure her, she loved me so much"— "*Je ne la pouvois souffrir, tant elle m'aimait.*"[35] Such is the incorrigible levity of the nation, that they have a dreadful legend current in the country, that the Methusalem of French Cupids did not live six days.

They are fond of characterising themselves by drawing ironical portraits of their serious brothers and sisters across the channel. They hate grave men. "Gravity is a mystery of the body invented to conceal the defects of the wit." "The English women," say the French, "have two left hands;" and they pity from their hearts those unfortunate English ladies who have never known how to dress themselves, but who also for the most part make excellent nurses.

The character of moroseness has been fixed on the English by French travellers, who, from Froissart, Voltaire, Lesage, Mirabeau, and Holbach down to the

---

33. Attributed to William Shenstone (1714–63), English poet (see *JMN*, 13:222).
34. Jean François Regnard (1655–1709), French writer of comedies.
35. Roger de Rabutin, comte de Bussy (1618–93), French soldier and author.

lively journalists of the *Feuilletons*, have spent their wit on the solemnity of their neighbors.[36] Gay conversation is unknown in this country. The Englishman finds no relief from reflection, except in reflection itself. When he wishes for amusement, he goes to work. His gaiety is like an attack of fever. Religion, the theatre, and the reading of the books of his country all feed and increase his natural melancholy. The police does not interfere with public diversions. It thinks itself bound in duty to respect the rare gaiety of this unhappy nation: and the well-known courage of the English is attributable entirely to their disgust of life.

But the high merit accorded to France, by the general voice of nations, is, to have created a brilliant social culture in advance of every other nation. I suppose, that there was never anything more excellent in its way, than the play of talent, wit, science, and epicureanism, in the French salons, at the best period. We are pretty faithfully supplied with specimens and fragments of it, in the voluminous memoirs of the time.

When M. de Bignon was made librarian of the Bibliothèque du Roi, Count d'Argenson said, "My cousin, here is a fine opportunity to learn to read."[37] But M. de Bignon did not profit by the occasion. He, however, became a member of the Académie; they said, he was chosen, because there needed a cipher to make the figure *40*. But this reason cannot pass, since, if it were necessary to count all the ciphers that belong to the Academy, their number would give not forty, but forty millions and more.

The curious in timing and placing everything have even traced the origin of what is now called by eminence, *society,* in any polite city, Boston, or New York, or London, back to the Hotel de Rambouillet, at about the date when the Plymouth Pilgrims landed in America. It is certain, that, until about 1600, very different manners and customs existed in France. France was feudal; the great lords were all soldiers; the men of the law, and the men of letters, were distinct from them, like inferior castes: and the manners of all were gross and rude. The king kept a poet as he kept a fool, and the *grandées* had some hired man of letters in the capacity of secretary. "*C'était déroger à noblesse que d'avoir de l'esprit.*" Even the houses were still feudal fortresses. The court or hall in the hollow square was the essential part, furnishing mainly accommodations for knights, their grooms, horses, and dogs. There was no room in the house for large companies of persons, or none for the convenience or luxury of such assemblies.

In 1600, Catherine de Vivonne married Charles d'Angennes, Marquis de

36. Jean Froissart (1338–ca. 1410), chronicler of French history from 1325 to 1400; Voltaire had traveled throughout Europe, spending time at various courts; Alain René Lesage (1668–1747), French novelist and dramatist; Baron Paul Henri Dietrich d'Holbach (1723–89), skeptical philosopher.

37. Possibly Abbé Jean Paul de Begnon de Blazy (d. 1743), who joined the Académie Française in 1693; Marc René Louis, marquis d'Argenson (1652–1721), general of police in Paris.

Rambouillet, and, some years later, built the Hôtel de Rambouillet in a style and with new dispositions of the interior, which she had borrowed from Italy. She made the doors wide. The windows reached from the ceiling to the floor. She threw the staircases to the side, which had once occupied the middle of the house; and so made wide and spacious saloons opening one into another. When this house was built near to the Tuileries, by these persons, allied to the royal family, yet independent of it,—they proceeded to fill it with friends. They brought thither Condé and Conti, Lauzun, Montausier, d'Enghien, and the high *noblesse;* they brought also the Marquis and Madame de Sévigné; they brought also Voiture and Saint-Evremond, and, in due time, Corneille, and Bossuet, and Balzac, and Vaugelas, and Mme de Maintenon, and whatever was distinguished in wit and genius and manners in France.[38]

The wonderful charm of Madame de Rambouillet, assisted by the grace and genius of her daughter and of de Sévigné, gave a new tone, rather a new life, to these circles, refined them in wonderful manners, and created a self-respect, and a rapid culture, in all the guests. Everything witty, elegant, and beautiful came thither. The court, which was before the only society, found a rival in this. At court, all was undisguised ambition and gallantry: at the Hôtel de Rambouillet, elegance, and letters, and character ruled the hour.

Everybody's ambition was to be admitted there: the women who resorted there, were called *précieuses* and *illustres*, titles at first bestowed in hearty honor;[39] the mode in speech, in manners, in books, in opinions, proceeded thence; the men of letters were elevated in manners, by association with the nobles, and these last refined by men of education; so that a new day dawned, and *conversation*, as a fine art, *conversation*, which, the men of the next generation declared, was not to be found out of France, was created. New circles were formed on the model of these; *soirées* of literary men and women: and Cardinal Richelieu, ambitious of

38. Catherine de Vivonne de Savelli, marquise de Rambouillet (1588–1665), and her husband, Charles d'Angennes, marquis de Rambouillet (1597–1652), leaders of society; "Condé" and "Conti" are, respectively, Henry II and his son Armand, prince de Conti (1629–68), involved in the Parisian theatrical world; Jean-Jacques-Régis, duc de Cambacérès (1753–1824), statesman, jurist, and friend of Napoleon; Charles de Sainte-Maure, duc de Montausier (1610–90), statesman who married Julie d'Angennes (1607–71), daughter of the marquis and marquise de Rambouillet; Henri, marquis de Sévigné (d. 1651), husband of Marie de Rabutin-Chantal, marquise de Sévigné (1626–96), epistolary writer; Vincent Voiture (1598–1648), poet and man of letters; Charles de Marguetel de Saint-Denis, seigneur de Saint-Evremond (1613–1703), French wit and man of letters; Pierre Corneille (1606–84), dramatist; Jacques Bénigne Bossuet (1627–1704), historian and theologian; Claude Favre, seigneur de Vaugelas (1585–1650), grammarian and original member of the Académie Française; Françoise d'Aubigne, marquise de Maintenon (1635–1719), mistress and then second wife of Louis XIV.

39. A *précieuse* is someone who exhibits excessive refinement and uses elegant language; an *illustre* is a society woman who defines proper language and social mores.

their influence, founded the French Academy, in 1635, which was the establishment of a kind of literary nobility in the kingdom.[40]

But I suppose, too, that this very triumph of the art of talking had its usual
effect. When talking came to be cultivated as an art, action and history came to
be valued only as they furnished topics. So it happened in France, at the approach
of the old Revolution, that great political events were less valuable to the salcons
for their substantial reforms, than for the new aliment and grander scope they
gave to conversation, weary of levities, and glad of new tones, new topics, new
affections, new eloquence, on this vast and grave event. "In the morning of the
Revolution, in spite of the truths which burst out in every discourse, society in
Paris resembled a grand troop of comedians playing republican personages;" and
civil liberty came to be painted a god-like, personal independence.

Of course, the conversation of this million of pleasure hunters can have nothing very serious. The only rule is that nothing serious shall be said. In all times,
a malignant gaiety jokes alike at the good and bad fortune of the public. The best
of kings is not less its butt than the worst tyrant. Epigrams, sarcastic sentences,
caricatures, puns, are forever the favorite toy of this infant people. Persiflage or
banter is the genius of the boulevard and the salon. It is the knife by which every
rival is cut down. To be once ridiculous is to be stone dead. And where everybody
talks incessantly, a bonmot flies with fatal effect. Is the new beauty slender? She
is the Venus of the Père La Chaise.[41] Is the Bishop of Autun fat?[42] He was created and placed on this earth merely to show to what extent the human skin might
be stretched. When the squinting man asked Talleyrand, "How things went
in the cabinet?" he replied, "As you see." When it was rumored once and again
M. Dupin's life was threatened, he was greeted, on entering the assembly, "*Comment vous assassinez vous, M. Dupin?*"[43]

These giddy talkers,—I fear, little good came of it. They went on pulling
down; rioting; sacrificing the public weal to private pleasure. The law of French
society came to be the coldest egotism. But none would deny them the pushing
the joys of sense to the highest point of refinement. They economize their pleasures, and despise nothing more than a greedy enjoyer. They possess an erudition of sensation; they have a civility of condiments, of wine and cigars. Their
philosophy ended in a dreary materialism. "The nerves," said one philosopher,

40. The Académie Française was established by Richelieu in 1634 and limited to forty members
charged with maintaining standards of literary taste and establishing the country's literary language

41. François d'Aix de La Chaise (1624–1709), French Jesuit priest and confessor of Louis XIV;
he approved the secret marriage of Louis XIV and Madame de Maintenon.

42. The bishop of Autun is Talleyrand.

43. André Marie Jean Jacques Dupin (1783–1865), president of the Chamber of Deputies
(1832–40).

"they are the man." "The heart," said another, "is one of the viscera." "The virtues," said a third, "are only a human institution, the passions are a divine institution." Voltaire said, "I would exchange a hundred years of immortality for a good digestion." 'Tis hunger, 'tis *le petit ventre,* said Napoleon, that moves mankind.[44] It had only the merit of frankness. There was sneering, but no cant. The desire of enjoying took the place of the desire of pleasing. Not to bore one another, became the only rule of politeness, and so down into selfishness pure, or absolute disregard of everybody's enjoyment but your own, which arrived, at last, at its natural superlative in Napoleon's famous instructions, "Your first duty is to me; your second to France."

Of course, the wits and braves carried this out with humour into sarcasm. The *Don Juan* of Molière and of Byron,—who braves the visible and the invisible world for his debauch, and invites the spectre that haunts him to take wine with him,—is the hero of the French salons.[45] He says with Louis XV, "After me, the deluge," and that is the reason not why I should forebear, but why I should enjoy.[46] And it was said in that flood of riot that preceded the revolution in France, that "Virtue had been so decried, that hypocrisy no longer existed."

This spirit of luxurious, clear-headed, witty, selfish saloons found no representative so faithful as Talleyrand. Napoleon derived immense advantage for commanding it, from not being of it: but Talleyrand represents its agreeable, finished, worldly, freezing glitter.

Talleyrand at fifteen years had discovered that the secret of governing men lay in self-command. "*Surtout, messieurs, pas de zèle, beaucoup de dîners.*"[47] Lannes said of him, "If any one gave him a kick on the posteriors, it would not make him change countenances."[48] "Sire," said he to Louis XVIII, "There is something in me which bodes no good to those governments which neglect me." "That lame rascal," said Chénier of Talleyrand, "resembles a sponge, which imbibes every liquid into which it is dipped, with this difference, that when the sponge is pressed it returns the liquid it has taken, whilst our limping friend makes it his own."[49] Of course, he was prudent, or of that class whose watches, he said, go faster than their neighbors', and had great respect for the real master, the com-

44. *Le petit ventre* is one's stomach.

45. Molière first produced *Don Juan* in 1665; Byron's *Don Juan* was published between 1819 and his death in 1824.

46. Madame de Pompadour attributed this statement—"Après nous le déluge" [After us the deluge]—to Frederick the Great, claiming that he said it to Louis XV (1710–74), the king of France whose policies set the stage for the French Revolution, after the defeat of the French and Austrian armies at the battle of Rossbach. Larousse attributed the saying to the king, but neither is correct; it's actually an old French proverb.

47. "And above all, gentlemen, let us not have too much zeal but rather have lots of dinners."

48. Jean Lannes, duc de Montebello and prince de Siévers (1769–1809), Napoleon's favorite general.

49. André Marie de Chénier (1762–94), poet of classical verse.

manding class: "*On peut être plus fin qu'un autre, mais pas plus fin que tous les autres.*"— "Who is," he said, "who is this people, this somebody who is cleverer than everybody?" But he had no respect for reputed wise men, like Sieyès: "*Il est profond,*" said Cambacères, "*profond!*" "Yes," replied Talleyrand, "a cavity, a perfect cavity."[50]

But he was troubled by no superstitions, for sham power in church or state, being himself the cripple of cripples—By means of my vices, I understand yours—and could detect a halt. When the Pope had interdicted Talleyrand, the latter wrote to M. de Biron, "You know the news, come and console me, and sup with me. Everybody is going to refuse me fire and water. We shall therefore have nothing this evening but iced meats, and drink nothing but wine."[51]

"Doctor Bourdois, an odd notion strikes me. I wish to give you a pension. Yes, I am serious, a pension of six thousand *francs*. But let us understand each other — It will not be for your life, but for mine."[52] It was therefore very naturally answered by one of the company at Paris, when it was asked whom they would have godfather to Rothschild's child: "Talleyrand."— "*Pourquoi, monsieur?*"— "*Parce qu'il est le moins Chrétien possible.*"[53]

Yet Nature, everlasting in beneficence, scatters here also beautiful and generous souls, and profound minds. Here was born Fénelon, the saint, a man whose nobilities were so apparent in his manners, that his contemporaries said, that you could not turn your eyes from his face without an effort. Here was Montesquieu, the wise, who "found the lost titles of the human race," and whose heart was as great as his head. Here was Pascal. Here were noble and beautiful women. Here was Guyon, the mystic and saint. Here, Sévigné and Mme de Rambouillet. Here, Madame Geoffrin, who, for thirty years, made a centre for letters and philosophy, where every illustrious European was domesticated, and whose head was never turned, and who presided over all, and tamed the petulances and vanity of the *philosophes,* and checked the sallies of the sensualist by her steady good sense and benevolence. Her house was one of the institutions of European civility. *Rien en relief. Voilà qui est bien.*[54] Madame de Staël, whose pure genius has made bright every height and depth of thought and sentiment which she has approached, but has also enlarged the known power of the sex in intellect. Madame de Récamier, her beautiful friend, the complement of her nature and genius, the angel of these evil years of vice and blood, whose innocence made all better, and when Canova

50. Emmanuel Joseph Sieyès (1748–1836), abbot and politician.
51. Armand Louis de Gontaut, duc de Biron (1747–93), French general and politician who fought in the American Revolution and represented the side of the nobility in the Estates-General; Talleyrand was suspended as bishop by the pope in 1791.
52. Bourdois de la Motte (d. 1835), friend and physician to Talleyrand.
53. "But why him, sir?" "Because he is the least Christian of them all."
54. "Now here is something nice. Nothing sticks out."

carved her in marble, he needed no ideal, for she was that. Here was the Princess of Vaudémont, of whom when someone asked in the presence of Talleyrand, where she lived, "Rue St. Lazare," he said.— "I have forgot the number,—But you have only to ask the first beggar you meet. They all know the house." Here was Madame Roland; and here for an hour of need, was Charlotte Corday.[55]

Levity, levity. It is, you know, told of Saint Denis, the patron saint of France, the singular accident interesting to anatomists, that, when his head was cut off, he took it up under his arm, and walked away; which gave occasion to the remark, "It is only the first step that costs." [56] Well, I can't vouch for the historical fact, and yet there is a little presumption in its favor to be drawn from the character, in all ages, of his people. Their head is not yet quite in the right place: something topsy-turvy still. One would say of the French, that they have levity, in the sense in which very serious men sometimes tax women with levity, as constitutionally not having a deep, but superficial interest only in things. Talent enough they have, but a Frenchman doesn't care for more than the look and air of the thing, and are in relation to English as a nation of women compared with a nation of men.

Thus, Théophile Gautier's remark, "wisest in pleasures, foolish in affairs." [57] Observe, in France, always, the opera is the first interest; and politics the second. They are not exact accountants: they rely on proclamations, on processions, on fêtes, on artificial prices; pay the bakers a premium to sell the bread at fixed rate; as if corn could be coaxed and complimented; suffer hysterical revolutions, and Cagliostro on the throne. A confusion of truth and false, right and wrong, in every man's mind. Talleyrand's friend Montrond said, "In God's name who can help liking him, he is so vicious." [58]

Even, in art, the same topsy-turvy. Boucher found Raffaelle insipid; Michael Angelo an artist of deformity; and nature wanting in harmony and attractiveness.[59] "Nature," he said,—"too green—badly managed as to light!" Louis XV had reason, when he took M. Bertin to counsel as to the best means of saving his

55. François de Salignac de La Mothe-Fénelon (1651–1715), prelate and author of an early utopian novel; Jeanne-Marie Bouvier de la Motte Guyon (1648–1717), mystic identified with quietism; Marie Thérèse Geoffrin (1699–1777), a leader of the literary society in Paris; Jeanne Françoise Julie Adélaïde Récamier (1777–1849), famous for her beauty, wit, and literary salon; Antonio Canova (1757–1822), Italian sculptor; Princesse de Montmorency Vaudémont (d. 1832); Madame Roland de la Platière (1754–93), Revolutionist who fell to the guillotine; Charlotte Corday (1768–93), sent to the guillotine after assassinating Jean Paul Marat (1743–93), Swiss-born French revolutionary politician.

56. Saint Denis, the patron saint of France, was an apostle to the Gauls who was beheaded in Paris ca. 250.

57. Théophile Gautier (1811–72), poet, critic, and novelist.

58. François Philibert Casimir, count de Montrond (1769–1843), soldier and agent for Talleyrand.

59. François Boucher (1703–70), French painter of historical and pastoral scenes and favorite of Madame de Pompadour.

light-headed and light-heeled lieges, and learned that, "what the French wanted was to be inoculated with the Chinese mind." [60]

Yet, one would say these traits which disparage the French are the salient traits which most strike the spectator, but not really the essential traits. For there is excellent sense in French science, excellent sense in French arts, and, to all good readers, in French books; conclusive proof of moderation, of culture, of practical judgment, of love of the best, or wisdom.

Formerly, men were sent to the Dorian race to learn the ascetic virtues. Men were sent to Rome to learn a haughtier style of patriot virtue than the world had seen. But, if the design were to teach a youth the secret of Christianity,—would you send him to France?—or of a wise ethics? or of heroic life? No: the French mind has certain defects. It wants veracity. When the French poet or romancer paints an elevated character, he is permitted to lie, when his convenience requires. The parole of a French officer is not a security. And in trade, I am informed by merchants they do not value the truth.

Then, I think the sense which the nation gives to the word *amour* is the serious bar to its civilization. The French ideas are subversive of what Saxon men understand by society. The nation has an exceptional temperament, and that is not more humane. I am far from thinking with M. Guizot that theirs is the most civil of civilizations.

There is a consciousness of this in the French mind, a penitence, which is expressed by their great minds: Montesquieu, Fourier, Mallet du Pan, Mirabeau, Montaigne.[61] Montesquieu said, There are no people of real good sense except those born in England. It was *Voltaire,* who characterised the mingled levity and ferocity of his countryman by calling him *singe-tigre,* half-monkey, half-tiger. It was *Condorcet,* who said, he is a mimic. It was *Fourier,* who said, "Would you make an abortion of one whom nature has moulded for a great man? It suffices to rear him in France, to fashion him on the taste of the arbitrary, of confusion, of imprudence, which make the national character of the French."

In their political history, the same levity appears. Bonaparte said, "They do not care for liberty. It is equality which tickles them." They are inconsequent, light-headed, stung to revolt by some petulance, not marching to it, like the logical English, year after year, through sun and shade, and never pausing until it is attained.

Chateaubriand has marked the curious coincidence of the disappearance of the French religious war of freedom, in the buffoon fighting of the Fronde, in time with the triumph of religious freedom in England, at the death of Charles I.[62]

60. Henry Léonard Jean Baptiste Bertin, controller general of France under Louis XV.
61. Jacques Mallet du Pan (1749–1800), Swiss journal editor.
62. François René Chateaubriand (1768–1848), author and statesman known as an early Romantic.

"While England passed to liberty with a severe brow, France ran laughing to despotism." The stability of England is the cornerstone of the modern world. If the English race were as mutable as the French, what reliance? But the English go for liberty, the conservative, money-loving, rank-loving, lord-loving, yet liberty-loving English go for freedom; and, therefore, freedom is safe. For, they have more personal force than any other people in the world. And, I suppose, notwithstanding the base tone of Boston and New York, that, when it came to the final choosing of sides, they too would be found firm for freedom. And they are capable, if hard should come to hard, of grand action.

These seakings may yet take once more to their floating castles, and swear anew, never to sleep under a smoky roof, nor to own a yard of land.—Up to this time, it appears, only the English race can be trusted with freedom. France has taken the yoke again. Yet on this point, it is always too early to despair. On the contrary, all the noble struggles of French patriots have not been vain. The very great social progress of France warrants a better future.

At the Diet of Tours, 1433, the clergy and nobility insisted that the Third Estate should pay the expenses of all three Estates incurred by travelling to and living at the Diet, because made to support the two other estates. As late as 1616, the Third Estate were forced to address the king on their knees, the others standing. In 1629, the grand judge of the monks of Saint Claude convicted Guillon, *écuyer*, of having taken some morsels from a dead horse thrown into the jakes, and, the next day, eaten the same in Lent: and he was beheaded the next day. In whole districts, the population were born serfs, were permitted only to offer their money on their knees; permitted only to die in the army; if at home, without law, victims of chicane, of feudal lords, of the clergy.

Such was the state of the law, that the people had better submit to wrong, than to make their case worse by seeking legal redress. M. Servan, a lawyer, who drew up (about 1789) an analysis of the criminal code, ends his labors with a bitter dedication to persons accused.[63] "*Messieurs les accusés!* I have the honor to offer you a digest of our criminal laws, to teach you a truth which it is well you knew, this, namely, that a good flight is much better than any trial. Abscond who can, and a prosperous voyage!" Napoleon gave them a code, and the law at least is fixed and may be known.

M. Simond says, "Before the Revolution, in some provinces of France a woman was yoked side by side with an ass to the plough or the harrow, and it excited no horror to see the driver distributing his lashes impartially between the woman and her brute yoke-fellow." The gardens of the Tuileries and of the Luxembourg were in principle, like the parks of St. Cloud and Versailles, des-

---

63. Joseph Michel Antoine Servan (1737–1807), reform-minded politician.

tined for the personal convenience of one man and his circle. Later, they admitted successively, with the people of the court, persons of fashion. In 1789, nobody yet entered the Tuileries without a sword at his side, unless it were an *abbé*. But, in 1839, there were sixteen peers in France who had no other claim to the peerage than that of intellect. Napoleon opened more doors than he had time to shut again, and he had reason to say that every French private soldier carries in his knap sack the materials of a marshal's baton.

It is notorious that the French Revolution has immensely aided France, destroyed the feudal service, newly distributed property, and given every man a right to vote when an opportunity shall once more return to use it.

Another measure of the substantial force of a nation is its foreign relations. Here France is wanting. The time was when England and France were contesting with equal advantage the possession of America. But France lost, and has never recovered. France lost; Spain lost; and now the French are lately discovering, with terror, that all the Latin nations are falling into a state of decay: Italy, Spain, Poland, even France itself. France, alone of them all, remains a first-class power, and France only at home. The young ambitious Frenchman attaches himself to some exploring expedition that carries him to the Poles, or to China, or to Australia, and finds that everywhere the English and American powers weave their net of commercial influence, and that France is nowhere, and a Frenchman in a ship is looked on as some amateur. Bonaparte saw this plainly enough and said, "in twenty-five years the United States of America will write the treaties of Europe."

Xavier Raimond publishes in Paris on his return from Canton, that everywhere there is an English ship, and everywhere an American clipper; and that, in all the parts of the world, these only watch each other, disdaining all other flags, as beneath notice. Seeing with his own eyes the gigantic aggression of these two branches of the Saxon Race, he draws the most melancholy inferences to the future of his countrymen.

In this kingdom of illusion, life is a dream. In the language of the ancient, We change only from bed to bed, from one folly to another, and what signifies, what becomes of such nobodies: they change from bed to bed, from the nothing of life to the nothing of death. They are not the true geniuses, not the creators. They are talkers, reasoners, jokers, critics. A bad picture gives occasion to a good pamphlet. They speak better of the arts than they shall ever do. Late and early, it will be found that they have reasoned best and best discussed what other nations shall have best done. They may then well cherish the *feuilleton,* the journal, as their part in the world.

Yet a trait of France is the immense vitality of a people whom famine cannot starve, not fire burn, nor war kill. Over and over again—a hundred times—that devoted land has been harried by war, oppressed by kings, sucked by taxation, filled with horror by revolution, and becomes again the ornament and joy of the world. Such is the blessing of the soil, or such the unextinguishable energy of the race, that in a year or two it is green and rich with grain, peopled by new and industrious millions. They have a great industrious population. Men of honor have appeared in their late crises who did not bow the knee, and there exist in the nation multitudes of individuals nowise implicated in their bad politics, and nowise infected with the old giddiness of the Gauls.

# "Seventh of March Speech on the Fugitive Slave Law, 7 March 1854"

Nearly three years after his "Address to the Citizens of Concord on the Fugitive Slave Law, 3 May 1851," Emerson delivered a second address on the Fugitive Slave Law on 7 March 1854 before the New York Anti-Slavery Society at the Broadway Tabernacle in New York City. He received $50 for the lecture ("Account Books").

The address was not completed to Emerson's satisfaction until the day of its delivery. On 3 March he told a friend that "I should speak more confidently . . . if I were quite ready to speak. At present I am far from it." And on the morning of his address, he wrote his brother William that "I am prisoner here of my papers" (*Letters*, 4:432). Emerson was unsure of the success of his talk. Writing in his journal, he says of the occasion: "I saw the great audience with dismay, & told the bragging secretary, that I was most thankful to those who stayed at home; Every auditor was a new affliction, & if all had stayed away, by rain, or preoccupation, I had been best pleased" (*JMN*, 13:47). Writing to his old friend William Henry Furness, Emerson commented, "I came home near three weeks ago, with good hope to write a plea for Freedom addressed *to my set;* which, of course, like a Divinity Collegian's first sermon, was to exhaust the subject & moral science generally; but I fared much as those young gentlemen do, got no answer to my passionate queries— nothing but the echo of my own cries, and had to carry to New York a makeshift instead of an oracle. . . . & I shall not cease to try" (14 March 1854, *Letters*, 8:397–98).

Accounts of the address were published in the *New York Herald* and *New-York Daily Tribune* ("The Seventh of March. A Lecture by Ralph Waldo Emerson," 8 March 1854, 1; "Last of the Anti-Slavery Lectures," 8 March 1854, 5). A report of the address, "compiled" from these two papers and described as "not perfect" but showing "the spirit and the substance of what the speaker uttered," was published in the *National Anti-Slavery Standard* ("Ralph Waldo Emerson's Lecture," 18 March 1854, 169). The address is summarized in a letter from "Delta," dated 8 March, published in the *Boston Evening Transcript* (11 March 1854, 1; reprinted as "Ralph Waldo Emerson at the New York Tabernacle," *Liberator*, 17 March 1854, 44).

The address was first published as "The Fugitive Slave Law" in *Miscellanies* in 1884 (*W*, 11:215–40). It was reedited as "The Fugitive Slave Law" in Emerson's *Antislavery Writings*, 73–89.

I DO NOT OFTEN speak to public questions; they are odious and hurtful, and it seems like meddling or leaving your work. I have my own spirits in prison, spirits in deeper prisons, whom no man visits, if I do not. And then I see what havoc it makes with any good mind—this dissipated philanthropy. The one thing not to be forgiven to intellectual persons is not to know their own task, or to take their ideas from others and believe in the ideas of others. From this want of manly rest in their own, and foolish acceptance of other people's watchwords, comes the imbecility and fatigue of their conversation. For, they cannot affirm these from any original experience, and, of course, not with the natural movement and whole power of their nature and talent, but only from their memory, only from the cramp position of standing for their teacher.— They say, what they would have you believe, but which they do not quite know.

My own habitual view is to the well-being of students or scholars, and it is only when the public event affects them, that it very seriously affects me. And what I have to say is to them. For every man speaks mainly to a class whom he works with, and more or less fitly represents. It is to them I am beforehand related and engaged,—in this audience or out of this audience,—to them and not to others.

I am not responsible to this audience for what I shall say; I am responsible to myself for now and forever for what I say to this audience. And yet when I say the class of scholars and students,—that is a class which comprises in some sort all mankind,—comprises every man in the best hours of his life:—and in these days not only virtually, but actually. For who are the readers and thinkers of 1854?

I say I consider myself bound to speak only to the reading and thinking class. But this class has immensely increased. Owing to the silent revolution which the newspaper has wrought, this class has come in this country to take in all classes. Look into the morning trains, which, from every suburb carry the business-men into the city, to their shops, counting rooms, work yards, and warehouses. With them, enters the car the humble priest of politics, finance, philosophy, and religion in the shape of the newsboy. He unfolds his magical sheets. Two pence a head his bread of knowledge costs, and instantly the entire rectangular assembly, fresh from their breakfast, are bending as one man to their second breakfast. There is, no doubt, chaff enough, in what he brings, but there is fact, and thought, and wisdom in the crude mass from all regions of the world.

Now, I have lived all my life without suffering any known inconvenience from American slavery. I never saw it; never heard the whip; I never felt the check on my free speech and action; until the other day, when Mr. Webster, by his personal influence, brought the Fugitive Slave law on the country. I say Mr. Webster, for though the bill was not his, yet it is notorious that he was the life and soul of it, that he gave it all he had: it cost him his life. And under the shadow of his great name, inferior men sheltered themselves, and threw their ballots for it, and made the law. I say inferior men; there were all sorts of what are called brilliant men, accomplished men, men of high office—a President of the United States, senators—and of eloquent speech, but men without self-respect, without character, and it was droll to see that office, age, fame, talent, even a repute for honesty, all count for nothing: they had no opinions; they had no memory for what they had been saying, like the Lord's prayer, all their lifetime; they were only looking to what their great captain did, and if he jumped, they jumped,—if he stood on his head, they did. In ordinary, the supposed sense of their district and state is their guide, and this keeps them to liberty and justice. But it is always a little diffi-cult to decipher what this public sense is: and when a great man comes, who knots up into himself the opinions and wishes of his people, it is so much easier to fol-low him as an exponent of this. He, too, is responsible. They will not be. It will always suffice to say,—I followed him.

I saw plainly that the great show of their legitimate power was in nothing more than in their power to misguide us. I saw that a great man, deservedly esteemed and admired for his powers and their general right direction, was able—fault of the total want of stamina in public men—when he failed, to break them all with him, to carry parties with him. He scattered terror which he and they manufac-tured together, the terror of southern bluster, amongst all the feeble, and timid, and unprincipled; and covered their own treachery by the panic they created. Everything went to the ground: it was a sadly instructive crisis: it showed that men would not stick to their professions, or parties to their platforms.

It showed much. It ended a great deal of nonsense we had been accustomed to hear and to repeat, on the twenty-second of December, the nineteenth of April, the seventeenth of June, and the fourth of July.[1] It showed what reputations are made of; what straws we dignify by office and title, and how competent they are to give counsel and help in a day of trial: the shallowness of leaders; showed the divergence of parties from their alleged grounds, and that men would not stick to what they had said: that the resolutions of public bodies, and the pledges never so often given and put on record, of public men,—will not bind them. The fact comes out more plainly, that you cannot rely on any man for the defence of truth who is not constitutionally, or by blood and temperament, on that side.

In what I have to say of Mr. Webster, I do not confound him with vulgar politi-cians of his own time or since. There is always base ambition enough, men who calculate on the immense ignorance of masses of men;—that is their quarry and farm,—they use the constituences at home only for their shoes. And, of course, they can drive out from the contest any honorable man. The low can best win the low, and all men like to be made much of. There are those, too, who have power

---

1. The Pilgrims' landing at Plymouth in December 1620 was usually commemorated on the twenty-second, which is also the anniversary day of the New-England Society; the Battles of Lexington and Concord were fought on 19 April 1775, and of Bunker Hill in Boston on 17 June 1775.

and inspiration only to do ill. Their talent or their faculty deserts them when they undertake anything right.

Mr. Webster had a natural ascendancy of aspect and carriage which distinguished him over all his contemporaries. His countenance, his figure, and his manners, were all in so grand a style, that he was, without effort, as superior to his most eminent rivals, as they were to the humblest, so that his arrival in any place was an event which drew crowds of people, who went to satisfy their eyes, and could not see him enough. I think they looked at him as the representative of the American continent. He was there in his Adamitic capacity, as if he alone of all men did not disappoint the eye and ear, but was a fit figure in the landscape. I remember his appearance at Bunker Hill.[2] There was the monument, and here was Webster. He knew well that a little more or less of rhetoric signified nothing; he was only to say plain and equal things,—grand things, if he had them,—and, if he had them not, only to abstain from saying unfit things;—and the whole occasion was answered by his presence. It was a place for behavior, much more than for speech; and Webster walked through his part with entire success.

His wonderful organization, the perfection of his elocution,—and all that thereto belongs,—voice, accent, intonation, attitude, manner,—we shall not soon find again. Then, he was so thoroughly simple and wise in his rhetoric,—he saw through his matter,—hugged his fact so close,—went to the principal or essential, and never indulged in a weak flourish, though he knew perfectly well how to make such exordiums, episodes, and perorations, as might give perspective to his harangue, without in the least embarrassing his march, or confounding his transitions. In his statement, things lay in daylight;—we saw them in order as they were. Though he knew very well how to present his own personal claims, yet in his argument he was intellectual, and stated his fact pure of all personality, so that his splendid wrath, when his eyes became lamps, was the wrath of the fact and cause he stood for. His power, like that of all great masters, was not in excellent parts, but was total. He had a great and everywhere equal propriety. He had the power of countenance and the gravity of a sachem. He worked with that closeness of adhesion to the matter in hand, which a joiner or a chemist uses, and the same quiet and sure feeling of right to his place that an oak or a mountain have to theirs.

After all his talents have been described, there remains that perfect propriety which animated all the details of the action or speech with the character of the whole, so that his beauties of detail are endless. He seemed born for the bar, born for the senate, and took very naturally a leading part in large private and in pub-

2. For Daniel Webster's appearance at Bunker Hill at the dedication of the monument, see *JMN*, 8:425, and *Letters*, 3:180–81, both of which use some of the language employed in this passage.

lic affairs; for his head distributed things in their right places, and what he saw so well, he compelled other people to see also. Ah! great is the privilege of eloquence. What gratitude does every human being feel to him who speaks well for the right,—who translates truth into language entirely plain and clear!

The history of this country has given a disastrous importance to the defects of this great man's mind. Whether evil influences and the corruption of politics, or whether original infirmity, it was the misfortune of this country that with this large understanding, he had not what is better than intellect, and the essential source of its health. It is the office of the moral nature to give sanity and right direction to the mind, to give centrality and unity.

Now, it is a law of our nature that great thoughts come from the heart, that the moral is the occult fountain of genius. It was for this reason I may here say as I have said elsewhere: the sterility of thought, the want of generalization in his speeches, and the curious fact, that, with a general ability that impresses all the world, there is not a single general remark, not an observation on life and manners, not a single valuable aphorism that can pass into literature from his writings.

Four years ago tonight, on one of those critical moments in history when great issues are determined,—when the powers of right and wrong are mustered for conflict, and it lies with one man to give a casting vote,—Mr. Webster most unexpectedly threw his whole weight on the side of slavery, and caused by his personal and official authority the passage of the Fugitive Slave Bill.

It is remarked of the Americans, that they value dexterity too much and honor too little, that the Americans praise a man more by saying that he is smart than by saying that he is right. Now, whether this defect be national or not, it is the defect and calamity of Mr. Webster, and it is so far true of his countrymen, that, namely, the appeal to physical and mental ability, when his character is assailed. And his speeches on the seventh of March, and at Albany, Buffalo, Syracuse, and Boston, are cited in justification.[3] And Mr. Webster's literary editor believes that it was his own wish to rest his fame on the speech of the seventh of March. Now, though I have my own opinions on this seventh of March discourse, and those others, and think them very transparent, and very open to criticism, yet the *secondary* merits of a speech, that is, its logic, its illustration, its points, are not here in question. The primary quality of a speech is its *subject*. Nobody doubts that

3. Webster's speeches supporting his position on the Fugitive Slave Law are, for 7 March 1850, *Speech of the Hon. Daniel Webster on the Subject of Slavery* (1850; also published in 1850 as *Speech of Hon. Daniel Webster on Mr. Clay's Resolutions*); the speeches in New York State in May 1851, *Mr. Webster's Speeches at Buffalo, Syracuse, and Albany* (1851; delivered 22, 26, and 28 May, respectively; the last one was published separately as *Speech of Hon. Daniel Webster, to the Young Men of Albany* [1851]); and 20 April 1850 in Boston.

Daniel Webster could make a good speech. Nobody doubts that there were good and plausible things to be said on the part of the south. But this is not a question of ingenuity, not a question of syllogisms, but of sides. How came he there? There are always texts, and thoughts, and arguments; But it is the genius and temper of the man which decides whether he will stand for Right or for Might.

Who doubts the power of any clever and fluent man to defend either of our parties, or any cause in our courts? There was the same law in England for Jeffries, and Talbot, and Yorke to read slavery out of, and for Lord Mansfield to read freedom.⁴ And in this country one sees that there is always margin enough in the statute for a liberal judge to read one way, and a servile judge another. But the question which History will ask is broader. In the final hour, when he was forced by the peremptory necessity of the closing armies to take a side, did he take the side of great principles, the side of humanity and justice, or the side of abuse, and oppression, and chaos?

Mr. Webster decided for slavery; and *that,* when the aspect of the institution was no longer doubtful, no longer feeble and apologetic, and proposing soon to end itself, but when it was strong, and aggressive, and threatening an illimitable increase; then, he listened to stale reasons and hopes and left with much complacency, we are told, the testament of his speech to the astonished State of Massachusetts. *Vera pro gratis.*⁵ A ghastly result of all those years of experience in affairs, this, that there was nothing better for the most American man in America to tell his countrymen, than, that slavery was now at that strength, that they must beat down their conscience and become kidnappers for it. This was like the doleful speech falsely ascribed to the patriot Brutus. "Virtue, I have followed thee through life, and I find thee but a shadow."⁶

Here was a question of an immoral law—a question agitated for ages, and settled always in the same way by every great jurist, that an immoral law cannot be valid. Cicero, Grotius, Coke, Blackstone, Burlamaqui, Vattel, Burke, and Jefferson do all affirm this, and I cite them not that they can give plainness to what is so clear, but because, though lawyers and practical statesmen, they could not hide from themselves this truth.

Here was the question: Are you for man, and for the good of man; or are you for the hurt and harm of man? It was a question, whether man shall be treated as

---

4. The English jurists George Jeffreys, first baron Jeffreys of Wem (1644–89), and Charles Yorke (1722–70).

5. "Vera pro gratis" [truth rather than pleasantness] appeared as part of a Latin passage as a preface to Webster's pamphlet publication of his Seventh of March speech.

6. Attributed to Dio Cassius (ca. 155–ca. 235), Roman historian who wrote an eighty-volume history of Rome in Greek, by Edward Waldo Emerson, who gives the Greek original and provides a translation and commentary (*W,* 11:590n).

leather? Whether the negroes shall be, as the Indians were in Spanish America, a species of money? Whether this institution, which is a kind of mill or factory for converting men into monkeys, shall be upheld and enlarged? And Mr. Webster and the country went for quadruped law.

Immense mischief was done. People were all expecting a totally different course from Mr. Webster. If any man had in that hour possessed the weight with the country which he had acquired, he would have brought the whole country to its senses. But not a moment's pause was allowed. Angry parties went from bad to worse, and the decision of Webster was accompanied with everything offensive to freedom and good morals.

There was something like an attempt to debauch the moral sentiment of the clergy and of the youth. The immense power of rectitude is apt to be forgotten in politics. But they who brought this great wrong on the country, did not forget it. They wished to avail themselves of the names of men of known probity and honour to endorse the statute. The ancient maxim is still true, that never was any injustice effected except by the help of justice. Burke said, "he would pardon something to the spirit of liberty,"—but the opposition was sharply called *treason* by Webster and prosecuted so. He told the people at Boston, "they must conquer their prejudices," that "agitation of the subject of slavery must be suppressed." He did, as immoral men usually do, make very low bows to the Christian Church, and went through all the Sunday decorums; but when allusion was made to ethics, and the sanctions of morality, he very frankly said, at Albany, "Some higher law, something existing somewhere between here and the third heaven,—I do not know where." And, if the reporters say true, this wretched atheism found some laughter in the company.

I said I had never in my life suffered before from the slave institution. It was like slavery in Africa or in Japan for me. There was a fugitive law, but it had become, or was fast becoming, a dead letter and, by the genius and laws of Massachusetts, inoperative. The new Bill made it operative; required me to hunt slaves; and it found citizens in Massachusetts willing to act as judges and captors. Moreover, it disclosed the secret of the new times: that slavery was no longer mendicant, but was become aggressive and dangerous.

The way in which the country was dragged to consent to this, and the disastrous defection on the miserable cry of *Union* of the men of letters, of the colleges, of educated men, nay of some preachers of religion, shows that our prosperity had hurt us, and we cannot be shocked by crime. It showed that the old religion and the sense of right had faded and gone out; that, whilst we reckoned ourselves a highly cultivated nation, our bellies had run away with our brains, and the principles of culture and progress did not exist. For I suppose that liberty is a very accurate index in men and nations of general progress.

The theory of personal liberty must always appeal to the most refined communities and to the men of the rarest perception and of delicate moral sense. For these are rights which rest on the finest sense of justice, and with every degree of civility, personal liberty will be more truly felt and defined. A barbarous tribe of good stock will by means of their best heads secure substantial liberty. But where there is any weakness in a race, as is in the black race, and it becomes in any degree matter of concession and protection from their stronger neighbors, the incompatibility and offensiveness of the wrong will, of course, be most evident to the most cultivated. For it is—is it not—the very nature of courtesy, of politeness, of religion, of love, to prefer another, to postpone oneself, to protect another from oneself? That is the distinction of the gentleman, to defend the weak, and redress the injured, as it is of the savage and the brute to usurp and use others.

It is an old story a thousand times told—we had all clung fast to our laws, and books, and usages, and the life that was in them had glided away. And there was no watchman on the walls. The spiritual class were not aware that we were wrong. In Massachusetts, as we all know, there has always existed a predominant conservative spirit. We have more money and value of every kind than other people, and wish to keep them.

The plea on which freedom was resisted was Union. I went to certain serious men who had a little more reason than the rest, and inquired why they took this part. They told me candidly that they had no confidence in their strength to resist the democratic party in this country; that they saw plainly that all was going to the utmost verge of licence; each was vying with his neighbor to lead the party by proposing the worst measure, and they threw themselves on the extreme right as a drag on the wheel; that they knew Cuba would be had, and Mexico would be had, and they stood stiffly on conservatism, and as near to monarchy as they could, only to moderate the velocity with which the car was running down the precipice: in short, their theory was despair; the whig wisdom was only reprieve, a waiting to be the last devoured. They sided with Carolina or with Arkansas, only to make a show of whig strength, wherewith to resist a little longer this general ruin.

Gentlemen, I have a respect for conservatism. I know how deeply it is founded in our nature, and how idle are all attempts to shake ourselves free of it. We are all conservatives; all half-whig, half-democrat, in our essences; and might as well try to jump off our planet or jump out of our skins as to escape from our whiggery. There are two forces in nature by whose antagonism we exist: the power of Fate, of Fortune, the laws of the world, the order of things, or, however else we choose to phrase it,—the material necessities, on the one hand; and Will, or Duty, or Freedom, on the other. *May* and *must:* the sense of right and duty, on the one hand; and the material necessities, on the other. *May* and *must.* In vulgar politics, the whig goes for what has been, for the old necessities, for the *musts;* the reformer goes for the better, for the ideal good, for the *mays.*

But each of these parties must of necessity take in, in some manner, the principle of the other. Each wishes to cover the whole ground, to hold fast, and to advance: only, one lays the emphasis on keeping; and the other, on advancing. I, too, think the *musts* are a safe company to follow, and even agreeable. But if we are whigs, let us be whigs of nature and science, and go for *all* the necessities. Let us know that over and above all the *musts* of poverty and appetite, is the instinct of man to rise, and the instinct to love and help his brother.

Now, Gentlemen, I think we have in this hour instruction again in the simplest lesson. Events roll, millions of men are engaged, and the result is some of those first commandments which we heard in the nursery. We never get beyond our first lesson; for really the world exists, as I understand it, to teach the science of liberty, which begins with liberty from fear.

The events of this month are teaching one thing plain and clear, the worthlessness of good tools to bad workmen. Papers are of no use, resolutions of public meetings, platforms of conventions—no, nor laws, nor constitutions any more. These are all declaratory of the will of the moment and are passed with more levity and on grounds much less honorable than ordinary business transactions in the street.

You relied on the Constitution. It has not the word "slave" in it, and very good argument has shown that it would not warrant the crimes that are done under it: that with provisions so vague, for an object *not named,* and which would not be suffered to claim a barrel of sugar or a bushel of corn, the robbing of a man and all his posterity,—is effected.

You relied on the Supreme Court. The law was right; excellent law for the lambs. But what if, unhappily, the judges were chosen from the wolves, and give to all the law a wolfish interpretation? What is the use of admirable law forms and political forms, if a hurricane of party feeling and a combination of monied interests can beat them to the ground? What is the use of courts, if judges only quote authorities, and no judge exerts original jurisdiction, or recurs to first principles? What is the use of guaranties provided by the jealousy of ages for the protection of liberty,—if these are made of no effect, when a bad act of Congress finds a willing commissioner?

You relied on the Missouri Compromise: that is ridden over.[7] You relied on state sovereignty in the free states to protect their citizens. They are driven with

7. Congress had passed the Missouri Compromise on 3 March 1820. It held that Arkansas would be admitted to the Union as a slave state and Maine as a free state, and no restrictions would be set on Missouri; also, no slavery would be allowed in the future north of a latitude of 36°30′. This was repealed by the passage of the Kansas-Nebraska Act on 30 May 1854, which gave the people in each state the right to determine whether that state would be slave or free.

contempt out of the courts, and out of the territory of the slave states, if they are so happy as to get out with their lives.[8] And now, you relied on these dismal guaranties infamously made in 1850, and before the body of Webster is yet crumbled, it is found that they have crumbled: this eternal monument at once of his fame and of the common Union, is rotten in four years.[9] They are no guaranty to the free states. They are a guaranty to the slave states: that as they have hitherto met with no repulse, they shall meet with none.

I fear there is no reliance to be had on any kind of form or covenant,—no, not on sacred forms,—none on churches, none on bibles. For one would have said that a Christian would not keep slaves, but the Christians keep slaves. Of course, they will not dare read the bible. Won't they? They quote the bible, and Christ, and Paul to maintain slavery.[10] If slavery is a good, then are lying, theft, arson, incest, homicide, each and all goods and to be maintained by Union societies.

These things show that no forms, neither constitutions, nor laws, nor covenants, nor churches, nor bibles, are of any use in themselves; the devil nestles comfortably into them all. There is no help but in the head, and heart, and hamstrings of a man. Covenants are of no use without honest men to keep them. Laws are of no use, but with loyal citizens to obey them. To interpret Christ, it needs Christ in the heart. The teachings of the spirit can be apprehended only by the same spirit that gave them forth.

These events are putting it home to every man, that in him is the only bulwark against slavery:

> "None any work can frame
> Unless himself become the same."

To make good the cause of Freedom, you must draw off from all these foolish trusts on others. You must be citadels and warriors, yourselves Declarations of Independence: the charter, the battle, and the victory. Cromwell said, "We can only resist the superior training of the king's soldiers, by having godly men." And no man has a right to hope that the laws of New York will defend him from the contamination of slaves another day, until he has made up his mind that he will

8. Samuel Hoar (1778–1856), Emerson's Concord neighbor and the commissioner of Massachusetts, had been expelled in 1844 from Charleston, South Carolina, when he went to inquire about black Massachusetts citizens who had been kidnapped there. Emerson comments on this event at length in his sketch "Samuel Hoar" in *Lectures and Biographical Sketches* (1884).

9. Webster had died on 24 October 1852.

10. "The sending back of Onesimus by Paul was a precedent precious in the eyes of the pro-slavery preachers, North and South, in those days, ignoring, however, Paul's message, 'Not now as a servant, but above a servant, a brother beloved, specially to me, but how much more unto thee, both in the flesh and in the Lord. If thou count me therefore a partner, receive him as myself' (*Epistle of Paul to Philemon*, I, 16, 17)" (Edward Waldo Emerson's note, *W,* 10:590n).

not owe his protection to the laws of New York, but to his own sense and spirit. Then, he protects New York. He only who is able to stand alone, is qualified for society.

And that I understand to be the end for which a soul exists in this world: to be himself the counterbalance of all falsehood and all wrong. "The army of unright is encamped from pole to pole, but the road of victory is known to the just "[11] Everything may be taken away, he may be poor, he may be houseless, yet he will know out of his arms to make a pillow and out of his breast a bolster. Why have the minority no influence? because they have not a real minority of one.

Whenever a man has come to this mind, that there is no church for him but his believing prayer; no constitution, but his talent of dealing well and justly with his neighbor; no liberty, but his invincible will to do right, then certain aids and allies will promptly appear. For the eternal constitution of the universe is on his side.

It is of no use to vote down gravitation or morals. What is useful will last; whilst that which is hurtful to the world will sink beneath all the opposing forces which it must exasperate. The terror which the *Marseillaise* thunders against oppression, thunders today,—*Tout est soldat pour vous combattre: "Everything that can walk turns soldier to fight you down."* The end for which man was made, is not stealing, nor crime in any form. And a man cannot steal, without incurring all the penalties of the thief; no, though all the legislatures vote that it is virtuous, and though there be a general conspiracy among scholars and official persons to hold him up, and to say, *Nothing is good but stealing.* A man who commits a crime defeats the end of his existence. He was created for benefit, and he exists for harm. And as well-doing makes power and wisdom, ill-doing takes them away. A man who steals another man's labor, as a planter does, steals away his own faculties: his integrity, his humanity, is flowing away from him.

The habit of oppression cuts out the moral eyes, and though the intellect goes on simulating the moral as before, its sanity is invaded, and gradually destroyed. It takes away the presentiments. I suppose, in general, this is allowed; that, if you have a nice question of right and wrong, you would not go with it to Louis Napoleon; or to a political hack; or to a slave driver.[12] The habit of mind of traders in power would not be esteemed favorable to delicate moral perception.

It is not true that there is any exception to that in American slavery, or that the system here has called out a spirit of generosity and self-sacrifice. No excess of good nature and of tenderness of moral constitution in individuals has been able to give a new character to the system or to tear down the whipping house. The

11. Attributed to Hafiz, *Divan*, Ode XXIX, ll. 11–12 (see *JMN*, 11:233).
12. Louis Napoleon (1808–73), ruler of France for about twenty years as Napoleon III.

plea that the negro is an inferior race sounds very oddly in my ear from a slave-holder. "The masters of slaves seem generally anxious to prove that they are not of a race superior in any noble quality to the meanest of their bondmen." And, indeed, when I hear the southerner point to the anatomy of the negro, and talk of chimpanzee,—I recall Montesquieu's remark, "It will not do to say, that negroes are men, lest it should turn out that whites were not."

I conceive that thus to detach a man, and make him feel that he is to owe all to himself, is the way to make him strong and rich. And here the optimist must find, if anywhere, the benefit of slavery. We have many teachers. We are in this world for nothing else than culture: to be instructed in nature, in realities; in the laws of moral and intelligent nature; and surely our education is not conducted by toys and luxuries,—but by austere and rugged masters,—by poverty, solitude, passions, war, and slavery,—to know that paradise is under the shadow of swords; that divine sentiments, which are always soliciting us, are breathed into us from on high and are a counterbalance to an universe of suffering and crime,—that self-reliance, the height and perfection of man, is reliance on God.[13] The insight of the religious sentiment will disclose to him unexpected aids in the nature of things. The Persian Saadi said, "Beware of hurting the orphan. When the orphan sets a crying the throne of the Almighty is rocked from side to side."[14]

I know that when seen near, and in detail, slavery is disheartening. But nature is not so helpless but it can rid itself at last of every wrong. An Eastern poet, in describing the world God made pure in the beginning, said, "that God had made justice so dear to the heart of nature, that, if any injustice lurked anywhere under the sky, the blue vault would shrivel to a snakeskin and cast it out by spasms."

But the spasms of nature are centuries and ages and will tax the faith of short-lived men. Slowly, slowly the avenger comes, but comes surely. The proverbs of the nations affirm these delays, but affirm the arrival. They say, "God may consent, but not forever."[15] The delay of the Divine Justice,—this was the meaning and soul of the Greek Tragedy,—this was the soul of their religion. "There has come, too, one to whom lurking warfare is dear,—Retribution,—with a soul full of wiles, a violator of hospitality, guileful without the guilt of guile, limping, late in her arrival."—[16] "This happiness at its close begets itself an offspring, and does not die childless, and instead of good fortune, there sprouts forth for posterity ever-ravening calamity."[17]

13. "Paradise is under the shadow of swords," quoted from Mohammed, was used as the epigraph to "Heroism" in *Essays: First Series* (1841).

14. The Persian poet Saadi, also known as Muslih-ud-Din (ca. 1184–ca. 1291), a longtime favorite of Emerson, who wrote a preface to an 1865 edition of *The Gulistan or Rose Garden*.

15. Attributed to a "Spanish Proverb" (see *JMN*, 13:82).

16. Quoted from *Choephoroi* by Aeschylus (525–456 B.C.), Athenian tragic dramatist.

17. Aeschylus, *Agamemnon*.

> For evil word, shall evil word be said,
> For murderstroke, a murderstroke be paid,
> Who smites must smart.

These delays,—you see them now in the temper of the times. The national spirit in this country is so drowsy and preoccupied with interest, deaf to principle. The Anglo-Saxon race is proud and strong, but selfish. They believe only in Anglo-Saxons. Greece found it deaf, Poland found it so, Italy found it so, Hungary found it so. England goes for trade, not for liberty; goes against Greece; against Hungary; against Schleswig-Holstein; against the French Republic whilst it was yet a republic.[18] To faint hearts the times offer no invitation, and the like torpor exists here throughout the active classes on the subject of domestic slavery and its appalling aggressions.

Yes, that is the stern edict of Providence, that liberty shall be no hasty fruit, but that event on event, population on population, age on age, shall cast itself into the opposite scale, and not until liberty has slowly accumulated weight enough to countervail and preponderate against all this, can the sufficient recoil come. All the great cities, all the refined circles, all the statesmen,—Guizot, Palmerston, Webster, Calhoun,—are sure to be found banded against liberty; they are all sure to be found befriending liberty with their words, and crushing it with their votes.[19]

It is made difficult, because freedom is the accomplishment and perfectness of a man. He is a finished man, earning and bestowing good equal to the world at home and in nature and dignifying that; the sun does not see anything nobler, and has nothing to teach him. Therefore, mountains of difficulty must be surmounted, wiles of seduction, dangers, stern trials met, healed by a quarantine of calamities to measure his strength by, before he dare say, I am free. And in the School of Providence, in the unknown paths of him who made and maketh us, him before whom ages, and dynasties, and Saxon races flee as snows before his forming wind, who knows but Nebraska and the calamities it is now menaced with are the schoolbooks, the pains, and the mortifications.

Whilst the inconsistency of slavery with the principles on which the world is built guarantees its downfall, I own that the patience it requires is almost too sublime for mortals and seems to demand of us more than mere hoping. And when one sees how fast the rot spreads,—it is growing serious,—I think we demand of superior men that they shall be superior in this, that the mind and the virtue give

18. Schleswig-Holstein, a province of Prussia, had recently engaged in a war with Denmark (1848–50).

19. Henry John Temple, Viscount Palmerston (1784–1865), English statesman and prime minister; John Caldwell Calhoun (1782–1850), South Carolina congressman, senator, and champion of states' rights.

their verdict in their day and accelerate so far the progress of civilization. Possession is sure to throw its stupid strength for existing power; and appetite and ambition will go for *that*. Let the aid of virtue, and intelligence, and education be cast where they rightfully belong. They are organically ours. Let them be loyal to their own. English Earl Grey said, on a memorable occasion, "he should stand by his order."[20] And I wish to see the instructed or illuminated class know their own flag, and not stand for the kingdom of darkness. We should not forgive the Clergy of a country, for taking on every issue the immoral side. Nor the Bench, if it throw itself on the side of the culprit. Nor the Government, if it sustain the mob against the laws.

It is an immense support and ally to a brave man standing single or with few for the right, to know, when outvoted, and discountenanced, and ostracised in that hour and place, yet better men in other parts of the country appreciate the service, and will rightly report him to his own age and to posterity. And without this assurance he will sooner sink; "If they do not care to be defended," he may well say, "I too will decline the controversy, from which I only reap invectives and hatred."

Yet the lovers of liberty may tax with reason the coldness and indifferentism of the scholars and literary men. They are lovers of liberty in Greece, and in Rome, and in the English Commonwealth, but they are very lukewarm lovers of the specific liberty of America in 1854. The universities are not now as in Hobbes's time, the core of rebellion; no, but the seat of whiggery.[21] They have forgotten their allegiance to the muse and grown worldly and political. I remember, I listened on one of those occasions when the university chooses one of her distinguished sons to return from the political arena, believing that senators and statesmen are glad to throw off the harness and to dip again in the Castalian pools.[22] But if audiences forget themselves, statesmen do not. The low bows to all the crockery gods of the day were duly made. Only in one part of the discourse the orator allowed to transpire, rather against his will, a little sober sense. It was this.

I am, as you see, a man virtuously inclined and only corrupted by my profession of politics. I should prefer the right side. You gentlemen of these literary and scientific schools have the power to make your verdict clear and prevailing. Had you done so, you would have found me its glad organ and champion. Abstractly, I should have preferred that side. But you have not done it. You have not spoken out. You have failed to arm me. I can only deal with masses as I find them. Abstractions are not for me. I go, then, for such parties and opinions as have provided me with a

---

20. Charles Grey, second Earl Grey (1764–1845), English statesman.
21. Thomas Hobbes (1588–1679), English philosopher.
22. The Castalian Spring on Mount Parnassus in Greece was sacred to the Muses and Apollo in ancient times.

working apparatus. I give you my word, not without regret, that I was first for you, and though I am now to deny and condemn you, you see it is not my will, but the party necessity.[23]

Having made this manifesto, and professed his adoration for liberty in the time of his grandfathers, he proceeded with his work of denouncing freedom and freemen at the present day, much in the tone and spirit with which Lord Bacon prosecuted his benefactor Essex.[24] He denounced every name and aspect under which liberty and progress dared show itself in this age and country, but with a lingering conscience which qualified each sentence with a recommendation to mercy: death, with a recommendation to mercy.

But I put it to every noble and generous spirit in the land; to every poetic; to every heroic; to every religious heart; that not so is our learning, our education, our poetry, our worship to be declared: not by heads reverted to the dying Demosthenes, Luther, or Wallace, or to George Fox, or to George Washington, but to the dangers and dragons that beset the United States at this time.[25] It is not possible to extricate oneself from the questions in which your age is involved. I hate that we should be content with standing on the defensive. Liberty is aggressive. Liberty is the crusade of all brave and conscientious men. It is the epic poetry, the new religion, the chivalry of all gentlemen. This is the oppressed Lady whom true knights on their oath and honor must rescue and save.

Now, at last, we are disenchanted and shall have no more false hopes. I respect the Antislavery Society. It is the Cassandra that has foretold all that has befallen, fact for fact, years ago,—foretold it all, and no man laid it to heart.[26] It seemed, as the Turks say, "Fate makes that a man should not believe his own eyes." But the Fugitive Law did much to unglue the eyes of men, and now the Nebraska Bill leaves us staring. The Antislavery Society will add many members this year. The Whig party will join it. The Democrats will join it. The population of the Free States will join it. I doubt not, at last, the slave states will join it. But be that sooner or later,—and whoever comes or stays away,—I hope we have come to an end of our unbelief, have come to a belief that there is a Divine Providence in the world which will not save us but through our own cooperation.

23. Edward Waldo Emerson notes that the "occasion alluded to was Hon. Robert C. Winthrop's speech to the alumni of Harvard College on Commencement Day in 1852. What follows is not an abstract, but Mr. Emerson's rendering of the spirit of his address" (*W*, 10:592n). Actually, much of this passage is based on Emerson's contemporaneous account in *JMN*, 13:71–73. Robert Charles Winthrop (1809–94), congressman and senator from Massachusetts.

24. Francis Bacon (1561–1626) was befriended early in his career by the courtier Robert Devereux, second earl of Essex (1567–1601), but later served as a witness for the prosecution in Essex's trial for treason.

25. William Wallace (ca. 1270–1305), Scottish national hero.

26. Cassandra, in Greek myth, was given the gift of prophecy by Apollo, but when she refused his advances, he cursed her by having no one believe her predictions.

# "An Address to the Adelphic Union
of Williamstown College,
15 August 1854"
*and*
"An Address to the Social Union
of Amherst College,
8 August 1855"
(1854–1857)

Emerson delivered his untitled discourse on 15 August 1854 before the Adelphic Union of Williamstown (now Williams) College in Williamstown, Massachusetts. He repeated it on 8 August 1855 before the Social Union as part of the commencement exercises at Amherst College in Amherst, Massachusetts. Titled "The Scholar," Emerson delivered the lecture on 1 May 1856 as the sixth in a series of six private lectures at the Freeman Place Chapel in Boston; on 5 February 1857 before the Adelphian Union at Antioch College in Yellow Springs, Ohio; on 6 February 1857 as the fourth in a series of four lectures at the Unitarian Church in Cincinnati, Ohio. This lecture has never been published.

Emerson wrote his address especially for the Adelphic Union; as of 28 July, it was still "not ready" (*Letters*, 4:454). He received $50 for expenses ("Account Books"). The *North Adams (Massachusetts) Weekly Transcript* described the oration as "Emerson all over" and its topic as "an examination of the scholar's duty" (17 August 1854, quoted in *Letters*, 4:455n), and the *Pittsfield (Massachusetts) Culturalist & Gazette* wrote that as "an orator, we think the less said of him the better; but as an essayist, we heartily acknowledge his power" (23 August 1854, 2). One member of the audience was a future president of the United States, James A. Garfield, who wrote of the occasion: "he is the most startlingly original thinker I ever heard. The bolt which he hurls against error, like Goethe's cannon-ball goes 'fearful and straight shattering that it may reach and shattering what it reaches.' I could not sleep that night after hearing his thunderstorm of eloquent thoughts. It made *me* feel small and insignificant to hear *him*"; and Garfield later told a friend that "he dated his intellectual life" from the time of Emerson's lecture (Theodore Clarke Smith, *The Life and Letters of James Abram Garfield*, 2 vols. [New Haven, Conn.: Yale University Press, 1925], 1:76). Similarly, the Unitarian minister Theodore Clapp noted that the "views of this great man on religion have been either grossly misunderstood, or misrepresented," for he was "not an atheist any more than Dr. Channing was." Indeed, he was "simply opposed to hypocrisy, cant, pretence, assumption, bigotry and humbug" (reprinted from the *New Orleans Picayune* in Kenneth Walter Cameron, "Theodore Clapp on Emerson's Williamstown Address," *American Transcendental Quarterly*, no. 2 [2nd quarter 1969]: 37–38).

A year later, Emerson was invited by James C. Parsons, secretary of the Social Union (a combination of the two undergraduate literary societies), to lecture at Amherst College during the commencement ceremonies; he accepted within the month (*Letters*, 4:511). The audience was disappointed because Henry Ward Beecher was unable to come as promised, but Frederick Dan Huntington substituted with a lecture on "Common Sense" (Emerson had also volunteered to substitute for Beecher; see *JMN*, 13:509). According to the *New York Times*, Emerson, who followed Huntington, "seemed to feel himself challenged. . . . [H]e amply avenged himself on common sense. His address is said to be the same he delivered a year or two since at Williams College." The audience's response was interesting: "All were astonished. Those who were sure they understood him certainly were mistaken. . . . Others waited for him to come to his subject—waited an hour, arose and walked out. Some wondered whether the loose leaves on which the oration was written were arranged by chance or by design. . . . But most regretted the leaves he passed without reading, and that the conclusion came so soon" ("Amherst College," 21 August 1855, 2). The *Hampshire and Franklin Express* described the subject as "A Plea for the Scholar" and said Emerson was "too comprehensive and metaphysical to be at all times easily understood. But there was one visible defect in his performance—it had neither beginning, nor middle, and so of every other part. It was a series of subtle-minded, comprehensive, epigrammatic, detached thoughts" (10 August 1855, reprinted in George F. Whicher, "Uriel in Amherst," *Amherst Graduates Quarterly* 23 [August 1934]: 285).

In Boston the lecture formed part of a financially successful series, from which Emerson garnered $772.36 ("Account Books"). He even asked one of the organizers to arrange for extra chairs to be placed in the aisles for latecomers (*Letters*, 5:20). When proposing the lecture series in March, Emerson offered as the final lecture either "The Scholar" or "'Stonehenge,' which describes an excursion with Mr Carlyle" (*Letters*, 8:476). He finally decided on "The Scholar," which, he felt, "did very well" (*Letters*, 5:54).

The following year, while on a midwestern lecture tour, Emerson was able to deliver "The Scholar" twice. He was scheduled to go to Cincinnati under the auspices of Moncure Daniel Conway for a series that would pay him $330 ("Account Books"). However, he did not decide on including "The Scholar" until 27 January, when he telegraphed Lidian to send the manuscript to him (*Letters*, 5:60). When he received the manuscript on 3 February, Emerson realized that the lecture would do well at nearby Antioch College, where his old friends Horace (the college's president) and Mary Peabody Mann had urged him to come (*Letters*, 8:521n). Thus, the lecture easily did double duty. Writing to the *Daily Cincinnati Gazette*, "Abracadabra" described Emerson as "one good looking Yankee, with a long nose, spouting pantheism, nonsense, mist and mud"; this attack was so personal that it called forth a defense of Emerson from "St. Dunstan" a few days later ("About Mr. Emerson," 7 February 1855, 1, 13 February 1855, 1). On the other hand, the *Cincinnati Times* found "The Scholar" to have given "true satisfaction" to the audience during its hour-and-a-half delivery (7 February 1855, quoted in Louise Hastings, "Emerson in Cincinnati," *New England Quarterly* 11 [September 1938]: 460–61).

James Elliot Cabot, with Ellen Emerson's assistance, mined Emerson's "Address" delivered before the Adelphi Union of Williamstown College on 15 August 1854 and before the Social Union at Amherst College on 8 August 1855 and "The Scholar" (1863) for major portions of an address that Emerson delivered at the University of Virginia in 1876. Cabot eventually printed the University of Virginia address as "The Scholar" in *Lectures and Biographical Sketches* in 1884 (see *W*, 10:259–89 and the headnote to "The Scholar").

G ENTLEMEN,
In obeying your invitation, I yield to the pleasant custom of the season. And now, when the fields admonish us that the year has turned, and is "hasting to the hollows where the frosts of winter lie," I join you in the gathering of the academic harvest. Nature looks kindly on. These are the best days of the year. The mountains stand around, like galleries; the old constellations climb the Zodiack;—

The grass is mown, the corn is reaped, autumnal stars arise.[1]

And if we, in our capacity of scholars, unroll the scrolls of fame; whisper to one another the old and awful secrets of our fraternity; blow aside the ashes, and read the handwriting that flames on the wall of memory; we shall be more truly in Nature, and speak at once for her and the Muse.

The United Societies, whose festival we keep, were formed "for the literary improvement of the members." So, I shall not travel out of my assigned path, if I read a lesson to Scholars, a *concio ad clerum* to the priests of the intellect.[2] And, though, in this country, where the State connects itself with no church, every man is a sect of one, and a man of the right religion in his own district may find himself a heretic in the next county,—Yet, I venture to premise, that you shall find me one of the true Catholic church in letters; orthodox as Milton, or Aristotle, or Plato, in my strict belief in the Intellectual Power,—and that I carry my faith in its attributes, to as high a point as any.

The Scholars are an organic caste or class in the State. They are paid to read, paid to think. Society has an obstinate persuasion, that there is a benefit to which all our works and livings tend,—some ulterior wisdom. For all the hypocrites, for all the charlatans, it has not relinquished the conviction, that the world exists to some good yet unknown and undescribed. Men toil and sweat; forge iron; dig

1. Emerson quotes himself (see *JMN*, 5:352).
2. The expression "concio ad clerum" is not accurate Latin. Emerson probably meant to imply "stir up the clergy."

the earth; sail the sea; earn money; save; consent to menial service and to servile compliance;—all to raise themselves out of the necessity of being menial and overborne; to put themselves on a plane where they can breathe, and look about them and above them, and judge of this believed good. For this, they educate their children,—to expiate their own short-comings. I serve, I am blind, I am dunce and slave; but my child shall be free to choose; he shall see and know; I adjourn my life, I will live in him.

Fine arts, libraries, colleges, churches, poetry, romance, music, and the love of these, attest the respect to what is ulterior;—to theism, to thought, which super-exist by the same elemental necessity as flame above fire, or as centre to sphere. Our Anglo-Saxon society is a great industrial corporation. It sees very well the rules indispensable to success. You must make trade everything. Trade is not to know friends, or wife, or child, or country: That were weak sentimentalism.— But this walking ledger, knows, that, though he, poor fellow, has put off his royal rights, somewhere the noble humanity survives, with head unshorn of its redun-dant locks, with heart undried of its rivers of generous blood,—and he keeps his eye on this distant hope

These men have a secret persuasion that, as little as they pass for in the world, they are immensely rich in expectancy and power. The best part of truth is cer-tainly not that which a man can define;—but that which hovers in gleams and suggestions unpossessed before him. His recorded knowledge is dead and cold. But this chorus of thoughts and hopes,—these dawning truths, like great stars, just lifting themselves into his horizon, they are his future, and console him for the ridiculous brevity and meanness of his street life.

He knows the conditions of vulgar success,—that a devotion to means with-out reference to any end, is the sole safe method. But he has not been able to hide from himself, that this is a kind of absurdity,—is prescribing amputation for headache,—is, for a livelihood, to defeat the ends of living: *Propter vitam vivendi perdere causas.*[3] And, it is out of the wish to preserve sanity, in time to come, to find out how the minor propositions may be established, without throwing over-board the major proposition; how not to lose the troop, in his care for the bag-gage; that he has said, Let there be schools, a clergy, art, music, poetry.

This is the foundation of the school and college,—this religion, in those who are not professionally religious,—the love and hope of learning, in those who are not learned,—this belief, that there exists a sphere outside of their sphere. They have put their beatitude in abeyance, and they testify their fealty by this spend-ing for the college and clerisy. Had they believed otherwise, had they disbelieved

3. Quoted from *Satura VIII,* l. 84, by Juvenal (ca. 60 – ca. 140), Roman satirist. The passage says that if you are called as a witness in a case whose outcome is uncertain, even if Phalaris the tyrant gives you the choice of lying or being burned alive, consider it the worst sin of all to prefer life to honor, and "for the sake of life to lose all the reasons for living."

in the intellect, they would have spent their money in a different way. They would have founded a hotel, a public garden, a riding-school, a bull fight, a cook-shop, or a Fourier phalanstery to secure the greatest possible amount of kissing.

Now, whether these men were right in their belief?—

It is true, that, while it is the distinction of man to think, few men think truly. But there are, in every society of well-born men, souls which apprehend things so correctly, that they seem to have been in the counsel of Nature. Their understanding seems to transform itself into the image of the thing understood, and *that*, not as a passive mirror, but as a living cause: so that, they cannot only describe a thing as it is, but can follow its genesis like a creator.

They have the generalizing and ascending effort, which, even in chemistry, finds not atoms, at last, but spherules of force;—which measures and differences minds, as they can take strides of advance,—as if one mind could only take one step; another could take two or three; another, many. And there are minds, which do not sit down in any finality; which neither gold, nor love of antiquity, nor old age can tame, or clip the wings of, but which, like Ulysses, sail the sea, and discover and project, as long as they remain in our sight.

For man does not love fences. Each farmer covets the land that joins his own: And, in mind, there is always a better thought waiting for us. What we call the bounds of nature, are only the limits of our organs: The microscope detects the eye of an invisible infusory; but it cannot reach to what the infusory sees. The microscope saw far; the infusory sees farther. There are no finalities in nature. The Torricellian tube was thought to make a vacuum. But no; over the mercury is the vapor of mercury. The pores of glass, the pores of gold, are as wide to the mysterious ether and the elemental forces, as the chimney of a volcano. Our arctic voyagers, as if obeying the laws of mind, are now seeking, beyond the polar barrier, a Polynia, or open sea, north of the north. And in the mind, every thought leads in another thought by the hand; every generalization shows the way to a larger: and every reform is only a cover under which a larger reform that dares not yet name itself advances.

Meantime, this costly result was to be obtained, according to the traditions of mankind, only by unbroken meditation, by solitude, and by exemption from toils and cares. "These applications of the wit and mind," says Milton, "are tender things: they do not fancy the sun and the crowd, but delight in shade and retirement. Like noble and delicate maidens, they must rather be kept safe at home, than brought forth into engagements and perils." And, therefore, the cloisters of the college were built.

The college is founded, the youths are assembled, the contests are prepared: But, lately, with this unlucky experience, that, the youths looking over the college-wall at the lives and houses of their founders,—and I mean by the *Founders* not only the donors of Halls and Libraries, but I call every poor man, who, in farm or shop, pinches himself to educate liberally his son, a founder,—make the mistake of imitating them: They are commercial. They are finer merchants, grammatical planters, Latin Democrats, Greek Whigs, philosophic brokers,—really steering in the same course, weaving the same web, selling Vermont Centrals and Erie bonds in a masquerade of college gowns and liberal professions.— To the no small disappointment of the good founders, who may well say, 'We paid you, that you might not be merchants. We bought and sold to the very end that you should not buy and sell, but reveal the reason of trade. We did not want apes of us, but guides and commanders!'

They wished piety,—inspiration, somebody who could climb where they could not,—could fly, if it were possible, to heavenly domes; could sing, as they had heard of singing; could talk better far than singing; people to love, people to die for; O, for such, they would spend money like water.— Not for these hucksters and jobbers.—

This treason in the counsellor, this atheism of the priest, this prose in the poet.— On what wheel shall they be broken? What gallows, heaven-high, shall hang them?

This false shame in the Scholars, this cowardice and succumbing before material greatness, which is nothing but the work of their own hands,—is a treason one knows not how to excuse.— The inventor recoiling before his invention.— Shall the gunsmith be afraid to fire his gun? Will the farmer run from the scarecrow he has stuck in his field? Shall the Scholar hold himself cheap, in a bank, or in a Senate? Let him stand by his order. They who put them there, knew what they did,—they followed a wise instinct,—and put them there for kings and priests, and not for mean men.

This dereliction is of so grave an effect on the literary class and on society at large, that, if it is not to be looked on as a piece of Fate,—I should think it the one sin that breeds all other sins: And I should address myself to the work of reform, by opening, as I could, the excellences of that power which the unworthy scholar betrays.

I have observed that the complexion of college festivals is not literary, but political; that the university plays a very pale and permitted part in its own halls. A man of letters would not feel attracted, and would find himself as much out of place as at the Board of Brokers. I share the disgust of society, in seeing our diplomas ridiculous, because they do not follow learning, but seem to be filled out at the suggestion of the Whig or Democratic Committee of the nearest county town.

And the tendency is to require a commonsense not of the high kind, but a low commonsense; a commercial education; to aim at vulgar power. The right scale is reversed. They wish to put the eternal to commercial uses. The talent that is cultivated for success, becomes a breadwinner, but no muse.

But I, Gentlemen, wish to see the college put on quite another foundation. I wish the college not to make you rich or great; No, but the reverse: The college is to show you the riches of the poor; to shame the vain; to show you that the common daylight is worth something; to show you that the material pomps and possessions,—that the cities, mills, farming, institutions, nations, history, are bubbles filled only and colored by the divine air which men blow into them, and that these, at their best, are poor things, which you will not prize at the same rate, when you have learned that you can create better: for day and night, the arch of the sky, and the balls that roll forevermore in space, nourishing all their kinds, are only bubbles blown by the same divine air which through men's organs made these secondary toys.

Until we have intellectual property in a thing, we have no right property. That is the law of the world. As to first coming and finding, there were comers and finders before you already in occupation. There was the bird, the beaver, the buffalo, and the fox. But there were meliorations these could not reach; obstructions they could not surmount: when nature adds difficulty, she adds brain. That gave a more penetrating possession of properties these could not reach. He has who uses: Not the man who plays with the loadstone, and draws tin fishes through a bowl of water, has it; but he who detects the directive faculty hid in that wise pebble, and steers by it on the stormy sea. He who sees new relations in old thoughts; he in whose hand the dry staff blossoms again. He who begins at home, dates from his own heart and mind, and proceeds outward. He who teaches that when you steer for Italy, and Athens, and the East, you unlearn what you know. He teaches that the spot of earth under the zenith and over the nadir of the universe is your own house, and that today is the age of ages.

I might show you the interest that attaches to the name of every poor mortal, whose lungs one breath of poetry dilated. To the traveller in Italy and Greece, who is it the horizon and the landscape speak of, day by day? They never mention their owner, or their digger. Superciliously, they forget these, and fill him with hints of men and women who owned no acre, and had no practical faculty, as we say. The poet cannot bring you in October a poor bushel of beans, yet he takes precedence of all the producers of the economist. I read, in Wood's *Athenæ Oxonienses*, a score of pages treating of learned nobodies, of whose once odoriferous reputations not a trace remains in the air; and I come to the name of some Lovelace, Carew, Herrick, Suckling, Chapman,—which is as fresh and modern as those of our friends in Boston and London; and all because they could turn a verse.[4]

4. Anthony à Wood, *Athenæ Oxonienses: An Exact History of All the Writers and Bishops Who Have Had Their Education in the University of Oxford from 1500 to 1690* (1691–92, 1721); the English Cavalier poets Richard Lovelace (1618–58), Thomas Carew (ca. 1595–ca. 1639), and Sir John Suckling (1609–ca. 1642); George Chapman (ca. 1559–1634), English poet, dramatist, and translator of Homer.

Everything is rushing to reality.— The air and water that stream invisibly around us,—are rushing to fix and solidify themselves in timber, in animals, in mineral forms: every thought of the heart hastens to be extended by the fingers' ends; every abstraction tends to become a fact.

If I should celebrate the functions of the scholar, I might show you,

First, All the feats of our civility are from them;

Second, That society cannot spare the cultivated man;

Third, The power and glory of poets;

Fourth, The realism of science,—its gravitation,—that the generalizers are *ipso facto* nobles.

Well, not to make you Cornelius Agrippas, not to kill you with ambition like Bulwer-Lytton. Above all, not to make low Englishmen of you. The brilliant but shallow Macaulay, who expresses the tone of the English governing classes of today, explicitly teaches that *good* means *good to eat*; that the true and shining merit of modern philosophy is fruit: to yield economical inventions, to avoid ideas, to avoid morals, but to make a better wine-whey for an invalid, and a better sick chair.[5] And, thus, the Intellect is believed to exist mainly as a stewpan. Another's wide-spread skepticism, it is easy to see in Europe and America.

It is certain that the order of the planets is not more exact than the order of thought; that water does not rise in the rose tree, or fall in the beds of rivers, by more sure law, than the gravitation of opinion and belief. Metternich said truly, "Revolutions begin in the upper classes, and descend to the lower." Yes, if he meant, in the best heads. Men do not go to the President of the Academy for their list of books. They read what they like. They learn what they do not already know. Only those above them can give them this. These also do likewise,—read only such as know more than they. Thus, we all depend, at last, on the few heads, on the one head, that is nearest to the stars,—nearest to the fountain-head of all science. And knowledge runs steadily down from class to class, down to the lowest people, from the highest, as water does.

I call those persons who can make a generalization, provided also they have an equal spirit, masters. All the rest, in palaces or in lanes, are journeymen. Thus Picard, who knows how to measure a degree on the earth's surface: Harvey, who alone in the world sees the motion of the blood; Vauban, who knows how to make a river and the rain irrigate Versailles; Adam Smith, who sees liberty in trade; Oken and Saint-Hilaire, whose thought classifies the animated creation; Archimedes, Copernicus, Laplace, in physics; Napoleon in government: these I call nobles, because they know something originally of the world.[6] All the grand

5. Thomas Babington Macaulay, first Baron Macaulay (1800–1859), English historian, essayist, and poet.

6. Jean Picard (1620–82), French Roman Catholic priest and astronomer who measured the arc of a meridian of the Earth; William Harvey (1578–1657), English anatomist and physiologist known for

*seigneurs* who prate after them, and do the thing in little, which they formulated and did once for all, are of no account. I call these nobles, because they know something originally of the world; are of that stem of which the world came. If the sun were extinguished, and the solar system deranged, there is that in these men's minds, which could begin to replace it. My proposition is, that all right masters are real by virtue of following their natural bias, and doing that which they can know and do better than other men.

That is the reason why, when a good book is published, though not ten people in the world are fit to read it, and though, perhaps, there never are more than ten people in the world at one time who can read its entire sense, yet it takes its right place in the libraries, and in public esteem, as surely as wheat does among grains, or perfect female beauty in any assembly of men.

Nay, you shall let me call to witness the neology of our times. I shall say that the extraordinary delusions of the day show that the spirit of the age, and its best thought,—the very night-mares, as they go, can read it. Nay, the very rats and mice seem to know which is the great religious genius of the last ages. For now, at these midnight mahogany tables at which people fumble all through the land,—whoever is questioned,—Plato, or Benjamin Franklin, or Beau Brummel, or Jeremy Bentham, or Doctor Channing, or Rammohun Roy,—Swedenborg always replies.[7] This is the cow from which all the milk comes. I mean that the new religious philosophy, which is all that is worth regarding in the thousand forms of folly,—is all of a piece, and can be traced home to him.

'Tis wonderful, the swift and secret channels, through which thought can pass, and appear at either pole, and at the antipodes. And, as I hold it certain, that men of aim ought to rule the aimless; that those who see the real order of things, ought to control the blind and fantastic persons; I remark with joy this natural ascendency.

Do you not see the great mystery of the world, this namely, that men are frail and casual receptacles,—that it is thoughts which make them great and strong? The power of one man over another man, over multitudes of men, is in the grasp he has of a thought, which is also in their minds, but less firmly held. It is vain to plant cannon, or navies, or cities, against it. It is vain to slay the believers. For they are only the frail and casual tents in which certain invulnerable, immortal beliefs lodge for a day. These flit from chief to chief, from army to army, from race to race. They persuade thousands to speak, and work, and fight for them.

---

his work detailing how the blood circulates; Sébastien Le Prestre, marquis de Vauban (1633–1707), the Frenchman who founded the first engineering corps.

7. George Bryan (Beau) Brummell (1778–1840), leader of fashionable society in early-nineteenth-century London; Jeremy Bentham (1748–1832), English reformer and utilitarian philosopher; Rammohun Roy (ca. 1774–1833), Indian religious reformer who corresponded with the American Unitarians.

The nimble thought turns all their heads in one direction, and sweeps them in an irresistible current to its will and aim. It seizes every man by his faculty; sparkles in his expression; flows into what talent he has, and exalts that. Can he build, or argue, or fight, or sail for it, or pour it into Tyrtaean songs, or *Marseillaise* ode, or strategize it into grim campaigns, or codify it into popular laws?

Therefore we say, that History is nothing but the fortunes of a few ideas; that the joyful beholding of some idea which a people were ripe to receive, brought up their action to more than they were yet capable of:—whether love for a hero and his line; or some dim sense of justice, or liberty; or theism, impure or pure; modern equality, and war against privilege; or a war of races;—it is still not a man, but a day-dream, which builds the fort, mixes sulphur and saltpetre, equips the colony, and writes the laws.

There is no pit of earth and no obscurity of time can hide you. You are dear and necessary to the human race. Every circumstance attached to you has light shed on it. Your loves, your quarrels, interest mankind. "The poet wounded," says Firdousi, "writes a satire, and it remains to the morning of the Resurrection." [8]

The poet writes his verse on a scrap of paper, and instantly the desire and love of all mankind take charge of it, as if it were Holy Writ. What need has he to cross the sill of his door? Why need he meddle with politics? His idlest thought, his yesternight's dream, is told already in the senate. What the Genius whispered him at night, he reported to the young men at dawn. He rides in them; he traverses sea and land. The engineer in the locomotive is waiting for him; the steamboat is hissing at the wharf, and the wheels whirling to go.

'Tis wonderful, 'tis almost scandalous, this extraordinary favoritism shown to poets. I do not mean to excuse it. I admit the enormous partiality. It only shows that such is the gulf between our perception and our painting; the eye is so wise, and the hand so clumsy,—that the whole human race have agreed to value a man according to his power of expression. Is it a belief that a power of expression betrays a deeper health, and a nearness to the fountain, and that he who can speak the unspeakable is nearer to God who doeth the impossible? But come how it will, here is the fact, and this fame or hospitality of all men to a poet's verse stands me in good stead—to illustrate the penetration and longevity of thought. Hafiz—

> "Go follow my sonnet's flight,
> Follow, who can, its fleet career,
> A child begot in a night,
> That lives to the thousandth, thousandth year."

8. Firdausi or Firdousi or Firdusi (ca. 941–1020), Persian poet.

There are many arguments against literature; but one verse of a poem will blow them all out of memory. Some men may fancy they do not like poetry; but they are poetically made; and whatever obstructions may stuff our ears for this present, each knows that tunes exist which his feet must obey. Every man will dance when the music reaches him. All the fables of Orpheus, or of Odin's songsmiths, or of the Pied Piper of Hamelin,—who, if Verstegan say true, piped not only the rats into the river, but the children and the men also must follow him as they might;—are only figures, under which the real power of poetry is described.[9] Ah! we all know more of it, than we care to own,—the oldest and severest,—let alone the graduates of tomorrow,—can remember what the morning woods and solitudes have sung to them,—what we hated, and what we preferred.

Yonder lone pastures, and springs, and mountain-heads, I am sure, could tell me many a tale of the youth who traversed them,—

> Slighting Minerva's learned tongue,
> Yet leaped with joy, when on the wind, the shell of Clio rung.[10]

And there is never a fine aspiration, not the first perception of likeness or difference in a poet's mind, but is on its way to its body or incarnation in history; and the only question is, when will your law get legs?

Society cannot do without cultivated men. They who build cities, and lay out the map of counties and of states, build and lay all out for the scholars and most accomplished men of their time. For they must have company; They cannot live with oxen. They want what you know; they want arts, languages, taste, perception, history, mathematics, wit. Palaces are nothing but stone barns, until they are animated and made majestic by great and educated men.

Is not an accomplished and cultivated man worth something? There is always, whispers the Muse, admittance for you to the great; since the nobles wish to be more noble.

Far be it from me to complain of aristocratic exclusiveness. Nobody wants dull people, after once they have tasted the joy of living with quick and fine persons. Where is the palace in England, that is not too happy if it can make a home for Pope, or Addison, or Swift, or Burke, or Canning, or Scott or Tennyson?[11]

It was said of Balzac what, to be sure, is partly to be credited to the prevalence of the French language, as well as the popularity of this novelist, that Europe was his park and pleasure-ground. When he travelled, he did not need the freedom of cities to be presented to him. In whatever kingdom or state he chanced to find

---

9. Odin, the supreme deity of Norse mythology; Richard Verstegan (pseudonym of Richard Rolands) (1565–1620), English antiquarian.

10. Emerson, "Fragments on the Poet and the Poetic Gift," *W*, 9:334.

11. Joseph Addison (1672–1719), English essayist, poet, and statesman.

himself, at the close of day, he had only to look around him and select the fairest mansion in sight, turn his steps thither, knock at the door, and announce his name, to be welcomed by bands of his friends and admirers. No matter what was the language of the country, in Bohemia, in Poland, in Sweden, in Germany, in Spain, they were *his* people who lived there.

How was it with Humboldt? If the French novelist would be greeted wherever French could be understood, Humboldt would find his friends and disciples wherever the name of science was known. Or, if wealth has humours, and wishes to shake off the yoke and assert itself,— O, by all means let it try! Will it build its fences very high, and make its almacles too narrow for a wise man to enter? Will it be independent? I incline to concede the isolation which it asks, that it may learn that it is not independent, but parasitical.

I might show you the scale, or order of degrees, through which society is fed with that wisdom it has. Such is the interest which attaches to particular men. The light by which we see in this world comes out from the soul of the observer. Wherever any noble sentiment dwelt, it made the faces and houses shine. Men perish by millions in Indostan, in China, like mice and rats, but, in those burning plains, when a school of profound hermits had reached the vast generalizations of the *Bhagvad Geeta*, which is the highest intellectual expression of theism—as the Hebrews had the highest moral—India is a mystery and a dwelling of gods. Every inch of Palestine is dear to human nature, because of the blessed feet which walked in its sands and rocks for a season. When we are wise, every book streams with universal light: Joy and sorrow are radiations from us. Nay, the powers of this busy shop of the brain are miraculous and illimitable. There are the rules and formulas by which the whole empire of matter is worked. It feels the antipodes and the pole as much as its limbs. Nay, the powers of the instrument, as measured by these dangerous indications, reach to the neighboring heavens, and the spheres of astronomy pre-exist in the spheres of the mind.

Now, Gentlemen, with all these fine facts,—which all accept as the commonplaces of literature, when they are said in college, and which yet are pale and cold compared with our private experience when we have been happy in thought, it is yet true what I said, that the scholar is worldly; the times are unspiritual; that this great ocean which, in itself is always equal and full, in regard to men ebbs and flows,—is now, for us, in ebb. The nobler generalizations which have marked the great men and great periods are not now made.

It is the decline of literature, when the throngs of frivolous gentlemen and ladies, without thought or aim, are suffered to assume a superiority, and take it as allowed,—that their houses and drawingrooms are anything but the conveniences and tributes of wisdom and virtue,—held to service. It is the vulgarity of this country,—it came to us with commerce out of England,—it is the vulgarity of England, to believe, that, naked wealth, unrelieved by any use or design, is merit, and may take place. And you shall hear civil and sensible persons, bred in all the culture of the times, congratulate themselves that they have put away their youthful fancies, and settled down into sensible opinions and practices;—meaning, that they have silenced every hope and faith, and settled down into fops and fribbles, as if a sane man could look respectfully at those illusions; as if that success they so admire, were anything but a drug to drown thought; an expedient of despair: as if we did not know too well what wealth is, and its poor uttermost;—expense breeding expense, aiming only at more of that they already have; impediments; from fine clothes to finer clothes; from slavery to slavery; and so downward to barbarism and imbecility. To speak truly, our civilization never grows to man's estate, remains always a child, never gets beyond its first nursery song,

> "Ride a cock horse to Banbury Cross
> To see what money can buy."[12]

The result is, it gives an inevitable bias to the course of education and to the social tone. Now, in this skepticism, if one turn to the literary class, it is curious to observe at what a zero point their faith stands. Who calls us, in these days, to glory and virtue?—who, in English or American poetry or philosophy? Where are the Stoics? Where is enthusiasm?

The student is badly counselled: he is told to aim at places and vulgar power. The right scale is reversed. He wishes to put the eternal to commercial uses. The talent that is cultivated for success becomes a breadwinner, but no muse.

Is it not true that out of a few heads come the mythology, divinity, law, and social machinery of the world? Whence came all these tools, inventions, books, laws, parties, kingdoms? Out of the invisible world, through a few brains. The arts and institutions of men are created out of thought. The powers that make the capitalist are metaphysical: the force of method and the force of will make trade and build towns. "All conquests that history tells of will be found to resolve themselves into the superior mental powers of the conquerors, and the real credentials by which man takes precedence of man and lays his hand on those advantages which confirm and consolidate rank are intellectual."

Who is accountable for this wide materialism, for this pettiness of counsel? Who, but the Scholars, or educated class? They are the thought, the light, the conscience. When they do not see principles; When the poets do not believe in their own poetry,—how should the bats and the swine?

There is always some proportion between the opinions of the majority and the

12. Emerson misquotes the second line of this famous nursery rhyme, which should be "To see a fine lady upon a white horse."

minority. The world is as bad as it dares to be. And if the majority are evil, it is because the minority are not good. If the South creates slavery, it is because the North permits it. If the great Whig party,—the so-called party of property and education,—has drivelled and huckstered away for party fear or advantage every principle of humanity and the dearest hopes of mankind;—if the public officers, national or local, are only energetic, when mischief can be done, and imbecile as corpses, when evil was to be prevented; it is because their leaders, whom they believed wise, staggered blindly, sneered at principles and higher law, and because the heart and the head of the literary class was apathized. If the heathen rage, 'tis because the Christians doubt. The avarice, the skepticism, the luxury, the sorcery, the table-trotting,—it is all yours. When the stones cry out, it is because the men are dumb. When slavery is rampant, it is because liberty is couchant. And if the influence of the minority loses and lessens until it is all gone, it is because there is not, at last, a minority of one, that is pure and grand in its aims.

For we are all, at last, of one party. We share the spirit of the age. These pull forward and those drag back, but all are in one boat, swept irresistibly onward, and it makes but a moment's difference who is radical, and who is conservative.

The educated class wish to be amused by thoughts; they wish to be amused by love of nature like travellers in Italy who wish Vesuvius to get ready an eruption, when they have dined and slept. They summon a lecturer or a poet, to read to them for an hour, and so they do with a priest. But the thoughts, could they once enter these frivolous bosoms, would break up this card house. They will not be patronised: they turn the patrons out of doors. The love of nature received and obeyed would break up the band-box of a parlor, shatter the rosewood pianos, end this card-case and amiable idiocy of morning calls. They think these elemental forces, like fire, like brandy and ether, pretty servants, but bad masters.

What is the moral of all these facts about Intellect?

Why, to revere and trust it evermore as the source out of which the worlds are made. Of all the foibles and frenzies of men, was there ever any like this of valuing practical life, and holding thought cheap? Thought! It is the thread on which the system of nature and the Heaven of heavens are strung. All that we see, or touch, or experience, came from it, as leaves from a tree. The world, the galaxy, is but a scrap before the metaphysical power. Nature is its rude realization; History, the first blotting down of a noble plan. But the Mind itself, all mixed and muddy as it is in us, is ever prophesying a grander future. There are more inventions in the thoughts of one happy day than ages could execute.

Let us think little of persons. Let us think little of history. Let us think nothing of masses. Let us obey the divine inspirations of secret thought above all the acclamation of nations.

We figure to ourselves intellect as an ethereal sea, which ebbs and flows, which surges and washes hither and thither, and carrying its whole virtue into every creek and inlet it bathes. To this sea every human house has a waterfront. But this great force, creating nature, visiting whom it will, and withdrawing from whom it will, making day where it goes, and leaving night where it departs, is no fee or property of man or angel: it is there, as the light, public and entire to each; and on the same terms. "It is ours whilst we use it; it is not ours when we do not use it."

I speak badly for the scholar and on a low platform. I speak badly, whilst I praise his faculty for the feats it can show; for the discoveries it can make; for the power, and fame, and money, which reward poets. This is a poor, popular, outside statement. Feats are no measure of the heaven of intellect. I do not wish to offer to your ambition a career. I own, it is profoundly solitary; it is unprofitable; it is to be despised and forgotten of men. If I recall the happiest hours of existence, those which really make man an inmate of truth, it is a lonely and undescribed state, but it is the door to joys that ear hath not heard nor eye seen.

All that is urged by the saint for the superiority of faith over works, is as truly urged for the highest state of intellectual perception or beholding, over any intellectual performance, as the creation of algebra, or of the *Iliad*. Under the spell of poetry in solitude, in deep conversation sometimes, we come out of our eggshell existence into the great dome and see the zenith over us and the nadir under us. It is like everything of a divine nature: it is simple, modest, sufficient. If it have this character of fate, and it must be obeyed, and not commanded, it has also its own joy and peace. I confide in it. If it ebb now, I know it will flow again. To it belongs an immense hope. Up and down swings the pendulum and tilts the pole of this world. But the lesson which thought teaches every wise man is "not to cramp his heart, or take half-views of men and things"—"that for some true result of good, all things must work together."

We all think alike, for we all think as this one sea washes through us. Every house has a waterfront to this great sea. The roar of this sea, is the common sense or public opinion of the world. It is because all have access to this one water, that men are found to hold one sentiment on the Thames, and the Ganges, and the Connecticut. It varies in form and tone with each age, but all the men of one age,—however differenced in training,—are animated by a similar spirit. What we call the Spirit of the Age leaps all boundaries and appears at the antipodes.

Whilst I say these things of the possibilities of the scholar, it is only in illustration of the popular folly of his shame. I should be ashamed to speak seriously to so low motives. I wish you better than to be scholars by ambition. Bulwer-Lytton is remarked among living writers as having steadily addressed himself to the worldly ambition of the student. His romances tend to fan these low flames.

But that way madness lies. I have seen the cheek of youth glow to hectic red with the love of college distinction. I have seen the grave close suddenly over those whom this daemon hath slain.

I do not wish you to be poets and geometers that you may have villas. This is Wall Street in disguise. O, no: for there is a nemesis not to be trifled with or out-witted that would deprive you and rightly of your crown. Poet ceases to be poet when he sits crowned. Fame follows who flies. It is for a poet's joys and powers, not a merchant's, that I wish you poets. I wish you for yourselves, for the sake of knowledge, to love knowledge, to know that knowledge is your healthy food which nourishes man to what is most human; that the deep mystery of nature is there; that men are as they think, men are as they believe; that history is nothing but the realization of certain thoughts.

In America, the geography is sublime, the men are not; the inventions are excellent, the inventors one is ashamed of; the means by which events so grand as the opening of California, Texas, Oregon, and the junction of the two oceans are affected are paltry: the filthiest selfishness, fraud, and conspiracy. As if what we find in nature that the animalcule system is of ferocious maggot and hideous mite who bite and tear, yet make up the fibre and texture of nobler creatures so all the grand results of history are brought about by these disgraceful tools. Grandeurs do not ultimate themselves in grandeurs, but in paltriness. The idea of God ends in a Methodist meeting house.

This great and beautiful landscape is made up of what particulars? Why of farms—of houses, barns, shops, and churches—built by very dull people, bought and sold with very mixed and with a preponderance of sordid motives, and filled with cattle which give system to the farm, and with men who are pulled down by the cattle which they tend into a like estate. The landscape remains grand, and thanks these accessories for so many beauties. So paltry are the agents in politics and colonization whose paltriness is wrenched and twisted by irre-sistible inner tendencies to proud historical results.

Religion is the perception of that power, which constructs the greatness of the centuries out of the paltriness of the hours.

> Ah, yet though all the world forsake,
> Though fortune clip my wings,
> I will not cramp my heart, nor take
> Half-views of men and things:
> Let Whig and Tory stir their blood,
> There must be stormy weather,
> But for some true result of good,
> All parties work together.

> This whole wide earth of light and shade
> Comes out a perfect round.[13]

Decomposition is recomposition. Cholera is organization. War and Despotism are rough benefactors.

Genius magnetizes, inundates armies, and impresses a whole generation with his own purpose which is irresistibly executed. When a man leaves his right task and adopts some short or fraudulent method, he is bringing society to bankruptcy. But nature watches over all this too, and turns this malfaisance to some good. For California gets peopled, and subdued, and civilized in this factitious way, and, on this fiction, a real prosperity is built. 'Tis a tub thrown to the whale, a decoy duck: real ducks, real whales are caught, and out of Sabine rapes and out of robbers' forays real Romes and their heroisms come in fulness of time. That absoluteness and deity that resides in it must make the rule of dealing with it. It comes and goes at its will. It is for us to apply ourselves. We are to treat it reverently as our beatitude, which, if it enters us, we live; if not, we die. Like Fate, it has its grand oceanic manners,—there is little we can do but observe and revere.

Nor do I fear any misapprehension because I am not in an assembly of poets. College gowns do not make scholars any more than the uniform makes heroes. This college is built on laws of the mind, laws of the world, and, if there are those here who are thinking only of Wall Street and State Street, and not of the eternal principles whose organs and servants we ought to be, the sooner they go to their own place the better for all.

I see the levity and condescension which listens to hints and suggestions of mental power. They think they stand on solid ground, and they are pleased to be amused by what they call imaginative and transcendental. I see in that conceit nothing but fat and foolishness. A college, a bible, reason, that built and builds the world forevermore: what have these fat hypocrites to do with a college, a bible, or the reason that upholds all? 'Tis all hypocrisy—a college, or the school book, or the name of intellectual culture—in the way these people live. I like people who can do things. The suggestions of power of new and highest kind— of the only real power—which come to two thoughtful men in conversation apprise me that we are rude and savage; that the Deity is offering us vast resources, and we are penny wise. I believe and know that the powers exist which these popinjays sniff at. Their conceited performance—the streets of cities, the ships, the mills, the harvests, the mines, all that feeds, clothes, or amuses—I receive and the whole existence of the poppinjays also as I do a bee hive: as a low piece of geometry and work, but surely as very humble end. I think of the wind, and not of the weathercocks.

13. Alfred, Lord Tennyson, "Will Waterproof's Lyrical Monologue," ll. 49–56, 67–68.

But, you shall not be partisan; you shall not be sectarian. Priests of the creative, beneficent power which out of evil makes good, you shall not take half-views of men and things, but leaning on real power, you shall be serene. For men are as they think: men are as they believe; and the thought and the belief are the very function and secret of the scholar. It is an established fact—not the less a fact that few men have penetration enough to see it—that the view of nature generally prevailing in a nation is the foundation of their whole science, and its influence spreads over every department of life. Does not the Indian medicine man know this? Does not the Jesuit know this? Do not Voltaire and Helvetius know this?[14] A gun, a steamboat, the telegraph, of course, necessitate a different view of nature from the savages yelling indecently to punish their gods for drying the ground. Not less, he who knows his way into nature, who sees how to make boiling water boil the world for him; who sees what the conditions are; that the reason why turnips cannot grow here, is for want of drainage, and, by cylindrical tiles and gutta-percha tubes, transforms a barren county into a garden.

Gentlemen, I too am an American, and value practical talent. I love results, and hate abortions. I delight in people who can do things. I prize talent,—perhaps no man more. I hold dear the poet who knows his art so well, that, when his voice vibrates, it fills the hearer with sympathetic song, just as a powerful note of an organ sets all tuned strings in its neighborhood in accordant vibration. I prize the novelist with his romance, the architect with his palace, the composer with his score.

Great is the immunity of the Scholar. Men think he would found a sect; he knows better. Society has no bribe for him. He sheds all unsuitable influences. Carlyle kept out of all these importunities of his readers, by the necessity of isolation which genius feels. He must stand on his glass tripod of insulation, if he would keep his electricity. He represented well: the literary man made good in his day the function of Erasmus, of Johnson, of Dryden, and of Swift.[15]

The Scholar is a collector of finer coins than the numismatologist, of finer shells than the conchologist. But the question is ever to what end: with what design, as the temptation is ever to desert the end for the means. The Scholar is measured by the end. Is he a method? Has he a future? Is the end elevating and unselfish? Is it vanity? Is it gain? Or, is he fired by a beauty above the reach of his eyes? an order detected in nature by the soul only, and which comes from the soul?

Ah, Gentlemen, I cannot praise the literary state of New England. The low state of public morality accuses the decline of thought. That does not feel itself

---

14. Claude Adrien Helvétius (1715–71), French philosopher.
15. Desiderius Erasmus (1455–1536), Dutch classical and theological scholar.

rebuked as it ought before the mind. The majority usually bears some relation to the minority: fears it, emulates it, adopts what it can. Why do the minority have no influence? Because there is not a pure minority, because there is not a minority of one that is grand in design. Things have been done in America within late years that will make this age dark in history. Our scholars were reading Demosthenes, our priests were reading in the Talmud, and whilst they wondered that the Romans should make a consul of Caligula's horse, the foremost freemen of mankind suffered themselves to be saddled, and bridled, and made to run and carry the offal of the dark ages into opening West of America.

But I am detaining you too long. I only wished to fill the hour your honoring kindness assigned me by a few counsels which are rather my perpetual observation than as counsels to be offered to you. I congratulate you on the happy fortune which, in this opening America, gives to you the white lot of the scholar, which makes the noblest offices of the human being your profession and calling in an age in which the whole world is looking to America for the lead, and puts the opportunity and obligation of taking that lead on you.

www.ingramcontent.com/pod-product-compliance
Lightning Source LLC
Chambersburg PA
CBHW051554100726
47898CB00001B/94